THE FRIAR AND THE MAYA

THE FRIAR AND THE MAYA

Diego de Landa and the
Account of the Things of Yucatan

MATTHEW RESTALL, AMARA SOLARI,
JOHN F. CHUCHIAK IV, AND TRACI ARDREN

UNIVERSITY PRESS OF COLORADO
Denver

© 2023 by University Press of Colorado

Published by University Press of Colorado
1580 North Logan Street, Suite 660
PMB 39883
Denver, Colorado 80203-1942

 The University Press of Colorado is a proud member of
the Association of University Presses.

The University Press of Colorado is a cooperative publishing enterprise supported, in part, by Adams State University, Colorado State University, Fort Lewis College, Metropolitan State University of Denver, University of Alaska Fairbanks, University of Colorado, University of Denver, University of Northern Colorado, University of Wyoming, Utah State University, and Western Colorado University.

∞ This paper meets the requirements of the ANSI/NISO Z39.48-1992 (Permanence of Paper).

ISBN: 978-1-64642-423-8 (hardcover)
ISBN: 978-1-64642-504-4 (paperback)
ISBN: 978-1-64642-424-5 (ebook)
https://doi.org/10.5876/9781646424245

Cataloging-in-Publication data for this title is available online at the Library of Congress

Cover illustration: Landa preaching to Maya elders, from Marianus de Orscelar, *Gloriosus Franciscanus redivivus sive chronica observantiae* (Ingolstadt, 1625). Reproduced with permission of the John Carter Brown Library, Brown University.

Contents

Illustrations

Tables

Preface and Acknowledgments

Diego de Landa is the archetypal spiritual conquistador. A sixteenth-century Spaniard, a Franciscan, a monastic inquisitor and bishop, he spearheaded the conversion of the Mayas of Yucatan, provoking trans-Atlantic controversy with his methods—both protecting the Maya from the new colonists and ordering "idolatrous" Mayas to be tortured.

His extensive writings on Maya culture and history, and on the tumultuous tale of the protracted Spanish effort to establish a colony in Yucatan, were lost in the seventeenth century and have never been found. When a fragment of those writings was discovered in the nineteenth century—the manuscript presented by us here—Landa's controversial reputation was reignited. That reputation burns as brightly today as it ever did; if the famous Dominican friar, Bartolomé de Las Casas, is the stereotype of the "good" missionary in the sixteenth-century Americas, then Diego de Landa is infamous as the "bad" one. Landa's legacy is thus complex and contested.

He and his Franciscan colleagues wrote a great deal in these tumultuous early decades of the Spanish-Maya encounter. But, like the Maya codices that the same Franciscans burned, almost none of it has survived. A rare exception is one small manuscript, attributed to Landa with the title *Relación de las Cosas de Yucatán* (*Account of the Things of Yucatan*). Lost for centuries, the Account reached near-biblical status in the twentieth century as the first "ethnography" of the Maya, used for generations of scholars as the sole eyewitness insight into an ancient civilization.

https://doi.org/10.5876/9781646424245.c000a

The Account is routinely consulted, cited, and used in the classroom, making Landa the best-known Spaniard to set foot among the Maya.

The Account of the Things of Yucatan has been published many times in many languages. But the better editions in English are not easily found, and most lack a full set of explanatory essays and notes, while those that are easily accessed in print or online are flawed in multiple ways. Our purpose here, therefore, is to replace all prior editions of this influential text for English-speaking readers.

To that end, we have spent over a decade creating a translation from the original manuscript held by the Real Academia de la Historia in Madrid, comparing our work with prior translations, all with a view to offering an English version that is readable and polished, yet also accurate in its reflection of the style and vocabulary of the original manuscript. As we shall explain, the original manuscript does not flow like a coherent book written by a single author—because it is no such thing; as a collection of excerpts made from a long-lost compilation of texts, it comprises various voices, authors, sources, and styles. We hope we have managed to convey that awkwardness, while also achieving some clarity. We have also chosen to sandwich our translation of the surviving manuscript between an introductory chapter and a set of seven essays that describe, explain, and analyze the life and times of Diego de Landa himself, the Account, and the role it has played in the development of modern Maya studies.

This project originated in conversations between two of us (Chuchiak and Restall) in the 1990s, both excited by our parallel reading of the original Account in the Real Academia—a tiny gem of an archive hidden on a small street in the beautiful Spanish capital—and our parallel realizations that the manuscript was not the 1566 book manuscript it was so often taken to be. Encouraged by the late Neil Whitehead, an article followed in 2002, along with a resolution to produce a new edition of the Account.[1] Over the decades, the project expanded and contracted, spurred on by countless conference papers and eventually entire panels, never abandoned but too often sidelined by other undertakings, and then finally rescued by the complementary expertise and energy of this volume's other pair of translators, editors, and authors (Ardren and Solari).[2]

Along the way, countless debts were incurred. We thank the Real Academia de la Historia for preserving Landa's Account so well for so long; Harri Kettunen

[1] Restall and Chuchiak, "A Re-evaluation."
[2] The contributions of the four authors of this project vary between the essays and segments of the translated text and notes, as one might expect. But all four of us have played roles in the creation of every page, through multiple meetings, exchanges, and drafts over many years. This book is thus very much a collaboration, and it would be neither possible nor agreeable to identify accurately the author order for each essay or other portions of the project.

for his generous permission to use the high-quality digital copy of the Account that he made with the RAH's blessing; our department heads/chairs, deans, and provosts at the University of Miami and at the Missouri and Pennsylvania State Universities, for making work like this possible; Penn State's History Department and its head, Michael Kulikowski, for crucial subvention funds; the gifted Penn State graduate students who served as editorial assistants, Scott Doebler, Samantha Davis, and Micaela Wiehe; and Laurent Cases, Tom Cohen, Kris Lane, Richard Leventhal, and Linda Williams for contributing solutions and suggestions to specific problems. We are also grateful to Darrin Pratt and Laura Furney, the University Press of Colorado's director and assistant director, to acquisitions editor Allegra Martschenko, and to her predecessors Charlotte Steinhardt and Jessica d'Arbonne, for giving us the contractual incentive to complete the project, as well as the space to include such scholarly accoutrements as essays and extensive endnotes; and we thank the press's production professionals for turning our manuscript into a beautiful book. Finally, forgive us for simply thanking in one sentence all our family members, friends, colleagues, sponsoring institutions, and other organizations for myriad other contributions and acts of support; with a project this long in gestation, you are all too numerous to list, but nonetheless invaluable to this book—and to us. Thank you.

THE FRIAR AND THE MAYA

Figure 0.1. The Landa Statue in Izamal. The friar stares at the Franciscan convent and church built in the sixteenth century on the platform of an ancient Maya pyramid and temple. Local Izamaleños ignore him; he's just part of the stonework. But tourists, like generations of scholars, often pause to try and make sense of his image and legacy. Photograph by the authors.

Introduction

The Landa Conundrum

Diego de Landa stands on a plinth in the small Yucatec town of Izamal. He looks toward a spectacular convent that sits on top of the base of what was once an ancient Maya pyramid. He appears to be frowning, his hands tightly gripping a long bishop's pastoral staff and a book of scripture (see figure 0.1). His very existence—a statue of a Spanish colonist in a nation where the invaders of the sixteenth century are seldom commemorated in public works—raises questions. Is this Franciscan friar celebrated in Izamal, revered as the founding father of the Christianized Maya town? Or does his grim expression convey a less happy reputation?[1]

In the 1620s, another Franciscan in the province of Yucatan, fray Bernardo de Lizana, noted how the Maya parishioners of the colony had reacted to Diego de Landa's death a half-century earlier: "The Indians of all Yucatan felt his death so greatly, that they not only showed it with tears, but wished to remain lamenting it forever."[2] Such a claim seems difficult to reconcile with the fierce friar standing in bronze beside Izamal's convent-church today, even more so when one considers the act for which Landa is now best remembered: a violent campaign to destroy Maya

---

[1]   Earlier passages of this introduction were delivered by Matthew Restall at the symposium on The Franciscans in Mexico: Five Centuries of Cultural Influence at the Mexican Cultural Institute (Washington, DC) in October 2017 and published as Restall, "The Landa Conundrum."

[2]   "*Los indios de todo Yucatán sintieron tanto su muerte, que no sólo lo mostraron con lágrimas, más quisieron quedarse en lamentaciones perpetuas*" (Lizana, *Historia de Yucatán*, 77r).

https://doi.org/10.5876/9781646424245.c000b

religion that terrorized the twenty-year-old colony in the summer of 1562. Thousands of Maya men and women were interrogated under torture, hundreds dying as a result. Yet Lizana's assertion was not pure invention; it simply told part of the story.[3]

A mere five years after the violent 1562 campaign, a group of Maya noblemen wrote to the King of Spain that they owed their conversion to Christianity—their very salvation—to Landa's "great benevolence [*tibilil*] and his goodness [*utzil*]." Yet others wrote in the very same year that just hearing Landa's name "causes our entrails to revolt."[4] Thus did Landa's Maya parishioners unwittingly evoke the friar-bishop's paradoxical reputation, whereby five centuries later he would remain both the most famous—and yet also the most infamous—of all the Franciscans, perhaps even of all the Spaniards, who came to Yucatan to proselytize, rule, and settle beside the Maya.

Of these competing opinions, these opposing reputations, pithily summarized by the Maya petitioners of 1567 as "great benevolence" versus "great cruelty," the former predominated during the three centuries of Spanish colonial rule in Yucatan. That is hardly surprising. He was loathed in his lifetime by other Spaniards in Yucatan, especially the colonists (Governor Francisco Velázquez de Gijón remarked in 1575 that he wished he could lock Landa and his fellow friar Gregorio de Fuenteovejuna "inside a room and leave them both to die of hunger").[5] But Landa's ghost had the likes of Lizana to promote his reputation, as well as the larger support of the Spanish chroniclers, secular and religious, who controlled the pro-colonial message. It was not until the modern era, whose birth coincided with the collapse of the Spanish Empire and the rise of Maya studies, when the latter Landa—the cruel one—returned and triumphed. Yet the negative reputation never completely eclipsed the positive one. In the skilled hands of an historian such as the late Inga Clendinnen, an evocative portrayal of Landa emerged, with the friar above all a monastic Inquisitor, utterly convinced of his own righteousness and just authority, of his divine mandate to torture Mayas in order to save them.[6]

Clendinnen also imagined that for Landa, his 1562 campaign to extirpate idolatry in Yucatan had a personal dimension to it. She argued that between his arrival

---

[3] DQAY; Scholes and Roys, "Fray Diego de Landa and the Problem of Idolatry in Yucatan"; Clendinnen, *Ambivalent Conquests*; Tedlock, "Torture in the Archives"; Timmer, "Providence and Perdition"; Restall, *Maya Conquistador*, 151–68; Chuchiak, "In Servitio Dei," 614–19; Enríquez, "Exuberant Imagination."

[4] Restall, *Maya Conquistador*, 151–68 (Restall's translations of Maya phrases on 157, 167).

[5] *Pleito entre Don Francisco Velázquez de Gijón, gobernador de Yucatán, y el obispo Fray Diego de Landa*, 18 de junio 1575, AGN, Ramo de Inquisición, Vol. 117, fs. 2–3.

[6] Clendinnen, *Ambivalent Conquests*, 66–92. Landa was a "monastic Inquisitor," not an "Inquisitor," as he never held a formal position in the Holy Office or Inquisition; he was accused of usurping Inquisition authority, and only once he became bishop could he exercise episcopal inquisitorial power.

in the newly founded province in 1549 and his appointment as Provincial of the Franciscans in Guatemala and Yucatan in 1561, Landa developed genuine friendships with Maya leaders that were possibly "the most emotionally rewarding of his life." Thus, his apparent discovery of "their secret persistence in idolatry" struck him as a profound and personal betrayal, for which the friar "proceeded to punish them, and to strive to wrench the last root of opposition out of them." In our view, Clendinnen tends to sympathize too much with Landa—or, striving to stay objective, she appears to do so. Yet, as she herself admits, he clearly manufactured evidence that recidivist Mayas had committed human sacrifice, in order to justify his campaign and its brutality to the newly arrived Bishop fray Francisco de Toral. Maya noblemen surely perceived Landa's true nature, understanding him to be a dangerous and duplicitous manifestation of a protracted invasion, one with whom genuine friendship was impossible.[7]

If Clendinnen's interpretation is problematic in some ways, it is nonetheless significant for its subtleties, and it rightly remains at the heart of academic discussion over Landa's legacy. Yet her nuances have tended to be lost in the popular imagination. With the twentieth century's growth of Maya studies and the Mexican Revolution's encouragement of a romantic view of the ancient Indigenous past, the popular view of Landa became increasingly and bluntly negative. This can be seen in various genres of expression, one of which is that of Landa portraits. Such paintings tend to use the infamous book-burning of 1562 as the favored visual trope for his image as the bringer of hell-fires to the Maya.[8] The best-known of these—as it has been on public display in the Palacio de Gobierno in central Merida since it was painted in the 1970s—is by Fernando Castro Pacheco (see figure 0.2). The friar's face, grim and unflinching, is a mask of determined cruelty as he throws codices and effigies on the fire. In another example (see figure 0.3), the long civil war of the nineteenth century is imagined as a kind of revenge against Landa and his iconoclasm.

The cruel, iconoclastic Landa also features in a cluster of literary genres. In poems, novels, and even guidebooks, he is a colonialist caricature. A particularly vivid example is a 1999 novel by Rikki Ducornet, titled *The Fan-Maker's Inquisition*, in which Landa is seen as a fitting subject for a book by the Marquis de Sade, who is fascinated by what is presented as the fear-driven perversity of the Inquisitor. Tainted by the Spanish Inquisition stereotypes of the Black Legend,[9] Landa becomes even more

---

[7] Clendinnen, *Ambivalent Conquests*, 88–92, 124–26 (quote on 123).
[8] See, for example, the 2007 painting by Leonardo Paz, chosen to illustrate the Wikipedia entry on Land, and a prominent section titled "Inquisition: Suppression of Maya and Destruction of Maya Texts" (en.wikipedia.org/wiki/Diego_de_Landa; accessed June 2018).
[9] As a term referring to the negative depiction of Spanish colonialism by Anglo historians, "the Black Legend" (*la leyenda negra*) was coined in 1914 by Spanish historian Julián Juderías y

Figure 0.2. Landa's Conflagration. The friar burning Maya books and religious statues (or "idols") in 1562, as painted by Fernando Castro Pacheco. Palacio de Gobierno, Merida, 1970s. Photograph by the authors.

twisted than the marquis after whom sadism is named. Ducornet's semi-fictional Landa is not a proselytizer and writer, but a destroyer and a purifier. The burning of books and the execution of Mayas become one: "So great was the stench of burning flesh, of deerskin curling up like fingers."[10]

Few Mayanists can (or should) write the way a novelist can, but Ducornet's phrase evokes for scholars of the ancient Maya something of the agony that accompanies the contemplation of Landa's bonfire of codices. That act has made the friar a figure of loathing in modern academia, especially among Mayanists. Yet those same detractors have for a century and a half treated Landa's writings as gospel, as a sort of bible on ancient Maya culture to be quoted and cited without thought

Loyot (Restall, *When Montezuma Met Cortés*, 245–46, 250–52).
[10] Ducornet, *The Fan-Maker's Inquisition*, 203.

Figure 0.3. Retribution. A mural painting by Marcelo Jiménez Santos, in the Caste War Museum, Tihosuco, Mexico, imagines the nineteenth-century war as a vengeful uprising against Landa and the cultural invasion he represents. Photograph by the authors.

for the nature of those writings. Extant descriptions of Indigenous life in the era of Maya-Spanish contact are precious few, to be sure. Landa and his Franciscan colleagues in Yucatan apparently wrote much about the Maya and their mission among them, but none of it was published at the time and almost all of it is lost.[11] The lone surviving Landa manuscript, the Account (as we call it, for convenience's sake), describes Maya history, society, and culture shortly before and during Maya-Spanish contact, making it understandable that Mayanists have long treasured the Account as an invaluable source of ethnographic information (discussed in chapter 3). But the age-old paradox of Landa's reputation has thereby been perpetuated and deepened, creating what we term "the Landa conundrum."[12]

---

[11] The earliest surviving *doctrinas* in Yucatec Maya date from c. 1620 (see Hanks, *Converting Words*, 242–76). Other late-sixteenth-century writings by Franciscans in Yucatan survive in the form of seventeenth-century excerpts or copies (e.g., within Cogolludo, *Historia de Yucathan*; or as *informes* such as the so-called Códice Franciscano, published in *Nueva Colección de Documentos para la historia de México*, 55–72). There are also letters and reports surviving archivally, a handful of them published (such as Francisco de Toral, *Avisos del Obispo Fr. Francisco de Toral* [1563], in DHY, vol. 2, 25–34).

[12] After Restall, "Landa Conundrum."

The Landa conundrum is two layers deep. The first layer relates to his actions and the motivations behind them. The core question is: Was Landa a monster, or was he simply a brilliant if overly zealous product of his times? Was he a leering, racist, sadist; or was his love for Maya converts and parishioners a sincere and spiritual one, albeit the impatient and unforgiving affection of a Franciscan caught up in the millenarianism of the sixteenth century?

The second layer connects his actions to his writings, specifically to his one surviving work—which modern scholars have consistently, but misleadingly, called a "book," attributed completely and unquestioningly to his authorship. The Account was not published in Landa's lifetime, but it has been available for the past century-and-a-half in numerous modern editions and languages, variously titled *Relación de las cosas de Yucatán*, *Relation des choses du Yucatan*, *Yucatan before and after the Conquest*, and—most commonly in English—*Account of the Things of Yucatan*. The questions here, then, are: How could he write so fondly of the Mayas having treated them so brutally? Why does his "book" fail to justify the events of 1562—indeed, to dismiss them so coldly? By better understanding what kind of manuscript the friar really wrote, what parts of it were truly authored by him, and why he wrote or copied what he did, might we come closer to solving the puzzle of his actions? And perhaps most importantly, can we, as scholars, use this source more responsibly to understand the sixteenth-century Maya and their ancestors?

*   *   *

Our suggested resolution to the Landa conundrum is presented gradually over the seven essays that comprise Part II of this book (and, to a lesser extent, the notes to the translated text that is Part I). But in order to introduce and contextualize those ideas, we outline here four ways to approach the friar and his manuscript.

The first approach involves a recalibration of our lens—a need both to zoom further in and to zoom further out. Let us explain. By narrowing our focus too tightly onto Landa and his writings and actions, we create the illusion of Landa as an exception, thereby fostering the conundrum. At the same time, there is a tendency to zoom back and attempt to understand Landa either as a medieval figure or as an early or proto-ethnographer (a similar debate has been conducted, but in far greater depth and detail, over Bernardino de Sahagún—and, to some extent, over Bartolomé de Las Casas).[13]

It may be more helpful, however, to analyze Landa as a sixteenth-century figure, without pushing him back into the Middle Ages or pulling him forward into

---

[13]   See, for example, as entry points into these substantial literatures, Schwaller, ed., *Sahagún at 500*; Clayton, *Bartolomé de las Casas*; and Orique and Roldán-Figueroa, eds., *Bartolomé de las Casas*.

modern times. He lived fifty-five years in the very middle of the sixteenth century (1524–1579), a time when almost the entire Franciscan order was swept up in a millenarian fervor, convinced that the conversion of the Indigenous peoples of the New World was the pressing precursor to the Second Coming of Christ. He took his profession as a Franciscan at the impressionable age of sixteen at the convent of San Juan de los Reyes in Toledo, which was controlled by the Observants—the fervently anti-Semitic, Joachimist, millenarianist branch of the Franciscan Order—and the point of origin for a great number of the most zealous missionaries to the New World. There, Landa was surely moved by the almost constant reports of Franciscan martyrdoms and their "wars against idols" (Landa's life and career is discussed in chapters 2 and 4).[14] Landa was not unique, but typical, in believing that his mission was ordained and urgent; he saw it as of his time, and he was right.

More specifically, in terms of his missionary vision, he was influenced by the Franciscans who a generation earlier had initiated the conversion of Nahuas in Central Mexico, such as that mission's founder, fray Martín de Valencia. That meant an emphasis on three goals: the baptism of converts; the development of two-way language learning (that is, young Indigenous noblemen should be taught Spanish and Latin, while friars should learn Indigenous languages so as to better proselytize "the Indians" and study the culture that they sought to erase); and the destruction of physical manifestations of Indigenous religion, such as temples, books, and effigies, combined with the punishment of backsliders.[15]

Viewed thus within the context of Franciscan ideology and practice in sixteenth-century New Spain, Landa's activities seem less contradictory. They seem even less so when compared to other sources—far less known than Landa's Account—that lend insight into how Franciscans in Yucatan perceived their mission in the late-sixteenth century. The so-called Códice Franciscano, for example, surviving only in the form of a later copy of excerpts (like the Account, but much shorter), is an *informe*, or a sort of friars' manual. Its emphases match many of Landa's own, such as

---

[14] The chronicle of the Convent of San Juan de los Reyes contains a record of the events in the convent during the period that Landa professed there, including reports of Franciscan martyrs like fray Juan de Espiritu Santo from 1538–1542; see *Memoriale libro ordinis minorum nostri ab anno divini 1506–1625, Convento de la orden de San Francisco de San Juan de los Reyes*, Toledo, AHN, Clero, Libro 15923, especially folios 27r–31v. For a persuasive argument that Landa equated the Maya with the Jews, see Davis, "Evangelical Prophecies."

[15] See the tidy summary in Nesvig, *Forgotten Franciscans*, 3–5. Classic works on the topic include Phelan, *Millennial Kingdom of the Franciscans*; Kobayashi, *La educación como conquista*; and Baudot, *Utopia and History*. For two versions of a book that is very far from being the definitive study of Franciscan millenarianism, but which succinctly ties the phenomenon to sixteenth-century Mexico, Yucatan, Landa, and the Maya, see Restall and Solari, *2012 and the End of the World*; and *Maya Apocalypse*. Also see Chuchiak, "*Sapientia et Doctrina*."

separating noble and commoner parishioners for preaching and teaching, as well as building vast churches and convent complexes (so that "the ornament and splendor of the churches" can fully replace "the sumptuous temples" of the past). The Códice Franciscano also notes that the Maya are

> like children, and in order to be well governed they need to have with them, as children do, their schoolmasters, who, should they fail or not take to the lesson, or commit a transgression, should therefore punish them with a half dozen lashes.[16]

This is not to say that all Franciscans in early Yucatan shared Landa's views; as Martin Nesvig has warned, it is important not "to flatten the considerable ideological diversity of the order" in New Spain. Indeed, the province's first bishop, fray Francisco de Toral, stopped Landa's extirpation campaign, successfully requested that he be recalled to Spain, spent 1563 conducting a *visita* of all the parishes, and wrote a set of *avisos* (notices) that heavily emphasized pedagogy over punishment. In Toral's vision of the mission, there is much rigor of teaching, ritual, and due process, but no violence.[17]

Landa and Toral can therefore be best appreciated as individuals whose particular emphases represented variants within the Franciscan ideology of sixteenth-century Mexico and Yucatan. But, while Landa cannot be said to stand for all his fellow friars, his vision prevailed; as William Hanks concluded, Toral "failed obviously" and, denied his petition to be relieved of his post in 1566, lived long enough to see Landa exonerated.[18]

For our second approach, we do not need to ponder Landa's putative sadism to understand how Indigenous peoples could be studied, valued, and protected while at the same time derided, abused, and even executed. That dichotomy had been at the heart of European reactions to the Indigenous population of the Americas beginning in the 1490s. (It is, arguably, at the heart of Western colonialism in the Age of Empire.) Most obviously it took the form of the division of Caribbean islanders into two invented races, the "good Indians" (passive converts) and "bad

---

[16] Códice Franciscano, 58–59 ("*el ornato y aparato de las iglesias . . . sumptuosos templos . . . porque ellos son como niños, y para bien regirse hanse de haber con ellos como los niños los maestros de las escuelas, que en faltando o en no dando la leccion, or en haciendo la travesura, luego los escarmientan con media docena azotes*"); also see Hanks, *Converting Words*, 63–66.

[17] Toral, *Avisos*; Nesvig, *Forgotten Franciscans*, 5. For the best coverage of the Landa-Toral affair, see González Cicero, *Perspectiva religiosa en Yucatán 1517–1571*. For a perspective on Toral's relationship with his Nahua parishioners in the 1540s and 1550s, see Townsend, *Annals of Native America*, 102–18.

[18] As we shall see, Landa was exonerated in 1569; Toral died in 1571, after which Landa was appointed to replace him (so Toral did not live to see Landa become bishop, despite Hanks's poetic claim; *Converting Words*, 67).

Indians" (the cannibals or Caribs, who resisted conversion and colonization).[19] That dichotomy was subsequently extended to the Maya of Yucatan, as Spaniards struggled to explain how their efforts to subdue the peninsula's "Indians" took so long and why the result remained incomplete (see figure 0.4). We have dubbed those protracted campaigns the Maya-Spanish Thirty Years' War, as it stretched from the first open battle between a Maya army and invading conquistadors in 1517 to the end of full-scale conquest violence in 1547 (that war, traditionally and misleadingly called "the Conquest of Yucatan," is discussed in chapter 1).[20] Most of the peninsula remained free from Spanish colonial control, and it would do so for centuries; the stereotypical bifurcation of Yucatec Maya into good/bad categories persisted into the modern centuries, when they were termed *pacíficos* and *bravos*.[21]

But the dichotomy—of "Indians" respected/abused, seen as good/bad—also functioned on a broader plane, being central to how Spaniards viewed and treated every ethnic group encountered in the Americas. The Nahuas, for example, were slaughtered and enslaved by the tens—perhaps hundreds—of thousands and yet admired and valued, their nobles taught Latin and (for a brief while, at least) appraised for the priesthood. Nor do we even need to stop with the Spaniards: the noble/ignoble, good/bad dichotomy extended to how Europeans and Euro-Americans have seen Indigenous peoples for centuries.[22]

To tackle this second way of resolving the Landa conundrum, then, we need to reorient our approach, placing Landa's perspective within the larger context of how "the Indians" were a conundrum in the minds of Spaniards. The highly complex Indigenous reaction to colonization—which has arguably been the primary focus of the entire field of ethnohistory for the past three generations—was not well understood by Spaniards, who so often distilled their own reaction down to a dichotomy of satisfaction and frustration. Therefore, Landa's gratification over his proselytizing and parish-building campaigns of the 1550s, combined with his vexation over apparent outbreaks of recidivism, placed him firmly in the center of the larger sixteenth-century phenomenon of how Spanish friars and priests, settlers, and administrators, responded to the paradox or conundrum of "the Indian."

A third way to contextualize Landa's life and the Account is to appreciate factional

---

[19] For an overview of the development of this dichotomy, see Whitehead, *Of Cannibals and Kings.*

[20] Restall, "Wars of Invasion."

[21] Good entry points for the relevant literature (especially on the Caribbean) are Bacci, *Conquest*; and Stone, *Captives of Conquest*; on Yucatan, see Restall, "Invasion: The Maya at War"; Restall, "Wars of Invasion"; Chuchiak, "Forgotten Allies"; and Chuchiak, "La Conquista de Yucatán, 1517–1542."

[22] It is also reflected, for example, in the art and sculpture of the United States Capitol in Washington, DC; see Restall, "Trouble with 'America.'"

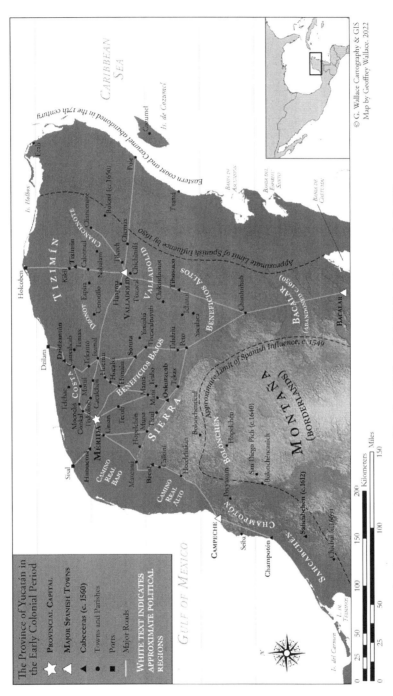

Figure 0.4. Map of Early Yucatan. Map courtesy of Geoffrey Wallace. © G. Wallace Cartography & GIS.

politics in late sixteenth-century Yucatan. Much of the history of the peninsula in the first colonial decades of the 1550s–1570s, a history which justifiably is often seen as heavily Landa-centric, is in fact a story of factional rivalries within the fledgling colony—more specifically, a nexus of rivalries spread across the Spanish and Maya communities.

Landa's Yucatan years were divided into two stints. The first stretched from 1549 until he left for Spain in 1563. The provincial capital of Merida had only been founded in 1542, and invasion warfare did not wind down until less than two years before Landa's initial arrival. Only eight friars had traveled to Yucatan before Landa, and they had only founded two convents (at Merida and Mani). So, although Landa and his seven or so colleagues were the second missionary wave, there were still fewer than twenty friars facing the enormous challenge in the 1550s of converting hundreds of thousands of Mayas, whose status as Christianized, colonial subjects was tenuous, if not imaginary.[23]

Landa's departure from the province fourteen years later was under a dark cloud of controversy; although he resigned as Provincial in early 1563 and voluntarily crossed the Atlantic,[24] an order was already on its way to have him detained and dispatched to Spain to respond to allegations by Bishop Toral and by conquistador-settlers that Landa had overstepped his authority.[25] He was eventually acquitted of all charges (on January 29, 1569),[26] and after Toral's death he was appointed bishop (on November 17, 1572).[27] He then returned to the province for a second stint in

---

[23] These early mission years are discussed further in our chapter 2. Also see DHY, vol. I, p. 4; Lizana, *Historia de Yucatán*, 43r–57r; Cogolludo, *Historia de Yucathan*, Libro V, Capítulos V–IX; Carrillo y Ancona, *El Obispado de Yucatán*, I, 276-77.

[24] The claim that Landa resigned and left on his own accord, before that order reached Yucatan, comes from Cogolludo, *Historia de Yucathan*, Libro VI, Capítulo VI, and it may thus be pro-Landa spin.

[25] The royal cedula for Landa's recall along with that of fray Pedro de Ciudad Rodrigo, fray Miguel de la Puebla, and fray Juan Pizarro was issued in Barcelona on February 26, 1564. See *Real cédula al alcalde mayor de las provincias de Yucatán que hallados los frailes los envie a estos reinos*, 26 de febrero, 1564, AGI, Audiencia de México, 2999, Libro 2, 3 folios. The documentation created by the Toral-Landa affair is massive, mostly found in several *legajos* in AGI, *Escribanía de Cámara*, 1009A, some of which was published in transcription in DQAY.

[26] See *Sentencia del padre Fray Antonio de Cordoba, Ministro Provincial de la Orden de San Francisco de la Provincia de Castilla, en el caso de Fray Diego de Landa*, Toledo, 29 de enero, 1569, AGI, Escribanía de Cámara, 1009A.

[27] Landa was recommended by Pope Gregory XIII to King Philip II on October 17, 1572 (*Bula de Gregorio XIII al rey Felipe II recomendando a Diego de Landa, electo obispo de Yucatán* 17 de octubre, 1572, AGI, Patronato, 3, N.16, R.2), and Philip made the appointment a month later. Just in case there were any doubts about his lingering guilt in the case that Toral and others had made against him, Landa's agents at the papal court had requested a separate bull of exoneration. Pope Gregory XIII issued the bull on the same date (see *Bula de Gregorio*

Figure 0.5. Landa as Bishop. This late-colonial portrait, likely copied from a damaged or fading earlier one in the Merida Cathedral, hung in the cathedral for centuries and is the closest we have to a likeness created from life. Two copies of uncertain date survive, one in the Sala Capitular of Merida's cathedral, the other in the Museo de Arte Sacro de Conkal, Yucatan. Photograph by the authors.

1573, where he resided until his death almost seven years later (on April 29, 1579; see figure 0.5).[28]

What was the significance of that chronology for understanding factional alliances and conflicts in the very early colony? In both 1549–1563 and 1573–1579, Landa benefited from and relied upon alliances with other religious officials and with conquistador-settlers—while, at the same time, he also faced enemies

---

XIII a Diego de Landa, electo obispo de Yucatán, absolviéndole de cualquier excomunión, suspensión, interdicto y censura eclesiástica en que pudiere haber incurrido, para evitar contradicción, 16 de diciembre, 1572, AGI, Patronato, 3, N. 16, R.2, f. 3).

[28] Fray Thomás de Cardenas, Franciscan visiting commissary in Yucatan, first officially reported the death of Bishop Landa in a letter dated May 8, 1579; see *Carta de Fray Tomas de Cardenas sobre la muerte de Don Fray Diego de Landa*, 8 de mayo, 1579, AGI, Audiencia de Guatemala, 170, 1 folio.

within the Church and among the colonists. Loosely speaking, the Church and the encomendero-settler establishment were in opposition throughout colonial Yucatan's history, with governors and bishops often tied up in bitter battles.[29] But as soon as one looks in detail at such conflicts, the battle lines multiply and shift, determined by individual personalities and relationships.[30] Yucatan's first two bishops, Landa and Toral, are good examples of this: they were political archrivals with differing interpretations of the Franciscan mission and the methods required to turn the Maya into Christians.[31]

At the same time, the Maya nobility were no more homogenous in their loyalties and political positions than were the Spanish colonists. To take Maya descriptions of Landa from petitions to the king and use them to underscore the Landa conundrum—as we did above—is in fact misleading. The Maya polities or small kingdoms that existed in the first half of the century more or less survived the protracted Spanish invasion—the period of that Maya-Spanish Thirty Years' War.[32] Those polities then functioned in the century's second half as clusters of *cahob* (Maya municipalities; *cah* in the singular) centered on regional capital towns ruled by dominant dynasties (the Pech, Xiu, Canul, Cocom, Chel, and so on; see our chapters 1 and 4). That survival was made possible by political gamesmanship, with Maya noblemen jostling for advantage both within their own dynastic networks and inside the world of Spanish factionalism. The Franciscans—Landa included—were part of that high-stakes political game, sometimes playing, and sometimes being played by, Maya dynastic leaders.[33]

*   *   *

The fourth and final way to approach Landa and the conundrum he embodies is to look more closely at the Account than previous editors of published editions have done. The details of that examination will unfold in the notes and essays to come. But it is worth reiterating here that there is no evidence that Landa ever saw the

---

[29] Encomenderos were the dominant Spanish settlers, usually former conquistadors in the first generations of settlement, who were granted groups of Indigenous villagers in encomienda ("trust"); those villagers were not slaves or serfs, but they were obliged to provide labor and pay tribute goods to their encomendero, in return for the benefits of "protection" and of the encomendero's support for a church and priest (for which Indigenous communities had also to pay).

[30] This was true of the whole colonial period in Yucatan: on such battlelines among the settlers, see the work of Manuela Cristina García Bernal and of Robert W. Patch, as well as, more recently and most evocatively, Lentz, *Murder in Mérida*.

[31] See Chuchiak, "Entre la cooperación y la usurpación."

[32] Restall, "Wars of Invasion."

[33] See Restall, *Maya Conquistador*; "People of the Patio"; Quezada, *Maya Lords and Lordship*.

Account, let alone wrote it—that is, no evidence that the manuscript presented here, and published many times as a self-contained book, was conceived and composed by him as such, or that the compiled version we have today existed before he died.

So, what did Landa write? Apparently, a great deal, of which almost nothing has survived, as far as we know. While working on his defense in Spain, Landa himself cataloged a long list of *memoriales, informes,* and other reports and compiled documentation on the Franciscan missions in Yucatan; he submitted the list to the Council of the Indies in 1565, and to his own Franciscan Order sometime in 1565–1569.[34] Much or all of this documentation would surely have remained in the possession of the Council of the Indies, as well as in the provincial archives of the Franciscan Order of Castile, in Toledo—where his formal ecclesiastical trial for censure occurred. It has not been found, however, and is likely no longer extant.[35]

There is also strong seventeenth-century evidence that the friar maintained a *recopilación,* a compendium or compilation of information on topics of interest, which ecclesiastics, chroniclers, and other intellectuals of the era often maintained. Landa's *recopilación* would have been a great compendium of passages written by him in Yucatan and in Spain, mixed with passages written or dictated to him by Yucatec informants, combined with passages copied by him from other books and manuscripts.[36] It probably dovetailed with the items in the abovementioned list. The *recopilación* must have been assembled between Landa's arrival in Yucatan in 1549 through to his death there in 1579, and it was probably steadily compiled over those three decades. He likely assembled some of it in Yucatan during the 1550s through to 1563, then took this work-in-progress with him to Spain and did further editing and composition there in the late 1560s. He was certainly working on part of it in 1566—the only date of authorship anywhere on the Account—in the Franciscan convent of San Juan de los Reyes in Toledo, Spain, where he had been a

---

[34] *Memorial de Fray Diego de Landa al Rey y al Consejo de Indias presentando varias probanzas y documentos para su defensa en el asunto de la idolatría de los indios,* Sin fecha, AGI, Escribanía de Cámara, 1009A.

[35] Unfortunately, little of these ecclesiastical archives survived the Spanish Civil War of 1936–1939. Diego de Landa's body itself was returned to Spain in the early eighteenth century, but his tombstone in his hometown of Cifuentes similarly was damaged during the Civil War. Reportedly, Juan Catalina García had found his tomb and bones in the later nineteenth century in the parish church of Salvador in his hometown of Cifuentes, where it was destroyed by artillery in 1936; see Catalina García, "Investigaciones históricas y arqueológicas en Cifuentes," 62–63. Catalina García claimed he discovered a funerary tombstone with the inscription: "Aqui estan colocados los guesos del Ill.mo Señor Don Frai Diego de Landa Calderon, Obispo del Yucatan. Murio año de 1572 [*sic*]. Fue sexto nieto de Don Iban de Quiros Calderon, que fundo esta capilla año 1342 como consta de la fundacion."

[36] Cogolludo repeatedly refers to Landa's various writings throughout his great *Historia de Yucathan.*

novice and where he served as Maestro de Novicios in the late 1560s. He no doubt continued to work on it, and to utilize his notes for his defense in the Franciscan order's trial for censure against him, while he served as the guardian of the distant convent of San Antonio de la Cabrera in Castile.[37] As Yucatan's bishop, from 1573 until his death in 1579, he continued working in Merida on his great *recopilación*. It has never been found.

There is hope that it may be found, as there is a chance that at least two copies existed, one in Spain and one in Yucatan. A smattering of references to a large Landa manuscript in Yucatan begin soon after his death, suggesting that it was deposited in 1579 or 1580 in the library of the Franciscan convent in Merida. Over the next century, Yucatan's Franciscan chroniclers mention it and clearly used it as a source. For example, fray Bernardo de Lizana, writing in 1633, drew information from Landa on Maya religion and the conversion campaigns (the "spiritual conquest"), also referring to many Franciscans and others who had written about Landa, his life, and his written works.[38]

By 1694, however, fray Francisco de Ayeta, who might be expected to mention the great *recopilación* just as his predecessors did, cites only another long-lost work of Landa's, his *Arte y gramática*. In the final decades of the century the *recopilación* may therefore have been destroyed or taken to Spain. If the latter was the case, it was very possibly fray Diego López de Cogolludo who took it. Cogolludo penned most of his massive *Historia de Yucathán* in the Yucatan peninsula itself beginning in the 1650s and then finished it in Madrid, where it was published in 1688. He appears to have drawn from Landa either directly or indirectly (through Lizana, for example), both from passages recognizable to us as they ended up in what we know as Landa's Account and from other passages that were very likely part of the *recopilación*.

Whether Cogolludo made copies of portions of the *recopilación* before he left Yucatan, or whether he simply transported the entire work from Merida to Madrid, he may have been—according to the written evidence currently available—the last person to use Landa's vanished magnum opus. As writers in Yucatan made no further references to the manuscript, it was likely no longer in the convent in Merida when the Franciscans were expelled in 1820; but if it was, it was either destroyed at that time or spirited away to sit in a dark box or on a dusty shelf, awaiting its discoverers. We like to think that it is buried today in a library or private collection

---

[37] The Council of the Indies turned the whole case against Landa over to the Franciscan Order to handle on January 30, 1565. See *Auto de Consejo Real de las Indias por el cual mandan que se remita al Provincial de Castilla el negocio de Fray Diego de Landa*, Madrid, 30 de enero, 1565, AGI, Escribanía de Cámara, 1009A.

[38] RHGY, Vol. I: 142–53 (entry discussed further in chapter 4; also see chapter 1; Lizana, *Historia de Yucatán*, 57v–77v; Pagden, *Maya*, 18, 20).

in Mexico, the United States, Spain, or Italy—in a Spanish attic, perhaps, or in the Vatican Library—but the chances of that are surely slim.

When we ponder the possibility that there were once two copies of the *recopilación*—identical or partial and different, both long lost—the plot thickens. In fact, it seems likely that Landa either left it in Spain in 1573, most likely in the convent of San Juan de los Reyes, as a copy of whatever he had compiled by that date, or he sent a copy to Spain of everything he had up to that point—prior to this death in 1579. This would no doubt have been the copy from which the royal historians extracted the excerpts that comprise our Account. There was certainly *some* written work of Landa's left in Spain, whether it was a copy of all or part of his *recopilación* or not. This is clear from the fact that several authors who never set foot in Yucatan consulted Landa's work in the decades after his death (and before Lizana's 1633 *Historia* provided readers in Spain with a biography of Landa). One of these authors was the royal chronicler Antonio Herrera y Tordesillas, whose *Historia general* was first published in Madrid in 1601–1615 and who drew on writings of Landa's that were in Spain.[39] Another was fray Antonio de Daza, whose *Cronica general de nuestro padre San Francisco y su apostolica Orden* was first published in Valladolid, Spain, in 1611. Daza consulted, at first or second hand, Landa's written accounts of his own activities—a smattering of which survive in the Account—and he cites Landa as an exemplary Franciscan in the New World.[40]

What does this tantalizing history of Landa's elusive magnum opus mean for the *Account of the Things of Yucatan*? It seems clear that the *recopilación* manuscript served as the source for the Account, which comprises a set of excerpts. But those excerpts were made by multiple scribes, in a seemingly haphazard way. They made no explicit reference to Landa's larger work, they left no clues as to its whereabouts, and they neither recorded their own identities nor told us where they did the copying work. To ferret out answers to the questions implied therein, we were obliged to analyze the object itself—its paper, handwriting, and binding—as well as its content. As we did so, we grew increasingly suspicious of the assumption of Landa's authorship by previous editors and readers of the Account. The more we pondered and uncovered the manuscript's history, in combination with its inconsistencies of content, the more our investigation turned to identifying alternative authors.

We present in detail in chapters 6 and 7 our analysis of the Account as a text that is wildly varied in topic, tone, and style, disjunctive in structure and lacking

---

[39]   Herrera y Tordesillas, *Historia General*.

[40]   Daza, *Qvarta parte de la Chronica general de nu[es]tro padre*, Book 2, Capítulo 49, f. 196–198 (Daza got his information about Landa from Francesco Gonzaga, *De origine Seraphica Religionis Franciscana ejusque progressibus, de regularis observancia institutione*, part 4, fs. 1306–1307).

cohesion or coherence as a single composition. But our conclusion is too important not to be revealed now, before presenting our translation. It is this. Much of the first half of the Account does appear to have been authored by Landa, but much of it comprises passages that were abbreviated, paraphrased, summarized, and even redacted from lost portions of the *recopilación*—portions that themselves were likely a mixture of Landa's writings and his summaries of writings by others, with the famous Dominican fray Bartolomé de Las Casas a likely source. Furthermore, the second half of the manuscript mixes passages likely written by Landa using Maya informants (on Maya religion and calendrics, for example) and with segments copied or summarized from writings by others. We have identified those others as including Francisco López de Gómara (hagiographer of Hernando Cortés). Most strikingly, it seems highly likely that two of the copyists who wrote down in their own hands many of the passages in the Account were none other than Juan López de Velasco, the royal Cronista and Cosmógrafo Mayor of 1571–1591, and Antonio de Herrera y Tordesillas, the Cronista Mayor of 1596–1625.

Behind the veil of Landa's authorship, then, lie multiple authors, copyists, sources, narrative voices, and intentions. Some portions are in the handwriting of royal historians, some in the hands of notaries—but none in Landa's own hand. The confounding manuscript that survived such a complex process was likely bound and given its cover in the eighteenth century, probably when it was deposited in the small library of Madrid's Real Academia de la Historia. It was still there in 1861, when it was found by a Frenchman styling himself the Abbé Brasseur de Bourbourg. It remains there to this day.

*   *   *

Landa's unpublished *magnum opus*, a *recopilación* that must have comprised the writings of others as much as those of the Franciscan himself, was therefore read and cited for a century and then ignored for the next two centuries, destroyed or consumed by fire or left to gather dust until a part of it was found in that little Madrid archive. That any of it survived at all seems miraculous.

Since its discovery and first publication—a partial French edition by Brasseur de Bourbourg in 1864—the Account has become one of the most widely read and oft-cited pieces of early modern Latin American writing, second only, perhaps, to the so-called Florentine Codex (produced by another sixteenth-century Franciscan, fray Bernardino de Sahagún). The Account has become a standard reference for students of Franciscan history, of the history of religious conversion, of colonial Mexican history, of the history of Yucatan, and above all of Maya history. Yet its messy and mysterious origins in a lost larger manuscript, its ambiguous authorship (revealed here, for the first time, as a manuscript only partly written by Landa), and its equally messy early publication history (to which we also turn in chapter 3), have only contributed to the Landa conundrum—and will continue to do so. This book is thus a response to our conviction that the Account deserves a reliable new translation, made directly from the manuscript in Madrid, with analytical packaging that explains the conundrum of how the friar—and the fragmentary manuscript wrongly attributed entirely to him—became so celebrated and reviled, so famous and infamous.

PART I

The Account

The original manuscript of the Account lacks chapters, section breaks, and subheadings (with a few exceptions, noted as they appear in our translation). As explained in the essays of our part II, the first translator of the Account, Brasseur de Bourbourg, created chapters with long descriptive titles, and other editors and translators followed him (using his or inventing their own), all contributing to the misreading of the Account as a coherent "book" written by Landa. We have sought to avoid that mistake and therefore only translated what is in the manuscript itself. However, to help readers familiar with earlier editions navigate the text, we have included the "section" numbers used by William Gates in brackets; for example, where *[Sec. 14]* appears in our translation, Brasseur, Gates, and others had created a break and a new chapter numbered XIV. We have also inserted the folio references to the original manuscript (although note that the folio numbers were probably added to the manuscript by Brasseur de Bourbourg); they appear likewise in brackets, as, for example, *[f. 11r]*.

These bracketed section or chapter numbers and folio numbers effectively serve as a concordance, allowing the reader to cross-reference our translation with the original manuscript and almost any published edition in any language. For quick reference, we also list here those section-chapter numbers with the titles used by Gates (and others) along with their folio concordance. Note that we have reproduced Gates's titles exactly, including his errors and the interpretations he borrowed from Brasseur (we list them *not* to endorse them, but for your historiographical convenience).

https://doi.org/10.5876/9781646424245.p001

Sec. 1. Description of Yucatan. Variety of seasons. [f. 1r–1v]

Sec. 2. Etymology of the name of this province. Its situation. [f. 1v–2r]

Sec. 3. Captivity of Gerónimo de Aguilar. Expedition of Hernández de Córdoba and Grijalva to Yucatan. [f. 2r–3r]

Sec. 4. Expedition of Cortés to Cozumel. Letter to Aguilar and his friends. [f. 3v–4v]

Sec. 5. Provinces of Yucatan. Its principle ancient structures. [f. 4v–5r]

Sec. 6. Cuculcan. Foundation of Mayapan. [f. 5r–6r]

Sec. 7. Government, priesthood, sciences, letters and books in Yucatan. [f. 6r–6v]

Sec. 8. The arrival of the Tutul-Xius, and the alliance they made with the lords of Mayapan. Tyranny of Cocom, the ruin of his power and of the city of Mayapan. [f. 6v–7r]

Sec. 9. Chronological Monuments of Yucatan. Foundation of the kingdom of Sotuta. Origin of the Chels. The three principal kingdoms of Yucatan. [f. 7r–7v]

Sec. 10. Various calamities felt in Yucatan in the period before the conquest by the Spaniards: hurricane, wars, etc. [f. 7v–8r]

Sec. 11. Prophesies of the coming of the Spaniards. History of Francisco Montejo, first Admiral of Yucatan. [f. 8r–9r]

Sec. 12. Montejo sails for Yucatan and takes possession of the country. The Chels cede to him the site of Chichen Itza. The Indians force him to leave. [f. 9r–10r]

Sec. 13. Montejo leaves Yucatan with all his people and returns to Mexico. His son, Francisco de Montejo, afterwards pacifies Yucatan. [f. 10r–11r]

Sec. 14. State of Yucatan after the departure of the Spaniards. Don Francisco, son of the Admiral Montejo, re-establishes the Spanish rule in Yucatan. [f. 11r–11v]

Sec. 15. Cruelties of the Spaniards toward the Indians. How they excused themselves. [f. 11v–12r]

Sec. 16. State of the country before the conquest. Royal decree in favor of the Indians. Health of the Admiral Montejo. His descendants. [f. 12r–12v]

Sec. 17. Arrival of the Spanish Franciscan friars in Yucatan. Protection they gave to the natives. Their contests with the Spanish military element. [f. 12v–13v]

Sec. 18. Vices of the Indians. Studies of the friars in the language of the country. Their teachings to the Indians. Conversions. Punishments of apostates. [f. 13v–14v]

Sec. 19. Arrival of Bishop Toral and release of the imprisoned Indians. Voyage of the Provincial of San Francisco to Spain to justify the conduct of the Franciscans. [f. 14v–15r]

Sec. 20. Construction of the houses of Yucatan. Obedience and respect of the Indians for their chiefs. Headgear and wearing of ornaments. [f. 15r–16r]

Sec. 21. Food and drink of the Indians of Yucatan. [f. 16r–16v]

Sec. 22. Painting and tattooing of the Indians. Their orgies, wines and banquets. Their comedies, music and dances. [f. 17v–18v]

Sec. 23. Industry, commerce and money. Agriculture and seeds. Justice and hospitality. [f. 18v–19r]

Sec. 24. Method of counting of the Yucatecans. Genealogies. Inheritances and tutelage of orphans. The succession of the chiefs. [f. 18v–19r]

Sec. 25. Divorces frequent among the Yucatecans. Nuptial customs. [f. 19v–20r]

Sec. 26. Method of baptism in Yucatan; how it was celebrated. [f. 20r–21v]

Sec. 27. Kind of confessions among the Indians. Abstinences and superstitions. Diversity and abundance of idols. Duties of the priests. [f. 21v–22v]

Sec. 28. Sacrifices and self-mortifications, both cruel and obscene, among the Yucatecans. Human victims slain by arrows, and others. [f. 22v–23v]

Sec. 29. Arms of the Yucatecans. Military chieftains. Militia and soldiers. Customs of war. [f. 23v–24v]

Sec. 30. Penalties and punishments for adulterers, homicides, and thieves. Education of the young men. Custom of flattening the heads of children [f. 24v–25r]

Sec. 31. Clothing and ornaments of the Indian women [f. 25r–25v]

Sec. 32. Chastity and education of the Indian women of Yucatan. Their chief qualities and their household economy. Their devotion and the special observances at the time of childbirth. [f. 25v–27r]

Sec. 33. Funerals. Burials of the priests. Statues to preserve the ashes of the chiefs, and the honors they paid to them. Their belief regarding a future life, with rewards and punishments. [f. 27r–27v]

[Sec. 1] [f. 1r]

FRAY DIEGO DE LANDA

THE YEAR MDLXVI

Yucatan is not an island nor a headland that enters into the ocean, as some have thought, but rather it is the mainland [*tierra firme*].[1] People were misled by the headland of Cotoch [Cape Catoche], which is made by the sea entering into the Bay of the Ascension towards the Golfo Dulce, and because of the other headland made on the other side towards Mexico [the northwest corner of the peninsula], towards the point or port of *la Desconocida* before arriving at Campeche,[2] or because of the extension of the lagoons made by the sea entering through Puerto Real and Dos Bocas.

The land is very flat and clean of any mountains,[3] and for that reason it cannot be spotted from ships until they are very near, except between Campeche and Champoton, where one can spot some small hills and a peak among them, called Los Diablos.

Coming from Veracruz towards the headland of Cotoch, it is less than twenty [XX] degrees, and near the mouth of Puerto Real it is more than twenty-three, and

---

[1] The Account includes two regional maps, both of which represent the Gulf of Mexico and the geographical expanse of Yucatan. We have included reproductions of these maps in our chapter 7, along with transcriptions and a modern map of the same region for readers' clarification. In the early years of the sixteenth century, many mistakenly understood Yucatan to be an island, not connected to the mainland; see Antochiw, *Historia Cartográfica de la Península de Yucatán*; and Restall, "Creating 'Belize.'"

[2] The only colonial-era evidence to support the common notions that the name Campeche is derived from Kinpech or Kimpech comes from fray Juan de Torquemada and Miguel León Portilla in Torquemada's *Monarquia Indiana*, where he called the Maya province *Kin Pech*. He also stated that the pre-colonial control was held by the Pech dynasty, whereas it was in fact Canul and Canche territory; see Okoshi Harada, "Los Canules," and Restall, *Maya Conquistador*, 82–103. More likely, the toponym was originally *Canpech* (*can*, serpent; *pech*, tick); the conquistador Pedro García reported on January 20, 1581 that the name for the province—Campech—came from "the name of an idol that wore a curled snake on its head as an insignia, with a tick on the snake's head [*el nombre de un ydolo que traia en la cabeza por insignia una culebra arroscada y en la cabeza de la culebra una garrapata*]" (RHGY, Vol. I: 146).

[3] The peninsula is a limestone shelf that juts northward into the Caribbean Sea. While there are very few sources of groundwater (only a handful of lakes and no rivers), the peninsula boasts the largest underground riverine system in the world. Occasionally, its upper crust breaks through to reveal this aquatic system, creating massive sinkholes, known in Mayan as *dzonotob* (*ts'ono'ob* in modern orthography) or in Spanish as *cenotes*. A distinctive ring of cenotes was created circa 65 million years ago when the earth was struck by a meteorite just off the coast of northern Yucatan. Today a village called Chicxulub marks this site of impact, giving its name to the resulting crater. Historically, Maya settlements have been clustered around this "ring of cenotes" and other natural water sources, such as the great precontact site of Coba, in modern Quintana Roo, which sits next to two naturally occurring spring-fed lakes.

it extends from one headland to the other over 130 leagues in length in a straight line.[4]

The coast is low-lying, and because of this, large ships must stay away from land.

The shore is very cluttered with crags and sharply pointed rocks that wear greatly at the cables of ships; but there is also much silt, so that even when ships run ashore few people are lost.

The ebb tide of the sea is so great, especially in the bay of Campeche, that many times half a league is left dry in some places.

These extensive tides leave behind in the seaweed, silt, and tide pools with many small fish that support a lot of people.

Yucatan is crossed from corner to corner by a small range of hills that begin close to Champoton and run to the town of Salamanca [Bacalar], which is at the opposite corner from Champoton.[5]

This range of hills divides Yucatan into two parts: the southern [*mediodía*] part, going towards Lacandon and Tah Itza [*Taiza*],[6] is uninhabited due to a lack of water,[7] of which there is none unless it rains. The other part, which is to the north, is inhabited.[8]

This land is very hot, and the sun burns fiercely even though there is no lack of fresh air such as the breezes and easterly winds that prevail there, as well as the afternoon sea breeze.

In this land people live a very long time, and a man was found who was one hundred and forty years old.

---

[4] In the colonial period, a league was equal to 4 kilometers and 190 meters in present day calculations. See Robelo, *Diccionario de pesas y medidas Mexicanas Antiguas y modernas y de su conversión*, 6. However, there have always been some discrepancies in the measurements and their modern equivalents. Some authors suggest that a league was equal to 5 kilometers and 570 meters (approximately three and one-half miles as Standard British Measurement).

[5] Today, this small range is known as the "Puuc Hills," a redundant phrase since "puuk" translates as "hill" in Mayan. In the precontact era, this region of the peninsula boasted dozens of cities, the largest being Uxmal, Kabah, and Labná, known for their distinctive architectural design and associated sculpture. In the modern era "puuc" became synonymous with the idiosyncratic mosaic patterning that adorned the facades of monumental structures in ceremonial centers. For a detailed discussion of this stylistic development and its relation to political history see Dunning, *Lords of the Hills*.

[6] For a history of the Tah Itza or Peten Itza region, centered on its eventual conquest by Spaniards from Yucatan and Guatemala in the 1690s, see Jones, *Conquest*.

[7] This region is outside of the "cenote zone," described in n3 and n45. Precontact inhabitants developed rainwater storage systems known as chultuns and *aguadas*.

[8] In the precontact era, the entire region of the Peninsula, including the area south of the Puuc hills, was inhabited; it continued to be lightly inhabited after Spanish colonization of the northwest corner, with the label of "*desplobada*" being a misnomer masking the Spanish failure to colonize it.

Winter begins on the day of San Francisco,[9] and it lasts until the end of March, because during this season the northerly winds blow and *[f. 1v]* cause harsh colds and fevers, since the people are poorly dressed.[10]

Around the end of January and February there is a brief warm spell with a harsh sun, and it does not rain during this season except at the waxing of the moon.

The rains begin in April and last until the end of September, and during this season they plant all their crops [*cosas*], which mature even though it is always raining. They also sow a type of maize around the day of San Francisco, which is quickly harvested.

[Sec. 2] This province is called in the language of the Indians *u luumil cutz yetel ceh*, which is to say, "land of turkeys and deer."[11] They also called it *Peten*, which is to say, "island," misled by the aforementioned creeks and bays.[12]

When Francisco Hernández de Córdoba arrived in this land, landing at the headland that he called the cape of Cotoch [Cape Catoche], he found several Indian fishermen and asked them what land it was; and they replied "*cotoch*," which is to say, "our houses and our country [*patria*]," and for that reason he gave this name to that headland.[13] And asking them further by signs what that land of theirs was like, they replied

---

[9]   The feast day of St. Francis of Assisi is still held in the Catholic Ritual Calendar on October 4. See Butler's *Lives of the Saints*, 329.

[10] Spanish colonists frequently blamed illness on these winds, which they termed "*nortes*." See Solari, "Contagious Stench of Idolatry," 489–90; for more information on what the Maya called *kakas ik*, see Chuchiak, "*Ah Mak Ikob yetel Ah Pul Yahob*," 149–50.

[11] The Maya words "*Ulumilcuz*," "*Etelceh*," and "*Peten*" also appear in the left-hand margin, written by a copyist as a notation or marking of the unfamiliar Maya words. This Mayan phrase was no doubt written correctly, as above, in Landa's original manuscript, but the late-colonial copyist wrote it as "*ulumilcuz, y Etelceh*," betraying his unfamiliarity with Yucatec and with sixteenth-century paleography. The phrase does occasionally appear in the more literary colonial records written in Maya, such as the primordial titles (combined histories and land records; see Restall, *Maya World*, chap. 21; and *Maya Conquistador*, chaps. 3, 5, 6; Herrera also cites this probably taken from the Account, Herrera, *Historia general de los hechos de los castellanos*, vol. 4, Decada IV, Libro III, Capítulo IV; also see note 14). The element for "deer" also appears in some Yucatec toponyms, such as the town of Acanceh and the district of Cehpech.

[12] Landa here does the Mayas a disservice in assigning them the same ignorance as early-sixteenth-century Spaniards: *peten* means "region" or "province" and can also mean "island," but not exclusively so. Note that in several of the Spanish-language Mexican editions of the text, most of this paragraph is displaced and wrongly transcribed. For instance, in the Porrúa edition of Garibay, this paragraph is truncated, with one of the sentences of the original transcription missing; Garibay transcribes this section as "*Que esta provincia se llama en lengua de los indios Ullumil cutz ensenadas y bahias dichas*" (*Relación*, 4), thus leaving out the part that reads "*y Etel Ceh que quiere decir tierra de pavos y venados y que tambien le llamaron Peten que quiere decir isla enganados por las*." There are omissions and missing paragraphs similar to this throughout the edition, yet it remains the most-used Spanish-language edition.

[13] *Cotoch* or *ca otoch* does in fact mean "our home."

"*ciuthan*," which is to say, "they say so," and so the Spaniards named it *Yucatan*.[14] This was learned from one of the old conquistadors named Blas Hernández, who went with the adelantado [don Francisco de Montejo the elder] the first time.[15]

In the southern part of Yucatan there are the rivers of Tah Itza [*Taiza*] and the mountain ranges of Lacandon, and between the south and the west lies the province of Chiapas [*Chiapa*].[16] To reach it one must cross the four rivers that descend from the mountains and join others to make the San Pedro y San Pablo, the river discovered by Grijalva in Tabasco,[17] and to the west are Xicalango and Tabasco, which are one and the same province.

Between this province of Tabasco and Yucatan are the two mouths that break the seacoast,[18] the larger of which has a great opening while the other is not very large.

The sea enters through these mouths with such fury that it forms a great lagoon abundant with all kinds of fish, and so full of little islands that the Indians place signs on the trees to indicate the way to come or to go navigating between Tabasco and

---

[14] This is not a very satisfactory explanation for the naming of the peninsula, although it is possible that the Mayas were saying "*ca than*" or "*cu than*," meaning "our language" (in other words, imploring the Spaniards to "speak our language!"). The colonial Maya histories of the Pech dynasty, the Titles of Chicxulub and Yaxkukul, offer a more convincing version of the story (the following is translated from the Maya of the Yaxkukul manuscript): "Then they [the Mayas of Campeche] were asked by the Christians and the *adelantado*, in the Castilian language, 'Where do you live?' As they did not understand the language, they could only reply, 'We do not understand what you are saying [*matan cub a than*].' Because of these words, they said that this land here of the wild turkey, this land of the deer, was 'Yucatan'" (Restall, *Maya Conquistador*, 122). Gaspar Antonio Chi, via the "Relación de Mérida" in RHGY, records a version of the story, while colonial Spanish chroniclers also repeat versions (Cogolludo, *Historia de Yucathan*, Libro 2, Capítulo I; Herrera, *Historia general de los hechos de los castellanos*, vol. 1, Decada II, Libro II, Capítulo XVIII; Lizana, *Historia de Yucatán*, 2v). An alternative (or parallel) explanation is that the word is a Spanish truncation of *Yukal Peten* ("the whole province") or *Yokol Peten* ("[on] this province"), both of which appear in the Pech histories as the ancient name for Yucatan (Restall, *Maya Conquistador*, 121).

[15] The Account uses "the first time" to refer to the first of Montejo's multiple invasion expeditions or *entradas*, that of 1527–1528, described and discussed starting in Sec. 12, f. 9. Here too the author, like most early chroniclers of these events, conflates the first two *entradas*, combining them into one in Secs. 12–13, fs. 9v–10v, with the third and final *entrada* found in Secs. 13–14, fs. 10v–11v. See Restall, "Invasion: The Maya at War"; "Wars of Invasion"; Chuchiak, "Forgotten Allies"; "Conquista de Yucatán"; and Clendinnen, *Ambivalent Conquests*, 20–31. See also our discussion in chapter 1.

[16] These places are all labeled on the Account's maps (fs. 67–68; our figures 7.7–7.10).

[17] This river is imaged on both maps. On the roles played by Grijalva and Córdoba in the Spanish invasions of Yucatan, see Díaz, *Conquest of New Spain*, 15–43; Chamberlain, *Conquest and Colonization of Yucatan*; Clendinnen, *Ambivalent Conquests*, 4–19; Restall, *Maya Conquistador*, 6–8.

[18] These river mouths are also noted on the Account's maps, as "*dos bocas*."

Yucatan.[19] And these islands, and their beaches and sandbars, are filled with such a diversity of seabirds that it is a thing of wonder and beauty; there is also an infinite quantity of game in deer, rabbits, the swine of that land, and monkeys—which are not found in Yucatan.

There are an astonishing number of iguanas. And on one of them [the islands] there is a town [*pueblo*] that they call Tixchel.[20]

To the north is the island of Cuba, and at sixty leagues right opposite is Havana; somewhat further on is a little Cuban island that they call de Pinos [the Isle of Pines].

To the east is Honduras, and between Honduras and Yucatan [*f. 2r*] there is a very large stretch of sea which Grijalva named the Bay of the Ascension, and which is so full of small islands that ships get lost among them, mostly those of the trade from Yucatan to Honduras. About fifteen years ago a boat was lost there with so many people and clothes that they capsized the ship. Everyone was drowned save for a certain Majuelas and four others who clung to a large piece of the ship's mast; and they traveled thus for three or four days, unable to reach any of the little islands, until, their strength failing them, they drowned—except for Majuelas, who escaped half-dead and recovered by eating snails and mussels; and from the little island he reached land on a raft which he made as best he could from branches; having made it to the mainland, he was looking for food along the shore, when he came across a crab that bit off his thumb at the first joint and caused him great pain. He then took a path through the forest [*áspero monte*] towards the town of Salamanca [Bacalar]; and at night he climbed a tree and from there saw a large tiger ensnare a doe; and he saw it killed and the next morning he ate what had been left.[21]

Yucatan also has at Cozumel, below and opposite the headland of Cotoch, a five-league channel formed by the sea between it and the island, with a very strong current.

---

[19] Here the Account describes the brackish estuary and lagoon system of Acalan-Tixchel. On the manuscript's maps, the small islands are depicted by a series of small circles.

[20] Clearly labeled on the Account's two maps (figures 7.7–7.10), Tixchel was the one-time precontact capital and colonial head-town of the Chontal Maya region of Acalan-Tixchel, ruled from Postclassic to early colonial times by the Paxbolon dynasty. The Chontals first accommodated the Spaniards in 1525, when they received Hernándo Cortés and his expedition (en route to Honduras) and when the ruler Paxbolon fatally betrayed the fallen Mexica ruler Cuauhtemoc; over successive decades Acalan-Tixchel was gradually incorporated into New Spain (see Scholes and Roys, *Maya Chontal Indians of Acalan-Tixchel*; Smailus, *Maya-chontal de Acalan*; Izquierdo, *Acalán y la Chontalpa*, chap. I; and Restall, *Maya Conquistador*, chap. 3).

[21] Since tigers are not indigenous to the Americas, this large feline was likely a jaguar (Spanish accounts of this century tend to use *tigre* or *trigre* to refer to most of the wild cats of Mesoamerica). We have not encountered in the archives or other sources a record of this shipwreck that would confirm the story and date it; but if such a record were to be found, it would help indicate whether this passage was written in 1566 or not.

Cozumel is an island fifteen leagues long and five wide, where there are few Indians, and they have the language and customs of those of Yucatan; and it is at twenty degrees latitude.

The Isla de las Mujeres is thirteen leagues below the headland of Cotoch and two leagues off the mainland in front of Ekab.

[Sec. 3] The first Spaniards to arrive in Yucatan, they say, were Gerónimo de Aguilar, a native of Ecija, and his companions, who in the year 1511 left Darién due to the dispute [*las revueltas*] between Diego de Nicuesa and Vasco Núñez de Balboa. They followed [Juan de] Valdivia, who was going in a caravel to Santo Domingo, in order to inform the Admiral and Governor [don Diego Colón] as to what had happened; and to bring twenty thousand ducats of gold for the King. This caravel, upon arriving off Jamaica, came upon the shoals that are called Las Víboras, where it was lost.[22] Only twenty men escaped with Valdivia in a raft without sails, and with some broken oars and without any supplies, they were adrift for thirteen days in the open sea; and after almost half of them died from hunger, they reached the coast of Yucatan, to a province "of the Maya," as they called it; the language of Yucatan is called *mayathan*, which is to say, "the Maya language."[23]

These poor people came into the hands of an evil cacique,[24] who sacrificed Valdivia

---

[22] The "twenty thousand ducats of gold" was the Crown's royal fifth from the conquest and exploration of Panama and the province of Darién. Vasco Nuñez de Balboa sent the gold and Capitan Juan de Valdivia in order to "bribe" the Crown and its royal officials to support his claim to the province. Unfortunately for Valdivia, Aguilar, and Balboa, the ship sank. Ironically, the Crown, not receiving its royal fifth, issued Pedro Arias Davila, the governor of Panama, an arrest warrant for Vasco Nuñez de Balboa; Davila subsequently executed Balboa. Aguilar's shipwreck and the loss of the treasure thus directly led to the beheading of the famous discoverer of the Pacific Ocean. Juan de Valdivia was also one of the most important officers of the Balboa expedition, also participating in the discovery and conquest of the Darién region. For a more detailed description of the events, especially involving the dispute between Balboa and Nicuesa, and the roles of Aguilar and Valdivia, see Martir de Angleria, *Decadas del Nuevo Mundo*, Tomo I, 221–330; also see Cervantes de Salazar, *Cronica de la Nueva España*, Tomo II, caps. XXV–XXXIX, 110–22. For more specific information on Aguilar, Valdivia, and the shipwreck's impact on the fate of Balboa, see Butterfield, *Jerónimo de Aguilar*; Herrera y Tordesillas, *General History*, 3–11, 170–85; Oviedo y Valdés, *Historia general de las Indias*, Vol. III, 160–90, 403–20; Las Casas, *Historia de las Indias*, Tomo III, 265–75. Also see various other books on the history of Panama and Balboa, including Verrill, *Great Conquerors*; and Parry, *Discovery of South America*, 114–36.

[23] The author is here correct in his translation of *mayathan; than* means "language" or "word" in Yucatec Mayan.

[24] The term "cacique" was appropriated early in Spanish colonial history from the Taíno term *kasike*, meaning "chieftain": Spaniards applied it to local Indigenous rulers throughout the Americas.

and four others to their idols,[25] and then made feasts of them for the people, keeping
Aguilar and [Gonzalo de] Guerrero and five or six others, in order to fatten them up;[26]
and these broke out of their prison and fled into the bush [*unos montes*],[27] and they
fell into the hands of another [*f. 2v*] lord, an enemy of the first and more merciful,[28]
who used them as slaves. The one who succeeded this lord treated them with kindness, but all the rest died from depression [*dolencia*], leaving only two, Gerónimo
de Aguilar and Gonzalo Guerrero. Of these, Aguilar was the good Christian and
had a book of hours by which he knew the feast days; and he was saved by the arrival
of the Marquis Hernando Cortés, in the year 1518 [1519],[29] while Guerrero, since he

---

[25] Throughout our translation we have transcribed the term "idol" from the Spanish *ídolo*, but
we recognize that this term is insufficient to relay the full scope and sophistication of precontact religious belief. The "idols" to which the author refers are three-dimensional sculptures
of various deities, essentially effigies, which often simultaneously functioned as incense
braziers. For more on this genre of artistic production see Solari, *Idolizing Mary*, 38–49; also
see Chuchiak, "*De Descriptio Idolorum*," 135–41; and *El castigo y la represión*, 41–58.

[26] We believe that this accusation of Maya cannibalism does not reflect actual practice—for
which there is no direct evidence and, indeed, no indirect evidence beyond Spanish prejudicial stereotypes regarding "Indians" (see Enríquez, "Exuberant Imagination," for example).

[27] The chronicler Fernando Cervantes y Salazar (Book II, Chapter XXVI), consulting various
relaciones de méritos y servicios of Aguilar and his daughter, wrote that Aguilar recounted
"I, together with six others, remained in a coop, in order that for another festival that was
approaching, being fatter, we might solemnize their banquet with our flesh ... We broke the
cage in which we had been placed and fled through the forest." Gerónimo de Aguilar, his
daughter Luisa, and his brother Juan de Aguilar all compiled several important *Relación de
méritos y servicios*, confirming details of his merits (see *Información de los méritos y servicios
de Jerónimo de Aguilar, que salió de Écija con don Diego Colón, y fue con Diego de Nicuesa al
descubrimiento y población de Tierra Firme, 1520*, in AGI, Patronato, 150; and *Información
de los méritos y servicios de Luisa de Aguilar, incluye también los méritos de su padre Jerónimo
de Aguilar en la conquista de Nueva España que fue intérprete para con los indios de México*,
1581, in AGI, Patronato, 78A). The Aguilar quote is evidence of Spanish belief in Indigenous
cannibalism, of course, not of the practice itself. Cogolludo (*Historia de Yucathan*, Libro 1,
Capítulo VIII), writing in the succeeding century, also reports that Valdivia and others were
"sacrificed," although Díaz just has them being killed or dying of disease (*Conquest of New
Spain*, 64–65). According to some chroniclers and Aguilar himself, two women also survived
the shipwreck and made it alive to the Yucatec coast. Herrera, for example, remarked that
"the two Spanish women were forced to grind corn into meal ... one of the women, who was
rumored to be the wife of an hidalgo, died not long after for she was not accustomed to the
hard work" (Herrera, *Historia general de los hechos de los castellanos*, 175).

[28] According to the later *Relación de los méritos y servicios de Gerónimo de Aguilar* (AGI,
Patronato, 78A), Aguilar stated that the Maya lord's name was Ah Kin Cutz, and he was the
cacique (in Maya, the *batab*) of the town of Xamanzama (perhaps the town later known as
Zama). Also see Butterfield, *Jerónimo de Aguilar*; Roys, *Political Geography*, 162.

[29] The Account (and a handful of English translations) mistakenly has Cortés reaching Yucatan
in 1518, not 1519; see Restall, *When Montezuma Met Cortés*, 161–71, and numerous other

understood the language, went to Chetumal,[30] which is now Salamanca [de Bacalar] of Yucatan. There he was received by a lord named Nachan Can, who gave him control over matters of war. In this he excelled, many times defeating the enemies of his lord. He taught the Indians to fight, showing them how to build forts and defenses. In this way, and by acting as an Indian, he won a great reputation; and they married him to a very high-ranking woman with whom he had children; and because of this he never tried to procure his salvation, as did Aguilar. Instead, he tattooed his body, grew out his hair, and pierced his ears in order to wear earrings like the Indians, and it is likely that he was an idolater like them.[31]

In the year 1517, during Lent, Francisco Hernández de Córdoba left Santiago de Cuba with three ships in order to collect [Indian] slaves for the mines, since in Cuba the people were becoming scarce; others say he left in order to discover new lands.[32] He took as his pilot [Antón de] Alaminos and arrived at the Isla de las Mujeres, giving the island its name for the idols he found there of the goddesses of that land, such as Aixchel,[33] Ixchebeliax, Ixbunic, Ixbunieta,[34] and they were dressed

---

studies of the Spanish-Aztec War or "Conquest of Mexico."

[30] The manuscript records this town as "Chectemal." Citing Lothrop, Tozzer argues that this town was probably located between the mouths of the Rio Hondo and the New River (Rio Zuluinic) (Tozzer, *Landa's* Relación, 8n36), in what is today northern Belize.

[31] Some of these anecdotal details about Guerrero are also included in Oviedo's *Historia general y natural de las Indias*, Vol. 2, Part 2, Book 32, Chapter 3, 232–33; also see Clendinnen, *Ambivalent Conquests*, 17–22; Restall, *Maya Conquistador*, 7, 180n8. While we might reasonably accept the basic elements of the story (that Guerrero willingly married into a local elite family), we should be suspicious of its condescending colonialist details (e.g., Guerrero—which means "fighter"—portrayed as a better warrior than all the Maya, friend or foe).

[32] The most complete account of the voyage collected from the writings of the early colonial chroniclers and other material is found in Saville, *Discovery of Yucatan*.

[33] No doubt Landa is referring to the Maya goddess Ix Chel, though the masculine prefix "A" is confusing in this case. Landa would know better than to use the masculine prefix for a goddess, so this error likely comes from another author or a copyist. Concerning the idols and the goddess Ix Chel, she was believed by the Maya to be the goddess of healing and childbirth. Concerning the pilgrimages and shrines to the goddess Ix Chel, see *Carta del gobernador de Yucatán, Francisco de Solis, sobre las ydolatrías de los yndios de la ysla de cozumel*, 11 de marzo, 1584, in AGI, México, 359, 4 folios; Ardren, "Mending the Past"; Palka, *Maya Pilgrimage to Ritual Landscape*; Patel, "Caves and Pilgrimage"; and Chuchiak, "Caves of Life," 82–84.

[34] According to Díaz (*Conquest of New Spain*, 66), this island was not discovered and named by Spaniards until Cortés landed there in 1519. However, there is indeed a reference to a landing on what appears to be Isla Mujeres during the Grijalva expedition, chronicled by the chaplain of the expedition, Juan Diaz, who records in his *Itinerario de la Armada* that they came to an island or point "*y anduvimos por la costa, donde encontramos una muy hermosa torre en una punta, la que se dice ser habitada por mujeres que viven sin hombres*" (4). A full discussion of this issue is in Saville, *Discovery of Yucatan*, 436–47. As for the images of Maya goddesses

from the waist down, with their breasts covered in the style of the Indian women. The building [housing the effigies] was made out of stone, which astonished them, and they found within it several things made of gold,[35] which they took. They then arrived at the headland of Cotoch and from there they turned back as far as the bay of Campeche, where they disembarked on the Sunday of St. Lazarus,[36] and because of this they called it Lázaro. There they were well received by the lord, and the Indians were astonished to see the Spaniards, and they touched their beards and their bodies.

In Campeche they found a building in the sea, close to land, square and completely terraced, and at the top of the building there was an idol with two fierce animals devouring its flanks and a large fat serpent made from stone that was swallowing a lion, and the animals were covered in the blood of sacrifices.[37]

---

reportedly discovered there, what Landa records as a variety of goddesses have unfortunately become subsumed in both academic and popular literature into the name *Ixchel*, who is widely referred to as the Maya goddess of childbirth, healing, and the moon. Careful review of the multiple sixteenth-century Spanish sources that mention a shrine on Cozumel shows that none of the early sources mention an association with the moon, only with childbirth and healing; see Ardren, "Mending the Past." None of these early accounts were accessible to the general intellectual community until after the late nineteenth century, when Landa's work was published for the first time. The association of *Ixchel* (and all the other goddess names mentioned by Landa in his description of Cozumel) with the moon was first suggested by the infamous Mayanist J. Eric S. Thompson, who in 1939 published a study entitled *The Moon Goddess in Middle America*. In this iconographic study of Mexican and Maya codices, Thompson stated that the Maya were "profoundly influenced by Mexican concepts even before the development of their specialized art and writing" (127). Despite the absence of any mention in any Spanish source for an association between Ixchel and the moon, Thompson drew analogies to Aztec moon goddesses and used a modern Mopan Maya myth describing the Moon as the wife of the Sun, to ascribe to Ixchel an association with the moon. He went on to conflate the various female deities mentioned by Landa and other Spanish sources into variations of a single moon goddess. These errors were repeated in his popular volume (still in print today) *Maya History and Religion*, and in the highly influential Spanish translation of the book, where he chose to illustrate his discussion of a universal moon goddess with a young earth goddess figure from the Dresden codex, now known as Ikik-Cab; see Vail and Stone, "Representations of Women." Although incorrect, Thompson's ideas were in keeping with intellectual trends of his time—between 1940 and 1960, many significant English intellectual contemporaries of Thompson, such as Jacquetta Hawkes and Gordon Childe, would offer interpretations of archaeological materials that relied upon the concept of a unifying great goddess cult. For additional information on these precontact deities see Knowlton, "Filth and Healing in Yucatán."

[35] Although we have no direct evidence of the gold artifacts taken from Isla Mujeres, precontact shrines on this island share typical Late Postclassic artifacts, which often include bells made of *tumbaga*, or gold mixed with copper. *Tumbaga* artifacts were produced at Mayapan (Paris, "Metallurgy").

[36] This would have been Sunday, February 23, 1517.

[37] The Account has *leon*, "lion," but the more accurate English term for this kind of large cat

[*Que*]³⁸ From Campeche they learned that there was a large town nearby, which was Champoton. Upon their arrival they discovered that the lord of the town was called Moch Couoh, a warlike man who called out his people against the Spaniards.³⁹ Francisco Hernández was distraught at this, seeing what was going to happen. In order not to reveal *[f. 3r]* his low morale, he also placed his men in order and had the artillery fire from the ships; and although the noise, smoke, and fire from the guns was new to the Indians, this did not stop them from attacking with great howls; and the Spaniards resisted, inflicting terrible wounds and killing many. But the lord so encouraged them [his people] that they forced the Spaniards to retreat, and they killed twenty, wounded fifty, and captured two alive whom they later sacrificed; and Francisco Hernández himself

---

in Yucatan is "jaguar." Rather than "swallowing a lion," it is more likely that this building housed architectural sculpture of a deified ancestor emerging from a serpent's mouth, a common trope in the precontact Maya world, associated with the pan-Mesoamerican cult of Quetzacoatl or Kukulcan, best known from the site of Chichen Itza. The building's location is easily explained by the enormous length of the tides on the coast at Campeche, whose vast mudflats at low tide are covered by shallow water at high tide. Based on recent research by William Folan and colleagues, this "structure in the sea" is likely a small island off the Classic-period site of Chakanputun, now largely buried under the modern city of Champoton; see Folan, Bolles, and Ek, "On the Trail of Quetzalcoatl/Kukulcan"; and Folan et al., "Chakanputun, Campeche 3,000 Años de Sustentabilidad." Many islands off Campeche were occupied in the Classic period, some with large architectural complexes that recall Landa's description of a square and terraced building. In the Terminal Classic and Postclassic period, a temple much like those on the east coast of Yucatan may have been built on the island site off Chakanputun, as part of the network of sites linked by the trade-based cult of Quetzalcoatl. During the 1950s, Edwin Shook and Tatiana Proskouriakoff visited Champoton and saw a small island off the Río Champoton with cut stone and other rubble remains of a structure; a few years later, Mexican archaeologist Alberto Ruz Lhuillier visited the same island and suggested it was the one mentioned by Landa (Ruz Lhuillier, *La costa de Campeche en los tiempos prehispánicos*). Jerald Ek confirms the island and architectural remains are still visible today in the bay off Champoton. Much of the carved stone Landa describes was repurposed in Champoton's colonial era. Note that this fantastical description was repeated in various accounts of the time, of which this was not the first and thus certainly not authored by Landa; it was also the basis for an even more fantastical engraving used in publications in multiple European languages for centuries.

³⁸ In the original manuscript, this section begins with a "*que*" indicating that the author was changing topic; the copyist mistakenly forgot to insert a line break after the previous sentence, so this section is simply a portion of the previous paragraph. We have included the omitted line break.

³⁹ The original reads *hombre belicoso el qual apellido su gente*; Garibay took the liberty in his Spanish edition of omitting the phrase "*el qual apellido su gente*" and adding a phrase of his own invention, "*el señor se llamaba Mochcouoh, hombre belicoso que lanzó*" right before "*su gente contra los españoles*" (*Relación*, 7).

emerged with thirty-three wounds and thus returned sadly to Cuba, where he announced that the land was very good and rich due to the gold found on the Isla de Mujeres.⁴⁰

This news prompted Diego Velázquez, the governor of Cuba, and many others, to send his nephew Juan de Grijalva with four ships and two hundred men; and with him went Francisco de Montejo, who had one of the ships, and they departed on the first of May 1518.⁴¹

They took along with them the same pilot, [Antón de] Alaminos, and they arrived at the island of Cozumel [*Cuzmil*], from which the pilot saw Yucatan.⁴² Because on the previous occasion, with Francisco Hernández, he had run along the right-hand side, he wanted to sail around it to see if it was an island, so he made a left-hand turn. They followed the bay, which they named the Ascension because on that day they entered it.⁴³ They then returned along the entire coast until arriving again at Champoton, where, while taking water, they [the Mayas] killed a man and they wounded fifty, among them Grijalva, from two arrows, and they shattered one and half of his teeth. And thus, they left, naming that port "The Port of the Bad Fight" [*Puerto de la Mala Pelea*]. On that voyage they discovered New Spain, and Panuco, and Tabasco, and to do this they spent five months. And they wanted to make landfall at Champoton, which the Indians denied them with such courage that in their canoes they came as far as the caravels to shoot arrows at them, and because of this they [the Spaniards] made sail and left them.⁴⁴

⁴⁰ See our chapter 1 in part II for brief discussion of this encounter and other episodes in the history of the Spanish invasions of Yucatan.

⁴¹ The Account is in error here; the expedition did not leave Cuba on May 1, 1518, but rather on April 8, 1518. Grijalva's *Itinerario* correctly states that they left on April 8, and came to the Island of Cozumel on May 3, 1518, the day of the Holy Cross. For that reason, the Spaniards earlier gave the island of Cozumel the name *Santa Cruz*. The four captains of the four Velázquez-owned ships were Grijalva himself, Montejo, and their fellow encomenderos on Cuba, Alonso de Avila and Pedro de Alvarado; the latter three went on to play major roles in Spanish conquests on the mainland. The documents of the Grijalva expedition were written by the notary and chaplain of the expedition and later published. The first publication occurred in García Icazbalceta's *Colección de documentos para la historia de Mexico*, 281 onward. For a more modern version, see Grijalva, *Itinerario de la armada del rey católico a la isla de Yucatán*.

⁴² The text here omits an episode recorded by Díaz, *Conquest of New Spain*, 28–29, in which Grijalva, Díaz, and some others went ashore but failed to make contact with the local Mayas, who had prudently fled their town. The Spaniards sent messages with two Maya men captured the previous year by Hernández; the Maya did not return, but there appeared instead an Indigenous woman from the island of Jamaica (presumably a Taíno), whom the Spaniards promptly seized and took with them.

⁴³ That date being May 3, 1518.

⁴⁴ Díaz states that seven men were killed, sixty wounded, and Grijalva received three arrow wounds, losing two teeth (*Conquest of New Spain*, 29–30).

When Grijalva returned from his discovery and trade in Tabasco and Ulua,[45] the great captain Hernando Cortés was in Cuba; and hearing the news of so much land and so many riches, he desired to see them and to win them for God and for his King, for himself, and for his friends.

[Sec. 4] [f. 3v; fig. A.1] Hernando Cortés left Cuba with eleven ships, of which the greatest was of one hundred tons.[46] And he placed on them eleven captains, himself being one of them. He brought five hundred men and some horses and merchandise for trade, and Francisco de Montejo, and the aforementioned pilot, Alaminos, chief pilot of the fleet. He put on the leading ship a flag with white and blue flames in honor of Our Lady, whose image, along with the cross, he always placed wherever he removed idols. On the flag there was a red cross with lettering around it, saying: *amici sequamur crucem, & si nos habuerimus fidem in hoc signo vincemus* ("Friends, let us follow the cross, and if we have faith in this sign, we will conquer!").

With this fleet and no other equipment, he set off and arrived at Cozumel [*Cuzmil*] with ten of the ships, because the other had been separated from him due to a quarrel [*refriega*], and he later caught up to it on the coast.[47] The arrival at Cozumel was on the north side, where he found good stone buildings for the idols and a fine town [*pueblo*];[48] and the people, seeing so many ships and the soldiers making landfall, all fled into the bush [*monte*].[49]

---

[45] San Juan Ulúa was the name Spaniards gave to a fort and island located near Vera Cruz, in Tabasco. According to Díaz, the Spaniards picked up the word from a local native man saying "Culua" ("But as he was slovenly in his speech he said, 'Ulua, Ulua' "; *Conquest of New Spain*, 38); *Culhua* was a name that Maya and other Mesoamericans called the Mexica or Aztecs (see Restall, *Maya Conquistador*, 87, 206–7).

[46] Díaz also states that there were eleven ships, giving the date of departure as February 10, 1519 (*Conquest of New Spain*, 57).

[47] The Porrúa transcription changed *refriega* to *tormenta* (Garibay, *Relación*, 9), thus inventing the ship being separated in a storm, and all subsequent English editions followed suit. But the text is clear: the problem was a spat of some kind, and indeed Bernal Díaz offers a possible explanation. According to him, "the ship commanded by Francisco de Morla had lost a rudder in bad weather, and it had to be provided with another from one of the other ships"; meanwhile "the pilot Camacho, who was in charge of our ship, paid no attention to Cortés' orders and went his own way, so that we arrived at Cozumel two days before Cortés" (*Conquest of New Spain*, 57). The *refriega* was thus between Cortés and Camacho.

[48] Today we know this Maya town is the site of Xamancab, renamed by the Spaniards San Miguel Xamancab, today known as San Miguel de Cozumel. For recent research on the archaeological sites of Cozumel see Batun, "Agrarian Production and Intensification."

[49] The events of the following six paragraphs—Cortés's sojourn on Cozumel—are recounted in greater detail by Díaz (*Conquest of New Spain*, 57–66) and by Cortés himself (in the letter "authored" in Vera Cruz by his associates; Pagden, *Hernán Cortés*, 11–17). It is likely that the author of the Account had read Cortés's letter, which had first been published in the 1520s and was widely available by 1550 (Restall, *When Montezuma Met Cortés*, 6–7).

Having reached the town, the Spaniards sacked it and took up their lodging in it; and searching for people in the bush, they came across the wife of the lord with her children; from whom they understood, through Melchor, the Indian interpreter who had been with Francisco Hernández and with Grijalva,[50] that she was the lord's wife. Cortés gave her and her children many gifts, and made them call for the lord, who, upon his arrival, was treated very well; he [Cortés] gave him some presents, returned to him his wife and children and all the things that had been taken in the town. And he urged him to make the Indians return to their homes, and when they came, he had each one given back whatever was his. And having thus reassured them, he preached to them on the vanity of their idols, and persuaded them to venerate the cross, and he placed it in their temples with an image of Our Lady; and thus, did public idolatry cease.[51]

There Cortés learned that some bearded men were in the power of a lord some six suns' [days'] journey away, and he persuaded the Indians to go and summon them; there was one who would go, although with some difficulty, because they were afraid of the lord of the bearded ones. He wrote them the following letter:

Noble sirs: I left Cuba with a fleet of eleven ships and five hundred Spaniards, and I arrived here, in Cozumel, from where I write [f. 4r; fig. A.2] you this letter. Those of this island have assured me that there are in this land five or six bearded men who are in every way very similar to us. They cannot give me other details, but from these I conjecture and feel certain that you are Spaniards. I and these noblemen who come with me to settle and discover these lands, we urge you to come to us without any delay or excuse within six days of receiving this. If you come, we shall acknowledge and reward the good services which this fleet will receive from you. I send a brigantine in which you may come, accompanied by two ships for security.[52]

---

[50]   Although Díaz confirms the role played here by Melchor, the Maya captured in 1517 by Hernández, he also states earlier in his account that Grijalva sent Melchor into the interior of Cozumel in 1518 and he never returned (Díaz, *Conquest of New Spain*, 28, 58).

[51]   Despite Cortés's desires, it is highly unlikely that any of the Mayas he contacted in Yucatan immediately adopted Christianity and stopped traditional religious practices, such as the production and ritualization of effigy figures. An abundance of scholarship exists on processes in Indigenous evangelism, but for the Maya in particular, see Early, *Maya and Catholicism*; Christensen, *Nahua and Maya Catholicisms*; Solari, *Maya Ideologies of the Sacred*; Chuchiak, "Indian Inquisition," 51–79; *El castigo y la represión*.

[52]   As figures A.1–2 (fs. 3v–4r) show, the letter is written in a different hand than the surrounding text (reflected in the font shift in our translation), and it was likely added after the rest of the manuscript had been copied. There is no suggestion in any of the sources that Cortés kept a copy of his letter, and it is thus very unlikely that the author of the Account had a copy.

The Indians carried this letter wrapped up in their hair, and delivered it to Aguilar; and the ships, because the Indians lingered beyond the deadline, thought that they were dead and returned to the harbor of Cozumel. Cortés, seeing that neither the Indians nor the bearded men had returned, set sail the next day. But that day one of the ships sprung a leak and obliged them to return to port; and as they were repairing her, Aguilar, having received the letter, crossed the channel between Yucatan and Cozumel in a canoe; and as he approached, those of the fleet went to see who he was, and Aguilar asked them if they were Christians, and when they replied yes, and Spaniards too, he wept for joy, and kneeling on the ground, gave thanks to God, and asked the Spaniards if it was Wednesday.[53]

The Spaniards took him, all naked as he came, to Cortés, who clothed him and showed him great affection; and Aguilar then told of his losses and his travails, and the death of his companions, and how it was impossible to notify Guerrero in so short a time, as he lived more than eighty leagues from there.

With the help of this Aguilar, who was a very good interpreter, Cortés returned to preaching the worship of the cross and removed the idols from the temples. It is said that this preaching of Cortés made such an impression on those of Cuzco [Cozumel][54] that they went out on the beach, calling out to the Spaniards who passed by, "María, María, Cortés, Cortés."

Cortés left there, touched in passing at Campeche, but did not stop until Tabasco, where, among other things and Indian women which those of Tabasco presented to

---

Although the general gist of the missive is clear enough, oral tradition must have produced various versions. Indeed, Díaz offers this one: "Gentlemen and brothers, here in Cozumel I have heard that you are captives in the hands of a cacique. I beg you to come to this place at once, and for this purpose have sent a ship with soldiers, in case you need them, also a ransom to be given to those Indians with whom you are living. The ship will wait for you eight days. Come as quickly as you can, and you will be welcomed and looked after by me. I am staying at this island with five hundred soldiers, and eleven ships in which I am going, please God, to a town called Tabasco or Champoton" (Díaz, *Conquest of New Spain*, 60).

[53] Again, at the start of this paragraph—and at the start of the subsequent two paragraphs—the copyist omitted intended line breaks, indicated in the original by a *Que* at the start of each paragraph.

[54] That the original text has *cuzco* (Peru) suggests that the copyist was gleaning this information from a source that also included accounts of the conquest wars between the Spaniards and the Inka, whose imperial capital was Cuzco. Likely candidates are López de Gómara's *La Istoria de las Yndias*, and Oviedo's *Historia general*, as both included synthesized accounts of the "conquests" of both viceroyalties of New Spain and Peru; the mythologizing here of Cortés as a preacher closely follows López de Gómara's hagiographic account. Note that none of the Spanish editions of the Account include the original "*cuzco*" in their transcriptions or notes (for example, see Pérez Martínez, *Relación*, 64; Garibay, *Relación*, 10).

him, they gave him an Indian woman who was afterwards named Marina.[55] She was from Jalisco [*Xalisco*], the daughter of noble parents, and had been stolen when she was little and sold in Tabasco, and from there she had also been sold in Xicalango and Champoton, where she had learned the Yucatecan language. By this means she came to understand Aguilar; and *[f. 4v]* thus, God provided Cortés with good and faithful interpreters, whereby he came to have news of and access to the affairs of Mexico, of which Marina knew much, from having talked with Indian merchants and élites who daily spoke of them.[56]

[Sec. 5] Some of the old men of Yucatan say that they have heard from their ancestors that this land was populated by certain people who came from the east, whom God delivered by opening for them twelve roads through the sea. If this were true, it necessarily follows that all of the peoples of the Indies are descended from the Jews,[57] because after passing through the Straits of Magellan they must

---

[55] The oft-repeated notion (see Tozzer, *Landa's* Relación, 16, for example) that *Marina* was derived from a Nahuatl name, *Malinal*, is not borne out by the evidence. Tens (perhaps hundreds) of thousands of Indigenous women and girls were given, exchanged, and sold as slaves in the sixteenth-century wars of Spanish invasion in the Caribbean, Mexico, and Central America, often preteens or teens (Marina was twelve or thirteen when given to Cortés in 1519) forced into sexual slavery (Restall, *When Montezuma Met Cortés*, 287–93, 305–11, 363; Chuchiak, "Human Plunder," 15–20). They were simply given Spanish names, without consideration of what their native names might have been; Marina was no different, until her skills as an interpreter permitted her social mobility, after which she was called doña Marina, the Nahuatl equivalent of which was *Malintzin* (Nahuas transposed the Spanish *r* and *l* sounds, and *-tzin* was a reverential suffix akin to the don or doña title); Spaniards in turn heard *Malinztin* as *Malinche*.

[56] Doña Marina, or Malintzin, went on to play a major role in Cortés's conquest of central Mexico—and to become a major cultural icon in Mexican history and in modern historiography; Cypess, *La Malinche in Mexican Literature*; Karttunen, "Rethinking Malinche"; Karttunen, *Between Worlds*, 1–23, 305–7; Townsend, *Malintzin's Choices*.

[57] According to Phelan, the myth that the "Indians were the descendants of the ten lost tribes of Israel" became prevalent among the early Franciscan missionaries; fray Geronimo de Mendieta, for example, a prominent proponent of the theory, believed that their "vague knowledge" of the great flood, as well as their conception of the Aztec god Quetzalcoatl as a promised savior who would return, gave evidence of Ancient Jewish origins (*Millennial Kingdom*, 24–25; also see Davis, "Evangelical Prophecies"). This theory of Jewish origins grew deeper roots as Franciscan belief and missiology took on an apocalyptic tone in the sixteenth century, while among Dominican friars the theory continued into the seventeenth century—with its greatest defender being fray Gregorio García, who wrote a defense of it in his 1607 *Origen de los indios de el nuevo mundo*. Other contemporaries, however, such as the Jesuit José de Acosta, called the notion of the Indians as the lost tribes a "frivolous conjecture" for which the negative evidence was overwhelming (*Historia*, 87–88). Franciscans of the later seventeenth century, like fray Juan de Torquemada, attempted to correct these earlier conjectures about Indigenous origins; Torquemada dedicated an entire chapter to

Que Hernando Cortez salio de cuba con onze navios que el mayor era de cien toneles y que puso
en ellos onze capitanes siendo el uno dellos y que
llevava quinientos hombres y algunos cavallos
y mercerias para rescatar y a Francisco de montejo por capitan y al dicho pedro alaminos mayor
piloto del armada y que puso en su nao capitana
una vandera de fuegos blancos y azules en reverencia de nuestra Señora cuya ymagen con la cruz po-
nia siempre donde quitava idolos y que en la vandera iva una cruz colorada con un letrero en latin q dezia amici sequamur cruzem, &, si nos
habueimus fidem in hoc signo vinceimus.
Que con esta flota y no mas aparato partio, y que
llego a Cuzmil con los diez navios porq el uno se le
aparto con una refriega y que despues le cobro en
la costa. Que la llegada a Cuzmil fue por la parte del norte y hallo buenos edificios de piedra para
los idolos y un buen pueblo, y que la gente viendo
tanta armada y salir los soldados a tierra huyo toda
a los montes.
Que llegados los Españoles al pueblo le saquearon
y se aposentaron en el y que buscando gente por
el monte toparon con la muger del señor y
con sus hijos de los quales con Melchior interprete Indio que avia ido con Francisco Hernandez
y con Grijalva entendieron que era la muger
del sr a la qual y a sus hijos regalo mucho Cortez
y hizo que embiassen a llamar al sr al qual
venido le trato muy bien y le dio algunos done-
zillos, y le entrego a su muger y hijos, y todas
las cosas que por el pueblo se avian tomado, y q
le rogo que hiziesse venir los Indios a sus casas
y que venidos hizo restituir a cada uno lo que
era suyo y despues de assegurados les predico
la vanidad de los idolos, y les persuadio que no los
casen la cruz, y que la puso en sus templos, co
una ymagen de nuestra señora y que con esto cesso
alla la idolatria publica.
Que Cortez supo alli como unos hombres barbados estavan camino de seis soles en poder de
un señor y que persuadio a los Indios que se
los fuessen a llamar, y que hallo quien fuesse
aunq con difficultad porq tenian miedo al señor
de los barbados. y escrivioles esta carta
Nobles sres. yo parti de cuba con onze navios de armada, y
quinientos Españoles, y llegue aqui a Cuzmil de donde os
escrivo

escriuo esta carta. Los desta isla me han certificado
que ay con esta tierra cinco o seis hombres barbados, y en todo a nosotros muy semejantes no me saben dar ni dezir
otras señas mas por estas conjeturas, y tengo por cierto
sois Españoles yo, y estos hidalgos que comigo vienen a po
blar y descubrir estas tierras os rogamos mucho que den
tro de seis dias que recibieredes esta os vengais para noso
tros sin poner otra dilacion ni escusa. Si viniéredes todos
conoceremos, y gratificaremos la buena obra q̃ de nosotros
recibira esta armada. Vn vergantin embio para en que
vengais, y dos naos para seguridad.   Que los Indios
llevaron esta carta enbuelta en el cabello, y la dieron
a Aguilar, y que los navios porque tardavan mas los
Indios mas del tiempo del plazo crecieren que los
aruian muerto y que se boluieron al puerto de
Cozumil y que Cortez viendo que los Indios no tor
navan ni los barbados se hizo otro dia a la vela,
mas aquel dia se les abrio vn navio y les fue necessa
rio tornar al puerto y que estando le adereçando
Aguilar recebida la carta atravesso en vna canoa
Con ciertos entre yucatan y cuzmil y que oviendo
te los del armada fueron a ver quien era y que
Aguilar les pregunto si eran Christianos y que res
pondiendo le q̃ si y Españoles lloro de plazer, y puestas
las rodillas en tierra dio gracias a Dios y pregun
to a los Españoles si era miercoles. Que los Espa
ñoles lo llevaron a Cortez assi desnudo como venia
al qual le vistio y mostro amorosso amor, y que
Aguilar conto alli su perdida, y trabajos, y la mu
erte de sus compañeros, y como q̃ de imposible
avisar a Guerrero en tan poco tiempo por estar
mas de LXXX leguas de alli.   Que vso
este Aguilar que era muy buen interprete
como Cortez a predicar la adoracion de la Cruz
y a quitar los idolos de los templos, y dizen que hizo
esta predicacion de Cortez tanta impression en
los del Cozoto que salian a la playa diziendo a los
Españoles q̃ por alli passavan maria maria
Cortez Cortez
Que partio Cortez de alli, y que toco de passo en Cam
peche y no paro hasta Tavasco donde entre otras co
sas y Indias que le presentaron los de Tavasco le
dieron vna India que despues se llamo marina
la qual era de xalisco hija de padres nobles, y hur
tada pequeña, y vendida en Tavasco y que de
ay la vendieron tambien en Xicalango, y Champ
poton, donde aprendio la lengua de yucatan con
la qual se vino a entender con Aguilar, y que

have spread out over more than two thousand leagues of land which today Spain governs.

The language of this entire land is all one, which was a great advantage for their conversion, although along the coasts there are several differences in vocabulary and in the tone of speech. Therefore, those of the coast are more polished in their manners and language, and the women there cover up their breasts, while those who live more inland do not.[58]

This land is divided into provinces subjected to the Spanish towns to which they are closest. The province of Chetumal [*Chectemal*] and Bacalar [*Bachalal*] is subject to Salamanca; the provinces of Ecab [*Ekab*] and Cochuah and that of Cupul [*Kupul*] are subject to Valladolid. That of Ah Kin Chel and Izamal [*Yzamal*], that of Sotuta [*Zotuta*], that of Hocaba and Homun [*Hocabaihumun*], that of Tutul Xiu [*Tutuxiu*], that of Ceh Pech and that of Chakan are subject to the city of Merida. Those [provinces] of Canul [*Camol*], Campech, Champoton [*Champutun*], and Tixchel are assigned to San Francisco de Campeche.

In Yucatan there are many buildings of great beauty, which is the most remarkable thing that has been discovered in the Indies. All are made of masonry that

refuting them (Torquemada and Portilla, *Monarquía Indiana*, Libro I, Capítulo IX, 36–43), dismantling earlier missionaries' contentions with his counterarguments. It appears that Landa, even though he hesitantly mentions the theory here, later disagreed with it; he took Oviedo to task over his misunderstanding of Maya penis-sacrifice rituals (the so called *xicin poy*) as a type of circumcision, a rite that many of the earlier friars saw as a Jewish remnant among Indigenous groups (see Account, Sec. 26, ff. 20r–21r; Sec. 28, ff. 22v–23r; Sec. 52, f. 66r; Chuchiak, "Colonial Maya Religion," 57).

58 Spaniards associated clothing with civilization, and here the author is judging a possible difference in clothing styles that, if it did exist, was more likely based on climate (the Yucatec coasts can be breezy). He then transfers that judgment onto perceived dialectal differences in the language, although the notion that one dialect can be more "polished" (*pulidos*) than another is not linguistically tenable. His essential point, however, is borne out by colonial and modern evidence; the peninsula is a single-language area marked by minor variations of dialect that are often hard to pinpoint (see Restall, *Maya World*, 293–303; Bricker, Po'ot Yah, and Dzul de Po'ot, *Dictionary of the Maya Language*). Although a general distinction between coastal and inland dialects is not well evidenced, there is certainly a clear difference between what linguists call Yucatec Maya and Chontal Maya—the latter being the now-extinct tongue of the Mayas of Acalan-Tixchel, in Campeche state's southwest corner, a language often classified as being in the Cholan group (e.g., Justeson and Broadwell, "Language and Languages in Mesoamerica," 380), but which we would argue is a Yucatecan language (based on Restall's translation of a sixteenth-century Chontal text; *Maya Conquistador*, 53–76). The root of the author's comment is very likely Spanish familiarity (predating even the conquest of Yucatan) with the Chontals of Acalan-Tixchel. If the author was a Maya-speaking person themself, this could also be understood as deeply rooted animosity towards other provincial lineage groups.

is very well carved without there having been any type of metal in this land with which they could have been cut.

These edifices are very close to one another, and they are temples, the reason for having so many of them being that the populations moved many times; and in every town they carved out a temple, due to the great abundance of stone and lime and a certain white clay excellent for [making] buildings.[59]

These buildings are not made by any peoples [*naciones*] other than the Indians, as is seen in the stone figures of naked men modestly covered by long strips of cloth that are called *Ex* in their language, along with other symbols that the Indians wear.[60]

While the present friar [*religioso*], the author of this work,[61] was in that land, he discovered in one of the edifices that they broke up a large urn with three handles, painted with silver-colored flames on the outside, and containing the ashes of a burned body and several arm and leg bones of a remarkable size, and three fine stone beads of the type that the Indians use for money.[62]

---

[59] The "white earth" is no doubt referring to what the Maya called "*sahcab*" ("white earth"), a pale, powdery clay which can be mixed with lime to create a mortar. Additionally, it is used as an inclusion in certain ceramic wares, and perhaps most importantly, was a component part of Maya Blue, a vibrant turquoise pigment that had religious meaning in the precontact era (see Solari and Williams, "Maya Blue and Franciscan Evangelism"). Note that there is an omitted line break after this paragraph.

[60] In the colonial period Maya men substituted these loincloths, characterized by a long frontal piece, with loose trousers that they likewise called *ex* or *es* (a dialectal variation) (Restall, *Maya World*, 127, 184, 367).

[61] This is the first of five times that the author is referenced, either as "the author" (four times) or "the present friar" (here only) or giving Landa's name (twice), or a combination of those; the total instances are on Sec. 5, f. 4v (this one here); Sec. 8, f. 6v; Sec. 11, f. 8v; Sec. 15, f. 11v; Sec. 30, f. 25r. On a sixth instance Landa is referenced, but not by name (only as "the Franciscan Provincial") and not as the author (Sec. 19, f. 14v).

[62] Precontact Maya burial practices varied regionally and by socioeconomic status, but certain commonalities were shared across the Maya area. Ancestral reverence was a cornerstone of Classic Maya culture and the dead were not segregated from the living. There were no cemeteries, and many burials were placed in close proximity to the living, either under residential floors or in small platforms within household groups. Elites planned their burial tombs during their lifetimes and often housed them within large funerary pyramids if they had the resources. Large urn burials became common in the Terminal Classic and Postclassic periods in Yucatan (see Ardren, *Social Identities*, 83–116; and Ruz Lhuillier, *Costumbres funerarias de los antiguos mayas*). One of the RHGY accounts also contains a description of the grave that so struck the Spaniards: "In the year '50, while the friars of [Izamal] monastery were tearing down one of those buildings [a Maya pyramid and temple], they found a grave of amazing size and near it a very beautiful earthen jar full of ashes and the fragments of an alabaster vase" (RHGY, Vol. I: 213–14). Maya burial practices changed little during the early colonial period and not until the mid-seventeenth century did they appear to adopt widespread Catholic

These buildings of Izamal [*Yzamal*][63] numbered eleven or twelve altogether, without there being any memory of their founders; on top of one of them, at the insistence of the Indians, a monastery was established in the year 1549, called San Antonio.[64]

The second most important buildings are those of Tecoh [*Tikoch*] [*f. 5r*] and Chichen Itza [*Chicheniza*], which will be drawn later.[65]

Chichen Itza is a very good site ten leagues from Izamal and eleven from Valladolid, where they say that three lords ruled, brothers who came to that land from the west. They were very religious and therefore they built very beautiful temples. They lived decently, without women,[66] and then one of them died or left, whereupon the others became partial and dishonest, and for this they were killed. We will paint a picture of the main building later, and we will write of the nature of the well where they threw living men and other precious things in sacrifice.[67] The well is more than seven

---

Christian burial practices in more isolated regions (see Chuchiak, "Yaab Uih Yetel Maya Cimil," 4–7, 10–15). Note that between this and the next paragraph, the copyist left a small space and then omitted the next line break.

[63] See our chapter 2 in Part II for a discussion of Landa's tenure in this town.

[64] The first mass at Itzmal (called Izamal by Spaniards and today) was recited on August 6, 1549, the feast day of the Transfiguration of Christ. This liturgical fact prompted the founding friars Bienvenida and Landa to name the structure atop which they preached "Mount Thabor," the supposed location of Christ's transfiguration to his apostles.

[65] These descriptions, along with accompanying sketches, are on Sec. 42, f. 46; given that on f. 46 the author describes and illustrates a structure from Tiho, not Tikoch, it is likely that the mentioning of Tikoch here is a mistake, and that Tiho was intended. A different place, named Tecoh, but written as *Tikoch*, is introduced in Sec. 9, f. 7r. Note that between this and the next paragraph, the copyist left a small space and then omitted the next line break.

[66] Here Tozzer (*Landa's* Relación, 19) is in error: he states that "their wives lived honestly" when in fact the original Spanish tells us that they lived without women (celibate), which would be very "religious" according to both Catholic and traditional Maya beliefs, as both encouraged priests and religiously devout men to live without sexual intercourse, at least for a period of time leading up to a ritual performance. Colonial evidence exists that the Maya priests, or *ah kinob*, and their ritual assistants called *chacs* (*chacob* in Mayan) practiced temporary ritual celibacy (see Chuchiak, "Pre-conquest Ah Kinob," 144–45).

[67] Found on Sec. 14, f. 11r, and Sec. 42, f. 49. For an overview of the archaeological investigation of this feature, see Coggins, *Artifacts*. Recent analysis of the skeletal remains from the Cenote of Sacrifice, recovered in 1904 by Edward H. Thompson and in the 1960s by Román Piña Chan, indicate that the majority of sacrificial victims were children, not adult men (Ardren, "Empowered Children"). Children were common sacrificial offerings throughout Chichen Itza, in architecture as well as the cenote; Ardren argues they were understood as one of the most precious offerings that could be given to the Underworld. Restall is skeptical of what he sees as the overly ready association made by scholars between child burial and "sacrifice"—the latter a term that is arguably distorted by cultural judgmentalism of the kind found in sources such as the Account—while recognizing Ardren's authority as a published scholar on the topic.

estados in depth down to the water and more than one hundred feet in width;[68] it is marvelously made of a rounded fissure in the rock and the water appears green—the cause of which, it is said, is the grove which encircles it.

[Sec. 6] It is the opinion of the Indians that with the Itzas who settled Chichen Itza a great lord named Kukulcan [*Cuculcan*] ruled, and showing this to be the truth, the principal building is called Kukulcan.[69] They say he came from the western side [of the peninsula], but they disagree as to whether he came before or after the Itzas, or with them.[70] They say that he was well disposed, that he did not have a wife or children, and that after his return he was considered in Mexico to be one of their gods, called Quetzalcoatl [*Cezalcouati*]. In Yucatan also he was considered as a god because he was a great statesman [*gran republicano*], and this is seen in the order he established in Yucatan after the death of the lords, to alleviate the dissension that their deaths caused in the land.

This Kukulcan returned to settle another city, arranging with the native lords of the land that he and they would live in it, and that there all matters and business would come. To this end they chose a very good site eight leagues farther inland from where Merida now lies, and fifteen or sixteen from the sea. They surrounded it with a very broad wall of dry stone some eighth of a league long, leaving only two narrow doorways, with the wall itself very low.[71] In the middle of the enclosure, they built their temples, they called the largest one Kukulcan, the same as at

---

68 As an *estado* was 1.85 yards or 1.7 meters, the depth of this cenote from the edge to the water level was—according to the author here—about 12 meters. For colonial-era measurements, see Villasana Haggard and McLean, *Handbook for Translators*.

69 This is the structure imaged in the manuscript on f. 48v.

70 This passage helped inspire a century of misunderstanding among scholars interested in the relationship of Chichen Itza to other Maya cities of the Classic period. Due to perceived similarities between the art and architecture of Chichen Itza and ancient cities in central Mexico, especially Tula, and in the absence of chronometric dating, early-twentieth-century scholars such as J. Eric S. Thompson and others proposed an invasion of "Itza" warriors from central Mexico to the Maya lowlands at the end of the Classic period. This model built upon Thompson's belief (since disproven) that the Classic Maya were peaceful astronomers, and that war was introduced from outside the Maya area. Although a few scholars still invoke the Itza invasion explanation for the rise of Chichen Itza, the last twenty years of research in the region surrounding this important Terminal Classic city has not produced any solid evidence of invasion. Rather, the artifacts, domestic architecture, and writing are wholly Maya—albeit influenced by other ninth- and tenth-century trends in Mesoamerica. In a series of breakthrough articles William Ringle, George J. Bey III, and Tomás Gallareta Negrón have shown that the leaders and occupants of Chichen Itza participated in a pan-Mesoamerican cult of Quetzalcoatl (the Nahuatl cognate of Kukulcan), elements of which can be seen in other key cities such as El Tajin, Cholula, and Tula.

71 The walls of Mayapan have been studied by Masson and Peraza Lope, *Kukulkan's Realm*; Pollock et al., *Mayapan, Yucatan, Mexico*; and Russell, "Fortress Mayapan."

Chichen Itza. They built another one, round and with four entrances, different from the many that are in this land,[72] and many others in a circle, all joined together.[73] Within the enclosure they built houses for the lords, exclusively among whom the land was divided, assigning towns to each according to the antiquity of their lineage and personal standing. Kukulcan named the city, but not after himself, as the Ah Itzas [*Ahizaes*] did at Chichen Itza, which means "Well of the Ah Itzas," but called it Mayapan, meaning "The Banner of the Mayas," because the language of the land they called Maya.[74] The Indians [today] call it Ichpa, meaning "Within the Enclosures."

This Kukulcan lived with the lords for some years in this city, and then leaving them in great peace and friendship he returned by the same road to Mexico. On the way he stopped at Champoton, and to memorialize himself and his departure he erected in the sea, *[f. 5v]* at a good stone's throw from the shore, a fine building similar to those at Chichen Itza. Thus, Kukulcan left a perpetual memory in Yucatan.[75]

[Sec. 7] Upon the departure of Kukulcan, the lords agreed that for the permanence of the state the house of the Cocoms should have the chief authority, it being the oldest or richest, or because its head was at that time the bravest man. This done, they ordained that within the enclosure [walls] there were only temples and residences of the lords and the high priest, they should thus build outside the walls houses where each of them might keep servants, and whither the people from their towns might come whenever they had business in the city. In these houses each one placed his majordomo, who bore as his sign of office a short thick baton, and whom they called the *caluac*. This majordomo kept account of the towns and those

---

[72] This round tower served as an astronomical observatory and, like much of the monumental architecture at Mayapan, it is a copy of the more finely wrought prototype at Chichen Itza, colloquially known—like this one at Mayapan—as the "Caracol" (the "Snail"), for the spiraling staircase that leads up to the tower's height (Ruppert, *Caracol at Chichen Itza*).

[73] This is likely an architectural feature created by the joining of a series of low-lying mounds, connected to create an interior patio space, a common feature of urban design in the Maya area and elsewhere in ancient Mesoamerica, typically used to delineate the domestic space of separate lineages (see Masson and Peraza Lope, *Kukulkan's Realm*).

[74] The author's definition is not convincing, as there is no evidence that Indigenous peoples of Yucatan called themselves "Maya" before the conquest period, and it was very rarely used as a term of ethnic reference in the colonial period. Rather, the colonial usage of the term was primarily to the language, and indeed Landa suggests above that the term named the language not the people. Restall has argued that the term "Maya" derived from the toponym "Mayapan" (and not vice versa, as is the conventional view, following Landa). He has published variously on the evolution of the term "Maya," most recently as Restall and Gabbert, "Maya Ethnogenesis" (also see Restall, *Maya World*, 14–15; *Maya Conquistador*, 177, 233).

[75] According to Herrera y Tordesillas, *Historia general de los hechos de los castellanos* (cited incompletely by Tozzer, *Landa's* Relación, 26), this temple was visible on a small island in the bay at the time of the Spanish invasions; it is still visible today.

in charge of them, to whom he sent notice as to what was needed in the lord's house, such as birds, maize, honey, salt, fish, game, clothing, and other things.[76] The *caluac* was always on duty at the lord's house, seeing what was needed and providing it promptly, as his [own] house functioned as though it were the office of his lord.

It was the custom to seek out in the towns the maimed and the blind, and to give them what they needed.

The lords appointed the governors and, if competent, confirmed the offices on their sons. They charged them [the governors] with the good treatment of the common people and the peace of the community [*pueblo*], and them [the people] with the task of supporting themselves and their lords.

All the lords took care to respect, visit, and entertain Cocom, accompanying and making festivals for him, and deferring to him in difficult affairs. They lived very much in peace with one other, and with their accustomed pastimes of dances, feasts, and hunts.

The people of Yucatan were as interested in matters of religion as in those of government. They had a High Priest whom they called Ah Kin May [*Achkinmai*], and whose name was also Ahau Can May [*Ahuacanmai*], meaning the Priest May, or the High Priest May. He was greatly revered by the lords; he had an allotment of Indians and, in addition to the offerings, the lords gave him presents, to which all the priests of the towns contributed. He was succeeded in office by his sons or closest relatives. In him lay the key to their sciences, to which they [the High Priest and his successors] greatly devoted themselves, giving counsel to the lords and answers to their questions. As to matters of sacrifices, they rarely dealt with them, except at great festivals or business of much importance. They appointed priests to the towns, when they were lacking, examining them in their sciences and ceremonies, charging them with the affairs of their offices and the setting of a good example to the people, and providing them their books which he sent them. They attended to the service of the temples, [*f. 6r*] teaching their sciences and writing books about them.[77]

---

[76]   There was tremendous organizational variability across the precontact Maya area in terms of how tribute and related economic systems functioned; we can no longer refer to a singular Maya "economy" but must refer to Maya "economies." What the author describes in this passage is the system of tribute paid in goods and services by subsidiary or dependent settlements to a local leader, who would in turn redistribute some portion of these products. But there is also strong evidence for reciprocity between households, market exchange, and long-distance trade during the time when Mayapan was occupied (see King, "Maya Commerce"; McAnany, *Ancestral Maya Economies*; Masson, Freidel, and Demarest, *Real Business*).

[77]   Before and after the conquest a hierarchical Maya priesthood continued to exist and function (Chuchiak, "Pre-conquest Ah Kinob in a Colonial World," 136–41). Ecclesiastical extirpators uncovered a significant number of these codices or "books of their sciences" in use by *ah kinob* as ritual formularies and calendars for ritual cycles from the 1570s through the 1690s

They taught the sons of the other priests, and the second sons of the lords, who were brought to them for this purpose when they were children, if they saw that they were inclined toward this profession.[78]

The sciences which they taught were the reckoning of the years, months, and days, the festivals and ceremonies, the administration of their sacraments, the terrible [*fatales*] days and times, their methods of divination, and their prophecies, events, remedies for sickness, antiquities, and the art of reading and writing with their letters and the characters with which they wrote, and drawings that illustrated the writings.[79]

They wrote their books on a long sheet doubled in folds, which was then enclosed between two boards that were finely decorated; and they wrote on both sides, in columns, according to where the folds were.[80] The paper they made from the roots of a tree, giving it a white finish, upon which one could write well.[81] Some of the

---

(Chuchiak, "Images Speak," 169–76; Chuchiak, *El castigo y la reprensión*, 603–39). This priesthood and their continued usage of Maya codices survived into the early eighteenth century in a type of "graphic pluralism" (Chuchiak, "Writing as Resistance," 90–92, 106–10).

[78] One is reminded in this description of the Maya priesthood of the organization and purpose of the Franciscans—the dispatch of friars like Landa out into the general population to set good examples, teach, write books, and educate the sons of the chiefs—to such an extent that one suspects Landa's interpretation is central to this description (on the role of the Maya *ah kinob* as keepers and makers of their hieroglyphic books see Chuchiak, "Images Speak," 167–71).

[79] Tellingly, this literary diversity is present in the handful of manuscripts composed by Mayas during the postcontact period known collectively as the Books of Chilam Balam. These texts were copied from precontact codices and then continually copied and retranscribed from the sixteenth through the nineteenth centuries. Today, the extant books are from the towns of Chumayel, Tizimin, Teabo, Tusik, Kaua, Chan Kan, Nah, Ixil, Tekax, and Mani (see Christensen, *Teabo Manuscript*; Love, "Que son los Libros de Chilam Balam?").

[80] Here, the author describes precontact codices, of which only four survive from the Maya region, three named for their current locations (Dresden, Madrid, and Paris) and the fourth for its repatriated location in Mexico (see Coe et al., "Fourth Maya Codex"). Thousands surely existed during the course of precontact history, but these books were specifically targeted for destruction by the missionaries. The four extant Maya codices all contain various combinations of both hieroglyphic writing and illustrative text. For recent studies on the plausible origins of these codices and the historical circumstances of their confiscation, see Chuchiak, "De Extirpatio Codicis Yucatanensis," 116–23.

[81] The "paper" was composed from the processed and then flattened interior bark of the amate tree, a species of the Ficus genus, which in turn is part of the same family of plants as the mulberry, from which paper was made in Asia and the Pacific. A labor-intensive process, the bark was soaked and then macerated with a specific stone tool (often our only indication of papermaking in the archaeological record of the Maya area). After repeated processing, the plant fibers form a mat that is polished and left to dry. In some cases, the resulting bark paper or cloth was covered with a thin coat of limestone plaster to create a less porous

principal lords were learned in these sciences, out of curiosity, and for this were more esteemed even though they did not make use of them in public.[82] *[Sec. 8]* The Indians relate that from the south there came into Yucatan many people with their lords, and it seems they came from Chiapas, although the Indians do not know this, but the author[83] conjectures thus because many words and verbal constructions are the same in Chiapas and in Yucatan, and there is much evidence in Chiapas of sites that have been abandoned.[84] They say that these people wandered forty years through the uninhabited regions of Yucatan,[85] without there being any water there except from the rains; that at the end of that time they reached the mountains that lie almost opposite the city of Mayapan [*Maiapan*], ten leagues from it, and here they began to settle and put up very fine buildings in many places.[86] The people of

---

surface before it was painted with hieroglyphic texts and imagery. Ficus trees have aerial root systems that spread far beyond the base of the tree and often become quite thick. Landa may have seen craftspeople harvesting bark fibers from "*las raices del palo*," which are not actually underground (Von Hagen, *Aztec and Maya Papermakers*). All four of the surviving Maya codices were painted on bark paper, but animal skin was also used as a writing and painting surface in the precontact era.

[82] The suggestion here that literacy was the preserve of the political and religious elite, and that it was a prestigious skill passed down within prominent families, is supported by archaeological evidence of precontact practices (Matsumoto and Carter, "Recent Developments") and historical evidence from the colonial period (Restall, *Maya World*; Christensen and Restall, *Return to Ixil*). See also Chuchiak, "Writing as Resistance," 106–10; and Chuchiak, "Images Speak," on the survival of hieroglyphic books many decades after Landa's campaign to destroy them in the 1550s throught the 1570s. On the confrontation between European alphabetic writing and the varied writing systems of Indigenous Americans, see Mignolo, *Darker Side of the Renaissance*. The copyist omitted the line break between "in public" and "The Indians."

[83] This is the second of five times that "the author" is referenced; the total instances are on Sec. 5, f. 4v; Sec. 8, f. 6v (here); Sec. 11, f. 8v; Sec. 15, f. 11v; Sec. 30, f. 25r.

[84] Chiapas is part of the Maya area, and its inhabitants spoke in Landa's time, as they do today, various Cholan and Tzeltalan languages of the Western Mayan language family (Justeson and Broadwell, "Language and Languages in Mesoamerica," 380); this fact alone does not suggest migration from Chiapas to Yucatan, nor does the existence of Maya sites already abandoned by the mid-sixteenth century. One such site, the most impressive in Chiapas, is Palenque, and although the site does not appear as such in Spanish records until it was visited in 1746 by the priest Antonio de Solís (Baudez and Picasso, *Lost Cities of the Maya*, 31–32), it is likely that Spaniards had heard about or seen Palenque before this and possible that such stories had reached Landa.

[85] This reference to "forty years" is reminiscent of Moses's forty-year wander through the desert.

[86] The question of the supposed non-Yucatecan origins of the Xiu and other dynasties is a controversial and complex one; Masson and Peraza Lope, who have conducted the most thorough recent research at Mayapan, argue there is ample material evidence that elites across the city had political and economic alliances with people from outside Yucatan, including those from Campeche, Tabasco, Peten, and the Caribbean (Masson and Peraza Lope, *Kukulcan's Realm*). However, they side with scholars such as Ringle and Bey, who argue that the Xiu are

Mayapan became very friendly with them and were pleased that they worked the land as if they were natives [*naturales*].[87] Thus, the people of Tutul Xiu subjected themselves to the laws of Mayapan; and they intermarried, and so the lord Xiu of the Tutul Xius, as such, came to be greatly esteemed by everyone.[88]

These people lived in such tranquility that they had no conflicts and used neither arms nor bows, even for the hunt, although today they are excellent archers; they only used snares and traps, with which they took much game. They ~~the priests~~[89] also had a certain technique of throwing darts using a stick as thick as three fingers, hollowed out for a third of the way, and six palms long; with this and some cords they threw with force and accuracy.[90]

They had laws against delinquents, which they rigorously applied, such as against an adulterer, whom they turned over to the offended one, so that he might kill him by throwing a large stone from a height down upon his head, or he might forgive him if he wished. For the *[f. 6v]* adulterous women, there was no punishment save infamy, which among them was a very serious thing. One who raped a virgin was stoned to death. They tell of a case of the lord of the Tutul Xius whose brother was accused of this crime; and he had him stoned and afterwards covered

---

an ancestral family of Yucatan, with strong ties to the western Puuc region around Uxmal (Ringle and Bey, "Post-classic and Terminal Classic Courts"). While precontact Maya cities of the Puuc area were a tight-knit group that shared distinctive architecture and artifacts, other western Yucatan cities such as Chunchucmil and Champoton had multiethnic and nonlocal trade contacts for millennia. Masson and Peraza Lope (*Kukulcan's Realm*) suggest the leaders of the Mayapan state were successful at muting ethnic differences in favor of a citywide, emblematic style of material culture. As we argue in chapter 1 of part II, these migration tales were likely myths that originated with elite, autochthonous Maya dynasties, but were then perpetuated as historical "fact" by colonial-era Spaniards (such as Landa) and modern scholars (taking Landa unquestioningly as an authority on the Maya).

[87] Throughout the Account, we translate *naturales* as "natives," and *los Indios* as "the Indians." Those are the only two terms used in the manuscript to refer to the Maya and to Indigenous peoples, although note that *natural* is not a race-specific term. As reflected in usage in the Account, "native" and "Indian" are colonialist terms that we therefore avoid.

[88] Landa insinuates that this lord's status was because he "intermarried" (*emparentaron unos con otros*). This may be a reference to the ancestor whom colonial-era Xius believed to be the founder of the dynasty, Hun Uitzil Chac Tutul Xiu, who married a woman from Ticul, a town near Mayapan, according to the Xiu Family Tree; the Tree was very likely drawn by Gaspar Antonio Chi, the Maya protegé of Landa's who was one of his sources of information and discussed in our chapter 1. Marriages between men from outside the peninsula and local elite Maya women have a long history in Yucatan, and they are attested in the inscriptions of Chichen Itza (Krochock, "Women in the Hieroglyphic Inscriptions").

[89] "The priests [*los sacerdotes*]" was written here and then crossed out.

[90] The dart thrower, common throughout Mesoamerica, was termed *hulche* in Yucatec Maya and *atlatl* in Nahuatl.

with a great mound of rocks. They also say that before the foundation of this city they had another law ordering that the entrails of adulterers be pulled out through their navels.[91]

The governor Cocom began to covet riches, and for this reason he made a deal with the garrison that the kings of Mexico kept in Tabasco and Xicalango, promising to turn over the city to them. Thus, he brought Mexican people to Mayapan,[92] oppressed the poor, and made many slaves. The lords would have killed him if they had not been afraid of the Mexicans. The lord of the Tutul Xius never consented to this. And those of Yucatan, seeing their situation, learned from the Mexicans the art of arms, and thus became masters of the bow and arrow, and of the lance and axe, with their shields and strong jackets made of quilted cotton,[93] together with other instruments of war, so that soon they no longer stood in awe of the Mexicans nor feared them, but rather paid them no account. In this way several years passed.

This Cocom was the first to make slaves, but from this evil came the use of arms with which they defended themselves so that they might not all become slaves.[94]

---

[91] Disembowelment was used in medieval and early modern Spain, but only as a civil or secular punishment for those condemned of regicide and other treasonous crimes, so it is unlikely that this punishment was imagined by Landa, drawing upon Spanish practice. Indeed, although this exact form of death sentence has not been verified in the ancient Maya world, the Maya interpreter and nobleman Gaspar Antonio Chi claimed in his own *Relación de Algunas Costumbres* of 1581 that the Maya before the conquest did execute adulterers: "the man or woman who committed adultery received the death penalty, and they killed them with arrows and by piercing them with a stake" (Strecker and Arcieda, "Relación de algunas costumbres," 15). The Spanish encomenderos on Merida's *cabildo* related in 1579 that before the conquest the Maya "punished adulterers with the death penalty" (RHGY, Vol. I: 73). Yñigo Nieto, the encomendero of Citilcum, added in 1581 that the death penalty was given to both men and women accused of adultery (RHGY, Vol. I: 183).

[92] It has been argued that merchants from central Mexico did reside in Mayapan, but for purely economic reasons; to "solidify their cacao and cotton trade" and also to guarantee large quantities of salt (Sabloff, "It Depends," 22).

[93] Landa's text has *sacos fuertes de sal y algodon*, "strong jackets of salt and cotton"; as Gates observes (*Yucatán*, 16), Landa probably heard his Maya informant say *tab* ("salt") when he actually said *taab* ("something tied or twisted"). The Nahuas called this cotton armor *ichcauipilli*, which passed into Mexican Spanish as *escaupil* when the Spaniards adopted the armor during the conquest period.

[94] The Cocom lineage was not solely responsible for the introduction of slavery as a social category in northern Yucatan; as briefly discussed in chapter 1, slavery had existed among the Maya for centuries, probably millennia, as it did elsewhere in the world, and was likely conceived as a more fluid category among the precontact Maya than it was in sixteenth-century Europe. Note that Spanish hypocrisy regarding the enslavement of Mayas and other Indigenous Mesoamericans—it was illegal, yet widespread—would have complicated the category for Mayas in sixteenth-century Yucatan. See Chuchiak, "Human Plunder."

Among the successors of the Cocom dynasty was another one, very proud and an imitator of Cocom, who made another alliance with the Tabascans and took in more Mexicans inside the city. He began to tyrannize and to enslave the common people. For this reason, the lords came together with Tutul Xiu, a great statesman like his ancestors, and they plotted to kill Cocom. This they did, killing all of his sons, leaving no more than one who was absent. They sacked his house and took the estates he had of cacao and other fruits, saying that in this way they repaid themselves for what he had stolen from them. The quarrels between the Cocoms, who claimed that they had been unjustly expelled, and the Xius, went on for so long that after having been settled in that city for more than five hundred years, they abandoned it and left it empty, each going to his own territory.[95]

[Sec. 9] According to the reckoning of the Indians it has been 120 years since Mayapan was abandoned.[96] In the plaza of that city are to be found seven or eight stones, each ten feet high, round on one side, well worked and containing several lines of the characters they use, so worn away by the rain as to be unreadable, although they are thought to be a record of the foundation and destruction of that city.[97] There are others [f. 7r] like them at Dzilan [Zilan], a town on the coast,

---

[95]   This account of Cocom-Xiu relations and the fall of Mayapan is a blatantly partisan one sympathetic to the Xiu dynasty at the expense of the Cocom. This bias is probably due to the identity of Landa's source for his history of Mayapan, the professional interpreter Gaspar Antonio Chi, who was a Xiu on his mother's side and was a young boy when his father was killed during the 1536 Cocom massacre of Xiu dignitaries at Otzmal (see Restall, "People of the Patio"). As discussed in chapter 1, Landa also had a Cocom source, but rather than reconcile contrary biases, Landa allowed the partisanship of both informants to color the passages and topics on which they provided the friar with information. Excavations at Mayapan in the last decade have produced tantalizing material evidence of widespread and escalating violence within the city, especially in the final century of occupation, that may corroborate what Landa recorded (Masson and Peraza Lope, *Kukulkan's Realm*; Paris et al., "Violence, Desecration, and Urban Collapse"). Landa's text can be seen less as offering insight into fifteenth-century Yucatec history and more as a window into the oral historical traditions circulating the Xiu region in the 1550s. Indeed, Sections VI–X of Landa's text reflect conquest-era Maya oral traditions in the same way that Sections II–IV reflect those circulating among the new colony's Spaniards.

[96]   In the next section Landa writes that this time span was 125 years.

[97]   While not as common as in earlier Maya cities, monumental stelae did litter the ceremonial core of Mayapan. Carnegie Institution publication reported thirteen carved and twenty-five plain stelae from Mayapan during their research in the 1950s, and Tatiana Proskouriakoff suggested that those found near round structures likely had historical information about Kukulcan, the legendary founder of Mayapan (Proskouriakoff, "Civic and Religious Structures"). Carlos Peraza Lope identified one additional stela in the city center, and some suggest the association between stelae and Puuc-style architecture may indicate stelae were erected by the Xiu elite (Ringle and Bey, "Post-classic and Terminal Classic Courts"). Although nearly all the

although they are taller.[98] The natives, when asked what they were, replied that they were accustomed to setting up one of these stones every twenty years, which is the number by which they count their time periods.[99] But this seems to be unfounded, for according to this there would be many more, especially as there are none of them in towns other than Mayapan and Dzilan.[100]

The most important thing that those lords who abandoned Mayapan took away to their territories were the books of their sciences, for they were always very subject to the advice of their priests, for which reason there are so many temples in those provinces.

The son of Cocom who had escaped death through being away trading in the land of Ulua, which is beyond the town of Salamanca, on hearing of his father's death and the destruction of the city, returned very quickly. He joined his relatives and vassals, and they settled a site which he called Tibolon [*Tibulon*], meaning "we have been played with."[101] They built many other towns [*pueblos*] in those forests,

---

hieroglyphs are eroded from Mayapan stelae, iconography and fifteenth-century dates are still visible. For details on these monuments, see Masson and Peraza Lope, *Kukulcan's Realm*.

[98] Landa likely means the stelae found at the archaeological site of Dzilam Gonzalez, directly north of Izamal toward the coast. Hieroglyphic inscriptions on Stela 1 from Dzilam mention a king of the nearby site of Dzibilchaltun. Stela 2 of Dzilam has a long count date of 10.1.3.0.0. or 852 CE, indicating it was an important site where literacy was preserved late into the Classic period. Most of the stelae were removed from this site in the early twentieth century, but Stela 2 can be seen in the Museo del Pueblo Maya at the site of Dzibilchaltun (Covarrubias Reyna and Burgos Villanueva, "Investigaciones arqueológicas"; Grube and Krochock, "Reading between the Lines," 210).

[99] The Account's Indigenous informants corroborate other lines of evidence when referring to the twenty-year katun cycle that chronologically oriented Late Postclassic ritual life in northern Yucatan. So pervasive was this calendrical cycle that it continued to be used to chart local history well into the colonial period, as passages from a handful of the Books of Chilam Balam attest. Rulers of Classic Period metropoles in the southern Maya world similarly used the katun cycle to mark the passage of time, frequently erected carved portrait stela (such as the sculptural cycle in Copán's Great Plaza), and built ritual complexes (such as Tikal's Twin Pyramid Complexes) to commemorate their completion.

[100] Of course, there are many stelae at archaeological sites across Yucatan, and this statement that they only exist at Mayapan and Dzilam must originate in information provided to Landa by his informants (who perhaps deliberately deceived the bishop in order to protect these monuments). The author's editorializing here is absolutely unfounded; this calendrical cycle, a subset of the longer haab calendar, which will be discussed below (Secs. 34–41; fs. 28r–45v), had been used throughout the Maya world since the Preclassic period.

[101] Yucatec toponyms are usually simple or compound nouns, not verbal phrases like the one Landa proposes here in spelling it *Tibulon* (as Gates observes; *Yucatán*, 17), and they often begin with the locative element *ti* (sometimes elided to *t*). *Tibolon* actually means "The Place of Nine" or "At the Nine." The Ulua mentioned in this paragraph is Ulúa in Honduras, not San Juan de Ulua on the Mexican coast.

and many families have sprung from these Cocoms. The province where this lord rules is called Sotuta [*Zututa*].

The lords of Mayapan took no vengeance on those Mexicans who helped Cocom, seeing that they had been persuaded by the governor of the land, and because they were foreigners. Thus, they left them alone, granting them the right to settle a town apart, for themselves alone, or else to leave the land. [If they stayed] they were not to marry among the natives of the land, but only among themselves. They decided to remain in Yucatan and not to return to the lagoons and mosquitoes of Tabasco, and they settled the province of Canul, which was assigned to them, and there they stayed until the second of the Spanish wars.[102]

[*Que*][103] They say that among the twelve priests of Mayapan was a very wise one who had an only daughter, whom he married to a young nobleman named Ah Chel [*Achchel*]; he had some sons who were named the same as their father, according to the custom of the land. They say that this priest warned his son-in-law of the destruction of the city, the latter knowing much about the sciences of his father-in-law, whom, they say, wrote on the broad part of his left arm certain letters of great importance and worthy of respect. With this honor, he went to live on the coast, until founding a settlement at Tecoh [*Tikoch*], a great number of people following him. Thus, the population there of the Chels became very significant, and they inhabited the most significant province of Yucatan, which they called, after their own name, the province of [*f. 7v*] Ah Kin Chel. It is that of Izamal [*Ytzamal*], where the Chels resided and multiplied in Yucatan until the invasion of the Adelantado Montejo.[104]

Between the three houses of the principal lords, those of the Cocoms, Xius, and Chels, there were great quarrels and enmities, and there still are today, even though they have become Christians. The Cocoms call the Xius foreigners, and traitors for murdering their principal lord and stealing his estate. The Xius say they are as good

---

[102] Because Landa elided the first and second Montejo campaigns of conquest into one, his reference to the "second wars" is actually to the third Montejo-led invasion, which began in 1540 and resulted in the foundation of a colonial capital at Merida-Tiho in 1542 (see chapter 1 in part II; and Restall, *Maya Conquistador*, 3–18). There is no evidence that those who inhabited the Canul region (the northern half of what is now the state of Campeche) were displaced in the 1540s; on the contrary, a colonial document from this region, dubbed by historians The Title of Calkiní, emphasizes continuity (Restall, *Maya Conquistador*, 82–103).

[103] Another omitted line break at the "Que."

[104] This last statement, that the Chels had resided in Izamal until the arrival of the Spaniards, throws into question Landa's authorship of this section of the Account. Landa knew that Izamal had been abandoned decades before the start of the Spanish-Maya Wars. Alternatively, this could be evidence of Landa's political savvy, as perhaps he was intentionally trying to exaggerate the precontact importance of his favorite mission town.

as the others, as ancient and as lordly, and that they were not traitors but libera-
tors of the land, having slain its tyrant. The Chel [lord] says that he was as good as
the others in lineage, being the grandson of Mayapan's most respected priest, and
that personally he was greater than the others because he had learned how to make
himself as much a lord as they were. Because of this, they have even disrupted each
other's food supply, because the Chel, who was on the coast, would not give fish or
salt to the Cocom [lord], making him go far for it; and the Cocom would not let
the Chel take any of their game or fruits.

[Sec. 10] These peoples enjoyed more than twenty years in abundance and health,
and they multiplied so much that the whole land seemed like a town. At that time,
they built the temples in such numbers as today can be seen everywhere, and if one
goes through the forests one can see in the groves the sites of houses and buildings
of amazing construction.

Following this prosperity, one winter night, there came at about six in the eve-
ning a storm that grew into a hurricane of the four winds.[105] This storm blew down
all the fully grown trees, causing great slaughter of all kinds of game. It knocked
down the tall houses, which being thatched and having fires within for the cold,
caught fire and burned a great many people. Some who escaped being burnt were
crippled by blows from [falling] timbers. The hurricane lasted until noon the next
day, when they saw that those who lived in small houses had escaped, among them
the newly married couples, whose custom was to build huts in front of the homes of
their fathers or fathers-in-law where they lived for their first years [of marriage]. In
this way, the land lost the name it had borne, that "of the turkeys and the deer," and
was left so treeless that today's trees, look as if they were planted together, all [f. 8r]
sprouting equally. Thus, to view the land from certain high points, it looks as if it
were all trimmed with a pair of shears.[106]

Those who escaped busied themselves building and cultivating the land and multiplied greatly during the following sixteen years of health and abundance, the last year
being the most fertile of all. Then when they were about to begin gathering the crops
there came upon the whole land a plague of pestilential fevers that lasted for twenty-
four hours, after which the sick swelled up and broke out full of maggoty sores; and
from this plague many people died and most of the crops were not gathered.

After the end of the plague, they had another sixteen good years, during which
they revived their passions and quarrels in such a way that 150,000 men were killed
in battle. With this slaughter they calmed down and made peace and rested for
another twenty years. After that there came again a pestilence, with great pustules

---

[105] On glyphic evidence of how precontact Yucatec Mayas viewed and experienced hurricanes,
see Dunning and Houston, "Chan Ik' "; also see Schwartz, *Sea of Storms*.

[106] Again, the copyist omitted the line break at the end of this paragraph.

that rotted the body with a foul odor, causing their limbs to fall to pieces within four or five days. Since this last plague more than fifty years have now passed, the mortality of the war was twenty years before that, the pestilence of the swelling and maggots was sixteen years before the wars, and the hurricane another sixteen years before that, which was twenty-two or twenty-three after the destruction of the city of Mayapan. Thus, according to this count, it has been 125 years since its overthrow,[107] within which time the people of this land have passed through the calamities described, as well as many others which began with the invasion of the Spaniards, both from the wars and other punishments sent by God.[108] It is thus a marvel that the present population exists at all, small as it is.

[*Sec. 11*] Just as the Mexican people had signs and prophecies of the coming of the Spaniards and the end of their power and religion,[109] so did also those of Yucatan some years before they were conquered by Adelantado [licensed invader] Montejo. In the hills of Mani, in the province of Tutul Xiu, an Indian named Ah Cambal, [*f. 8v*] of the office of *chilan*,[110] that is, "he who has charge of giving out the responses of

---

[107] The Account's tally here of 125 years of events is the primary basis for historians and archaeologists dating the fall of Mayapan to 1441. However, the time periods detailed in this passage add up to 123 or 124 years, not 125, if one includes the fifteen years mentioned after the description of the hurricane earlier in the section; to arrive at the latter number, "more than fifty" must be 51 or 52. Based on this chronology, the fall of Mayapan should be dated c. 1440 or even just mid-fifteenth century. Current models based on extensive new excavations and radiocarbon dating put the fall of Mayapan circa 1400 CE, essentially confirming the ethnohistoric sources (Masson and Peraza Lope, *Kukulkan's Realm*; Peraza Lope et al., "Chronology of Mayapan"). This research has also documented material evidence of escalating violence within the city, such as burning episodes and mass graves, perhaps as a result of the conflict between rival lineages (see Paris et al., "Violence, Desecration, and Urban Collapse").

[108] With respect to sixteenth-century "calamities" and Maya demographic collapse, note how deftly (and typically) the author deflects blame away from his fellow Spaniards and onto divine providence, as though the diseases that accompanied the Spanish invasion and devastated the native population were no more connected to human action than the hurricane of the previous century. The Maya appeared frequently to conflate illness with human-made and natural disasters (see Chuchiak, "Yaab Uih Yetel Maya Cimil," 7–13; Kashanipour, "World of Cures," 43).

[109] Most scholars no longer believe that these omens and prophecies occurred in precontact Mexico, or they believe that, if any did, they were interpreted as anticipations of the Spanish invasion; on the contrary, they were developed by Franciscan friars and Christianized Indigenous men as post-invasion explanations. See Fernández-Armesto, "'Aztec' Auguries"; Restall, *Seven Myths*, 114, 117, 137. This may also be the case with these alleged Maya prophecies too; or the colonial-era record of such prophecies, be they recounted by the likes of Landa or by Maya scribes in the Books of Chilam Balam, are derived from Maya-Franciscan cultural interaction.

[110] A *chilan* or *ah chijlan* was, according to the sixteenth-century Diccionario Motul, an *interprete* ("interpreter"), revealing the author's inability to comprehend Indigenous religion as

the devil [*demonio*]," told them publicly that they would soon be ruled by a foreign people who would preach of one god and the great power of a wooden post which in their tongue he called *uahom che* [*Vamonché*], meaning "a wooden post lifted up, of great power against the devils."[111]

The successor of the Cocoms, called don Juan Cocom after his baptism, was a man of great reputation and very learned in their affairs and very wise and knowledgeable about the natives.[112] He was very familiar to the author of this book, fray Diego de Landa,[113] recounting to him many ancient things, and showing him a book, which had belonged to his grandfather, the son of the Cocom whom they killed at Mayapan. In this was painted a deer, and his grandfather had told him that when there should come into the land large deer—for so they called the cows—the worship of the gods would cease; and this had been fulfilled, because the Spaniards brought along large cows.

The Adelantado Francisco de Montejo was a native of Salamanca, and he came to the Indies after the settling of the city of Santo Domingo and the island of Hispaniola, after having first lived for a time in Seville, where he left an infant son whom he had there. He came to the city of Cuba, where he gained a livelihood and made many friends through his fine circumstances [*buena condición*]. Among these were Diego Velásquez, the governor of the island, and Hernando Cortés. The governor decided to send his nephew Juan de Grijalva to trade in [*rescatar*] the territory of Yucatan and to discover new lands, after the news brought by Francisco Hernández de Córdoba when he discovered the land, of how rich it was.[114] He

---

anything other than a demonic intervention (Ciudad Real, Diccionario de Motul, f. 15r); Gates has *ah cambal* as "one who learns, a pupil" and *chilan* as "orator."

[111] On Landa's use of *demonio*; see Tozzer, *Landa's* Relación, n213. Here, as throughout our translation, we have followed the original text in showing, for example, *uahom che* styled as *Vamonché*, indicating inconsistencies in spelling, spacing, and capitalization by the copyists of the Account.

[112] Don Juan Cocom was called Nachi Cocom before he was baptized; as head of the Cocom polity (arguably king of the small Cocom kingdom), he led part of the resistance against the Spanish invasion of 1540, suffering defeat outside Tiho (Merida) on June 11, 1541 (Restall, *Seven Myths*, 71; Chamberlain, *Conquest and Colonization of Yucatan*, 211–17; Chuchiak, "La Conquista de Yucatán," 53–54); also see our chapter 1.

[113] This is the third of five times in the Account that an author is referenced; the total instances are on Sec. 5, f. 4v; Sec. 8, f. 6v; Sec. 11, f. 8v (here); Sec. 15, f. 11v; Sec. 30, f. 25r. In two of these instances (here and in Sec. 15), Landa himself is named as author; the phrase could be self-referential, with Landa referring to himself in the third person, or more likely, the copyist—who was familiar with Landa's personal biography and native sources—is here simply reiterating with whom Juan Cocom was "very familiar."

[114] This brief summary of the Grijalva expedition is very similar to its coverage in Oviedo y Valdés, *Historia*, Bk. 17, Ch. 9, and in López de Gómara's *Conquista de Mexico* and his *La Istoria*

[Velásquez] decided to have Montejo go with Grijalva. He [Montejo] being wealthy, he supplied one of the ships and much provisioning, and was thus one of the second party of Spaniards that discovered Yucatan. Having seen the coast of Yucatan, he felt a desire to enrich himself there rather than in Cuba. Seeing the determination of Hernando Cortés, he followed him with his estate and his person *[f. 9r]*, Cortés giving him the responsibility of a ship and making him its captain. In Yucatan they rescued Gerónimo de Aguilar, from whom Montejo acquired knowledge of the language of the country and its affairs. Having landed in New Spain, Cortés began at once to found settlements, calling the first town Vera Cruz, after the blazon of his banner. In this town Montejo was appointed as one of the *alcaldes del rey* [royal judges], in which role he acquitted himself discreetly. He was publicly deemed as such by Cortés when he returned from the trip he made around the coast. For this he was sent to Spain as one of the *procuradores* [representatives] of that republic of New Spain, that he might convey to the king his fifth,[115] together with an account of the lands discovered, and the things they had begun to do there.[116]

When Francisco de Montejo arrived at the court of Castile, Juan Rodríguez de Fonseca, Bishop of Burgos, was president of the Council of the Indies. He was wrongly informed about Cortés by Diego de Velásquez, the governor of Cuba, who likewise claimed New Spain. The majority of the Council were against Cortés's dealings, thinking that he seemed to be asking money of the king instead of sending it, and because the emperor was in Flanders, the negotiations went badly.[117] He [Montejo] persevered for seven years from the time he left the Indies, which was in the year MDXIX [1519], until he re-embarked, which was in XXVI [1526], and by this persistence he had the president recused from the case, and he spoke with Pope Adrian, who was regent for the kingdom, and he talked with the emperor, who gave his strong approval and justly [*de razon*] disposed of the affairs of Cortés.[118]

---

de las Yndias, and is likely drawn from the latter.

[115] Beginning in 1504, 20 percent of the value of all precious metals acquired in the New World by Spanish conquistadors and colonists had to be paid to the Crown; this *quinto real* or "royal fifth" was sometimes applied to other sources of wealth, especially booty from conquest expeditions; in 1723 it was reduced to 10 percent.

[116] "XXV" (25) written in the left margin here, slightly above the paragraph break that precedes "When Francisco . . ."

[117] The king and emperor mentioned here are the same—King Charles I of Spain was also Charles V, the Holy Roman Emperor—and Flanders was one of his many European territories.

[118] Upon reaching the shores of central Mexico, Cortés had betrayed his patron in Cuba, Governor Diego Velásquez, and appealed directly to the king; this action initiated a Cortés-Velásquez feud that was played out politically both in Mexico and Spain, with Cortés's eventual triumph, despite Velásquez's powerful allies, due mainly to his destruction of the Aztec empire and founding of a wealthy colony in its place (Restall, *When Montezuma Met*

[Sec. 12] During the time that Montejo was at court he negotiated for himself the conquest of Yucatan, although he could have negotiated for other things, and received the title of *Adelantado*. So, he then went to Seville, taking with him a nephew, thirteen years old, bearing the same name [Francisco de Montejo]. In Seville he also found his son, who was twenty-eight [XXVIII] years old, whom he took along with him. He exchanged marriage vows with a lady of Seville, a rich widow,[119] and was thus able to gather five hundred [D.] men whom he embarked in three ships. And *[f. 9v]* setting off on his voyage he made port at Cozumel [*Cuzmil*], an island of Yucatan, where the Indians did not oppose him, having been tamed [*domesticados*] by the Spaniards under Cortés. There he learned many words of their language in order to make himself understood by them. From there he sailed to Yucatan and took possession of it, telling a second lieutenant [*Alférez*] with the banner in hand: "In the name of God I take possession of this land for God and for the king of Castile."[120]

In this way he went down the coast, which was then well populated, until arriving at Conil,[121] a town of that coast; the Indians were alarmed at seeing so many horses and men, and they sent warning to all the people of what was happening, watching the purpose of the Spaniards.

The Indian lords of the province of Chauaca [*Chicaca*] came to the adelantado to visit him in peace and were well received. Among them was a man of great strength,

---

Cortés, 161–81). The author's purpose here seems to be to emphasize Montejo's unswerving loyalty to Cortés from the moment of that betrayal on the Veracruz shore, with his loyalty the reason why Cortés (and "reason") prevailed. Note that Adrian, along with the Cardinal Francisco Jimenez de Cisneros, served as co-regents of Spain. When Charles V left Spain for the Netherlands in 1520, he appointed Cardinal Adrian Regent of Spain. He was not made Pope until January 9, 1522.

[119] Montejo married the recently widowed Beatriz de Herrera. The author is correct that this union allowed Montejo to be able to afford the furnishing of a ship with five hundred men and provisions. The Account provides further details of Beatriz de Herrera in the following pages (also see Chuchiak, "La Conquista de Yucatán").

[120] The *alférez* in question was Gonzalo Nieto, the second lieutenant of the first *entrada*, who recounts this moment in September of 1528 slightly differently, claiming that "in the post of Alférez of the Spanish Infantry, it was [my] banner that was first raised in this province in symbol of the taking of the possession of it for Your Majesty" (*Relación de los meritos y servicios del Capitán Gonzalo Nieto en la primera entrada en Yucatán*, in AGI, México, 244, N.34, fs. 567v–568r). Having joined the expedition in Santo Domingo, Nieto quickly became close to the Adelantado Montejo.

[121] The early colonial port and settlement of Conil was located immediately south (inland) from the precontact archaeological site of Chiquilá (and the modern town of the same name), on the Yalahau Lagoon in northern Quintana Roo (Andrews, "El antiguo puerto Maya de Conil"). The port was located in an area important for the colonial export of *palo de tinte* and served a strategic military purpose for the Spanish.

who took a curved sword from a young Black man who was carrying it behind his master, and tried to use it to kill the adelantado, who defended himself until the Spaniards reached them and the outburst quieted. They learned it was prudent to proceed on their guard.

The adelantado sought to learn what was the largest settlement and found it to be Tecoh [*Tekoch*], where the Chels were lords, situated on the coast further down along the route the Spaniards were taking.[122] The Indians, thinking they were on their way to leave the country, did not oppose or hinder their journey. In this way they came to Tecoh, and they found it a much larger and finer city than they had expected. It was fortunate that the lords of that country were not the Couohs of Champoton, who were always more courageous than the Chels. The latter, with their priesthood, which still exists today, were not as proud as the others, and thus conceded to the adelantado that he could make a settlement for his people. And for this purpose, they gave him the site of Chichen Itza [*Chicheniza*], an excellent place seven [*VII*] leagues away. From here he conquered [*f. 10r*] the land, which he was able to do easily because those of Ah Kin Chel did not resist and those of Tutul Xiu helped him—and thus the rest offered little resistance.

In this way the adelantado requested men to build at Chichen Itza, and in a short time he built a town, making houses of wood and roofs of certain palms and strands of long straws used by the Indians. And so, seeing that the Indians served without distress, he counted the people of the land, who were many, and divided the towns [in encomienda] among the Spaniards. They say the smallest of these allotments contained two or three thousand Indians. And in this way, he began to give order to the natives as to how they should serve that city, which did not much please the Indians,[123] although they hid their feelings for a while.

[*Sec. 13*] The Adelantado Montejo did not settle the land as he had planned,

---

[122] This does not necessarily contradict an earlier statement that the Chel lineage was located at Izamal at the time of Spanish contact; coastal Tecoh and Izamal are in the same region where the Chels were prominent.

[123] The scribe wrote the nonsensical *pluho* for *plugo* ("please" in the preterite). Despite the impression given here by the author that the Spanish settlement at Chichen Itza had all the makings and potential of a real colony, Montejo was clearly being set up by the Maya rulers of the region. Chichen Itza was ideal for Maya purposes because (a) it was no longer settled, yet remained a major ceremonial and pilgrimage site, so its geography was well known to those who would attack the Spanish settlement; (b) it was located more or less between regional polities, facilitating some cooperation among Maya rulers in the campaign to expel the invaders; and (c) as the author observes below, it was too far from the coast for the Spaniards to acquire reinforcements or make a rapid escape; see Restall, "Invasion: The Maya at War," for this argument (also see Chamberlain, *Conquest and Colonization of Yucatan*, 132–50; Chuchiak, "Forgotten Allies," 178–81).

because he had enemies there, as it was very far from the sea for easy entry from
and departure to Mexico, and for receiving things from Spain. The Indians, feeling
it to be a hardship to serve foreigners where they had been the lords, ~~and thus~~[124]
began to be hostile in all ways. Although he [Montejo] defended himself with his
horses and men, and killed many, the Indians grew stronger every day, so that he
found provisions failing. At last, one night, he left the city, leaving a dog tied to the
clapper of the bell, with a piece of bread nearby but where he could not quite reach
it. The same day he wearied the Indians with skirmishes so that they might not
follow, and the dog in trying to reach the bread kept the bell ringing, catching the
attention of the Indians who thought they were going to come out and attack them.
When they discovered the trick, they were furious at what had been played on them,
and sought to pursue the Spaniards in all directions, not knowing which road they
had taken. Those that followed in the direction they had gone caught up with the
Spaniards, shouting a great deal at them as people do in a chase. Six of the horse-
men waited for them in the open and lanced many of them. One of the Indians
seized hold of a horse by the leg *[f. 10v]* and stayed him as if he were a sheep. The
Spaniards [then] came to Dzilan [*Zilan*], a beautiful town whose chief was a youth
of the Chels, already a Christian and a friend of the Spaniards, whom he treated
well. Dzilan was near Tecoh, which along with all the other towns of that coast, was
under the control of the Chels. Here they remained safe for several months.

The adelantado seeing that here they would be unable to receive the aid of supplies from Spain, and that if the Indians were to attack them [the Spaniards] again
they would lose, decided to go to Campeche and [from there to] Mexico, without
leaving any [of his] people. From Dzilan to Campeche it was forty-eight leagues,
densely populated. When he told his intention to Namux Chel [*Namuxchel*], the
lord of Dzilan, he offered to secure the road and to accompany him. The adelantado
also arranged with this lord's uncle, who was the lord of Yobain, that he would give
him two of his willing sons, who would accompany him. In this manner, with these
three young cousins, he of Dzilan leading on horseback and the other two seated
behind [*en coupe*], they arrived safely at Campeche where they were received in
peace. The Chels took their leave, and on their return to their towns he of Dzilan
fell dead. From there they departed for Mexico, where Cortés had assigned an allotment [*repartimiento*] of Indians to the adelantado, despite his absence.[125]

---

[124] Written but crossed out here is "*y que assi.*"

[125] Montejo left Campeche at the end of 1534. He was granted in encomienda the Nahua town of
Azcapotzalco, many of whose warriors participated in the final Montejo-led invasion of Yucatan
(see Chuchiak, "Forgotten Allies," 186–205). The campaign described above by Landa was in
fact far more complex than his narrative suggests; as mentioned earlier by us (and see chapter 1
in part II), Landa omits most events in the campaign and folds two distinct invasions into one.

The adelantado having arrived in Mexico with his son and nephew, there came in search of him his wife, doña Beatriz de Herrera—by whom he had a daughter named doña Catalina de Montejo[126]—and whom he had secretly married in Seville. Some say that he disowned her, but don Antonio de Mendoza, the viceroy of New Spain, intervened and as a result he [Montejo] received her, and that same viceroy sent him to be governor of Honduras, where he married his daughter to the *licenciado* Alonso Maldonado, president of the Audiencia de los Confines.[127] Then after some years they moved to Chiapas, from where he sent his son, duly empowered, to Yucatan, which he conquered and pacified.[128]

[*f. 11r*] This don Francisco, son of the adelantado, was brought up at the court of the Catholic king, and his father brought him along when he returned to the Indies, to the conquest of Yucatan, from where he went with him to Mexico. The viceroy don Antonio and the marquis don Hernando Cortés liked him very much, and he went with the marquis on the journey to California [*Caliphornia*].[129] On his return the viceroy appointed him to rule Tabasco and married him to a lady named doña Andrea del Castillo, who had come to Mexico as a maiden [*doncella*] with her parents.[130]

---

[126] In a copyist's error, doña Catalina's name was omitted, and doña Beatriz's was repeated as the scribe moved onto the phrase about the clandestine marriage.

[127] Montejo's jurisdiction as governor and captain-general of Honduras-Higueras included the as-yet-unconquered Yucatan peninsula (as well as Tabasco and Chiapas). Montejo's choice of husband for his daughter was a shrewd one, as all of these claimed territories (save for Tabasco) fell under the jurisdiction of the newly created Audiencia de los Confines, founded in 1543, otherwise known as the Audiencia de Guatemala. Alonso de Maldonado, descended from one of the most prominent families in Salamanca, allies of the Montejos during the fifteenth-century struggles of the *bandos* (political family factions) in Salamanca, held the power while he was president of the Audiencia (from June 14, 1543, until 1548) to facilitate Montejo's conquest plans. Note that even with all the legal issues that plagued the Montejos, it was not until Maldonado left the presidency of the Audiencia in Guatemala that the Montejos suffered a fall from grace and the loss of their encomiendas and lands in Yucatan. By 1550, the control over the province of Yucatan would be transferred from the Audiencia of Guatemala to that of Mexico (Chamberlain, *Conquest and Colonization of Honduras*, 43–47; Chamberlain, "Governorship of the Adelantado").

[128] "XXX" written in left margin here, slightly below the line break. That could be a reference to a planned chapter 30, but more likely it marks where the copyist paused in writing his summary of the passages from the *recopilación* that he was redacting. After "*y las conquisto, y pacifico*" there is space for one- or two-and-a-half lines of text, which were never added; instead, the copyist turned the page and started a new paragraph summarizing the early life of Montejo the younger.

[129] See AGI, Patronato 21, no. 2, ramo 4; Restall, *When Montezuma Met Cortés*, 271–76; León-Portilla, *Hernán Cortés y la Mar del Sur*.

[130] Francisco de Montejo y León married doña Andrea del Castillo in 1539, the year he was granted the title of Governor and Captain General of the province of Tabasco, which he held until he left it for the third and final entrada campaign into Yucatan.

[*Sec. 14*] After the departure of the Spaniards from Yucatan, there was a drought in the land, and, the corn having been consumed during the wars with the Spaniards, they suffered a great famine; it was such that they were reduced to eating the bark of trees, especially one called *kuumche* [*cumche*], the inside of which is soft and tender.[131] On account of this famine the Xius, the lords of Mani, resolved to make a solemn sacrifice to the idols, taking certain male and female slaves to throw into the well at Chichen Itza. Because they had to pass through the town of the Cocom lords, their mortal enemies, and thinking that in such times old passions would be put aside, they sent to ask that they be left to pass through the territory. The Cocoms tricked them with a favorable answer; and having lodged them all together in one great building, they set fire to it and killed those who escaped.[132] From this followed great wars. There was also a plague of locusts for five years, that left them not one green thing. Such a famine ensued that they fell dead on the roads, so that when the Spaniards returned, they did not recognize the country, even though in the four good years after the locusts, things improved somewhat.

This don Francisco set out for Yucatan along the rivers of Tabasco, and he entered by the lagoons of Dos Bocas.[133] The first place he touched was Champoton, whose lord, named Moch Couoh, had badly treated Francisco Hernández and Grijalva. As he was now dead, there was no resistance there like before. [On the contrary], those of this town sustained don Francisco and his people for two years, during which time he could not advance further because of the resistance that there was [elsewhere]. Later he went on to Campeche, where he came to establish much friendship with those of that town. In this [*f. 11v*] way, with their help, and that of the

---

[131] Although that previously had been identified as *Leucopremna mexicana* (*bonete* in Spanish), we believe this is *k'uum che*, the "wild papaya" (*Jacaratia mexicana*) (also *bonete* in Spanish), so named due to the soft nature of its inner bark. There are accounts in Maya-authored texts of this tree being used as food during other moments of famine (Dine et al., "Famine Foods").

[132] This was the infamous massacre at Otzmal of 1536; see Restall, *Maya Conquistador*, 204n13. The massacre is described from the Xiu viewpoint by Gaspar Antonio Chi in his 1581 *relación de meritos*: "In a place called Otzmal, which is on the line that borders between the town of Mani and the town of Sotuta and its province, on the way to the seat of Chichen Ytza, the lord of the town of Sotuta and his province, Nachi Cocom, having given the insurance of safe and secure passage through his lands for which they necessarily had to go through to reach the city, Nachi Cocom while under said insurance did betray them and thought of treason, and there they killed the said Ah Kulel Chi and Napot Xiu and other principal men for having sworn obedience to his majesty and having received the Spaniards in peace and helped them in the conquest and pacification, and Ah Kulel Chi, father of Gaspar Antonio in particular, they cut off his head and tongue and took out his eyes, all of them dying and suffering for having served their King and lord" (*Probanza de Gaspar Antonio intérprete general de las provincias de Yucatán y vecino de ellas sobre su ayuda de costa*, 12 de octubre de 1581, in AGI, México, leg. 105b, r. 4, f. 8r).

[133] "Dos Bocas" is clearly labeled in the Account's maps (fs. 67–68; our figures 7.7–7.10).

people of Champoton, he accomplished the conquest, promising them that they would be rewarded by the king for their great loyalty, although to this day the king has not fulfilled this promise.

The resistance was not strong enough to prevent don Francisco and his army from reaching Tiho, where he founded the city of Merida [_Medina_].[134] Leaving the equipment in Merida, he set out to continue the conquest, sending captains to different places. Don Francisco sent his cousin Francisco de Montejo to the town [_villa_] of Valladolid to pacify the villages [_pueblos_] that had rebelled somewhat, and to settle the _villa_ as it now is. He founded in Chetumal [_Chectemal_] the city of Salamanca [de Bacalar]; Campeche he had already occupied. He put in order the services of the Indians and the government of the Spaniards until the adelantado, his father, came from Chiapas with his wife and household to govern. He was well received in Campeche, calling that _villa_ San Francisco after his own name. He then went on to the city of Merida.

[_Sec. 15_] The Indians took the yoke of servitude grievously. Although the Spaniards had divided well the towns that covered the land, still the Indians were not lacking for those who kept stirring things up. Such very cruel punishments were inflicted, resulting in the diminution of the population. They burned alive several principal men of the province of Cupul, and others they hanged. Accusations were made [_hizo se informacion_] against the people of Yobain, a town of the Chels, and so they [Spaniards] seized the principal men, put them in stocks in a house and then set fire to it, burning them alive with the greatest inhumanity in the world. And this Diego de Landa[135] says that he saw a great tree near the village in which a captain hanged many Indian women from the branches, with their infant children hanged from their feet. At this same village, and in another called Verey,[136] two leagues from it, they hanged two Indian women, one a maiden [_donzella_] and the other recently married, not because they took them to be guilty of anything, but because they were very beautiful, and they feared a disturbance in the Spanish camp on their account—and in order to show the Indians that the Spaniards were indifferent to the women. The remembrance of these two is strong among the Indians and the Spaniards due to their great beauty and the cruelty with which they were killed.

---

[134] The original has _Medina_, underlined, with "Merida" written in the left margin after the next mention of Merida, correctly rendered on the same line.

[135] This is the second time that Diego de Landa is mentioned by name in the Account. Other English translators (e.g., Tozzer, _Landa's_ Relación; Gates, _Yucatán_, 25) translated this clause as "I, Diego de Landa," but the manuscript clearly demonstrates the third person: "_dize este Diego de Landa que el vio._"

[136] There is no Yucatec village called Verey, presumably a copyist error, and the correct toponym remains unclear.

The Indians of the provinces of Cochuah and Chetumal rose up, and the Spaniards pacified them in such a way that those two provinces went from being the most settled and populous to the most wretched in the whole land. They committed *[f. 12r]* unheard-of cruelties, cutting off noses, arms, and legs, and the breasts of the women; throwing them into deep lagoons with gourds tied to their feet; stabbing at the children with spears because they could not walk as fast as their mothers. If some of those who had been put in chains fell sick or could not walk as fast as the rest, they would cut off their heads rather than stop to unfasten them.[137] They also kept a great number of women and men captive in their service, with similar treatment. It is asserted that don Francisco de Montejo did not commit any of these cruelties nor approve of them; on the contrary, they seemed very wicked to him, but he could do nothing.[138]

The Spaniards excused themselves by saying that being so few they could not have subjected so many people without making them afraid of such terrible punishments. They offer the example from the history of the passage of the Hebrews to the land of promise and the great cruelties committed by the command of God.[139] On the other hand, the Indians had a right to defend their liberty and trust in the valor of the captains they had among them, and they thought they would be thus against the Spaniards.[140]

---

[137] A similar account of Spanish atrocities in Yucatan was written by fray Bartolomé de Las Casas as part of his *The Devastation of the Indies: A Brief Account* (Las Casas, *An Account*, 47–53; also see Restall, *Maya Conquistador*, 31–37), which was first published in Seville in 1552 and was very likely read by Landa and his fellow Franciscans before the various sections of the Account were composed.

[138] Landa's assertion of Montejo's innocence is not entirely convincing, surely reflecting Landa's positioning within conquistador politics rather than an accurate appraisal of conquistador actions. That said, it was not the Montejos, but the Pachecos, father and son, who conquered the southwestern provinces of Cochuah and Chetumal—and it was the Pachecos who were reputed to have committed similar atrocities in earlier campaigns against the Zapotecs. Fray Lorenzo de Bienvenida, in a letter to the Crown, complained bitterly about the Pachecos' abuses in Chetumal; describing Alonso Pacheco, the friar wrote that "Nero was not more cruel than this man" (f. 2v in *Carta del franciscano fray Lorenzo de Bienvenida al príncipe D. Felipe, dándole cuenta de algunos asuntos referentes a la provincia de Yucatán y quejándose de abusos, 10 de febrero, 1548*, in AHN, Diversos-Colecciones, 23, n. 16, 3 folios).

[139] Here the author is referring to the Biblical book of Deuteronomy (7:1–16), to God's commands to the Israelites to "smite" all those who occupied their Promised Land. According to this passage, God commanded Joshua: "When the Lord your God brings you into the land you are entering to possess and drives out before you many nations—the Hittites, Girgashites, Amorites, Canaanites, Perizzites, Hivites and Jebusites, seven nations larger and stronger than you and when the Lord your God has delivered them over to you and you have defeated them, then you must destroy them totally. Make no treaty with them and show them no mercy" (7:1–2).

[140] On numerous occasions, including in several of his earlier treatises, fray Bartolomé de Las Casas defended Indigenous peoples' rights to resist a violent conquest, arguing that

They tell of a Spanish crossbowman and an Indian archer, who being both very expert, sought to kill each other, but neither could take the other off guard. The Spaniard, feigning to be off guard, put one knee to the ground, whereupon the Indian shot an arrow into his hand that went up his arm and separated the arm bones [*canillas*] from each other. But at the same moment the Spaniard shot his crossbow and struck the Indian in the chest; feeling himself mortally wounded, and so it might not be said that a Spaniard had killed him, he cut a vine like a liana only much longer, and he hanged himself with it in sight of everyone. Of such acts of valor there are many examples.

[*Sec. 16*] Before the Spaniards conquered this land the natives [*naturales*] lived together in orderly towns [*con mucha policia*]. They kept the land very clean and cleared of noxious vegetation and they planted very good trees. Their habitation occurred in this manner: in the center of the town were the temples with beautiful plazas and around the temples stood the houses of the lords and the priests and then those of the leading men. The houses of the richest and most esteemed stood closest to these and on the outskirts of the town were the houses of the common people. The wells, where there were a few, were close to the houses of the lords. They had their cultivated lands planted with the trees from which they made wine[141] and they sowed cotton, pepper, and maize. They lived together in these communities out of [*f. 12v*] fear of their enemies who captured them, but after the wars with the Spaniards they disappeared into the forests [*montes*].

Either driven by their vile customs or by the harsh treatment of the Spaniards, the Indians of Valladolid conspired to kill the Spaniards when they split up to collect their tributes. In one day, they killed seventeen Spaniards and four hundred servants belonging to those who were killed and those left alive. Then they sent several arms

---

conquistadors had routinely violated the Crown's prohibitions against waging war on "the Indians" (see, for example, Proposition XXII of his *Tratado Cuarto* in *Tratados de Fray Bartolomé de las Casas*, 485; also see Orique, *To Heaven or to Hell*). In few other conquests did Las Casas see more abuses than in Yucatan, specifically naming Montejo and his invasions of Yucatan as among the most egregious. In the document known as the Kraus Manuscript #139, Las Casas directly lays the blame for this violence on the *adelantado*, claiming that the Maya "always retain the horror and fear and enmity of the said Montejo and Spanish soldiers for the said great evils and injuries and dimunition which they received from them" (Capítulo 29, 23 of the "Petition of the Bishop of Chiapas," in Parish and Las Casas, *Las Casas as a Bishop*).

[141] The author here is referring to the balche tree (*Lonchocarpus violaceus* Pittier, although sometimes cited as *Lonchocarpus longistylus* Pittier or *Lonchocarpus yucatanensis* Pittier; note that there are 163 species of *Lonchocarpus*; balche or balché is *balche* in colonial orthography, *baalche'* in modern). For a description of and information on the balche tree, see Bricker, Po'ot Yah, and Dzul de Po'ot, *Dictionary of the Maya Language*, 26. For the significance of this Maya "wine" and its role in Maya religion and ritual, see Chuchiak, "It Is Their Drinking," 141–47; Vail and Dedrick, "Human-Deity Relationships."

and feet throughout the whole country as a sign of what they had done so that the others would rise up. The others, however, did not wish to do this, so the adelantado was able to come to the aid of the Spaniards of Valladolid and punish the Indians.[142]

The adelantado had disagreements with the Spaniards of Merida and still greater troubles on account of the emperor's decree that deprived the [holding of] Indian [*encomiendas*] to all the governors.[143] A commissioner came to Yucatan and took the Indians away from the adelantado and placed them under the administration of the Crown. After this the Royal Audiencia of Mexico conducted a *residencia* trial and sent him to the Royal Council of the Indies in Spain, where he died full of years and labors.[144] In Yucatan, he left behind his wife, doña Beatriz, who was much richer than he when she died; his son, don Francisco de Montejo, who married

---

[142] The surviving encomenderos gave the most detailed account in 1579, writing: "In the year of 1544 in the month of November, the natives of these provinces of Valladolid rose up against the Royal Crown and killed eighteen Spaniards who were scattered throughout their villages, burning two sons of Magdalena de Cabrera, roasting them in copal in the town of Chemax, whom they found there studying and learning their first letters in the company of a conquistador who taught them, named Juan López de Mena. And one of them they burned alive and to the other Spaniards they made great cruelties, taking out their hearts while alive, also killing more than six hundred Indians in the service of the Spanish. And among those who they killed, the Alférez and Alcalde Ordinario Bernaldino de Villagómez and Juan de Villagómez, his brother, and Hernando de Aguilar, all prominent persons, leaving behind in this town of Valladolid no more than twenty-two residents" (*Relacion del cabildo de la villa de Valladolid*, May 8, 1579, RHGY, Vol. II: 36).

[143] For the series of royal *cédulas* and other documentation compiled against the *adelantado* (Montejo the elder), see *Relación de la residencia que tomo el doctor Blas Cota al Adelantado Don Francisco de Montejo*, 1549–1550, AGI, Justicia, 244. The original *Real Cédula* that stripped Montejo the elder of his office and transferred his family's encomiendas into direct Crown control is found in *Pleito del Adelantado Don Francisco de Montejo con el Fiscal*, AGI, Escribanía de Cámara, 1006A. For the next two centuries the Crown used the proceeds from the encomiendas confiscated from the Montejos to reward loyal descendants of the conquistadors and settlers (*pobladores*) with pensions and stipends. Records of the values of the tributes and monies gained from these confiscated encomiendas exist in the AGN (Mexico City); a good example is *Cuentas de la provincia de Yucatán tocante a la cuenta de la administración de los tributos que se quitaron al Adelantado Francisco de Montejo para dar ayudas de costa*, 1666, AGN, Ramo de Tributos, Vol. 60, Exp. 2, fs. 53–75.

[144] A *residencia* was a formal "judicial review of an official's conduct at the end of his term of office," in which a specially designated judge, known as the *juez de residencia*, traveled to the region and took formal control over the government, holding a trial which began with a formal proclamation of the date on which the tribunal of the *residencia* began taking complaints or accusations against an official (see Haring, *Spanish Empire*, 149–53, quote on 149). As the formal ruler of more than one province, the Adelantado Montejo faced numerous costly and lengthy *residencia* trials for his actions in Tabasco, Chiapas, Honduras, and Yucatan, starting in 1539, and remained embattled with the Council of the Indies and the Crown until his death in 1553 (Chamberlain, *Conquest and Colonization of Yucatan*, 310).

in Yucatan; and a daughter, doña Catalina, who married the *licenciado* Alonso Maldonado, President of the *Audiencias* of Honduras and Santo Domingo in the island of Española. He also left don Juan Montejo, a Spaniard, and don Diego, a mestizo, whom he had by an Indian woman.

This don Francisco, after he had given up the government to his father, the adelantado, lived in his own home as a private citizen, as far as the government was concerned, although much respected by all for having conquered, parceled out the towns, and ruled the country. He went to Guatemala for his *residencia* trial and then returned to his home.[145] He had three children: don Juan de Montejo, who married doña Isabel, a native of Salamanca; doña Beatriz de Montejo, who married her uncle, the first cousin of her father; and doña Francisca de Montejo, who married don Carlos de Arellano, native of Guadalajara.[146] He died after a long illness, after having seen all his children married.

---

[145] Yucatan was administratively under the control of the Audiencia in Guatemala until 1550. Unlike his father, Francisco de Montejo the younger emerged mostly unscathed from his *residencia* proceeding, allowing him to return to civilian life following a brief trip to the Audiencia in Guatemala; he never held high colonial office again, but remained a prominent conquistador-settler for the rest of his life (Chamberlain, *Conquest and Colonization of Yucatan*, 310).

[146] Tozzer (*Landa's* Relación, 67) transcribes the last name in error as "Avellano." The don Carlos de Arellano mentioned here is also not to be confused with don Carlos de Luna y Arellano, who would become the governor of Yucatan (1602–1612), although the two were distant relatives. This Carlos de Arellano was not a conquistador, but rather one of the first *pobladores*, or colonists in the province, though initially not a willing one. A native of Guadalajara, Spain, illegitimate son of Iñigo de Arellano (brother of the Second Count of Aguilar, who was father of doña Juana de Zuñiga, Hernando Cortés's second wife) and of doña Ana de las Ruelas (see Garcia Carraffa, *Diccionario heraldico*, 19–24). Carlos de Arellano was a member of the entourage of the Second Marqués del Valle, don Martín de Cortés y Arellano, who arrived and stayed in Campeche for three months. He apparently had an unplanned, illicit relationship with the youngest daughter of Montejo the younger, causing a scandal when her pregnancy was revealed (Rubio Mañe, *Notas y acotaciones a la historia de Yucatan*, 438–439). Landa was very close to the Montejos, and under his advice and that of the newly arrived bishop, fray Francisco de Toral, the Montejo family resolved to remedy the scandal with an acceptable marriage: a dowry was created (largely by using what would have been part of the the inheritance of Francisca's brother, Juan de Montejo—the encomiendas of Conkal, Cholul, and Dzitilpech); and Carlos de Arellano married Francisca de Montejo Castillo on December 29, 1562, in the Sagrario of the Cathedral of Merida (with both Landa and Toral present). Even though he was well connected with the Cortés family, the link to the Montejo clan served Arellano well; as the son-in-law of Montejo the younger he was able to use his influence to become an encomendero and later a member of the Cabildo of Merida (see *Titulo de Encomienda a favor de Carlos de Arellano*, 11 de marzo, 1569, AGI, Escribanía de Cámara, 304B). A few years later, he became a wealthy merchant and producer of *añil* (indigo), arguing for the expansion of its cultivation in order to "aid the economy of the Indians" (*Carta de Carlos de Arellano, vecino de Mérida de Yucatán, con memoria sobre la siembra y beneficio del añil*, AGI, Indiferente General, 1530, N. 17, 6 folios). He would have been well

[Sec. 17] Fray Jacobo de Testera, a Franciscan, came to Yucatan and began the indoctrination of the sons of the Indians.[147] The Spanish soldiers, however, wanted to use the services of the young boys to such an extent *[f. 13r]* that they did not have time left to learn the Christian doctrine. They also hated the friars when they rebuked them for the evil that they did to the Indians. For this reason, fray Jacobo returned to Mexico, where he died. Afterwards, fray Toribio Motolinia sent friars from Guatemala and fray Martin de Hojacastro sent more from Mexico, and all of them settled in Campeche and Merida with the approval of the adelantado and his son don Francisco. The friars built a monastery in Merida,[148] as it is said, and they made sure to learn the native language, which was very difficult. The man who knew the language the best was fray Luis de Villalpando. He began to learn it by means of signs and the use of small stones and he reduced it to a sort of grammar *[alguna manera de arte]*, and he wrote a Christian Catechism in that language.[149] Still, he

---

known to Landa in his later life, as he served as the procurator of the city government of Merida in a 1578 case against the *"Defensor de Indios"* Francisco de Palomino—who fearlessly attacked the abusive use of Maya labor by Arellano and other encomenderos (see *Don Carlos de Arellano, procurador de la provincia de Mérida de Yucatán, con Francisco Palomino, defensor de aquellos indios, sobre los agravios que supuso a Su Majestad en deshonor de dicha provincia,* 1578–1589, AGI, Justicia, 1016, n. 6, r. 2).

[147] The Viceroy Antonio de Mendoza, in a letter to the Crown, described a report that Testera and his fellow missionaries sent him from Campeche in 1537 (published in CDI, vol. II, 195). Bartolomé de Las Casas, a friend and companion to Testera, in their return to Spain to petition together for the New Laws from 1539–1542 also recounts his discussions of these events with the Dominicans who arrived in Campeche in 1544 ("Platica que dio el Obispo de Chiapa en Campeche, 1545," in Remesal, *Historia de la prouincia,* Libro V, Cap. IV, fs. 239–45).

[148] Both Tozzer and Gates interpret this clause to mean that Montejo and his son built the monastery, but that is a clear mistranslation; they merely supported the monastery financially in its early construction and deeded the Franciscans the lands on which it was constructed. Built atop one of Tiho's largest Maya mounds, this structure was used as the primary religious house of the Franciscans in the region, even after it was fortified in 1667 and renamed La Ciudadela de San Benito. In 1821, with the introduction of the Spanish constitution, the Franciscans were forced to abandon the site, which eventually fell into ruins. These three historical and superimposed structures—the vast Maya pyramid, the monastery, and the fort—were razed nearly to street level, and today Merida's Lucas de Gálvez municipal market and post office stand on the site. The description of the pyramidal structure in the Account begins on f. 47; on the remaining traces of the pyramid, monastery, and fort, see Escalante Carrillo, "Reconocimiento y Análisis Arqueológico."

[149] According to the Franciscan chronicler fray Diego López de Cogolludo, Villalpando was the first to systematically study the Mayan language. Once he memorized "variations of their nouns and verbs, [he then] reduced the language of these Indians to a full grammar, ordering it into an *arte* to enable others to learn it" (*Historia de Yucathan,* Libro V, Capítulo I). In 1573, while he was in Mexico City to be consecrated as Yucatan's bishop, Landa requested

met with many obstacles on the part of the Spaniards who were the absolute masters of the country and who wished everything to be done with an eye to their own gain and tributes; as well as from the Indians who wanted to persist in their idolatries and drunken feasts. Mainly, the labor was greater because the Indians were scattered throughout the forests.[150]

The Spaniards were displeased to see that the friars had built monasteries, so they frightened away the sons of the Indians of their *repartamientos* so that they could not come to [learn] the Christian doctrine. Twice they burned the monastery-church of Valladolid that was made from wood and straw so that it became necessary for the friars to go live among the Indians. When the Indians of that province rose in rebellion,[151] [the friars] wrote to the Viceroy Don Antonio [de Mendoza] that they had revolted out of love for the friars. The viceroy investigated and found out that at the time of the rebellion the friars had not yet arrived in that province.[152]

---

permission to print a small run of this Maya grammar, with additions by other friars. For a further discussion of these early printed works on the Mayan language, see Rene Acuña, "Escritos Mayas inéditos y publicados."

[150] For the next two hundred years, the friars and bishops of Yucatan complained that the frequent movement of the Maya population across the colonial boundary served as the main cause of their continued "idolatries." For example, in 1606, Bishop Diego Vasquez de Mercado wrote that the Maya had to be forcibly removed from the forests so that they could "be better indoctrinated and have the sacraments more easily administered to them, and so that they can be removed from their occasions to commit their idolatries and other ordinary sins which they easily commit in their solitary homes within the heavily wooded forests, since they cannot be easily monitored there" (*Carta del obispo don Diego Vásquez de Mercado al rey sobre la idolatría de los indios y el estado general de su iglesia*, 10 de octubre, 1606, AGI, México, 369). The colonial governors also lamented the Mayas' dispersed settlement across the peninsula and their tendency to flee into the forests to continue with their traditional ritual practices. In 1601, Governor Diego Fernández de Velasco echoed the bishops' concern in a letter to the Crown: "Concerning their idolatries, I wish to inform your Majesty now of the very grave damage that the Indians commit when they flee to live as they did during their gentility hidden in the forests and mountains [*Al particular de las ydolatrías quiero Aora ynformar a V mag^d por constarme El grandisimo daño que Hazen los yndios que viben como en su gentilidad escondidos en montañas fraguosas*]" (*Carta del gobernador Don Diego Fernández de Velasco al rey sobre los indios idólatras y lo que convenga a su remedio*, 1 de octubre, 1601, AGI, México, 359, ramo 8, no. 42).

[151] As argued in our chapter 1, these final years of the wars of invasion in northeast Yucatan were styled "rebellion" by Spaniards in order to justify and legalize (under Spanish law) violence, slaving, and other conquest activities.

[152] The first Franciscan friars did not arrive until fray Lorenza de Bienvenida and his companions came to Valladolid in early 1548 (see *Carta de Fray Lorenzo de Bienvenida a S. A. el Príncipe Don Felipe, dándole cuenta de varios asuntos referentes a la provincia de Yucatán*, 10 de febrero de 1548, AHN, Diversos-Colecciones, 23, N.16, 3 fs.; and Lino Canedo, "Fray Lorenzo de Bienvenida").

[The encomenderos] kept watch over the friars, spying on them at night, scandalizing the Indians by making inquiries [*hazian inquisicion*] into their lives, and they took their alms from them.

The friars, seeing this danger, sent a friar [*un religioso*] to the very excellent judge [Alonso López de] Cerrato, president of the Audiencia of Guatemala, who gave him an account of what had happened. Seeing the disorder and unchristian conduct of the Spaniards who absolutely took all of the tributes and whatever they could without an order from the King and who obligated the Indians to give personal services of all types of work, even renting them out to carry heavy burdens, he [Cerrato] established a rate of taxation which, though high, [*f. 13v*] was still bearable.[153] In this he specified which things belonged to the Indians after they paid the tribute to their encomendero, and that everything did not absolutely belong to the Spanish. The encomenderos appealed this and out of fear of the tax quota they took more from the Indians than before. The friars returned to the Audiencia and complained in Spain, and they succeeded to such an extent that the Audiencia sent a Judge [*Oidor*], who decided the taxes to be paid in that land and abolished the personal services. He obliged some [Indians] to marry [only a single woman] and took away from them the houses that they had filled with women.[154] This judge was Licenciado Tomás López, a native of Tendilla.[155] All this made the Spaniards despise the friars even more. They spread infamous libels against them and ceased to hear their masses.

This hatred caused the Indians to become attached to the friars, considering all the work that they undertook without any personal interest in order to give them their freedom. This went so far that they did nothing without informing the friars and consulting their advice. And all of this gave cause to the Spaniards to say out of

---

[153] This visit resulted in the *Tasación de Tributos* (ca. 1550), which Francisco del Paso y Troncoso published in his series *Epistolario de Nueva España, 1505–1818*. This valuable document describes and lists by name each major encomienda town that existed in 1550. It also enumerates the amount of tribute due twice a year, on the Día de San Juan (June 23) and on Navidad (December 25). For a longer discussion of tributes and taxation in colonial Yucatan, see Chuchiak, "*Ca numiae, lay u cal caxtlan patan lae*," 107–218.

[154] There are multiple references in the Account to polygamous relationships or, more precisely, to polygyny or the practice of a man having more than one wife. Polygyny among Maya elite is attested in the hieroglyphic record at ancient cities such as Yaxchilan and Calakmul, where marriage often solidified political alliances between dominant and dependent polities (see Ardren, "Strange and Familiar Queens"; Guenter and Freidel, "Warriors and Rulers"). As discussed further in chapter 5, sixteenth-century Maya elite did not share the same perception of conjugal monogamy as Landa.

[155] The decrees set forth by Tomás López only survive in transcription, as a section of Cogolludo's account on the history of Yucatan (Cogolludo, *Historia de Yucathan*, Libro V, Capítulo XVI).

envy that the friars had done this in order to govern the Indies and enjoy the things that they had taken from them.[156]

[Sec. 18] The vices of the Indians were idolatries, divorce, public drunkenness, and the buying and selling of slaves; and over separating them from those things, they came to hate the friars. But apart from the Spaniards, the ones who gave most trouble to the friars, albeit secretly, were the [Maya] priests,[157] as people who had lost their offices and the benefits of them.

The manner in which they began to indoctrinate the Indians was to collect the small children of the lords and leading men, placing them around the monasteries in houses that each town built for that purpose. Here all the children of each place were gathered together, and their parents and relatives brought them food to eat.[158] With these children they gathered those who came to the catechism. From this frequent contact many asked for baptism out of devotion. These children, after they were taught, informed the friars of the idolatries and drunken feasts. They broke the idols, even those belonging to their parents, and they urged the divorced women and the orphans, if they had been made slaves, that they should complain to the friars. Even though [these children] were in danger [f. 14r] from their own people, they did not cease because of this, but instead they responded that they did it to honor them, and it was for the good of their souls. The adelantado and the officials of the king always had given fiscales [to the][159] friars in order to oblige the Indians to attend catechism and punish those who returned to their old life. At first the lords sent their sons unwillingly, thinking that they wanted to make them slaves as the Spaniards had done. For that reason, they sent many younger slaves in place of their sons; others understood the matter and sent their sons willingly.

---

[156] Hostility between conquistador-settlers and Franciscan friars was not unusual in the early Spanish colonies, and it was persistent in colonial Yucatan—manifest most notably in centuries of governor-bishop conflict—as discussed in chapter 2 and elsewhere.

[157] Likely due to a copyist's slip at the start of the sentence (where he wrote *entre* instead of *aparte*), there was debate among previous editors over as to whether *sacerdotes* meant the Spanish secular clergy (e.g., Tozzer, *Landa's* Relación, 73) or the *ah kinob* or Maya priests (Gates, *Yucatán*, 29). As the Account uses *sacerdotes* numerous times to refer to Maya priests, and as the secular clergy were not active in the Diocese of Yucatan until the 1560s—after the arrival of the first resident bishop, fray Francisco de Toral—the meaning is clearly the latter, as we have translated it.

[158] Here the author is describing the earliest Franciscan Mission schools, where the friars gathered elite Indigenous children to be schooled in alphabetic literacy and the Catechism; although this system seems similar to Aztec schooling practices, there is no evidence that Franciscan practice in Yucatan was in any way based on precontact Maya practice. For more detail on Franciscan education of Mayas, see Chuchiak, "Sapientia et Doctrina."

[159] The original reads *fiscales a* [document damage]-*rayles*.

In this manner, so many of the young boys in the schools and the other people in the catechism benefited, which was a remarkable thing.

They [the friars] learned to read and write in the language of the Indians which was reduced to such a grammar [*arte*] that they studied it like Latin. It was discovered that they did not use six of our letters, which are D, F, G, Q, R, S, nor did they need them for anything. Still, they needed to double others and to add other letters in order to understand the many meanings of some words, because *Pa* means "to open" and *Ppa*, tightly compressing the lips, means "to break," and *Tan* is "lime" or "ash," and *Than* uttered forcibly between the tongue and upper teeth, means "word" or "to speak," and so on with other expressions.[160] Because they had different characters for these things it was not necessary to invent new forms of letters, but rather make use of Latin letters so that the use of them became common to all.[161] Orders were given so that they left their homes in the forests and gathered as formerly in proper settlements so that they could be more easily taught and so that the friars did not have so much work.[162] For the support of the friars, they gave alms at Easter and other festivals and also contributed alms to the churches by means of two aged

---

[160] The author is correct here in his definition of *tan* and *than*, but he reverses the meanings of *pa* and *ppa*.

[161] On the rapid Maya acquisition of the Spanish alphabet, its adaption to Yucatec Mayan (which, despite the assertion here, did in fact include the invention of "new forms of letters"), and the persistence of the Maya culture of writing in the colonial period, see Restall, *Maya World*, 229–303; Hanks, *Converting Words*; Chuchiak, "Writing as Resistance"; and Bricker, Po'ot Yah, and Dzul de Po'ot, *Dictionary of the Maya Language*.

[162] These forcible relocation programs were known as "*congregación*" (congregation) and "*reducción*" (reduction); they were used throughout the entirety of the Spanish American colonization campaign, beginning with the colonization of the Caribbean in the first decade of the sixteenth century. First codified by the Law of Burgos in 1512, and later expanded in 1542 and again in 1552, the policy's original intent was to facilitate Christianization and to prevent the mistreatment of Indigenous peoples by Spanish settlers. In reality, the policy allowed for a much more systematized method of population control, which in turn, allowed for the institutionalized exploitation of Indigenous communities through high tribute demands by resident encomenderos. It also made Indigenous people more vulnerable to physical and sexual abuse at the hands of friars; and indeed, the encomenderos tended to blame the friars for all problems related to *congregación*, such as overwork and population decline. The *cabildo* of Valladolid, for example, complained in 1579 that the friars "burn their villages and settle them where they wanted, in places not as healthy or comfortable as those in which they lived before; forcing them to work in the very sumptuous monasteries they have built, to build and rebuild them as each new religious *guardián* undoes them and has them rebuilt in his own way, and never ceasing their work, taking no consideration in stopping the work during the time when the Indians have to go to their fields, of which the natives have complained because it has caused them to lack supplies for their own sustenance" (RHGY, Vol. II, 40). There is a large literature on *congregación* in Spanish America, but for Yucatan, Hanks, *Converting Words*, is the most comprehensive study.

Indians named for that purpose. By means of these alms they supplied the needs of the friars when they went about visiting them and they adorned the churches with ornaments.[163]

After the people had been instructed in religion, and the young boys advanced in their studies, as we said, they were corrupted by the priests because of their idolatries, and by the lords, into returning to their idolatries and making sacrifices not only of incense [*sahumerios*] but also of human blood. Concerning this, the friars held an inquisition and asked for the aid of the Alcalde Mayor, arresting many. They held formal trials [*processos*] [*f. 14v*] and celebrated an *auto* in which they placed many on the scaffold[164] wearing *corozas*, and they whipped them, and they were shorn, and some of them wore *San Benitos* for a while.[165] And others, out of sadness and deceived by the devil, hung themselves. In general, they all showed much repentance and a willingness to become good Christians.[166]

[*Sec. 19*] At this time, don fray Francisco Toral, a Franciscan, arrived in Campeche. A native of Ubeda, he had been in Mexico for twenty [*XX*] years and he came as Bishop of Yucatan.[167] Based on the information of the Spaniards and on the complaints of the Indians he undid what the friars had done and ordered the release of the prisoners. Because of this affront, the Franciscan Provincial [Landa][168] was

---

[163] This is the only indication in the Account of the Maya contribution to the colonial-era production of visual, cultural, and architectural design in the Americas.

[164] Here, the copyist wrote "*cada balços*," but clearly intended "*cadalsos*," which is to say, "scaffolding."

[165] The *sanbenito* [alt. sambenito] (or *saco bendito*) was a "distinctive garment, a 'sacred cloth' worn by those reconciled or condemned by the Inquisition. The term refers to the penitential garments worn in public by the condemned at the various public penance rituals called *autos de fé*. The garment usually consisted of a long, one-piece tunic made out of either white or yellow cloth" (Chuchiak, *Inquisition in New Spain*, 353). The fact that Landa and his friar commissary judges ordered some of the convicted idolaters to use *sanbenitos* served as evidence against him in the accusation of his usurping the "trappings and symbols of the formal inquisition" (*Cargos hechos contra Fray Diego de Guzman*, 6 de marzo, 1565, AGI, Escribanía de Cámara, 1009A).

[166] This paragraph describes the events for which Landa has become most infamous, the auto-da-fé of 1562, described in our chapter 2. Extracts from the primary source material for the auto-da-fé can be found in translation in Clendinnen, *Ambivalent Conquests*, and a significant number of the documents were published in DQAY; also see Scholes and Roys, "Fray Diego de Landa"; Restall, *Maya Conquistador*; Chuchiak, "In Servitio Dei."

[167] On Toral, see our discussion in chapter 2, and also Toral, *Avisos*; González Cicero, *Perspectiva religiosa*; Hanks, *Converting Words*; and, on Toral's relationship with his Nahua parishioners in the 1540s and 1550s, Townsend, *Annals of Native America*, 102–18.

[168] Once again, Landa is referred to in the third person (but not by name), suggesting that this section was not written by him, but either copied from another source or redacted by copyists from his longer writings on this topic.

determined to go to Spain after complaining first in Mexico. Thus, he came to Madrid, where the members of the Council of the Indies censured him severely for having usurped the office of bishop and inquisitor. In his defense he alleged the powers that his [religious] order had in those parts, conceded by Pope Adrian at the request of the emperor and the aid ordered to be given by the Royal Audiencia of the Indies, the same as that given to the bishops.[169] The members of the Council grew more angered by these excuses, and they resolved to send him with his papers and those that the bishop had sent against the friars to fray Pedro Bobadilla, the Franciscan Provincial of Castile, to whom the King had written, ordering him that he see the papers and decide justice.[170] And this fray Pedro, being ill, submitted the examination of the proceedings to fray Pedro [Francisco] de Guzmán,[171] of his own order, a wise and experienced man in matters concerning the Inquisition. They presented the opinions and testimony of seven learned men from Toledo, who were: fray Francisco de Medina; fray Francisco Dorantes, of the order of San Francisco; the master fray Alonso de la Cruz, friar of the order of San Agustín who had been in the Indies for thirty years;[172] Licenciado Tomás López who was an *Oidor* in the

---

[169] At the heart of the issue of Landa's supposed usurpation of the inquisitorial jurisdiction was the question of whether, as the provincial of the Franciscan order, he served as a legal prelate—that is, an ecclesiastical official with the "ordinary powers" of a bishop, such as the authority to initiate an "inquisition" into Indigenous "idolatry." Landa argued that he had such powers and rights, because he was the only prelate in the province before the arrival of the first bishop, and that the 1517 papal decree known as the Omnimoda bull gave the religious prelates of the orders permission to administer corporal punishments to their "spiritual children" for backsliding or disobedience. The Franciscans systematically applied ecclesiastical justice based on these extraordinary powers, granted to them in the absence of an established bishopric, and Landa likewise used Omnimoda in defense of his actions as provincial. The enquiry in Spain exonerated him, finding that while he had usurped the jurisdiction of a bishop through his creation of a monastic ecclesiastical court, his actions were condoned because at that time there was no resident bishop within three days' journey as stipulated by the Omnimoda bull. When he returned to Yucatan as its second bishop (1573–1579), he continued his extirpation of Maya "idolatry" (Chuchiak, "Indian Inquisition," 72–79, 92–95; *El castigo y la represión*, 203–15.)

[170] It is likely that some of the "papers" used in Landa's defense were included in his lost *recopilación*, as argued in our chapter 2.

[171] This is a copyist's error: the friar entrusted with the case was fray Francisco de Guzmán; the copyist accidentally duplicated the first name of the Provincial fray Pedro de Bobadilla, named several times on this page, including immediately above this mention of Guzmán.

[172] Fray Alonso de la Vera Cruz (1509–1584) studied grammar and rhetoric in Madrid and liberal arts and theology at the University of Salamanca under the tutelage of fray Francisco de Vitoria. He arrived in New Spain in 1536, and he took the habit of an Augustinian in Mexico City on July 20, 1537, in the Augustinian convent of Santa María de Gracia. Considered the founder of the study of philosophy in New Spain, he became one of the first friars to establish colleges and libraries for his order. More than a scholar, fray Alonso learned

New Kingdom of Guatemala and was a Judge in Yucatan;[173] the Dr. [*el D.*] Hurtado, a professor of Canon Law; the Dr. Méndez, a professor of Sacred Scriptures; and the Dr. Martínez, a professor of Scoto in Alcalá, all of whom said that the provincial had acted justly in the matter of the *auto* and in the other things pertaining to the punishment of the Indians. When fray Francisco de Guzmán saw this, he wrote at great length about it to the Provincial fray Pedro de Bobadilla.[174]

[*f. 15r*] The Indians of Yucatan deserve that the King favor them for many reasons and for the good will that they have shown in his service. When he was in need in Flanders, he sent the princess doña Juana, his sister, who was then the regent in the kingdom, a decree requesting aid from those of the Indies. An *oidor* from Guatemala [Tomás Lopéz] took the decree to Yucatan, and he gathered all the lords and ordered that a friar preach about what they owed to his Majesty and what he was requesting. When the sermon ended two Indians stood up and responded that

---

Tarascan, and he served as an Augustinian missionary in Michoacán, where he founded in Patzcuaro one of the first colleges in the Americas, El Real Colegio de San Nicolas Obispo (Prometeo Cerezo, *Alonso de Veracruz y el derecho de gentes*; Gómez Robledo, *El magisterio filosófico y jurídico de Alonso de la Vera Cruz*). Well-versed in the mission methods and nature of ecclesiastical justice in mission regions, he served as a key defender of Landa's actions in his *auto-da-fé* in Mani, asserting that "I have experience there, and I can certify that it is true that in those parts wherever there does not exist a bishop, the religious friars are held as prelates and that those who exist there have very ample commissions based on the papal bull of Pope Adrian VI *omnimoda* . . . and they have cognizance in cases of heresy." In fray Alonso's official opinion, "based on all of this, the said friar has not exceeded his authority here" (*Carta y Parecer de Fray Alonso de la Veracruz al padre Fray Pedro de Bobadilla, Provincial de la Orden de San Francisco en Castilla*, 6 de febrero, 1565, AGI, Escribanía de Cámara, 1009A, 2 folios).

[173] This is the same Tomás López mentioned earlier (Sec. 17; f. 13v).

[174] Although this section appears to recount trivial matters, it helps us to date when this section of the manuscript was written. Provincial fray Pedro de Bobadilla was ill when in 1565 he handed the case over to fray Francisco de Guzmán, and he had died by the end of January 1569, when fray Antonio de Córdoba became Provincial Minister of Castile. Guzmán's initial findings did indeed go before Bobadilla, but he too died before issuing a final sentence (see *Informe de fray Francisco de Guzmán al Provincial de Castilla*, 6 de mayo, 1565, AGI, Escribanía de Cámara, 1009A). Fray Antonio de Cordoba then issued his final sentence in the case early the next year (see *Sentencia del padre fray Antonio de Cordoba, Ministro Provincial de la Orden de San Francisco de la provincial de Castilla*, 29 de enero, 1569). As the manuscript here clearly states that the documentation at the time of writing had already passed from Guzmán to Bobadilla, without a final sentence mentioned, we surmise that Landa wrote this section (of his *Recopilación* and of the Account) between late May 1565 and the end of 1568. This would place him in the convent of San Juan de los Reyes in Toledo, as he resided there in 1565–1568, before being transferred late in 1568 to serve as Guardian of the convent of San Antonio de la Cabrera. This explains why a copyist wrote on title page of the Account the date MDLXVI (1566).

they well knew that they were obligated to God for having given them such a noble and Christian king, and that they regretted that they didn't live where they could serve the king with their persons, and thus they would serve him with whatever they had in their poor possessions [*su pobreza*] that he may want, and if that was not enough, they would sell their children and wives.[175]

[*Sec. 20*] The way in which they built their houses was to cover them with straw, of which they have of a very good quality in great abundance, or with the leaves of palm trees,[176] which are so well suited for this that when there are great torrents of water, it does not enter. After this they place a wall in the middle that divides the house lengthwise. In this wall they put some doors in the middle which [lead to what] they call "the back of the house" where they have their beds. They finely whitewash the other half of the wall with lime and the lords have them painted very charmingly.[177] This half serves as the reception and lodging of guests and has no doorway. It is open along the whole length of the house. The roof drops down very low in front because of the sun and rain.[178] They also say that it is better to defend themselves from within against their enemies in times of need. The common people built at their own expense the houses of the lords. Because they did not have doors, they took it as a grave offense to do harm to the houses of others. They had a small door behind the house for the necessary service and beds made from rods on top of which they placed straw mats where they slept covered by their cotton *mantas*. In the summer they sleep in the whitewashed part of the house on those mats, especially the men. In

---

[175] This passage refers to the desperate lack of resources that the Emperor Charles V faced at the beginning of the Italian War of 1551–1559, a.k.a. the Habsburg-Valois Wars. While in Flanders, Charles discovered that the French King Henry II had made a secret alliance with the Ottoman Turks. Shortly after, in 1551, Henry II of France declared war against Charles. Facing conflicts throughout the Holy Roman Empire and in Italy, Charles thus sent word to the Indies with requests for contributions to the war effort. The visiting Judge Tomás López Medel received specific instructions to have the friars in Yucatan preach to their new converts of "the king's need" and to solicit contributions from them to help in the war. Landa may have been the friar who accompanied the judge and translated for him, as this reads like a firsthand account of the Maya reaction to this request. The Maya reaction may also be apocryphal, as Landa's inclusion of it to prove his loyalty to the crown—and his success at nurturing such loyalty among Maya converts—is transparent.

[176] *Sabal yapa* (*palma de guano* in Spanish and *xa'an* in Yucatec Maya) were intensively managed by precontact Maya farmers. Each tree produces only six to twelve leaves per year, but a sizeable Maya center needed millions of leaves at any given moment (Ardren, "Savanna Products and Resource Abundance").

[177] Very few examples of precontact wall painting have survived, all of which come from elite contexts, not the humbler domestic structures described here. For a recent summary see Hurst, "Maya Mural Painting."

[178] Again, Tozzer makes an error of translation. He states that "the roof comes down very low in front on account of their *love* of sun and rain" (Tozzer, *Landa's Relación*, 86).

addition to building the house,[179] the entire town also sowed, planted, and harvested the fields for their lords' benefit, giving them all that was necessary for themselves and their household. When there was hunting and fishing, or when it was time to bring salt, they always [f. 15v] gave a part of it to the lords since they did these things communally. If the lord died, although the oldest son succeeded him, the other sons were also honored, assisted, and regarded as lords. They also aided the other secondary elites [los demas principals inferiors del señor] according to who they were or the favor that the lord gave them. The priests lived from their jobs and offerings. The lords ruled the town, settled disputes, ordered and settled the affairs of their republics all through the hands of the leading men who were obeyed and esteemed especially by the rich people whom they visited. The lords held court in their houses, where they settled all matters and business, principally at night. If the lords left the town, they were well accompanied; it was the same when they left their homes.

The Indians of Yucatan are a people of good physique, tall, robust, and with great strength and commonly all bow-legged because during their infancy their mothers carried them astride their hips from one place to another. They took it as a sign of beauty to be cross-eyed, and their mothers brought this about intentionally during their childhood by hanging a small thing [pegotillo] from their hair that reached down between the middle of their eyebrows. As they went about playing, their eyes were attracted to it and they came to be cross-eyed.[180] They also had their heads and foreheads flattened on purpose from infancy by their mothers.[181] They had their ears pierced for ear pendants and very mutilated from their sacrifices.[182] They did not grow beards and they said that their mothers burned their faces with hot cloths to prevent the growth. But now they grow beards even though they are rough, and the hairs are thick like horsehair.

They wore their hair long like women, and on the top, they burned a space like a good tonsure. Thus, it grew long below but was short on the crown. They braided their hair and wound it about their head like a wreath leaving a little tail behind like a tassel.

---

[179] In translating this sentence, both Tozzer and Gates are in error. The sixteenth-century word *allende* means "in addition to or besides," not (as those editors glossed it) "away from" or "beyond" (for complete contemporary definitions of colonial Spanish words see the six volumes of the *Diccionario de autoridades*, published from 1726–1739).

[180] Head-shaping practices may have caused strabismus and cross-eyed appearances, although there is not yet any archaeological or visual evidence for the suspension of a bead in order to cause a cross-eyed appearance (Tiesler, *Bioarchaeology of Artificial Cranial Modifications*).

[181] There is strong evidence in the archaeological record for cranial modification practices, not just among the Maya people but throughout the Americas. Again, see Tiesler, *Bioarchaeology of Artificial Cranial Modifications*.

[182] There is a change in hand here, which continues until f. 17v, when it reverts to the previous.

All of the men used mirrors, while the women did not.[183] In order to call themselves cuckolds, they said that their wife had placed the mirror in the hair at the back of their heads.

They bathed frequently without bothering to cover themselves from the women, except what they could cover with the hand.[184]

[f. 16r; figure A.3] They were great lovers of perfumes and for this they used bouquets of flowers and other odorous herbs curiously arranged with care.

They had the custom of painting their faces and bodies red, and although unsightly, they took it as a mark of beauty.[185]

Their clothing consisted of a strip of cloth about a hand's length across that served them for a loincloth and breeches that they wound about their waists in such a manner that one of the ends hung down in front and the other behind. These ends were made by their women with care and adorned with feather work. They wore large, square-shaped mantles and they tied them over their shoulders. They wore sandals of hemp or of dry untanned deerskin and they used no other garments.[186]

[Sec. 21] Their principal staple is maize, from which they make various foods and drinks. Even drinking it as they do, it serves them as their food and drink. The Indian women soak the maize in lime and water the night before. On the following morning it is soft and half-cooked, and in this way, they take off the thin skin and the nib and then they grind it on stones.[187] They give the workers, travelers, and sailors large balls or loads made of this half-ground maize and this lasts several months except for souring. From this they then take a small ball and dissolve it in a vessel or gourd formed by the shell of a fruit that grows on a tree from which God has provided them with vessels.[188] Then they drink this substance, and they eat the rest, and it is savory and of great nourishment. From the maize that is more fully ground they take out the milk and condense the liquid over a fire and make a type of gruel in the mornings and they drink it hot. With whatever is left over from the morning

---

[183] The precontact Maya certainly had mirrors, but there is no evidence to substantiate this particular claim.

[184] There is a blank folio page inserted here; between the folios labeled 15 and 16.

[185] Colonial dictionaries mention *chak tahal* or *ix tahate* as "skin red," a pigment prepared with hematite (Magaloni, "El arte en el hacer").

[186] This description of typical male clothing is remarkably consistent with depictions of Maya men from the Classic and Postclassic period.

[187] The author here is describing the "nixtamal" process whereby corn kernels are soaked in lime (or wood ash) and water for a period of time, boiled, steeped, rinsed, and then ground. In addition to making the corn softer for grinding and pliable for the production of dough, this also allows for a healthier food staple.

[188] This is the calabash tree, *Crescentia cujete*, or *luch* in Maya. It is used today in Yucatan to create cups, bowls, and canteens (*jícaras* in Spanish).

que con muchos de buenos olores, y que por esto vsan de
mjlletes, se flores y jeruas olorosas, y muy carposos, y labrados.
Que vsauan pintarse de colorado el rostro, y cuerpo, y les parecia muy
mal pero tenianlo por gran gala.

Que su vestido era vn liston de vna mano en ancho que les seruia
de bragas y calcas, y que se dauan con el algunas bueltas por la
cintura de manera quel vn cabo colgaua delante, y el otro detras
y que estos cabos les hazian sus mugeres con curiosidad, y labores
de pluma, y que traian mantas largas, y quadradas, y las atauan
en los ombros, y que traian sandalias de cañamo o cuero de venado
por curtir seco, y no vsauan otro vestido.

Que el mantenimiento principal es maiz del qual hazen di
versos manjares y beuidas, y avn beuido como lo beuen les sir
ue de comida, y beuida, y que las Indias echan el maiz a re
mojar vna noche antes en cal, y agua, y que a la mañana esta
blando, y medio cozido, y desta manera se le quita el hollejo, y
peçon, y que lo muelen en piedras, y que de lo medio molido dan
a los trabajadores, y caminantes, y nauegantes grandes pelotas
y cargas, y que dura con solo azedarse algunos meses, y que de
aquello toman vna pella, y deslian la en vn vaso de la corteza
ra de vna fruta que cria vn arbol por el qual les proueyo Dios
de vasos, y que se beuen aquella substancia y se come lo demas
y que es sabroso, y de gran mantenimiento, y que de lo mas moli
do sacan leche, y la cuajan al fuego, y hazen como poleadas
para las mañanas y que lo beuen caliente y que sobre lo que so
bra de las mañanas echan agua para beuer entre dia, por
no acostumbrar beuer agua sola, y que tambien lo tuestan y
muelen y deslian en agua que es muy fresca beuida, echa
dole vn poco de pimienta de Indias o Cacao

Que hazen del maiz y Cacao molido vna manera de espuma
muy sabrosa con que celebran sus fiestas, y que sacan del Cacao
vna grasa que parece mantequillas, y que desto y del maiz
hazen otra beuida sabrosa, y estimada, y que hazen otra beuida
de la substancia del maiz molido assi crudo que es muy fresca
y sabrosa   que hazer pan de muchas maneras bueno
y sano, saluo que es malo de comer quando esta frio, y assi procuran las
Indias tostarlo en lo hazer dos vezes al dia. que no lo ha podido
acauar a hazer quanto que se muelle como la oblea. y que si alguna
vez se haze como pan de trigo no vale nada.

que hazen guisados de legumbres y carne de venados y aves mon-
teses y domesticas que ay muchas, y el pescado que ay muchos. y que
assi tiene buenos mantenym.to principalmente despues que vino
plantado y ves de Castilla.

que por la mañana toma la bebida caliente con pimienta como
esta dho. y entre dia las otras frias. y a la noche los guisados.
y que si no ay carne hazen sus salsas de la pimienta y legumbres
que no acostumbravan comer los hõbres con las mugeres. y que ellos
comian por si en el suelo, o quando muchos sobre vna sevilla por mesa.
y que comian bien quando lo tienen, y quando no sufren muy bien la
hambre y passan con muy poco. y que se lavan las manos y la boca
despues de comer. Labravan se los cuerpos, y quanto mas
tanto mas valientes y braviosos se tenian porq el labrarse era gran
tormento que era desta manera. Los oficiales dello labravan
la parte q querian con tinta, y despues se javan le delicada
mente las pinturas, y assi con la sangre y tinta quedava
en el cuerpo las señales. y q se labran poco a poco por el tormento grande, y tambien se despues malos porq les encona-
van las labores, y hazia se materia, y q con todo esso se mofa-
van de los q no se labravan, y que se preciavan muchos de ser
requebrados, y tener graçias, y habilidades naturales, y q ya
comen y beven como nosotros.

que los Indios eran muy dissolutos en bever, y emborachar-
se de q les seguian muchos males como matarse vnos a otros
violar las casas pensando las pobres mugeres recebir a sus
maridos, tambien con padres y madres como en casa de sus
enemigos, y pegar fuego a sus casas, y q todo esso se perdian
por emborracharse, y q quando la borrachera era general, y
de sacrificios contribuian todos para ello porq quando era particular hazia el gasto el q la hazia. con ayuda de sus parientes
y que hazen el vino de miel y agua, y cierta raiz de vn
arbol q para esto criavan con lo qual se hazia el vino
fuerte, y muy hidiondo, y que con vaisles y regozijos
comian sentados de dos en dos, o de quatro en quatro, y
que despues de comido, sacavan los escançianos, los quales
no se solian emborrachar, de vnos grandes artezones del
bever hasta q se hazian vnas cimitarras, y q las mugeres
tenian

they add water so as to drink it during the day because they were not accustomed to drinking water alone. They also toast maize, grind it, and dissolve it in water, and it makes a refreshing drink, putting into it a little Indian pepper and cacao.

Out of maize and ground cacao they make a type of foaming drink that is very delicious with which they celebrate their feasts. From the cacao they extract a type of grease which resembles butter and from this and maize they make another esteemed savory drink. Another drink is made from the substance of uncooked ground maize which is also fresh and tasty.[189]

They make different kinds of bread, good and healthy, except that it is bad to eat when it is cold. Thus, the Indian women are kept busy making it two times a day. They have not succeeded in making flour that they can knead like wheat flour, and when they do make it like wheat flour it is good for nothing.

[f. 16v; figure A.4] They make stews of beans [*legumbres*] and the meat of deer and wild and domestic fowls, of which there are many, and of fish, which there are plenty. Thus, they have good provisions, especially after they began to raise Spanish pigs and poultry.

In the morning they take their drinks hot with chili pepper, as has been said, and during the day they take the others cold and at night the stews. If there is no meat, they make sauces out of peppers and beans.

The men were not accustomed to eating with the women, but rather they eat by themselves on the ground or at most over a mat that serves as a table. They eat well when they have food, and when they do not have food they suffer through the hunger, getting along on very little. They wash their hands and mouths after eating. *[Sec. 22]*[190] They tattooed their bodies, and the more they did it, the braver and more valiant they were considered, because tattooing was a great torment. And it was done in this manner: the craftsman [*los officiales*] first painted the part that they wanted to tattoo with ink, and after they delicately cut in the paintings, and with the blood and the ink the marks are left on the body. They tattooed themselves little by little due to the great pain that it caused. Also, afterwards they became ill because the area worked would inflame and fester.[191] Despite all of this they made fun of those

---

[189] There is a space in the text line, and instead of a line break, the section continues with a change in handwriting (see figure A.3, five lines up from the foot of the page).

[190] Again, the expected line break is omitted and a change in handwriting occurs.

[191] Many elite Mayas were also shown with tattoos in the precontact iconographic record. Although outlawed in the colonial period, the Maya continued to engage in ritual tattooing, and in their rituals, they paid homage to *Ah Cat* as the Maya deity of tattooing, piercing, scarification, and body painting. Cogolludo confirmed that "they also had idols for the Indians who painted and tattooed their bodies, saying that they converted themselves into flowers, they called these idols Acat" (Cogolludo, *Historia de Yucathan*, Libro IV, Capítulo VIII). Although the friars rigorously punished those who continued to scarify and tattoo

who were not tattooed. They also well appreciated being complimented and having social graces and natural talents, and today they eat and drink as we do.

The Indians were very dissolute in drinking and becoming intoxicated, from which many bad things arose, such as killing one another; violating the [conjugal] beds, the poor women believing that they were receiving their own husbands; also treating their fathers and mothers as if they were in the house of their enemies; and setting their houses on fire. Despite all of this they ruined themselves in order to get drunk; and when the drunken feast [la borrachera] was communal [general] and accompanied by sacrifices, everyone contributed to it, because when it was private [particular] the one who threw the feast paid for it with the help of his relatives. And they make wine out of honey and water, and with the root of a certain tree that they grew for that purpose, which made the wine strong and gave it a very disagreeable odor.[192] And with dancing and rejoicing they ate seated either two by two or four by four. After eating, the cupbearers, who did not usually get drunk, brought out large wooden tubs filled with drink until all the guests made a ruckus and their wives had [f. 17r; figure A5] to take much trouble getting their husbands home.

Often, they spend on one banquet what it takes them many days of trading and bargaining to earn. They have two methods of making these feasts. The first, which is that of the nobles and leading men, obliges each one of the guests to return an invitation to his host and they give each guest a roasted fowl, bread, and a cacao beverage in abundance; and at the end of each feast they used to give each guest a cotton *manta* to cover themselves, and a small wooden bench and a cup, the most beautiful that the host can afford. And if one of the guests dies, his household or his relatives are obligated to pay for the reciprocal feast.[193] The other method of giving feasts occurs between relatives when one of their children marries or when they celebrate the memory of their ancestors' deeds. This method does not oblige the guests

themselves, the worship of this deity continued into the later colonial period, as the Maya continued to engage in these activities. One interesting case of the continued worship of the god *Ah Cat* occurred in 1676, when authorities discovered a Spaniard who had pierced his own nose and offered sacrifices in an idolatrous ritual to *Ah Cat* (see *Proceso de idolatría contra un español Juan de Sosa, par ofrecer sacrificios a los ídolos*, AGN, Inquisición, Vol. 639, exp. 7, 20 folios).

[192] Maya honey wine, or balche, may have been made with the root at some point in the past, but the bark was surely also used—and today balche is made from water, honey from the native stingless bee, and the bark (not root) of the balche tree (*Lonchocarpus violaceus*). Balche was an important libation to the gods in the Postclassic and colonial periods, and balche rituals are depicted in the Maya codices (see Chuchiak, "It Is Their Drinking"; Vail and Dedrick, "Human-Deity Relationships").

[193] There are many colonial documents that mention and describe the continuation of these ritually reciprocal drinking feasts; on the feasts and their social nature, see Chuchiak, "It Is Their Drinking," 148–54.

to give a feast in return, except when one has been invited to other similar feasts; in that case when he holds a party or marries his children, he is obliged to invite everyone who invited him previously.[194] They highly value friendship and they conserve it even when far apart from one another with these feasts. At these feasts beautiful women serve the drink and after giving the cup, they turn their backs on the person who took it until the cup is emptied.

The Indians have very agreeable entertainment, principally comedians who act with great humor, so much so that the Spaniards hire them only to watch the jokes that the Spaniards pass between them and their girls [*moças*], between married couples or among themselves concerning their good and bad service, which these comedians then retell [*representar*] with as much skill as extraordinary [*curiosos*] Spaniards. They have small drums that they beat with their hands and another drum made from hollow wood that gives a deep mournful sound. This drum they play using a long stick capped with sap [*leche*] from a certain tree placed on its tip. They have long thin trumpets made from hollow wood with, at the end, long *[f. 17v]* twisted gourds. They have another instrument that they make out of a whole tortoise with its shells, and removing the flesh, they play it with the palm of their hand and its sound is melancholy and sad. They have whistles made from the shank bones of deer, and large conch shells, and flutes made from reeds.[195] With these instruments they make music for the dancers, and they have two dances in particular that are very manly [*de hombre*] and watchable. The first is a game of reeds and thus they call it *Colomche*, which has that meaning.[196] In order to play it they gather together

---

[194] This passage reads in the original (f. 17r; see figure A.4) "*y este no obliga a restitucion salvo que si ciento han convidado a un indio a una fiesta asi a todos cuando el hace fiesta o casa sus hijos combida.*" Previous English editions have translated it in different ways. Our translation here keeps with the sense of this original passage. Tozzer (*Landa's* Relacion, 92) translated it as "and this does not oblige the guests to give a feast in return, except if a hundred persons have invited an Indian to a feast, he also invites them all when he gives a banquet or marries his children." Gates (*Yucatán*, 36) opted for "This does not have to be returned, except that if a hundred Indians have invited one to a feast, all are invited by him when he makes a feast or marries his children." Pagden (*The Maya*, 69) chose "This does not require repayment, but when a hundred people have invited an Indian to a celebration he has to invite them all in return when next he holds a celebration or his children marry."

[195] Many of these instruments are visible in the processions depicted in the murals of Bonampak; precontact Maya music is a sorely neglected topic. Note that the term used for "shank" and "reed" is the same, *cañas*, reflecting the limited vocabulary of much of the Account; we have tried to remain faithful to those limitations with a fairly literal translation, but this is an example of where the English language effectively forces the translator to make use of its extensive lexicon.

[196] *Colomche*, or more accurately *colomte*, means "dance of reeds," "game of reeds," and "woodpecker."

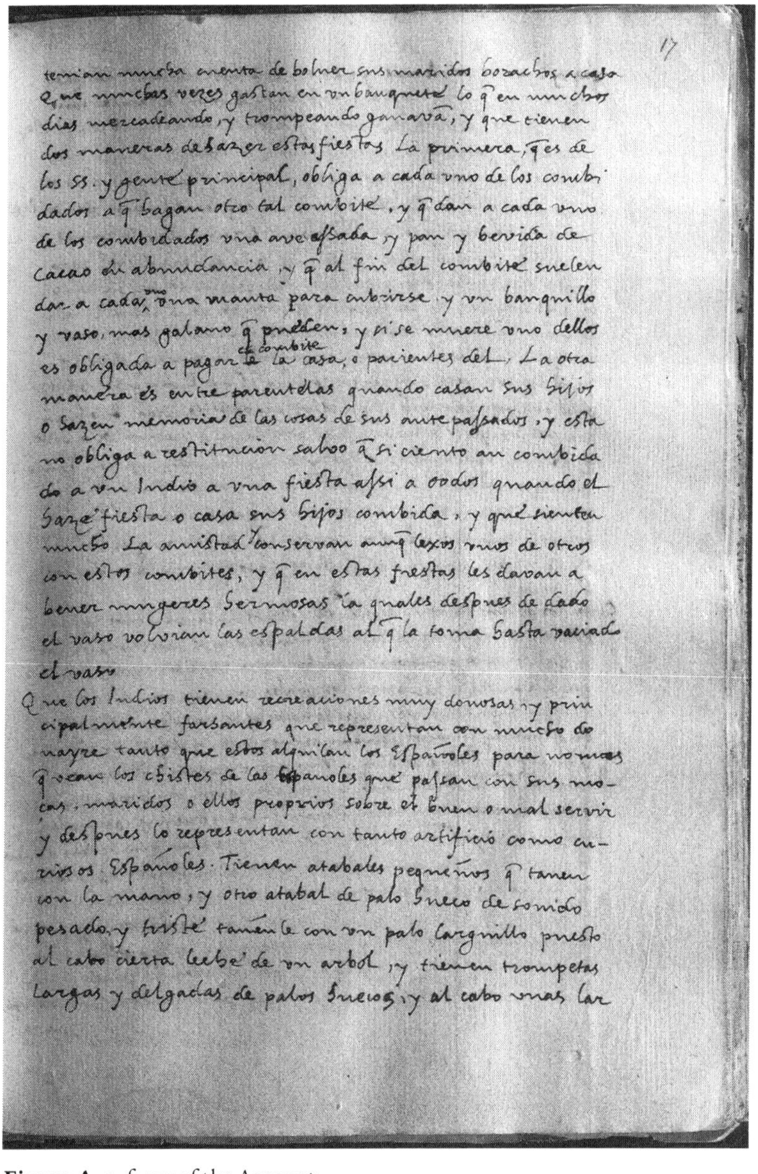

temian mucha cuenta de bolver sus maridos borachos a casa
que muchas vezes gastan en un banquete lo que en muchos
dias mercadeando, y trompeando ganava, y que tienen
dos maneras de hazer estas fiestas. La primera, que es de
los ss. y gente principal, obliga a cada uno de los combidados a que hagan otro tal combite, y que dan a cada uno
de los combidados una ave assada y pan y bevida de
cacao en abundancia, y que al fin del combite suelen
dar a cada, una manta para cubrirse, y un banquillo
y vaso, mas galano que pueden, y si se muere uno dellos
es obligada a pagar el convite la casa, o parientes del. La otra
manera es entre parientes quando casan sus hijos
o hazen memoria de las cosas de sus antepassados, y esta
no obliga a restitucion salvo que si ciento an combida
do a un Indio a una fiesta assi a todos quando el
haze fiesta o casa sus hijos combida, y que sienten
mucho. La amistad conservan aunque lexos unos de otros
con estos combites, y que en estas fiestas les davan a
bever mugeres hermosas las quales despues de dado
el vaso volvian las espaldas al que la toma hasta vaciado
el vaso

Que los Indios tienen recreaciones muy donosas, y prin
cipalmente farsantes que representan con mucho do
nayre tanto que estos alquilan los Españoles para no mas
que oyan los chistes de las españoles que passan con sus mo-
cas, maridos o ellos proprios sobre el buen o mal servir
y despues lo representan con tanto artificio como curiosos Españoles. Tienen atabales pequeños que tañen
con la mano, y otro atabal de palo hueco de sonido
pesado y triste tañenle con un palo larguillo puesto
al cabo cierta leche de un arbol, y tienen trompetas
largas y delgadas de palos huecos y al cabo unas lar

Figure A.5. f. 17r of the Account.

a great circle of dancers, with their music they make a pleasant sound[197] and as partners they come out of the circle, one of them with a bundle of reeds [*manojo de
bohordos*], and he dances rigidly [*en hiesto*] with them, and the other one dances
squatting [*en cuvillas*]; both move as partners around the circle, and the one with
the reeds throws them with all his might at the other, who deflects them with great
dexterity with a small stick, and then having thrown them, the couple returns to the
middle of the circle, and others come out to do the same. There is another dance
in which eight hundred Indians, more or less, dance with small flags to a pleasant
sound in a rapid [*passo largo*] martial dance that they have, and among them there
is not one who leaves their partner; and their dances are very tedious because they
don't stop dancing for the entire day, and because of this food and drink are brought
to them. The men were not accustomed to dancing with the women.

   [*Sec. 23*] The occupations of the Indians were potters and woodworkers, who in
the making of idols of clay and wood made many observances and much fasting.
There were also surgeons, or better said, sorcerers, who cured with herbs and many
superstitions; and thus equally [superstitious] were all the other occupations.[198] The
occupation to which they were most inclined was that of trade, carrying salt, clothes,
and slaves to the lands of Ulúa and Tabasco, and trading it all for cacao and stone
beads, which were their money. With this they were used to buying slaves or other
beads, which were really fine and good and worn by the lords like jewels at their
festivals.[199] They had other handmade objects of certain red shells that they used as
money and bodily jewelry, and they carried them in netted bags that they had.[200] In
the markets they traded in everything that existed in that land. They financed with
credit, loaned, and paid courteously and without usury. And most of them were

---

[197] We have glossed *son* as sound, but in case others read this as the *son* dance (anachronisti-
   cally, in our view): the *son* is today associated less with Spain and more with its many
   variants in Spanish America (the *son Mexicano*, the *son Cubano*, and so on), and is broadly
   viewed by ethnomusicologists as a product of Spanish, African, and Indigenous American
   elements; it is fascinating to see it clearly assigned to Maya dancers here and again a few
   lines down.
[198] On the many types of *hechiceros* (the term used here), *curanderos*, and other healers that
   existed in colonial Yucatan, see Tozzer, *Landa's* Relación, n414; Restall, *Black Middle*, 115–34,
   144–45, 154–55, 247–49, 270–76; Chuchiak, "It Is Their Drinking"; "*Ah Mak Ikob yetel Ah
   Pul Yahob*"; "*Yaab Uih yetel maya cimil*"; Kashanipour, "World of Cures"; Gubler, *Yerbas y
   Hechicerías*; and the *Libro de Yerbas y Hechicerias de Yucatán* housed in TULAL.
[199] The author has made a distiction between beads (*cuentas*) that were merely stone (*de piedra*)
   and fine and good (*finas y buenas*). The former were likely limestone or shell carved to appear
   like cacao beans, as discovered in the tomb of Ukit Kan Le'k Tok', a king of Ek Balam, and
   mentioned by Sahagún as the mark of a bad cacao seller. The fine beads worn by lords were
   jade. For more on the use of cacao as a currency, see Baron, "Making Money in Mesoamerica."
[200] The spiny oyster or Spondylus genus was the source of these red beads.

occupied as farmers [*labradores*] and those who collected maize and other seeds that they kept in fine granaries and bins for sale in their season. [*f. 18r*] Their mules and oxen were the people themselves [lacking pack animals]. According to custom each married man with his wife sowed a measure of four hundred [*CCCC*] feet [of land], which they called *hun uinic* [one man], measured with a rod twenty [*XX*] feet long, twenty measures wide, and twenty measures in length.[201]

The Indians have the good custom of helping one another in their labors.[202] At planting time, those who have no people of their own to do it, join together in groups of twenties [*XX en XX*], more or less, and together they do all their planting, each one doing his assigned share, and they do not stop until everyone's field is planted. Today the lands are held in common, and thus whoever is the first to occupy the land possesses it.[203] They also plant in many places so if one plot should fail another supplants it. In working the land, they do nothing more than gather the brush [*vassura*] and burn it in order to sow afterwards.[204] From the middle of January until April they work on the land and then they sow it when the rains come, which they do by carrying a little bag of seeds hung at their side [*cuestas*], and with a well-sharpened stick they make a hole in the ground, and put in it five or six grains, which they then cover up with the same stick. When it rains it is surprising how they grow. They also join together when they hunt in groups of fifties [*L. de L.*], more or less, and they roast the deer meat on grills so that it doesn't waste. And when they arrive back in the town, they first make their presents to the lord and then distribute the rest among themselves as friends, and they do the same with fish.

The Indians, in making visits, always take a gift with them according to their quality and the person's station, and the one visited gives a gift in return satisfying the other. During these visits, third parties speak and listen attentively, paying attention to the status of the person speaking. Nevertheless, they informally call each

[201] The Maya counted in a vigesimal (base-twenty) counting system, so these units of twenty are to be expected. For more details on Maya agriculture in the late post-Classic and colonial times, and on these fields called *hun uinic* and their productivity, see Chuchiak, "*Ca numiae, lay u cal caxtlan patan lae*," 111–15.

[202] On the colonial-era Maya culture of work, see Restall, *Maya World*, 121–40, 178–87, 256–59.

[203] While the author may be oversimplifying ancient Maya property rights, his assessment does resonate with Okoshi Harada's argument that the modern concept of private property cannot be applied to ancient Maya land use. Instead, he has suggested that uninhabited lands (the *monte*) were communally owned, and their variable states of use, disuse, growth, and regrowth precluded the possibility of defining secure boundary lines (Okoshi Harada, "Otra lectura"). Also see Restall, *Maya World*, 189–216.

[204] The author here refers to the common "slash and burn" technique, which is still preferred among contemporary Yucatec Maya populations. However, in the past, as today, farmers have a diverse array of cultivation techniques at their disposal, including terrace farming and forest gardening.

other "you" during the course of their talks, for the younger, out of attentiveness [*curiosidad*], usually repeats the title of office or status of the older, using it a lot, encouraging [*ayundando*] the speaker who brings news [*los mensajes*] by making a sound made from an aspiration in the throat—as if saying "indeed" or "so it is." The women are slow [*cortas*] in their reasonings and are not accustomed to conduct business because of it, especially if they are poor. For this reason, the lords mocked the friars for listening to both rich and poor without distinction.

[f. 18v] For offenses committed by one against another, the offense was satisfied by the lord of the town of the transgressor, and if he did not, it bred more passions. And if they were from the same town, they informed the judge who was the arbitrator, and examining the damage he ordered the recompense. If [the transgressor] did not have sufficient means to satisfy the judgment, his friends and relatives helped him. The causes in which they used to make such judgments were in instances of involuntary murder, or when a wife or husband hanged themselves due to the spouse's blame for having given them occasion to do so, or when someone was the cause of the burning of someone else's homes, lands, beehives, or maize granaries. The other more serious offenses committed with malice they satisfied with blood or blows.

The Yucatecans are very generous and hospitable, for no one enters their houses without being given some of the food and drink. During the day they offer them from their drinks, and at night from their foods, and if they do not have any, they search for it in the neighborhood. When traveling on the roads, if they meet fellow travelers, they share with everyone, even if by sharing they are left with little for their own needs.

[Sec. 24] Their method of counting is by fives until twenty and by twenties until one hundred, and by hundreds to four hundred, and by four hundreds up to eight thousand. This method of counting was very useful for the commerce of cacao. They have other very long counts which they extend into infinity [*in infinitum*], counting twenty times eight thousand, which makes 160,000, and then they multiply this by twenty and so on until they reach an uncountable number.[205] They do all their counting on the ground or on a flat surface.

---

[205] The manuscript uses a mixture of Roman and Arabic numerals here, which we have not included in brackets so as to avoid cluttering the text. This passage describes (albeit not very well) the Maya long count and base-twenty numerical system, both aspects of the Maya worldview since the Preclassic period, playing significant roles in the political and ideological system that supported ancient Maya kingship. This and the later passage that includes Maya day names provided crucial information for the initial decipherment of the Maya calendrical and epigraphic systems in the nineteenth century. The day names recorded in the Account are sixteenth-century versions of names that are remarkably consistent over the two thousand years of Maya calendrical inscriptions on stelae and painted texts. The long count operated in

They also admire knowing the origin of their lineages, especially if they came from one of the noble houses of Mayapan. This they learn from their priests, since it is one of their sciences, and they frequently boast about the distinguished men that they have in their lineages, as has been pointed out. Father's names are always passed on to the sons, but not to their daughters. Both their sons and daughters are always named for the last name of their father and their mother, with the father's name being their proper name and their mother's name the given one. ["So"], the son of Chel and Chan was called *[f. 19r]* Na Chan Chel, which means son of so-and-so.[206] This is the cause for the Indians saying that those who have the same name are related and treated as relatives. For this reason, whenever they come to a new unknown place and they are in need, they use their names and if there is someone of the same name, they receive them with all goodwill and charity. Thus, no woman or man marries another of the same name because among them this was a great disgrace. Today they call themselves by their baptismal names and by the others.

The Indians do not allow their daughters to inherit equally with their brothers except out of piety or goodwill [*por via de piedad o voluntad*]. Then, they are given something from the accumulated goods [*del monton*], and then the brothers divide the rest equally except in the case of the brother who most notably helped to increase the estate, they gave him his due [*equivalencia*]. If the children were all daughters, then the father's brothers or other nearest male kin inherited.[207] If the heir was not of sufficient age to receive the property, they entrusted it to a tutor or to another close relative who gave it to the mother to raise them, because they were not used to leaving anything in the mother's power. Or they took away the children from their mothers, principally if the tutors were the brothers of the deceased. These tutors gave the heirs what they were entitled to when they became of age and not doing so was a great ugliness [*fealdad*] among them and the cause of many quarrels. When they did transfer the goods [to the heirs] they did it in the presence of the lords and leading men, deducting from it the quantity that they had spent raising them. The tutors received nothing from the harvests of the inherited lands [*cosechas*], except when they came from beehives or some cacao trees, because they said that it was difficult to keep them up.[208] If the lord died and there weren't sons

---

parallel to the 260-day tzolk'in, and the 365-day haab calendars, and was capable of expressing both short and immense periods of time with tremendous accuracy. The tzolk'in is still in use in highland Guatemala today. For a recent overview of Maya timekeeping, see Stuart, "Maya Time"; also see Restall and Solari, *The Maya*, 16–17, 25–27, 47–50.

[206] On the Maya naming system, see Restall, *Maya World*, 41–50; Thompson, *Tekanto*, 194–96, 288–300.

[207] Both Tozzer and Gates reduced "other nearest of kin" [*u mas propinquos*] to "cousins."

[208] Again, both Gates and Tozzer translate this passage differently, and both are in error, making the passage state that heirs were not given the harvests of the lands, hives, and cacao groves;

to reign and he had brothers, the eldest of the brothers ruled or the most capable. These brothers taught the true heir their customs and festivities so that he [could rule] when he became a man. These brothers commanded him all his life. If there were no brothers, then the priests and leading men elected a man fit to hold office.[209]

[Sec. 25] [f. 19v] In the past they married at the age of twenty [XX] and now at the age of twelve or fourteen [XII o XIIII]. For this reason, they repudiate their marriage [se repudian] now more easily since they marry without love and are ignorant of married life and the duties of spouses. If the parents cannot convince the men to return to their wives, they search to find them another, and others and others. With the same ease, men left their children with their mothers, without fear that another man might take them as their wives, or later return to them. Nevertheless, they are very jealous, and they cannot bear with patience that their wives may be unfaithful to them, and now that they have seen that the Spaniards kill their wives for their infidelity, they have begun to mistreat them and even kill them. If they repudiate the marriage when the children are young, they leave them with their mother; if the boys are older, [they go] with their fathers, and older girls with their mothers.

Although it was a common and frequent thing to repudiate marriage [repudiar], the old people and those of better customs condemned it as a bad thing. There were many who never had more than one wife. These wives were never taken from members of their father's family, because this was a wicked thing among them. And if someone married one of his sisters-in-law, wives of their brothers, this was also taken as wrong. They did not marry their stepmothers, nor their sisters-in-law, sisters of their wives, nor their maternal aunts, and if one did so he was taken as wicked. With all the remaining relatives on their mother's side they could contract [legitimate marriage] even if she was a first cousin.

The parents took great care in searching for wives of good status and condition for their sons, and if they could, in the same town [el mismo lugar]. It was undignified for a man to seek his own wife or for parents to seek marriage for their daughters.[210] In order to conduct marriage negotiations, they agreed upon the dowry or

---

the original plainly states that "with the exception of the harvests of beehives and some cacao trees" the tutors received no harvests from the inherited lands. This means that the tutors did not receive any "maize," but they *did* receive the more valuable commodities, due mostly for the labor and costs of their upkeeping until the heir reached the age of maturity.

[209] Classic-era inscriptions make clear that patrilineal descent (as described here) was the norm, but royal mothers sometimes ruled as regents for their sons, or royal daughters ruled alongside a nonroyal husband (see Restall and Solari, *The Maya*, 35–38, 49). On succession patterns among Maya noblemen from the fifteenth to eighteenth centuries, see Quezada, *Maya Lords and Lordship*; Quezada and Okoshi Harada, *Papeles de los Xiu*; Restall, *Maya World*, 51–83; Thompson, *Tekanto*.

[210] The copyist seems to have dropped a word in this sentence (*y poquedad era entre ellos buscar*

settlement, which was small. The father of the boy gave the gift to the girl's father. [In addition], the boy's mother made new garments for her daughter-in-law and her son. When the [wedding] day came, they gathered together in the house of the father of the bride and there they prepared the food. The guests [*combidados*] and the priest came together with the young couple and their in-laws. The priest made sure all were in agreement, so that the in-laws had examined it [the arrangement] well, and everything being good, they gave the woman to the young man that night, if she was for him [*si era para ello*]. Later they had the meal and banquet, and from then on, the son-in-law lived in the house of his wife's father, working for his father-in-law for five or six years [*f. 20r*]. If he did not do so, he was thrown out of the house. And the mothers worked hard so that the wife always had something to give her husband to eat and drink as a symbol of the marriage. [Marriages between] widows and widowers took place without any festival or solemn ceremony. The men simply went to live in the house of the women, and if the women admitted them and gave them something to eat, they were married. The result of this was that the men could leave their wives just as easily as they had taken them. The Yucatecans never took more than one wife, as was the custom in other parts, where they had many partners [*juntas*]. Sometimes, parents contracted marriages for their young boys, [waiting] until they were of age, and the children treated [their intended spouse's parents] as in-laws.[211]

[Sec. 26][212] Baptism[213] is not found in any part of the Indies except in Yucatan. It

---

las mujeres para, si, . . .).

[211] This passage (fs. 19v–20r; Sec. 25) on Maya marriage is notable for being relatively uncritical of traditional practices; in fact, the worst tendency, that of wife beating and murder, is presented as a recent development due to the bad example set by Spanish colonists. It is likely, therefore, that this bears the strong influence—or authorship—of Chi or another of Landa's informants. An example of a less sympathetic attitude by a Spanish ecclesiastic is the 1604 report by Pedro Sánchez de Aguilar, parish priest in Chancenote, that some of his parishioners "have fled [the village] because I tore them from badly contracted marriages and returned women to their first and true husbands" (AGI, México, 299, f. 1v).

[212] Although transcribed in the same hand, at this point of the manuscript there is a shift in rhetorical style. The author no longer relies on the "*Que*" formulation. The "*Que*" is picked up again following this lengthy description of the "baptism" rite, so it is likely that this description was directly culled from another source.

[213] Here the author misinterprets an ancient Maya ritual for a Catholic-like baptismal ceremony, due to the young age of the ritual participants and the use of water during the rite. This event is more likely a ritual in which certain children of a Maya *cah* (municipal community) advanced to a higher age grade, socially marking their transition into adolescence. Once these participants had been ritually transformed, they were eligible for marriage and likely accepted increased social responsibility within their communities. The use of water, typically that which hadn't been touched by human hands before its use in ceremony, is well documented in the colonial period, during which time it is referred to as *suhuy haa*, or "ritually

is even known by a word that means "to be born anew or again," which is the same as the word *renascos*[214] in the Latin language, because in the language of Yucatan *zihil* means "to be born anew or again." It is only used in compound words such as *caputzihil* which means "to be reborn." We[215] have not been able to find out its origin other than it is always used and that they have such devotion to it that no one failed to receive it. They held it in such reverence that those who had sinned or those who knew those who had sinned, they were to especially speak out about them to the priests. And they had so much faith in it that they did not repeat the sin in any way. What they thought they received in baptism was the prior aptitude [*previa dispusicion*] to be good in their habits, not to get damaged by the earthly things of the devils, and to come, by means of it [baptism] and their good life, to obtain the glory for which they hoped, in which, according to Mohammad, they had enjoyed delicacies and drinks.[216] They therefore had this custom of preparing for baptism: the Indian women raised the children to the age of three, on the crown of boys' heads they always had attached to their hair a small white stone. The little girls wore cinched very low from their waists a small shell attached to a thin cord, hanging down to the top of their private parts [*la parte honesta*].[217] Among them, it was sinful [*f. 20v*] and something very ugly to remove those [small shells] from the little girls before they were baptized, which they always received between the ages of three and twelve. And they were never married until baptized. Whenever someone desired to have his child baptized, he went to the priest and gave him notice of his intention. The priest announced the baptism to the town and ensured that the date he performed it would not be unlucky. With this done the person who made the feast, the same one who gave notice of his intentions, chose a town elder [*un*

---

pure water." *Caput zihil*, reasonably glossed in this passage as "to be reborn," comes to refer to baptism in the colonial period.

[214] This should read "*renascitur.*"

[215] "We" is used here, suggesting that this section of the manuscript originated on a report, drawn up by now anonymous Franciscan friars, that centers on the customs and religious practices of the Mayas.

[216] Here, the author is making a direct link between the precontact practices of the Mayas and those of Islam. This is a common trope, whereby all "non-Christians" would be conceptually conflated as equally deceived by the Devil. This may also be evidence of Landa's intellectual training, as argued below in our chapter 4.

[217] There is a widespread pattern in precontact burials of marine shell ornaments found in the pelvic area of juvenile individuals (Ardren, *Ancient Maya Women*, 76). Numerous scholars have drawn a connection between this passage in the Account and the depiction of Classic-period royal women wearing the *xoc* girdle in royal portraiture, which consists of a spondylus bivalve worn over the pelvis; marine shell pendants are indicators of reproductive power (Ardren, *Ancient Maya Women*, 76; Joyce, *Gender and Power*; Looper, "Women-Men [and Men-Women]," 179).

principal del pueblo] of his choice to help him in this matter and everything pertaining to it. After this, it was customary to elect four other elderly and honorable men who would help the priest with the ceremonies on the day of the feast. These were elected in consultation with the priest, and in these elections the parents of all the children who were to be baptized participated together, since the feast belonged to all, and the chosen men were called *Chaçes* [Chacs]. Three days before the feast, the fathers of the boys and the officials fasted and abstained from women. On the day of the baptism, they all assembled in the house of the man who gave the feast, and they brought all the children who were to be baptized, placing them all in the patio or plaza of the house, which had been cleaned and covered with fresh leaves, putting them in ranked order with the boys on one side and the girls on the other.[218] They gave them godparents [*padrinos*], and the young girls were placed in the care of an old woman as their godmother, and the boys had a man who had charge of them. After this was done, the priest undertook the purification of the patio, casting out the devil[219] in the four corners of the patio on which the four Chacs [*chaces*] sat with a cord extended from one to another. In this manner the children were corralled together in the middle or inside of the cords. Afterwards, all the fathers of the children who had fasted had to enter the enclosure, passing over the cords. Before or after they placed another small bench in the middle, where the priest sat with a brazier that burned with a little bit of ground maize and ~~a little of~~ [*un poco*] some incense. The boys and girls came to the brazier in turns and the priest gave them each a little ground maize [*f. 21r*] and incense in their hands and they threw it into the brazier. Each of them did this and when they finished their incense offerings, they took the brazier in which they had made them, and the cord with which the Chacs had enclosed them; and pouring some wine into a cup they gave it all to an Indian so that he could take it outside of the town, warning him not to drink it or look behind him, and with this they said that the devil had been cast out. When he [the *Indio*] had left, they cleaned out from the patio the leaves of the tree that they called *Cihom* [*çihom*, soapberry tree] that they had put there, and they placed others that they called *copo* [ficus], and they laid down mats while the priest changed his vestments. He came out dressed in a coat of large red feathers decorated with feathers of many colors with other longer plumes that hung down from the ends of

---

[218] Fresh tree leaves from specific species feature in many Yucatec Maya rituals today; see Flores and Kantun Balam, "Importance of Plants"; and Gubler, *Yerbas y Hechicerías*.

[219] What the authors here viewed as "casting out the devil [*hechando al demonio*]," was—and remains—a well-documented mode of ritual preparation, used during a variety of Maya rites from the precontact period until today. For a ritual to be properly performed, ritual specialists ensured that the stage was cosmologically marked out in microcosm, evident in the placing of benches at a patio's four corners.

the coat. He also wore a type of *coroza* [miter] on his head made from the same feathers, and underneath his coat hung many strips of cotton that reached the ground like tails. He also held a hyssop in his hand made from a well-decorated short stick, and for the hairs or bristles of the hyssop it had the tails of certain snakes that are like bells.[220] He showed no more nor less gravity than a pope shows in crowning an emperor, and it was remarkable to see how much serenity these vestments gave to them. Later the Chacs went to the children and placed white cloths that their mothers had brought for that purpose. They asked the older children if they had committed any sin or ugly act, and if they had done so they confessed it and were separated from the others.[221] After this was done the priest ordered everyone to keep silent and sit down, and he commenced with great serenity to bless the children with many prayers and to bless them with his hyssop. When his benediction had ended, he sat down, and the elder that the parents had selected for this festival stood up and with a bone that the priest had given him he went to each of the children and threatened to hit them nine times over the forehead. Afterwards without saying a word he wet the bone in a vessel of water that he had in his hand and anointed them on their foreheads, their faces, and between the fingers and toes of their hands and feet. They made this water out of certain flowers and ground cacao dissolved into virgin water, as they called it, brought from the water collected in the hollows of the trees or of the stones in the forest. When the anointing finished, the priest rose and took the white cloths from their heads and others that they had hanging at their backs behind them, to which were attached *[f. 21v]* a few small feathers from very beautiful birds tied to them along with several cacao beans, all of which one of the Chacs collected. Then with a stone knife the priest cut the small white bead that the boys had attached to their heads. Behind him the priest's other assistants went with a handful of flowers and a pipe that the Indians used to smoke. They passed each one nine times before each of the children, and after that they gave each one the flowers to smell and the pipe to suck the smoke. Then they collected the presents that the mothers had brought, and they gave each boy a little to eat from them, because these presents were food, and they took a good cup of wine and the rest of the presents and offered it to the gods with devout petitions, begging them to receive that small offering from the boys. Then they called another official who assisted them, called *cayom* [chanter], giving him the wine to drink, which he did without stopping to take a breath, for they say to stop is a sin. When this was done the girls were sent away with their mothers to remove the cord and the shell protecting their purity which up to now they had tied low around their

---

[220] Clearly not a real hyssop plant, but a ritual object using a stick and rattlesnake tails to imitate one.

[221] This reference is to the Maya prayers known as *kamathan*.

waists, and this act gave them a license to marry when they and their parents desired. After that they sent the boys away, and the fathers came bearing the heap of mantles that they had brought, and they partitioned them by hand to all the assistants and officials. After this the festival ended with feasting and much drinking. They called this festival *Imku* [*emku*], which meant "the descent of God." Then the one who had borne the cost of the ceremony, after being celibate and fasting for three days, now remained celibate for nine more days; and this they observed strictly.

[*Sec. 27*] The Yucatecans naturally knew what they had done wrong, because they believed that due to wrongdoing and sin, deaths, sicknesses, and torments would come for them. They had a custom of confessing when such things were happening to them. In this way, whenever they were in danger of dying due to sickness or another reason, they confessed their sins, and if they neglected it, their close relatives or friends reminded them. And thus, they publicly confessed their sins to the priest if he was there, and if not, to their fathers and mothers, the women to their husbands and the husbands to their wives. The sins of which they commonly accused themselves were those of theft, homicide, the flesh, and bearing false witness [*f. 22r*]. With this, they believed they were saved. Many times, if they escaped [death], there would be quarrels between husband and wife for the disgraces that had befallen them and with those who had caused them. They confessed their weaknesses except for those that occurred with their female slaves, because those who had them [slaves] said that they committed [these sins] because it was permitted to use one's things as one pleased.[222] They did not confess the sins of intention, even though they are evil, and managed to avoid them in their meetings and sermons.

The abstinences which they commonly made were of salt in their stews, and of pepper, which was a very hard thing for them, and abstaining from [intercourse with] their wives for the celebration of all their festivals.[223] They did not marry again for up to a year after becoming widowers, nor did they know [carnally] either man or woman during that time. Those who violated this [abstinence] were considered

---

[222] Precontact Maya sexual customs are not well understood, and there are few iconographic sources of data for this topic and period. The rare depiction of an unclothed Classic period Maya body that displays primary or secondary sexual characteristics is usually within a ritualized or mythologized context, such as a cave setting (where ritual was conducted) or depicts deities (such as the naked snake woman scenes on codex pottery vases). From this we can conclude, for the precontact period at least, that the Maya, like Nahua, acknowledged the potency of sexual connection, and that sexual behavior was often situational; in ritual, on certain calendrical days, or at certain times in life, sexual behaviors might have been acceptable or indicated that did not necessarily carry over into other circumstances (see Ardren, "Strange and Familiar Queens"; Chuchiak, "Sins of the Fathers," 72–77).

[223] Gates leaves this whole sentence out of his translation.

intemperate and they believed that some evil would come to them. In several of
the fasts for their festivals they did not eat meat nor know [carnally] their women.
They always received the offices of their festivals with fasting and the same with the
offices of the state [*republica*]. Some were so long that they lasted three years and it
was a great sin to break them. They were so given to their idolatrous prayers that in
times of necessity even the women, boys, and girls did this by burning incense and
praying to God to free them from evil and repress the devil that had caused them it
[the affliction]. Even the travelers took incense with them on the road and a small
plate on which to burn it. Thus, by night wherever they arrived, they erected three
small stones and placed on each of them a small amount of incense. In front of these
they put three other small flat stones on which they placed incense, praying to the
god whom they called Ek Chuah.[224] They did this each night until they returned to
their own houses, where there was always someone who did the same for them and
sometimes even more.

They had a great multitude of idols and temples, sumptuous in their own way.
Besides these communal temples the lords, priests, and principal men had oratories
and idols in their houses for their prayers and private offerings. They also held them
at Cozumel [*Cuzmil*] and the well at Chichen Itza [*Chicheniza*] in the same veneration that we hold for the shrines of Jerusalem and Rome.[225] Thus, they went to
visit them and offer gifts, especially at Cozumel, like we do at sacred places. When
they could not go, they always sent their offerings. Those who would go also had
the custom of entering abandoned [*derelictos*] temples when they passed by them
to pray and burn copal. They had so many idols, yet there were still not enough for
all of their gods, for there was not *[f. 22v]* an animal or reptile of which they did not
make a statue, and they made all of these in the image [*la semenjança*] of their gods
and goddesses.[226] They had a few idols made from stone; others, small ones made
of wood and polychromed [*de bulto*],[227] but not as many as those made from clay.[228]

---

[224] On the Ek Chuah deity and image, see Vail, "Yearbearer Rituals and Prognostications"; and
"Gods of the Madrid Codex."

[225] So many Mayas made the pilgrimage to Cozumel during the colonial period that even Governor Francisco de Solis complained of it in a letter to the Crown; he remarked that countless
numbers of Maya even from remote interior villages of the province went on idolatrous pilgrimages to the island shrines (*Carta del gobernador Don Francisco de Solis sobre los ydolatrias
de los indios de la ysla de Cozumel*, 1584, AGI, México, 283, 4 folios).

[226] The author is careful here not to assert that the Mayas believed their effigies *were* the supernatural entities they venerated, but rather, were understood as mere representations of them.

[227] In the early modern Iberian world, "*imagenes de bulto*" typically referred to statues of saints
that were carved of wood and painted with polychromatic pigments.

[228] Both Gates and Tozzer strangely leave out one of the more common "idols," which were
"small bundles" that contained sacred objects such as shark bones, stingray spines, stone beads,

The idols made of wood were so cherished that they were inherited as a principal part of an inheritance. They did not have idols made from metal, because no metal existed there. They well knew that the idols were works of their own hands, dead and without divinity,[229] but they held them in reverence for what they represented and because they had made them with many ceremonies, especially those made of wood. The greatest idolaters were the priests, *chilanes*, sorcerers, physicians, *chaces*, and *nacomes*.[230] The job of the priests was to discuss and to teach their sciences, to announce their hardships and the remedies for them, to preach and host the festivals, make sacrifices, and administer their sacraments. The job of the *chilanes* was to give the people the replies of their devils [*demonios*],[231] which were held in such high esteem that they often carried them on their shoulders. The sorcerers and physicians cured by bleedings made of the parts that hurt the afflicted person.[232] They cast lots to divine the future in their offices and in other things. The Chacs [*Chaces*] were four old men, always newly elected to assist the priest in the proper and full celebration of the festivals. The Nacoms [*Nacones*] had two offices: one was perpetual and of little honor since it was he who opened the chests of persons whom they sacrificed; the second position was elected for a term of three years as a captain for war and other festivals, and this was of great honor.

[Sec. 28] They made sacrifices with their own blood, only sometimes, cutting themselves around in pieces, leaving them like this as a sign.[233] Other times they

---

and so on (nonetheless, see Tozzer, *Landa's* Relación, n502–n505). Based on inventories of "idols" confiscated by Provisorato officials, the clay or terracotta idols were by far the most common.

[229] Here the author explicitly compares the Maya sculptural tradition to that of medieval and coeval Europe whereby some statues of sacred Christian personages were understood *not* to have been crafted by artisans, but instead were miraculously produced by God. Termed "*acheiropoietos*" ("Αχειροποιετός" or "not made by human hands"), these images seemed particularly holy and were understood to have an inherent divinity because of their miraculous origins (see Bynum, *Christian Materiality*).

[230] Note that the Account uses the Spanish plural (*-s* or *-es*) instead of the Maya plural (*-ob*), although these are Maya office titles (those we have translated are the Spanish "*sacerdotes*," "*hechizeros*," and "*medicos*").

[231] The phrase implies that precontact statuary served an oracular function in Maya communities.

[232] Bleeding a patient, or phlebotomy, was standard medical procedure in medieval and early modern Europe; there is no evidence of it being similarly common among the precontact Maya. This example serves as a reminder that we cannot assume any assertions made in the Account regarding Maya culture are accurate, or even close to accurate, just because they appear here.

[233] Timothy Knowlton has suggested this represents an Indigenous practice of cupping as part of a medical bloodletting rite, later documented by Redfield and Villa Rojas in the 1930s (Knowlton, "Perinatal Rites," 730; Redfield and Villa Rojas, *Chan Kom*).

pierced their cheeks, other times the lower lip. Others scarify parts of their body, while others pierce their tongues across from side to side and with great pain passed blades of straw [*pajas*] through the holes. Others pierce the unnecessary part [foreskin] of the virile member [*se harpavan lo superfluo del miembro vergonçoso*], leaving it pierced like the ears.[234] On account of this, the Historian General of the Indies was deceived into saying that they practiced circumcision.[235] Other times they conducted a vile and shameful sacrifice, gathering themselves in a temple where, formed in a line, they each made holes across their virile member from side to side. When the holes were made, they passed through them the largest amount of thread that they could, staying like that, all caught up together, strung together, and they also smeared the blood from all these [their] parts on the [statue of the] devil. The man who did this the most was considered the bravest. Their sons from the earliest age [*f. 23r*] began to practice this and it is a horrific thing to see how devoted to it they are. The women did not practice this [blood] shedding, even though they took good care of the statues [*eran harto santeras*], of all the things there could be, of the birds of the sky, animals of the land, or fish from the waters. Always they smeared the faces of the devils [*los rostros al demonio*] with their blood and other things that they had; from some animals they took out the heart and offered it, while others they offered whole, some alive and some dead, some raw and some cooked [*guisado*]. They also made great offerings of bread and wine and of all other types of food and drink that they made.

In order to make these sacrifices, there were tall logs, carved and adorned, very close to the stairs of the temple. They had a wide, round pedestal and in the middle

---

[234] Bloodletting from the penis was also widely practiced before and after the conquest (see Ardren and Hixson, "Unusual Sculptures of Telantunich"). The symbol of the pierced penis (or its foreskin), according to colonial documents called *xicin poy* in Maya, became associated with idolatry and was acquired through a Maya sacrificial ritual. So many instances of penis sacrifice occurred that the Crown issued royal ordinances that no Maya found to have his virile member so mutilated could hold public office (See *Real Cedula* mentioned in AGN, Inquisición, vol. 213, exp. 10). In a 1587 case, a Spanish encomendero named Juan de Loria apparently cut his own penis and offered the blood. His accusers charged him with having participated in this "rite and ceremony, in which the Indians cut their genital member, slicing it with sharp knives in many parts of the said member as a means of sacrifice" (see *Denuncia de Martin Ruiz de Arze contra Juan de Loria por ydólatra y haberse retajado su miembro genital en sacrificio*, 15 de octubre, 1587, AGN, Inquicisión, vol. 213, exp. 10, fs. 10r–11v). Upon examination by the ecclesiastical authorities, they discovered that his penis was indeed scarred and marked by the ritual.

[235] The Historian of the Indies is often a reference in the sixteenth century to Gonzalo Fernández de Oviedo y Valdés, but we believe that Landa does not refer here to Oviedo (his 1535 *Historia general de las Indias* did not cover Yucatan, which was as yet unconquered), but instead to Francisco López de Gómara and his *La Istoria de las Yndias*.

a rather thin stone of four or five palms in height, adorned. At the top of the stairs there was another such pedestal.²³⁶

Apart from the festivals in which they sacrificed animals, they also sacrificed persons during some tribulation or calamity when ordered to do so by the priest or *chilanes*. For this everyone contributed so that they could purchase slaves. Or some, out of devotion, handed over their own little children who were well treated [*regalados*] and very protected until the day of the festival, so that they would not escape or tarnish themselves with some carnal sin.²³⁷ All the while they took them from town to town with dances. The priests, *chilanes*, and other officials fasted. When the day arrived, they gathered themselves in the courtyard of the temple and if they were to be sacrificed by arrows [*asaetadas*], they stripped him entirely and smeared his body with a blue pigment and placed a miter [*coroza*] on his head. After [thus] invoking [*alancado*] the devil, the people performed a solemn dance with him, everyone with bows and arrows, all around the pole. Dancing, they tied him to it, raised him up, continuing to dance and looking at him. The obscenely costumed priest rose up [*Subia el suzio del sacerdote vestido*], and with an arrow he wounded him, whether man or woman, in the private parts [*la parte verenda*], drawing blood; and he lowered himself and smeared it on the faces of the devil. Giving particular signals to the dancers, they started to shoot arrows in order as they danced, quickly shooting at the heart, which had been marked with a white symbol. In this way, they all put into his chest a single point, like a hedgehog of arrows. If the heart was to be taken out, a large company of people brought him to the courtyard with great ceremony. Smearing him in blue, with his miter on, they carried him to the round pedestal that was for sacrifice. Afterwards, the priest and his officials smeared that stone with the color blue, they cast out the devil [*demonio*], purifying the temple. The Chacs took the poor one [*f. 23v; figure A.6*] that they were sacrificing, and with great anticipation quickly threw him down on his back upon that stone. They tied him by the legs and arms, all four [limbs] drawn away from

---

²³⁶ This entire paragraph is written in the right margin of f. 23r. Apparently, precontact Maya temples had tall sculpted wooden posts for the burning of incense, although these have not been documented archaeologically. In one instance in 1575, Captain Francisco Sánchez de Cerdan discovered a public Maya temple in the jungle south of Campeche, describing the temple as a wooden structure which "had eight large wooden pillars. At the base and tops of these pillars were ceremonial braziers which had small cakes of copal incense burning in them and around them were raised pedestals with idols placed on them" (*Memoria y relación que presenta Francisco Sánchez Cerdan sobre la reducción y expedición que hizo contra los ydólatras y apóstatas el año de 1575*, AGI, México, 138, 12 folios).

²³⁷ Child sacrifice was practiced in parts of the precontact Americas, arguably because children were one of the most precious offerings that could be given to the gods (see Ardren, "Empowered Children"). But the rituals described in this section are not well corroborated by other sources of evidence on Maya practices (as noted later).

the middle. At this point, the executioner *nacom* arrived with a stone razor, and with great skill and cruelty stabbed him between the ribs on the left side below the nipple. He stuck in his hand and pulled his hand out with the heart, like a rabid tiger, ripping it from him alive, and put it on a plate that he gave to the priest, who very hastily smeared the faces of the idols with that fresh blood. Sometimes they conducted this sacrifice on the stone at the top of the temple stairs and then they threw the body, now dead, rolling down the steps. At the bottom the officials took it and flayed the skin from it entirely except for the hands and feet. Then the naked priest dressed in that skin and the others danced with him, which was something of great solemnity for them. They commonly buried those sacrificed in the temple courtyard, or if not, they ate them, distributing him between those who could reach and the lords. The hands, feet, and head belonged to the priest and officials. They held those sacrificed as saints [*por santos*]. If they were slaves captured in war, their captor [*el señor dellos*] took the bones in order to bring them out as insignia at their dances as a symbol of victory.[238] Sometimes they threw people alive into the well at Chicheniza, believing that they came out the third day even though they never appeared again.[239]

---

[238] Three of us (Ardren, Restall, and Solari) believe that much of this section is drawn from accounts of central Mexican (i.e., Nahua) rites, with only the final sentence appearing to be localized to the Maya area with the mention of Chichen Itza; one of us (Chuchiak) disagrees and reads it as mostly about the Maya, arguing that there is evidence of the Maya practice of taking bones and trophies. Either way, many of the details here (such as the accusation of cannibalism) are evidence not of Maya practice, but of the Spaniards' prejudicial stereotyping of Indigenous cultures—a deeply rooted trope used to justify slaughter, enslavement, colonization, and forced conversion. For a discussion of "bone" (*baak* in Mayan, and the most common term for "captive" in Classic period hieroglyphics), see Tokovinine, "Bundling the Sticks," 289; and for the use of bone trophies even among the Postclassic and early colonial Maya, see Chuchiak, "The Burning and the Burnt," 164–72.

[239] The human remains dredged from the depths of Chichen Itza's "Sacred Cenote" (what used to be called, misleadingly, "Cenote of Sacrifice") show little evidence of trauma. As much as popular imagination wants to see the human bones from the cenote—along with comments by the likes of Landa—as evidence of the Maya practicing "human sacrifice" on a regular basis, there is actually no strong evidence to show whether those thrown into the cenote went in alive (as Landa states) or were ritually executed, drugged, or wounded first (or had died beforehand from battle wounds, illness, or old age). Recent reanalysis of the human remains does prove juvenile people were more often found in the cenote than adults (Ardren, "Empowered Children"). For this reason, as discussed in our chapter 5, three of us believe child sacrifice was practiced here (with Restall the holdout), although we all remain skeptical of the descriptions given by Landa and his contemporaries. One of us (Restall) suggests the passing reference to the belief in resurrection after the third day has clear allusions to the sacrifice, burial, and eventual resurrection of Jesus Christ, suggesting strongly that the informant here was Christianized; one of us (Ardren) sees ample evidence in precontact Maya culture for the belief that contact with the dead could occur as soon as three days after death. As this passage reminds us, the Account is an invaluable source on colonial-era Maya culture, and

[Sec. 29] They had both offensive and defensive weapons. The offensive ones were bows and arrows that they wore in their quivers tipped with flint or the very sharp teeth of fish, which they shoot with a great skill and force. Their bows were made of a beautiful strong yellow wood, the color of a lion's mane [*leonado*], straighter than the cords of canvas [*las cuerdas de su canamazo*]. The length of the bow is always slightly smaller than [the stature of] the one who carries it. The arrows are made from very thin reeds that grow in the lagoons and more than five palms long. They insert a very strong, thin piece of wood into the reed, and into that they will insert the flint. They did not know of or use poisons even though they have enough to do so. They had small axes made from a certain type of metal made in this form.[240] These they fit together with a wooden handle, and they served as weapons and alternatively for the carving of wood. They strike the cutting edge with a stone that is like soft metal. They had small, short lances one estado in length with their points [*hierros*] [*f. 24r; figure A.7*] made from a strong flint.[241] They had no other weapons than these. They had shields for their defense made from split and tightly woven reeds rounded and covered with deerskins. They made jackets of quilted cotton and salt quilted in two parts or layers, and these jackets were very strong. A few lords and captains wore helmets made out of wood, like *moriones*,[242] but these were few. With these weapons they went to war, and those who had them wearing also feathers and the skins of tigers and lions. They always had two captains: one of them was for life, inherited; the other one, with many ceremonies, was elected every three years in order to host the festival that they celebrated in their month *Pax*, which fell on the twelfth of May, or to serve as captain of the other band [of warriors] in war. This latter they called Nacom [*Nacon*], and for those three years he could not know [carnally] a woman, not even his own, nor eat meat. They held him in great reverence and gave him fish and iguanas, which are a type of lizard, to eat. During the same time, he could not get drunk, and he kept his [eating and drinking] vessels and the articles of his personal use separate. No woman served him, and he interacted little with the people. At the end of these three years, he returned to live as before. These two captains dealt with matters pertaining

---

on colonial-era perceptions of the precontact past, but it is unreliable on precontact culture itself.

[240] In the right margin of f. 23v, the author drew a small illustration of this kind of hatchet (see figure A.5); a different hand labeled it "*hastil*" ("handle" in Spanish), marking the handle.

[241] As defined in n68 to part I, the Spanish measurement of an *estado* was roughly equal to two *varas* or 1.85 yards (1.7 meters).

[242] The *morion* was the standard high-combed steel helmet now commonly associated with Spanish conquistadors. It was standard issue in most European armies of the sixteenth century, and it can still be seen today in the Swiss honor guard of the Pope in the Vatican. The high comb was used to deflect the blows of swords and other weapons, similar to the function of the wooden helmets of the Maya.

que sacrificauan, y con gran presteza le ponian de espaldas en
aquella piedra, y asian le de las piernas, y braços todos quatro, y el q̃ le
partian por medio, en esto llegaua el señor nacon con un navajo̅
de piedra, y dauale con mucha destreza, y crueldad una cuchilla-
da entre las costillas del lado izquierdo debaxo de la tetilla, y
acudia le alli luego con la mano, y sacaua le mano del coraço̅
con, como rabioso tigre, y arrancaua selo vivo, y puesto en un
plato lo daua, al sacerdote el qual iua, muy a prissa, y untaua
a los idolos los rostros con aquella sangre fresca. Algunas veçes
hazian este sacrificio en la piedra, y grada alta del templo, y
estonces echauan el cuerpo ya muerto las gradas a baxo a rodar
y tomauan le abaxo los officiales, y desollauan le todo el cuero
entero salvo los pies, y las manos, y desnudo el sacerdote en
cueros vivos se aforraua de aquella piel, y vailauan con el
los demas, y era cosa de mucha solemnidad para ellos esto. A
estos sacrificados comunmente solian enterrar en el patio
del templo, o sino comian se le repartiendo por los q̃ alcançar
van, y los señores, y las manos pies, y cabeça eran del sacerdote, y officiales, y a estos sacrificados tenian por santos. Si eran
esclavos captivados en guerra el señor dellos tomaua los huessos
para sacar por divisa en los vailes en señal de victoria. Algunas veçes echavan personas vivas en el poço de Chichen iza, creyen-
do q̃ salian al tercero dia aunq̃ nunca mas parecian.

Q̃ no tienen armas offensivas, y defensivas. Ofensivas eran arcos, y flechas q̃ llevavan en su cargaçe con pedernales por cax
illos, y dientes de pescados muy agudos las quales tiran con
gran destreza, y fuerça. son los arcos de un hermoso palo les
nado, y armadura fuerte, mas derechos que corvos las
cuerdas de su cañamo. La longura del arco es siempre
algo menos q̃ el q̃ la trae. Las flechas son de cañas muy del
gadas q̃ se crian en lagunas, y largas de mas de a cinco
palmos, y enxieren le a la caña un pedaço de palo delgado del
gado muy fuerte, y en aquel va esperido el pedernal. No
usavan poner ponçoña, aunq̃ tiene harto de q̃
temian sacbuelas de cierto metal, y esta hechura las quales
encaxavan en un bastil de palo, y les servia de armas, y buelta
de labrar la madera. Davan le filo con una piedra a poder, q̃
q̃ es el metal blando. Toman cançuelas ciertas de un estaño con los fierros
de

de fuerça pedernal, y no tenian mas armas q̃ estas. Tenian para su
defensa rodelas q̃ sozian de cañas sentidas, y muy texidas redondas
y guarnecidas de cueros de venados. Hazian sacos de algodon colchados
y de sal por moler colchada de dos tandas, o colchaduras, y estos eran
fortissimos. Tenian algunos como 15. y capitanes moriones de palo
y estos eran palos, y con estas armas iuan a la guerra, y con pluma-
jes y pellejos de tygres, y leones puestos los q̃ los tenian. Tenian siempre dos capitanes vno perpetuo y se eredava otro elegido, con muchas cerimonias para tres años para hazer la fiesta q̃ hazian en
su mes de Pax, y este a doze de Mayo, o para capitan de la otra
banda para la guerra. a este llamavan Nacon no avia en
estos tres años conocer muger ni aun la suya, ni comer carne
tenianle en mucha reverencia y davanle pescados, y yguanas
q̃ son como lagartos, a comer no se enborachava en este tiempo,
y tenia en su casa la vasijas, y cosas de su servicio aparte, y
no le servia muger y no trataua mucho con el pueblo. Passados los tres años como antes. Estos dos capitanes tratavan la
guerra, y ponian sus cosas en orden, y para esto avia en pueblo
gente escogida como soldados q̃ quando era menester con sus
armas acudian, los quales llaman holcanes, y no bastando esso
recogian mas gente, y concertavan, y repartian entre si, y
guiados con vna bandera alta salian con mucho silencio del
pueblo, y assi iuan a arremeter a sus enemigos con grandes
gritos, y crueldades donde topavan descuidos, en los caminos y passos
los enemigos les ponian defensas de flecheros de varacon y madera, y comunmente destos despredra. Despues de la vitoria
quitavan a los muertos la quixada, y limpia de la carne ponian sela en el braço. Para sus guerras hazian grandes
ofrendas de los despojos, y si captivavan algun hombre señalado luego le sacrificavan porq̃ no querian dexar quien
les dañasse despues. La demas gente era captiva en poder
del q̃ la prendia.
Que a estos holcanes sino era en tiempo de guerra no davan sol-
dada, y q̃ estonces les davan cierta moneda los capitanes, y poca
porq̃ era del suyo, y sino bastava el pueblo ayudava a ello. Davan les tambien el pueblo la comida, y essa aderecavan las mugeres pero ellas la llevavã a cuestas por carecer de bestias, y assi

to war and put everything in order. In each town there existed people chosen as soldiers, and when they were called upon, they came with their weapons. They were called *holcanes*.[243] If these were not enough, they collected more people and set them up and divided them up, and, issuing forth with a tall banner they left the town in great silence. Like so, they went to charge their enemies with loud cries and cruelties when they came across them unprepared. On the roads and paths, the enemies put up barricades of stakes, tree trunks, and commonly others made from stone. After the victory they took the jawbone from the dead and cleaning it of the flesh they put it on their arm. For their wars they made great offerings of the spoils, and if they captured some important man, they sacrificed him later because they did not want to leave alive those who could harm them later. The remaining people remained captives in the power of the person who captured them.

Except for when it was a time of war, these *holcanes* were not given any salary. When there was war, the captains gave them a certain type of money, but only a little since it came from their own belongings. If this were not enough, the town helped them out. The town also gave them the food, which their women prepared for them. They carried this on their backs since they were lacking in beasts of burden, and thus *[f. 24v]* the wars were of short duration. When the war was over, the soldiers greatly harassed the people in their towns while the smell of war lasted, compelling others to serve them and give them gifts. And if one of them had killed some captain or lord, he was much honored and feasted.

[Sec. 30] Since the fall of Mayapan, these people have had the custom of punishing adulterers in this manner:[244] once the investigation was made and someone was convicted of adultery, the leading men came together in the house of the lord and brought the adulterer and tied him to a pole and handed him over to the husband of the delinquent woman. If he forgave him, he was set free. If not, he killed him by throwing a large stone down upon his head from a high place. For the woman, the great disgrace served as sufficient punishment and commonly they left their wives for this crime. The penalty for homicide was death at the hands of the relatives, and if it was unintentional *[casual]*, [the murderer] had to pay the dead person's [family]. For theft, they paid and were punished by enslavement, however small the theft. For this reason, there were so many slaves, especially during times of famine. It was because of

---

[243] As with other Maya titles of office given in the Account, the Mayan term is here given a Spanish plural ending (in Maya it would be *holcanob*). Literally meaning "snake head," *holcan* meant warrior or soldier, as the Account states, and as an adjective could also mean "brave."

[244] As is the case with a number of topics, the Account repeats itself here, reflecting its multiplicity of sources and authors; f. 24v (Sec. 30) repeats slightly differently the punishments for adultery in f. 6r–6v (Sec. 8) (which are also mentioned by Gaspar Antonio Chi in his own *Relación*).

this that we friars worked so hard baptizing them in order to give them their liberty.[245] If the thief was one of the lords or principal men, the people came together after having apprehended the delinquent and in punishment they tattooed his face on both sides from the chin to the forehead and this they considered a great disgrace.

The young men respected the old men very much and they took their advice. Thus, they boasted of being old and told the boys of what they had seen, and that since they had seen more, they had to believe them. The boys gave them more credit for their advice when they did so. They were so esteemed that the young boys did not associate with the old men except when it could not be avoided such as when the boys were to be married. The young boys also associated with married couples very little. Because of this they used to have in each town a large, white-washed house, opened all around, in which the young boys gathered together for their recreations.[246] They played ball and a kind of game with beads like dice and many others. They slept together there almost all of the time until they married. I[247] have heard that in other parts of the Indies they used such houses for sodomy [nefando peccado].[248] In this land, I have not learned that they did such a thing; nor do I believe that they do it, because those plagued with this pestilential vice say that they are not fond of women like those people were. They brought into these places the bad public women, and they used them. The poor women who among these people fall into this job, although they receive some recompense [gualardon], die because there were so many boys who came to them and pursued them relentlessly. They [boys] painted themselves the color [f. 25r] black until they married, and they did not usually tattoo themselves until they were married, except a little. In all other things they accompanied their fathers, and thus they became as great idolaters as them and they helped them greatly in their work.

---

[245] "We friars" is clear evidence of Franciscan authorship here. The implication that baptism automatically emancipated a slave in the Spanish American world is not to be read into this line (it did not, either for Indigenous or African slaves; see Restall, Black Middle, 23–26, 47–59, 101–18; Reséndez, Other Slavery, 279, 293, 313).

[246] Men's houses are known from other colonial period descriptions of the Maya area, such as J. Eric S. Thompson's analysis of sixteenth- and seventeenth-century reports on the Chol Maya written by Spanish explorers, which provide little additional data except that men were in the custom of sleeping in the men's houses from the fifth month of pregnancy to twenty days after birth (Thompson, "Sixteenth and Seventeenth Century Reports"; Tozzer, "Spanish Manuscript Letter"). Thompson also drew parallels to the male-only spaces of contemporary Kekchi and Lacandon Maya god houses and ritual performances. The identification of possible men's houses in the archaeological record has been attempted by a few authors: e.g., Ardren, Social Identities; Houston, "Splendid Predicament"; and Joyce, "Pre-Columbian Gaze."

[247] The author here uses the first person.

[248] The pecado nefando or nefarious sin refers to sodomy.

The Indian women raised their small children with all of the harshness and nakedness of the world, because on the fourth or fifth day after birth they placed the newborn stretched out on a little bed made of wooden rods. Face down [*alli boca*], they placed their head between two boards, one at the back of the head and the other on the forehead. Between them they squeezed their heads tightly, and they left them there for several days enduring it, until their heads remained flat and modeled, like all of them used to be.[249] So great was the distress and the danger to the poor children, that some were placed at risk of their life. The author[250] of this [account] saw the head of one pierced behind the ears and this must have occurred to many. They were raised entirely naked [*en cueros*], except at the age of four or five they gave them a small mantle for sleeping and several cloth strips to cover their private parts like their parents. The young girls began to cover themselves from the waist down. They breastfed them for a long time. If they could, they never stopped giving them milk, even though the children were three or four years old. On this account, they had among them so many people of great strength. They were brought up for the first two years of their life marvelously cute and fat. Afterwards, due to the sun and to their mothers bathing them continuously, they became dark complexioned, but during their entire childhood they were darling [*bonicos*] and mischievous, for they never ceased from going about with bows and arrows and playing with one another. Thus, they were raised until they began to follow the lifestyle of the young men [*mancebos*], increasingly holding themselves that way and leaving behind the things of boys.

[*Sec. 31*] The Indian women of Yucatan are in general better put-together [*dispusicion*] than Spanish women, larger and well formed, lacking the large haunches of Black women. Those who are beautiful pride themselves on it, and on the one hand, they are not ugly, [although] they are not white, but of a brown color, caused more by the sun and by constant bathing than from their nature. They do not make up [*adoban*] their faces as our nation does, considering this trivial. They had a custom of filing their teeth, leaving them like saw teeth, and this they viewed as charming. Old women did this job, filing them with certain stones and water. They pierced their noses through the cartilage that divides the nostrils, in order to put [*f. 25v*] in

---

[249] Bioarchaeologist Vera Tiesler has conducted extensive study of the physical evidence for head shaping, which varied by region and family. Performed by older women within an extended lineage, this process was perhaps one of the most powerful means by which family membership was signaled and reproduced. See more in Tiesler, *Bioarchaeology of Artificial Cranial Modifications*.

[250] Again, the writer of the manuscript included a self-referent, presumably to add validity to the claim of what he has seen.

the hole a stone of amber,[251] which they considered finery. They pierced their ears in order to put in earrings, in the manner of their husbands. They tattooed their bodies from the waist up, leaving their breasts for nursing, with patterns more delicate and beautiful than those of the men. They bathed often in cold water, like the men, but they did not do it with very much modesty, for they went undressed to the skin to the well where they go to [bathe in] water.[252] They were also accustomed to this: bathing in hot water, heated by fire, but this was seldom, more for reasons of health than cleanliness. They were accustomed to smearing themselves with a certain red ointment, like their husbands. Those who were able to, added a concoction of a fragrant gum,[253] very sticky, which I[254] think is liquidambar, in their language called *iztah-te*. They smeared themselves with this concoction, [formed] into a sort of brick, like soap, decorated with lovely designs. With this they smeared their breasts, arms, and shoulders, leaving themselves elegant and fragrant, or so it seemed to them. It lasted many days without fading, according to how good the ointment was. They wore their hair very long, which they arranged very smartly, and still do, divided into two parts. They braid them into each other, making another hairstyle. When young girls are ready to be married, their caring mothers used to arrange it for them [*curarselos*] with so much care that I have seen many Indian women with hair as well-cared-for [*curiosos*] as well-cared-for Spanish women. The little girls, up until they are somewhat grown up, braid their hair in four buns [*cuernos*] and in two, which to them seems pretty. The Indian women of the coast and of the provinces of Bacalar and Campeche are very modest in their dress, because beyond the covering that they wore from the waist down, they covered their breasts, tying a double-folded cloth [*manta*] under their armpits. Most of [the Indian women] didn't wear more than a dress like a large, wide sack, open on the sides, drawn in at the waist, drawn together by a single cord.[255] They didn't have clothing other than

---

[251] Amber is found only in the Simojovel region of Chiapas, where it ranges in color from white to yellow, red, pink, and green.

[252] Although the author uses the Spanish term for well, *pozo*, this is clearly a reference to the large watering holes characteristic of Yucatan, called *dzonot* in Maya and *cenote* in Yucatecan Spanish (as discussed earlier).

[253] Texts of this period often used the word "gum" to describe what are actually resins, or oils made from the distillation of resin, which has led to much confusion about the binding agents used with precontact pigments. Today scholars believe *itztah-te* was actually obtained from a Mexican conifer known as *Pinus oocarpa schiede ex schlechtendal*, although whether the author refers to a resin or an oil obtained from the resin is unclear (see Vázquez de Ágredos Pascual, Doménech Carbó, and Doménech Carbó, "Resins and Drying Oils").

[254] Note the use of the first person here.

[255] Connections to the precontact, colonial-era, and contemporary women's dress of Yucatan, the white cotton *huipil*, are obvious.

the *manta* in which they always slept. They used it when they went on the road, bringing it doubled up and rolled, and like that they went.

[Sec. 32][256] The women prided themselves on being good and they had good reason to, because before they knew our nation, according to the old men who are complaining of it today, they were a wonder. Of this I will give two examples. Captain Alonso López de Ávila, brother-in-law of the Adelantado Montejo, had captured *[f. 26r]* a young Indian woman, who was both beautiful and charming, when he was engaged in the war of Bacalar. Being afraid that her husband would die in the war, she had promised him not to know [carnally] anyone except him. Because she would not risk being defiled by another man, he [Ávila] could not manage to persuade her to not give up her own life, on which account they had her put to death by dogs [*aperrear*]. An Indian woman came to me to be baptized, and complained of an Indian, already baptized, who was falling in love with her, for she was beautiful. He was waiting until her husband was absent, and went one night to her house, and declared his intent with many words of love. It was not enough, so he proved it to her by giving her gifts, which he had brought for this purpose. But as this did not succeed, he tried to force her. And though he was gigantic and struggled all night to accomplish his purpose, he obtained nothing more from her than enraging her so much that she came to me to complain to me of the wicked attempts of the Indian. And it was just as she said. They had the habit of turning their backs on the men whenever they met them anywhere, and of stepping aside to let them pass. They did the same thing when they gave them drink, until they had finished drinking. They teach what they know to their daughters, and bring them up in their good way, for they scold them and teach them and make them work, and if they commit any fault, they punish them by giving them pinches on their ears and arms. If they see them raise their eyes, they scold them well, and rub their eyes with their pepper, which causes them great pain. And if they are indecent, they beat them and rub another part of their body with the pepper as a punishment and insult.[257] To badly disciplined girls, they say as a great disgrace and serious rebuke that they seem like women raised without a mother.[258] They are very jealous, and

---

[256] The manuscript does not include a paragraph break here; all the information about Maya women is one continuous paragraph. The author, using the first person to stress personal observation, here seems to us to be Landa himself.

[257] This description of the creative uses for chili pepper, deployed on a man rather than a woman, is immortalized in an early scene in the 2006 Mel Gibson feature film *Apocalypto*. This type of punishment using the chili peppers is also evidenced in the sources of the Nahua, especially in the Codex Mendoza and the Florentine Codex.

[258] The phrase "like women raised without a mother [*que parecen mugeres criadas sin madre*]" is written in a different hand as though a space was left in the manuscript and this clause was added later.

some so much so that they lay hands on the women of whom they are jealous. And they are so bad-tempered and angry, even though they are extremely meek, that some tended to twist their husband's hair, which the men rarely do. They are great workers and frugal [*vividoras*] since the greatest part of the most important work, for the maintenance of their houses, the education of their children, and the payment of their tribute all depends on them.[259] And despite all this, if there is need for it, they sometimes carry an even greater burden, cultivating and sowing their fields [*mantenimientos*]. They are wonderful farmers, working at night for a little, in order to be of service to their households, they go to the markets to buy and sell their little things. They raise fowls for sale—both the Castilian and their own [breeds] [*f. 26v*]—and to eat. They raise birds for their own pleasure, and for the feathers from which to make their fine clothes. They raise other domestic animals, and they give their breasts to deer, by which means they raise them to be so tame that they do not know to go into the woods ever, even though they take them and carry them into the woods and raise them there. They have the habit of helping each other in weaving and spinning, and they repay each other for these kinds of work as their husbands do for work on their lands. And on these occasions, they always have their teasing jokes and telling news and from time to time, a little gossip. They considered it as a very improper thing to look at men or to laugh at them, so much so that this alone was sufficient to constitute impropriety and, without anything more, could be the first stage of bringing her to ruin. They danced their dances among themselves, and some with the men, as for instance, one that they called *naual*, which is not very decent. They are very fertile and give birth early. And they are excellent nursemaids [*criadoras*] for two reasons: first, because the warm drink which they take in the morning creates a lot of milk; and secondly, the continual grinding of the maize does not allow them to keep their breasts cramped, making them be very large ones, from which come a lot of milk. They also used to get drunk with their guests, even though they eat by themselves,[260] but they did not get as drunk as the men. They are a people who want a lot of children, and she who does not have them petitions her idols with gifts and prayers and now they ask them of God. They are prudent, polite, and sociable, with those who understand them, and they are extremely generous. They are not secretive, and they are not very clean personally, nor in their houses, even with how much they wash like weasels. They were very

---

[259] On women's labor and the degree to which women carried the family and community tribute burden, see Hunt and Restall, "Work, Marriage, and Status"; Restall, *Maya World*, 121–40; Patch, *Maya and Spaniard in Yucatán*, 86–90, 131, 182, 193, 253; and Chuchiak, "*Ca numiae, lay u cal caxtlan patan lae,*" 131–33.

[260] This last clause—"*aunque por si como comian por si*"—is a confusing statement whose exact meaning is not clear.

devout and caretakers of their idols [*santeras*], and because of this had many acts of devotion with their idols, burning incense to them, offering them gifts of cotton clothing, food, and drinks, and fearing them. It was their job to make the offerings of food and drink that they offer during the festivals of the Indians. But with all this they did not have the habit of shedding their blood to the demons; this they never did. Nor did they allow them to go to the temples for the sacrifices, except on a certain festival, at which they admitted certain old women for its celebration. For their childbirths the female shamans [*hechizeras*] came, who made them believe their lies. They put under their beds an idol of a demon called Ix Chel, whom they said was the goddess of making infants. When their children were born, they washed them at once. When they were once through with the torment of flattening the foreheads and heads, they went with them to the priests, so that they might see [the child's] destiny, and state which profession they were going to have, and to give the name he was to have [*f. 27r*] during his childhood because they were accustomed to call their children by different names until they were baptized, or until they grew up. Afterwards they gave up these [names] and began to call them by the name of their fathers until they were married, and then they were called by the name of their father and of their mother.

[*Sec. 33*] This people had a great and excessive fear of death, and they showed this by the fact that all the services that they performed for their gods were for no other purpose nor for any other thing except they should give them health, life, and sustenance. But when it came time to die, it was indeed a thing to see the sorrow and the cries that they made for their dead, and the great grief it caused them. During the day they wept for them in silence, and at night with loud and very sad cries. What a shame it was to hear them. And they spent many days in deep sorrow. They were abstinent and fasted for the dead, especially the husband or wife, and they said that the devil had taken him away, since they thought that all evils came to them from him, and above all death. The dead, they wrapped up in a shroud, filling their mouths with ground corn, which is their food, and a drink which they call *koyem*, and with it some of the stones that they use for money, so that in the other life they would not be without something to eat. They buried them inside or behind their houses, casting into the grave some of their idols, and if he was a priest, some of his books. If he was a sorcerer [*hechicero*], they buried with him some of his sorcerer stones and tools of his trade [*pertrechos*]. Usually, they abandoned the house and left it deserted after the burials, except when there were a lot of people living in it, because with their company they lost some of the fear that remained of the death. As for the nobles and people of high esteem, they burned their bodies and placed their ashes in great urns, and they built temples above them as has been shown to have been done in ancient times, like the ones they found in Izamal. Now in this period, it has been found that they put their ashes in hollow clay statues. The other principal people made wooden statues, of which the back of the neck was left hollow, for their parents. They burned some part of the body and placed its ashes [in the hole] and sealed it up. Afterwards, they stripped from the dead body the skin of the back of the head and glued it there [on the seal], burying the rest as they were accustomed to do *[f. 27v; see figure A.8]*. They preserved these statues with a great deal of veneration among their idols. They used to cut off the heads of the ancient lords of Cocom, when they died, and after cooking them they cleaned off the flesh. Afterwards, they sawed off half the crown from the back, leaving the front part with the jaws and teeth. To these half-skulls they substituted the flesh that had been taken off with a kind of stucco [*betun*], which gave to them a perfect appearance of those whose skulls they were.[261] They kept these together with the statues with the ashes, all of which they kept in the oratories of their houses with their idols, in very great reverence and respect. And on all of their festival days and celebrations they made offerings of food to them, so that they should not lack for food in the other life, where they thought that their souls lay, and where their gifts were of use to them.

These people have always believed in the immortality of the soul, more than many other nations, although they have not lived in such an orderly and civilized manner. After death, they believed that there was another and better life, which the soul enjoyed when it separated from the body. They said that this future life was divided into a good and a bad life, into a painful one and one full of rest. The bad and painful one was for the vice-ridden [*viciosos*], while the good and pleasurable one was for those who had lived well according to their manner of living. The pleasures which they said they were to obtain, if they were good, were to go to a delightful place, where nothing would give them sorrow and where they would see an abundance of foods and drinks of great sweetness, and a tree which they call there *yaxche*, very cool and giving great shade, which is the ceiba [*zeyva*], under the branches and the shade of which they would rest and forever cease from labor. The sorrows of a bad life, that they said the wicked would suffer, were to go to a place lower than the other, which they called *mitnal*, which means "hell,"[262] and there to be tormented by the devils and by great need of hunger, cold, fatigue, and grief. There was also in this place a devil, the prince of all the devils, whom all obeyed, and they call him

---

[261] Skulls of this kind, and others very similar, have been uncovered in various parts of the Maya region; a 3-D photographic image of one can be seen at https://p3d.in/53q1E.

[262] The Christianized nature of this theology suggests that Maya beliefs have been passed through Franciscan filters here. We are reminded, yet again, that the Account is authoritative on early colonial Maya culture (and on early colonial Franciscan-Maya views of precontact Maya culture), but *not* simply on precontact Maya culture *per se*. For a good discussion of how Christian teachings may have crept into our conceptions of the Mesoamerican underworld see Jesper Nielsen, "How the Hell."

in their language Hunhau.[263] They said that these lives, bad and good, had no end, because the soul has none. They also said, and held it as absolutely certain, that those who hanged themselves went to this heaven of theirs [*a esta su gloria*]. Thus, there were many whom on little moments of sadness, troubles, or illnesses, hanged themselves in order to escape these things and to go and rest in their heaven, where they said that the goddess of the gallows, whom they called Ix Tab,[264] came to fetch them. They had no knowledge of the resurrection of the body and gave no account from whom they learned of this heaven and hell of theirs.

[*Sec. 34*] [*f. 28r; see figure A.9*][265] The sun of this land of Yucatan does not hide

---

[263] Interestingly, this is also the name of one of the primordial deities of the Maya, recorded in the K'iche' manuscript, the Popol Vuh, in which the father of the Hero Twins, Hunahau ("One Hunter"), is sacrificed by the Lords of the Underworld but is reborn as the Maize deity. This passage must have been influenced by one of Landa's Christianized Maya informants (like Chi, Euan, or Cocom).

[264] Although Ix Tab is not recognized as a precontact Maya deity in Maya scholarship today, like Ix Chel, this name has come to have significance within modern popular culture, unfortunately in a way that exoticizes contemporary Maya people and the high rate of suicide in Yucatan. The association between Ix Tab and the figure from the Dresden Codex that appears to show a female figure hanging from a noose (but in fact is a representation of a lunar eclipse) was erroneously made by Tozzer in the notes to his translation of the Account (Tozzer, *Landa's* Relación, n619). The "goddess of the gallows" is not mentioned in other colonial documents from Yucatan and there does not seem to be evidence beyond Landa's writings for either an association between the image in the Dresden Codex and Ix Tab, or for the existence of a deity of suicide in the precontact corpus. Beatriz Reyes-Foster has explored how the consumption of archaeological knowledge, specifically Tozzer's association of Ix Tab with what appears to an untrained eye to be a suicide, by the contemporary Mexican press, has created an urban myth of an Indigenous Maya suicide goddess (Reyes-Foster and Kangas, "Unraveling Ix Tab"; Reyes-Foster, "He Followed the Funereal Steps"). That said, Landa was for some reason convinced that the Maya had a "goddess of the gallows" or "of the hanged," as he repeats this in his 1565 testimony in Spain, stating that he is drawing upon his "*Copilación*"; responding to charges that his actions caused Mayas to hang themselves from fear of interrogation under torture, he claimed "that they do that [hang themselves] casually and with little cause, because they say that they will go to rest with Ixtab, the goddess of the hanged" (*Y esto solianlo ellos hacer muy fácilmente y por pocas cosas, porque decian iban a descansar con Ixtab, la diosa de los ahorcados ...*) (*Respuesta de Fray Diego de Landa a los cargos hechos por Fray Francisco de Guzmán, Ministro Provincial de la Orden de San Francisco de la provincia de Castilla*, AGI, Escribanía de Cámara, 1009B). That claim could either be interpreted as corroborating evidence to support the Account, or as circular evidence from the same source (Landa's *recopilación*), and a distortion of Maya belief and practice by a self-defensive Landa. If the latter (as we believe), this is an example of how the misuse of the Account can have far-reaching and pernicious (let alone, in this case, cruelly ironic) implications.

[265] Here begins a thirty-four-page section solely dedicated to Maya calendrics. It neatly begins at the top of f. 28r (Sec. 34) and ends at the bottom of f. 45v (Sec. 41), mid-sentence; clearly, a

itself nor move away often, so the nights never ever come to be longer than the days. And when they come to be at their longest, they are usually of the same length [*ser iguales*] from San Andrés until Santa Lucía,[266] and then the days begin to grow. The night sky guided them to know the time, which was by the [movement] of Venus [*el lucero*], Equuleus and Pegasus [*las cabrillas*], and Castor and Pollux [*astilejos*]. For the day, they had discrete names, from dawn until midday and from midday until sunset, with which they understood and guided their work. They had a perfect year, like ours, of 365 days and six hours. They divided it into two kinds of months, those of thirty [xxx] days are called *U*, which is to say "moon," which they count from when it came out new until it disappeared again.[267] The other kind of month had twenty days, those which they call Uinal Hunekeh. The whole year has eighteen of these [months], plus five more days and six hours.[268] Of these six hours they add a day every fourth year, and in this way in four years they have a year of 366 days.[269] For these 360 days they have twenty letters or characters by which they call them, leaving out a name for the other five because they take these as ill-fated and evil.[270] The letters are those that follow and each one carries its name above in order so as to be understandable by ours [letters]. ∞[271]

portion of the original manuscript is missing. It seems to be a discrete intellectual project, as it addresses a single topic and in the most anthropological detail furnished in the entire manuscript. The level of specificity is so precise it is unlikely that Landa authored this on his own, if at all. Interspersed throughout this section are thumbnail drawings of Mayan hieroglyphs that denote particular days and months of the 260- and 365-day calendars. In some cases, the copyist reserved blank spaces for these images and later returned to draw them; in others, he drew the glyphs first and then surrounded them with the accompanying text. Each circular form is of identical size, revealing that the copyist traced a small coin during their production.

[266] This would be between the feast days of St. Andrew (November 30) and St. Lucy (December 13), the weeks immediately preceding winter solstice.

[267] The author provides here a partially correct description of the tzolk'in, a pan-Mesoamerican calendrical system consisting of twenty day signs that were interdigitated with thirteen numbers to complete a cycle of 260 days. Scholars are as yet unaware of what this calendar is based upon, but one theory has held that it is somehow tied to the observation of astronomical phenomena, such as certain segments of the Venus cycle. This is perhaps where the author came up with his reference to the moon. Alternatively, it has been surmised that 260 days approximates the time between the acknowledgment of a missed menstrual cycle and the birth of child, thereby linking this calendrical system to human gestation.

[268] This second calendrical cycle is termed the haab. As suggested by the author here, it is composed of eighteen months of twenty days each with a small month of five days added to the end.

[269] Although the author claims that the Maya had knowledge of the astronomical year's true orbital of 365.2422, scholars have been unable to substantiate this fact.

[270] Indeed, each month was referred to by a singular name, but the author is incorrect here in his assertion that the short month of five days was unnamed; in fact, it was known as Uayeb.

[271] This is the place on this folio where the twenty month glyphs were drawn (plus one scratched

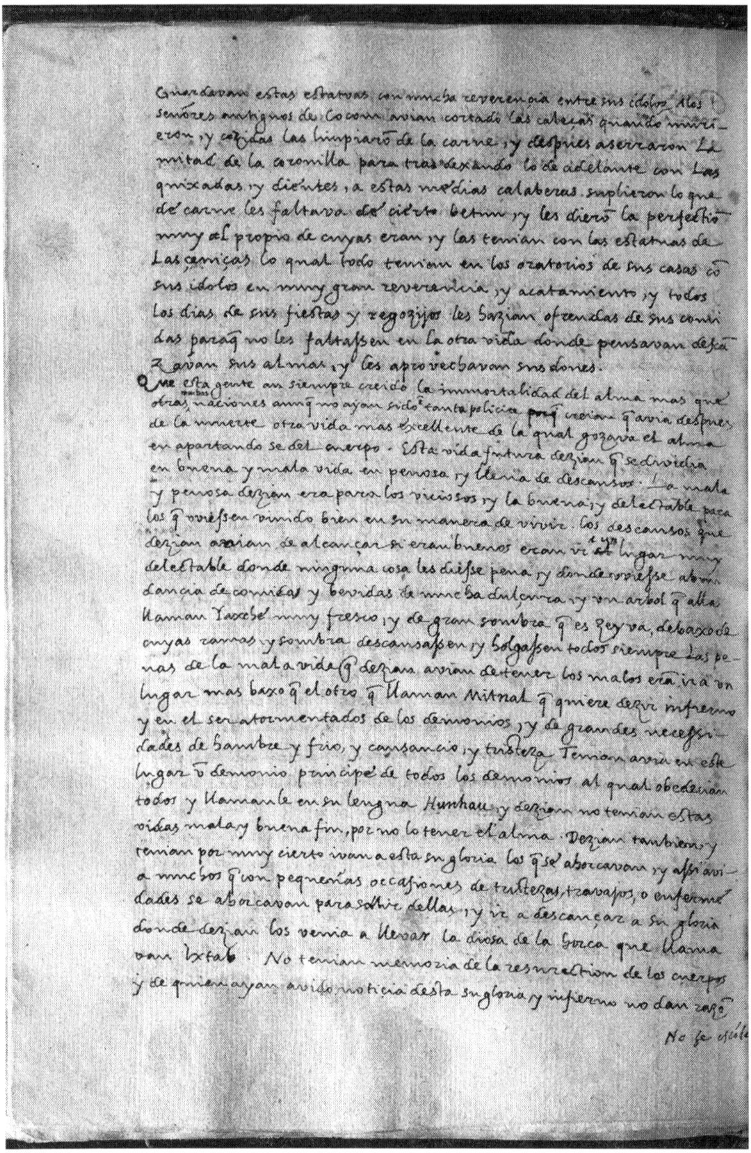

Guardavan estas estatuas con mucha reverencia entre sus idolos y los
señores antiguos de Cocom avian cortado las cabeças quando murie-
ron y cozidas las limpiaron de la carne, y despues aserraron la
mitad de la coronilla para tras dexando lo de adelante con las
quixadas y dientes, a estas medias calaveras suplieron lo que
de carne les faltava del cierto betun, y les dieron la perfectió
muy al propio de cuyas eran, y las tenian con las estatuas de
las cenizas lo qual todo tenian en los oratorios de sus casas có
sus idolos en muy gran reverencia, y acatamiento, y todos
los dias de sus fiestas y regozijos les hazian ofrendas de sus comidas paraq no les faltassen en la otra vida donde pensavan des[c]a
zavan sus almas, y les aprovechavan sus dones.

Que esta gente an siempre creido la immortalidad del alma mas que
otras naciones aunq no ayan sido tanta policia porq creian q avia despues
de la muerte otra vida mas excelente de la qual gozava el alma
en apartando se del cuerpo. Esta vida futura dezian q se dividia
en buena y mala vida, en penosa y llena de descanso. La mala
y penosa dezian era para los viciosos y la buena y deleitable para
los q uviessen vivido bien en su manera de vivir. los descansos que
dezian avian de alcançar si eran buenos eran ir a ün lugar muy
deleitable donde ninguna cosa les diesse pena, y donde uviesse abundancia de comidas y bevidas de mucha dulçura, y un arbol q alla
llaman Yaxche muy fresco, y de gran sombra q es ceyva, debaxo de
cuyas ramas y sombra descansassen y holgassen todos siempre. las penas de la mala vida q dezian avian de tener los malos era ir a un
lugar mas baxo q el otro q llaman Mitnal q quiere dezir infierno
y en el ser atormentados de los demonios, y de grandes necessidades de hambre y frio, y cansancio y tristeza. Tenian avia en este
lugar un demonio principe de todos los demonios al qual obedecian
todos, y llamanle en su lengua Hunhau, y dezian no tenian estas
vidas mala y buena fin, por no lo tener el alma. Dezian tambien, y
tenian por muy cierto ivan a esta su gloria los q se ahorcavan, y assi avi-
a muchos q con pequeñas occasiones de tristezas, trabajos, o enfermedades se ahorcavan para salir dellas, y ir a descansar a su gloria
donde dezian los venia a llevar la diosa de la horca que llama
van Ixtab. No tenian memoria de la resurrection de los cuerpos
y de quien ayan avido noticia desta su gloria y infierno no doy razó

No se escrib[e]

Figures A.8–A.9. fs. 27v–28r of the Account.

No se esconde ni aparta tanto el sol desta tierra de Yucatan
que vengan las nochos jamas a ser majores que los dias, y quando majores vienen assi suelen ser iguales desde s.t andres a
s.ta Lucia, que comiencan los dias a crecer. Regian se de noche
para conocer la hora que era por el luzero, y las cabrillas, y los
astilejos. De dia por el medio dia, y desde el al oriente, y poniente, tenian puestos a pedazos nombres con los quales
se entendian, y para sus trabajos se regian. Tienen su año
perfecto como el nro de ccc y lxv dias y vi horas. Divi-
denlo en dos maneras de meses, los unos de a xxx dias q
se llaman V, q quiere dezir luna, la qual contavan desde
q salia nueva hasta que no parecia. Otra manera de
meses tenian de a xx dias a los quales llaman Vinal Hunekeh. Destos tenia el año entero xviii, y mas los cinco dias
y seis horas. Destas seis horas se hazian. hazianse q cada quatro años un dia, y assi tenian de quatro en quatro años
el año cc lxvi dias. Para estos ccclx dias, tenian xx letras
o caracteres con q los nombran, dexando de poner nombre
a los de mas cinco, porq los tenian por aciagos, y malos.
Las letras son las que se siguen, y llevara cada una
su nombre encima porque se entienda con las nuestras.

Kan Chicchan Cimi Maia Lamat Muluc Oc

Chuc Eb Been Ix Men Cib Caban Zanab

Cauac Ahau Ymix Ik Akbal

Ya e dicho que el modo de contar de los indios es de cinco
en cinco, y de quatro cincos hazen veynte, assi en estos
sus caracteres que son xx sacan los primeros de lo quatro cincos de los xx, y estos sirven cada uno dellos por
año de lo que nos sirven a nosotros nras letras dominicales para comencar todos los primeros dias de los
meses de los de a xx dias. Kan Muluc Ix Cauac

Entre la muchedumbre de dioses, que esta gente adorava ado-
ran quatro llamados Bacab, cada uno dellos. Estos dezian era

I have already said that the Indians' manner of counting is five by five, and with four fives they make twenty. In this way, they have individual characters for the sets of XX [twenty days]. They take a day of the [set] of four fives of XX, and each one of them serves for a year, like our Dominical letters stand in,[272] in order to begin all of the first days of the months of the XX days. ∞[273]

Among the many deities that these people adore, they adore four called Bacab each one of them. These they say were *[f. 28v; figure A.10]* four brothers who God placed, when he created the world, at the four parts [corners] of it to hold up the sky so it didn't fall down. They also say that these Bacabes escaped when the earth was destroyed by the flood.[274] They name each one of these individually, signifying which part of the world that the deity had been put, holding the sky. They adapted one of their four Dominical letters to each [deity] and the cardinal direction [*parte*] where it is. They have signaled the misfortunes or happy occurrences that they said were to happen in the year of each one of them, and with their letters. And the devil, who deceives them in this as in other things, points out to them the rites [*servicios*] and offerings [they should perform] in order to avoid the misfortunes that he has made for them. In this way, if no misfortunes arrived, they say that it was because of the rites [*servicios*] that they had done. And if they did come, the priests made the people understand and believe that was because of the fault or lack of the rites [*servicios*] or something they had done. ∞ The first, then, of the Dominical letters is Kan. The year that this year serves was the omen of the Bacab who, among other names, they call Hobnil, Kanalbacab, Kanpauahtun, Kanxibchac. This one marks the south [*medio dia*]. ∞ The second letter is Muluc; he marks the east, and his year was the omen of the Bacab that they call Canzienal, Chacalbacab, Chacpauahtun, Chacxibchac. ∞ The third letter is Ix. His year was the omen of the Bacab that they

out); see figure A.9. We have inserted a ∞ in the text to show where glyph drawings appear on f.28 (figures A.9 and A.10).

[272] Developed in the ancient Roman era, Dominical letters were used during the early modern period as a way to determine which date of any given calendar year would correspond with a particular day of the week. Each year would be given a designation of A, B, C, etc., depending upon which weekly day January 1 fell. In this passage, the author tries to compare the Maya tradition of yearbearers with the European practice of using Dominical letters to refer to any given year in the Gregorian calendar.

[273] In this convoluted sentence, the author describes what scholars have termed the "yearbearers." For a detailed discussion, see Vail, "Yearbearer Rituals and Prognostications." The final four glyphs on this folio appear here, after "*los de a xx dias.*"

[274] Interestingly, colonial Maya textual courses, such as the Book of Chilam Balam of Chumayel, recount a flood destruction myth, during the course of which the Bacabs were not eliminated. Although the author conflates this Maya tale with the Biblical flood of the Old Testament, it seems clear that these are two discrete mythological traditions (see Knowlton, "Maya Creation Myths").

call Zaczini, Zacalbacab, Zacpauauhtun, Zacxibchac and he marked the north. ∞ The fourth letter is Cauac. His year's omen was of the Bacab they call Hozanek, Ekelbacab, Ecpauahtun, Ekxibchac. He marks the west.[275] In each festival or ceremony that these people make for their gods, they always begin by casting out the devil in order to improve the event. Sometimes they cast him out with prayers or petitions that they had and other times with favors, offerings, and sacrifices that they do for this reason. In order to observe the celebration of the new year, more joyfully and more dignified according to their humble opinion,[276] these people understood the five ill-fated days that they had as an entryway [*portales*] before the first day of their new year.[277] During these days they performed very grand rites for the aforementioned bacabes and to the devil [*f. 29r; figure A.11*] whom they called by four other names, he was known as Kanuuayayab, Chacuuayayab, Zacuuayab, Ekuuayab.[278] And when these rites and festivals were finished, the devil venerated in this way, they started their new year and the festivals of it.

[*Sec. 35*] All the towns of Yucatan used and had made two piles of stones, one in front of the other, at the entrance to the town for its four directions [*partes*], as is known, the east, west, north [*septentrion*], and south. For the celebration of the festivals of the ill-fated days, they held in this way each year: The year that the Dominical letter was Kan was the omen of Hobnil and according to them they say they both reigned on the southern side. In this year they made an image or figure of hollow clay of the devil that they called Kanvuayayab,[279] and they carried it to the piles of drystone that they had made at the southern part [of town]. They elected an elder of the town in whose house the days of the festival were celebrated. To celebrate it, they made a statue of a devil that they called Bolonzacab, which they put in the suitable elder's house in a public place, so everyone could come [to see it].[280] This done, the lords, the priest, and the men of the town gathered, remaining clean.

---

[275] In addition to orienting each of the four Bacabs with one of the cardinal directions, the prefixes of the various names given for the Bacab also uphold the color associations with each direction: "Kan" (yellow), "Chac" (red), "Zak" or "Sac" (white), and "Ek" (black).

[276] This phrase "in their wretched" or "humble opinion," reveals that the author was garnering the information included in this lengthy calendrical section from Maya informants.

[277] The author is here referring to the five-day mini-month that ends the tzolk'in calendar, called Uayeb.

[278] Each of the Bacabs is here referenced according to their associated color combined with the name of the 5-day period, so "Kanuuayayab" (Yellow Uayeb), "Chacuuayayab" (Red Uayeb), "Zacuuayab" (White Uayeb), and "Ekuuayab" (Black Uayeb).

[279] As just noted, the yellow color (*kan*) of the *uayeb* image was associated with the south.

[280] The Ah Bolon Dzacab deity has been identified as Schellhas God K; literally "he of the nine generations," the deity appears to be have been a Postclassic Yucatec form of God K, known in Classic times as K'awil (Taube, *Major Gods of Ancient Yucatan*, 73–78).

quatro hermanos a los quales puso Dios quando crio el
mundo a las quatro partes del sustentando el cielo no
se cayesse. Dezian tambien destos Bacabes que escaparon
quando el mundo fue del diluvio destruido. Ponen a
cada vno destos otros nombres y señalanle con ellos a
la parte del mundo que Dios le tenia puesto teniendo
el cielo y apropriandole vna de las quatro letras dominicales a el y a la parte que esta, y tienen señaladas las
miserias o felices sucessos que dezian avian de suce-
der en el año de cada vno destos y de las letras con
ellos. Y el demonio que en esto como en las demas cosas
los engañava. Les señalo los servicios y offrendas que
para evadirse de las miserias le avian de hazer. Y assi
sino les venian dezian era por los servicios que
le hazian, y suspomian hazian entender, y creer al
pueblo los sacerdotes era por alguna culpa o falta de
los servicios o los que los hazian. La primera pues
de las letras dominicales es Kan el año que esta letra
servia era el agüero del [figura] Bacab que por otros
nombres llaman Hobnil, Kan [figura] nalbacab, Kanpauahtun
Kanxibchac a este señalavan a la parte de medio dia
La segunda letra es [figura] Muluc señalavan le al
oriente su año era [figura] agüero el Bacab que llaman
Canziennal Ebacab Cansicnalbactun Chacxib chac. La ter-
cera letra es Ix su año era agüero el Bacab que llama
Zaczini ac [figura] albacab Zacpauahtun Zacxibchac de
la banda [figura] a la parte del norte. La quarta letra
es Cauac su año era agüero el Bacab que llaman Hoza
nek [figura] Ekbacab Ecpauahtun Exibchac a este señalavan a parte del poniente en qualquiera fiesta o
solemnidad que esta gente hazian a sus dioses. Comen-
cavan siempre del cesar de si al demonio para mejor
la hazer. Y el cesarte vnas vezes eran con oraciones
y ponderaciones que para ello tenian otras con sacrificios y offrendas y sacrificios que le hazian por estar ya
con para celebrar la solemnidad de mano muero
esta gente con mas regozijo y mas dignamente, se
[...] opinion tomavan los cinco dias
acyagos que ellos tenian por tales antes del primero
dia de su año nuevo y en ellos hazian muy gran
des servicios a los Bacabes de arriba y al demonio
que

que llamauan por otros quatro nombres como a ellos
es a saber Kanuuayayab, Chacuuayayab, Zacuuayayab, Ekuuayayab. y estos seruicios y fiestas acabadas, y alança-
do de si como veremos el demonio començauan su año
y las fiestas del.

V so era en todos los pueblos de Yucatan tener hechos dos montones
de piedra vno enfrente de otro a la entrada del pueblo por
todas las quatro partes del pueblo, es a saber a oriente, poniente, septentrion, y medio dia. Para la celebracion de
las dos fiestas de los dias aciagos los quales serian desta
manera cada año. El año que la letra dominical era
♦Kan era el aguero Hobnil, y segun ellos dezian rey-
nauan ambos a la parte del medio dia. Este año pues
hazian vna imagen o figura hueca de barro del demonio que llamauan Kanuuayayab, y lleuauanla
a los montones de piedra seca que tenian hechos a la
parte de medio dia. Elegian vn principe del pueblo
en cuya casa se celebraua estos dias esta fiesta, y para
celebrarla hazian vna estatua de vn demonio que llamauan Bolonzacab al qual ponian en casa del principal
aderecada en vn lugar publico, y que todos pudiesen
llegar. Esto hecho se juntauan los ss. y el sacerdote, y
el pueblo de los hombres, y teniendo limpio, y con arcos y frescuras aderecado el camino desde el lugar de
los montones de piedra donde estaua la estatua, iuan
todos juntos por ella con mucha de su deuocion. llegados
la saumaua el sacerdote con quarenta y nueue gra-
nos de maiz molidos con su encienso, y ellos lo repartia
en el brazero del demonio, y le saumauan. llamau-
al maiz molido solo Zacah, y a lo de los ss. Chahalte. sa-
umada la imagen degollauan vna gallina, y se la presentauan o offrecian. Esto hecho metian la imagen en
vn palo llamado Kante, y poniendole acuestas vn angel en señal de agua, y que este año avia de ser bueno.
y estos angeles pintauan y hazian espantables, y assi
la lleuauan con mucho regozijo y bayles a la casa del
principal donde estaua la otra estatua de Bolonzacab
sacauan de casa deste principal a los señores, y al
sacerdote al camino vna beuida hecha de cccc. y x v

With arches and fresh flowers, they decorated the road that led to the place of the stone piles where the statue had been. All together they went via the road;[281] with much devotion they arrived. The priest incensed [the statue] with forty-nine grains of corn ground with his incense. They shared the devil's brazier, and they incensed him. They called the ground corn only Zacah and that of the lords [*señores*] Chahalte'. They incensed the image, slit the throat of a chicken, and presented or offered it. This done, they put the image on a pole named Kante' and an angel[282] they placed on its shoulder as a symbol of water and that this year would be good. And these angels, they painted and made frightful, and they carried it [the statue] with much joy and dances to the elder's house where the other statue of Bolonzacab was. They left the house of this elder to take to the lords and the priest along the road a beverage made from 415 [*cccc y xv*] [*f. 29v*] grains of toasted corn, which they call Picula Kakla, which they all drank. Arriving at the house of the elder, they put the image in front of the statue of the devil that they had there. Then they made many offerings of food and drink, of meat and fish, and these offerings they distribute to the strangers [*estrangeros*] that they found there.[283] They give the priest a deer leg. Others let blood, cutting their ears, smearing it with a stone that they had there of a demon, Kanalacantun. They make a heart out of bread and another bread with pumpkin seeds and offer them to the image of the devil, Kanvuayayab. In this way, they leave this statue and image for the ill-fated days. They incense them with their incense, and with their corn ground with incense. They believed that without doing these ceremonies they would have had certain illnesses that they have had in this past year [during] those ill-fated days.[284] They carried the statue of the devil

---

[281] Some scholars suggest *sacbeob*, or white roads, of the Classic period were used for these sorts of new year ritual processions (see Ardren, "Procesiones y *sacbeob* de las Tierras Bajas del norte," 25).

[282] The use of the term "angel" in this sentence likely refers simply to a winged supernatural being, not the angels of early modern Catholicism. For example, it could be referring to the bird messenger of the god of creation, Itzamna, or Itzamna Yeh, who is often seen on top of trees (such as in the murals of San Bartolo), and who is prominently displayed in the murals of Tulum in the presence of the goddess consort of Itzamna, Ix Chebal Yax, who performs rituals with rain-god Chac imagery throughout. This bird deity (known to scholars as the Principal Bird Deity—PBD) was the "omen" or messenger of the creator god (see Chuchiak, *Indian Inquisition*, 256–60; Bardawil, "Principal Bird Deity," 195–209).

[283] The presence of "foreigners" at the new year's rituals suggests that these events were regionally conceived, meaning that elites from distant provinces may have attended the events, thus making them diplomatic exchanges as much as calendar-marking rituals ("foreign" did not mean non-Maya; after all, a common Maya patronym, Dzul, meant "foreigner," and a Maya kingdom in southeastern Yucatan was called Dzuluinicob, which literally means "foreigners").

[284] These illnesses could have been any one of the several epidemics that plagued Indigenous

Bolonzacab to the temple and the image to the eastern [entrance of town] in order to be by it another year. They placed it there and went home, understanding that that each one [of the statues] had to stay there in order for the celebration to take place the next year. With the ceremonies done, the devil was cast out. Owing to his deception, this year was good because it was reigned over by the letter Kan, and the Bacab Hobnil, who they said was not sinful like his brothers. For this reason, misfortunes won't come during it. Since the devil has supplied them [with misfortunes] many times, they would do rites for him. So, in this way they would always stay deceived and blind, because when there were [misfortunes] they were [blamed on] the fault of the rites and ritual practitioners [servidores]. They would be ordered to make an idol that they called Izamnakavil, that they should put in their temple.[285] They would burn in the patio of the temple three balls of milk or resin that they call Kik.[286] They would sacrifice to it a dog or a man, that whichever they made, keeping the order that in chapter 100[287] I said they did with those that they sacrificed. Except that the mode of sacrifice in this festival was different because it was performed in the patio of the temple on a great pile of rocks. They put the man or dog that they had sacrificed [f. 30r] on something taller than himself, casting the bound sacrificial victim [patiente] down, they threw him from the highest of the stones. Those officials snatched him up and with great swiftness, they removed his heart. They carried it to the new idol, and they offered it between two plates. They offered other gifts of foods. In this festival the old women of the town danced. For this they had been elected, dressed in certain vestments. They said that an angel descended and received this sacrifice.[288]

---

communities during the early colonial period (see Hoggarth et al., "Drought and Its Demographic Effects"). As a major epidemic of hemorrhagic fever ravaged the colony in 1566 (see Chuchiak, "Yaab Uih yetel maya cimil," 6; and Kashanipour, "World of Cures," 5–56), it is tempting to surmise that this section of the Account was written or amended in 1566–1567, when Landa was preparing documents for his defense before the Ordinary of the Franciscan Order. The passage here also tantalizingly reveals that even as late as the 1560s the Maya maintained their calendar and count of days with the knowledge of the friars.

[285] This deity, Itzamna Kauil, has been associated with Schellhas God D, known as Itzamna; Taube, *Major Gods of Ancient Yucatan*, 31–41; "*kauil* being a Yucatec term referring to abundance and sustenance" (39).

[286] *Kik* translates as "blood," and is a common colloquial name for the sap of the ceiba tree.

[287] Here the author reveals that there were at least one hundred chapters or sections in his original manuscript (and probably many more), evidence that he had at least thought of preparing it for publication. If so, the later notaries copied sections verbatim, but did not include all of the materials or the chapter or paragraph numbers that appear to have been in the original manuscript. As discussed in our part II, this is just one of the many tantalizing clues as to how extensive the friar's lost *recopilación* was.

[288] This "angel" likely refers to the winged Principal Bird Deity (PBD) of Itzamna, Itzam Yeh,

[*Sec. 36*] The year in which the Dominical letter was Muluc was the omen of Canzicnal, and in his time they elected lords, the priest, and the principal man to host his festival. Whoever was elected made the image of the devil like that of the past year, they called it Chacvuayayab. They carried it to the stone piles that had been set up in the eastern part [of the town] where they had made it last year. They made a statue of the devil called Kinich Ahau [*Kinchahau*] and put it in the house of the principal man in a communal place.[289] From there, the street having been being clean and decorated, all together they went with their accustomed devotion with the image of the devil, Chacvuayayab. Arriving, the priest incensed it with fifty-three [*liii*] grains of ground corn and with their incense that they call Zacah. The priest gave [it] to the lords and they put in the brazier more incense that we[290] call Chahalte'. Afterward, they slit a chicken's throat like the year before and put the image on a pole called Chacte'. They carried it accompanied by everyone with devotion, dancing some war dances that are called Holcanokot Batelokot ["warrior dance, war dance"]. On the road, the lords and principal men drank a beverage of 380 [*ccc y lxxx*] [grains of] toasted corn like that described before. Arriving at the

---

who is often portrayed descending down to receive offerings (Taube, *Major Gods of Ancient Yucatan*, 30–36).

[289] The deity here named Kinich Ahau has been identified by Maya scholars as Schellhas God G, the Sungod (Taube, *Major Gods of Ancient Yucatan*, 50–56).

[290] The conjugation form shifts dramatically here to the third person plural, "we." This means that the person composing these sections is Maya, for only an Indigenous person would include themselves as someone who called a particular kind of incense "*chahalte*'." This "slip," combined with the mention of their "humble opinion" near the bottom of f. 28v, strongly suggests that these new year's ceremony pages were *not* written by Landa or another Spaniard, as previously assumed, but instead by a Maya man. However, it is important to note that throughout this section, the Maya writer repeatedly differentiates between the Maya of the ancient past, the "they" in the text, and himself, as would be expected for a Christianized Maya man working with the Franciscan clergy. A strong candidate is don Juan (né Nachi) Cocom, who would have been familiar with these rituals. Gaspar Antonio Chi, also the son of an Ah Kin (Maya priest), may have had a more general understanding of the religious rituals, but he was very young when they were still practiced on a public scale like this, whereas Cocom was older. Another more probable candidate is don Francisco Euan, the ruler of Caucel, whom Landa mentions by name as one of his informants later in the Account. As discussed in our chapter 4, after receiving his own instruction, Euan became a "very faithful assistant of the religious friars in the conversion of his other native peers . . . who learned to read and write, and due to his good persuasion, he spoke to the other natives teaching them some things of our faith"; this was according to fray Bernardo de Lizana, who described Euan as "very wise among them in their sciences, since he had been a high priest of their idols before the friars arrived, and as they believed it to be true what he told them . . . many flocked to the doctrine because of his work as a teacher among them" (Lizana, *Historia*, 51r). Another possible candidate is don Diego Nah, who allegedly was also an Ah Kin before his conversion, and who resided and worked with Franciscans in Conkal and Izamal, including Landa.

principal man's house, they put his image in front of the statue of Kinich Ahau [*Kinchahau*] and they made all their offerings, those which they distributed like the others. They offered the image bread made with egg yolks, others with deer hearts, and another made with their mild pepper. There were many who let blood, cutting their ears, and smearing the blood on a stone that they had of the devil they called Chacancantun. Here they took boys, and they drew *[f. 31v]* blood by force from their ears, putting knives to them. They kept this statue and image until the inauspicious days had passed. All the meanwhile they burned their incenses. After the days had passed, they took the image to be in the northern area [of the town], where they had left to be received the other year. The other image [they brought] to the temple and afterward they went to their homes to think about the setting up [*aparejo*] of their new year. They had to do so because if they did not do these said things [they would be] jinxed [*mucho mal de ojositos*]. In this year the Dominical letter was Muluc. Bacab Canzienal reigned, and they took it for a good year, and they said so because he was the best and oldest of those Bacab deities. So, they put him first in their prayers. But [in light] of everything the devil could do to them, they would make an idol called Yaxcocahmut and they should put it in the temple. They would throw out the old images and on the patio in front of the temple they would make a stone statue,[291] on which they would burn their incense and a ball of resin or milk [called] Kik. They did there a prayer to the idol asking for a remedy for their misfortunes that they had had that year, such as having little [rain]water, and the corn sprouting [too] many shoots, and things like that. For the remedy, the devil commanded them to offer squirrels to him and an unworked textile [*paramento*], which the old women weave as a trade. They dance in the temple to appease Yax Cocah Mut [*Yaxcocahmuti*].[292] They had many additional misfortunes and bad omens even though the year was good, without performing the rites that the devil commanded, which was to hold a festival during which to dance a dance with many tall lances, offering to him turkey heads, bread, and corn beverages. They had offered dogs made of clay with bread on their backs, and the old women performed dances with them in their hands and they sacrificed to him a puppy with a black back who was a virgin. And those devoted to this let blood and smeared it on the

---

[291] It is notable that they used the Spanish term *bulto* here, a term typically reserved for Catholic statues of Mary, Jesus, or the saints; the same term is used in a previous passage (on f. 31r) to describe precontact deity effigies.

[292] The Franciscan friar Andres de Avendaño mentioned a stone column at the late-seventeenth-century town of Tah Itza, which he said was a "first tree of the world"; it had a sculptured face at the base that, according to the friar, the Itza revered as the god Ah Cocah Mut (Avendaño, *Relación* [1696], f. 29v). Also known as Yax Cocah Mut, the deity has been argued by Tozzer, Taube and others to be an aspect of Itzamna (Tozzer, *Landa's Relación*, n695; Taube, *Major Gods of Ancient Yucatan*, 36).

stone of the demon Chacacantun. They held this rite and sacrifice for the pleasure of their god Yax Cocay Mut [*y Axcocahmut*].[293]

[*Sec. 37*] In the year that was of the Dominical letter Ix and the omen of [*f. 31r*] Zaccicci an election was made for the principal man who would host the festival. They made the image of the demon called Zacuuayayab and carried it to the hills of stone [pyramids] in the northern part of town, where the previous year they had placed it. They made a statue of the demon Ytzamna [*Yzamna*] and they put it in the house of the principal man. All together they went along the decorated road devotedly with the image of Zacuuayayab. Arriving, they incensed it as was done before and cut the chicken's throat and put the image on a pole called Zachia.[294] They carried it with their devotion and dances which are called Alcabtan Kamahau.[295] They drank the accustomed beverage on the road back, and arriving at the house they put this image in front of the statue of Ytzamna, and there they offered it all of their offerings, distributing them, offering to the statue of Zacuuayayab a turkey head, quail empañadas, other things, and their drink.[296] Others let blood and they smeared it on the stone of the demon Zacacantun. They kept the idols like this for the [inauspicious] days until the new year, and they incensed them with their incense burners until the arrival of the next day. They carried Ytzamna to the temple and Zacuuayayab to the western part of town, depositing it there so it could welcome the next year. The misfortunes that they had during this year if they were negligent in their rites were dejection [*desmayos*], fainting spells [*amorteçimientos*], and eye problems. They had for that year crop failure [*ruyn añor de pan*], but good cotton. This was the year in which the Dominical letter was Ix and the Bacab Zacciui reigned.[297] They had a year of crop failure because, they said, they have had many misfortunes, for they said they have had a great drought and too much sun which dried out the corn shoots. A great famine followed and because of the famine, theft, and the theft of slaves, and the selling [of people] to those who could afford them. Because of this, there followed discords [*f. 31v*] and wars among themselves and other towns. They also said that there was a change in the authority of the lords

---

[293] Here, as with many of these deities and other Maya names, the copyist has trouble; Yax Cocay Mut (literally Blue-Green Firefly Bird, likely an aspect of the deity Itzamna) is miswritten both times, the second time its initial *Y* seemingly read by the copyist as the Spanish "and."

[294] *Zac ya* is the sapodilla tree (Achras sapota, L.).

[295] Probably originally written as *alcab tankab ahau*, "procession around the ruler's patio."

[296] This "drink" could refer to any of the various beverages the Maya prepared for ritual events, though it is most likely referring to balche, which the priests and friars called "their drink" (see Chuchiak, "It is their drinking that hinders them," 138–142).

[297] With this sentence, the copyist may have mistakenly partially repeated the opening sentence of this section [37].

or of the priests due to the wars and discord. They also had a prognostication that said that some of them who wanted to be lords wouldn't prevail. They said they had also locusts, and many of the towns were depopulated because of the famine. That which the devil had commanded them to do, in order to remedy these misfortunes that came to all, or as some of them understood it, they came to make an idol that they called Cinchahau Yzamna.[298] Placing it in the temple where they made much incense, many offerings and prayers, and the letting of blood which they smeared on the stone of the Zacacantun demon, they performed a lot of dances, and the old women danced as they were accustomed to. In this festival they once again made a prayer, or they renewed one, to the devil. During it they gathered to perform sacrifices and offerings to the devil, and they had a solemn drinking binge [*una solemne borrachada*], because it was a public festival and obligatory. There were some holy men who of their own volition and due to their devotion made another idol, as that described above, and they put it in other temples where they made offerings and got drunk. These drunken festivals [*borracheras*] and sacrifices they had for the great pleasure of the idols and for the remedy to save themselves from misfortunes prognosticated.

[*Sec. 38*] The year of the Dominical letter was Cauac and the oracle was Hozanek. The election for the principal man was held. In order to celebrate the festival, they made the image of the demon called Ekuuajayab [Ek U Uayab Hab] and they carried it to the stone hills of the western part [of town], where they had left it since the last year. They also made a statue of the demon called Uacmitunahau and put it in the house of the principal man, in an appropriate place. [*f. 32r*] From there they all went together to the place where the image of Ekuuayayab [Ek U Uayab Hab] was and for that they had the road very decorated. Arriving at it, the priest and the lords incensed it as before, and they slit the throat of a hen. This done, they put the image on a pole that they called Yaxek. They put on the shoulders of the image a skeleton and a dead man, on top with a roasted bird called Kuch [vulture] as a symbol of a great loss of life, for this year had great evil. They carried it thus in this manner with their feeling and devotion, dancing some dances, during one of which they danced over crackling embers [*cazcarientas*], so they called it Xibalbaokot, which is to say, dance of the devil. The pourers carried the lords' drink through the streets. Those who drank arrived at the place of the statue of Uacmitunahau and put there in front of the image what they brought. Later they began their offerings, incensings, prayers, much bloodletting from many parts of the body, smearing the blood at the foot of the demon called Ekelacantun. In this way they spent those ill-fated days which passed. They carried Uacmitunahau to

---

[298] Actually, two separate names for the same deity: Kinich Ahau and Itzamna.

the temple and Ekuuayayab to the southern part of town to welcome the new year. This year in which the letter was Cauac was governed by the Bacab Hozanek. In addition to the prognostication of deaths, they had devastation because they said they had too much sun and it killed the young corn. Many ants and birds ate what they planted. Because of this there would not be enough food anywhere, and that which they had they only had because of much work. They made the devil in order to remedy these misfortunes, making four devils called Cichacchob, Ekbalamchac, Ahcanuolcab, Ahbulucbalam, and putting them in the temple where they incense them with their *[f. 32v; figure A.12]* incense. They offered them two balls of milk or resin from a tree that they call Kik in order to be burned, certain iguanas, bread, a miter, a bunch of flowers, and one of their precious stones. Other than this, for this festival's celebration they make a large wooden vault in the patio. They filled it to the top with firewood, leaving doorways in the walls so they could go in and out. Afterwards, more men each took tied bunches of sticks, very dry and long, and placed them at the top of the firewood. A singer sang, accompanied by a drum of theirs. Everyone danced below in concert and with much devotion, entering and exiting that wooden vault through the doorways. Like this they danced until the afternoon, each one staying there with their bunches. They returned to their houses to rest and eat. At night, rising, they returned with a lot of people because among them the ceremony was very esteemed. Each one lit their torch and with them, in turn, held them against the firewood. It blazed a lot and quickly burned. After everything was in embers, they razed it, and they spread out, very widely, and together those who had done it danced, some setting out barefoot and naked like they are. They walked to the top of the embers, one side to the other. Some walked on them without a mark *[lesion]*, others hugging each other, and others half-burnt. This they believed was the remedy for their misfortunes and bad omens, and they thought this was a very appeasing rite for their deities. This done, they went on to drink and they drank until they passed out, as this was required by custom of the festival and the heat of the fire.

   [Sec. 39] [f. 33r; figure A.13] With the letters of the Indians discussed before in chapter 110 they write the names of the days of the months.[299] All together the months made a kind of calendar by which they managed themselves, for their festivals, as well as their accounts, trades, and businesses, like we are guided by

---

[299] The words "the days of [*los dias de*]" are written in the left margin. The extant manuscript has no chapter 110 [*cx*], again underscoring the incomplete nature of this section of the manuscript and its status as an independent intellectual project. However, these chapter references strongly suggest that Landa's original *recopilación* was a more structured and larger work with chapter and paragraph organization throughout.

our knowledge. It turns out that they do not begin the first day of their calendar on the first day of their year, but instead much later, because of the difficulty with which they count the days of the months all together, as you will see in the typical calendar [*kalendario*] that I included here [below].[300] For even though the letters and days for their months are twenty [XX], they have the habit of counting them from one until thirteen [XIII], then they return to start at one until thirteen [XIII]. And so, they would divide the days of the year into twenty-seven thirteens plus nine [IX] days without the ill-fated ones.[301] Given these ambiguities and the awkward counting, it is something to see the fluency [*liberalidad*] of those who know how to count, and they always understand, and notably so, which is the Dominical letter on the first day of their year, without error or fault, nor coming out with another of the twenty [day names]. They also use this manner of counting in order to work out with these letters a certain way of counting that they use for ages and other things, although, odd even for them, they [the calendars] are not explained in more detail by us a lot for that purpose here [*no nos hazen aqui mucho al proposito*]. And for that reason, they kept saying that the character or letter that started the count of the days or calendar [*kalendario*] called Hunimix is this [symbol] ∞,[302] which does not have a specific day nor symbol on which it falls. Because each one changes his own count, and despite all of this, the letter that serves as the Dominical [letter] does not fail to start off the first day of the year that follows.

The first day of the year of these people is always the sixteenth [XVI] day of our month of July, and it is the first day of their month of Popp. It is not a thing of

---

[300] The spelling of *calendario* as *kalendario* was a conventional way in the early modern centuries to render the Latin term *kalendarium* in the dative case, showing that the author was trained in Latin—and thus was a Franciscan friar or was trained by Franciscans. The spelling thus likely made sense to the copyist, who repeats it three more times below. However, it would also have resonated with a Maya informant or coauthor. Obvious candidates are Chi, Cocom, or a Chel informant, although we suggest here that don Francisco Euan, formerly the senior Ah Kin or Ah Kin May of Caucel, was one of the major sources for this religious and ritual information. Although he died in 1560, Euan was the only close collaborator with Landa and other friars whom we know for sure was a precontact *ah kin may*. He lived in Caucel while Landa served as the Guardian of the nearby convent of Conkal (1551–1553), offering them ample chances to collaborate. Later in the 1550s, Euan served as an interpreter and informant (including as interpreter during inquisition trials held by Landa in 1558–1560 while he was Custodian), earning him the right to be "buried in the ancient church of the Franciscan convent in Merida, which was located just underneath the principal dormitory of the convent today" (Cogolludo, *Historia de Yucathan*, Libro V, Capítulo VI).

[301] The Porrúa edition of the Account erroneously transcribes this nine as eleven days (prompting confusion among some commentators).

[302] Here the Imix glyph is inserted (see figure A.13).

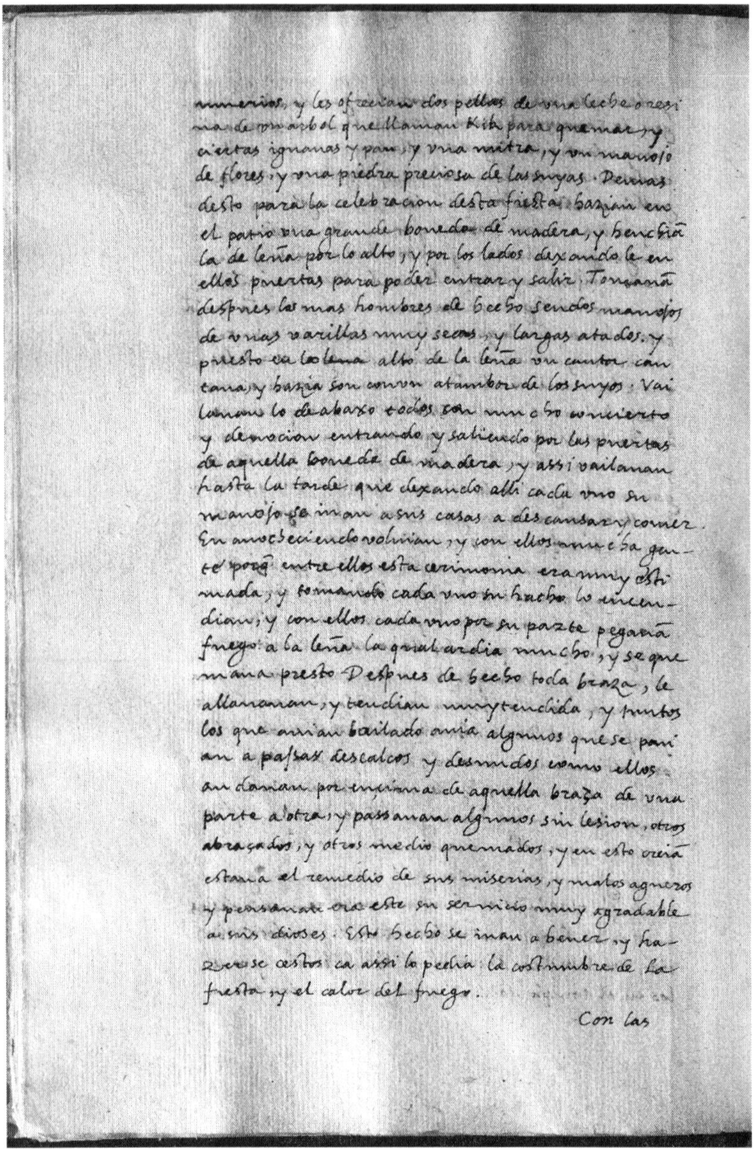

numerias, y les ofrecian dos pellas de una leche o resi-
na de un arbol q[ue] llaman Kik para quemar, y
ciertas iguanas y pan, y una mitra, y un manojo
de flores, y una piedra preciosa de las suyas. Demas
desto para la celebracion desta fiesta hazian en
el patio una grande boueda de madera, y henchian
la de leña por lo alto, y por los lados dexando le en
ellos puertas para poder entrar y salir. Tomauan
despues los mas hombres de Cecho sendos manojos
de unas varillas muy secas y largas atados, y
puesto en lo alto de la leña un cantor con
cana, y baxia son con un atambor de los suyos. Vailauan lo de abaxo todos con mucho concierto
y deuocion entrando y saliendo por las puertas
de aquella boueda de madera, y assi vailauan
hasta la tarde que dexando alli cada uno su
manojo se ivan a sus casas a descansar y comer
En anocheciendo voluian, y con ellos mucha gente porq[ue] entre ellos esta cerimonia era muy estimada, y tomando cada uno su hacho lo encendian, y con ellos cada uno por su parte pegaua
fuego a la leña la qual ardia mucho, y se que-
maua presto Despues de hecho toda braza, le
allanauan, y tendida muy tendida, y puntos
los que auian vailado auia algunos que se ponian a passar descalços y desnudos como ellos
andauan por encima de aquella braza de una
parte a otra, y passauan algunos sin lesion, otros
abraçados, y otros medio quemados, y en esto oria
estaua el remedio de sus miserias, y malos agueros
y pensauan era este su seruicio muy agradable
a sus dioses. Esto hecho se ivan a beuer, y hazian se cestos ca assi lo pedia la costumbre de la
fiesta, y el calor del fuego.

Con las

Figures A.12–A.13. fs. 32v–33r of the Account.

con las letras de los Indios puestas atras en el capitulo
X los dias de ex ponian a sus meses nombres, y de todos juntos los me-
ses hazian vn modo de calendario con el qual se regia
assi para sus fiestas como para sus cuentas, y tratos, y
negocios como nosotros nos regimos con el nro saluo
que no comencauan el primero dia de su calendario
en el primero dia de su año, sino muy adelante, lo
qual hazian por la difficultad con que contauan los
dias de los meses todos juntos, como se vera en el
propio kalendario que aqui porne, porque aunq las
letras, y dias para sus meses son xx tienen en costum-
bre de contarlas desde vna hasta xiii, tornan a comen
çar de vna despues de las xiii, y assi reparten los dias
del año en xxxii trezes, y ix dias sin los aciagos. con
estos estrauelanos, y embaraçosa cuenta es cosa de
ver la liberalidad con los que saben encentar, y se
entienden, y mucho de notar que salga siempre la
letra que es dominical en el primero dia de su año
sin errar ni faltar sin venir a salir otra de las xx
alli v a nar tambien deste modo de contar para
sacar destas letras cierto modo de contar que tenia
para las edades, y otras cosas que aunq son para ellos
curiosas no nos hazen aqui mucho al proposito, y
por esso se quedaran con dezir q el carater o letra
de q comencaua su cuenta de los dias o kale
dario se llama Kunimix y es este el qual no tie
ne dia cierto ni señalado en q caiga. Porq cada vno
le muda la propia cuenta, y con todo esso no falta el
salir la letra q viene por dominical el primero del
año q se sigue
El primero dia del año desta gente era siempre a
xvi dias de nro mes de Iulio, y primero de su mes
de Popp, y no es de marauillar q esta gente aunq
simple que en otras cosas les emos hallado curio-
sidad en esta la tuuiessen tambien, y opinion
como la an otras naciones tenido cerca la

marvel that these people, even though they are simple, would have things curious to us, but also in this they also had opinions like other nations according to the *[f. 33v; figure A.14]* gloss on Ezekiel.[303] January is, according to the Romans, the beginning of the year; according to the Hebrews, April; according to the Greeks, March; and according to the Asians [*orientales*], October. But even though they start their year in July, I did not write their calendar [*kalendario*] like that here, but instead in the order of ours. And together with our method, they will be indicated [below] using our letters and our months, and theirs and their count of the thirteens discussed above put in a numerical count. Since there is no need to write down in one part the calendar [*kalendario*], and in another the festivals, I put in each one of the months their festivals, the observances, and the ceremonies that are celebrated. With this, I will complete what I said above I would do, making their calendar [*calendario*], and in it talking of their fasts, the ceremonies that they performed for their idols, and other things, all of them, and of even more of these people treated here. It is not my intention for this to serve as anything more than as a basis for praising the divine kindness that has suffered too much, and has done so for the good of remedying our times; for in warning of it with Christian soul [*entranas*], we have begged for their salvation, the intention of good Christianity, and for those who are in charge to maintain it, encourage it, and help with it; so that neither for these people, because of their sins, nor for our own, may there be lacking help; nor may they fail in what has started and thus return to their miseries and the vomitings of errors, for worse things would happen to them than in the beginning, the household devils returning to their souls, out of which with such laborious care we have tried to cast them out, cleansing them of it, and sweeping away their vices and bad ancient customs. It does not take a lot to see the ruin that has happened for so many years in the great and very Christian Asia, and in the good, Catholic, august Africa, and the miseries and calamities that today are happening in our Europe, in our *[f. 34r; figure A.15]* nation and houses. For this we could say we have completed the evangelical prophesies about Jerusalem, which our enemies besiege and stain with blood. They will grip it so much that they will crush it to earth. All of this God has permitted according to who we are, and as such his Church and all of it cannot be missing, for it is said, "*Nisi d[omi]n[u]s reliquisset semen, sicut sodoma fuissemos.*"[304]

---

[303] In this context, "glossa" or "gloss" (the manuscript uses *glossa*, but the word is butchered by the copyist, as if he were not familiar with it) means marginalia or explanatory notes in the margins of a Bible passage. Landa here may be referring to his reading of the glosses and commentaries on Ezekiel that he had access to in the conventual library of San Juan de los Reyes (see our chapter 4 below).

[304] The Latin phrase quoted here is from Romans 9:29: "*et sicut praedixit Esaias nisi Dominus Sabaoth reliquisset nobis semen sicut Sodoma facti essemus et sicut Gomorra similes fuissemus*"

[Sec. 40][305]

THE ROMAN CALENDAR [*KALENDARIO*], AND YUCATECAN ONE, BEGINS[306]

According to what is said, they are very apprehensive about creating and completing gods, and perfectly making them into idols. The owner of them gave the best gift he could of birds, game [*caças*], and their money in order to pay he who did the work of making them. They removed them from the little house and put them in another thatched house [*ramada*] that had been made on the patio. There a priest blessed them with much ceremony and an abundance of particular prayers. Doing this first, the officials removed the soot from their bodies because they say that they had fasted so much during the making [of the idols]. They were anointed and cast out the devil like they were accustomed to, and they burnt the incense. Blessed in this way, they put them [the idols] in a small basket, wrapped in a cloth, and they handed them over to the owner, and he with much devotion received them. Later, the priest preached of the goodness and a little of the excellence of the official who made the new gods, and about the danger that they had in making them if they had not abided their abstinences and fasts. After they ate very well and even better got drunk.

In either of the months of Chen and Yax, on the indicated day, the priest holds a festival that they called Ocna, which is to say, renovation of the temple in honor of the Chacs, who are the gods of the maize fields. During this festival they looked for the prognostications of the Bacabs, as was said in greater detail in chapters 113, 114, 115, 116 [cxiii, cxiiii, cxv, cxvi] and according to the order in their *[f. 34v; figure A.16]* place. It was said that each year they held it and during others they renewed the clay idols and their braziers, for it was customary to have in each idol a little brazier in which they would burn their incense and if it was a new duty, they built the house anew, or they renovated it, and they put on the wall the memory of these things in their characters [glyphs].

("It is just as Isaiah predicted: 'Unless the Lord Almighty had left us descendants, we would have become like Sodom, we would have been like Gomorrah.'") Either Landa (or the author) or the copyist included here a somewhat garbled, partial version of the quote. Pagden (*The Maya*, 108n65) misattributes it to Isaiah 1:9.

[305] Although Brasseur de Bourbourg provided a verbatim translation of fs. 34r–43v (Sec. 40), both Tozzer and Gates reordered this section's discrete parts in an attempt to validate the claim made above that the beginning of the Maya new year began in our calendar's July. We have selected to follow Brasseur de Bourbourg's lead and simply translate this portion according to the order outlined in the original manuscript (see figure A.14).

[306] This is the first included heading in the manuscript. Our translation follows the right-hand column on f. 34r (see figure A.15).

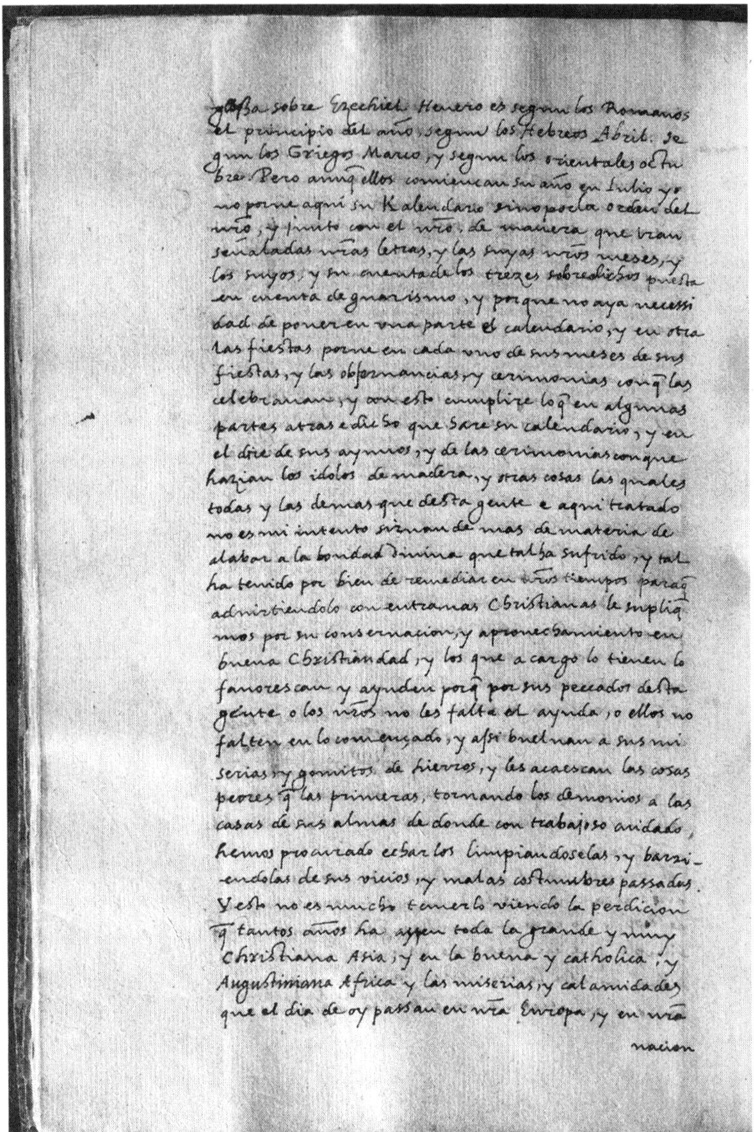

...ssa sobre Ezechiel. Henero es segun los Romanos
el principio del año, segun los Hebreos Abril. Se
gun los Griegos Marco, y segun los orientales octu
bre. Pero aunq ellos comiencan su año en Iulio yo
no porne aqui su Kalendario sino por la ocdan del
nro, y junto con el nro. de manera que vean
señaladas nras letras, y las suyas nros meses, y
los suyos, y su cuenta de los trezes sobredichos puesta
en cuenta de guarismo, y porque no aya necessi
dad de poner en una parte el calendario, y en otra
las fiestas, porne en cada uno de sus meses de sus
fiestas, y las obseruancias y cerimonias conq las
celebrarian, y con esto cumplire lo q en algunas
partes atras e dicho que hare en calendario, y en
el dize de sus aynios, y de las cerimonias conque
hazian los idolos de madera, y otras cosas las quales
todas y las demas que desta gente e aqui tratado
no es mi intento sino dar mas de materia de
elabor a la bondad divina que tal ha sufrido, y tal
ha tenido por bien de remediar en nros tiempos para q
admistiendolo con entrañas Christianas le suplica
mos por su conseruacion, y aprouechamiento en
buena Christiandad, y los que a cargo lo tienen lo
fauorescan y ayuden porq por sus peccados desta
gente o los nros no les falte el ayuda, o ellos no
falten en lo comencado, y assi buelvan a sus mi
serias y gomitos de hierros, y les acaescan las cosas
peores q las primeras, tornando los demonios a las
casas de sus almas de donde con trabajoso cuidado,
hemos procurado echar los limpiandoselas, y barri
endolas de sus vicios, y malas costumbres passadas.
Y esto no es mucho tenerlo viendo la perdicion
q tantos años ha aypen toda la grande y muy
Christiana Asia, y en la buena y catholica, y
Augustimana Africa y las miserias, y calamidades
que el dia de oy passan en nra Europa, y en nra
nacion

Figures A.14–A.15. fs. 33v–34r of the Account.

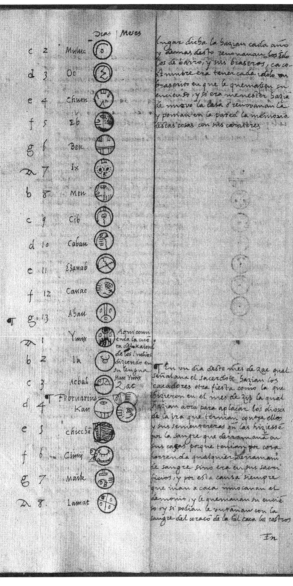

Dias			Meses
c	2	Muluc	
d	3	Oc	
e	4	Chuen	
f	5	Eb	
g	6	Ben	
a	7	Ix	
b	8	Men	
c	9	Cib	
d	10	Caban	
e	11	Ezanab	
f	12	Canac	
g	13	Ahau	
a	1	Ymix	
b	2	Ik	
c	3	Acbal	
d	4	Februarius Kan	
e	5	chicchā	
f	6	Cimi	
g	7	Manik	
a	8	Lamat	

Aqui comiença la cuenta delos kalendarios delos Indios diziendo en su lengua Hun Ymix 2 ac

lugar dicha la hazian cada año y demas desto renovavan los idolos de barro, y sus braseros, que por costumbre era tener cada idolo su brasserito en que le quemassen su encienso, y si era menester hazian de nuevo la casa ó renovavanla y ponian en la pared la memoria destas cosas con sus caracteres

En vn dia deste mes de zac qual señalava el sacerdote hazian los caçadores otra fiesta como la que hizieron en el mes de zip la qual hazian aora para aplacar los dioses de la ira que tenian contra ellos y sus sementeras pq las hiziesse por la sangre que derramavan en sus caças porque tenian por cosa horrenda qualquier derramar de sangre sino era en sus sacrificios, y por esta causa siempre que iuan a caça invocavan el demonio y le quemavan su encienso y si podian le vntavan con la sangre del coraçó de la tal caça los rostros

En

nacion, y casas por lo qual podriamos dezir se nos an
cumplido las euangelicas prophecias sobre Iherusalem de
que la cercarian sus enemigos, y ensangostarian, y
apretarian tanto que la derribassen por tierra. Y esto
ya lo auria Dios permitido segun somos, sino que no
puede faltar en yglesia ni lo del que dixo Nisi dns
reliquisset semen, sicut sodoma fuissemus.

Comienca el kalendario Romano, y Yucatanense

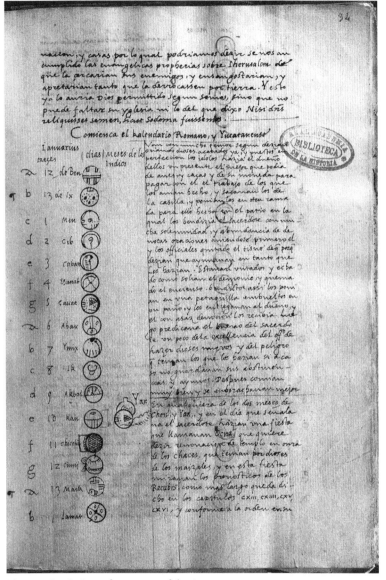

Ianuarius meses	dias	Meses de los Indios
℞	12	de Ben
b	13	de Ix
c	1	Men
d	2	Cib
e	3	Caban
f	4	Ezanab
g	5	Cauac
℞	6	Ahau
b	7	Ymix
c	8	Ik
d	9	Akbal
e	10	Kan
f	11	Chicchan
g	12	Cimi
℞	13	Manik
b	1	Lamat

Non con mucho temor segun dezian
seruian dioses acabados ya, y que los
en perfection los idolos hazian el dueño
dellos un presente, el mejor que podia
de aues, y caças, y de su moneda para
pagar con el el trabajo de los que
los auian hecho, y sacauan los de
la capilla, y ponianlos en otra rama
da para ello hecho en el patio en la
qual los bendezia el sacerdote con mu
cha solennidad, y abundancia de de
uotas oraciones auiendose primero el
y los officiales quitado el tizne de que
dezian que ayunauan en tanto que
los hazian. Estando untado, y ecba
do como solian el demonio, y quema
do el encienso bendeziase assi los poni
an en una petaquilla embueltos en
un paño, y los entregauan al dueño, y
el con asaz deuocion los recibia. Lue
go predicaua el bueno del sacerdote
le con poco de la excellencia del off.º de
hazer dioses nueuos, y del peligro
que tenian los que los hazian si aca
so no guardauan sus abstinen—
cias, y ayunos. Despues comian
muy bien, y se emborrachauan mejor

En qualquiera de los dos meses de
Chen, y Yax, y en el dia que señala
ua el sacerdote hazian una fiesta
que llamauan Ocna, que quiere
dezir renouacion de templo en onra
de los chaces, que tenian por dioses
de los mayzales, y en esta fiesta
mirauan los pronosticos de los
Bacabes como mas largo queda di
cho en los capitulos cxiii, cxiiii, cxv,
cxvi, y conforme a la orden en su

días / meses

b	9	Muluc
c	10	Oc
d	11	Chuen
e	12	Eb
¶f	13	Ben
g	1	Ix
a	2	Men
b	3	Cib
c	4	Caban
d	5	Eçanab
e	6	Cauac
f	7	Ahau
g	8	Ymix
a	9	Ik
b	10	Akbal
c	11	Kan
d	12	Chicchá
¶e	13	Cimi

en qualquier dia q cayesse este
septimo de Ahau hazian una muy
gran fiesta que dvrava tres
dias de sahumerios y offrendas; y
en gentil vayle y poesia; y por esto
es fiesta movible tenian los sacerdotes cuidado de abisar-
la con tiempo paraq se ayunasse
devidamente

35

HERE BEGINS THE COUNT OF THE CALENDAR [*KALENDARIO*] OF THE INDIANS, SAYING IN THEIR LANGUAGE *HUN YMIX*[307]

¶[308] On one day of this month of Zac, which was selected by the priest, the hunters hosted a festival like the one they held in the month of Zip. They hold it now in order to appease the gods and the ire they had against them and their field plantings that they would make, because of the blood spilled in their hunts, as they took it as a horrible thing for any blood to be let except in their sacrifices. For this reason, when they went to hunt they invoked the devil and they burnt incense to him, and if they could, they anointed their faces with the blood of that game's heart.

[*f. 35r; figure A.17*] On whatever day that fell on this 7 Ahau, they held a very big festival that lasted three days of making incense and offerings and their gentile drunkenness. And since this is a moveable festival, they have the priests in charge take care to throw it on time, so the fasting can be dutifully done.

[*f. 35v; figure A.18*] ¶ On any day of this month of Mac the oldest and most ancient people hold a festival to the Chacs, gods of the fields, and to Itzamna [*i Zamna*]. A day or two before, they performed the following ceremony, which they called in their language, Tuppkak.[309] They had looked [*f. 36r; figure A.19*] for all the animals and insects of the fields that they could find and that this land has, and they put them all together on the patio of the temple. There the Chacs and the priest sat in the corners, in order to cast out the devil as they used to, each one with a pitcher of water that they each carried. In the middle they placed upright a big bunch of dried and tied-up straw [*varillas*]. First burning incense in the brazier, they ignited the straw and while it burned, they quickly removed the hearts of the birds and animals, and they threw

---

[307] This "title" is actually written between the column of hieroglyphs and the Spanish text (see figure A.16).

[308] We insert this symbol whenever the copyist used it; his written version is almost identical to the one that is standard on modern keyboards. Called a "pilcrow," the ¶ was the early modern book printer's symbol for "paragraph," and was derived from the scribal symbols that monastic scribes used in liturgical and scholastic manuscripts to divide the text into manageable and logical units of reading. The inclusion of pilcrows here suggests that not only did the original (lost) manuscript have "chapter numbers" (i.e., 100, 101, 110, etc.) but that within the chapters there were paragraph markings of the kind common in sixteenth-century published works. This is further suggested toward the end of the Account (Sec. 52, f. 66r), when Landa refers the reader to the exact paragraph numbers of several chapters in which he refutes the statements of contemporary Spanish chroniclers. The copyist of those sections also attempted to make the initial letter of the paragraph a "bold capital letter," likewise a common printer or scribal mark to denote the beginning of sections of a manuscript being prepared for publication.

[309] This festival, U Tupic U Kak [He Puts Out the Fire], was not held on "any day," but on 11 Chic Chan, 11 Oc, 11 Men, and 11 Ahau.

them into the fire. And if they did not have large animals, like tigers, lions, or lizards, they made hearts out of their copal incense, but if they could kill them, they carried their hearts to that fire. The hearts all burned, the Chacs extinguished the fire with their pitchers of water. They hold this one and the following festival to bring about a good year of rains for their fields. Later, they celebrate [another] festival. This festival they celebrate differently than the others, for they did not fast for this one, except the host [*muñidor*], who fasted his fast. Coming to celebrate the festival, the town, priest, and officials gathered in the patio of the temple where they had made a pyramid [*monton de piedras*] with a staircase, all very clean and freshly decorated. The priest gave prepared incense to the host, who burned it in the brazier, and thus, they say, the devil fled. This done, with their usual devotion [*f. 36v; figure A.20*] they smeared the first step of the pyramid with mud from the well, and the other stairs with blue pigment [*betun azul*]. And they threw many incense sticks and invoked the Chacs and Itzamna with their prayers and devotions and offered gifts to them. This finished, they took comfort in eating and drinking what they offered, and they remained confident of a good year with their ceremonies and invocations.

❡ In the month of Muan, those who had cacao fields [*cacauatales*] held a festival for the gods Ekchuah, Chac, and Hobnil, who were their advocates [*abogados*]. They went to a plot of land [*heredad*] of one of them, where they sacrificed a male dog, with chocolate-colored spots. They burned incense to the idols, offering to them blue-skinned iguanas, certain [*f. 37r; figure A.21*] feathers of a bird, and other game; and each one of the officials gave to them a cacao pod [*mazorca de la fruta del cacao*]. They finished the sacrifice and their prayers, ate the gifts, and each one drank, it is said, no more than three sips [*vezes*] of wine, and they did not imbibe more. They went to the house of the festival's host and did some joyful things [*unas passas con regoçijo*].

❡ In this month of Pax they held a festival called Pacumchac, for which the lords and the priests of the minor towns gathered with those of the major towns. Thus gathered, [*f. 37v; figure A.22*] they stayed up for five nights in the temple of Citchaccoh, saying prayers, giving offerings and incense like it is said they did in the festival of Kukulcan in the month of Xul in November. Before these days passed, they went to the house of the war captain called Nacon, who was treated in chapter 101 [*CI*]. They treated him with great pomp, incensing him like an idol at the temple upon which he sat, and they burned incense to him like an idol. Like this he sat until the five days passed, during which they ate and drank the gifts they were offered in the temple. They danced a dance in the manner of a martial *passo largo*, and so they called it in their language Holkanokot, which is to say, dance of the

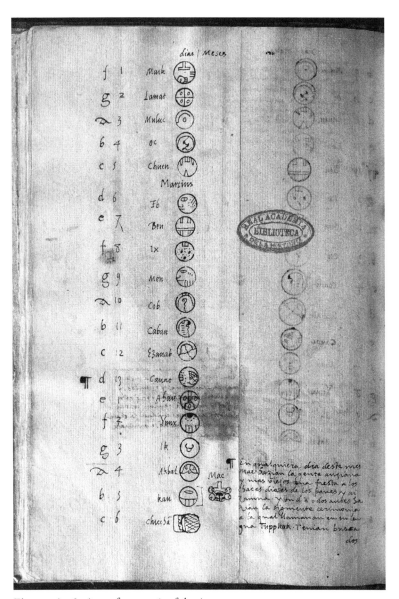

Figures A.18–A.19. fs. 35v–36r of the Account.

días y meses

d	7	Cimix
e	8	Manix
f	9	Lamat
g	10	Muluc
A	11	Oc
b	12	Chuen
c	13	Eb
d	1	Ben
e	2	Ix
f	3	Men
g	4	Cib
A	5	Caban
b	6	Eznab
c	7	Canac
d	8	Canac
e	9	Ahau
f	10	Ymix

Abriles

g	11	Acbal
A	12	Kan
b	13	Chicchã

Kankin

dos todos los animales, y sa
uandijas del campo, que po
dian auer y en la tierra mia
y con ellos se juntauan en el
patio del templo, en el qual
se ponian los chacnes, y el sa
cerdote sentados en las esqui
nas como para echar el demo
nio solian con sendos cantaros
de agua que alli les trayan a
cada uno. En medio ponian
un gran manojo de varillas se
cas atadas y enhiestas, y que
mando primero de su encien
so en el braçero pegauan fue
go a las varillas y en tanto que
ardian sacauan con liberalidad
los coraçones a las aues, y ani
males, y echauan los a quemar
en el fuego, y sino podian auer
los animales grandes como ti
gres, leones, o Lagartos, hazian
los coraçones de su encienso, y
si los matauan, trayanles los
coraçones para aquel fuego.
Quemados los coraçones todos
matauan el fuego con los can
taros de agua los sacaces. Esto
hazian para con ello y la sigui
ente fiesta alcançar buen año
de aguas para sus panes, luego
celebrauan la fiesta. Esta fi
esta celebrauan differentemen
te de las otras ca para ella no
ayunauan saluo el munidor
della, que este ayunaua su ayu
no. Y venidos pues a celebrar
la fiesta se juntauan el pue
blo y sacerdote y officiales en
el patio del templo donde se
nian hecho un monton de
piedras, con sus escaleras, y
todo muy limpio y aderesçado
de frescuras. Lleua el sacerdote
se encienso preparado para
el munidor, el qual lo que
mana en el braçero, y assi
dez q̃ huia el demonio. Esto
hecho con su devoción acostum

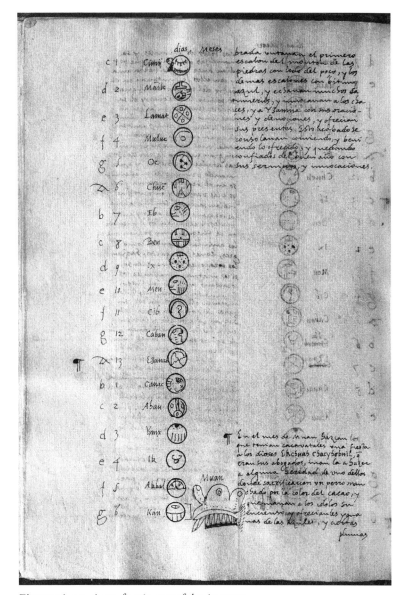

Figures A.20–A.21. fs. 36v–37r of the Account.

dias		meses
g	1	Chicchan
ç	2	Cimi
b	3	Mamk
c	4	Lamat
d	5	Muluc
e	6	Oc
f	7	Chue
g	8	Eb
ç	9	Ben
b	10	Ix
c	11	Men
d	12	Cib
¶ e	13	Caban
f	1	Ezanab
g	2	Cauac
ç	3	Ahau
b	4	Ymix
c	5	Ik
d	6	Acbal
	Iunius	
e	7	Kan

velauan cinco noches en el
templo de cuchaobob en oraçio-
nes, y ofrendas y sahumerios
como esta dicho hizieron en
la fiesta de Kukulcan en el mes
de Xul en noviembre antes
de estos dias passados, yuan to
dos a casa del capitan de sus guer
ras llamado nacon del qual
trate en el capitulo ci. y trayan
le con gran pompa sahumandole
como a idolo al templo en el
qual le sentauan y quemauan
encienso como a idolo, y assi estauan el, y ellos hasta passados los
cinco dias; en los quales comian
y beuian de los dones que se offrecian en el templo, y baylauan
vn bayle a manera de passo largo de guerra, y assi le llamauan
en su lengua Holkanokot que quiere dezir baile de guerreros. Pasa
dos los cinco dias venian a la fiesta
la qual porque era para cosas de
guerra y assi le llamauan en
su lengua, y alcançar victoria
de sus enemigos era muy solemne. Hazian pues primero
la cerimonia y sacrificio del fue
go como dixe en el mes de Mac.
Despues echauan como solian
el demonio con mucha solemni
dad. Esto echo andauan el oxar, y
ofrecer dones y sahumerios, y en
tanto que la gente hazian estas
sus ofrendas y oraciones, tomauan los ss. y los q ya les auian
echo al Nacon en hombros, y trayan le sahumando al rededor
del templo, y quando boluian
con el sacrificauan los chaces
vn perro, y sacauan le el co-
raçon, y embiauanle al de
monio entre dos platos, y los
chaces quebrauan sendas ollas
Kanab grandes llenas de beuida, y
con esto acabauan su fiesta
Acabada comian, y beuian
los

warriors.[310] After those five days had passed, they came to the festival, and because it was for things of war, ~~they called it in their language,~~[311] and to have victory over your enemies it was very solemn. First, they held the ceremony and sacrifice of fire, as I said, in the month of Mac. Afterwards, they cast out the devil like they do, with much solemnness. This done, they gave the oration and offered gifts and incense. While the people did their offerings and prayers, the lords picked up the Nacon on their shoulders and carried him smoking to the periphery of the temple. When they got back there, the Chacs sacrificed a dog, removed his heart, and presented it to the devil between two plates. And the Chacs each broke open a jar full of a beverage, and with this they completed the festival. They finished it by eating and drinking the *[f. 38r; figure A.23]* gifts that there they had offered, and they brought them to the Nacon with a lot of solemnity, to his house without scents. There they had a great festival, during which the lords, priests, and principal people got drunk. The other people left for their towns except for the Nacon, who did not get drunk. On another day later, the wine ingested, all the lords and priests of the pueblos gathered so they could imbibe. They remained in the house of the lord where they distributed a great quantity of incense that they had prepared there and had been blessed by some priests. Together with it a big speech was made. With much efficiency they entrusted the festivals to be made in the towns to the gods so that it would be a year prosperous with much support [*mantenimientos*]. The speech done, they all said goodbye, one to the others, with much love and staggering. Each one left for their town and home. There they began to hold their festivals, those which lasted according to those which were held until the month of Popp and which they called the Zabacilthan. They were held in this way: they watched in the town for the richest ones who wanted to host the festival, and they granted to them their day because they had more to give [*mas gasajo*] those three months than they had had since the new year. And those who held it held gathered in the house of the festival's host, and there held the ceremonies of casting out the devil, burning copal, and making offerings of little gifts, dancing, and making some wineskins [*botas de vino*] *[f. 38v; figure A.24]*. And for this they stopped everything. The excess of these festivals was so much these three months that it was a great shame to see it, for while some scraped by, others were wounded, others with bloody eyes because of the great drunkenness, and they were lost in all this love of wine.

¶ It remained to be said in the past chapters that the Indians started their years

---

[310] This martial *passo largo* or long-step dance is also mentioned earlier in the Account (f. 17v, Sec. 22; and f. 31r, Sec. 36), with notable descriptions of Maya dances in various sections of the text.

[311] Apparently unable to provide (or read) the Mayan term for this festival, this phrase was then crossed out by the copyist.

with the nameless days,[312] preparing themselves during them with vigilance for the celebration of their new year festival. In addition to the preparation, they held a festival for the devil U Uayab Hab [*Uuayayab*], for which they left their houses. The other preparation was to leave the house very infrequently during those five days to offer the donations for the public festival, payments to their devils and to others of the temples. These payments that they offered like this were never returned for other uses, nor for anything other than offerings to the devil. They bought them the incense that they burn. During these days they did not chop firewood [*pinavan*], wash, the men and women did not delouse themselves, neither doing any menial nor laborious work, because they feared something bad would happen if they did.

[*f. 39r; figure A.25*] ¶ The first day of Popp is the first month of the Indian new year. Among them, it was a much-celebrated festival because it was public for everyone. So, all the town held this festival together for all the idols. In order to celebrate it with more solemnness, they renewed all their homeware like plates, cups, little cups, shoes, their old clothing, and the little mantles worn by the enshrouded idols. They changed around their houses, and the trash and these old supplies they threw out outside of the town in a garbage dump. And even if they needed them, no one would touch them. For this festival, the lords, the priest, the principal people, and those who most wanted to [do it] out of devotion, begin to fast and abstain from women, even before it seemed fit, for some began it three months before, other two, and others as it seemed fit, but no one less than thirteen [*XIII*] days. During those thirteen days, they added to their abstinence from women by not eating delicious food, salt, nor peppers, which they took as a great penitence among them. During this time, they elected the Chac officials in order to assist the priest. He freshly prepared many little balls of their incense on some little tables that the priests had for it. For the abstinences and fasts, they would burn [incense] to the idols. Those who were fasting continued to, because they would not dare to break it, because they believed some evil would come [*f. 39v; figure A.26*] to their person or house. The new year arrived, and only the men all gathered together in the patio of the temple, because there is no single sacrifice or festival during which women can be found in the temple except the old women when they do their dances. In the other festivals that they hold in other parts, they can attend, and women can be found here now that they are clean and in their elegant, colored clothes, and the black soot that they used to smear themselves with. All congregated with many gifts that they carried of foods, drinks, and a lot of wine they had made. The priest purged the temple, seated in the middle of the patio pompously [*pontifical*] dressed, inserting

---

[312] By the "nameless days," the author means the five days of Uayeb, which technically were the last days of the previous year.

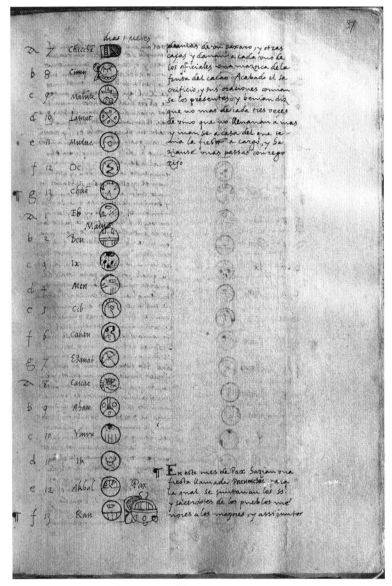

Figures A.22–A.23. fs. 37v–38r of the Account.

		dias / meses
f	8	Chicchan
g	9	Cimi
a	10	Manik
b	11	Lamat
d	13	Oc
e	14	Chue
f	2	Eb
b	3	Ben
a	4	Ix
b	5	Men
c	6	Cib
d	7	Caban
e	8	Izanab
f	9	Cauac
b	10	Ahau
a	11	Ymix
a	12	Ik
c	13	Akbal	Cumku
d	1	Kan

presentes, que alli se auian
ofrecido, y llenauan al Nacon
con mucha solemnidad a su casa
sin perfumes. Alla tenian gran
fiesta, y en ella se emborachauan
los señores, y sacerdotes, y los
principales, y mas la demas
gente a sus pueblos salvo que
el Nacon no se emborachaua. Otro
dia despues de digerido el vino
se juntauan todos los ss. y sacerdotes de los pueblos que se auī
an enbeuado, y quedado alli en
casa del Sõr, el qual les repartia
mucha cantidad de su encienso
so que tenia alli aparejado, y
bendicho de aquellos benditos
sacerdotes, y junto con ello les
hazia vna gran platica, y con
mucha eficacia les encomen-
daua las fiestas que en sus pue
blos ellos auian de hazer a los
dioses paraq fuesse el año pro
spero de mantenimientos. La
platica hecha se despidian todos
vnos de otros con mucho amor
y tababla, y se uan cada vno
a su pueblo, y casa. Alla trata
uan de hazer sus fiestas, las
quales durauan segun las ha
zian hasta el mes de Popp, y
llamauan las Zabacilthan, y
hazian las desta manera. Jū-
tauan en el pueblo de los mas
ricos quien queria hazer esta
fiesta, y encomendauan le su
dia por tener mas gasajo estos
tres meses que auia hasta su
año nuevo, y loque hazian era
juntarse en casa del que la
fiesta hazia, y alli hazer las
cerimonias de echar el demonio, y quemar copal, y
hazer ofrendas con regosijos,
y uailes, y hazerse vnas botas

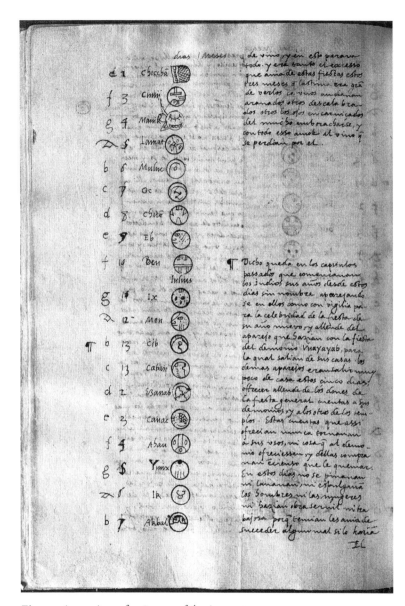

Figures A.24–A.25. fs. 38v–39r of the Account.

dias / meses

c	8	
d	9	
e	10	
f	11	
g	12	Pop
a	13	Kan
b	13	Chicçan
c	1	Cimiz
d	2	Manik
e	3	Lamat
f	4	Muluc
g	5	Oc
a	6	Chuen
b	7	Eb
c	8	Been
d	9	Ix
e	10	Men
f	11	Cib

El primero dia de Popp que es el primero mes de los yndios era su año nuevo, y entre ellos fiesta muy celebrada porque era general y de todos, y assi todo el pueblo junto hazian fiesta a todos los idolos. Para celebrarla con mas solemni dad renovavan en este dia to das las cosas de su servicio como platos, vasos, vanquillos, serillas, y la ropa vieja, y las mantillas en que comian los idolos embuel tos. Varrian sus casas, y la vasura y estos pertrechos viejos echava lo fuera del pueblo al mula dar, y nadie avnque lo oviesse menester tocava a ello. Para esta fiesta começavan a ayunar y abstenerse de las mugeres los [13] y sacerdote, y la gente principal, y los que mas que rian por su devocion, el tiem po antes que les parecia, ca algunos la començavan tres meses antes, otros dos, otros co mo les parecia, y ninguno menos de XIII dias, y [en] estos XIII dias añadian a la abstinencia de la muger no comer en los manjares sal ni de su pi mienta que era tenido por grave penitencia entre ellos. En este tiempo elegian los officiales chacs para ayudar al sacerdote, y el aparejava muchas pelotillas de su en cienso fresco en unas tabli llas que para ello tenian los sacerdotes para q los abstinetes y ayunantes quemassen a los idolos. Los que esto ayu nos començavan no los osa van quebrantar porq creia les vendrian algun mal

the incense pellets into the brazier. The Chacs sat in the four corners, and they tied a new cord, one to the other, inside of which everyone who had fasted to cast out the devil entered, like I said they did in chapter 96 [*XCVI*]. With the devil cast out, they all started their particular prayers, and the Chacs took out the new fire. And they lit the brazier that in the public festivals they lit communally, and with the new fire they burned the incense to the devil. The priest started to throw his incense into it, and everyone came by in order, beginning with the lords, to receive incense from the priest's hand, which he gave them with as much courtesy and devotion as is given to [*f. 40r; figure A.27*] reliquaries. They throw it into the brazier, little by little, and they wait for it to be finished burning. After the incensing, between them they eat all of the donations and presents, and the wine flows until they are blind drunk [*se hazian unas uvas*]. This was their new year, a ritual very appeasing to their idols. It was afterwards, during this month of Popp, that some others celebrated this festival because of their devotion with their friends and with the lords and priest. Their priests were always first in their great rites [*regrosorios*] and holinesses [*benvidas*].

❡ In the month of Uo, they began to prepare with fasts and their other things. In order to celebrate this other festival, the priests, doctors, and sorcerers, which were all the same thing, hunters, and fishermen came to celebrate it on the seventh of Zip. Each one celebrates on their day. First, the priests celebrated theirs, which they called Pocam, and together in the house of the lord with their accessories, they first cast out the devil like usual. Afterwards they took out their books and they laid them out on top of fresh leaves [*frescuras*] that they gathered for this. Invoking with prayers of devotion an idol that they called Cinchau Yzamna [Kinich Ahau Itzamna], he which they say was the first priest, they offer to him his donations and presents and ignite with the new fire [*f. 40v; figure A.28*] the little balls of their incense. Among so much they dissolve in the cup a little verdigris,[313] with virgin water that they say they brought from the *monte* where no women had been. They smeared it on the covers of their books for their cleansing. This done the most learned of the priests opened the book and looked for the prognostications of that year. He declared to those who were present, preaching to them a little, and granting them the remedies. This festival was thrown for another year by the priest or lord who had hosted it, and if he who prognosticated it died, his sons were obligated to complete it for the deceased. This done, they ate all the donations, and food that

---

[313] The author uses the Spanish term for verdigris, *cardenillo*, a green pigment that results from the intentional corrosion of copper, brass, or bronze. Although known in Eurasia since the Classic period, Indigenous Americans did not use this method of producing green paint; the author is thus likely referring to Maya Green, a pigment produced by heating a combination of palygorskite and indigo dye to high temperatures (see Solari and Williams, "Maya Blue and Franciscan Evangelism").

had been brought, and they drank until they turned into drunkards [figuratively wineskins; *zaques*]. Like so, as the festival finished, they sometimes danced a dance called Okotvil.

❡ The following day, the doctors and sorcerers gathered together in one of their houses with their wives. The priests casted out the devil, and then they took out the wrapped medicine bundles [*emboltorios*], in which they carried many silly things in each one, little idols of the medicine god that they called Ixchel, and in this festival they called her Ihcilixchel,[314] some of the little divinatory stones that they cast which they called Am. With much devotion they invoked with prayers the gods of medicine, which they said were Yzamna, Citbolontum, and Ahauchamahez. Giving to them the incense, the priests burned it in the new fire braziers. Meanwhile, the Chacs smeared the idols and little stones with another blue pigment [*betun azul*] like [*f. 41r; figure A.29*] that of the priests' books. This done, each thing of their office they wrapped and taking the wrapped bundle on their shoulders, they all danced a dance that they called Chantuniab. The dance finished with the men sitting by themselves, and the women by themselves. The festival was done for another year. They ate the gifts, and they got very drunk without embarrassment except for the priests, whom I said were ashamed and saved the wine in order to drink it by themselves and at their pleasure.

❡ The next day the hunters gathered in one of their houses and filling it together with their wives like the others, the priests came and cast out the devil like before. This done, they put in the middle the adornments for the sacrifice of incense, new fire, and blue pigment. The hunters invoked the devil and the gods of the hunt, Acanum Zuhuyzipi tabai [Acan Zum, Zuhuy Zip, and Ah Tabay] and others, and they distributed the incense, which they put into the brazier. While it burned, each one took out an arrow and a deer skull, which the Chacs smeared with the blue pigment. Anointed, they danced, some with them in their hands, while others punctured their ears, others their tongues, and passed through the holes seven leaves of a plant, somewhat wide, that they called Ac.[315] The priest had done this first, and the festivals' officials later offered donations, and so, dancing, the wine was poured, and they got drunk until passing out.

❡ Later the following day, the fishermen hosted a festival in the manner of the others except [*f. 41v; figure A.30*] that they smeared the fishing gear and did not puncture their ears, instead nicking them all around the upper part [*a la redonda*]. They danced a dance called *chohom*, and everyone was blessed with a tall and fat pole that they put upright. After they held this festival, they had the custom in the

---

[314] This would be Ichcil Ixchel, the bathing or cleansing of Ixchel or Ix Chel.

[315] This may be a tall grass sometimes used for thatch (Millspaugh, Chase, and Standley, *Plantæ Yucatanæ*, 211–13) or beardgrass (*Andropogon* sp.).

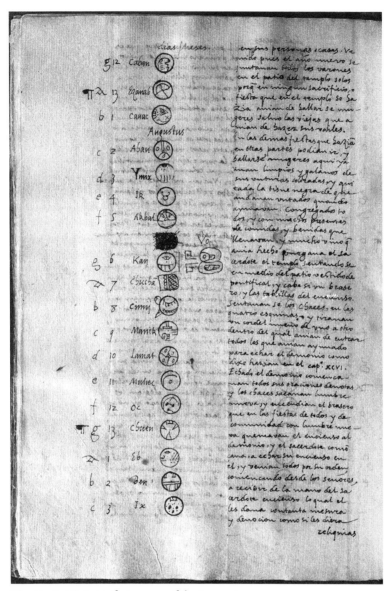

dias / meses

E	12	Caban
ꝑ	13	Eçanab
b	1	Canac

Augustus

c	2	Abau
d	3	Ymix
e	4	Ik
f	5	Akbal
g	6	Kan
	7	Chicchan
b	8	Cimi
c	9	Manik
d	10	Lamat
e	11	Muluc
f	12	Oc
g	13	C'been
	1	Eb
b	2	Ben
c	3	Ix

unas personas y casas. Venido pues el año nuevo se
juntavan todos los varones
en el patio del templo solos
porq̃ en ningun sacrificio o
fiesta que en el templo se ha
zia avian de hallar se mu
geres salvo las viejas que a
vian de bazer sus bayles.
En las demas fiestas que hazia
en otras partes podian ir, y
hallarse mugeres aqui ya
avian limpios y galanos de
sus venturas coloradas y aqui
toda la tiñe negra de q̃ se
andavan untados quanto
ayunavan. Congregados to
los, y con muchos presentes
de comidas y bevidas que
llevavan, y mucho vino q̃
avia hecho poniga ana el sa
cerdote el campo, sentando se
en medio del patio vestido de
pontifical, y cabe si un brase
ro, y las tablillas del encienso.
Sentavan se los chaces, en las
quatro esquinas, y tiravan
un cordel unos de unos a otro
dentro del qual avian de entrar
todos los que avian ayunado
para echar el demonio como
dixe hazian en el cap. XCVI.
Echado el demonio començavan todos sus oraciones devotas
y los chaces sacavan lumbre
nueva, y encendian el brasero
que en las fiestas de todos y de
comunidad con lumbre nue
va quemavan el encienso al
demonio, y el sacerdote como
carça a echar su encienso en
el, y venian todos por su orden
començando desde los señores,
a recevir de la mano del sa
cerdote encienso lo qual el
les dava con tanta mesura
y devocion como si les diera
                              reliquias

Figures A.26–A.27. fs. 39v–40r of the Account.

Dias		meses
d	4	Men
e	5	Cib
f	6	Caban
g	7	Eznab
	8	Cauac
b	9	Aʒau
c	10	Ymyx
d	11	Ik
e	12	Akbal
f	13	Kan
g	1	Chicchan
	2	Cimiy
b	3	Manik
c	4	Lamat
d	5	Muluc
e	6	Oc
		September
f	7	Chuen

reliquias, y ellos lo echauan en el brasero poco a poco, y aguardan do se fuesse acabado de quemar. Despues deste saumerio comian entre todos los dones y presentes, y andaua el vino hasta que se hazian vnas vuas, y este era su año nueuo, y seruicio muy ac cepto a sus idolos. Auia despues otros algunos que dentro deste mes de Popp celebrauan esta fiesta por su deuocion con sus amigos, y con los sus y sacerdote, q sus sacerdotes siempre eran pri meros en sus regocijos y be uidas.

En el mes de Vo se començaua a apareiar con animos y las demas cosas para celebrar otra fiesta los sacerdotes, los medicos y hechizeros que era todo vno Los cacadores, y pescadores ve nian la a celebrar a siete de Zip, y celebrauan la cada vno dellos por si en su dia. Primera mente celebrauan la suya los sa cerdotes a la qual llamauan Pocam, y juntos en casa del señor por sus ... Sechauan pri mero al demonio como solia despues sacauan sus libros, y tendian los sobre las frescuras que para ello venian y invo cando con oraciones y su de uocion a vn Idolo que llama Cinchau Yzamna el qual dizen fue el primer sacerdote ofrecia les sus dones y presentes, y que man aule con la lumbre

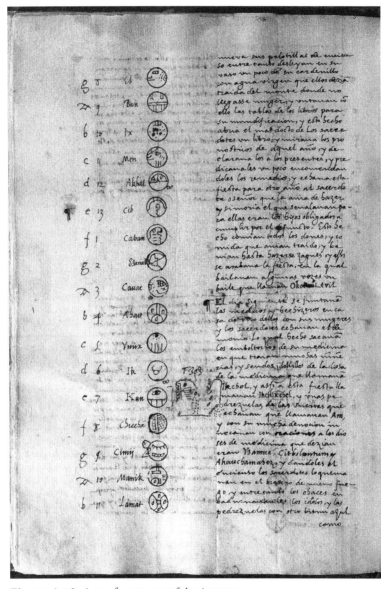

Figures A.28–A.29. fs. 40v–41r of the Account.

c	12	Muluc	
d	13	Oc	
e	1	Chuen	
f	2	Eb	
g	3	Ben	
a	4	Ix	
b	5	Men	
c	6	Cib	
d	7	Caban	
e	8	Ezanab	
f	9	Cauac	
g	10	Ahau	Octobez
a	11	Yimix	
b	12	Ik	
c	13	Ahbal	Tzec
d	1	Kan	
e	2	Chicchã	

el de los libros de los sacerdo
tes. Esto hecho emboluia cada
vno las cosas de su off.º y tomã
do el emboltorio a cuestas bai
lauan todos vn vaile q̃ ella
mauan Chantunyab, acabado
el vaile se sentauan los varo
nes por si, y por si las mugeres,
y echando la fiesta para otro
año comian los presentes, y
emborrachauan se muy sin
asco saluo los sacerdotes que
diz que auian pquerguença, y
guardauan les del vino para
bever a sus solas, y a su plazer.—

El dia siguiente se juntauan los
caçadores en vna casa de vno de
ellos, y lleuando consigo sus
mugeres como los demas re
nial los sacerdotes y echauan
el demonio como solian. Echa
do po̅nian en medio el adereço
para el sacrificio, de encien
so, y fuego nuevo, y el betun
azul, y con su denocion inuo
cauan los caçadores a los dio
ses de la caça: Acanum zuhuyzipi
tabai, y otros, y repartian les el
encienso, el qual echauan en
el brasero, y entanto que ardia
sacaua cada vno flecha, y vna
cababeza de venado, las qua
les los cħaces vntauan con el
betun azul, y vntadas vai
lauan con ellas en las manos vnos,
y otros se horadauan las orejas
otros las lenguas, y passauan
por los agujeros siete hojas de
vna yerua algo anchas que
llaman Ac. Auiendo echo esto
primero el sacerdote, y los ofi
ciales de la fiesta luego ofrecia
los dones, y assi bailando se
escanciauan el vino, y se em
borrachauan se hechos vnos cestos.

luego el siguiente dia hazia
su fiesta los pescadores por el
orden q̃ las demas saluo que

towns to go to the coast, the lords and many people. There they had great fishing feasts and joys, for they brought a big collection of loosely woven dragnets, fish-hooks, and other fishing tools. The gods who were the patrons of this festival were Ahkaknexoc, Ahpua, Ahcitzamalcum.

❡ In the month of Tzoz, the lords prepare the beehives in order to celebrate the festival in Tzec. And even though the main preparation was the fast, it was not required by more than the priest and the officials who fasted; for the others it was voluntary. The day of the festival arrived, and they gathered in the house where it was to be celebrated, and they did all the same as in the others [festivals] except that they did not let blood. The Bacabs were the patrons, especially Hobnil. They made many special offerings to the four Chacs, and gave them four plates, each one with incense ball in the middle of each one, painted all around with figures of honey, which there was in abundance in this festival. They concluded *[f. 42r; figure A.31]* it with wine, as usual, and a great deal of it, in order for the owners of the beehives of honey to have it in abundance.[316]

In the tenth chapter, the arrival of Kukulcan in Yucatan was related, after which there were some among the Indians who said that he had gone to heaven with the gods.[317] Because of this, they took him for God, and they marked time for him in which they would celebrate this festival for him and the whole region celebrated it, until the destruction of Mayapan. After this destruction, only the province of Mani celebrated it, and the other provinces, in recognition of what they owed to Kukulcan, held it one year, and the next another [province hosted it], and another year Mani four or five times. Very elegant, feathered flags were made for the festival, and it was celebrated in this manner, not like the past ones. By sixteenth of Xul all the lords and priests gathered together in Mani, and with them a great crowd from the towns, who came already prepared having fasted and abstained [from women]. That day in the afternoon, they came out in a great procession of people and with a lot of the jesters of the lord's house, where they had been gathered. They went in a great silence to the temple of Kukulcan, which they had well decorated. Having arrived, doing their prayers, they put the flags at the top of the temple. Below in the patio they had placed each one of their idols on tree leaves that they had for this. And taking out a new fire, they started to burn incense in many areas, and to make offerings of cooked food without salt or pepper, and of *[f. 42v; figure A.32]* drinks

---

[316] For more detail on the beekeeping rituals of this month, see Vail and Dedrick, "Human-Deity Relationships."

[317] Here again the copyist is including information to help us understand the structure of the original manuscript Landa had written, from which this Account was copied; this planned, original tenth chapter would refer to fs. 5r–6r (Sec. 6) above. Gates wrongly glosses *decimo* (the chapter number) as "twelfth" (*Yucatán*, 73).

made of their beans and pumpkin seeds. Always burning copal, the lords and those who had fasted spent five days and five nights doing these offerings there without returning to their homes, in prayer and performing certain dances. Until the first day of Yaxkin the jesters [*farsantes*] came to the principal houses making their jokes [*farsas*] and picking up the gifts that had been given them, and they carried it all to the temple, where at the end of the five days the donations were divided among the lords, priests, and dancers. They took down the flags and idols, returned them to the lord's house, and each one to their own house. They said, and it was strongly believed, that Kukulcan came down from heaven on the last of those days, and he collected his nightly rites and offerings. They called this festival Chicchahau.

❡ In this month of Yaxkin they start getting ready, as they were accustomed, for a festival for all of the gods, that they hold publicly on Mol, on the day indicated by the priest. They called it Olob-Zab-Kamyax. After gathering at the temple and doing the ceremonies and incensing that they had done in the past, all the tools of all the trades, from the priest's to the women's spindle whorls and the house posts, were smeared with blue pigment. For this festival, they gathered all the boys and girls of the town, and instead of anointments *[f. 43r; figure A.33]* and ceremonies, they gave them on the outside part of the wrist joints nine little taps. The girls were given over to an old woman dressed in an outfit of a feathered habit who brought [the girls] there. Because of this they called her [the old woman] Ixmol, which is to say, she who gathers. They gave them those taps so they would leave as expert officials in the offices of their mothers and fathers. The conclusion was done with a great drunken party, the offerings were eaten except those which were thought to have been gathered for the old devout woman who instead went to get drunk in her home so as not to lose the feathers of her cloak of office in the street.

❡ In this month the beekeepers return to hold another festival like that which they held in Tzec, for the gods who protect the flowers of the bees.

❡ One of the things that these poor people did, arduously and with difficulty, was the making of idols out of wood, which they call making gods. So, in order to make them, a particular time had to be indicated, and it was this month of Mol, or another if the priest told them that it was sufficient. Those who wanted to make them consulted the priest first and sought his council. They went to their officials, and they say that the officials always avoided them because death or deadly sicknesses could come upon their houses [in the making of the gods].[318] Having accepted, the Chacs

---

[318] The risk described here is due to the highly charged nature of creating ritual items, which in precontact periods were seen as animate and holding potentially dangerous life force. This view of personhood as more than the domain of humans indebted the craft specialist to the object and created lifelong ties. Miguel Astor-Aguilera ("Maya Rites, Rituals, and Ceremonies," 648) notes that like other Indigenous people, Maya personhood extends to ancestors,

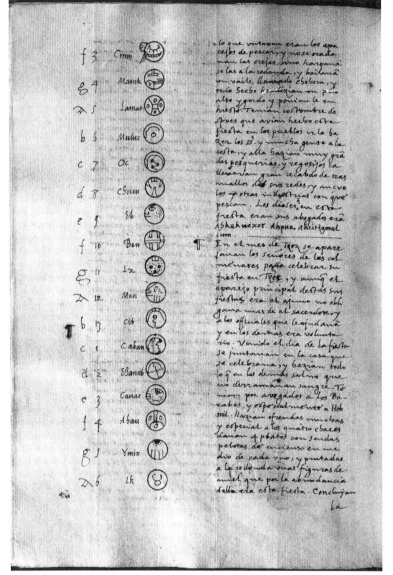

Figures A.30–A.31. fs. 41v–42r of the Account.

b	7	Akbal	
c	8	Kan	
d	9	Chicchã	
e	10	Cimij	
f	11	Manik	
g	12	Lamat	
	13	Muluc	
b	1	Oc	

Nouembre

d	3	Eb	
e	4	Ben	
f	5	Ix	
g	6	Men	
	7	Cib	
b	8	Caban	
c	9	Eßnab	
d	10	Cauac	
e	11	Ahau	

XIII. La con vino como solian, y harto porq̃ dauan para ello los dueños de las colmenas miel en abundancia.

En el dezimo capitulo que da cuenta la yda de Kukulcan de Yucatan despues de la qual vos entre los indios algunas que di xeron se auia ydo al cielo con los dioses, y por esso le tuuieron por dios, y le señalaron tiem po para q̃ como a tal le celebra ssen en fiestas y se la celebro toda la tierra hasta la destruy cion de mayapan. Despues desta destruicion se celebraua en la prouincia de mani solamente y las demas prouincias en re conoscimiento de lo q̃ deuian a Kukulcan presentauan vn a ño vnas y otra otro a mani qua tro, y a las vezes sino a muy gala nas vanderas de pluma con las quales hazian la fiesta en esta manera y no como las passadas. A diez y seis de Xul se juntauan todos los ss. y sacerdotes en mani y con ellos gran gentio de los pue blos los quales venian ya prepa rados de sus ayunos y abstinen cias aquel dia en la tarde salian con gran procession de gente, y con muchos de sus farsantes de casa del señor donde juntos estauan y yuan con gran sosie go al templo de Kukulcan el qual tenian muy aderecado y llegados hazian sus oraciones ponian las vanderas en lo alto del templo y abaxo en el patio tendian todos cada vno sus ydolos sobre hojas de arboles q̃ para ello auia y sacada lumbre nueua comen cauan a quemar en muchas partes de su enciensso, y a hazer ofrendas de comidas guisadas sin sal ni pimienta y de be

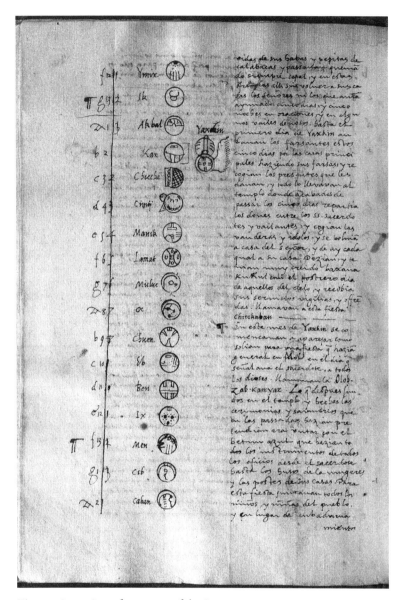

Figures A.32–A.33. fs. 42v–43r of the Account.

b	23	Eçanab
c	24	Cauac
d	25	Ahau
e	26	Ymix

December

f	27	Ik
g	28	Akbal
a	29	Kan

Mol

b	30	Chicchan
c	1	Cimi
d	2	Manik
e	3	Lamat
f	4	Muluc
g	5	Oc
a	6	Chuen
b	7	Eb
c	8	Ben
d	9	Ix

mientos, y cerimonias les
vntauan en las coyunturas
de las manos por la parte de
fuera cada vna de ellos golpe
zillos, y a las niñas se les vntaua
vna vieja vestida de vn habi-
to de plumas que las traia alli
y por esto la llamauan Ixmol
que quiere dezir la allegadera.
Dauan les estos golpes paraq
saliessen expertos officiales
en los officios de sus padres y
madres. La conclusion era
con buena borrachera co-
midas las offrendas saluo q
es de creer que aquella cien-
ta vieja allegadora con que se em-
paro otra en casa por no per-
der las plumas del officio en
el camino

¶ En este mes tornauan los
colmeneros a hazer otra fiesta
como la que hizieron en
Tzec paraq los dioses prove-
essen de flores a las auejas

¶ Vna de las cosas que estas pobres
tenian por ardua, y
difficultosa era el hazer idolos
de palos lo qual llamauan
hazer dioses, y assi tenian pa
ra hazer los señalado tiempo
particular y era este mes
de Mol o otro si el sucedia te-
las dezia buen otra. Los q lo querian hazer consultauan
el sacerdote primero y toma
do su consejo yuan al official
dellos, y dizenque se escusauan
siempre los officiales porque
temian se avrian ellos o algu
nos de sus casas demorir o
venir les enfermedades de a-
morecimientos, y acceptan
dos comẽçauan los q ações
que para esto tambien elegian

started, who were also elected *[f. 43v; figure A.34]*, with the priest and the official, to fast. While they fasted, he whose idols they were sent for the wood to the *monte*, which was always cedar.[319] The wood having arrived, they built a little enclosed thatch house where they dragged the wood and an earthenware jar in which they prepared the idols. There they were covered up as they were making them. They placed the incense that they burned to the four devils called Acantunes, which they brought and put in the four cardinal directions. They placed [inside] what they used to draw blood from their ears and the tool they used to carve the black gods and with these implements, the priest, the Chacs, and the officials were locked up in the house and they started their godly work *[su labor de dioses]*, occasionally cutting their ears and smearing the blood on those devils and burning their incense. In this way they persisted until they were done, [the future owner] giving them food or whatever was necessary. They did not know [carnally] their wives, nor think of it, nor did anyone come to that place where they were.

[Sec. 41] [f. 44r; figure A.35] Not only did the Indians have an account of the year and of the months, as stated and pointed out before, but they also had a certain way of recounting the times and their other things by ages, which they calculated in twenty by twenty years, counting thirteen *[XIII]* cycles of twenties along with one each of the twenty *[XX]* letters of their months that they call Ahau, without any regular order, but instead immediately one followed by another in an inverted order as they appear in the following circle *[see figure A.35]*. They call these in their language Katunes, and with them they have, in a marvelous way, an account of their ages. It was thus easy for the old man whom I mentioned in the first chapter to recount events that occurred three hundred years before. For if I did not know about these counts, I would not believe that they could recount things that occurred so long ago in this way.[320]

---

objects, creatures, and places.

[319] Sometimes known in English as Spanish cedar, *Cedrela odorata* (*kulche*, or *ku'che* in Maya), this is of the Mahogany or Meliaceae family, and is not an evergreen like European cedar. Spaniards likely called it *cedro* (as the text does here) due to its reddish, resinous wood, which smells strongly like pine. An imposing tree that can grow a hundred feet tall in Yucatan, the wood is highly prized because it is not susceptible to insects. The Maya name itself evokes the sacredness of the tree, as it can be translated as *kulche* or *ku'che* ("holy tree" or "god tree").

[320] Here the author is referring to the old man that he reported was "one hundred and forty years old" in the first section of the Account (f. 1r–1v; Sec. 1. f. 1r–1v); this could be one of his older informants, who must have been named in his original *Recopilación*, since Antonio de Herrera (Scribe B of the Account) gave his name in his later published history as Juan Na from the town of Homun (Herrera de Tordesillas, *Historia general de los hechos de los castellanos*, folio 44). The details of the man's name and his town could have only come from the original source, whose information Herrera copied into the Account. Although this man Juan Na may have been one of his oldest informants, the most probable candidate as the

Whoever ordered this count of Katunes, if it was the devil or not, did so as to order it in his honor.[321] If its designer was a man, he must have been a great idolater because with these Katunes he added all the major deceptions, omens, and tricks with which these people went about in their miseries completely duped. And so, this was the science to which they gave the most credit and the one to which they held the most, and the one which not all of their priests knew how to give account.[322] The order that they had in recounting their things and making their divinations with this count was that they had [*f. 44v; figure A.36*] two idols in the temple dedicated to two of these characters. They adored the first, according to the cross contained in the upper part of the circle above; they made services and sacrifices [to the image of 11 Ahau] in order to remedy the plagues of their twenty[*XX*]-year periods. In the ten years that remained of their first twenty years, they did nothing more than burn incense to the idol and revere it. After the completion of [the remaining ten years of the] first twenty-year period, the fates of the second [idol] were followed, making sacrifices to him. That first idol was removed, and they put up another one which they venerated for another ten years. For example [*Verbi gratia*]: the Indians say that the Spaniards first arrived in the city of Merida in the year of the Nativity of the Lord 1541 [*MDXLI*], which was precisely the first year of the era of *Buluc Ahau* [11 Ahau], which is the one which is in the house where the cross is. They arrived in the same month of Popp, which is the first month of their year. Without the arrival of the Spaniards, they would have worshiped the idol of Buluc ahau until the year

---

informant for most of this ritual and religious information must have been the Ah Kin Francisco Euan of Caucel, discussed earlier, who was in his late fifties when the Spaniards arrived, according to Cogolludo (*Historia de Yucathan*, Libro V, Capítulo VI). The Adelantado Montejo was his godfather, hence his baptismal name of Francisco. Landa likely consulted with him often at the convent in Merida in 1556–1559, when both men were living and working there. According to Molina Solís, Euan was "famed to be intelligent and wise for having been a priest of their idols, and the principal leader of the cacicazgo of Chakán" (Molina Solís, *Historia del descubrimiento y conquista de Yucatán*, 821). Certainly, he would have been an expert witness on the calendar and Maya religion in general, as he had served as one of the chief priests of precontact Maya religion before the conquest. Euan died in 1560, probably in his eighties (but not 140 as reportedly was the age of this Juan Na).

[321] Above this line is inserted the black cross and the katun wheel (see figure A.35). The caption inside the wheel reads: "They called this count in their language Vazlazonkatun, which is to say, the war of the Katunes"; the term butchered by the copyist (or not well grasped by the author) is *u azaklom katun*, "the katun wheel." Note that *katunes* is a Hispanized plural; the Mayan plural is *katunob*.

[322] Again, this strongly suggests that one of Landa's informants had been a Maya priest, such as an Ah Kin May (see Chuchiak, "Pre-conquest Ah Kinob," 137–39), and Francisco Euan is again a likely candidate; if so, Euan is here hinting, through Landa, that this kind of specialized knowledge of the calendar and the ritual cycle was not common even among the other Ah Kinob.

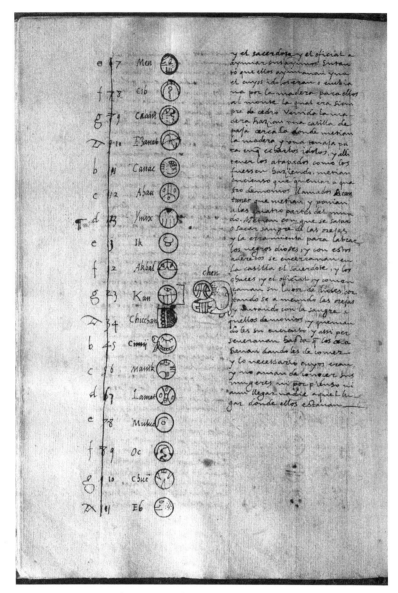

Figures A.34–A.35. fs. 43v–44r of the Account.

44

No solo tenian los Indios cuenta en el año y meses como queda dicho y señalado atras pero tenian cierto modo de contar los tiempos y sus cosas por edades, las quales hazian de veynte en veynte años contando xiii veyntes con una de las xx letras de los meses que llaman Ahau, sin orden sino retruecanados, como parecerán en la siguiente raya de donda. llamaban ellas a estos en su lengua Katunes, y con ellos tenian a maravilla cuenta con sus edades, y le fue assi facil al viejo de quien en el primero capitulo dixe avia trezientos años acordarse dellos. Ca si yo no supiera estas sus cuentas yo no creyera se pudiera assi acordar de tanta edad.

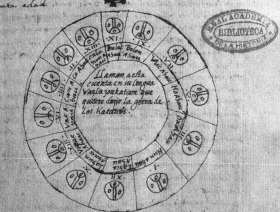

Llaman a esta cuenta en su lengua Vazlazonkatum que quiere dezir la cuenta de los Katunes.

Quien esta su cuenta de Katunes ordeno si fue el demonio hizo lo que suele hordenandolo a su honor o si fue hombre devia ser buen idolatra porq con estos sus Katunes añadio todos los principales engaños, y agueros, y embaymientos conq aquesta gente andava allende de sus miserias del todo enbaucada, y assi esta era la sciencia a que ellos davan mas credito, y la q tenian en mas, y de la q no los sacerdotes todos sabian dar cuenta. La orden que tenian en contar sus cosas y hazer sus divinaciones, con esta cuenta era que se—

1551 [*LI* ('51)], which makes ten years, and in the tenth year they would have placed another idol, to Bolon ahau, and honored him, following the prognostications of Buluc ahau until the year 1561 [*LXI* ('61)]. Then they would have removed him from the temple and put the Uuc ahau idol, and followed the prognostications of Bolon ahau for another ten [*X*] years. So, like this they gave all of them a turn, in this way worshipping their Katunes of twenty [*XX*] years, and the ten [*X*] years of which were governed by their superstitions and deceptions, which were so many and so great as to deceive simple people easily lost in amazement, but not to those who know natural things and the experience that the devil has of them.

These people also used certain characters or letters, with which they wrote in their books their ancient things and their sciences. And with these, and figures, and some symbols in the figures, they understood their things, and they allowed them to understand, and they taught them. We discovered a large number of these books of their letters, and because they contained nothing but superstition and falsehoods of the devil, we burned them all, which astounded them and caused them pain.[323] Concerning their letters, I will place here an *A, b, c*, which does not allow for their difficulty [*pesadumbre*] mostly because they use one character for all the pronunciations [*aspiraciones*] of the letters, and then they join them together [in one part] to *[f. 45r; figure A.37]* the parts of another, and thus they continue in infinitum [*sic*], as one can see in the next example: *Le*, which is to say "noose" or "to hunt with one." To write "*le*" with their characters, after we had made them understand that it has two letters, they wrote it with three, adding to the pronunciation [*aspiracion*] of the *L* the vowel *e*, placing another in front of it, and in doing so they do not err, even though they would use [an additional] *e*, if they wanted to, out of diligence. For example: *[see fig. A.37]*. Then, at the end, they join the parts together. *Ha*, which is to say "water," and because their *h* has an *a* before it, they put an *a* at the beginning, and also at the end of it in this way: *[see fig. A.37]*.[324] They also write in parts, but in one way and another I could not put or explain it here without giving an entire account of the things of these people. *Main kati*, which is to say, "I do not want,"

---

[323] This is the second time in the Account—and an oft-quoted sentence—when Landa references his iconoclastic destruction of an unknown number of codices in Mani in 1562. The final, resonant phrase is "*lo qual a maravilla sentian, y les daua pena.*"

[324] Landa here errs in his understanding of how the Maya "spelled" words with their "alphabet." This error came most probably from the fact that he asked his informants to spell the word in their own characters, but he elicited the word in the form of the pronunciation of the letters as they sounded in the Spanish alphabet, which he no doubt pronounced out loud. Maya informants would have heard *Ha* spelled out as "a-ché, ah," and thus hearing the "a" pronounced before a "che" they wrote it as seen here (on figure A.37): *ah-che-ha*. For a complete study of the phonetics and glyph drawings of Landa's alphabet, see Robinson, *Landa Alphabet Reconsidered*; and also Stuart, "Glyph Drawings from Landa's *Relación*."

they write it in parts in this way: *[see fig. A.37]*. Their *a*, *b*, *c* follows: *[see fig. A.37]*. The letters that are missing here do not exist in this language, and they also have others added in addition to ours for other things of which they have need, and now they no longer use these characters, especially the young people who have learned our own.[325]

[Sec. 42] [f. 46r][326] If Yucatan could earn a name and reputation due to the great number and beauty of its buildings, like other parts of the Indies have achieved with gold, silver, and riches, it would be known about as much as Peru and New Spain. This is because its buildings and the large number of them are one of the most remarkable things that have been discovered up until today in the Indies, for there are so many of them spread throughout all the parts of this land which are and so well built of masonry in their style, they are astonishing. And to explain why this land is not so at present, even though it is good land as it seems to have been in the prosperous time, during which they built so many and such distinguished buildings, built without having any kind of metal with which to work, I will put down here the arguments that I have seen given by those who have seen them.[327] They are that these people must have been subject to some certain lords, who wanted to keep them busy, occupied in this work. Or that, since they have been such idol worshippers, they distinguished themselves in their communities by making temples to them. Or, for some other reasons, the populations moved and so everywhere they settled themselves they always newly built their temples, sanctuaries, and houses as is their custom for their lords, for which they always had used wood covered with thatch, or that the great abundance that there is in this land of stone, lime, and a certain kind of white earth—excellent for the buildings that had been made for them—presented the occasion to make so many it would seem that those who had seen them had spoken in jest. Or this land has some secret that up until now has not been discovered, nor have the native people of this era yet discovered it. Because it is said that there were other nations who forced these Indians to build. But this is

---

[325] Coe, *Breaking the Maya Code*, 99–122, has a full description of the crucial role this passage of the Account played in the modern decipherment of Maya hieroglyphic writing. The reference to young Mayas no longer using "these characters" means glyphic writing, not the "letters" that were "added"—those invented alphabetic letters were used in Yucatan from the sixteenth through nineteenth centuries (detailed in Restall, *Maya World*, 297–300).

[326] Note that f. 45v is absent here because it contains no text; it is a blank page containing only the red stamp of the Real Academia de la Historia.

[327] The "I" here may be Landa, distinguishing himself from other people ("those"), likely his Maya informants, who have seen more of the many thousands of ancient buildings scattered across the peninsula (by the time he left Yucatan in 1562, he had only served as a friar in Merida, Izamal, Conkal, Mani, Ticul, Oxkutzcab, Yaxcaba, Sotuta, Dzitaz, and Tizimin). But it could also be another Franciscan author, with "those" including Landa.

rian en el templo dos idolos dedicados a dos destos carate-
teres. Al primero conforme a la cuenta desde la cruz de
la raya redonda arriba contenida adoravan, y hazian
servicios, y sacrificios para remedio de las plagas de sus xx
años, y a los x años que faltavan de los xx del primero no
hazian con el mas de quemarle encienso, y reverenciarle
complidos los xx años del primero comencava a seguir-
se por los dados del segundo, y a hazerle sus sacrificios, y
quitado aquel idolo primero ponian otro para venerarle
otros x años. Verbi gratia. Dizen los Indios que acaba-
ron de llegar los Españoles a la ciudad de Merida el año
de la Natividad del señor ✠ D xlı que era en punto
en el primero año de la era de Bulc Aban que es el que
esta en la casa donde esta la cruz, y llegaron el mesmo
mes de Pop que es en el primero mes de su año. Si no viera Españoles adoraran ellos el idolo de Bulu aban hasta
el año de li. que son diez años, y al año decimo pusieran
otro idolo a Bolon aban y honrraranle, siguiendose por los pronosticos de Buluc aban hasta el año de Lxı y estonces qui-
taran le del templo, y pusieran a Vaxac aban idolo, y siguie-
ran se por los pronosticos de Bolon aban otros x años, y assi davan a todos buelta de manera que veneravan a estos su[y]os
Katunes xx años, y los x se regian por sus supersticiones
y engaños, las quales eran tantas y tan bastantes para en-
gañar a gente simple que admira aun q no a los que sabe
de las cosas naturales, y la experiencia que dellas el demonio tiene
Vsavan tambien esta gente de ciertos carateres o letras con
las quales escrivian en sus libros sus cosas antiguas, y
sus sciencias, y con ellas, y figuras, y algunas señales en
las figuras entendian sus cosas, y les davan a entender y
enseñavan. Hallamos les grande numero de libros destas
sus letras, y porq no tenian cosa, en que no uviesse super-
sticion, y enga[ñ]os falsedades del demonio se los quema-
mos todos, lo qual a maravilla sentian, y les dava
pena. De sus letras porne aqui un A,b,c, que no permi-
te su pesadumbre mas porq usan para todas las aspiraciones de las letras de un carater, y despues al juntar
                                                              de

de las partes otro, y assi viene a hazer in infinitum, como
se podra ver en el siguiente exemplo. Le, quiere dezir laço
y caçar con el, para escrivirle con sus caracteres aviendo
les nosotros hecho entender que son dos letras lo escrivian
ellos con tres puniendo a la aspiracion de la .l. la vocal .e.
que antes de si trae, y en esto no yerran aunque vsen ei si
quisieren ellos de su curiosidad. Exemplo.
despues al cabo le pegan la parte junta. Ha. que quiere dezir
agua porq̃ la hache tiene a. h. ante de si lo ponen ellos al
principio con a. y al cabo desta manera Tambie
lo escriuen a partes, de la vna y otra manera, y
no pusiera aqui ni tratara dello sino por dar cuenta entera
de las cosas desta gente. Mainkati quiere dezir no quiero. ellos
lo escriuen a partes desta manera

Siguese su a, b, c.

De las letras que aqui faltan carece esta lengua
y tiene otras añadidas de la nuestra para otras
cosas q̃ las ha menester; y ya no vsan para nada destos
sus caracteres especialmente la gente moça q̃ an aprendido
los nuestros

not so, because there are carvings [*señales*] that have been built into the structures of Indian people, naked, as one can see on one of the buildings. Many very large ones are there on the walls of the bastions, still remaining markings of naked men [*hombres de carne*], and some of them modest with long loincloths which they call in their language *ex*, and with other insignias [*divisas*] that the Indians of these times wear.[328] All made of very strong plaster. And while I dwelt there,[329] in a building that we demolished there was found a large urn with three handles and painted on one of them silver-plated flames on the outside, inside of which were the ashes of a burned body. And among them we found three good stone beads, the type of which the Indians now use as currency. This all shows that it had been Indians [who built everything]. Well, if indeed it was so, they were a superior people [*gente de mas ser*] than those [*f. 46v; figure A.38*] of today, and of much larger bodies, and stronger. And one can even still see this here in Izamal, more than in any other part, in the stucco half-relief sculptures of large grown men that I say today are fixed on the bastions; just like the length of the extremities of the arms and legs of the man, whose ashes were in the urn that we found in the structure, were a marvel to burn and very thick. Also, this can be seen on the structure's staircases, which are more than two good palms in height, and this here only in Izamal and in Merida. There is here in Izamal a building among all the others, of such height and beauty that it astonishes, which will be seen in this figure [*see fig. A.38*] and this is a plan [*razon*] of it:[330] It has twenty [*XX*] steps of more than two good palm spans in height and

---

[328] This is the second time these building materials and plaster carvings are described; the first is f. 4v (Sec. 5).

[329] The first person here is not necessarily evidence of Landa's authorship of this section, as he would have seen all these buildings; as noted above, it seems as likely to have been another of the friars, especially as the earlier mention of this urn's discovery states that "he" found it (f.4v, Sec. 5). This large burial urn was discovered as the friars, under Landa's direction as Guardian of Izamal in 1553–1556, excavated and demolished the stone pyramid upon which they built the convent of San Antonio de Padua. Large urn burials became common in the Terminal Classic and Postclassic periods in Yucatan (see Ardren, *Social Identities*, and Ruz Lhuillier, *Costumbres funerarias de los antiguos mayas*). That said, the descriptions of Izamal would appear to have been drafted by Landa while he served there; at the Franciscan Capítulo held in Merida in 1553, he was elected as the Guardian of the Convent of Izamal for a three-year term (Cogolludo, *Historia de Yucathan*, Libro V, Capítulo XIV).

[330] The drawing here in the Account is of the pyramid of Kinich Kak Mo, the location of the original chapel at Itzmal, but the great convent that Landa began in 1553 was built on top of the city's second largest pyramidal mound, known as Ppap Hol Chac (Lizana, *Historia de Yucatán*, 5r); in 1561, it was completed by fray Francisco de la Torre (later also the Franciscan provincial; on the convent's early history, see Solari, *Maya Ideologies of the Sacred*). The captions inside the Kinich Kak Mo drawing read (from top to bottom): "chapel," "stairway," "landing, or plaza," "Very large, and beautiful, plaza," and "Stairway very hard to climb."

width each, and each of which extends more than one hundred feet in length. These steps are of very large carved stones, although over time and having been exposed to water, they are now ugly and misused. Then it was carved around, as shown by this round line, carved in masonry into a very strong wall, upon which, at about a fathom-and-a-half high, rises a cornice of beautiful stones, all [carved] in the round. From these the building terraces inward [*se torna despues*] following the construction [*obra*] until it becomes equal to the height of the plaza that was made at the top of the first staircase. Above this plaza, another staircase was made, like the first one, but not so large nor of so many steps, always following the construction of the rounded wall, all the way around.[331] On top of these steps another good small plaza was made, and on that, stuck against the wall, a rather high hill is made, with its staircase to the south, where the large staircases lead down [*caen*], and on top of that there is a beautiful masonry chapel well carved. I climbed on top of this chapel and, as Yucatan is a flat land, one could see from it so much of the land that the view can be wondrous, and one could see the ocean. These buildings of Izamal were eleven [*XI*] or twelve [*XII*] in all, although this one is the largest, and they are very close to each other. There is no memory of the founders, so it they would seem to have been the first inhabitants [*los primeros*]. It is eight [*VIII*] leagues from the sea in a very beautiful site, and [is] good land and a region with people. Because of this, [*f. 47r; figure A.39*] the Indians made us, with great pestering, inhabit a house on the top of one of the structures, which we call San Antonio, in the year 1549 [*MDXLIX*]. On account of which and all around [*en todo lo de a la redonda*] this has assisted them greatly in their Christianity. So, they have inhabited on this site two good towns, one apart from the other.[332]

*   *   * [333]

The second [set of] buildings in this land are more important and so old that there is no memory of their builders. They are those of Tiho. They are thirteen

---

[331] Here, the copyist repeats *redonda* with *la redonda*; three lines later, he repeats the word *donde*.

[332] After the founding of the Franciscan convent in Izamal, the Franciscan friars, led by Landa, re-congregated a number of smaller Maya towns in the region into the central town of Izamal, which had a population of 370 tributaries (approximately 1,200 people) in 1579. A smaller settlement, named Santa María, was established by groups of Nahuas and other Indigenous peoples from Tabasco, Chiapas, and Guatemala who had been allies and dependents of the Spanish conquistadors who settled in Yucatan ("founded by *indios naborios*, servants of the Spaniards, who found the site a good one and came to live there, now comprising thirty-four tributaries"; RHGY, Vol. I, *Relación de Izamal y Santa Maria*, 304). By 1579, this "town" of Santa María, comprising some 120 residents, was simply across a street from the Maya neighborhoods of Izamal.

[333] The copyist here left two line-breaks in the text.

leagues from those of Izamal, and eight leagues from the sea like the others. There are signs today that there had been a very beautiful road from one to the other.[334] The Spaniards populated here a city and they called it Merida because of the exoticness [*estraneza*] and grandeur of the buildings.[335] The most important and principal of which I will indicate here, as I can and did with Izamal, because it is better for one to be able to see what it is.

*   *   *[336]

This is the rough sketch [*boron*] that I have been able to produce of the building.[337] For one's own understanding, you have to know that this is on a square-shaped site of much grandeur, as it is more than two *carreras de caballo*.[338] From the eastern edge the stairway then begins from the ground. This stairway will be of seven terraces of the height of those of Izamal. The other parts at [*f. 47v*] the south, the west, and the north, rise from a sturdy, wide wall. The top of that square-shaped massive construction [*hechimiento*] is paved of dried stone. On the flat and level surface another staircase begins on the same eastern part of the structure, it seems to me it rises twenty-eight [*XXVIII*] or thirty [*XXX*] feet, within as many steps, so big. On the southern side, I drew the same slope as on the north side, but not the western, on which the strong walls rise until the meeting or joining with the square part on the western side. And in this way, they support the weight of the staircases, making the whole massive construction in the middle of drystone, which is astonishing being so tall and so grand, given that it is handmade construction. Beyond, on the flat upper part, the buildings begin in the following manner: On the eastern part, rises a room that is ultimately cozy, inside up to six feet, and it does not reach the ends, carved of very good masonry, and all of cells on one side, and the other is

[334] No archaeological evidence survives of a Maya road between Izamal and Tiho, although Izamal is connected to the smaller sites of Ake and Kantunil by the ancient white roads called *sacbeob* (note that the text above reads, in the plural, "*de los unos a los otros*").

[335] The Spanish conquistadors renamed the city *Merida* because its numerous stone structures, some but not all looking like ancient ruins, reminded them of the Spanish city of the same name, where ancient Roman ruins are present even today.

[336] Here is inserted the drawing of the great pyramid in Tiho-Merida (see figure A.39).

[337] For recent archaeological investigations into the remains of Tiho, see Escalante Carrillo, *Reconocimiento y análisis arqueológico*, and Rogers, *From Ichcanzihoo to Merida*.

[338] The measurement of a *carrera de caballo* was similar to the old Roman measurement of a *cursus*, roughly equivalent to the colonial measurement of four hundred *varas*, or the modern measurement of 1,200 meters; the base of this monument thus ran 2,400 meters in length. After the reduction of the structure in colonial times, and its final demolition in the nineteenth century, all that is left today is the foundation on the eastern side (visible beneath the portales of Calle 54a) and the foundation on the western side (likewise visible beneath the portales of Calle 56a).

twelve [*XII*] feet in length, and eight [*VIII*] in width. The doorways have no sign of doorframes in the middle of each one, nor any kind of doorjamb in order to close them, except with flat pieces of highly carved and polished stone, and the work had been wonderfully done, so all of the doors closed at the top with tiles of solid stone. It had in the middle a passage shaped like an arch of a bridge, and above the doors of the cells rose a relief in stone carved along the whole room lengthways, above which they rose until the height of the pillars, half of them carved rounded, and half adjoined to the wall, and they continued until the height of the springing of the vaults [*piden las bovedas*] of which the cells were made and closed above. On top of these pillars rose another stone relief around the whole room. The top was a terraced roof, very heavily whitewashed, as they do there with a particular tree sap.[339] On the northern side there was another block of cells, such as the others, except that the room that was almost in the middle was not as long. To the west followed once again cells, four or five, and there was an arch that went through like the one that was set in the middle of the eastern room, [through] the whole building, beyond it a circular building, somewhat tall and beyond the other archway, and the rest were cells like the rest. This room extended across the large patio [*f. 48r*], with a good part less than halfway, and so it created two patios, one in the back at the west, and the other on the east, becoming surrounded by four rooms, the last of which is very different because it is a room made to the south of two chambers enclosed in a vault, like the others, but longer. The chamber in the front has a corridor made of very thick pillars capped at the top with single pieces of very beautifully carved stone. A wall runs through that, bearing the loads of the vaults of both rooms, with two doors in order to enter the other room. [In this] way everything is capped above and covered with whitewash. This building has, two good stones'-throw away, another very tall and beautiful patio in which there are three masonry mounds [* çerros*]; they were well carved, and on top have very good, vaulted chapels that they used to have and knew how to make. There was quite apart from this a rather larger and beautiful mound, out of which was built a large part of the city that settled around it; I do not know if it will ever be seen to be finished. The first building with the four rooms, the Adelantado[340] Montejo gave to us [the Franciscan order]; it had become rugged with vegetation, we cleaned it, and we have built on it, with its own stones, a reasonable monastery built all of stone, and a good church

---

[339] The author's use of "there" to refer to Yucatan implies that this section was written outside of the province.

[340] As discussed elsewhere in these notes and in our chapter 1, the term *adelantado* refers to a military and political title granted by means of a charter and contract to a person legally commissioned to undertake a military conquest of a specific region.

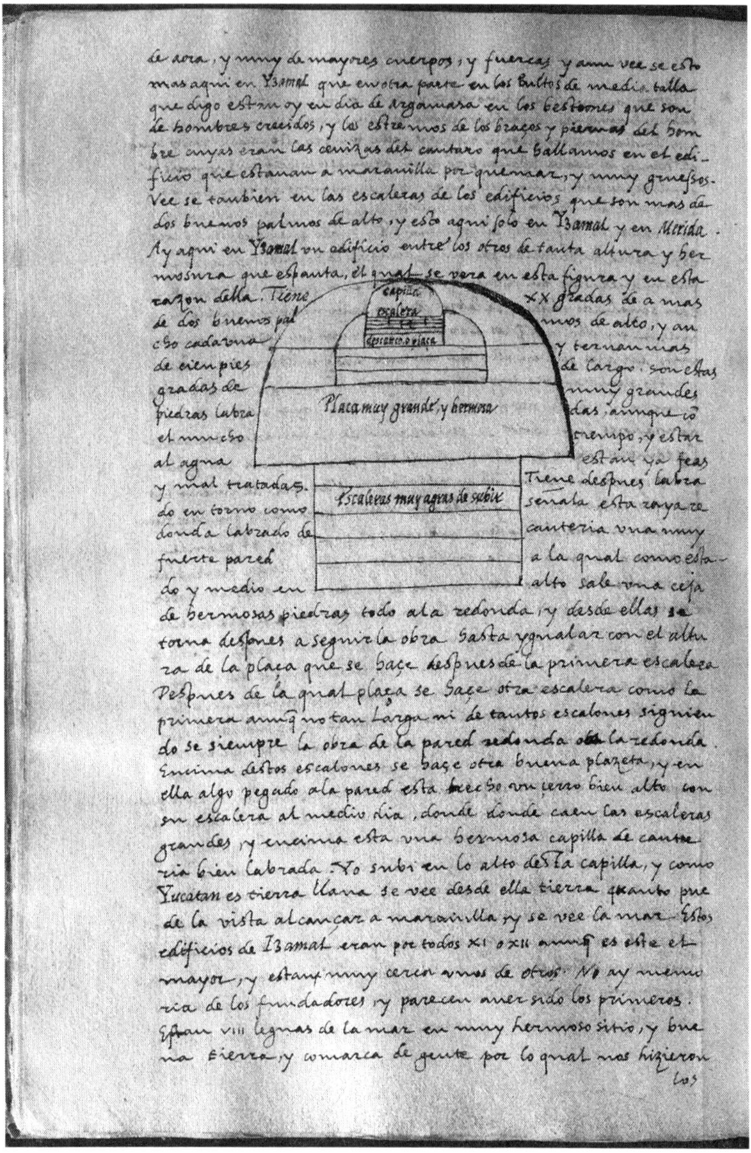

de aora, y muy de mayores cuerpos, y fuerças, y aun vee se esto
mas aqui en Yzamal que en otra parte en los bultos de media talla
que digo estan oy en dia de argamasa en los bestiones que son
de hombres crecidos, y los estremos de los braços y piernas del hombre cuyas eran las cenizas del cantaro que hallamos en el edificio que estauan a marauilla por quemar, y muy gruessos.
Vee se tambien en las escaleras de los edificios que son mas de
los buenos palmos de alto, y esto aqui solo en Yzamal y en Merida.
Ay aqui en Yzamal un edificio entre los otros de tanta altura y her-
mosura que espanta, el qual se vera en esta figura y en esta
razon della. Tiene ____ XX gradas de a mas
de dos buenos pal- ____ mos de alto, y aun
esso cada una ____ y ternan mas
de cien pies ____ de largo son estas
gradas de ____ muy grandes
piedras labra- ____ das aunque o
el mucho ____ cuerpo, y estar
al agua ____ estan ya feas
y mal tratadas. ____ Tiene despues labrado en torno como ____ senala esta raya ra
honda labrado de ____ canteria una muy
fuerte pared ____ a la qual como esta
do y medio en ____ alto sale una ceja
de hermosas piedras todo a la redonda y desde ellas se
torna despues a seguir la obra hasta ygualar con el altura de la plaça que se haze despues de la primera escalera
Despues de la qual plaça se haze otra escalera como la
primera aunque no tan larga ni de tantos escalones siguien-
do se siempre la obra de la pared redonda a la redonda
Encima destos escalones se haze otra buena plazeta, y en
ella algo pegado a la pared esta hecho un cerro bien alto con
su escalera al medio dia, donde donde caen las escaleras
grandes y encima esta una hermosa capilla de canteria bien labrada. Yo subi en lo alto desta capilla, y como
Yucatan es tierra llana se vee desde ella tierra quanto puede la vista alcançar a marauilla y se vee la mar. Estos
edificios de Yzamal eran por todos XI o XII aunque es este el
mayor, y estan muy cerca unos de otros. No ay memoria de los fundadores y parecen auer sido los primeros.
Estan VIII leguas de la mar en muy hermoso sitio, y buena tierra, y comarca de gente por lo qual mas hizieron

los

Figures A.38–A.39. fs. 46v–47r of the Account.

Los Indios poblaro con harta jmportunacion vna casa en vno
destos edificios que llamamos St Antonio el año de MDXLIX
en la qual y en todo lo de a la redonda se les ha mucho ajn
dado a su christiandad, y assi se an poblado en este assiento
dos buenos pueblos a parte vno del otro.

Los segundos edificios que en esta tierra son mas princi
pales y antiguos tanto que no ay memoria de sus fun
dadores son los de Tiho, estan treze leguas de los de Bamal
y ocho de la mar como los otros y ay señales oy endia de
auer auido vna muy hermosa calcada de los vnos a los
otros. Los Españoles poblaron aqui vna cibdad, y llama
tonla medida por la estrañeza y grandeza de los edifi
cios. el principal de los quales señalare aqui como pu
diere, y hize al de Bamal para que mejor se pueda ver lo que

Poniente
patio — capilla — patio
patio hermosisimo
Norte
io dia
Oriente
mas escaleras
descanso de mas de treinta pies
escalera

Este es el borron que se podia sacar del edificio para cuyo en
tendimiento se ha de entender que este es vn assiento qua
drado de mucha grandeza porq tiene mas de dos carreras
de caballo desde la parte del oriente comienca luego la
escalera desde el suelo. Sera esta escalera de siete esca
lones del altor de los de Bamal. Las demas partes de

that we call the Mother of God [*Madre de Dios*].³⁴¹ There was so much stone in the rooms that the southern wing and parts of the other sides are still intact. We gave a lot of stone to the Spaniards for their own houses, especially for their doorways and windows; so much was the abundance of the stone. The buildings in the town of Tikoh³⁴² are not as many or as sumptuous as some of these others, although they were also good and sound in their construction. And here I would not have made mention [of it], except due to it having had a large population, of which it has been necessary to talk about later, and because of this I will leave it for now. These buildings are three leagues from *Izamal* to the east, and seven [*VII*] from Chicheniza.

[f. 48v; figure A.40] Chicheniza is therefore a very good site, ten [*X*] leagues from Izamal and eleven [*XI*] from Valladolid, in which, according to what the ancients among the Indians say, three lords reigned who were brothers. According to those [ancient Indians], they remember having heard about [the brothers'] histories. They came to that land from the west and they gathered together in these sites a large population of villages and peoples, which they governed for some years in much peace and justice. They were very dutiful worshippers of their god and so they built many buildings, very elegant ones, especially one, the oldest, whose figure I will paint here like I painted it while I was in it, so that it can be better understood.³⁴³ They say these lords lived without women,³⁴⁴ in great modesty, and the whole time that they lived like that they were very esteemed and obeyed by all. Then, as time passed, one of them went missing, and he must have died, although the Indians say that he left the land from close to the region of Bachalal.³⁴⁵ The absence of this one, however that it happened, [was] such a loss for those who ruled after him, that they

---

³⁴¹ The main convent house of the Franciscan order in the Province of San Joseph de Yucatán, which served as the order's headquarters and main religious house, was dedicated to the Virgin Mary of the Assumption in 1547.

³⁴² The existence of more than one Tecoh and the effects of colonial *reducciones* have complicated identification of this precontact site occupied by Spaniards in the sixteenth century. Archaeologists believe the Tecoh referenced by Landa is located approximately ten kilometers east of Izamal. This Tecoh has ample precontact architecture (such as ten-to-twelve-meter-high pyramids) as well as colonial constructions, including a huge tank for the extraction of *añil*, a church, and Spanish-style living structures. See Millet, Ojeda M., and Suárez A., "Tecoh, Izamal"; and Garcia Targa, "Analisis histórico y arqueológico."

³⁴³ Here the author reveals that the drawing he includes in the Account was directly based on another sketch he had drawn while on site at Chichen Itza.

³⁴⁴ As can be seen from the facsimile (see figure A.40), *vivieron* could be read as *vinieron* (and thus "the lords came without women"), although in view of the subsequent line about their modest living the distinction would seem moot.

³⁴⁵ Landa hints here at the legend of Kukulkan, or Quetzalcoatl, who for some reason left Chichen Itza heading to the east and, as he states here, near Bacalar (as Bakhalal became in colonial times, and remains today).

started later to be in divided republics. Their habits became so dishonest and unrestrained that the people came to hate them in such a way that they killed them, and they dismantled and depopulated the buildings. And the site [remains] very beautiful because it is near the sea, ten [X] leagues. All around, it has very fertile lands and provinces. The figure of the main building is the following: *[see figure A.40]*.

[f. 49r; figure A.41] This building has four staircases that face the four directions of the world.[346] They are twenty-three [XXXIII] feet in width and have ninety-one steps each, so it is deadly to climb them. The steps have the same width and height that we give to our own. Each staircase has two low balustrades, equal to the steps of two feet in width, of good stonework as is the whole building. This building is not sharp cornered because starting from the ground level they are carved from the balustrades to the contrary one, as is painted, with some rounded blocks that go upwards for a stretch and narrowing the edifice in a very pleasing manner. There was, when I saw it, at the foot of each of the balustrades, a fierce mouth of a serpent, or one piece [of stone], rather curiously carved. The staircases ended in this way: meeting at the top a little flat plaza on which there is a building built of four rooms. Three of them go through the entire building without impediment, and each has a doorway in the middle, and they are vaulted. The northern room goes like this with a corridor of thick pillars. [The pillar] in the middle, so it had to be like a little throne room [*patinico*], that put in order the drapes of the building, having a doorway that led to the hallways to the north, and above it is closed with wood, and it was used to burn incense. There is at the entrance of this door or the corridor, a sort of coat of arms sculpted in a stone which I have not been able to understand well.[347] This building had surrounding it, and still does today, many other buildings, very well made and large, and all the ground between it and them is plastered,[348] so that still there are in parts signs of the white plaster, so strong is the mortar that they make there.[349] In front of the northern staircase, somewhat apart, it had two small masonry theaters, [each] with four staircases, paved with stone at the top, on which they say were

---

[346] From this description, we know Landa refers to the radial pyramid on the Gran Nivelación of Chichen Itza, known as El Castillo.

[347] Tozzer (*Landa's* Relación, 179n942) noted that no such coat of arms like that described by Landa existed in the early twentieth century, but that in the northern room of the Castillo, "here described by Landa, there are thirty different bas-reliefs on door jambs and pillars." In fact, none of these bas-reliefs appear to contain the design described by Landa, although Tozzer was arguably right to see one of the bas-reliefs as resembling a "sort of coat of arms."

[348] Excavation has documented the use of white plaster floors across the plaza, which is exactly what Landa reports here.

[349] Another instance of Yucatan being referred to as "there," revealing that this section was composed by someone who was not in the peninsula at the time (e.g., Landa in 1562–1570).

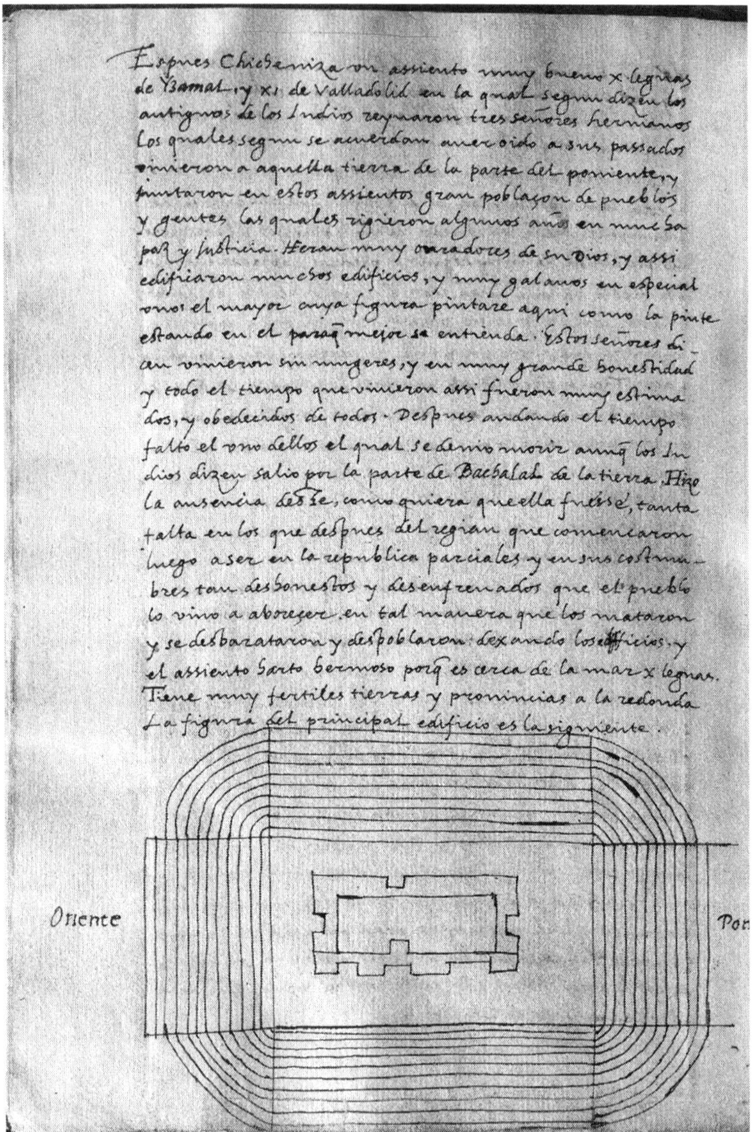

Es pues Chicxeniza vn assiento muy bueno x leguas
de Ysamal, y xi de Valladolid en la qual segun dizen los
antiguos de los Indios reynaron tres señores hermanos
los quales segun se acuerdan auer oido a sus passados
vinieron a aquella tierra de la parte del poniente, y
pintaron en estos assientos gran poblaçon de pueblos
y gentes las quales rigieron algunos años en mucha
paz y justicia. Heran muy onrradores de su dios, y assi
edificaron muchos edificios, y muy galanos en especial
vnos el mayor cuya figura pintare aqui como la pinte
estando en el para q mejor se entienda. Estos señores dizen vinieron sin mugeres, y en muy grande onestidad
y todo el tiempo que vinieron assi fueron muy estima-
dos, y obedecidos de todos. Despues andando el tiempo
falto el vno dellos el qual se dexo morir avnq los Indios dizen salio por la parte de Bachalal de la tierra. Hizo
la ausencia deste, como quiera que ella fuesse, tanta
falta en los que despues del regian que començaron
luego a ser en la republica parciales, y en sus costumbres tan desonestos y desenfrenados que el pueblo
lo vino a aborecer en tal manera que los mataron
y se desbarataron y despoblaron dexando los edificios, y
el assiento Santo, hermoso porq es cerca de la mar x leguas.
Tiene muy fertiles tierras y prouincias a la redonda
La figura del principal edificio es la siguiente.

Oriente   Pon...

Figures A.40–A.41. fs. 48v–49r of the Account.

Este edificio tiene quatro escaleras que miran a las quatro
partes del mundo. tienen de ancho a xxxIII pies y a noven
ta y vn escalones cada vna que es muerte subirlas. Tienen en los escalones la mesma altura y anchura que
nosotros damos a los nuestros. Tiene cada escalera dos
passamanos bajos a ygual de los escalones de dos pies de
ancho de buena canteria como lo es todo el edificio. No
es este edificio esquinado porque desde la salda del
suelo se comiencan a labrar desde los passamanos
al contrario, como estan pintados, vnos cubos redondos
que van subiendo a trechos y estrechando el edificio por
muy galana orden. Avia quando yo le vi al pie de
cada passamano vna fiera boca de sierpe de vna pie-
ca bien curiosamente labrada. Acabadas de esta ma
nera las escaleras, queda en lo alto vna placeta lla
na en la qual esta vn edificio edificado de quatro quar
tos. Los tres se andan a la redonda sin impedimiento
y tiene cada vno puerta en medio, y estan cerrados de
boueda. El quarto del Norte se anda por si con vn cor
redor de pilares gruessos. Lo de en medio que avia de
ser como el patinico que haze el orden de los paños
del edificio tiene vna puerta que sale al corredor del
norte, y esta por arriba cerrado de madera y servia
de quemar los sahumerios. Ay en la entrada desta
puerta o del corredor vn modo de armas esculpidas
en vna piedra que no pude bien entender. Tenia este
edificio otros muchos, y tiene oy en dia a la redon
da de si bien hechos y grandes, y todo su suelo della
ellos encalado que aun ay a partes memoria de los
encalados tan fuerte es el argamasa de que alla los
hazen. Tenia delante la escalera del norte algo
a parte dos teatros de canteria pequeños de a qua
tro escaleras, y enlosados por arriba en que dizen re-

performed *[f. 49v; figure A.42]* the farces *[farsas]* and comedies for the amuse-
ment of the people.[350] A beautiful and wide road goes from the patio in front
of these theaters to a well, two stone-throws in the distance. Into this well they
have had, and had then, the habit of casting men alive as sacrifices to the gods in
times of drought, maintaining that they did not die even though they were never
seen again. They also cast many other things, valuable stones and things that they
had prized. And so, if this land had possessed gold around, this well would have
contained most of it, according to how the Indians had been so devoted.[351] This
well has a depth of seven *[VII]* long estados down to the waterline, and a width
of more than one hundred feet, and is rounded, and is of sheer rock down to the
water, which is a wonder to behold. It seems that the water is very green, and I
think that the tree groves that surround it cause this, and it is very deep. It has on
the top, close to the mouth, a small building where I found idols made in honor
of all the principal buildings of the land, almost like the Pantheon of Rome.[352] I
do not know if this was an ancient creation or done by modern people who came
across their idols when making offerings at that well. I found carved sculptures
of lions and jars and other objects, so that I do not know how anyone could state
that these people did not have any tools. I also found two images of men of great
stature, carved out of stone, each one made out of a single piece, naked save for
the covering of their honesty [privates] in the way the Indians covered themselves.
They had their heads as so, with earrings in the ears just as the Indians wore them,

---

[350] These two structures are today known as the Platform of the Eagles and the Platform of
Venus. Both small-scale radial pyramids, as described by the author, they were likely used as
ritual stages.

[351] On this point the author is correct—some of the only gold artifacts from the Maya area were
recovered from the Great Cenote (see Coggins, *Cenote of Sacrifice*).

[352] Note that the author is again using the first person to describe his eyewitness account of
Chichen Itza. Also in this sentence, the copyist wrote *edificios* (buildings) where we imagine
he meant to write *dioses* (gods) or *demonios* (devils). Landa (presumably the author here)
must have seen this temple shortly after his arrival in the province as a younger friar in
August of 1549. He may also be offering us an example of his earlier life and a trip to Rome:
as a youth, he served as a page (1534–1541) to the IV Count of Cifuentes, don Fernando
de Silva, residing in the count's household in Cifuentes, Toledo, Madrid, and likely Rome
too. The *maestresala* of the count's household, don Pedro de Ludeña, later testified in the *probanza* of the bishop elect that "when he was a young boy, I knew him well, [and I] dealt with
him frequently since [we] both lived together in the household of the said Illustrious Count,
don Fernando, for whom [I] served as his *maestresala*" (*Testimonio de Pedro de Ludeña, Maestresala del IV Conde de Cifuentes Don Fernando de Silva, en la probanza de hidalguía de Fray
Diego de Landa, Obispo Electo*, 19 de junio, 1573, AHNob, Condado de Almodovar, caja 40,
doc. 8). As most of the count's household followed him to Rome where he was Ambassador
to the Pope on behalf of Charles V, Landa may well have seen the Pantheon there.

with a spike connected to the heads from behind in the neck that fit into a deep hole made for it in the same neck, and when fitted, made the sculpture complete.

*   *   *³⁵³

[f. 50r; figure A.43] [Sec. 43]

FOR WHAT THINGS THE INDIANS MADE OTHER SACRIFICES

The festivities in these people's calendar were put down before. They showed us which and how many there were, and for what, and how they celebrated them. But because these feasts served only to be pleasing and favorable to their gods, except when they were afraid of the angry ones, they did not hold more nor crueller. And they were believed to be angry when they had problems of pestilences, disagreements, or infertility, or other similar problems. Therefore, they did not try to placate their devils by sacrificing animals to them, nor by making them only offerings of their food and drinks, or by letting their blood and afflicting themselves with night vigils, fasts, or abstinences. Instead, forgetting all natural piety and all laws of reason, they made sacrifices of human beings as easily as if they sacrificed birds, and as many times as their evil priests or the Chilanes told them it was necessary, or what the lords wished, or seemed [right]. Given that the population of this land is not great as that of Mexico, and that now since the destruction of Mayapan they are not ruled by one head but by many, there was not therefore such a wholesale slaughter of men. Regardless, they gave them up for dead most miserably, for each town had the authority to sacrifice those according to the priest, or *chilan*, or their lord. They had their public places in the temples for doing this, as if it were the most necessary thing in the world for the conservation of their state [*republica*]. Besides merely killing them in their towns, they also had those two nefarious sanctuaries of Chichen Itza and Cozumel [*Chichenyza y cuzmil*], where they sent an infinite number of poor wretches for sacrifice—in the one by throwing them down from a height, and in the other by taking out their hearts. From those miseries they have been forever freed by the merciful lord [*f. 50v*], who for goodness had himself sacrificed on the cross to the father for us all.³⁵⁴

---

³⁵³ Like the discrete section on Maya calendrics that begins with fs. 28r (sec. 34), the passages that begin here—fols. 50r–58v (secs. 43) through the first half of sec. 48, discussed as Segment F in our chapter 6—appear to be a single, discrete intellectual project, transcribed by a different scribe (the handwriting is remarkably different; we call him Scribe B and suggest he may have been the royal chronicler Antonio Herrera y Tordesillas). This is the only part of the Account that furnishes its own title (*Porque cosas hazian otros sacrificos los Indios*; see figure A.43), although that only applied to one folio; this is the first of thirteen paragraph spaces left for subheadings or titles, with all but the first, ninth, and tenth left blank (we use three asterisks [*] to mark all thirteen).

³⁵⁴ One of us (Restall) views this passage (f. 50r) as a blatant exaggeration of Maya practices of

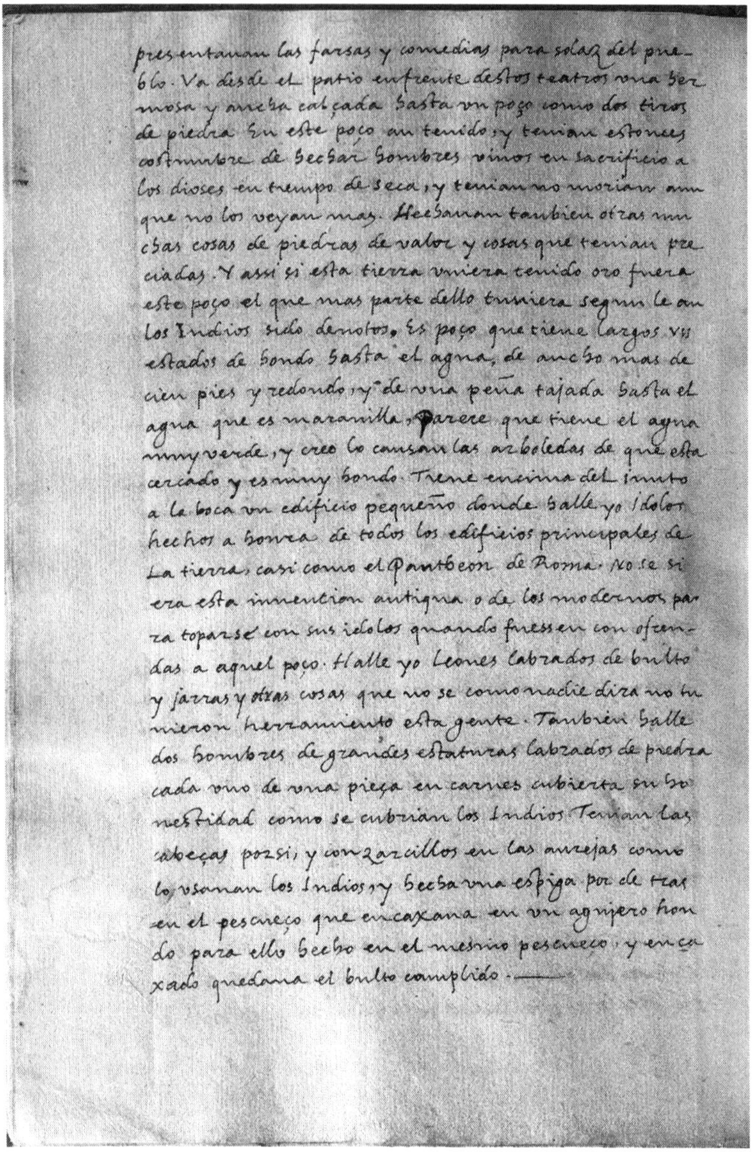

presentauan las farsas y comedias para solaz del pueblo. Va desde el patio enfrente destos teatros vna hermosa y ancha calçada hasta vn poço como dos tiros
de piedra en este poço an tenido y tenian estonçes
costunbre de hechar hombres vinos en sacrificio a
los dioses en tiempo de seca y tenian[?] morian aun
que no los veyan mas. Hechauan tanbien otras muchas cosas de piedras de valor y cosas que tenian pre-
ciadas. Y assi si esta tierra vuiera tenido oro fuera
este poço el que mas parte dello tuuiera segun le an
los Indios sido denotos. Es poço que tiene largos vij
estados de hondo hasta el agua, de ancho mas de
cien pies y redondo y de vna peña tajada hasta el
agua que es marauilla. Pareçe que tiene el agua
muy verde, y creo lo causan las arboledas de que esta
cercado y es muy hondo. Tiene encima del junto
a la boca vn edificio pequeño donde halle yo idolos
hechos a honrra de todos los edificios principales de
la tierra casi como el Pantheon de Roma. No se si
era esta inuençion antigua o de los modernos para toparse con sus idolos quando fuessen con ofrendas a aquel poço. Halle yo leones labrados de bulto
y jarras y otras cosas que no se como nadie dira no tuuieron herramiento esta gente. Tanbien halle
dos hombres de grandes estaturas labrados de piedra
cada vno de vna pieça en carnes cubierta su ho-
nestidad como se cubrian los Indios. Tenian las
cabeças por si, y con zarcillos en las orejas como
lo vsauan los Indios y hecha vna espiga por de tras
en el pescueço que encaxaua en vn agujero hondo para ello hecho en el mesmo pescueço, y enca-
xado quedaua el bulto cumplido. ——

Figures A.42–A.43. fs. 49v–50r of the Account.

Porque cosas hazian otros sacri-
ficios los Indios.

Las fiestas que enel calendario desta gente atras puesto quedan, nos muestran quales y quantas son eran y
para que, y como las celebrauan. Pero porque eran sus fiestas solo para tener gratos y propicios asus dioses sino era
temiendo los ayrados no hazian mas nimas sanguientas.
y creyan estar ayrados quando temian necessidades de
pestilencias /o dissensiones /o esterilidades /o otras seme-
Jantes necessidades, entonces no curauan de aplacar los
demonios sacrificandoles animales ni haziendoles solas offre-
das desus comidas y beuidas /o derramando su sangre y
affligiendose con velas y ayunos y abstinencias, mas olui-
dada toda natural piedad y toda ley de razon les hazian
sacrificios, depersonas humanas contanta facilidad como si
sacrificasan aues, y tantas vezes quantas los maluados sacerdotes /o los Chilanes les dezian era menester /o alos señores
seles antosaua /o parecia. y dado que eneta tierra por no
ser mucha la gente como en Mexico ni regirse ya despues
dela destruycion de Mayapan por vna cabeça sino por muchas, no auia assi tan Junta matança de hombres, no por
esso dexauan de morir miserablemente artos, pues temia
cada pueblo auctoridad desacrificarlos queal sacerdote /o
al chilan /o señor parecia, y para hazerlo toman sus publicos
lugares enlos templos como si fuera la cosa mas necessaria
ala conseruacion desu republica del mundo. Despues dema-
tar ensus pueblos temian aquellos dos descomulgados sanctu-
arios de Chichen yça y cuçmil, donde infinitos pobres embiaua
asacrificar al vno a deffeñar y al otro asacar los coraçones,
delas quales miserias tenga por bien siempre librarlos el S.

*   *   *³⁵⁵

Oh Lord, my God, the light, being, and life of my soul, holy guide and true path of my habits, consolation of my afflictions, inner joy of my sorrows, refreshment and rest from my labors! Why do you command me, Lord, to do what is better called work than rest? Why do you oblige me to do that which I cannot complete?[356] By chance, Lord, do you ignore the capacity of my cup [*la medida de mi vaso*], the quantity of my limbs, and the quality of my strength? In fact, Lord, are you absent from my labors? Are you not the helpful father to whom I spoke, you the holy prophet in the psalm, "with him I am the tribulation and the labor, and I will free him from it, and I will glorify him?"[357] Lord, if you are him, if you are the one of whom the prophet, full of your most holy spirit, speaks, they who feigned your commandment: labor. And so, Lord, those who have not enjoyed the gentleness of keeping and completing your rules, they find labor in them, but Lord, it is false labor, a torrid labor, it is a fainthearted labor, and the men who fear it are those who have never finished putting their hands to the plow to complete them. Those who set out to keep them, find them to be sweet, they go after the smell of their ointments, and their sweetness refreshes them at every step. They experience many more delights each day than anyone knows how to discern, like another Queen of Sheba. And so, Lord, I beg you, please give me the grace of your example, leaving behind the house of my sensuality and the reign of my vices and sins. Make everything the experience of serving you, protecting your holy commandments, because that, more than anything, will teach me the experience of their obedience and in only reading them and addressing them, I found [*f. 51r*] the good of your grace for my soul. So, as I believe your yoke

---

ritual execution, tantamount to the invention of widespread "human sacrifice" among the Maya, and one of the many roots of the prejudicial distortion of Maya civilization seen most blatantly in Mel Gibson's film, *Apocalypto* (2006)—all designed to justify the violence with which Landa sought to destroy all vestiges of Maya religious practice; the other three of us are less dismissive of the passage. Far from the ethnographic observation that might wrongly be seen here, the passage's final line reveals its purpose: to twist Maya culture into a negative image of Christianity, a diabolistic mockery of the "good" human sacrifice made by Christ.

[355] The polemic of the previous passage is followed here by a somewhat sudden shift to a prayer, or address to God, underlining the atypical nature of this segment (marked by the second of the segment's thirteen paragraph spaces; this one is two lines deep).

[356] Here Landa (who is presumably the author here) laments his difficult labor in the conversion campaigns in the face of the continued idolatry of the Maya, perhaps as part of his self-defense against the accusations of abusively usurping episcopal jurisdiction in holding autos-da-fé. In a moment of self-doubt, questioning, and lament here, he offers us a very quick glimpse of Landa and his missionary glimpse of Landa and his missionary mentality.

[357] Most probably Psalm 130, which speaks of tribulations and labors of the soul, and the easy yoke of the Lord, is referenced here. See our table 4.2.

to be soft and light, I thank you for having put me underneath your obligation of obedience, and free from that which I see many groups of people who walk and have walked, commanding them to hell, that which is for them a great pain. I do not know anyone whose heart does not break to see the mortal grief and intolerable burden with which the devil has always carried and led the idolaters to hell. And if this, on the part of the devil who procures and does it, is a great cruelty on the part of God, then it is justly permitted, because if they do not want to govern themselves by the light of reason that he has given to them, they should start to be tormented in this life; they should deserve arduous services that they are continually given by the devil, with their very long fasts, vigils, and abstinences, and with the incredible offerings and presents of their property and other things, and the continuous spilling of their own blood, with heavy pains and wounds of their bodies, and with what is worse and more serious, with the lives of their neighbors and brothers. With all this the devil is never satiated and satisfied with their torments and labors, nor with carrying them off to hell where he will eternally torment them. Surely, God is placated better, for with fewer torments and deaths he is satisfied. For he loudly speaks and commands the Great Patriarch Abraham not to extend his hand to take the life of his son, because His Majesty is determined to send his own son to the world and let him lose his life on the cross, truly, so that men may see that for the son of eternal God the commandment of his father is heavy; even though it is very sweet to him, for men it is a false labor. Therefore, let men now leave behind the tepidness of their hearts and the fear of the labor of this holy law of God, since their labor is false and it turns in a short time to the sweetness of their souls and bodies, and so much the more, that besides that it is honorable for God to be well served, we also owe him a just debt, and it is all for our own benefit, and not only eternally, but also even temporally. And they will see *[f. 51v]*, all Christians, especially the priests, that in this life it is a great shame and confusion, and in the future it will be better to see that the devil finds those who serve him with incredible labors, in order to go to hell in recompense for it. God barely finds anyone who, in keeping such gentle commandments, faithfully serves him in order to go to the eternal glory.[358] Therefore, you, priest of God, tell me if you have carefully looked at the job of these sad priests of the devil, and if all those we find in the divine writings were so in past times, how engaging, enduring, and many were their fasts more than yours? How much more constant were their vigils and in their miserable prayers than yours; how more curious and careful in the things of their ministry, than yours? With how much more carefulness and care of the things of their jobs, than you are of yours? With how much greater zeal than you

---

[358] Here, in a veiled manner, Landa may be criticizing Bishop Toral and all the other clergy who did not aid him in his extirpation campaigns, opposing his methods and efforts, which to Landa were "the labor and work of God."

did they engage in teaching their perfidious doctrines? And if you will find yourself in some fault or guilt, remedy it and see that you are a priest of the high lord who to that job alone, obliges you to make sure to live in purity and care, the purity of an angel, more so than a man.

*   *   *

[Sec. 44] Yucatan is a land with the least amount of soil that I have ever seen, because all of it is one living slab.[359] It is astounding how little soil it has, so much so that there are few parts of this land where one can go down an estado without yielding great layers of very large [limestone] slabs. The stone is not very good for delicate carvings, because it is hard and coarse, nevertheless, even as it is, it has been [used], so they have made out of it a great number of buildings that are in that land. [The stone] is very good for [making] lime, of which there is a lot. It is a wonderful thing that the soil is so fertile above and between these stones. Everything that there is in this land grows, and it grows better and more abundantly among the stones than in the poor soils, because around the soils that exist in some parts, trees do not grow, nor does anything grow *[f. 52r]*, nor do the Indians sow their seeds in it; there is nothing there except grass. Among the stones and on top of them,[360] they sow and plant all of their seeds and they raise all the trees, some rather tall, beautiful ones, which are marvelous to see. The cause of this I think is that among the stones there is more moisture, and it is retained better in the stones than in the soil.

*   *   * [361]

In this land so far, no kind of metal has been found that she has of her own; and it is shocking it does not have it, considering they have built so many buildings, because the Indians have no clue as to the tools with which they were built. Nevertheless, since they lacked metals, God provided them with a mountain range made out of flint, which runs contiguous to the mountains that I talked about in the first chapter, which cuts across the land;[362] from which they extracted stones of which they made the points of their lances for war, the large knives for their sacrifices (those

---

[359] The author writes here in the first person, giving testimony to his experience in Yucatan. That does not mean this is Landa's original work; see our chapter 6 below for an argument that he more likely redacted the natural history sections that follow from another source.

[360] The author describes the widespread practice of planting maize, beans, and squash on top of precontact mounds, which retain moisture and contain richer soils due the organic materials left by precontact inhabitants.

[361] The paragraph break here, like the four that follow (the fourth through eighth), is equivalent to three or four lines of text.

[362] The author refers to the Puuc hills which are a natural source of high-quality flint, one of the features of the Chicxulub crater.

which the priests had in good supply),[363] they made the points for their arrows and they still use them. In this manner flint functions as their metal. They had a certain type of soft brass and by mixing some of it with gold, they cast little hatchets, some little bells with which they danced,[364] and a certain kind of little chisel with which they made their idols and with which they pierced their blowpipes like this figure in the margin here,[365] for they use the blowgun often and they shoot it well. This brass, along with sheets or harder plates, those from Tabasco brought to trade for their idols. There was no other kind of metal among them.

*   *   *

According to the sage,[366] one of the most necessary things to the life of man is water, and it is so necessary that without it neither the earth produces its fruits, nor can men sustain themselves. Having lacked in Yucatan the abundance of rivers that their neighboring lands have [*f. 52v*] in great abundance, because it has only two, and one is the River of Lagartos that goes from one of the land's capes at the sea, and the other is that of Champoton, both brackish and of bad waters. [But] God provided the land with many very beautiful waters, some [created] through ingenuity [*industria*] and others provided by nature. Nature worked on this land more differently with respect to rivers and springs than with the rivers and springs in the whole

---

[363] The phrase "those which the priests had in good supply" is enclosed in parentheses in the original manuscript.

[364] Bells made of *tumbaga*, or a mixture of gold and copper, are found at many Terminal Classic and Postclassic archaeological sites in Yucatan. There are no local sources of either mineral, but the discovery of crucibles and sprues at Mayapan strongly suggests metal objects were produced by at least the Postclassic period (Paris, "Metallurgy") (see n35 in part I).

[365] No figure exists in the manuscript.

[366] Pagden translates this term for sage as "the Philosopher Aristotle," but there is no internal evidence here to support this; Tozzer, Gates, and Genet all simply translate this as "Sage, or Wiseman." We believe the Account is referring here to the "sage" or philosopher Thales (636–546 BCE), born in Miletus, considered one of the founders of Greek Philosophy and one of the so-called "seven sages." One of his two major philosophical propositions was that water was the principal material and cause of all things, that all things come from water, and to water all things return. Here and in other passages, Landa and the other original authors of the text offer us insight into their education and studies of the classics. Landa and other Franciscans would have studied advanced theology, philosophy, and the other liberal arts. The author is here at pains to show how well-educated he is because, as Landa noted in his 1572 *Probanza de Hidalguia*, "in the Franciscan order the friars are not accustomed to, nor do they use, or receive, nor take, the formal titles of the grades of *bachiller*, nor *licenciado*, nor any other licenses for what they have studied and learned" (question number 6 in the interrogatory composed by Landa himself, in *Probanza de Hidalguia del reverendísimo padre Fray Diego de Landa, Obispo Electo de la Provincia de Yucatán*, 9 de junio, 1572, AHNob, Condado de Almodovar, Caja 40, Documento 8, f. 4r).

world, where springs flow on top of the land, yet in this one, they all run via secret channels underneath it.[367] And all of this has taught us that almost the entire coast is full of freshwater springs that are born in the sea and from which you can, in many places, collect fresh water (as has happened to me)[368] when the ebbing of the water and the tides leaves the shore somewhat dry. God provided sinkholes [*quebradas*] that the Indians call Zenotes.[369] They are created from rock collapsed into pieces down to the water, and in some of which there are very furious currents, and livestock that fall into them are often swept away. All of these freshwater currents go out to sea and serve as the source of the aforementioned springs. These Zenotes have very beautiful waters and [are] very spectacular to see, for there are some with sliced rock all the way to the water, and others with some mouths that God made for them, caused by some accidents of lightning which usually falls often or by another cause, and inside are beautiful vaults of sliced living rock, and trees on their surfaces, so at the top it is forest and below Zenotes. And there are some that one can fit and sail a caravel, and others more or less [large]. The ones that could be reached, they drank from them because they did not have wells, and due to their lack of metal tools needed to build them, they were very meager. But now, not only have we given them the skill to make good wells, but also very nice waterwheels with watertanks where, just like the springs, they take the water. There are also lagoons, and they are all brackish and meager to drink and they are not of [water] currents like Zenotes. In terms of the wells, this land has one marvelous thing, and that is that wherever one digs, out comes good spring water, and some of these are so fine that a lance is swallowed up in them. And in all of the places where they have dug, at about half an estado before reaching the water, there have been found a bank of conch shells and small seashells, of so many varieties *[f. 53r]* and colors, big and small, like those

---

[367] The author displays a relatively sophisticated understanding of the hydrogeology of the Yucatan peninsula in this passage. Prior to modern coastal development, a nearly continuous dune ridge could be found along the coast, broken only by subterranean outflows of fresh water. This fresh water, in the form of springs (what the author calls "wells") and brackish rivers, provided drinking water prior to, and through, the colonial period. For a thorough overview of the complex karst system of the Yucatan peninsula, see Perry, Velazquez-Oliman, and Socki, "Hydrogeology of the Yucatan Pennsula."

[368] In the manuscript, "as has happened to me [*como me ha a mi acaescido*]" is in parentheses. This aside most likely came from Landa, or another friar from Yucatan as neither of the two identified copyists of the manuscript ever traveled to the New World.

[369] In fact, the Maya call these *dzonot* (pl. *dzonotob*); *cenotes* is the Hispanized plural rendering, now also used in English. Given the reliance of Maya people on fresh water from cenotes in the historic and even modern periods, there is a vast literature on the hydrogeology of cenotes. In the 1990s, scholars discovered that these unique features are the surface expressions of an asteroid or comet that struck the earth 65 million years ago (see Pope et al., "Surface Expression") (today a widely known event due to its connection to the dinosaur extinction).

on the shore of the sea and the sand, now already formed into hard white rock. In Mani, a town of the king [*pueblo del Rey*], we[370] dug a large well in order to make a waterwheel for the Indians and after having dug seven or eight estados in the living rock, we found a good long, seven-foot tomb, full of very fresh, reddish earth and with human bones,[371] and they were already nearly turned to stone. It took another two or three more *stadia* to reach the water, before which there was a hollow vault created by God, so that the tomb was shoved inside the rock, and you could walk underneath it to where it was. We could not understand how this could be, unless, like we said, that the tomb was built there with that part inside, and then, with the humidity of the cave and with the passage of a long time, the rock began to harden and grow around it and thus enclose the tomb. In addition to the two rivers that I have said there is in this land, it also has a spring three leagues from the sea, near Campeche, and it is brackish. There are no other waters in all the land, nor other kinds of water sources. The Indians from the hills, because they have very deep wells, during the rainy season tend to carve out concavities in the rocks near their houses and collect the rainwater there,[372] for it rains greatly, and intensely, strong downpours, sometimes with a lot of thunder and lightning. All the wells, and especially those that are close to the sea, rise and fall every day when the ocean rises and falls, which shows very clearly that all the river waters run under the ground to the sea.

*   *   *

There is a swamp in Yucatan worthy of mention that extends more than seventy leagues in length, all made of salt water. It starts from the coast of Ekab, which is near the Isla de mugeres [Isla Mujeres], and it follows very close to the coast from the sea, in between the same coast and the forests [*montes*], until close to Campeche. It is not deep because there is no space for it due to the lack of soil, but it is very bad

---

[370] The author here states that "we" dug a well in Mani. He may have meant "we" as a generic reference to the Franciscans, but it is also possible that Landa himself witnessed the digging of the well, as he visited Mani in 1550 or 1551 while missionizing the Maya of the region. From 1553 on, he was resident in Conkal, then Izamal, and finally in Merida, but we know he was back in Mani late in 1561, taking testimony there in an early monastic inquisition case—having been elected that September as the provincial of the new Province of San Josef (recently separated from the Franciscan province of Guatemala).

[371] The author may be referring here to a possible royal Maya burial with the red earth being red cinnabar powder which the Maya often imported and placed over the burials of their prominent people. For more on the use of cinnabar in elite Maya burials see Fitzsimmons, *Death*. He may also have encountered the reddish soil Yucatec speakers now call *k'an kab*, which is found in depressions across the peninsula (Bautista and Zinck, "Construction").

[372] The precontact Maya had a variety of water storage technologies. The concavities described here, known as "chultuns" (*chultunes* in Spanish, *chultunob* in Maya), are common in the Puuc hills area (Dunning, *Lords of the Hills*).

to pass through, going from the towns to the coast or coming from it to the villages, due to the trees that it has and a lot of mud. This swamp is salty such that God has created there the best salt that I have seen in my life, because when ground it is very white and, for salt, says those who *[f. 53v]* know, half a bushel of it is as good as a whole one from other areas.[373] Our Lord created the salt in this swamp out of rainwater and not water from the sea, for it does not enter it, because between the sea and the swamp runs a thin strip [*ceja*] of land, the entire length of it, dividing it from the sea. Over time, then, this swamp swells with rainwater and the salt settles inside the same water, in large and small lumps so that it looks like nothing but pieces of sugar candy. After the rainy season has lasted for four or five months, and once the lagoon is somewhat dried up, the Indians in ancient times had a custom of going to extract the salt, which they extract by removing those clods in the water and extracting them to dry outside. They had for this their designated places in the lagoon itself, which were the most abundant with salt and had less mud and water. They used not to make this harvest of salt without the permission of their lords, whom they had there, because of their control over these places. A principal Indian lord attested to this, a native of the town of Caucel [*caukel*], called Francisco Euan, and he attested that the government of the city of Mayapan had put his ancestors on the coast in charge of it and of the distribution of salt.[374] Based on this, the Audiencia of Guatemala ordered that all those who went to those regions to collect salt should even now do the same.[375] A great deal of salt is collected now in this era

---

[373] The northern and western coasts of the Yucatan peninsula have large natural evaporative saltworks. The pure salt crystals, easily raked up from ground surface, were highly prized in precontact times and traded throughout Mesoamerica. During the colonial period, the salt works proved to be second only to the massive number of tribute cloth *mantas* in terms of wealth generated by the colony. So important were the salt works for the economics of the colony, that a royal *cédula* of 1603 placed them under complete royal control as "*patrimonio real*" (*Real cédula sobre las Salinas de Yucatán dada al gobernador Don Carlos de Luna y Arellano*, 3 de julio, 1603, AGI, México, 72, R.7, N.91, f. 3r); in response, the governor don Carlos de Luna y Arellano compiled information and testimonies on all the various *salinas* in the peninsula, their value, and production in 1604–1605 (*Testimonio de autos sobre las salinas de Yucatán*, 5 de enero, 1605, AGI, México, 72, R.7, N.91, fs. 4–40). Las Coloradas saltworks on the northern coast remains in use today (see Andrews, *Maya Salt Production and Trade*).

[374] This is a reference to a possible *probanza* by the batab of Caucel, don Francisco Euan, claiming his lineage's centuries-long control of the salt works. The twenty-five salinas in the region of Caucel alone produced 43,100 *fanegas* of salt in 1604, valued at ninety pesos for every twelve *fanegas*, making it one of the most productive salt works in the colony. The entire salt production of the colony at the same time amounted to approximately 150,700 *fanegas*, worth 12,558 pesos (*Capítulos de los autos de posesion sobre las Salinas*, AGI, Mexico, 72, R.7, N.91, f. 40r).

[375] If the *probanza* of don Francisco Euan was sent and approved by the Audiencia of Guatemala, it was sent very early (1550–1559) and may still exist in the archives of Guatemala. As detailed

to be taken to Mexico, Honduras, and Havana. This swamp also produces, in some parts of it, very beautiful fish, and although not large they taste very good.

* * *

[Sec. 45] Not only are there fish in the lagoon but there is such a great abundance of fish on the coast that the Indians almost never catch the lagoon fish, except if they are those who do not have fishing nets, and those who are used to using arrows; since there is little water, a lot of fish are killed. The others make their very big fishing catches from which they are able to eat and sell fish throughout the entire land. They are accustomed to salting, drying, and roasting [the fish] in the sun without salt, and they have their own calculation of which of these methods benefits each kind *[f. 54r]* of fish as needed.[376] The roasted fish are preserved for several days, and they can be transported in this way twenty [*XX*] and thirty [*XXX*] leagues to sell. In order to eat them, they cook them again, and it is tasty and healthy. The fish that they kill, and which are there are on that coast, are very excellent filefishes, smooth and very fat, like trout neither more nor less in their color, spots, and flavor, and they are fatter and tastier to eat. They are called in their language *uzcay* [gnat fish]. [There are] very good sea bass, sardines, and along with them they also have sole,[377] swordfish, mackerels,[378] two-banded sea bream, and an infinite diversity of other small fish. There are very good octopuses on the coast of Campeche, three or four types of very good and healthy spotted dogfish sharks, and especially some special healthy yellow ones, very different in the heads from the others, for some have rounded ones and very flat, astonishingly so, inside the mouth and around the edges of the eyes: they call these *ahpechpol* [tick head]. They also kill some very big fish that look like blankets, and they cut them in pieces in salt and they die along the shoreline, and it is a very good thing; I do not know if this fish is a type of ray. There are many manatees on the coast between Campeche and [the point or port of] La Desconocida, from which they get so much fish or meat that they have made a lot of lard, and it is excellent for cooking food. They recount many marvelous things about these manatees, especially the account by the author of the *General History of the Indies* of an Indian

---

earlier, Euan had been a Maya priest, or *ah kin*, in Caucel, and after his conversion became very close to the Franciscans and Landa. He is mentioned in the tribute lists in 1549, and Cogolludo noted that he died later in 1560, making this statement here evidence that this section of the text was written between 1553 and 1560, when Francisco Euan was still alive.

[376] For a recent archaeological study into native fish salting and processing technology, see McKillop and Aoyama, "Salt and Marine Products."

[377] Called *lenguados* in Spanish (*Solea solea*), and sole fish in English, this type of flat fish looks like a tongue.

[378] *Mojarras*: commonly known as the Spanish mackerels or seerfishes.

noble from the Island of Española, who raised one in a lake, so domesticated that when he called him by the name he had given him, "Matu," he came to the water's edge.[379] What I can say about them is that they are so large that they get from them much more meat than is taken from a good large calf, and a lot of lard. They breed like other mammals, and they have their genitals like a male and female, and the female always gives birth to no more or no less than two [calves], and they do not lay eggs like the other fish. They have two large wings like strong arms with which they swim. Their face is very similar to an ox, and they can reach out of the water with it to graze on the grass along the banks. They are usually bitten by bats all along their round flat snout which wraps all around the face. From these bites they die since they are marvelously bloody and with any wound they bleed out in the water. Their meat is good, especially when fresh and eaten with mustard; it is almost as good as beef. The Indians hunt and kill them with harpoons in this way: first they look for them in the estuaries *[f. 54v]* and shallow parts (since it is not a fish that knows how to exist in the deeper parts)[380] and they carry their harpoons tied onto ropes with buoys at the end. Once they have found them, they harpoon them and release their ropes and buoys and the manatee will try to escape due to the pain of the wounds, fleeing to the shallow parts of the water, since they never venture out into the depths of the sea because they do not know how to submerge themselves. They are so large that they stir up the mud and silt and they are so filled with blood that they bleed profusely until they bleed to death. And so, with a sign of the mud, the Indians follow on their trails. After they find them, they extract them with their buoys. Fishing them is great sport and beneficial, as they are all meat and lard. There is another fish on this coast that they call *ba*, wide, round, and very good to eat, but it is very dangerous to kill or even come across it, because it knows little of the deep and likes coming up to the mud where the Indians kill him with the bow and arrow. If they are careless walking on it or tread on it in the water, it comes up quickly with its tail, which is large, thin, and so fiercely wounds with a saw blade that you cannot extract without making the wound much bigger, because the teeth [of the blade] are turned upside down,

---

[379] Although Pagden, in his own edition and translation of the Account (*The Maya*, 173n54, 176n84), attributes this story to the work of Oviedo y Valdés, *Historia general y natural de las Indias*, it would have been difficult for Landa to have seen this work, as it was unpublished in Landa's lifetime. The only work of Oviedo's that Landa could have accessed was his *Natural historia de las Indias* (1526), which does not contain this story. Instead, the work that is being cited here is surely Francisco López de Gómara's *La Istoria de las Yndias* (chapter XXXI, 50), which recounts this story in great detail, adding how the manatee's Indigenous keeper, the cacique Caramateji, had given him the name of Matu (or Mato), and how he interacted with the Indigenous islanders of Hispaniola.

[380] The phrase is in parentheses in the original text.

such as the way it is painted here.[381] With these little saw blades the Indians used to cut their own flesh in their sacrifices to the devil, and it was the priest's job to have them, and so they often had many.[382] They are very pretty, for they are of very white bone, a curiously made saw so sharp and delicate that they cut like a knife. There is a small little fish, so poisonous that no one who eats it escapes from dying. It swells up very quickly and often tricks people even though it is well known.[383] It lasts a long time without dying out of the water and inflates himself entirely. There are also very fine oysters in the Champoton River and a great many sharks along the coast.

*   *   *[384]

Besides the fish whose abode is the waters, there are other things that together they make use of, and they live in water and on land, such as *[f. 55r]* there are many iguanas, which are like Spanish lizards in shape and size, and in color, although they are not as green. These lay eggs in great quantities, and always stay near to the sea and to where there are waters, and inevitably they take shelter in the water and on the land because the Spaniards eat them in times of fasting, and they have been found to be a very unique and healthy food. There are so many of them that they help everyone during Lent. The Indians hunt for them with raised bows up in the trees and in their hollows. It is an incredible thing how they endure hunger, for it happens that even having spent twenty and thirty days after their capture they remain alive without eating a bite, and without losing weight. And I have heard that it has been observed that if they rub sand over their bellies, they [iguanas] are fattened a lot. Their excrement makes an admirable medicine; to cure the clouding of the eyes, you put it fresh in them. There are tortoises of a marvelous great size that are much bigger than large bucklers.[385] They are good to eat and they have much on

---

[381] Although the author refers to an illustration of this fish tooth, the manuscript does not include such an image. This description leaves little doubt that the author is here referencing a stingray. The Maya appear to have called both gophers and stingrays *ba*, presumably as both are burrowers.

[382] Archaeological evidence has indeed revealed that stingray spines were often interred in elite graves, leading many to assume that they were used as instruments for auto-sacrifice. However, given their toxicity, these may have been more symbolic that functional, much like the eccentric flints which are also found as elite grave goods. (Haines, Willink, and Maxwell, "Stingray Spine Use and Maya Bloodletting Rituals.")

[383] This is, of course, the puffer fish (*Sphoeroides nephelus*).

[384] This is the eighth of the thirteen paragraph breaks used by Scribe B (explained in a note at the first of them, and in our chapter 6).

[385] Five species of sea turtles nest on the shores of the Yucatan peninsula; hawksbill (*Eretmochelys imbricata*), green (*Chelonia mydas*), loggerhead (*Caretta caretta*), Kemp's ridley (*Lepidochelys kempii*), and leatherback (*Dermochelys coriacea*). See Valverde and Holzwart,

them. They lay eggs as big as a hen's, and lay one hundred and fifty or two hundred, making a big nest in the sand away from the water, and covering them afterwards with sand, and from there the little tortoises come out. There are other different turtles on the land in the dry forest and in the lagoons. A few times I saw a fish on the coast entirely in a shell, and I left it in order to describe it here: it is, then, of the size of a small turtle, and covered on the top with a delicate, round shell of beautiful craftsmanship, very bright green; it has a tail that is the same as the shell, very thin that seems like a bodkin, but a handspan [*xeme*] long, with a face below. It has many feet and is all filled with small eggs. It has nothing edible on it except the eggs, and the Indians eat a lot of those. They call it in their language, *mex*.[386] There are very fierce lizards; even though they walk in the water, they leave it and often go on land.[387] They eat on land or with their heads sticking out of the water because they lack gills and cannot chew under water. It is a heavy animal and is not away from the water often. It has a furious force in *[f. 55v; see figure A.44]* attacking something or wounding it. It is very gluttonous, and they tell very strange things about it. I know this is so because an Indian killed one for us close to a monastery; he was bathing in a lagoon, and a little bit further from there a priest went with the Indians to kill one. In order to kill one, they took a dog not much bigger, and shoved through it a handmade strong stick with points from its mouth to its anus, and they tied around the guts of the dog a very tough rope; and throwing the dog into the lagoon, the lizard came out and grabbed it by its teeth and gulped it. And having swallowed it, the people speared it, and so the friar went, and they captured it with a great effort and difficulty, forcing the stick through the body. They opened it up and they found in it half of a man in its belly as well as the little dog. These lizards breed like the animals and lay eggs, and in order to lay them they make big nests in the sand very close to the water. They lay three hundred eggs and more, bigger than those of birds. They keep them there until nature tells them it is time for hatching [*salir*], and thus they walk by there waiting, and the little lizards come out in this way: they come out of the egg, as big as a palm span, and they wait for an ocean wave that crashes close to them; and so, as they feel it, they spring from their place into the water, and all that cannot reach it are left dead in the sand, since they are so tender, the sun is so very hot it scorches them, then killing them; those that do reach the water

---

"Sea Turtles of the Gulf of Mexico." The term "buckler" refers to a large rounded steel shield commonly used by Spanish soldiers of the sixteenth century, which measured up to forty-five centimeters (eighteen inches) in diameter.

[386] This is likely the horseshoe crab (*Limulus polyphemus*).

[387] Although he introduces them with the generic term *lagartos*, the author goes on to describe crocodiles, of which there are two species native to Yucatan, the American crocodile (*Crocodylus acutus*) and the Morelet's crocodile (*Crocodylus moreletii*).

all escape, and they then begin to swim about until their parents flock there, they follow them in this way. Very few [of them] escape, even though they lay so many eggs. It is not without divine providence that we seek also more what benefits us than what damages us, and still we can suffer harm like these beasts, if we all come out into the light.[388]

* * *

PARAGRAPH VII. ON THE KINDS OF SERPENTS THERE ARE AND OTHER POISONOUS ANIMALS.[389]

[Sec. 46] The diversity of snakes or serpents is great; they are [f. 56r; figure A.45] of many colors and not harmful, except for two kinds of them that are very poisonous and much larger than those here in Spain; they call them *taxinchan*. There are also others very poisonous and very large, with rattles in their tails, and others so large that they can swallow a rabbit, or two, but they are not harmful. It is said that some Indians can easily grab the one kind or the other without being harmed. There is a kind of lizard, larger than the ones here, of which the Indians have an amazingly great fear, for they say that when a person touches one, it sweats a small sweat that is a deadly poison. There are many scorpions among the rocks, but they are not as poisonous as those here in Spain. There is a type of large ant whose bite is very bad, and which hurts and suppurates more than that of the scorpions; its suppuration is such that it lasts twice as long as that of a scorpion, as I myself have experienced.[390] There are two types of spiders, one small and very pestiferous, and the other very large and all covered with very fine black spines that look like down and which contain poison; and thus, the Indians take great care not to touch them. There are many other reptiles, but not harmful ones. There is a small red worm from which they make a good yellow ointment that is excellent for swellings and sores, needing

---

[388] An odd coda to this section, and a sharp change of voice; this may reflect that the material on natural history was copied by Landa from another source, but he then added this veiled lament for having come under attack from fellow Franciscans like Bishop Toral and under the scrutiny of the Crown, the Council of the Indies, and his own Order, all for what he saw as just defense of the faith and rigorous punishment of Maya idolatry.

[389] This subheading is in the Account as *Parrapho VII. de la manera que ay de serpientes y otros animales ponçónolos*, revealing that these paragraphs were copied from a much larger work (either Landa's or, as he was relatively disinterested in natural history, copied or paraphrased by Landa, or a scribe of his, from another author's work). Some previous editors of the Account rolled this "Paragraph VII" subheading (and the "Paragraph VIII" that follows) into the chapter or section titles (e.g., Gates, *Yucatán*, 100–101), thus completely eliminating this feature of the manuscript.

[390] Note the use of the first person (not necessarily clarifying issues of authorship mentioned in this previous note).

el acometer a algo lo en la huyda, es muy tragon q̃ cuentan
del cosas estrañas, y lo que yo se es que nos mato vno cerca de
vn monest.º vn frayle vañandose en vna laguna y fue luego de
alli avn rato vn religioso con los yndios a matarle a el y para
matarle tomaron vn perro no muy grande, y metieronle vn
fuerte palo por la boca hasta el sieso hechizo consus punta
y ataronle por las tripas del perro vna muy rezia soga y he
chando en la laguna el perro salio luego el lagarto y lo to
mo en los dientes yselo tragó, y tragado tiro la gente lo con el
frayle yua y le sacaron congran trabajo y difficultad atra
uessandosele el palo enel cuerpo, abrieronle y hallaronle
la mitad del hombre enel buche, y mas el perrillo. estos la
gartos engendran como los animales y ponen huebos, y pa
ra ponerlos hazen grandes hoyos enel arena muy cerca del
agua y ponen trezientos huebos y mas grandes mas q̃ de
aues y dexanlos alli hasta el tiempo que les a naturaleza
enseñado que han de salir yentonces andanse por alli agua
dando ysalen los lagartillos de tamaño. Salen del huebo
tan grandes como vn palmo yestan aguardando la ola de
la mar que bate cerca dellos, y assi como la sienten saltan
desu lugar ala agua y todos los que no alcançan quedan
muertos enel arena que como son tan tiernos y ella esta muy
caliente del sol abrasansse, y mueren luego: los q̃ alcançan
al agua escapan todos y comiençan luego a andar por alli
hasta que acudiendo los padres los siguen desta manera
escapan muy pocos aunq̃ ponen tantos huebos, no sin diuiª
prouidencia que quiere sea mas lo q̃ nos aproueche q̃ lo que
nos daña y podria tanto perjudicar como estas bestias si to
das saliessen aluz.

     Parrapho VII. dela manera que q̃ ay de serpi-
      entes y otros animales ponçoñolos.

De culebras / o serpientes es grande la diuersidad que ay de

de muchas colores y no dañosas: saluo dos castas dellas
las vnas son muy ponçoñosas biuoras y mayores mucho que
las de aca de España llamanlas texinchan y otras ay tan
bien muy ponçoñosas y muy grandes y con cascabel en las
colas. otras muy grandes que se tragan vn coneso y dos y no so
dañosas y es cosa de desech ay judios que con facilidad
toman las vnas y las otras sin reçibir dellas perjuyzio.
Ay vna casta de lagartissas mayores q̃ las de aca de las q̃
les es marauilla grande el temor q̃ los judios tienen porq̃
segun ellos disen entoccandola la persa suda vn sudorcillo
el qual es mortal ponçoña. Ay muchos alacranes entre las
piedras y no son tan ponçoñosos como los de aca de España.
Ay vn genero de hormigas grandes cuya picada es muy
peor y duele y encona mas q̃ la de los alacranes, y tanto q̃
dura su enconaçion mas al doble que la del alacran como
he yo experimentado. Ay dos generos de arañas, la vna
pequeña y muy pestifera; la otra es muy grande y toda
cubierta de essirintas muy delicadas negras q̃ parecen bello
y tienen en ellas la ponçoña y assi se guardan mucho de
tocarlas los judios donde las ay. otras muchas sabandi
jas ay, pero no dañosas. Ay vn gusanito colorado del qual
se hase vnguento muy bueno amarillo para hinchazones
y llagas con no mas de batirlos, o amasarlos juntos y sirue
de olio para pintar los vasos y hase fuerte la pintura.

Parrapho VIII. de las auejas y su miel y cera.

Ay dos castas de auejas y ambas son muy mas pequeñas
q̃ las mas, las mayores dellas crian en almenas las quales
son muy chicas, no hazen panal como las mas sino ciertas
bexiguitas como nuezes de cera todas juntas vnas a otras
llenas de la miel, para castrarlas no hazen mas de abrir la
colmena y rebentar con vn palito estas bexiguitas y assi corre

no more than to crush and knead them together; it also serves as oil for painting vases and strengthening paint.[391]

* * *

PARAGRAPH VIII. OF THE BEES AND THEIR HONEY AND WAX.[392]

[Sec. 47] There are two kinds of bees and both are much smaller than ours; the larger of these breed in hives that are very small, and do not make a comb as ours do, but instead certain little sacs like wax-nuts, all close together, one on top of the other, full of honey. To harvest them they only have to open the hive and with a small stick break the little sacs and thus out runs *[f. 56v]* the honey, and they remove the wax when it suits them. The others breed in the bush *[montes]*, in the hollows of trees and rocks, and there they look for the wax; of that and of honey this country is very abundant, and the honey is very good save for the fact that it comes out somewhat watery because the food of the bees is very fertile, so it is necessary to heat it over fire, and that makes it very good and very hard. The wax is good, save for it being very smoky, the reason for which I have never been certain; and in some provinces it is much yellower due to the flowers. These bees do not sting, nor do harm when they are harvested.[393]

* * *

[Sec. 48] Great and notable is the diversity of herbs *[yervas]* and flowers that adorn Yucatan in their seasons, both in the trees and among the herbs, many of them being marvelously lovely and beautiful, of many colors and fragrances; which, beyond the adornment with which they dress up the hills *[montes]* and fields, they give the

---

[391] See Lee, *Amphibians and Reptiles*.

[392] Original subheading again; *Parrapho VIII. de las avejas y su miel y cera.*

[393] This passage describes two means by which Maya people harvested honey and other products from the native stingless bee known as *Melipona beecheii*, or *xunan kab'* (sometimes *colel kab'*) in Maya. In precontact centuries, bees kept by Maya farmers contributed to the success of maize-based agricultural systems, and honey was used for making the ceremonial drink balche as well as for medicinal treatments. Wax was used for batik cloth and for decorating ceramic vessels, as well many other purposes for which we have less material evidence. Many beekeeping activities are depicted in the Madrid Codex, which has twenty-eight almanacs dedicated to apiculture and its role in Postclassic ritual life. The creator deity Itzamna is shown near beehives and offering balche, and on pages 103c–104c Itzamna is named as the owner of bees (Vail and Dedrick, "Human-Deity Relationships"). Beekeeping expanded in the colonial period due to high Spanish demand for wax (see Wallace, "History and Geography of Beeswax Extraction," and Patch, *Maya and Spaniard in Yucatán*, 81–92, 155–61). Maya beekeeping continues today in Yucatan, with both European and native bees kept by household producers and a number of state-sponsored programs to encourage production (see Anderson and Medina Tzuc, *Animals and the Maya*, 43–46).

most abundant sustenance to the bees for their honey and wax. Among these I shall mention here but a few,[394] both for their precious fragrance and beauty, and for the benefits derived from them by the inhabitants of that land. There are sages much fresher and more fragrant than those here, and with longer and slenderer leaves; and the Indians cultivate them for their odor and pleasure, and I have seen that the Indian women make them more beautiful by putting ashes around the base. There is one herb with broad leaves and tall, thick branches, of a singular freshness and fertility; because from cuttings from the branches they grow as they do in profusion, the same as does wicker, although not as much in comparison; rubbing the leaf a little between the hands it has a real odor of clover, although it loses this after drying; it is very good for freshening the temples at fiestas, and for this it is used. There is also much sweet basil found in the hills [*montes*] and roads, full of it in some places, and growing in those [*f. 57r*] rocks it is very fresh, beautiful, and odorous; although not comparable with what is grown in the orchards, imported from here,[395] it is something to see how it grows and spreads everywhere. There is a flower they call *tixzula*, of the most delicate odor I have ever smelled, much more so than jasmines; it is white, and there is a light purplish one too, and because it sprouts from fat bulbs, it could be brought to Spain. It then grows this way: its bulbs sprout tall, thick, and very fresh shoots that last the year around, and once a year produce in the center a green stem as thick as three fingers, and as fat and long as the shoots; at the end of these emerge the flowers in a bunch, each being some six inches long with the stem; when open, they have five little leaves, long and open and connected at the base by a delicate white membrane [*tela*], and in the middle they have little yellow membranes [*telitas*], marvelously beautiful in white and yellow; when the stalk is cut and put in a vase of water, it lasts with a gentle odor for many days, as the flowers do not open together, only little by little. There are certain small lilies, very white and odorous, which last long in water, and would be easy to bring here, since they are also from bulbs and are very similar to our lilies, except that the odor is gentler and does not give headaches, and it lacks the yellow center of the lilies. There is a rose they call *ixlaul*, which they tell me is of great beauty and odor. And also, a type of tree they call *nicte*,[396] that produces many white roses, and others half-yellow, and

---

[394] Note that the first person is used here, and again a few lines below. For detailed identification of the plants and trees is this section, see Tozzer, *Landa's* Relación, n1030–n1100; also see Anne Bradburn's "Botanical Index" in Bricker, Po'ot Yah, and Dzul de Po'ot, *Dictionary of the Maya Language*, 320–28.

[395] This section is clearly being written in Spain, as evidenced here and a few lines later, by an author (possibly Landa himself) who uses the first person and refers to his observations in Yucatan.

[396] Likely the flowering plumeria tree *Plumeria rubra*, known as *sac nicte* (white flower) in Maya. This tree remains an important part of many contemporary rituals in Yucatan.

others half-purplish; these are of great freshness and odor, and of them they make flat corsages, and those who wish to make rosewater.[397] There is a flower they call *kom*, that is very odorous and gives a burning heat when smelled; it could easily be brought here, and its leaves are marvelously fresh and broad. Besides these flowers and odorous herbs there are many others most beneficial and medicinal, among them two varieties of nightshade, fresh and very pretty. There is much ceterach, and also maiden's hair; also, an herb whose leaves boiled and removed from the water are a wonderful remedy for swollen feet and legs. There is another herb very good for the cure of sores, which they call *yax halal che* [*yaxpahalche*]. Another herb *[f. 57v]* has the flavor of fennel, and it is eaten, and is very good for boiling water and for curing sores, put on raw like the last one. There is around Bacalar [*bayhalar*][398] sarsaparilla [*çarçaparrilla*]. They have a certain herb that grows in the wells and in other places, three-cornered like the sedge [*Juncia*], but much fatter, out of which they make their baskets, and they stain them with colors, making them so marvelously pretty. Also, they have an herb that grows wild and is also cultivated in their houses, which is better, of which comes a kind of hemp [*cañamo*], from which they make infinite things of use. Again, there grows on some trees without cultivation a certain type of herb that produces fruits like small cucumbers, out of which they make their gums or glues with which they stick together whatever they need.

*   *   *

The seeds they have for human sustenance are very good maize, of many different kinds and colors, of which they harvest much and make granaries and keep them in silos for the barren years. There are two kinds of small beans, one black and the other of various colors, and others brought over by the Spaniards are small and white. Their peppers have many different pods, some of which are for removing the seeds to make seasonings, others for eating baked or boiled, and others for cups for household use. They now have fine melons, and very good gourds [*calabaças*] from Spain. We[399] have set them to raising millet, which yields marvelously well and is good as food. They have a yellow fruit, fresh and delicious, which they sow, and the root, which grows like a short, fat, and round turnip, is the fruit, which they eat raw with salt. The other root that grows under the earth, by being sown, is great as food, and is of many kinds; for there are purplish, yellow, and white ones, eaten boiled or

---

[397] The original term used is *lectuario*, or "electuary," which usually refers to a medicinal, herbal drink, but which we suspect is what we would call rosewater and what Mayas would call *nicte ha* (*ha* meaning water) (Gates [*Yucatán*, 102] and Tozzer [*Landa's* Relación] opted for "lectuaries" and "marmalade," respectively).

[398] Bakhalal, renamed Bacalar by the Spaniards, was presumably unfamiliar to the copyist.

[399] "We" presumably used here to refer to the Franciscan order.

roasted, and they are good eating, and taste somewhat like chestnuts *[f. 58r]*, and roasted can be drank. There are two other kinds of good roots that are foods of the Indians: [these] two other roots are wild and seem somewhat salty, of which I have spoken before, and which help the Indians in times of hunger, for otherwise they do not care for them. They have a small tree with soft branches containing much milk, whose leaves they eat cooked, and are like cabbages to eat, and good with plenty of fat bacon. The Indians plant it wherever they wish to make their homes, and the whole year round they have the leaves for gathering.[400] There is much fresh chicory grown in the gardens, but they do not know how to eat it.

*   *   *[401]

Something for which God is to be much praised, with the prophet who said "wonderful is your name, Lord, in all the earth," is the abundance of trees that in this land His Majesty created, and all so unlike ours that up to now I have seen and of which I know—I speak of Yucatan, as elsewhere I have seen some that all have their uses and benefits for the Indians and the Spaniards alike.[402] There is a tree whose fruit is very much like round gourds from which the Indians make their cups; they are very good, and they make them very well painted and handsome.[403] Of this same type [*casta*], there is another which produces fruit smaller and very hard, from which they make other small cups for ointments and other purposes. There is another type that bears a little fruit with pits like filberts [*del cuexco*], from which they make fine beads, and whose shell is used for washing clothes as with soap, for thus it makes a lather. They cultivate greatly the incense tree for the devils [*demonios*], and they extract from it by cutting the bark with a stone, so the gum or resin runs out.[404] This tree is fresh, tall, and with fine leaves and shade, but its flower turns the wax black when there is any. There is a tree that grows in the wells, very handsome in height, fresh in leaves, and is marvelous the way it spreads its branches, which sprout from its trunk in a very orderly way, for it sprouts thrice *[f. 58v; figure A.46]*, in threes or

---

[400] Likely bush spinach (*Cnidoscolus chayamansa*) or *chaya* in Maya. These long-lived bushes produce highly nutritious dark, leafy green leaves.

[401] This is the thirteenth and final paragraph gap left by Scribe B, about four lines deep, surely intended for the insertion of a subheading that was forgotten. Atop the next folio (59r; Sec. 48), Scribe A resumes copying, and he seldom leaves paragraph breaks (there are only two, a single line deep each, over the rest of the manuscript).

[402] First person used in this sentence.

[403] Likely the calabash tree (*Crescentia cujete*) known in Maya as *luch*, still grown in Yucatan house gardens today in order to make hand-carved tortilleras and canteens.

[404] Copal trees, or *pom* in Maya (*Protium copal*), yield a golden-colored sap that burns readily.

more, around the tree, and thus they go on extending and growing their shoots.[405] There are also cedars, although not fine ones. There is a type of yellowish tree [*palo*], with veins like an oak, marvelously strong and very hard, and so stout that we have found them in the doors of the houses of Izamal, placed as lintels [*por vatientes*] and supporting all the weight on them.[406] There is another, very strong, from which they make bows and lances, and it is tawny in color. There is another, dark orange in color, from which they make staffs; it is very strong, and I think it is called brazil-wood [*brasil*]. There are many trees which they say are good for sickness of buboes, which they call Zon. There is a tree whose sap is poisonous and hurts when touched, and its shade is pestilential, especially if one sleeps under it. There is another which is covered in pairs of thorns, long and very hard and thick, where there are no birds, as they never rest on it nor can they even sit there. These thorns are all hollow at the trunk and always full of ants. There is a tree of great height and size, which bears a fruit like carob beans, filled with certain black pinenuts, that in time of need the Indians make into food, and from its roots they make buckets for drawing water from the wells and waterwheels [*norias*]. There are other trees from whose bark the Indians make small cups for taking water individually, and others from which they make ropes, and others whose bark they crush to make a broth to polish plastered walls and make them hard. There are very beautiful mulberry trees, which is good wood; and they have so many other trees for all purposes and uses, that it is astonishing. They have in the fields and the hills [*montes*] many different kinds of long wicker, although they are not the kind of wicker from which they make baskets; anyway, using these they secure their houses, and whatever else they need, and it is very useful and a marvelous thing. There is a tree whose sap is a singular medicine for taking care of teeth. There is another that bears a large fruit filled with a wool better for pillows than tow from the Alcarría.[407]

---

[405] The strangler fig, or *Ficus cotinifolia*, was the source of soft malleable bark that ancient Maya people processed into paper for codices.

[406] The mention of Izamal suggests strongly that this passage contains the observations of a Franciscan, and thus likely Landa himself, at least in part; it also confirms that the Account informs us about Maya culture in the sixteenth century—not in precontact times, despite the impression the manuscript often gives. If the Maya had indeed used wooden lintels in precontact Yucatan, and Izamal was indeed uninhabited by the early sixteenth century, such lintels may have been made of mahogany (*Cedrela odorata* or *kuyche'* in Maya) or chicozapote (*Manilkara zapota* or *cuyche* in Maya), both of which might have survived from the Classic period until the sixteenth century. We suggest the author refers to chicozapote, which has a lighter color than mahogany.

[407] Likely kapok, or *yaaxche* in Maya (*Ceiba pentandra*). The fruit pods of a mature kapok produce a silky fiber that can be spun into thread or used as batting in clothing, pillows, and beds. The reference to Alcarría region is possible evidence of Landa's authorship here, as his hometown of Cifuentes was in that region of Spain.

[f. 59r; figure A.47][408] Fearing to give insult to the fruit or to their trees, I have decided to put them by themselves. First, I will speak of the wine, as it is something that the Indians esteem highly, and therefore almost everyone planted it in their enclosures or in spaces around their houses. It is an ugly tree, and without more than its roots, with honey and water, they make their wine.[409] There is in this land certain wild vines bearing edible grapes, and there are many on the Cupul [*Kupul*] coast. There are plums of many kinds, some of them very tasty and healthy, and extremely different from ours, for they have little meat, and a large pit, the reverse of those that are here, by comparison. This tree produces its fruit before the leaves, and without flowers save for the fruit. There are many bananas, these having been brought by the Spaniards, as they did not have them previously. There is a very large tree that bears a large, longish fruit, and fat, whose meat is reddened, and very good to eat; it does not produce a flower, but only its fruit, very small and growing little by little. There is another tree, very leafy and beautiful, whose leaves never fall, and without producing a flower it produces a fruit, so much sweeter than the one above, small, very dainty, delicious to eat, and very delicate; and some are better than others, so much better that they would be much valued if brought over here; they call them *ya* in their language. There is another very beautiful and fresh tree that never loses its leaves, and it produces some small, delicious figs that they call *ox*.[410] Another tree is marvelously beautiful and fresh, producing a fruit like large eggs. The Indians pick it green and ripen it in ashes, and once ripe it lasts marvelously and is sweet to eat and cloys like egg yolks.[411] Another tree produces another yellow fruit also, but not as large as the one above, and softer and sweeter; *[f. 59v]* this one, when eaten, leaves a pit like a soft hedgehog, which is worth seeing. Another fresh and beautiful tree produces a fruit more or less like hazelnuts, with its husk—inside the husk—is a fruit like cherries, with a large pit. The Indians call these Uayam, and the Spaniards Guayas. There is a fruit which the Spaniards brought, good to eat and healthful, which they call Guayavas [guavas].[412] In the sierras there are two types of trees. One bears a fruit as large as a good pear, very green, with a thick skin; these they ripen by

---

[408] Here Scribe B stops and Scribe A returns, being the copyist for the remaining eight folios (fs. 59–66; secs. 48–52).

[409] The *baalche'* or balche tree, or *Lonchocarpus violaceus* (as detailed in previous notes; also see Chuchiak, "It Is Their Drinking"; Vail and Dedrick, "Human-Deity Relationships").

[410] The *ya* and *ox* described here are likely *Achras sapota* L. (a species of sapodilla) and *Brosmium alicastrum* Swartz (breadnut), respectively.

[411] Likely eggfruit, or canistel (*Pouteria campechiana*).

[412] Still called *uayam* and *guaya* (in Spanish and English) today, this is the *Talisia olivaeformis*.

entres / omas, a troços a la redonda del arbol, y assi se va
cada estendiendo y la guia creciendo. Ay cedros aunque
no de los finos. Ay vna casta de palo algo amarillo y da-
ñetoso como enzina amarauilla fuerte y de mucha dura
y tan rezio q. lo hallamos en las puertas de los hedificios de
y çamal puestos por vatientes y cargada la obra toda sobrellos.
Ay otro fortissimo y hazian del los arcos y las lanças y es de
color leonado. Otro ay de color naranjado escuro de que hazian bordones, es muy fuerte, y creo se dize esbrasil. Ay muchos arboles de los que dizen son buenos para la enfermedad
de buas llamanle Zon. Ay vn arbol que lleua leche la qual
es rejalgar y llaga quanto toca y su sombra es muy pestifera
especial si duermē a ella. Ay otro que todo el esta lleno de
pares de espinas largas y muy duras y gordas que no ay aue
q enel sarnas repose ni se puede enel assentar, tiene aquellas
espinas todas agujeradas por el tronco y llenas siempre de hormigas. Ay vn arbol de muy grande altura y grandeza lleua vna fruta como algarrouas llena de vnos piñones negros
y q en tpo de nescesidad hazen della los Indios comida y
hazen de sus rayzes cubos para sacar agua de los pozos y
las norias. Otros arboles ay de cuyas cortezas hazen los Indios cubillos para sacar agua para si, y otros de q hazen las so-
gas y otros de las cortezas de los quales majadas hazen vn
caldo para bruir conel los encalados y hazelos muy fuertes. Ay muy hermosas moreras y es buena madera y tienen tantos otros arboles y de todo seruij. y prouecho q espa-
ta. Tienen en los campos y montes muchas differencias de
mimbres muy largos aunque no son mimbres de los quales
hazen cestas de todas maneras y con los quales atan sus
casas y quando son menester, y es muy grande el seruicio
q desto tienen amarauilla. Ay vn arbol cuya leche es singular medicina para enxarinar los dientes. Ay otro q lleua
cierta fruta grande llena de lana mejor para almohadas
q las estopas del alcarria.

Temiendo hazer agrauio a la fruta, o a sus arboles
los e acordado poner por si. y primero dire del vino
como cosa que los Indios mucho estimauan, y por eso
lo plantauan casi todos en sus corales, o espacios de sus
casas. Es arbol feo, y sin mas fruta de hazer sus raizes, y miel
y agua. Ay en esta tierra ciertas parras siluestres, y
llaman comestibles unas, y ay muchas en la costa de
Kupul. Ay ciruelos de muchas diferencias de ciruelas
y algunas muy sabrosas, y sanas, y differentissimas
de las nuestras, ca tienen poca carne, y gran cuesco
al reues de los que aca ay aunque lo compararon eesa. este
arbol las fruras, antes que las hojas, y sin flor sino la
fruta. Ay muchos platanos, y aun los llamado los Españoles que no los auia antes. Ay vn arbol muy grande
el qual lleua vna fruta grande algo larga, y gorda
cuya carne es colorada, y muy buena de comer, no
echa flor sino la propia fruta muy pequenita, y va
cresciendo su poco a poco. Ay otro arbol muy frondo
so, y hermoso, y que nunca se le cae la hoja, y sin echar
flor echa vna fruta de tanta y mas dulcura que
la de arriba pequeña, muy golosa, y gustosa de comer
y muy delicada, y ay vnos mejores que otros, y tan
to mejores que serian muy preciados si aca los tuui
essemos. llamanles en la lengua Ya. Ay otro muy hermoso, y fresco arbol que nunca pierde la hoja, y
lleua vnos higuillos sabrosos que llaman Ox. Otro arbol
ay a marauilla hermoso, y fresco, y lleua la fruta
como guebos grandes. Cogen la verde los Indios, y ma-
duran la en cenizas, y madura queda a marauilla
y al comer es dulce, y empalaga como yemas de
guebos. Otro arbol lleua otra fruta essi amarilla
y no tan grande como estotra, y mas blanda y dulce

beating them all on a stone, after which they have a very singular flavor. The other bears fruit very large, the size of pineapples, and they are delicious to eat, for they are juicy and acidic, and have many small pits which are not healthful. There is a tree that grows only in the open, never among other trees, only alone, whose bark is very good for tanning hides, and serves as sumac [*çumac*]; it bears a small tasty yellow fruit, greatly coveted by the women. There is a very large and fresh tree that the Indians call *on*. It bears a fruit like small gourds, largish, most soft and with the taste of butter; it is fatty and is of great sustenance and nourishment.[413] It has a large pit, a delicate husk, and is eaten sliced like a melon, and with salt. There are some thistles, very spiny and ugly, always growing on stems attached to other trees, and winding around them. These bear a fruit whose skin is red, shaped something like an artichoke, and soft to open, and without any spines.[414] The flesh inside is white, with many small [*f. 6or*] black seeds; it is sweet and marvelously delicious, and so watery that it melts in the mouth. It is eaten in rounds like an orange, and with salt, and as many as the Indians find in the forests [*montes*] the Spaniards eat. There is a spongy tree, ugly but very large, that produces a sort of large fruit full of very delicious yellow innards, with little pits like hemp seeds but larger; these are healthy for the urine. From this fruit, they make a good jam; the tree drops its leaves after the fruit has passed. There is a small, rather spiny tree that produces a fruit shaped like a slender cucumber, somewhat long; it is somewhat similar in taste to the thistle, and is likewise eaten with salt, in slices, and the seeds are like those of cucumbers, very small and many and tender. If by some accident a hole is made in the fruit while still on the tree, a little gum collects, smelling slightly like civet. It is also a good fruit for the monthly sickness of women. There is another tree whose flower is full of a gentle odor, and whose fruit is like what we here in Spain call blancmange; and there are many different kinds of it, bearing fruit that is good or better.[415] There is a little tree that the Indians cultivate in their houses, which produces certain spiny husks like chestnuts, but not so large nor so rough. They open when ripe and contain small seeds which they use—as do the Spaniards too—to color their stews, as one does with saffron; the color is fine and stains a great deal.[416] I am certain that there remain yet other fruits, but I shall however speak of those of the palms, of which there are two types. The leaves of one are used to cover [thatch] the houses, and they are [*f. 6ov*] very long and slender; they produce great bunches of a much-coveted

---

[413] Likely the avocado (*Persea americana*) (sometimes cited as *Persea gratissima*).

[414] Likely dragonfruit, or pitaya (*Hylocereus undatus*). The fruit is known as *wob* in Maya.

[415] Likely the annonaceae family, including soursop or guanabana (*Hylocereus undatus*), cerimoya or anona (*Annona reticulate*), and sugar apple or saramuyo (*Annona squamosal*).

[416] The annatto shrub, known as achiote (*Bixa Orellana*) or *ku'u up* in Maya.

black fruit like chickpeas, of which the Indian women are very fond.[417] The other kind is a low, very spiny palm whose leaves serve no purpose as they are very short and thin; they produce great bunches of a round green fruit, as big as pigeons' eggs. When the husk is removed, there remains a very hard pit, inside of which is a round seed the size of a hazelnut, very tasty and useful in times of famine; they make of it a hot food which they drink in the mornings, and if needed, one could flavor anything with its milk as with that of almonds.

*   *   *[418]

They gather a marvelously great amount of cotton, and it grows in all parts of the land, there being two types.[419] One is sown every year, and its little tree does not last each year, and it is small. Of the other, its tree lasts five or six years; and they all produce fruit in the form of pods like nuts, with a green husk that opens in four parts when its time comes, and there inside is the cotton. They used to gather cochineal, which is said to be the finest in the Indies, as the land is dry; and the Indians still gather in some parts a little of it.[420] There are colors of great diversity made from the dyes of certain trees, and of flowers; but because the Indians did not know how to perfect them with gums which give them the medium [*temple*] they need in order not to fade, so they fade. But those who gather the silk have now discovered remedies, and it is said that they make them as perfect as in the places where they make them most perfect.

---

[417] Note that the author reserves the term *golosa* or *golosilla* exclusively for the taste that Maya women (*las Indias*) have for certain fruit; it implies a strong craving driven by a sweet tooth, and thus on both occasions we have glossed the term with the verb "covet." The leaves used for roof thatching are a type of palm (*xa'an* in Mayan; *Sabal yapa*), as detailed in an earlier note.

[418] Unlike the large and frequent paragraph spaces used by Scribe B, Scribe A employed small and few such spaces; this is his penultimate one here.

[419] Cotton was a fundamental component of the precontact economy of Mesoamerica, and Yucatan was a primary area of production. Low genetic divergence among domesticated pools supports the hypothesis of domestication of *G. hirsutum* in northern Yucatan, and indicates both the chronological depth and intensity with which Maya people utilized cotton (Coppens d'Eeckenbrugge and Lacape, "Distribution and Differentiation"). Production of cotton cloth is indicated primarily by the presence of ceramic spindle whorls during the precontact period, and the frequency of these artifacts increased throughout the Postclassic period, suggesting intensified production of cloth in household contexts (Ardren et al., "Cloth Production"). Finding that a lively trade in cotton existed when they arrived, Spanish colonists made cotton *mantas* (blankets used to make clothing) a tribute item, and cotton thus became a core part of the economy in the colonized regions of the peninsula where it grew (see Patch, "[Almost] Forgotten Plants"; *Maya and Spaniard in Yucatán*, 81–91, 173–81).

[420] The Yucatec Maya called cochineal *mukay*. For Tozzer's comments on items from cochineal to the house mouse, see *Landa's* Relación, n1100–n1147.

[Sec. 49] [f. 61r] The abundance which this land has in birds is a great marvel, and so diverse that he is to be praised who filled it with them as a blessing. They have domestic fowls, which they raise in their houses like their hens, and cocks in great quantities though they are troublesome to raise. They have taken to raising Spanish birds, hens, and they do raise many wonderfully and at all times of the year there are chickens from them. Some people raise doves, as tame as ours, and they multiply greatly. They raise a certain kind of large white mallard duck, which I think came to them from Peru, for the plumage, for which they frequently pluck their breasts; and they want that plumage for the embroidery of their clothing.[421] There is a great diversity of songbirds [*paxaros*] and many are very pretty, and among them there are two types of very attractive little turtledoves, and some are very small indeed, and domesticated for raising tame. There is a little bird of as sweet a song as the nightingale, which they call Ixyalchamil. It hangs around the walls of houses that they have in the orchards and in the trees of the orchards. There is another large bird, of a very pretty dark green color, its tail does not have more than two long feathers, and with no more than the middle, and to the end [they have] hairs on them.[422] Its home is in the buildings, and it does not come out except for in the mornings. There are other birds that in their mischief and body are like magpies, great yellers at the people who pass by on the roads so that they are not left to go in secret. There are many house martins, or swallows, and I have thought that they were martins because they do not grow up in houses like swallows. There is a big, very beautiful, multicolored bird, who has a big, very strong beak and *[f. 61v]* it is always around the dry trees, making holes in the bark with its nails, accosting it with its beak so toughly that one can hear it a good distance away, in order to extract woodworms, which they eat. These birds make so many holes in the trees that a sieve is made, so the woodworms breed up high. There are many field birds, all for eating, for there are three kinds of very pretty, small doves. There are some birds that are all similar to the partridges of Spain, except they have very tall legs; although red, they are not good to eat; they are nevertheless marvelously tame, if they are raised in one's house. There are wonderfully many quail, and they are somewhat bigger than ours, and they are particularly [good] for eating. They fly infrequently and the Indians catch them perched in the trees, with dogs and with lances, and they

---

[421] There are frequent mentions of birds, plumage, and feather work in the Account: see folios 16r (sec. 11), 21r–v (sec. 26), 24r (sec. 29), 26v (sec. 32), 36v–37r (sec. 40), 42r (sec. 40), 43r (sec. 40), and the passage that follows on f. 61r (sec. 49). The repetition of the topic, with the same comments made slightly differently in different sections of the manuscript, reflects its multiple authors and sources.

[422] The turquoise-browed motmot (*Eumomota superciliosa*), famous for plucking all its own tail feathers out save those at the very end, is known as *toh* in Maya.

remove them by the neck. It is very tasty game. There are many brownish pheasants, and spotted ones of a reasonable size. They are not as good to eat as the Italian ones. There is a big bird like the hens from there [Yucatan] that they call *kanbul* [*Cambul*], a very great beauty, very fearful, and good to eat. There is another that they call *Cox*, equally big, with a violent step and shimmy, and the males are all black like a coal tit, and they have some very pretty crowns of curly feathers. Their eyelids are yellow and very pretty. There are many turkeys, and even though they do not have as beautiful plumage as those of Spain, the ones they have [in Yucatan] are very smart, of a great beauty, as big as the roosters of the Indians, and they are as good to eat. There are many other birds that even though I have seen them, I do not remember them.

[f. 62r] All the large ones the Indians kill with arrows in the trees, they steal the eggs, and they take the hens and raise them to be very tame. There are three or four kinds of parrots, small ones and large ones, and so many flocks of them that they do a lot of damage to the sowed fields. There are other nocturnal birds, like owls, little owls, and blind hens. It is an amusing thing to walk at night, for they go long stretches in the road taking flight in front of the men. It greatly vexes the Indians, who take it as a bad omen, and it is the same with other birds. There are some very carnivorous birds that the Spaniards call turkey buzzards, and the Indians *Kuch*, which are black and have necks and heads like the hens of there [Yucatan]. The beak is long with a hook. They are very dirty, as they always go into the stables, and in places for the purging of their belly, eating it, and looking for dead meat to eat. It is an established thing that their nest has not been found and it is not known where they grow up, for they say that some live lives of two hundred years, or more. Others think that they are actually crows. They smell dead flesh so well that when the deer that the Indians are killing run away from them wounded, they have no better solution than climbing into tall trees to look where these birds have gone, and it is certain that they will find their kill there. So great is the diversity of birds of prey that it is a marvel. There are small eagles, very pretty goshawks, and very great hunters. There are very beautiful sparrow hawks, larger than those here in Spain. There are fanners and sakers and others; since I am not a hunter, I have no memory [of them]. On the sea, the infinity, variety, and diversity are something to admire, and the *[f. 62v]* masses that there are of game birds and other kinds of birds, as is the beauty of each of the types. There are some birds as big as brown ostriches and with a larger beak. They always go in the water looking for fish, and so when they sense the fish, they rise up in the air and fall down with great momentum onto the fish with a peck to its neck; they never make a shallow attempt; and they keep swimming during the fight. They swallow the fish alive without cooking or scaling it.[423] There are some large, skinny birds that fly a lot and very high, with

---

[423] Although it is never explicitly stated, the author seems to have transitioned in this sentence

tails divided into two points. Their fat is marvelously medicinal for scars from wounds and for tetanus of the limbs, caused by wounds. There are some ducks that can stay under the water for a very long time in order to fish for their food. They are very fluffy, and they have on their beaks a hook with which they fish. There are other small, little ducks of great beauty that are called Maxix; they are very docile and if they are raised in a house they do not know how to run away. There are many kinds of heron and egret, some white and others brownish grey, some large and others small, and [they are found] in the Laguna de Términos [*las lagunas de terminos*]. There are many very bright red ones that seem to be the color of ground cochineal, and so many kinds of little birds, tiny and big, that their masses and diversity is admirable. Moreover, to see them all carefully looking for something to eat on that beach, some entering the waves of the bubbling spring of the ocean, and afterwards running away from it, others looking for food in the waves, some taking it from others by getting to it more quickly, it is so amazing to see that all the things that God has provided, I am filled with blessings.

[*Sec. 50*] [*f. 63r*] [The] Indians have lacked many animals, and they have especially lacked those which are more necessary for the service of man; but they had others, most of which they used for their sustenance, and none of them were domesticated save for the dogs—the ones that neither know how to bark nor do harm to men; but in hunting, yes, *ca*, they raise partridges and other birds, and follow deer a great deal and some of them are great trackers. They are small and the Indians ate them at feasts, and I think now they are ashamed and consider it lowly to eat them. They say that they taste good.[424] There are tapirs in only one corner [*cornejal*] of the country, that which is behind the sierras of Campeche, and there are many, and the Indians have told me that they are of many colors—that there are silver-gray, and dappled, bay, and chestnut, and very white, and black. They go more in that piece of the country than in all the rest, because it is an animal very fond of water, and around there are many lagoons in those hills [*montes*] and sierras. It is an animal of the size of medium-sized mules, very fleet, and has a cloven hoof like the ox, and a little trumpet on its snout in which it keeps water. The Indians considered it an act of great bravery to kill them, and they preserved as a trophy [*memoria*] the hide, or parts of it, down to the great-grandsons—as I saw myself. They call it Tzimin and from these they have given their name to horses. There are small lions and tigers,[425] and the Indians kill them with a bow, lying in wait up in the trees. There is a certain

to talk about Indigenous customs, not those of the seabirds.

[424] The general Mayan term for dog is *pek*, but this species was *kikbil* (*Canis familiaris*), raised for food all over Mesoamerica.

[425] We translate the Spanish terms to their English cognates, but these wild cats are actually cougars and jaguars (the *Felis concolor Mayensis* and the *Felis onça goldmani*; the latter the Maya called *balam*).

kind of bear, or whatever it is,[426] marvelously fond of robbing the hives; it is brown with black spots, and *[f. 63v]* long in body, and short in legs, and round-headed. There is a certain type of little wild goat, small and very light and darkish in color. There are pigs, small animals, and very different from ours, for they have their navel on their backs, and they really smell.[427] There are so many deer it is marvelous, and they are small, and the meat is good food. There is an infinite number of rabbits, like ours in every way except for the snout, which is long and not at all blunt, but like a sheep. They are large and good to eat. There is a little animal, very sad in nature, which always goes in caverns and little hiding places and by night, and for hunting it the Indians set a certain trap in which they catch it; it is similar to a hare, and goes by leaps, and is timid. It has front teeth that are very long and thin; its little tail is even smaller than a hare's and is of a dark greenish color. It is wonderfully tame and amiable and is called Zub. There is another small little animal, like a newly born piglet, like so in its forepaws and snout, [it is] a great rooter. It is completely covered with funny shells so that it seems like nothing except a horse in complete armor, with only the ears, front and back paws outside [the armor] and its neck, and forehead covered with the shells [also].[428] It is very good and tender to eat. There are other animals like little dogs. They have heads that are made like pigs, a long tail, and are the color of smoke and marvelously slow, so much so that they are often caught by their tail.[429] They are very greedy and at night they go into the houses, and the chickens don't escape *[f. 64r]* their little-by-little [advance]. The females give birth to fourteen to eighteen young like little weasels, without any coat of fur, and they are marvelously clumsy. God provided the mothers with a strange pouch in their bellies in which they protect [the babies], because a hide-like thing *[cuero]* sprouts long across the belly, reaching between the teats. When it joins one to the other the teats remain closed, and when she wants to open it, there each one of babies latches on to the teat's nipple in their mouth. When they have all been latched on, those flanks or hides overlap, and [the mother] squeezes them strongly so that no one will fall out. With them loaded so, she goes around there to look for food. She raises them like this until they have fur and can walk. There are foxes that are in every way like those here except that they aren't as large, nor have such a

[426] Landa is right to be unsure of the name of what is popularly known as a honey bear or *oso colmenero* ("hive bear"), called *zamhol* in Mayan, and actually a tayra (*Tayra barbara senex*).
[427] This small peccary is named after the peninsula which was originally its only native region: collared peccary; *Pecari angulatus yucatanensis*.
[428] This is clearly the armadillo that is native to Yucatan (*uech* in Mayan).
[429] This, again, is a clear description, and refers to the native possum (*och* in Mayan; or as they are typically mostly white, *sacoch* or *zacoch*; *Didelphis yucatanensis*).

beautiful tail.[430] There is an animal they call *chic*, marvelously mischievous, as large as a dog and with a snout like a suckling pig. The Indian women rear them, and they don't leave anything that they don't root out or disturb. It is an incredible thing that they are marvelously good at getting past the Indian women. They delouse them and they always reach for the women, and they can't see anything in a man other than death. There are a lot of them, they always walk as a herd in a row, one after the other, with their snouts placed underneath the tail of the other. They very much destroy the maize fields where they enter. There is a little animal like a white squirrel, with dark yellow stripes around it which they call *pay*.[431] It defends itself from those who follow or harm it by urinating on itself, and [the urine] that it makes is of such a horrible smell that there is no one who could endure it nor [*f. 64v*] [can] anything that [it touches] be worn again. They have told me that it is not urine but instead a little perspiration that it carries in a little pouch [on its] back. Whatever it is, their arms defend it [so well] that it is a wonder [when] the Indians kill one of them. There are many pretty little squirrels, moles, weasels, and many rats like those of Spain except they have very long snouts.[432]

The Indians have not lost, but instead have gained a lot with the coming of the Spanish nation, even in that which is less, even though it is a lot, advancing for them many things of which have arrived, the time comes to enjoy them in earnest. And now they have started to enjoy and use many of them. There are a lot of good horses, and many female and male mules, donkeys do not propagate well, and I think it is so [because] they are too gentle with them, because without fail they are a stubborn beast [that needs to be] controlled, and too much coddling does them harm. There are a lot of beautiful cows, many pigs, sheep, ewes, goats, and our dogs that are worth their service; and in the Indies they have counted them among the beneficial things. The cats are very beneficial and necessary there, and the Indians love them a lot. Hens, pigeons, oranges, limes, citrons, grapevines, pomegranates, figs, guava trees, date trees, bananas, melons, and the rest of the vegetables. Only the melons and squashes are grown from their own seeds, as the others require new seeds from Mexico. Now, silk is produced, and it is very good.[433] Tools have been brought to

---

[430] For identifying notes on these animals, from fox to ferrets, see Tozzer, *Landa's* Relación, n1141–n1146.

[431] The author refers here to a skunk, which was native to Yucatan. The encomendero Juan de Aguilar, writing in 1580, succinctly described this skunk: "There is an animal they call *pay* and we skunk [*zorrillo*], colored black and white; these, when something is trying to catch them, give off a perverse and foul smell which no one can withstand" (*Relación de Mama y Kantemo*, 1580, in RHGY, Vol. 1, p. 115).

[432] After this word, the copyist started on the next line accidentally or for some unclear reason.

[433] Note that the experiment in silk production in colonial Yucatan was begun at the end of the 1540s but lasted only into the 1570s.

them to be used in the mechanical tasks and they produce them for themselves very well. The use of money and of many other Spanish things, even though they have existed and could have existed without them, is no comparison, [that] they live more like men with them and with greater assistance in their manual labors and for the relief of them, which according to the statement of the philosopher, "Art assists nature."⁴³⁴

[f. 65r] [Sec. 51] Not only has God given increase to the Indians by means of our Spanish nation in the above things, which are so necessary for the service of man; but they do not pay for them only with what they give and will give to the Spaniards, for there have gone to them without payment those things which cannot be bought or earned, which are justice and Christianity, and the peace in which they now live, for which they owe more to Spain and to its Spaniards and principally to its most Catholic kings, who with such continual care, and with such great Christianity have provided them and still provide them with these two things, than they do to their first founders, evil fathers who spawned them; since we know that their fathers spawned [*engendraron*] them in sin, as sons of wrath, and that Christianity spawns them in grace and to enjoy eternal life, their first founders did not know how to give them order that they might avoid so many errors, and such great ones, like those in which they have lived.⁴³⁵ Justice has removed them from those [errors], by means of preaching, and she must ensure that they not return to them, and if they should return, to remove them from them. With good reason, then, can Spain glory in God, since God has chosen her among other nations as the remedy [*remedio*] of so many peoples, for which they owe her much more than they do their own founders or progenitors; for as indeed the blessed Saint Gregory says, it would not do us much good to be born unless we were to be redeemed by Christ's blessing. We might say more or less the same with Anselmo; what does being redeemed bring us, unless we obtain the fruit of the redemption, which is our salvation, and thus they err much who say because the Indians have received injustices, vexations, and bad examples from the Spaniards, it would have been better not to *[f. 65v]* have discovered them, since the injustices and vexations were greater which they were continually inflicting on

⁴³⁴ Here Landa may reference his knowledge of M. Fabio Quintiliano, an Iberian Roman philosopher during the age of the Emperor Domitian, who wrote "There is nothing perfect, except for when Art assists nature" (Fabio Quintiliano, *Instititionum*, 1527, Libro 11, Capítulo 3). Fabio Quintiliano himself was influenced by Cicero's statement that "*Notatio naturae, et animadversio perperit artem*" [Art is born of the observation and investigation of nature] (Marcus Tullius Cicero, *De oratore*, 183).

⁴³⁵ In order to best retain a sense of the original half-page-long sentence—which one might imagine as part of a sermon by Landa (whom we presume is the author here), with "they" as "you"—we have kept this as one sentence, adding only a few additional punctuation marks.

each other, killing each other, enslaving each other, and sacrificing each other to the devils [*demonios*]; if they have received a bad example, or from some are receiving it now, the king has remedied it and remedies it each day with his magistrates [*justicias*] and with the continual preaching and persevering opposition by the friars [*religiosos*] to those who have given or are giving it [bad example], all the more because scandals and bad examples are necessary to evangelical doctrine; and thus I believe it [bad example] has been among this people so that they can tell the gold apart from the clay, the grain from the chaff, to esteem virtue as they have done, seeing with the philosopher how virtues shine among vices, and the virtuous among the vicious, and he who has given them the bad example or scandal has his own terrible affliction, unless he atones for them with good deeds. And thou, dearest reader [*carissimo lector*], ask it also of God for yourself, and receive my modest work [*mi poco de trabajo*], pardoning its defects, and remembering when you find them that not only do I not defend them—as St. Augustine says that Tullio said of himself,[436] who said that he had never uttered a word which he wished to revoke, and this does not please the saint, since error is so natural to men—but in the beginning, before you find them, you will find them in my introductions or prologues revoked and confessed, and thus you will judge, as the blessed Augustine did in his epistle to Marcella, the difference between him who confesses his error or fault, and he who defends it, and you will pardon mine, as the prophet says, as God pardons mine and yours, saying, "Lord, I said that I will confess my wickedness and injustice, and immediately you have pardoned it."[437]

*   *   *[438]

[*Sec. 52*] The historian of the things of the Indies,[439] to whom [*f. 66r*] much is due for his labor and the light he shed on them, said, speaking of the things of Yucatan, that they used slings in warfare, and fire-hardened spears; but of the things that

---

[436] Tertullian (according to Tozzer, *Landa's* Relación); Tullius (according to Gates, *Yucatán*, 112). We think Gates was right, and this likely refers to Marcus Tullius Cicero, as St. Augustine indeed uses Cicero as an important source for his own work on rhetoric.

[437] After this sentence, and above the final line of this folio (f. 65) there is a blank line or one-line space, suggesting that the scribe had copied out the final page of Landa's *recopilación*, but then found another page of Landa's notes—the passage that follows (65v–66v; Sec. 52), in which Landa argues with "the historian of the things of the Indies" and refers the reader back to numbered chapters and paragraphs of the lost larger work.

[438] Scribe A's final, small paragraph break.

[439] The historian to whom he refers (later in the section "our historian") is possibly Gonzalo Fernández de Oviedo, but more likely Francisco López de Gómara—as we have noted earlier when the "Historian General of the Indies" is mentioned in the text (Sec. 28; f. 22v).

they used in warfare, I left them said in chapter 101 [*CI*],[440] and I am not surprised that it seemed to Francisco Hernández de Córdoba and Juan de Grijalva that the stones the Indians threw at them when they were at Champoton were discharged from slings, since they retreated. But they [the Maya] did not know how to pull on a sling, nor did they know of them, although they throw a stone very hard and fast, and they aim by throwing with the left arm and [pointing] the index finger where they are throwing. He also says that the Indians are circumcised, and how this is will be found in chapter 99 [*LXXXXIX*].[441] He says that there are hares, and what those are like you will find in paragraph 15 [*XV*] of the last chapter. He says there are partridges, and what kinds, and what they are like you will find in paragraph 24 [*XIII*] of the last chapter.[442] Our historian moreover says that they found at the Cape of Cotoch [Cape Catoche] crosses among the dead, and idols, but he does not believe it, because if they were from Spaniards who were migrating from Spain when it was lost, they would surely have touched on other lands first, as there are many.[443] I do not—for this reasoning does not convince me—I do not believe it, because no other places are known where it could have happened, and to where they could have arrived before coming to Yucatan, whether they arrived or not, not even as little [is known] as [about this place] of Yucatan. But also, why I do not believe it is because when Francisco Hernández and Grijalva arrived at Cotoch, they did not walk about digging up the dead, but went looking for gold among the living. And also I believe in the virtue of the cross, and in the malice of the devil, who could not bear to see

---

[440] This reference to a "chapter CI" or "101" appears to be to a numbered chapter in Landa's own larger work, suggesting at the very least that his *recopilación* was organized in that way, possibly in preparation for a publication that never happened (there is no chapter 101 on warfare or on Yucatan in any of the possible published sources for this section, such as López de Gómara's *La Istoria de las Yndias*).

[441] Landa already pointed out López de Gómara's error here, on f. 22v (Sec. 28) of the Account ("the Historian General of the Indies was deceived into saying that they practiced circumcision"); he is likely referencing Gómara's *La Istoria de las Yndias* (Vol. 1, Chapter LIV, *Costumbres de Yucatan*). Oviedo does briefly mention circumcision ("this abomination is better forgotten so that it may not be held in memory") but in Bk. 17, Ch. XVII of his *Historia general*, not yet published in Landa's lifetime. Thus, the reference to a "chapter 99" above must be to Landa's own lost larger work.

[442] Here Landa is referencing the fact that his original manuscript was divided into chapters and had paragraph markings and numbers.

[443] We gloss *despoblarse* as "migrate," but Tozzer chose "exile" and adds "(by the Moors)" to "when it was lost" (Gates, presumably confused by the reference, mistranslated and reduced the phrase to "when they perished" [*Yucatán*, 113]); Tozzer was probably right that Landa was thinking in terms of deep Iberian history, when Muslim invasions of the eighth century defeated Christian kingdoms across the peninsula (for a discussion of all the things Landa does *not* say about crosses in Yucatan, see Tozzer, *Landa's* Relación, n1153).

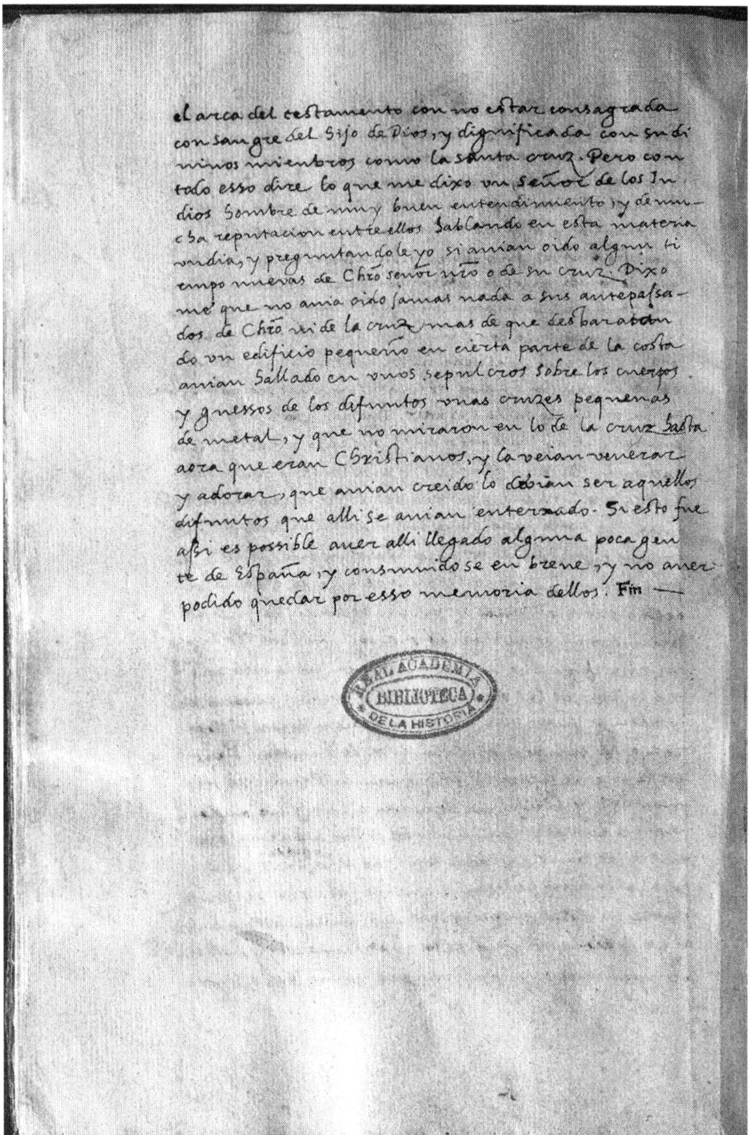

el arca del testamento con no estar consagrada
con sangre del hijo de Dios, y dignificada con sus divinos
miembros como la santa cruz. Pero con
todo esso dize lo que me dixo un señor de los Indios
hombre de muy buen entendimiento y de mucha
reputacion entre ellos hablando en esta materia
yndia, y preguntandole yo si avian oido algun tiempo
nuevas de Christo señor nuestro o de su cruz. Dixo
me que no avia oido jamas nada a sus antepassados
de Christo ni de la cruz mas de que desbarataron
do un edificio pequeño en cierta parte de la costa
avian hallado en unos sepulcros sobre los cuerpos
y guessos de los difuntos unas cruzes pequeñas
de metal, y que no miraron en lo de la cruz hasta
aora que eran christianos, y la veian venerar
y adorar, que avian creido lo debian ser aquellos
difuntos que alli se avian enterrado. Si esto fue
assi es possible aver alli llegado alguna poca gen
te de España, y consumidose en breve, y no aver
podido quedar por esso memoria dellos. Fin ——

Figure A.48. f. 66v, the final textual page of the Account.

a cross amongst the idols, in fear that miraculously one day its virtue would break them, and he would be chased away and vanquished [*confundiera*], as was done to Dagon [*f. 66v; figure A.48*] by the Ark of the Covenant [*testamento*], despite neither being consecrated with the blood of the son of God, nor dignified by his divine limbs as was the holy cross. But beside all this, I will say what a lord of the Indians told me, a man of fine understanding and much reputation among them. Speaking on this matter one day, and I having asked him whether he had heard at any time news of Christ our lord, or of his cross; he told me that he had never heard anything from his ancestors about either Christ or the cross, except that once while dismantling a small building on a certain part of the coast, they found in some graves, on the bodies and bones of the dead, some small metal crosses. But as they had not seen anything of the cross until now, when they became Christians, and saw it venerated and worshipped, they believed that those dead men that had been buried there must also have been [Christians]. If that was so, it is possible that a few people from Spain arrived there and died out so quickly that no memory of them could be left behind. The end.[444]

---

[444] A different copyist added "*Fin*——" at the end of the line here (roughly halfway down f. 66v); this passage (f. 66v; Sec. 52) is, of course, not much of an ending, and appears to have been tacked on by copyists, with the previous passage (f. 65v; sec. 51) serving more effectively as some kind of end to the manuscript.

PART II

Essays

The seven essays that follow are designed both to provide context for readers unfamiliar with sixteenth-century Yucatan and the history of the Landa-attributed Account, and to offer some analysis for scholars who may be very familiar with that context. Our solution to what we call "the Landa conundrum" in our Introduction is effectively further fleshed out in these essays. At the same time, we hope to persuade specialists that the Account is not the book by Landa for which it is has long been taken, but that its true nature makes it a far richer source—albeit on the sixteenth-century Maya and the dynamics of early colonialism, rather than on the precontact Maya (an argument we hope holds interest for Landa novices too). We have slotted our most technical essays, on the nature of the Account, at the end.

https://doi.org/10.5876/9781646424245.p002

I

The Maya of Yucatan and the Spanish Invasions

When the Spanish Conquest of Yucatan finally happened, it happened quickly. That statement could hardly be further from the truth, but it is the impression given by the Account. Some twenty pages into the manuscript (as it is currently sequenced and bound), the author picks up the narrative of Spanish efforts to establish a colony in the peninsula. What amounts to a little more than a page of handwritten text was converted by Brasseur and others into a chapter, titled (in Gates's version) "State of Yucatan after the Departure of the Spaniards. Don Francisco, Son of the Admiral Montejo, Re-establishes the Spanish Rule in Yucatan."[1] Aside from an odd error—Montejo the elder was not an *almirante*, but an *adelantado*, holder of a royal license to invade, conquer, and settle[2]—the modern editors put some spin on the narrative by using the verb "re-establishes." Does the page that follows justify that word choice? What impression does the passage give of the Spanish-Maya encounter? And how does that impression differ from our understanding of that encounter?

[1] Gates, *Yucatán*, 23; Account, f. 11r (Sec. 14).
[2] Gates consistently mistranslates *adelantado* as "admiral." For the original title and concession of a "conquest contract" or *capitulación*, with its powers and limitations, to Montejo the elder, see *Real Cédula de capitulación con Francisco de Montejo, vecino de México para la conquista de Yucatán*, AGI, Indiferente General, 415, libro 1, fs. 86v–94v. Although very dated, Hill, "Office of Adelantado," remains an important work on the *adelantado* system. As Hill (656) and others noted, Montejo received the title of *adelantado* for him and his heirs in perpetuity; most conquistadors only received the title for the limit of one or two lifetimes.

Before turning in detail to explore and explain how and why the Account is often a misleading and easily misunderstood source on the history of early-sixteenth-century Yucatan—despite the fact that Landa lived there in the same century—let us summarize the essential events. In the following three paragraphs, one for each *entrada*, we stick to incontrovertible facts (e.g., the holder of the peninsula's *adelantado* license was Francisco de Montejo the elder). Those three paragraphs are followed by a more interpretive, analytical summary.

Spanish efforts to conquer the peninsula thus comprised three invasion campaigns or *entradas*. Prior to the three *entradas*, Yucatec Mayas experienced less intrusive contact with Spaniards, ranging from a 1511 shipwreck on the northeast coast (from which one survivor was rescued eight years later, as discussed in the Account) to battles on the western coast in 1517 and 1518—followed by a more peaceful encounter with the Cortés-led expedition on Cozumel in 1519, marred by Pedro de Alvarado's plundering of one of the island's towns. The first *entrada*, led by Montejo the elder as *adelantado* and Alonso Dávila, began in 1527 at Cozumel, and ended in failure and retreat of the survivors in 1528; when Montejo sailed to Mexico, he left Dávila with a small contingent on the eastern coast.[3] The expedition had not made it further than a relatively small region in the northeast, and most died from sickness or from wounds acquired in battles at the Maya cities of Ake and Chauaca.

The second *entrada* was launched from the other side of the peninsula, with Xicalango established as a base in 1529 by Montejo the elder, now joined by his son, and Dávila. In 1530, the expedition moved up the coast to Champoton, and then in 1531 to Campeche. There Montejo the elder remained, while the *entrada* was fully launched by his son, who sailed to the north coast in 1532—and from there marched into the well-populated northern territories, apparently facing little resistance, founding a colonial capital named Ciudad Real in the center of the vast but largely abandoned Maya city of Chichen Itza. When the Maya did finally attack the invaders, Montejo's company suffered heavy casualties and retreated to the coast. There, at Dzilam, he was joined by his father, and in 1534 the two re-founded Ciudad Real on that coastal site. They later claimed that from there they subdued much of northern Yucatan. But when word reached Spaniards at Dzilam and Campeche of the discovery of the Inka Empire—and of the great distribution of gold at Cajamarca—they abandoned the Montejos to join the Peruvian expedition that Pedro de Alvarado was assembling in Guatemala. By the end of 1534, no Spaniards remained in Yucatan.

---

[3]   Dávila and his men were retrieved by ship the following year; they had survived, even prospered, by maintaining a rather active slave trade with the islands (discussed in a chapter titled "The Currency of Conquest—Juan de Lerma and Forced Maya Slavery, 1528–1530" in a book manuscript in progress by Chuchiak, with the working title of *Unfinished Conquests: The Adelantado Francisco de Montejo and the attempted Conquest of the Yucatec Maya, 1527–1535*).

After two failed *entradas*, the Montejos needed time to recruit men for a third. Montejo the elder also redirected his energies to Honduras, where he was appointed governor of a minimal Spanish colony in 1537, and where he brought some five hundred Nahuas from his *encomienda* in Azcapotzalco. That same year, his nephew (another Francisco de Montejo) reoccupied the small Spanish base at Champoton. But Alvarado was soon able to persuade crown officials to transfer Honduras to him. Awarded the governorship of Chiapas (and, briefly, Alvarado's lucrative *encomienda* of Xochimilco) as a consolation, Montejo the elder moved to Chiapas, bringing the Azcapotzalco warriors and their families. There Montejo the younger received the Nahuas—along with invasion instructions from his father—and took them, along with several thousand additional Indigenous warriors and support personnel, to Champoton; from where, in 1540, the third *entrada* moved to Campeche.[4] There was no violence (apparently), and the town was re-founded by the younger Montejos as San Francisco de Campeche. In 1541, the expedition—its small Spanish and large Nahua contingent, along with a significant number of other Mesoamerican auxiliaries, and supplemented by a large Maya force—marched north to Tiho, making the Maya city a base for raids into the surrounding country. In January 1542, Tiho was re-founded as the Spanish city of Merida.[5] Spaniards considered their conquest or "pacification" of Yucatan now complete, although there was fighting for a further five years, and the colony centered on Merida primarily comprised only the peninsula's northwest.[6] The Montejos would go down in local history as the celebrated conquerors, commemorated in everything from beer to buildings, street names to monuments (see figure 1.1).

By sticking to the basic facts, corroborated in Spanish sources, the summary above gives the impression of Spanish perseverance and the apparent inevitability of a Spanish conquest. That Hispano-centric perspective leaves Mayas with passive roles, disunited if not disorganized, only able to react to the invaders; the implication is one of civilizational inferiority. To correct those impressions, three interpretive points are worth emphasizing.

First, the Mayas of the sixteenth century were the heirs to a highly complex civilization that was thousands of years old.[7] Across an area that today stretches from

---

[4] On these Indigenous allied forces, see Chuchiak, "Forgotten Allies," 178–205.

[5] The city that Spaniards initially (and Mayas throughout the colonial period) called Tiho, was the ancient Maya city of *Ichcaansiho*, abandoned as a major residential center by the 1540s. A copy of the original act of the founding of Merida on January 6, 1542, is in AGI, México, 299 (see Chuchiak, "Documentos Históricos-Pilares de la Memoria," 13).

[6] For a similar summary, viewing the entire Maya area, see Restall, "Invasion: The Maya at War"; for secondary sources focusing on these events in Yucatan, see Chamberlain, *Conquest and Colonization of Yucatan*; Chuchiak, "La Conquista de Yucatán"; "Forgotten Allies"; Clendinnen, *Ambivalent Conquests*, 3–37; Love and Yoshida, *Chilam Balam*.

[7] A recent overview of major aspects of the Classic period is Hutson and Ardren, *Maya World*.

Figure 1.1. Monumental Montejos. The monument to the Franciscos de Montejo, father and son, on the Merida avenue named after them—the Paseo Montejo. Photograph by the authors.

southern Mexico to Honduras, including Yucatan, Guatemala, and Belize, well-fed Maya populations lived in and around spectacular cities. Their achievements in art and architecture were matched by the development of an 800-glyph writing system whose creativity we are still attempting to grasp in its totality, and by a profound knowledge of calendrics, mathematics, and astronomy. All this was accomplished with unique environmental resources, in particular domesticable and load-bearing animals and arable land, very different than those available to people of contemporary Old World cultures in western and southern Europe. Mayas had forged a civilization that differed from that of Spain and western Europe, but to classify it as inferior is simply absurd—an attitude rooted in the prejudicial ignorance with which conquistadors viewed the people they sought to subdue and exploit.[8]

---

[8]   We are drawing here upon Restall and Solari, *The Maya*, although there is of course a vast

Second, the Maya also built their civilization without centralized control. Small proto-empires rose and fell over the millennia, but none came even remotely close to controlling the entire Maya area and its dozens of ethnic groups and languages. Indeed, classifying them all as "Maya" is a convenient invention of modern scholarship; the Mayas themselves had no equivalent term of self-identity, neither one that was area-wide nor one that encompassed regions like Yucatan. Thus, to call the Maya disunited or divided falsely implies that there were historic reasons for them to be united, and unreasonably suggests they failed to unite in response to outside invasion. Their decentralization did mean that, at a regional level, invaders were able to play off one kingdom against another; obvious examples are the hostility between the K'iche' and Kaqchikel, exploited by Alvarado in highland Guatemala,[9] and the rivalry between the Xiu and Cocom in Yucatan—to which we shall turn shortly. But if we view the Maya area as a whole, and the larger history of Spanish invasions in that area (what we call here the Maya-Spanish Thirty Years' War of 1517–1547), it is clear that Maya decentralization hindered conquest and colonization. Efforts to establish colonies were restricted to four regions: two of those failed permanently (Tamactun in Yucatan's southwest corner, only nominally "pacified"; and Belize, where the sole Spanish settlers were friars, and before long they left too); the other two, in highland Guatemala and northwest Yucatan, became permanent colonies but left most of the Maya area outside direct colonial rule.[10]

Third—and focusing back on Yucatan alone—the Hispano-centric perspective on the wars of 1517–1547 and the three *entradas* of 1527–1547 only makes sense if one assumes Spanish superiority—manifest in astonishing resilience, persistence, righteousness, and inevitable victory—and Maya inferiority, manifest in disunity, duplicity, passivity, and ultimate defeat. Spanish sources from the time are, not surprisingly, infused with such assumptions, as are subsequent Spanish chronicles, the histories written by other Europeans and North Americans from the early modern period into the twentieth century.[11] Removing those assumptions reveals a narrative of Spanish conquest that makes no sense. Take, for example, the *encomiendas* of thousands of unconquered Maya families distributed by Montejo the elder on

---

literature of hundreds of books and thousands of articles on the Maya past. Note that Las Casas, ever the contrarian, argued (in his *Historia apologética*)—against his contemporaries—that the Maya had developed the same two hallmarks of civilization that Spaniards had: cities and writing.

[9] See Restall and Asselbergs, *Invading Guatemala*.

[10] On the role of Franciscan friars in bringing areas outside the peninsula's northwest under the nominal (and sometimes temporary) control of the "church and crown," see Scholes and Roys, *Maya Chontal Indians of Acalan-Tixchel*; and Chuchiak, "Fide, Non Armis," 119–42.

[11] The last, unabashedly Hispano-centric such account was Chamberlain, *Conquest and Colonization of Yucatan*, first published in 1938, but its legacy persisted long after that.

the eastern coast in 1527 from his new "town"—a fantasy of colonial settlement by a couple of hundred sickly foreigners who barely knew where they were, and who were utterly dependent for their very lives on the Maya lords who were feeding and observing them. Or consider the two "cities" named Ciudad Real, founded in the early 1530s at Chichen Itza and Dzilam, with their imaginary control of swaths of Maya territory, all evaporating as soon as local Mayas took up arms.[12]

Those events do make sense, however, when one permits Maya people agency and an active role in the story. In effect, they make sense when one reverses the traditional perspective, and when one thus views the Spanish invaders as able to do little more than react to Maya decisions and actions, to be manipulated by Maya rulers, and to do their best to spin the results as victories. In other words, Spaniards remained in the peninsula in 1527–1528, in 1531–1534, and from 1540 onwards because Maya rulers allowed it. In some cases, they allowed it because prior experience had shown them that Spaniards were quick to resort to extreme violence, but that accommodating and supplying them could more quickly result in them leaving without slaughtering local families; this was surely the thinking of Ah Naum Pat, Cozumel's ruler, in 1527. In other cases, feigning surrender was part of a deep-rooted Maya strategy of ambush; that is, fostering in the enemy a false sense of security through apparent victory, while local leaders were able to put aside their differences and negotiate a coordinated attack. That was likely why the two Ciudad Real "cities" were permitted and then destroyed by Maya leaders. In time, Spanish captains began to realize that Maya leaders were infuriatingly effective strategists, and they would rant over this "evil plan," that "treacherous plan," and how these "very bellicose people" raised their children "from birth in warfare" and insidiously "forced us into many battles."[13]

Finally, in other cases, Maya dynastic rulers determined that forging alliances with Spanish invaders—even to the extent of initiating those agreements—would preempt and prevent warfare in the towns and villages they controlled. The Xiu and Pech

---

[12] Montejo's quickness to found "towns" and "cities" was more than wishful thinking; it was designed to meet the specific clauses and requirements of his conquest contract (*capitulación*). To retain the royal grant of authority, and then use it to distribute land and encomiendas, that formal act of town creation was needed—even if the physical existence of a town, let alone its thriving, was fiction: "And in order to comply with such creations of towns and neighborhoods you should populate at least four towns where they should live in that land; and once those are completed, you can sell and make land grants as you wish" (*Real Cédula de capitulación con Francisco de Montejo, vecino de México para la conquista de Yucatán*, AGI, Indiferente General, 415, libro 1, fs. 85r–85v). On seven occasions during the *entradas*, Montejo founded towns named after his hometown of Salamanca (Tozzer, *Landa's* Relación, 127).

[13] The phrases refer to specific events by Pedro de Alvarado, his cousin Gonzalo de Alvarado, Cortés, and the first cabildo of Merida (see Restall, "Invasion: The Maya at War," 99, 103, 93, 113, respectively).

leaders seem to have taken such decisions in the early 1540s, if not in the 1530s.[14] In the short term, such decisions spared Maya families enslavement, sexual abuse, or slaughter, at a time when periodic warfare and the spread of epidemic disease had caused great hardship in the peninsula. They also strengthened the political positions of those leaders with respect to local rivals and regional enemies. In the long run, and in retrospect—considering the centuries of exploitation that Mayas would suffer under Spanish rule and, even worse, under the regimes of the nineteenth century—it is easy for us to judge those leaders for letting wolves into the chicken coops. But what else could they have done?

*   *   *

Let us now return to that section in the Account with which we began this chapter—the moment when Montejo the younger "re-establishes the Spanish rule in Yucatan," as early editors of the text described it—in order to understand how the Account is both glaringly Hispano-centric and yet, at the same time, misleadingly Maya-centric.[15]

Although no date is given, the story of the protracted and sporadic Spanish invasion is here picked up in the middle of the 1530s, when the invasion has failed for the second time: "After the departure of the Spaniards from Yucatan."[16] While we might imagine Mayas rejoicing at such a turn of events, the Account presents a grim picture of life in the peninsula without Spanish would-be colonists. The catastrophes were almost apocalyptic, both natural and cultural: first drought, then famine due to lack of corn (the Maya dietary staple), then a plague of locusts, then more famine as a result. Meanwhile, two royal lineages and "mortal enemies," the Xiu and the Cocom (rulers of their own small kingdoms, polities, or states), rekindled

---

[14] See Love and Yoshida, *Chilam Balam*, for an extensive and persuasive argument along these lines.

[15] Account, f. 11r (Sec. 14). Gates's interpretation was not unique: most early editors echoed this belief that the younger Montejo brought the "return" to Spanish rule and the definitive conquest; e.g., Brasseur (*Relation de choses*, p. XI), who argued that "he returned there a few years later, preceded by his eldest son, to whom Spain was indebted for the final conquest of this country [*il y retourna quelques années après, précédé de son fils aîné, à qui l'Espagne fut redevable de la conquête définitive de cette contrée*]," and Tozzer, whose notes detail the so-called return to Spanish rule ushered in by Montejo the younger (*Landa's Relación*, 54–57, n272–n285).

[16] That vagueness led previous editors of the Account to claim varying dates for the Spaniards' abandonment of the peninsula after the second *entrada*: Brasseur asserted, ". . . having abandoned Yucatan in 1532" (p. xi); Genet (Vol. I, 110) gave the date as 1534 (correctly, as we stated above); Perez Martínez insisted it was 1535, "when Yucatan remained free of the Spaniards" (p. 89, n58); while Tozzer (pp. 52–53, n256–n260) explained in great detail that the withdrawal of the Spaniards occurred in 1535, and that "this withdrawal of the Spanish forces from Yucatan marks the end of the First [*sic*] Conquest" (p. 53, n.257).

"old passions [*las passiones viejas*]," and, following a massacre, "great wars [*grandes guerras*]" broke out. One imagines Spanish (especially Franciscan) readers reading between the lines: here is evidence of the Devil doing his dirty work among the heathens while he still can and of a tough-love God preparing the way for redemption.

There is, in other words, hope (for Spaniards) on the horizon. The mention of "four good years that followed after the locusts" at the end of the paragraph is a providential prompt: don Francisco then returned. Obstacles to his advance are brushed aside and buried in the narrative (his company spends two full years in Champoton, on the southwest coast of the peninsula, barely a toehold on the region, "because of the resistance that there was"; no details provided). By and large, Montejo encounters either open friendship or insignificant resistance, and the four Spanish towns that mark the corners of Spanish Yucatan are quickly and easily established: the ruler of Champoton who had "badly treated" earlier invasion companies under Hernández de Córdoba and Grijalva (the abovementioned battles of 1517 and 1518) is now dead; the people of Campeche welcome the Spaniards; Montejo the younger has easily "reached" Tiho, where he has apparently founded Merida without a fight; his cousin founds Valladolid, years of conquest warfare reduced to a pacification of "villages that had rebelled somewhat"; Salamanca (Bacalar) has simply been "founded"; and Campeche, "already occupied," is dubbed "San Francisco" in honor of Montejo the elder upon his triumphal entry.

With six or seven years of invasion warfare (1540–1547) reduced to one paragraph, dramatically reimagined as a quick and complete victory, almost every word plays a role in the spinning of events. The following line, squeezed in between mentions of Campeche, is weighty with the political purpose of the narrative: "He put in order the services of the Indians and the government of the Spaniards until the adelantado, his father, came from Chiapas with his wife and household to govern." In a nutshell, the assertion is that the younger Montejo achieved the entire mandate of conquest and settlement—in order that his father, holder of the adelantado license, can fulfill that mandate. The message, and its phrasing, could have come directly from any of the numerous *probanza de méritos* ("proof of merit") reports that Montejo men filed with the Crown in the sixteenth century in order to consolidate royal approval and fend off rivals.[17]

The *probanza* reports submitted by Spanish conquistadors and officials underscored much of the "mythistory" of the Spanish invasions, in Yucatan as throughout the Americas. Historical accounts, ranging from conquistador reports to histories by ecclesiastics (like Landa) to crown-sponsored chronicles, tended to depict conquest and colonization in ways so distorted and purposeful as to constitute a kind

---

[17]   On *probanzas* as a genre of document, see Restall, *Seven Myths*, 12–14, 18, 37; Chuchiak, "Toward a Regional Definition," 142–49; and Macleod, "Self-Promotion," 25–42.

of mythology. The page under discussion here, for example, illustrates what one of us (Restall) has called "the myth of exceptional men," with Montejo the younger swiftly and boldly succeeding where others fell, and all out of loyalty to his father (and thus, by extension, the king). It also illustrates "the myth of the white conquistador," as there is no mention at all of the Nahua and other Indigenous warriors and support personnel brought from Mesoamerica in 1540; they greatly outnumbered the Spaniards, and without them, the invaders would have been ejected from the peninsula for a third time.[18]

Most strikingly, the passage encapsulates "the myth of completion," including its characteristic features of a conquest that is rapid and that leads immediately to the establishment of colonial rule.[19] Such rule is marked by "Indians" reduced to giving "services," the institutions of Spanish "government" implanted, and the invaders settled in "households" (complete with wives, family dependents, and non-Spanish servants and slaves). By asserting that a conquest is complete—Montejo is described as having "completed the conquest [*acabo la conquista*]," as well as "founding/settling (*poblarse*)," "pacifying (*pacificar*)," and "putting in order (*dar orden*)"—the conquistadors and their historians pulled a simple but devastatingly significant trick: they turned Indigenous families defending their homes and resisting invasion into "rebels [*rebeldes*]." Under Spanish law, Indigenous peoples of the Americas were subjects of the crown, and thus protected from indiscriminate violence; but once classified as rebels, they could be slaughtered or enslaved, in order to "pacify" them.[20]

Such a legalistic trick is played on the Mayas in northeastern Yucatan, who "had rebelled somewhat" in this page of the Account. The notion that Mayas were duplicitous and prone to violence is introduced earlier in the passage, where the Cocoms "trick" their "mortal enemies," the Xius, burning some alive and killing the rest, starting "great wars." No wonder—the reader is primed to think—such people rebel.

Reclassifying resistance to invasion as rebellion was thus a legalistic loophole that justified enslaving Indigenous peoples, while also relying on claims of conquest completion.[21] Those two topics and their treatment in the Account are worth

---

[18] The quoted phrases are subtitles to chapters in Restall, *Seven Myths*; see 1–26, 44–63. On Montejo's Nahua and other Indigenous allies, see Chuchiak, "Forgotten Allies," 205–13.

[19] Restall, *Seven Myths*, 64–76.

[20] Restall, *Seven Myths*, 68–75, 124–27; *When Montezuma Met Cortés*, 296–311, 339; "Wars of Invasion"; Reséndez, *Other Slavery*.

[21] Montejo's *capitulación* granted him specific permission to enslave those Maya servants and slaves already in captivity among the Maya (*esclavos de rescate*), and to enslave any Maya rebels against the crown (*esclavos de guerra*): "I give license and authority to you and the people there to enslave the Indians who are or become rebels, who after being reprimanded and required, you may take as slaves, keeping and obeying all laws past, present, and future

brief comment. The first two decades of the sixteenth century saw the rapid rise of Spanish slave-raiding expeditions across the Caribbean; the earliest moments of Spanish-Maya encounter were tied to that history, as the ship that wrecked on the Yucatec coast in 1511 was likely carrying Indigenous slaves as part of its cargo of loot, as was the expedition led by Francisco Hernández de Córdoba in 1517. The Account does in fact mention in passing that Spanish expeditions were slavers, noting that Hernández de Córdoba left Cuba "in order to collect slaves for the mines" (f. 2v, Sec. 3). But slavery had already been introduced into the narrative of the Account, with the Spanish castaways of 1511 "used as slaves" by a Maya ruler. A few folios later, the Cocom are accused of introducing slavery into Yucatan, then the Xiu are mentioned as owning slaves in the middle of the invasion wars, and slavery is identified as one of "the vices of the Indians." Enslaving by Spaniards is mentioned once more, but in the context of Maya lords distrusting the friars who were asking to educate their sons; some lords, fearing the friars were slavers like "the Spaniards" (meaning the conquistador-settlers with whom Landa often quarreled), sent "younger slaves in place of their sons." There follow half a dozen further references in the first half of the Account to Mayas owning slaves.[22]

The Account thus raises two basic facts: slavery existed as a social category among the Maya; and Spanish conquistador-settlers enslaved Indigenous people. But the two facts are presented very differently from each other. The impression given is that slavery was significant in the Maya world. But Spaniards exaggerated, misrepresented, and often invented patterns of slavery among Indigenous peoples, beginning in the Caribbean in the 1490s and continuing to do so on the mainland throughout the sixteenth century. In fact, among the Maya, as among the Nahuas of central Mexico, slavery was relatively fluid and temporary compared to its conception in the early modern Atlantic world; slaves "were not simply gained by raiding, but were obtained through warfare, tribute payment, punishment, and debt."[23] On the other hand, slaving by conquistadors is mentioned in the Account merely in passing, when it was in reality endemic to conquistador campaigns throughout the sixteenth century; as mentioned above, despite repeated edicts and laws banning

concerning what is ordered and contained in our other instructions and provisions that we may give" (*Cédula de capitulación con Francisco de Montejo, vecino de México para la conquista de Yucatán*, AGI, Indiferente General, 415, libro 1, fs. 92r–93r). It was, of course, the Montejos, not the Mayas, who classified individuals as meeting the criteria of exception. The family was also tripped up by the clause that required any enslavement of the Maya by the Montejos to conform to all laws present *and* future, as the 1542 New Laws thereby invalidated the slave license of the *capitulación*.

[22] References to slaves in the Account are on folios 6v (sec. 9), 11r (sec. 13), 13v (sec. 17), 14r (sec. 18), 17v (sec. 22), 22r (sec. 27), 23r (sec. 28), 23v (sec. 29), 24v (sec. 29), and 31r (sec. 37).

[23] Stone, *Captives of Conquest*, 22; also see Chuchiak, "Human Plunder."

the enslavement of Indigenous subjects of the Spanish Crown, loopholes were maintained, used, and abused. Indeed, the Montejos, praised in the Account as exceptions to any admissions of conquistador abuse in Yucatan, engaged heavily in slave-trading, especially of Mayas in Yucatan.[24] Landa would have known that the Montejos were notorious slavers, but he (or the original author of these passages) essentially covers that up by simply mentioning that the Mayas of Montejo the elder's *encomiendas* were transferred to the crown, while both his son and nephew enjoyed successful *residencia* trials (these were not criminal trials, but investigations into conduct during a term of office, standard procedure for all high officials in the empire). Arguably, the *residencia* of Montejo the elder was not a success, as he thereby lost his *encomiendas* and slaves, but the younger two Montejos were found innocent of wrongdoing, despite their more egregious slaving activities. In other words, the Montejos got away with selling Mayas as slaves, as Landa would have known. That dark fact is not only absent from the Account, but it is hidden by the way in which the manuscript otherwise treats the topic of slavery.

The passage discussed at the start of this chapter, styling the third Montejo *entrada* as a rapid triumph, effectively disguises the protracted nature of the invasion— the Maya-Spanish Thirty Years' War (1517–1547).[25] While it does mention the events both at the start and end of that period—the 1517 battle on a beach outside Champoton between Hernández de Córdoba's men and those of Moch Couoh, the town's ruler; and so-called revolt in the peninsula's northeast, in 1546–1547—they are placed outside the Montejo campaign of conquest. So how complete was the so-called Spanish Conquest of Yucatan (and did it justify such a phrase, with its implications of finality)? In one paragraph of that passage, the founding of four Spanish municipal settlements is declared—the provincial capital and sole city, Merida, and the three *villas* (towns) of Campeche, Valladolid, and Salamanca (Bacalar)—as if they are the four corners of a square that defines Spanish Yucatan, conquered, pacified, put in order.[26] That impression is false, an illusion of conquest. Spanish Yucatan was never a square that filled the peninsula, neither in 1547 nor at any point

---

[24] Indeed, Las Casas used the examples of the Montejos' abuses as direct evidence of the need for the New Laws. During his discussions before the Council of the Indies, he was accompanied by fray Jacobo Testera, who gave eyewitness testimony of slave-raiding and related atrocities in Yucatan. The sum of all the Montejos' abuses served as powerful evidence of the need to outlaw finally and fully the enslavement of Indigenous peoples (see *El parecer de los que se han juntado por mandado de vuestra magestad a entender en las cosas de las Yndias después de hayer oydo al padre fray bartolome de las casas y fray Jacobo de tastera y el licenciado Salmeron asy de palabra como por escrito*, June–July, 1542, Hans P. Kraus Collection of Hispanic American Manuscripts, LoC, 14 folios).

[25] Account, fs. 2v–3r and 11v (Secs. 3–4 and 13).

[26] Account, f. 11v (end of Sec. 14).

until the peninsula became part of independent Mexico in 1821. It was more of a crescent that curved from the northeast across to the southwest, with Merida at the fattest point (see the map that is figure 0.4). Bacalar was a tiny outpost that was abandoned a century later due to a combination of a successful Maya rebellion in the region and frequent pirate attacks, and it was not reoccupied for almost a century after that; the unconquered center and south of the peninsula actually grew in the seventeenth century, shrinking the colony.

If we place Spanish efforts to conquer Yucatan in the larger context of the Spanish invasions in the whole Maya area, the pattern is similar; the Thirty Years' War period encompassed over a dozen Spanish invasions, most of them failing to establish colonial settlements but causing massive mortality through violence, slaving, disruption of trade and food supply, and the introduction of epidemic disease. Spanish towns, colonies, and mission settlements failed everywhere, with only two permanent self-sustaining colonies founded by 1547, both comprising a small portion of the Maya area, both requiring multiple invasions and the deployment of tens of thousands of Indigenous auxiliaries from Mexico: the three Montejo-led campaigns in Yucatan; and the two campaigns into highland Guatemala led by the Alvarado brothers. Not all Mayas, therefore, experienced the period of the Thirty Years' War in the same way. For some, invasion forces, warfare, sexual violence, slave-taking, and disease ravaged their hometowns and broke apart their families—even repeatedly. There were surely others who never saw a single invader, either Spanish or Nahua, although the arrival of displaced refugees, epidemic outbreaks, and disruptions to trade routes meant every Maya community was impacted in some way by the invasions.[27]

The passage upon which we have mostly focused thus far is not, of course, the only one in the Account to describe the Montejo-led invasions, the Maya kingdoms they encountered, the Maya response to invasion, and the aftermath leading up to Landa's own decades in Yucatan. In fact, some twenty-one pages, roughly 16 percent of the manuscript, cover those topics (folios 2r–13r, Secs. 3–17).[28] But, like so much of the Account, those pages do not constitute a narrative that is coherent in terms of topic, style, or interpretation. That inconsistency reflects—and is evidence of—the fact that much of it was not composed by Landa himself but copied from other Spanish sources, or drawn from information provided, orally or in writing, by Landa's Maya informants. How are Mayas and Spaniards portrayed in

---

[27] Restall, "Wars of Invasion," 149–53.

[28] We are counting the pages from the 1511 shipwreck of the first Spaniards to set foot in Yucatan, roughly halfway down f. 2r (Sec. 3), to the arrival of the first Franciscan, fray Jacobo de Testera, at the bottom of f. 12 (Sec. 16), and the settler-friar conflict of the 1540s on f. 13r (Sec. 17); see our chapter 5 below for a description of the style in these pages.

that 16 percent of the Account, and how do such portraits reflect the sources and authorship of those sections?

The sudden shifts in topic and tone are partly the result of the copyist making decisions as to what paragraphs or sections to copy from Landa's larger *recopilación* or compendium. We have no way of knowing how much the copyist skipped or jumped around, but the impression given is almost that of a *découpé* or cut-up text (albeit unintentionally).[29] One imagines that the long-lost *recopilación*, being a collage of copied sources and original compositions, must have lacked the smooth transitions, coherence of tone, and narrative logic of a polished book; those rough edges are made rougher by the copyists in the manuscript they left to us.

Those shifts in topic and tone, then, also stem from the varying sources that underpin the part of Landa's writings from which the copyist made these passages. For example, in the first of these pages (fs. 2r–4v; Secs. 3–4), the Mayas are portrayed as generic, stereotypical "Indians"—as idolaters, sacrificers of humans, cannibals, and generally savage and simpleminded (see figure 1.2). These are not Landa's Mayas, and almost certainly these pages were not authored by Landa; the only "Indian" stereotype found here that runs all through this twenty-one-page portion of the Account is their bellicose or warlike nature. Likewise, the Spaniards are brave and bold, with Cortés given heroic treatment as a devout proselytizer. Again, these are not really Landa's Spaniards, as subsequent pages show. The tone of these pages, then, is consistent with conquest accounts such as that of Francisco López de Gómara. His *La Istoria de las Yndias*, first published in 1552, was a hagiography of Cortés that trafficked heavily in "Indian" stereotypes; these pages are likely a redaction of similar passages in López de Gómara's book.[30]

In the subsequent pages (fs. 4v–12v; Secs. 5–16), the Spaniards receive a more complex treatment, and the perspective is more consistent with that of the

---

[29] The cut-up or *découpé* literary technique involved cutting up texts and rearranging the words or sentences to create new texts; it originated with the Dadaists in the 1920s, was popularized in the 1950s and 1960s by William S. Burroughs (a more apposite connection than one might imagine, as the Maya of Yucatan play central roles in several of his novels), later being used by lyricists such as David Bowie and Thom Yorke.

[30] Both López de Gómara's *Conquista de México* and the larger *La Istoria de las Yndias* of which it was a part were banned in 1553 for overly glorifying Cortés and overly criticizing the Pizarros and their actions in Peru (see Restall, *When Montezuma Met Cortés*, 237, 437n10; Roa-de-la-Carrera, *Histories of Infamy*; AGI, Indiferente General, 425, Libro 23, f. 8). The passage above is similar to Bernal Díaz's coverage of these events, but as Díaz's account was not published until 1632, that similarity reflects the common sources upon which Landa and Díaz drew—such as López de Gómara. We disagree with Pagden (73n54) that Landa was easily able to access Oviedo, and that the references in the Account to the *Historia General de las Indias* are to Oviedo's book; it was actually called *Historia General y Natural de las Indias*, and most of it was not published until the 1860s.

Franciscans and Landa himself. There are three elements to that perspective worth noting. First, the presence of the Spaniards is providential; evidence that the invasion is guided and blessed by God ranges from moments of Spanish success or good fortune to the calamities that the Maya suffer between invasions, to the prophecies of their arrival and victory by a Maya *chilam* or priest. This perspective is generally in line with the larger view of "the Spanish Conquest" that had become well established by the late sixteenth century, described above as a kind of myth-based history—and illustrated in the paragraphs summarizing the invasion of the 1540s that are towards the end of this passage.

Second, while God has guided the Spanish conquistador-settlers to Yucatan with purpose, and they display a perseverance that borders on the heroic, their behavior rapidly deteriorates. The descriptions here of Spanish atrocities in the wars of invasion are positively Lascasian—a short but disturbing litany of torture, mutilation, and butchery, with women and children as highlighted targets, the atrocities categorized as "unheard-of cruelties," "terrible punishments," and "the greatest inhumanity in the world." Indeed, the language used may reflect the influence of Bartolomé de Las Casas and his *Account, Much Abbreviated, of the Destruction of the Indies*—which included a similar passage of atrocities committed in Yucatan (published in 1552, the book was surely familiar to Landa).[31] At the same time, there are two direct references to Landa in these pages, both in the third person (he is once named as author, once as eyewitness source), evidence that the copyist was redacting material that appeared to be the friar's own account of things.

The third element of the perspective towards Spaniards in these pages is the attitude towards the Montejo family; if not quite hagiographic, it is relentlessly positive, with Francisco Montejo the younger in particular given heroic treatment.[32] That

---

[31] Las Casas, *An Account*, 47–53; Landa also had access to the Dominican friar's *Historia de las indias* and perhaps even a manuscript version of his *Historia apologética*. Note that the title of Las Casas's *La Brevísima relación* has been translated variously by its English-language editors.

[32] The larger passage we are still discussing here is fs. 4v–12v (Secs. 5–16), but the pro-Montejo paragraphs are peppered across fs. 8v–12v. It was important for Landa to positively refer to Montejo the younger, as he would have needed his support should he eventually return to Yucatan (as he did), and he knew this. Furthermore, Montejo had been a key player and ally of Landa during the early 1562 idolatry trials, at least until the arrival of Bishop Francisco de Toral. After his arrival, with the Maya protesting the rigor of the Inquisition, Toral gave the younger Montejo a commission to clean up the mess he believed Landa had made. As Toral later wrote to the Alcalde Mayor don Diego de Quijada, "Your Lordship should know that I have given a commission to the lord don Francisco de Montejo and to Joaquin de Leguizama so that they should take over cognizance of the extirpation of idolatry" (*Carta del Obispo Fray Francisco de Toral al Doctor Don Diego Quijada*, Campeche, 27 de octubre, 1562, AGI, Justicia, 249, 2 folios). This action would severely test the alliance between Landa

Figure 1.2. Montejo's Conquest. The first Montejo invasion of Yucatan, fancifully rendered as an encounter of civilization and barbarism by Theodor de Bry (to accompany the 1595 Frankfurt edition of Girolamo Benzoni's *Historia del Mondo Nuovo*, Image gallery, p. XIX, in Bry's *Americae pars quinta nobilis & admiratione plena Hieronymi Bezoni* [*sic*]). Reproduced with permission of the John Carter Brown Library, Brown University.

stance is contrary to Las Casas's position—his *Account, Much Abbreviated* names very few of the captains leading the invasions of Yucatan and other regions of the Americas, calling them all "tyrants" responsible for excessive violence, but Montejo is one of the exceptions identified by name. The pro-Montejo passages in the Account are thus very much Landa's spin on conquest events, and the text lacks even a hint of ambiguity here. Landa, with his allies among the Franciscans in Yucatan, established from the start a clear and consistent political alliance with the Montejo family and their faction among the new settlers. In a sense, Landa inherited the alliance when he arrived in 1549, but he chose to strengthen and stick to it doggedly, even

and the Montejos, along with the fact that Montejo the younger insisted the new bishop stay as his guest in his home.

after later receiving slights and apparent wrongs from the younger Montejo during the Toral affair. The Account therefore presents the Montejo men as consistently persistent and hardworking, dedicated and loyal to the crown, strong and respected leaders. The Montejos are faultless in contrast to "the Spaniards of Merida," with whom don Francisco the elder had "some disagreements"—an arch reference to the factional divide between the dominant family and a group of conquistador-settlers who controlled the new city's cabildo or council.[33] And at the end of the description of conquistador atrocities, Landa adds this artless and unconvincing caveat: "don Francisco de Montejo did not commit of any of these cruelties nor approved them; on the contrary, they seemed very wicked to him, but he could do nothing."[34]

Just as the portrayal of Spanish conquistadors shifts from straightforward to more complex and contradictory as we move through the twenty-one pages of pre-contact and conquest history, so does a parallel transition take place in the depiction of Mayas. But in the case of the Maya, there is evidence of multiple sources or voices—competing perspectives from at least three Maya informants, as well as from Landa himself. Mayas are still portrayed as worshiping their "idols" and practicing "sacrifice," but far more words are devoted to detailing how precontact rulers were educated and cultured, governing well-ordered kingdoms. Such a view surely reflects the influence of those Maya informants who, in effect, slipped into Landa's ink their veneration of their own ancestors. But one can also detect the cultural intrusion of Landa and his Franciscan view of the world, with model Maya rulers of the past given friar-like—even Christ-like—qualities.

Much of the narration of Maya history right before, during, and after the wars of invasion is told through accounts of specific male Maya leaders and their *chibalob* or patrilineages. That style of history is how Landa, or any male Spaniard of the time, would have framed the past—the privileging of the Montejo family is a vivid example—but it is also a reflection of the specific identity of Landa's Maya informants and the political alliances he established among the Indigenous elite. Three royal Maya lineages are, in turn, promoted and their perspectives included—almost certainly directly, through testimony that was written down by informants from those lineages, or by a notary or by Landa himself, and then copied later into the Account.

The first such royal patrilineage is that of the Cocom. A series of paragraphs (f. 5;

---

[33] Landa himself felt that most of the conquistador-settlers betrayed him during his conflict with Bishop Toral. In fact, upon his return as succeeding bishop, Landa began a systematic campaign of revenge, attacking many of the same Spaniards who had testified against him; he launched episcopal trials and denounced many of them to the new tribunal of the Inquisition, especially those who were also enemies of the Montejo clan (see Chuchiak, "In Servitio Dei," 611–19; Clendinnen, *Ambivalent Conquests*, 108–11).

[34] Account, f. 12r (Sec. 15).

Secs. 6–7) that present the role of the Cocom in Maya history in a highly flattering light begins, "The opinion of the Indians is that . . ."; it is surely in large part the testimony or work of Ah Nachi Cocom, baptized as don Juan Cocom (see figure 1.3). Among Landa's Maya informants, don Juan Cocom is one of only two informants explicitly identified as such (the other being the *ah kin may* or chief priest of Caucel, don Francisco Euan). Cocom makes a brief appearance a few pages later (f. 8v; Sec. 11) as "very wise and knowledgeable" about the Maya, "very familiar to the author of this book, fray Diego de Landa, recounting to him many ancient things, and showing him a book, which had belonged to his grandfather."[35]

Despite that praise, right after the Cocom have been described as wise and peaceful rulers, the attitude towards the lineage shifts, as another lineage appears on the scene: the Xiu. It is now the Xiu who receive all the flattery, and the subsequent Xiu-Cocom conflict is presented as entirely the fault of the Cocom—who are accused of introducing slavery and violence, and of betraying the Maya to militaristic people from central Mexico. The influence here is surely Gaspar Antonio Chi, who was a Xiu on his mother's side (his pre-baptismal name was probably Ah Na Xiu Chi); he was Landa's primary Maya informant. We know this for two reasons. First, we know a fair amount about Chi's life and how closely it was intertwined with Landa's. Chi was one of the young Maya noblemen whom the first Franciscans in the new colony targeted for education and Christianization. Chi not only learned to speak and write Spanish, but he also mastered Latin as well as some Nahuatl, and became Landa's personal notary and interpreter for many years (1550–62). He went on to work in the same position for Landa's successor, Bishop Toral, soon rising to become the highest-ranked Indigenous interpreter in the colony, still notarizing documents through to 1610 (dying in that year or very soon after).[36]

The second reason why we know Chi was one of Landa's primary informants is that Gaspar Antonio wrote his own *relación*, only a small fraction of which has survived in a very damaged document in Spain.[37] The longer original is lost, but portions survived in various other ways. For our purposes, the two most notable survivals are passages in the Account, and passages that Chi ghost-wrote in twelve of the reports compiled by the 25 encomenderos of Merida between 1579 and 1581,

---

[35] On the larger history of the Cocom lineage, see Pérez de Heredia and Bíró, *La Casa Real de Cocom*; on Nachi (don Juan) in particular, 38–39, 78, 152–62, 176–95. On the portions of the Chi petition that mention don Juan Cocom (AGI, México leg. 105B, r. 4,), see the transcription in Quezada and Torres Trujillo, *Tres Nobles Mayas*, 60–83.

[36] Restall, "Gaspar Antonio Chi"; Karttunen, *Between Worlds*, 84–114; Jakeman, "Historical Recollections"; Quezada and Torres Trujillo, *Tres Nobles Mayas*, 15–27, 39–134; Clendinnen, *Ambivalent Conquests*, 94, 119, 132, 164. Mark Lentz is currently (2023) working on a monograph on interpreters in colonial Yucatan that gives considerable attention to Chi.

[37] It is in AGI, México, leg. 110, as *Relación de algunas costumbres de los indios de Yucatán*, 1582.

Figure 1.3. Cocom Revived. A statue to "Nachi Cocom, Señor de Sotuta," in front of his house (expanded since the sixteenth century) on the central plaza of Sotuta, the Cocom capital. Photograph by the authors.

in response to questionnaires sent by the king to every province of the empire.[38] In one, Chi wrote of Maya prophecies that predicted the coming of Spaniards and Christianity,[39] and in another he wrote of the Xiu-Cocom feud—both topics included in the passages of the Account discussed here.

Indeed, the presentation of that feud in both the Merida *relación* and the Account is built around a key incident, depicted very much as a Cocom atrocity, that was of deep significance to Chi: the ambush and massacre of the Xiu embassy by Cocom hosts at Otzmal in 1536; the head of the Xiu delegation was Chi's own father, the *ah kulel* or *ah kin* (priest) Ah Na Puc Chi, executed when the future

---

[38] King Philip II's *Relaciónes Geográficas* project (RHGY); Jakeman, "Historical Recollections"; the other two ways in which Chi's writings survived are a 1581 manuscript in AGI, México, leg. 105B, r. 4 (see Quezada and Torres Trujillo, *Tres Nobles Mayas*, 55–100) and passages borrowed by Cogolludo (*Historia de Yucathan*, Libro IV, Capítulo IV).

[39] *Relación de la Ciudad de Mérida* (by Martín de Palomar and Gaspar Antonio Chi, Feb. 18, 1579) in RHGY, Vol. I: 44–45; Account (f. 8r–8v; sec. 11).

Gaspar Antonio was six years old.[40] This event remained central to Gaspar Antonio Chi's later submission of his own *probanzas de méritos*. Its mention by Spaniards in various reports—from the Account to the responses to the *Relaciones Históricos* (RHGY) questionnaires—helped bolster Chi's own future claims, and around the same time that those questionnaires were being filled out, Chi began to submit his own *probanzas* (1579–1581).[41] To highlight the claim that Chi's father's assassination was a sacrifice in service to the Spanish crown, and thus that the Xiu dynasty's merits were deserving of royal recognition, Chi created a type of apocryphal coat of arms that commemorated the event (see figure 1.4).[42]

Gaspar Antonio Chi's influence is thus heavy in parts of the Account, and to him we might reasonably credit both the extensive mentions of the Xiu lineage or dynasty, as well as the unwaveringly flattering treatment that every Xiu nobleman and the dynasty in general receives—especially in relation to the Cocom.[43] Chi and Landa fell out in 1562, and remained estranged for over a decade, with Chi understandably siding with Bishop Toral.[44] But Landa was in Spain for most of those years, and after he returned as bishop, within a few years he forgave his old informant, once again seeking him out as an interpreter. As conquistador-settler Alonso de Rojas noted, "fray Diego de Landa occupied him in many affairs of the Indians since he had such confidence in him."[45]

---

[40] In the Account (f. 11r; Sec. 14), Chi's father is not named; he is named, and his death detailed, in the *Relación de Tiab-y-Tec y Tisculum* (by Juan Bote and Chi, Feb. 20, 1581) in RHGY, Vol. I: 288–89.

[41] For example, the first question that Chi answers in his 1580 *probanza* details his father's killing (*Presentación del interrogatorio de Gaspar Antonio sobre los servicios que sus familiares habían hecho*, Valladolid, 27 de mayo de 1580, AGI, México, leg. 105B, ramo 4, fs. 7v–8r).

[42] Chi's shield or coat of arms may have been what he sought to receive from the crown in recognition of the Xiu family's merits; see Chuchiak, "Anhelo de un escudo de armas," 284–291; Restall, *Maya Conquistador*, 40, 81, 144, 149; "People of the Patio," 366–67; and Solari, *Maya Ideologies*, 75–78.

[43] Mentions of the Xiu begin on f. 4v (Sec. 5), and they are frequent throughout the history segment of the Account discussed above (fs. 4v–12v; Secs. 5–16), specifically on f. 6r–6v (Sec. 8), f. 7v (Sec. 9), f. 8r (Sec. 11), f. 10r (Sec. 12), and f. 11r (Sec.14). Although Chi's influence on the passages on Maya culture is arguably evident, as we shall discuss later, there are no further mentions of the Xiu.

[44] As Toral never learned Maya (he was fluent in Nahuatl), he relied almost exclusively on Gaspar Antonio Chi for translations in the episcopal court and during his preaching and pastoral visits, appointing him to the privileged and salaried position of Maestro de Capilla in Merida's cathedral ("During the time of the Revered Bishop don fray Francisco de Toral, [I] was Maestre de capilla in the Cathedral Church of this bishopric," confirmed Chi in *Testimonio de Diego Briseño vecino de esta ciudad de Mérida defensor de los naturales de estas provincias en la Probanza de Gaspar Antonio*, 24 de diciembre de 1579, AGI, México, leg. 104, ramo 3, f. 11v).

[45] *Testimonio de Alonso de Rojas, vecino y escribano público del número de esta dicha ciudad de esta*

Figure 1.4. The Otzmal Shield. The Otzmal Memorial Shield or Apocryphal Coat of Arms of the Xiu Lineage of Mani, engraved for Cogolludo and Rubio Mañé's *Historia de Yucathan* (1688, Libro III, Capítulo VI, f. 133), from a lost original of c. 1580s by Gaspar Antonio Chi (the death of whose father by arrow is depicted at top). Reproduced courtesy of the John Carter Brown Library, Brown University.

The third elite lineage that is given particular attention in the Account is that of the Chel. We cannot assign the dynasty's influence in the Account to any specific Chel informant (there is no Chel equivalent to Gaspar Antonio Chi and Nachi Cocom, at least that we know of). But there were likely several Chel noblemen who informed and influenced Landa, for it was in the very heart of the old Chel kingdom that he built his convent and centered his campaign to convert the Maya and crush their old religious culture. Itzmal—or Izamal, as it became in Spanish—was a large, ancient city that by the 1540s had been abandoned as a major residential center (exactly when is not clear, but likely early in the Postclassic period). But, like Chichen Itza to its southeast, it remained a sacred center and a pilgrimage destination, its landscape dominated by vast pyramidal structures topped by small temples. The Chel role in Landa's decision to make Izamal his primary residence (even though Mani was technically the mission headquarters) is not detailed in the Account, but the Chel are arguably given the most positive coverage among all the ruling lineages mentioned.[46]

The introduction of the Chel reads like a synopsis of the dynasty's own historical mythology, complete with a founding priest-nobleman from Mayapan, updated to reflect the impact of Christianization and the re-centering of the Chel kingdom on Izamal. According to what was presumably deep-rooted Chel mythistory, that founding father was a prophet and leader, whose descendants occupied two capital cities—Tecoh (then Tekoch or Tikoch) near the north coast, and Izamal inland—continually up to Landa's time (f. 7r–7v; Sec. 9). The end of that passage (the final paragraph of Sec. 9) seems to be an attempt at objectivity, giving all three major dynasties—Xiu, Cocom, and Chel—equal roles in their regional rivalry. That suggests that the author of this synthesis of dynastic positions was Landa himself, preserving something of the accusatory indignance that must have permeated the original testimonies.

And yet one cannot help but hear Chi's voice in here, given his familial hostility to the Chel dynasty. Similarly, when the Chels return to the narrative a few pages later (fs. 9v–10r, Sec. 12), there are some subtle anti-Chel digs that are surely Chi's in origin: the Chels were less "courageous" than the Couohs, for example, and their priests less "proud" than those of other dynasties; their virtue is a passive one, the failure to "hinder" and "resist," whereas that of the Xiu is an active one—they "helped" Montejo to settle at Chichen Itza, and thereby offered a positive example to other Mayas.

That said, the treatment of the Chel role at the end of what was in fact the second

---

ciudad de en la *Probanza de Gaspar Antonio*, 24 de diciembre de 1579, AGI, México, leg.104, ramo 3, f. 23r.
[46] See Solari, *Maya Ideologies of the Sacred*. On Itzmal (Izamal), also see chapters 2 and 7 below.

Montejo *entrada* (although, as noted above, that is not made clear in the Account) is more than positive; it turns the Chel ruler of Dzilan into an apostle-like figure. He is Ah Na Mux Chel, "a youth" and "already a Christian," and he not only gave the Spaniards a safe haven in Dzilan, but—according to the Account—guided them for forty-eight leagues down to Campeche, riding with two other Maya noblemen on the same horse. Upon his return, "he fell dead," a Christian martyr to the cause of the Spanish conquest. That suggestion of martyrdom by Christianized Chel lords returns a few more pages on, with Landa's denunciation of Spanish conquistador-settler methods of violence. This is the section we described earlier as Lascasian (Sec. 15; fs. 11v–12r), in which Landa catalogues Spanish atrocities—including the placing of the Chel rulers of the town of Yobain "in stocks in a house," to which the Spaniards then set fire, "burning them alive with the greatest inhumanity in the world."[47]

Such an incident would have been remembered a generation later with outrage and anger, as much by the Chel of Yobain as by those of Izamal, as much by Chi as by Landa—whose conversion efforts were aided by Xiu and Chel collaboration, hindered by conquistador-settler violence. As Las Casas lamented in a 1544 petition to the crown that condemned the "many unjust and oppressive wars" that the Montejos had started and waged in Yucatan: "The Indians always retain the horror and fear and enmity of the said Montejo and Spanish soldiers for the great evils and injuries and diminution which they received from them."[48]

*   *   *

The Account therefore tells us a great deal about Maya history in the centuries before the Spanish invasion of Yucatan (the period that archaeologists call the Late Postclassic), about the invasion itself, and about the Maya experience of the invasion decades. But there is a catch: what it tells us is enormously unreliable and misleading. It is mythistory: historical facts twisted and wrapped and blended with legends and stories and bits of "fake news" designed to promote particular political and cultural agendas, some very local and others empire-wide, some deep-rooted

---

[47] This atrocity was confirmed by Spanish eyewitnesses who testified to it in the *residencia* trial of the Montejos held in 1547, just two years before Landa's arrival. According to one, Juan Farfán, it occurred in 1542, when the Spanish captain Pedro Alvarez mistook a peaceful embassy of Maya warriors from the town of Yobain as a raiding party: Alvarez and his men rushed toward the confused group of Maya warriors, who quickly "threw down their bows and arrows on the ground"; nonetheless, the Spaniards treated the prisoners with contempt, tying them together inside a wooden hut and burning them alive (*Testimonio del conquistador Juan Farfán en la residencia de Francisco de Montejo*, AGI, Justicia, 300, 7 folios). For an interpretive study of this event as a cultural misunderstanding see Chuchiak, "Burning and the Burnt," 177.

[48] See *Capítulo* 29 of the "Petition of the Bishop of Chiapas," published in Parish and Las Casas, *Las Casas as a bishop*, 23.

and others sprung from Yucatan's turbulent sixteenth-century present. It is a cut-up mix of contradictory Spanish and Maya perspectives, one elbowing the other aside to squeeze its bias into the next paragraph, its multiple authors and sources only declaring themselves through their partialities.

As such, the opening dozen folios of the manuscript are not that different from the rest of it. The challenge to readers of the Account is to sift, sort, and see through the filters and abridgments; to identify and analyze authorial perspectives; and to stack the claims of the Account up against other evidence. Above all, our challenge is to remember that the Account is *not* a source of information on the Maya or the Spanish invasions or any topic that it purports to tell us about; it is a rich but complex source on what its numerous late-sixteenth-century authors and informants (Landa, Cocom, Chi, and various Spanish, Maya, and possibly Nahua men) thought or had heard about those topics, or what they imagined should be said about them.

2

Landa's Life and the Franciscans in Yucatan

Unfortunately—and perhaps tellingly—the Account furnishes no biographical details about its author. This is regrettable, simply because the manuscript would have surely told us more about Landa's interaction with the Maya had the friar himself appeared in it more as a protagonist. But the lack of autobiographical comments in the Account does not mean we know little of Landa's life, particularly after his arrival in Yucatan. On the contrary, the friar left a trail of archival records, many of which have survived in Seville and elsewhere in Spain. That trail is light up to 1561, but relatively heavy from 1562 until his death seventeen years later.

Furthermore, two of his successors as Franciscans in Yucatan, fray Bernardo de Lizana and fray Diego López de Cogolludo, composed hagiographic accounts in the seventeenth century that detail both Landa's early life in Spain and his years spent in the peninsula. Other ecclesiastics in the seventeenth century—such as Marianus (see figure 2.1) and Francisco Cárdenas y Valencia—also mention Landa in glowing terms, supplying a smattering of biographical information.

* * *

Born Diego de Landa Calderón on 12 November 1524, in the small Spanish town of Cifuentes, in the Alcarría region of the archbishopric of Sigüenza, he was a son of the noble lineage of the Calderones on his mother's side, and a member of the

https://doi.org/10.5876/9781646424245.c002

Figure 2.1. Landa at Work. Landa preaching to Maya elders, from Marianus de Orscelar, *Gloriosus Franciscanus redivivus sive chronica observantiae* (Ingolstadt, 1625). Reproduced with permission of the John Carter Brown Library, Brown University.

Viscayan lesser nobility of hidalgos on his father's side.[1] Landa's mother, María Melendez Calderón, was the daughter of a prominent and wealthy nobleman, "the *Alcaide* Juan Ortiz Calderón and doña María Meléndez de Orozco."[2] His father's family were in the service of the Mariscal de Castilla, don Pedro de Ayala y Rojas, in the province of Álava in the region of Ayala. His great-grandfather, Diego de Landa, later served as *merino*, or administrator and judge, of the Valley of Llodio for the Mariscal, and in this capacity was caught up in Basque factional feuding—and in 1508 was murdered by the rival Ugarte faction. When his grandfather, Sancho de Landa, a local scribe, and his uncle Lope de Landa, sought justice for the murder, the subsequent factional fighting forced Landa's father, Diego López de Landa, to flee the region and migrate to Cifuentes to seek employment with the Count of Cifuentes.[3]

Landa's parents met in Cifuentes around 1518. They had at least one son older than Landa, a Juan López de Landa, who continued his father's profession as a scribe in the town of Amurrio. Juan and Diego had at least two sisters: María married a man named Juan Huidobro; and Juana married Geronimo de Funes.[4] A

---

[1]   A witness in Landa's *probanza* testified that he had seen "an official *probanza* that had been done in the land of the grandparents of the said reverend father fray Diego de Landa, on the part of his father, which confirmed that they had been *hijosdalgos*" in the Viscayan town of Amurrio in the province of Ayala (*Testimonio de Francisco de Espada, vecino de esta villa de Cifuentes en la probanza de fray Diego de Landa, obispo electo*, 18 de junio, 1572, AHNob, Condado de Almodovar, caja 40, doc. 8, f. 13r; also see *Carta real de privilegio aprobando y confirmando una concordia hecha entre Don Pedro de Ayala y los hijosdalgo de la tierra de Ayala*, 7 de noviembre, 1490, AGS, Registro General del Sello, 4 folios, in which Landa's great-grandfather, Diego de Landa, signed as an *escudero hijodalgo*).

[2]   *Interrogatorio de preguntas en la probanza hechos por el reverendo padre fray Diego de Landa, obispo electo*, Cifuentes, 9 de junio, 1572, AHNob, Condado de Almodovar, Caja 40, doc. 8, f. 1r. Ortíz Calderón served the IV Count of Cifuentes, don Fernando de Silva Alvarez de Toledo (1480–1546) as his Alcaide, or Warden, of the Castle of Atienza, a prestigious position that made him briefly the jailor of the rebel nobles of the Kings of Navarre (1516) and later of King Francis I of France after he was imprisoned there after the battle of Pavia. He had also served as the agent for the III Count of Cifuentes, don Juan de Silva, when Queen Isabella gifted him the Castle of Atienza in 1508 (*El escribano de Atienza testimonia la presentación por parte de Juan Ortiz Calderón, procurador y representante de Juan de Silva, Conde de Cifuentes*, 30 de junio, 1508, AHNob, Condado de Cifuentes, caja 9, doc. 45, 4 folios; Ortíz Calderon held the post of alcaide for the rest of his life, with the position reconfirmed under the IV Count of Cifuentes—who was Landa's patron).

[3]   See *Pleito litigado por Lope de Landa y Sancho de Landa, vecinos de Ayala con Juan de Ugarte de los Llanos, vecino de Gordejuela sobre el asesinato de Diego de Landa su padre*, 13 de enero, 1509, ARCV, caja 231, 21, 8 folios.

[4]   At least two of his nephews (one from each sister) migrated to Yucatan to take advantage of Landa's patronage network when he was bishop: Geronimo de Funes and Juan Huidobro Barahona. The latter acquired a lucrative treasury position, while a great-nephew, also called

few years before Landa was born, his father and his maternal grandfather, Ortíz Calderón, followed the forces of the Count in his defense of the new king, Charles I, during the *comunero* revolt of 1521.[5] Landa's father thus seems to have vindicated his family for their early support of the rebel Pedro de Ayala; as the Calderons and his father's branch of the Landa family became supporters of the new king, the families rose in prominence through royal service.

While little is known of Landa's earliest years, it is certain that as a member of two prominent families he would have received his education in first letters and literacy in Cifuentes. The Franciscan Monastery of Santa Cruz, financially supported and patronized by the Counts of Cifuentes, offered the sons of prominent families in the region a basic education.[6] Landa thereby became acquainted with the Franciscan order at a young age. This contact must have left an impression on him, as he later visited the convent in Cifuentes often, frequently accepting invitations to give sermons on special feast days.[7]

Landa's family connection with the Count of Cifuentes heavily influenced his future and that of his family. At eight or ten years old, Landa joined the count's household as a page, along with his cousin Diego Ortiz Calderón de Quiros.[8] The

---

Gregorio de Funes, eventually became an encomendero in Yucatan (*Relación de Méritos y servicios de Juan Huidobro Barahona, quien sirvió en la administración de alcabalas y rentas reales de Palencia*, AGI, Indiferente General, 161, núm. 558, 2 folios). A third great-nephew from his father's family in Amurrio, also named Diego de Landa, came over after Landa became bishop in 1578, serving as a secular clergyman in Landa's bishopric shortly before his death (*Información de la limpieza de sangre de Diego de Landa, clérigo residente en Mérida, Yucatán, para notario del comisario de Yucatán*, AGN, Ramo de Inquisición, vol. 189, exp. 16).

[5] Testimonies on the Count of Cifuentes and his actions in the region of Toledo are in a legal case seeking compensation for *comunero* destruction of the count's property (see *Pleito de Hernando de Silva, conde de Cifuentes, alférez mayor de Su Majestad y del Consejo, con Alonso del Castillo, Antonio de Dueñas, Luis de la Cruz, Juan Hurtado y otros muchos consortes, vecinos de Toledo y comuneros, sobre la reclamación de una indemnización por los daños que el conde recibió en tiempos de las Comunidades*, 1524, ARCV, Pleitos Civiles, caja 294, doc. 297).

[6] Santa Cruz was founded in 1484 by the III Count of Cifuentes, don Juan de Silva, in response to his liberation from the Muslims of Granada after a brief captivity; his son, the IV Count, spent lavish amounts of money to expand the monastery by paying for the "construction of the lower and upper cloisters, and the creation of an infirmary, and he walled off the groves and gardens, paying such attention to them that with his own hands he planted many of the trees in the convent's gardens" (see Salazar, *Historia genealógica de la Casa de Silva*, f. 343).

[7] For example, according to the Guardian of Santa Cruz, "on his urging and request" Landa preached a celebratory sermon "in the presence of the Count and Countess of Cifuentes" on the feast day of Corpus Christi on June 11, 1572, while he was in Cifuentes attending to family business (see Landa's *Probanza*, AHNob, Condado de Almodovar, caja 40, doc. 8, f. 22v).

[8] The Maestresalas of the Count's household, don Pedro de Ludeña, later testified in the

young cousins would have followed the count as he moved between his primary residence, the family's palace in Toledo, and a smaller castle in Cifuentes, as well as regular visits to Arevalo, Ocaña, and Madrid; and he likewise would have accompanied him to Rome when the count took up the position of Ambassador to the Pope on behalf of Charles V (and, as mentioned earlier, this would have allowed the young Landa to see the Pantheon, as he hints in the Account; Sec. 42, f. 49v).[9]

Through his service (1534–1541) as a page of the highly influential Count of Cifuentes, Landa would come to know the most prominent people at court, establishing personal connections that would aid him well in the future. Upon returning from Rome in 1537, the count was appointed as Mayordomo Mayor to the Empress Isabella (until her death in 1539), later holding the same position running the household of the young princesses, doña Maria de Austria and doña Juana de Austria, residing with them from 1538–1545 in the towns of Arevalo, Ocaña, and the city of Toledo. During this period, Landa thus lived in the same household where the future King Philip II's sisters, Maria and Juana, resided. No doubt Landa would have met Prince Philip while in Ocaña and Toledo, as he paid visits to his sisters in 1540 and 1541; this, of course, was the very prince who, as king, would name Landa as Bishop of Yucatan in 1572.[10]

*   *   *

Don Fernando de Silva, a great patron of the Franciscan Order, must have looked with pride on Landa's decision sometime in late 1541 to leave his employ and join

---

probanza of the bishop elect that "when he was a young boy I knew him well and dealt with him frequently since they both lived together in the household of the said Illustrious Count, Don Fernando, for whom this witness served as his *maestresala*" (*Testimonio de Pedro de Ludeña, maestresala del IV Conde de Cifuentes Don Fernando de Silva, en la probanza de hidalguía de fray Diego de Landa, obispo electo*, 19 de junio, 1573, AHNob, Condado de Almodovar, caja 40, doc. 8, fs. 8r–10r).

[9] For a listing of the properties, palaces, and estates owned by the Counts of Cifuentes, where Landa may have occasionally resided, see Begoña Riesco de Iturri, "Propiedades y fortuna de los condes de Cifuentes," 146–51. The count frequently complained about the lack of payment of his royal stipend while in Rome and the high cost of having transported, and having to maintain, his household (*Carta de Fernando de Silva, conde de Cifuentes, embajador en Roma, al secretario Francisco de los Cobos, solicitando su salario y la ayuda de costa que se le debe*, 13 de diciembre, 1533, AGS, legajo 1366, fs. 85r–86v).

[10] For information on the household of the princesses and the royal visitations that Landa may have witnessed as a page of the count in Arevalo, Toledo, and Ocaña see Carlos Morales et al., "El servicio de las casas castellanas del emperador," 129–42. The Emperor Charles V and his son Philip met and spent the Christmas holidays with Maria and Juana on December 18–27, 1540; Landa had turned sixteen the month before, and thus as an older page of the count he would likely have interacted with the emperor and the prince.

the Order.[11] He could have chosen no better monastic house to make his profession as a friar; the magnificent Gothic monastery of San Juan de los Reyes was the first great structure seen by anyone entering Toledo. Together with its cathedral and the royal palace or *alcázar*, the monastery was one of the three greatest monuments that dominated the skyline of the city, a testament to the power of the Franciscan Order there. King Philip II himself later exclaimed upon visiting and admiring the convent, "there is no doubt that this one brings us the most glory!"[12]

Landa entered San Juan de los Reyes at the age of sixteen, in 1541. Built by the *reyes católicos*, Ferdinand and Isabella, in 1477, almost since its inception the convent had been under the control of the Observant wing of the Order of St. Francis. The Observants were the most ardent advocates of the seraphic role that they believed Franciscans had in hastening the apocalyptic Second Coming of Christ, and thus by the time Landa took his vows at age eighteen, he was well immersed in millenarian ideology.[13] Any prospective Franciscan friar had to begin as a novice and, according to the Regula of St. Francis, the period of the novitiate lasted at least a year.[14] As a novice, Landa passed his time in prayer and conducting services and daily chores in the monastery. During the novitiate, Landa would have been indoctrinated in Franciscan culture by receiving a formal education and immersion in the life under the rules of St. Francis. Part of his day would have included sitting in and "listening" to the lectures and courses of the Franciscan teachers, or *lectores*, of grammar and rhetoric. He would have also set time aside to read and consult the major works on the life of St. Francis and other biblical sources and commentaries. San Juan de los Reyes held one of the largest convent libraries in Spain, an exceptional collection of volumes that would have afforded Landa access to all the classics and patristic volumes that were later used with erudition in various sections of the Account.[15]

---

[11] The Count of Cifuentes likely aided Landa with a small donation as required for a dependent or *criado* to enter into a monastic order (Salazar, *Historia de la Casa de Silva*, fs. 333–49).

[12] "*No hay duda, que este nos lleva la gala!*" (Álvarez, *Memorial illustre de los famosos hijos*, f. 23).

[13] Fray Juan de Yepes, Landa's older companion from his novitiate in Toledo, stated in 1572 that "it was about thirty years ago that he [Landa] professed the habit of our Lord San Francisco, and he did so in the company of this witness;" that would have been 1542, the year the Spaniards founded Merida in Yucatan (*Testimonio del padre fray Juan de Yepes, fraile del convento de la Santa Cruz de la villa de Cifuentes*, 18 de Junio, 1572, AHNob, Condado de Almodovar, caja 40, doc. 8, fs. 25r–25v; also see Davis, "Evangelical Prophecies," 93).

[14] On the noviate of Landa's day see "*Capítulo XLIIII: En el qual prosiguiendo la explicación del dicho capítulo segundo de nuestra Regla se trata de la forma del hábito de los Novicios, y del año del Noviciado*," in Miranda, *Exposición de la Regla de los Frayles Menores*, fs. 261–68.

[15] The library contained all of the main texts of the time and even a large collection of manuscripts and books donated to it by the Catholic Monarchs themselves. Unfortunately, in 1808 the famed library and its archives were lost to a fire that consumed much of the monastery, destroying any documentation on the young friar Landa. The clergyman Francisco Barrilero

As a member of the observant branch of the Franciscan order, Landa would have pursued a mystic path of emulating the life of St. Francis. As a novice, his spiritual transformation into a Franciscan friar necessitated a purging of his worldly pursuits and the shunning of all vanity—so much so, that even in the education he gained he could not receive or use any formal degrees or titles. Landa himself later noted, in reference to his lack of the use of the title of "Doctor of Theology," a course of study that he had pursued in various Franciscan schools:

> when a friar of the order is skillful and sufficient enough to preach and declare the Holy Gospel and teach the word of God, he appears before the chapter of his province and there they examine him and see his skill and science, and this being sufficient they give him leave and a license to preach, and none who do not have such a license can preach or teach, and such a license serves for us in our order, like what in other religions are the degrees of bachelor, licentiate [*licenciado*], and doctor.[16]

Landa undoubtedly pursued advanced study. Moreover, he and the other Observant Franciscans viewed this gradual mystical transformation through reading, education, and meditation as a marriage of their soul to God. Part of this mystical connection the Franciscans manifested in a longing for Christian self-sacrifice and martyrdom, modeled on the sufferings and crucifixion of Christ.[17] By emulating the life of St. Francis, each young friar sought their own "stigmata" or crown of martyrdom.

If Landa came to desire martyrdom, as many young friars did, there was no better convent in Spain to achieve this mystical education, or perfect the desire for martyrdom, than San Juan de los Reyes. The years of 1541–1542 at the convent were filled with momentous visits of friars from the New World, bringing news of the Franciscan conversions in Mexico, Yucatan, and elsewhere in New Spain.[18] These

---

wrote in the official *Relación sobre el incendio de San Juan de los Reyes* (1808): "*Se quemó toda el 19 de Diciembre de 1808 en la quema general del convento y quedan reunidos bastantes volúmenes, de los que no se ha podido formar su índice por la cortedad del tiempo.*" For a partial inventory of what the library once contained, see Abad Pérez, "La biblioteca franciscana de Toledo (1284–1808)," 18–36 (which includes the Barrilero quote).

16   See question number 7 that Landa himself presented for the taking of witness testimony on his merits and qualities as a Franciscan friar, in *Interrogatorio de preguntas en la probanza hechos por el reverendo padre fray Diego de Landa, obispo electo*, Cifuentes, 9 de Junio, 1572, AHNob, Condado de Almodóvar, caja 40, doc. 8, f. 4r–4v.

17   For the origins of this Franciscan desire for Christian martyrdom, see Daniel, "Desire for Martyrdom," as well as the recent study by MacEvitt, *Martyrdom of the Franciscans*.

18   A surviving chronicle of the Convent of San Juan de los Reyes contains a record of the events in the convent during the period that Landa professed there: *Memoriale libro ordinis minorum nostri ab anno divini 1506–1625, Convento de la orden de San Francisco de San Juan de los Reyes*, Toledo, AHN, Clero, Libro 15923; it also contains reports of various Franciscan

visitors would have filled the minds of the novices with desires to fight idols and perhaps achieve the "crown of martyrdom." Fray Jacobo de Testera, the first missionary to the Maya (as mentioned in the Account; Sec. 17, f. 12v), stayed at the monastery for several weeks during Landa's novitiate, and surely spoke to Landa and others about the Maya script and culture based on his own missions there from 1537–1539.[19]

Sometime in 1542, after ending his novitiate and early studies, Landa made his full profession as a friar in Toledo. Recognizing his aptitude for further study, the guardian of the monastery at the time, fray Pedro de Bobadilla (who ironically would later serve as the Castilian Province's judge in the case against Landa for usurping the powers of an inquisitor) nominated him for further study at the Franciscan province of Castilla's center for higher education: the convent of San Antonio de la Cabrera in the rocky region of Buitrago.

As the chroniclers of the order noted, "this convent, placed as it was in the mountains, was very propitious for contemplation, and for studies, little frequented by any laypeople."[20] Here Landa began his intensive studies of Latin, grammar, and rhetoric. As he quickly excelled in Latin, his Franciscan *lectores* advanced him there to the study of philosophy and theology. One of his closest friends, fray Agustín de Moragón, later noted his aptitude for his studies and testified that he had "resided there with him together in that monastery," that they had studied together their *latinidad* since they were of the same age, and that they were "very devoted friends."[21] Landa's early years as a friar there (1543–1548) were filled not only with a passion for learning, but also with this Franciscan zeal, as Moragón and other colleagues later testified. Fray Agustín saw in Landa the sanctity and dedication "during his youth there which showed him to be a good religious friar," describing his dedication to prayer and study "five or six o'clock in the morning until twelve noon"—claiming that the other younger friars commonly said that "Landa must be a saint, because they all said that he was always more advanced in his studies and the things of truth and religion."[22]

In 1548, aged twenty-five, having completed his advanced education and served as a friar at the convent of San Antonio de la Cabrera, Landa gained permission to join a missionary expedition to Yucatan. As Moragón later remembered, Landa

---

martyrs in Mexico, like fray Juan de Espiritu Santo, from 1538–1542 (fs., 27r–31v).

[19] See *Memoriale libro ordinis minorum*, f. 28r.

[20] Álvarez, *Memorial illustre de los famosos hijos*, f. 111.

[21] See *Testimonio del reverendo padre fray Agustín Moragón, Guardian del convento Franciscano de la Santa Cruz de Cifuentes*, Cifuentes, 19 de junio, 1572, AHNob, Condado de Almodovar, caja 40, doc. 8, fs. 22r–23r.

[22] *Testimonio del reverendo padre fray Agustín Moragón*, fs. 18r–22v.

"gained license to pass over to the Indies with fray Nicolás de Albalate, and he went with great zeal to go and convert the Indians." Landa and the others who left with Albalate were missed at the convent, Moragón added, but they also knew that Landa and his colleagues would "go and gain great fruit in the conversions of the gentiles because they would serve as a great example, and they went only for God."[23]

*   *   *

Fray Diego was thus still a young man—only twenty-five—when he first landed, full of missionary zeal, in the newly founded colonial province of Yucatan. The year was 1549, just seven years after the Maya city of Tiho had been claimed and renamed as Merida, the colony's capital and its only Spanish city. Landa was not among the first Franciscans in Yucatan; at least eight had come from Guatemala and Mexico in 1544.[24] But he was part of the second generation, and the first to come from Spain, one of between seven and nine recruited by fray Nicolás de Albalate. Albalate was one of the original eight, and he had sailed back to Spain in 1548 to convince others that Yucatan was a land of opportunity for a friar interested in saving souls by the thousands.[25]

When Landa arrived in the province the following year, the Yucatan mission was very much in its fledgling stage. There were just two completed convents, in Merida and Mani, and another in Valladolid (Sisal) currently under construction. The total number of friars in the entire colony in 1549—after the arrival of Landa and his fellow travelers, added to those had come in 1544, plus a few more arrivals from Guatemala, but minus two deaths—was still only nineteen. The conquistador-settlers controlled but a corner of the peninsula and numbered only in the hundreds. The mission's challenge was thus considerable. Despite a dramatic fall in population, there remained several hundred thousand Mayas scattered in small villages across a region held in check mostly by violence or its threat.

---

[23] *Testimonio del reverendo padre fray Agustín Moragón*, fs. 20v–21r.

[24] According to fray Bernardo de Lizana, the first Franciscan friars who arrived as permanent missionaries from Guatemala included fray Luis de Villalpando (as Comisario y Prelado), fray Melchior de Benevente, fray Nicolás Albalate, fray Ángel Maldonado, fray Juan de Herrera (as Lego); coming from Mexico, and arriving earlier, fray Lorenzo de Bienvenida arrived in time to join the expeditions of conquest to the Bacalar region (Lizana, *Historia de Yucatán*, 43v–45r). These earliest friars soon after were joined by fray Juan de la Puerta and five other friars (Lizana, *Historia de Yucatán*, 56r).

[25] Cogolludo names six (Cogolludo, *Historia de Yucathan*, Libro V, Capítulo IX); Villalpando told the king in 1550 there were seven (DHY, Vol. I:4). Along with Albalate, a group of six Franciscan friars arrived in Campeche in late 1549 (Lizana, *Historia de Yucatán*, 43v). Included among the six were fray Diego de Landa, fray Francisco Navarro, fray Antonio de Valdemoro, fray Antonio de Figueras, fray Pedro de Noriega, and fray Alonso de Alvarado (see Carrillo y Ancona, *El Obispado de Yucatán*, Vol. I, 276–77).

Spaniards were as much a part of the proselytizing challenge as were Mayas. The first Franciscans were convinced that violence by Spanish settlers was a barrier to conversion. The head of the mission, fray Luis de Villalpando, wrote letters to the crown denouncing his compatriot colonists. As mentioned earlier, the first generation of conqueror-settlers were granted groups of Maya villages in trust, or in encomienda, from which they could draw labor and tribute payments. These encomenderos, obligated to facilitate the conversion of their encomienda "Indians," tended to be more interested in their exploitation. Thus, in Yucatan, as elsewhere in the Spanish American provinces, friar-encomendero hostility was inevitable and common. Villalpando's letters, including a notorious one of 1550 that detailed the specific atrocities of ten of the colony's prominent settlers, helped lay the foundation for an antagonistic relationship between church and state in Yucatan that would persist for centuries.[26]

Landa appears to have shared Villalpando's abhorrence of abuses by conquistador-encomenderos. The passage in the Account that details such abuses (Sec. 15, fs. 11v–12v), while absolving the three Montejos, was likely copied by the colonial-period editor from a larger section that Landa probably compiled during the 1550s as he heard these stories from Villalpando, other friars, and Maya neophytes. He may also have found Las Casas's writings on these atrocities worth summarizing. Landa likewise shared Villalpando's view—at least during the 1550s—that a successful campaign of conversion should be guided by a spirit of compassion and a commitment to protecting the "Indians" from Spanish settlers as much as from their own "vices."

Shortly after Landa's arrival in 1549, the order held a Capítulo Custodial, a kind of "chapter meeting" for the administrative region—which remained a part of the Franciscan Province of Guatemala—to elect friars to leadership positions and to strategize the next stage of their evangelical campaign.[27] It was decided that Landa would accompany his more senior brother, fray Lorenzo de Bienvenida, into the eastern territories of the peninsula, which had yet to be proselytized. There they were to establish a new mission town. The two men's route from Merida into the largely unconquered eastern regions of the peninsula likely took the same roads the Maya had used for centuries—raised causeways paved with white stucco and

---

[26] AGI, *Diversos-Colecciones*, 23, no. 55 (1550-10-15).

[27] The Franciscan Order, in terms of its governance, held "councils" or chapter meetings every three years in order to decide upon the election of officials and *guardianes* for their monastic houses for the next triennium (three-year period). The *Diccionario de autoridades* defines these *capítulos* as the "regularly held meetings which the members of various military orders or religious orders hold so as to conduct elections of officials, and deal with other matters relating to their orders and institutions" (Vol. 2, 1729). When the Franciscan Order held elections for the selection of their general, the highest-ranking official of the order, these meetings were called a Capítulo General.

called *sacbeob*, or "white roads," in Yucatec Maya. About forty-five miles due east of the provincial capital, they came across a vast set of ancient Maya buildings. These structures were mostly in disrepair, but the settlement among and around the buildings was still inhabited. The local residents included a handful of Maya religious specialists who oversaw a local cult dedicated to the deity of health, sacred knowledge, and writing, the powerful Itzamna. The Maya called the city Itzmal.

On August 6 of that year, Bienvenida and Landa recited mass on top of the largest pyramid in the city, later recorded as Kinich Kakmo. The Account includes a sketch of this structure that, while simple, is remarkably accurate in its architectural details. We can assume that the manuscript's copyists never traveled to the peninsula, so had no firsthand knowledge of these three structures; and yet the Spanish scribes seem to have reproduced Landa's images with remarkable fidelity (we shall return to these drawings, as well as the maps in the Account, in chapter 7). Within weeks the friars had co-opted a neighboring structure, the Ppap Hol Chac, to use as their base of missionary operations. Although their evangelical journey was far from over—Izamal was only halfway between Merida and the settlers' eastern outpost, the new town of Valladolid—the friars decided to use this Maya pilgrimage site as a base. The ancient cult of Itzmanaaj would be replaced by a new cult, that of the True Faith.[28]

The next four years, Landa intermittently spent considerable periods of time in Maya villages that had no other European presence, some many days' walk from Izamal. It was likely during this time that he became fluent in Yucatec Mayan, and he made many of the observations that would later surface as quasi-anthropological details in passages of the Account.

At the chapter meeting of 1551, held in the monastery at Merida, Landa was named the fourth *Difinidor* (a prestigious position that made him a member of the Provincial's governing council) and he was selected to reside in the convent at Conkal. In 1553, the Franciscan Order held another Custodial Chapter meeting, and fray Lorenzo was summoned back to Merida to serve as the convent's custodian. This left Landa fully in charge of a nascent Izamal (the Hispanized name given to Itzmal by the mission's guardian friar). So, although his appointment to Conkal had been for a three-year term, he was actually in Izamal by 1553. Between then and 1559, Landa and Izamal's resident Maya population worked to transform the site's second largest structure, what was later called Ppap Hol Chac, into a functioning monastic complex. The structure seems to have mimicked that of the Kinich Kakmo in that it was composed of a monumental base, here reaching at least sixteen feet high, that served as a kind of platform for pyramid mounds, plazas, and other structural forms. Unlike the Kinich Kakmo, however, the Ppap Hol Chac's summit structures

---

[28] For an overview of this remaking, see Solari, *Maya Ideologies of the Sacred*, 127–44.

fortuitously mimicked the design of European monasteries in that they included a series of inward-facing rectilinear range structures. In this way, the Izamal pyramid was nearly identical in design to the great pyramid in Tiho, described by Bienvenida, which similarly served as the base for Merida's Franciscan convent.[29]

By all accounts, Landa was one of the most driven and energetic of the Franciscans who labored in Yucatan in the 1550s. During that decade he devoted himself to the creation of a Yucatec church in the form of a network of convents, village churches, and converted Maya parishioners. But his crowning achievement—if one puts aside the loss of the Maya buildings thereby destroyed—was the transformation of the precontact Maya metropolis of Izamal into one of the most impressive monastic complexes in the Americas, and the most extraordinary in the whole Maya area. Today visited by thousands of tourists and pilgrims alike, Izamal retains the city plan first outlined by Landa, as well as much of its colonial architecture and associated painting. As such, it is a kind of architectural and urban time capsule, and it is certainly the most substantial material imprint that Landa left in his bishopric.

Although Landa's refashioning of this ancient city can only be gleaned from the later accounts of his Franciscan brothers and the surviving architectural remains, there is little doubt that the town reflects his evangelical vision; that is, he was the mastermind behind not only the town's monastery but its urban design as well. For most of the decade that it took for the Maya city to be transformed into a proper Christian town, Landa was resident (see figure 2.2). Even after his religious duties required him to spend time in Merida, he preferred to be in Izamal and resided there whenever possible.

In 1557, Landa was elected Custodian of the Franciscan province of Yucatan, and by 1561 he had become Provincial, or head of the order in the colony. The following year, however, Landa's career took a less felicitous turn—as did the Maya experience of Franciscan missionary methods. Frustrated and angered by evidence of "idolatrous" activities in the region of Mani, where the dominant dynasty of the Xiu had more or less collaborated in the imposition of colonial rule, the resident friar Pedro de Ciudad Rodrigo, six visiting Franciscans (Juan Pizzaro, Francisco Aparicio, Antonio Verdugo, Francisco Miranda, Francisco de Santa Gadea, and Miguel de la Puebla), and the local encomendero instituted a violent campaign of extirpation—with Landa's knowledge and approval. Landa joined them in Mani a few weeks later with written formal authorization from the province's governor,

---

[29] Writing to Prince Philip in 1548, Bienvenida described the largest structures in Tiho as "at the height of five steps, of worked stone, and on top of the buildings, four quarters all of cells like those for friars, of 20 feet in length and 10 in width. All of the doorways are carved of a single stone at the height of the door and of the vault . . . the friars took these buildings for the site of the house of St. Francis" (Bienvenida, "Carta a S.A. el Principe Don Felipe," 71).

Figure 2.2. Glimpsing Landa. A likely portrait of Landa from a badly faded mural located on the façade of the Franciscan convent of Saint Anthony of Padua, Izamal. Photograph by the authors.

don Diego Quijada. For Landa, there was no hypocrisy in his actions; his continued use of "torment" was legal, regulated, and sanctioned by its higher purpose, categorically different in his mind from the arbitrary, extrajudicial violence that he had condemned in his description of conquistador behavior. Within a few months, over 4,500 Maya men and women had been questioned under torture, another 6,300 given various punishments (including ritual humiliation, public flogging, and forced servitude), at least 157 (and possibly several hundred) had died at the hands of their interrogators, 32 were permanently maimed, and dozens had committed suicide—all as the campaign spread menacingly across the colony. It was, in short, a war of terror against a subject population. Then, to the relief of Mayas and Spanish settlers alike, Yucatan's first resident bishop—a Franciscan friar named Francisco de Toral—finally reached the colony. Landa's extirpation campaign was immediately halted.[30]

The campaign was, as one scholar concluded, "an extraordinarily brutal affair."[31] It violated even the norms of an era steeped in violence and prejudice; it flouted the Council of the Indies's 1543 prohibition against counterproductively severe inquisitorial measures; it gave Landa the infamous reputation that still persists; and it continues to demand, and often confound, explanation. Was Landa's unflinching use of torture merely the action of "a missionary priest first and last," determined "to advance the Christian faith" at all costs (as France Scholes asserted)? Was his motivation more specifically a commitment to the authority of the Franciscans—over both Mayas and Spaniards in the colony (as Chuchiak has argued)? Was he enraged by a personal sense of betrayal (as Clendinnen suggested)? Was his extremism driven by an apocalyptic vision of the crucial nature of his mission, with the Franciscans and converted Mayas "the last hope of Christendom," and the very salvation of humanity at stake (as Davis argues)?[32]

These explanations are surely all valid and mutually compatible, as is a further point stressed variously by a number of scholars: that the chillingly vicious nature of the torments applied in 1562 to Maya men and women, young and old, prompted the victims to admit to the beliefs and practices that were fed to them by their interrogators.[33] Those men were more familiar with European convictions regarding the diabolistic perversion of Christianity by witches, Jews, Muslims, and Nahuas than they were with Maya religion, thus generating a grimly imaginative feedback loop featuring such details as heart-sacrificed children and crucified pigs. Two of us (Restall and Solari) are persuaded that all the confessed and offending practices of the Maya, beyond the simple hiding of codices and sacred objects, were unwittingly imagined and invented by Landa and his fellow interrogators. As Alejandro Enríquez notes, "tales of blasphemous ritual murder were an integral part of Franciscan lore";[34] they were, in Yucatan in 1562, Franciscan fiction. True or not, Landa believed the confessions, and that drove the campaign into greater excesses.

[30] Gonzalez Cicero, *Perspectiva religiosa en Yucatán*, 180–208; Clendinnen, *Ambivalent Conquests*, 72–92; Tedlock, "Torture in the Archives"; Timmer, "Providence and Perdition"; Restall, *Maya Conquistador*, 151–68; Chuchiak, "In Servitio Dei," 614–19; Enríquez, "Exuberant Imagination."

[31] Davis, "Evangelical Prophecies," 97.

[32] Scholes, "Franciscan Missionary Scholars," 415; Chuchiak, "In Servitio Dei"; Clendinnen, *Ambivalent Conquests*, 123; Davis (who also summarizes the above interpretations), "Evangelical Prophecies," 100.

[33] Tedlock, "Torture in the Archives"; Timmer, "Providence and Perdition"; Enríquez, "Exuberant Imagination."

[34] Enríquez, "Exuberant Imagination," 280; see also Hsia, *Myth of Ritual Murder*.

Toral's arrival prevented that loop of imagination and violence from resulting in further excesses planned by Landa—such as the burning alive of Maya leaders. By 1563, Landa was back in Spain, under a cloud of accusations of improper action, eager to defend himself. Because there is a page in the Account that claims an authorial date of 1566, some scholars have seen the entire manuscript as an important part of that defense. Others have seen it as an act of contrition and restitution for the wrongs done to the Mayas in the summer of 1562. Another suggestion is that Landa wrote "the book" as "part and product of his recruiting campaign" to attract more Franciscan volunteers to Yucatan, on the assumption that he would be vindicated and allowed to return. These proposals as to motive all have merit and in addition are mutually compatible, but they are complicated by the fact that the Account is not what most scholars have taken it to be. Clendinnen's comment that the Account is "a very odd document" is an accurate evaluation of its *form*. But for that very reason, it is not a useful description of its *content*. In other words, the text cannot be used to explore Landa's thinking about 1562, for example (emphasizing what he omitted from his "book," as Clendinnen does), because the Account is a multi-authored, copied document marked by numerous omissions created by others; it was not entirely made by Landa himself. That said, parts of the Account clearly stem from the five-year period (1564–1569) when Landa was working on both his great *recopilación* and his defense—a defense that vindicated him completely. Not only was he exonerated from any wrongdoing, but he was now poised for a triumphant final chapter to his life in Yucatan.

*   *   *

With Yucatan's first bishop, Toral, dead, Landa—vindicated and in Spain—was well positioned to succeed him. Sure enough, in 1572, he was appointed as Yucatan's next bishop, and he left Spain with thirty friars recruited to bolster Franciscan efforts in the province. He landed at Campeche in the autumn of 1573 and immediately renewed his efforts to strengthen the church. He did so with little compromise until his death in Merida on April 29, 1579, from complications caused by pneumonia.[35] News of his death quickly filled the correspondence of civil and religious officials. Fray Thomás de Arenas, the visiting Franciscan commissary to the province in 1579 who had arrived shortly before Landa's death, offered a eulogy to the friar-bishop. He wrote to the Crown:

---

[35] Landa's fatal case of pneumonia appears to have been aggravated by preexisting poor health, especially a form of asthma, "which bothered him since his youth" (Lizana, *Historia de Yucatán*, 87v).

While engaged in the visitation of the religious friars of San Francisco in this bishopric and province of Yucatan, the death of fray Diego de Landa occurred, a saint and
true servant of God, and a very true chaplain of Your Majesty in all of the things he
had done to remedy the royal conscience of Your Majesty, and his own, in his works
he was always a true padre and defender of the natives, and all here in the republic
have felt his loss greatly as they have told me in the various places through which I
have passed after news of his death.[36]

Landa was a controversial and pugnacious bishop, but the Franciscan Order
in Yucatan did not clash with him in the 1570s, and he in turn held the friars
close—even at the hour of his death, preferring to die in a friar's cell in the convent of Merida rather than in the episcopal residence next to the cathedral. Landa
insisted he was always a humble Franciscan, and though then a bishop, he did not
turn his back on his colleagues; upon returning to Merida in 1573, he had kneeled
before his fellow friars at the Convent of the Madre de Dios and proclaimed:

My dear spiritual brothers and fathers, you whose relationship to me is closer than
that of my own blood . . . Even though my present position as bishop might appear to
separate me from you, I swear that it cannot divide me from you, because I have and
always will be a son of our Father Saint Francis . . . Now that I have returned, I come
to you not as bishop, but rather as a son of this holy Province into whose brother-
hood I once again seek to incorporate myself.[37]

But as close as he may have remained with his fellow friars, Landa was widely
loathed by the Spanish settlers. His drive to expand the powers of the episcopacy
was often met with staunch resistance by the province's civil officials and by its
encomendero-colonists. As one lieutenant governor wrote, "the person who has
so scandalized the province here is none other than the bishop . . . and this is very
notorious because he does not guard the peace with any of the citizens here, nor
does he wish to have peace with the secular justices, nor will he ever have peace with
anybody because of his unbridled ambition and desire to control everything."[38]

Many examples can be given of a zeal that the settlers saw as conflictual and

---

[36] See *Carta de fray Tomas de Arenas, Comisario visitador de la provincia franciscana de Yucatan,
con noticias de la muerte del Obispo Fray Diego de Landa*, AGI, Audiencia de Guatemala, 170,
2 folios.

[37] Fray Bernardo de Lizana, *Historia de Yucatán*, 116v; and recounted in Cogolludo, *Historia
de Yucathan*, Libro VI, Capítulo XV.

[38] See *Carta del teniente del gobernador de Yucatán a los Inquisidores de México con su parecer
sobre una competencia de jurisdicción entre el Dean Lic. Cristobal de Miranda y el obispo
Fr. Diego de Landa*, 20 de julio 1577, AGN, Inquisición, vol. 83, exp. 4, fs. 6–7.

Figure 2.3. Survivors. Page 39a from the Dresden Codex (*left*), one of only four Maya codices that survived codex-burning campaigns by Franciscans and other religious in colonial Yucatan, and a page from the Book of Chilam Balam of Chumayel (*right*), one of about a dozen extant colonial-era alphabetic copies made by Maya notaries of disappearing glyphic books.

controlling. His efforts to extirpate "idolatry" continued, for example, despite the enormous controversy that his autos-da-fé of 1562 had prompted. The campaign of the 1570s actually featured more public rituals of mass humiliation than had been held in 1562, but this time he had the power as bishop to conduct them.[39] Landa and his Franciscan commissary judges held so many public displays of punishment that the governors and Spaniards complained bitterly. Governor don Guillén de Las Casas wrote to the Inquisitors in Mexico City that "the worst thing is that the Bishop is giving the friars commissions as Inquisitors of the Holy Office of the Ordinary, and they carry along with their commissions, prosecutors and notaries,

---

[39]   See Chuchiak, *El castigo y la represión*, 195–220; and Chuchiak, "La iglesia evangelizadora," 183–91.

and they have hung, tortured and punished a large number of Indians."[40] Even the Inquisition commissary complained of their rigor, and Landa's procedures in naming his judges and himself "ordinary inquisitors."[41]

The irony of the attention given to the 1562 campaign, both then and now, is that it has tended to overshadow the fact that Landa, his colleagues and rivals (even Toral), and his successors for generations continued to hunt, gather, and destroy the material vestiges of non-Christian Maya religion. That included glyphic books or codices, which were evidently not *all* burned during that violent summer. We cannot know exactly how many were lost or how many survived.[42] But the dramatic, cinematic image of Landa enacting a cultural conflagration was in reality the start of a far more protracted process of destruction, survival, and cultural evolution. After all, some of the Maya codices were also transcribed into alphabetic books, copied and maintained by the elite in each *cah*; more than a dozen of those have survived, most of them known to us as the Books of Chilam Balam (see figure 2.3).[43]

The Spanish colony in the peninsula would outlive Landa by almost two-and-a-half centuries. Meanwhile, to this day the Roman Catholic Church is still based in the same spot on the main square where the early cathedral of Merida stood in Landa's day, and it is arguably as significant an institution in Yucatan as it ever was. Yet Landa remains better known—certainly more infamous—than any of the bishops that have succeeded him. His legacy is complex, contradictory, and controversial and is unlikely to get any less so in the near future.

---

[40] *Carta del gobernador de Yucatán, don Francisco Velázquez de Gijón a los inquisidores de México sobre la usurpación del obispo de la jurisdicción del Santo Oficio en el castigo de la idolatría*, julio, 1577, AGN, Ramo de Inquisición, vol. 83, exp. 4, fs. 8–9.

[41] Chuchiak, "In Servitio Dei," 635–38.

[42] Chuchiak has documented that there were scores more destroyed through the seventeenth century ("Images Speak"; and especially Chuchiak, *El castigo y la represión*).

[43] The historical literatures here are extensive, but good starting points on the colonial-era campaigns to locate and destroy religious statues and books are Chuchiak, "Toward a Regional Definition"; "Images Speak"; and "In Servitio Dei." On the Books of Chilam Balam and colonial-era Maya-made books in related genres, see Knowlton, *Maya Creation Myths*; and the publications of Christensen (e.g., *Teabo Manuscript*).

3

The History of the Account and Maya Studies

Landa did not write the Relación, or Account. That is, as outlined earlier, copyists at a later time created the Account from a larger manuscript, a *recopilación* that long ago disappeared. Furthermore, as we shall detail in chapter 6, much of both the Account and its lost parent, the *recopilación*, comprised material copied or summarized from manuscripts and books written by others—most notably copied by the Cronistas de las Indias working in the scriptoria of Madrid. After his death in 1579, Landa left copies of his writings both in Spain and in Merida. Most likely a great *recopilación* was placed in the Franciscan convent in Merida, Yucatan, where it was read and cited in the seventeenth century—at the end of which, it was either lost or taken to Spain. Either way, it has never been found. The Account that we know was compiled in Spain as a selection of excerpts or notes taken from the larger work, presumably amounting to a fraction of the lost *recopilación*.[1]

Unfortunately, previous scholars knew little about the circumstances under which those excerpts were copied out. It is tempting to ignore the entire copyist stage, and simply imagine Landa himself composing the Account as part of his

---

[1] Landa himself alluded to this much longer "*relación*" about the missionary work and "idolatry" of the Maya, which he had prepared for presentation before the King; in his response to the ninth charge against him, Landa wrote: "concerning the lack of doctrine of the Indians, I respond with what I have written in the *relación* that I have made to give to His Majesty, and in all of this I remit the information I have presented" (*Respuesta de fray Diego de Landa a los cargos hechos por fray Francisco de Guzmán*, AGI, Escribanía de Cámara, 1009A).

https://doi.org/10.5876/9781646424245.c003

battle to defend his actions of 1562. Indeed, Clendinnen suggested that, in 1566 "after the committee had entered its judgement, in the quiet of a Spanish monastery, he wrote his *Relación*."[2] Such an image is appealing, but very misleading. The "committee" did not reach a final verdict in Landa's case until 1569; the final letter of exoneration was notarized on January 30 of that year.

It is true that what Landa did write was designed in part to defend himself before the Council of the Indies and before the Provincial of his own order in Castile (fray Francisco de Guzmán, whom the Council charged with proceeding in a case against Landa within the order in 1565). And Landa's *recopilación* on the Maya and on his mission served him well, helping him to eventually be exonerated for "having proved your intensions well," as fray Antonio de Córdoba, the Order's Provincial Minister in Castile, concluded; "and we find that you have no fault nor exceeded in your office in the things that you are accused of having done."[3]

Still, this verdict notwithstanding, it was his connections at the papal court that allowed Landa to acquire a papal bull in 1572 confirming his total exoneration—thereby removing all doubt about his actions as an ordinary inquisitor while serving as the Franciscan prelate in Yucatan a decade earlier.[4] In a *memorial*, Landa described the types of writings and "evidence" he presented, including an extensive "information which will confirm for Your Majesty that the Indians have been preached to and instructed very well in the things of Our Holy Catholic faith, and that they have not erred in ignorance."[5] As is clear from the varied nature of the Account, Landa wrote his original *recopilación* of *probanzas*, *relaciones* and other supporting documents about the Maya missions, their conversion, and their "idolatries" in various places and times, including but not limited to 1566, in Toledo; and his agenda of portraying his actions and those of his fellow Franciscans in a positive light was a constant. The excerpts that comprise the Account were copied and assembled from these varied sources, placed in the care of the archivists housed within the

---

[2] Clendinnen, *Ambivalent Conquests*, 116–19, 125–26.
[3] *Sentencia del padre Fray Antonio de Cordoba, Ministro Provincial de la Orden de San Francisco de la Provincia de Castilla*, Toledo, 29 de enero, 1569, AGI, Escribanía de Cámara, 1009A.
[4] Pope Gregory XIII issued this bull on November 16, 1572, stating in Latin: "We absolve you and commute any sentences, censures, or ecclesiastical penalties or punishments opposed upon you … and warn, under censure of excommunication, that no one should oppose this nor impugn your honor, nor attribute to you, our servant, any of these condemnations" (*Bula de Gregorio XIII a Diego de Landa, electo obispo de Yucatán, absolviéndole de cualquier excomunión, suspensión, interdicto y censura eclesiástica en que pudiere haber incurrido, para evitar contradicción*, Roma, 16 de noviembre, 1572, AGI, Patronato, 3, number 16, ramo 2, 1 folio).
[5] *Memorial de Fray Diego de Landa al Rey y al Consejo de Indias presentando varias probanzas y documentos para su defensa en el asunto de la idolatría de los indios*, Sin fecha, AGI, Escribanía de Cámara, 1009A.

chambers of the Royal Council of the Indies, in Madrid's Royal Palace (again, see chapter 6). Those extracts remained there until 1744, when by royal proclamation all of the papers and notes of the royal historians and chroniclers were transferred to the newly created Real Academia de la Historia.[6]

What the eccentric French antiquarian Abbé Brasseur de Bourbourg found in Madrid's Biblioteca de la Real Academia de Historia in 1861 was a manuscript written by different hands at different times, at some point (or points) between the last decades of the sixteenth century and the turn of the seventeenth century; some parts may have been copied in the later seventeenth and perhaps early eighteenth centuries. That manuscript has very little integrity as a cohesive book. Not only is it a contrivance stitched together by anonymous copyists, but the manuscript's very authorship is inconsistent. Some of it is in the first person, some in the third; some of it was clearly authored by Landa himself, but other passages are equally clearly taken from manuscripts—and, in one segment, a published book or a manuscript set for publication—written by other authors.[7]

Yet although Brasseur recognized that different hands had written the manuscript, he assumed that these were simply those of multiple copyists working from a more or less identical original, single, coherent work written by Landa. Brasseur immediately saw the value of the manuscript, and published part of it for the very first time. But his decision not to highlight and explore its disjointed nature, rather to disguise it with a heavy editorial hand, was one with long-lasting implications. His work was not without early critics. Daniel Brinton, in 1887, noted that "the freedom with which he dealt with his authorities, and the license he allowed his imagination, have always cast an atmosphere of uncertainty about his work."[8]

---

[6]   The post of Cronista Mayor de las Indias was created in 1571 by Philip II, shortly before Landa's nomination as Bishop of Yucatan. Previously, the post of Chief Cosmographer of the Indies combined the duties of both geographer and historian. Both of these officials were salaried staff of the Council of the Indies. The new post was appointed for life, with a mandatory residence at the court in the chambers of the Council of the Indies—until 1744, when King Philip V ordered the Cronista and his office to be transferred to the Real Academia de la Historia. According to that royal order, the Council of the Indies had to give access to the Cronista and "give and turn over to him all of the histories, and relations, information, memorials, letters and other books and papers that exist and which would be necessary to comply with the said office." For complete details of the duties and responsibilities of the Cronista Mayor to "compile and make the General History of the Indies," see *Real Provisión concediendo a Juan López de Velasco el título de cronista y cosmógrafo mayor de Indias especificando sus derechos y obligaciones*, AGI, Indiferente General, 426, Libro 25, fs. 126r–127v.

[7]   It even seems to two of us (Restall and Solari) that one passage describes Nahua practice in central Mexico, not a practice of the Mayas, but the other two of us are either somewhat skeptical (Ardren) or disagree (Chuchiak); see the notes to our translation of the Account.

[8]   Brinton, "Critical Remarks," 1. Pagden, in his own edition, noted these anomalies in the text

Although he was an amateur and somewhat eccentric scholar, Brasseur has arguably been misunderstood and given insufficient credit for his discoveries and extensive work on numerous Mesoamerican topics (most scholars of his day were technically "amateurs" by our day's reckoning).[9] That said, his relevance here is that he discovered the sole extant Landa manuscript and shared it with the world—publishing a partial transcription in 1861, then a fuller but still incomplete transcription and French translation in 1864 (see figure 3.1)—while at the same time inserting an editorial hand that altered how the world would read and understand those writings. His contribution was itself a positive/negative contradiction (yet another little paradox within the Landa conundrum): he founded the field of Landa studies, at the same time he misled it from the very start.

Brasseur did that by taking an annotation from the first page, or cover page, of the Account (see figure 3.2). It reads "Account of the things of Yucatan taken from the writings of the padre fray Diego de Landa of the order of St. Francis"—two dashes followed in the original manuscript, then—"Here is another account of the things of China" (meaning "the Far East"). From that Brasseur created a title. He then reordered the fragments into a sequence that made sense to him, giving them all chapter numbers (in Roman numerals) and titles. Brinton was scathing in his condemnation of this fabrication just a few decades later:

> In Brasseur's edition the text is divided into numbered sections, each with an appropriate heading. No such arrangement is in the original. What is more objectionable, many of the paragraphs and even sections as arranged by Brasseur are entirely arbitrary, and do not correspond at all with the paragraphing of the original. Sometimes they begin in the midst of a phrase, cutting it in two, and destroying its meaning.[10]

Brinton's words fell on rocky ground; almost all editions have treated Brasseur's imposed structure as integral to the original, maintaining and translating the chapter titles along with the rest of the text. In short, it was Brasseur who created a book by Landa.

*   *   *

The impact of Brasseur's Landa on the first generation of scholars to read it was massive. The timing was just right: in the final decades of the nineteenth century, international scholarship was assuming its modern form, with its multiplicity of disciplines and built-in institutional growth; and at the same time, there developed

---

(*The Maya*, 19–20).
[9]   The argument is made in Brasseur de Bourbourg, *Manuscript Hunter*.
[10]   Brinton, "Critical Remarks," 2.

RELATION

DES CHOSES

DE YUCATAN

DE DIEGO DE LANDA

TEXTE ESPAGNOL ET TRADUCTION FRANÇAISE EN REGARD

COMPRENANT LES SIGNES DU CALENDRIER

ET DE L'ALPHABET HIÉROGLYPHIQUE DE LA LANGUE MAYA

ACCOMPAGNÉ DE DOCUMENTS DIVERS HISTORIQUES ET CHRONOLOGIQUES,

AVEC UNE GRAMMAIRE ET UN VOCABULAIRE ABRÉGÉS FRANÇAIS-MAYA

PRÉCÉDÉS D'UN ESSAI SUR LES SOURCES DE L'HISTOIRE PRIMITIVE
DU MEXIQUE ET DE L'AMÉRIQUE CENTRALE, ETC., D'APRÈS LES MONUMENTS ÉGYPTIENS
ET DE L'HISTOIRE PRIMITIVE DE L'ÉGYPTE D'APRÈS LES MONUMENTS AMÉRICAINS,

PAR

L'ABBÉ BRASSEUR DE BOURBOURG,

Ancien Administrateur ecclésiastique des Indiens de Rabinal (Guatémala),
Membre de la Commission scientifique du Mexique, etc.

PARIS

ARTHUS BERTRAND, ÉDITEUR

21, RUE HAUTEFEUILLE

LONDON, TRÜBNER AND CO., 60, PATERNOSTER-ROW

1864

Figure 3.1. The First Edition. The title page to the Abbé Brasseur de Bourbourg's 1864 edition of the *Relación*; note that beneath the title the book claims to include "The Spanish Text and Facing French Translation / Comprising the Signs of the Calendar / and the Hieroglyphic Alphabet of the Maya Language." The catalogue entry to this copy, owned by the Library of Congress, glosses that claim as "includes a Mayan grammar and dictionary." The edition included only forty-nine of the sixty-six folios of text; its appendices did include a twenty-six-page Maya-French vocabulary (and, bizarrely, a five-page Haitian vocabulary).

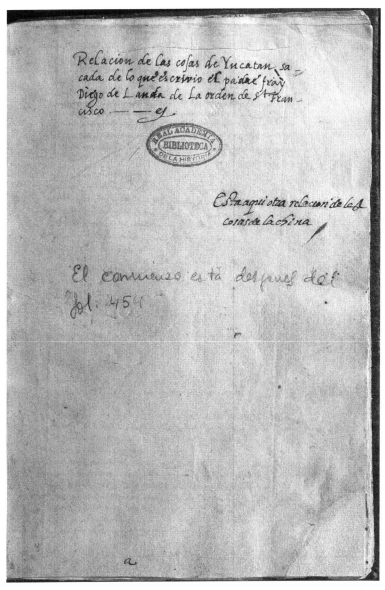

Figure 3.2. The First Page. The title page of the Account. Facsimile pages of the Account reproduced courtesy of Harri Kettunen and the Real Academia de la Historia, Madrid.

an intense interest in the ancient civilizations of the Americas—with the Maya prominent among them—a phenomenon of which Brasseur was a part.

These early Mayanists tended to be men of means; Stephen Salisbury III was no exception. A wealthy Massachusetts landowner, banker, state senator, and collector of Maya artifacts, Salisbury would eventually serve as president of the American Antiquarian Society—to whom he spoke in 1876 on the topic of Landa's Account. "Among the historical records relating to the aborigines of Spanish America, there is none more valuable than the manuscript of Diego de Landa," declared Salisbury.[11] By way of proof, he then quoted extensively from Brasseur's edition, as if the book's details on Maya life were themselves evidence of Landa's objective observations and unfiltered knowledge. Salisbury enthused:

> More than all, the manuscript of Bishop Landa, an eyewitness of expiring Mayan civilization, with its detailed account of the political and social relations of the Indians of that country, is strong testimony to the correctness of the generally accepted theories regarding their social and political systems. The truthfulness of Bishop Landa's account is attested by its conformity to other accounts, and to the customs and usages of the Yucatan Indians of to-day, as described by recent travelers.[12]

Men like Salisbury laid the foundation for a view of the Account as a book crafted by the friar-bishop himself, with its "truthfulness" fully corroborated, to be consulted and quoted as gospel—a view that has survived to the present day, underpinning how the Account has been used by generation after generation of Mayanists and other scholars. Even in the Spanish-language literature on Landa, his manuscript is credited with offering a "complete schematic of the civilization of Yucatan"—as Manuel Serano y Sanz put it in 1942, echoing Salisbury, and adding that "it refers minutely to all of the beliefs, laws and customs of the inhabitants, their agriculture, their weapons, both defensive and offensive which they used, and their vices . . . all of which makes the book of primary importance for the history of the said nation."[13]

There have always been countervailing opinions, cautioning how Landa is used. As early as 1880, the pioneering archaeologist Adolph Bandelier warned the American Antiquarian Society (with Salisbury in attendance) that "the picture which Landa gives us of the customs and organization of the Mayas is completely at variance with some of his other statements. Much close attention is required."[14] He was followed soon after by Brinton and his above-quoted attempt to hold editions

[11] Salisbury, *Mayas*, 32.
[12] Salisbury, *Mayas*, 46.
[13] Serano y Sanz, "Vida y escritos de Fray Diego de Landa," 448–49.
[14] Bandelier, *Notes*, 6.

of the manuscript to a higher scholarly standard.[15] But such voices have tended to be drowned out by the sheer weight of ready references to the Account as an unquestionable "eyewitness" source. Bandelier had spotted the internal contradictions of the Account. Yet from Bandelier's day to the present, most scholars have missed those contradictions, because they have tended to use the manuscript as if it were a bible or encyclopedia, to be consulted on a particular topic or passage cited.

Mayanists could hardly be blamed; as archaeologists more than archival researchers, they understandably tended to rely on the slow but steady emergence of printed editions of the Account, unaware that Brasseur's assumptions had become an integral part of it. At first, the reaction of the scholarly world to the 1864 French edition of part of the manuscript was slow, as the disciplines and fields that would come to embrace Landa's work were still in their infancy. Then, in 1884, the first Spanish edition appeared; it was initially well received, with some crediting it as a "literal and faithful copy of the original" under the "competent supervision of don Juan de Dios de la Rada y Delgado."[16] Yet it too was heavily influenced by Brasseur's edition and lacked any notations. Its flaws were repeated in another Spanish edition included in a multivolume presentation of primary sources, the *Colección de documentos inéditos*. Landa's Account may have been considered important enough to include in this 1900 collection, but it was effectively lost among the hundreds of other sources contained therein.

In fact, it was not until well into the next century, over fifty years after Brasseur's discovery, that the Account saw genuine and sustained scholarly interest and an accompanying spate of editions in various languages. Yet still Brasseur's legacy persisted. Another French version was published in 1928–1929, but because all four of the earliest editions included only part of the manuscript unearthed by Brasseur de Bourbourg, the full body of that manuscript and its length remained unknown and unavailable. Furthermore, Brasseur's invented chapters and chapter titles were again copied and presented as if they were Landa's own creations.

Because of the patchy history of the Account, there had not developed by the twentieth century a long mythology or historiography on Landa and his work—to compare, for example, to what Francisco Palou did for Junípero Serra.[17] Furthermore, as a Franciscan writing about a Mesoamerican civilization, and at the very same time that the manuscript attributed to Landa was discovered and made available, Landa faced competition from Bernardino de Sahagún and his twelve-volume, bilingual, richly illustrated study of the Aztecs. Like the Account, Sahagún's "La historia universal de las cosas de Nueva España" (as he called it) was a manuscript that remained

---

[15] Brinton, "Critical Remarks."
[16] Brinton, "Critical Remarks," 2.
[17] Palou, *Relación histórica de la vida y apostólicas tareas*.

unpublished and effectively unknown until the closing decades of the nineteenth century, when it acquired a modern name—the Florentine Codex—even more misleading than "the Account." Although it took far longer for the Florentine Codex to see full publication in multiple languages, its sheer length and richness (its parallel texts in Nahuatl and Spanish are fully illustrated) inevitably drew more scholars—from the very late nineteenth to the early twenty-first centuries—than Landa's little, and scantily illustrated, manuscript.[18]

Meanwhile, the emerging wealth of unexcavated, ancient Maya sites ensured that twentieth-century Maya studies would be overwhelmingly oriented towards archaeology. As the Account became increasingly available in translation, archaeologists mined it casually as a reference work; Landa himself, usually dismissed in passing, was seen in the context of the new Hispanophobic tradition that had in 1914 prompted that Spanish historian (mentioned earlier) to coin the phrase, in protest, "the Black Legend."[19]

By the 1920s, then, the foundation for the Landa conundrum had been laid. A clear, early expression of that paradox—whereby Landa's knowledge of the Maya was unequaled, yet so was his destruction of Maya knowledge—was in an early textbook on the Maya, by legendary early Mayanists Thomas Gann and J. Eric Thompson (first published in 1931). "Landa, Bishop of Yucatan soon after the Conquest," they wrote, "probably knew more" about the Maya "than any other European. To his bigotry, unfortunately, we owe an irreparable loss of the great mass of aboriginal Maya literature, burned in Merida by his order."[20]

That single sentence is packed with some of the errors that would reappear in textbooks and other sources over the next century. In fact, Landa was not a bishop until 1572, arguably not "soon after the Conquest," and thus not a bishop during the 1562 campaign; the burning of codices took place in Mani, not Merida, and we now know that "the great mass" of such literature was destroyed over the course of centuries, not in 1562. But, more significantly, here is the tone of how Landa would be represented in textbooks: a brutal, hypocritical Landa, who "protests in his book of the horrors perpetrated" by the conquistadors, yet "himself was not

---

[18] Although it took thirty years, for example, for the first English edition (by Arthur J. O. Anderson and Charles E. Dibble) to see publication, the Codex—all 2,400 pages and over 2,000 illustrations—was placed online at the World Digital Library in 2012 (www.wdl.org). There is no digital version of Landa's Relación on the website of the library that owns the original manuscript (the RAH) or available anywhere else. Still, the Account offers tantalizing clues to what may have been a better-illustrated and -organized original manuscript, with references to missing images, sections, paragraphs, and line-number callouts that may have existed in the original the copyists consulted.

[19] See note 11.

[20] Gann and Thompson, *History of the Maya*, 14.

overly squeamish" in his willingness to torture recidivist Maya parishioners; and at the same time a Landa whose writings offer "full descriptions" of Maya civilization and are "of great importance" to our understanding of it.[21]

In the wake of the Gann-Thompson textbook came the most concentrated period of interest in Landa's (supposed) work to date, with a series of new editions, all published between 1937 and 1941. They began with the first English edition of the Account, which was also the first edition of the full Real Academia manuscript—edited by Mayanist William E. Gates (1863–1940). But he offered virtually no notes and little commentary, remarking in passing that "the original manuscript of Landa's Relation has long disappeared . . . [and] must have been materially longer. The copy we have is a shortened transcript." Although this edition was published in limited numbers by Gates's own press in Baltimore (see figure 3.3), it was reprinted in 1978 by Dover, who have kept it in print ever since; it is today the only English version in print and is probably the single most widely read version of Landa's work. Thus, Gates's assumption of the textual integrity of the Account, and his use and extension of Brasseur's chapters and division of the work into two "parts," is more significant than Gates could have imagined.

The following year (1938) saw two Spanish editions, the first by editors Rosado Escalante and Ontiveros with an introduction by Barrera Vásquez, and the second edited by Pérez Martínez. All these editors likewise followed Brasseur de Bourbourg and his invented chapters—the text broken into sections, each numbered and titled, giving the impression that they were created by Landa himself. They observed that the surviving manuscript was an incomplete text, yet they otherwise accepted and treated it as a single work produced by Landa in 1566.

This run of Landa publications climaxed in 1941 with Alfred Tozzer's edition, the first and only truly scholarly presentation of the manuscript, with footnotes greatly outnumbering in words the translated text itself. Tozzer removed Brasseur's chapter headings and commented in his brief introduction on the nature of the Real Academia manuscript, mentioning some of its irregular features (as we detail in chapter 6) and describing the efforts by France Scholes to find in Spain "the original or another version" of the Account. However, Tozzer never elaborated upon the implications of the nature of the manuscript, as though its features were a curiosity that did not undermine its integrity—the latter reinforced by his presentation of a single, unbroken translated text. A few further comments on the manuscript's irregularities are buried in the voluminous footnotes.

More problematic is Tozzer's translation. His declared method would resoundingly fail modern smell tests: he used a team of assistants, with the base translation

---

[21] Gann and Thompson, *History of the Maya*, 15, 94, 118.

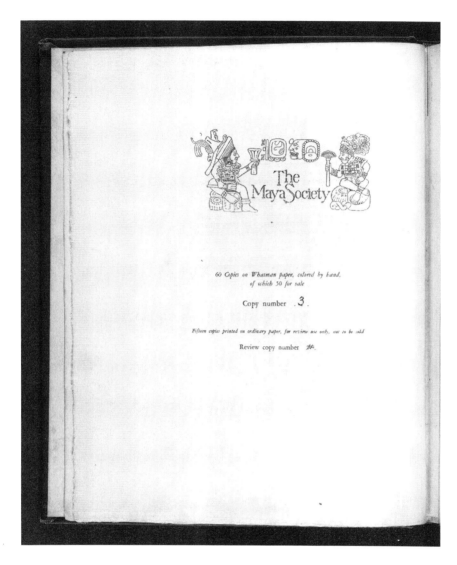

The
MayaSociety

60 Copies on Whatman paper, colored by hand,
of which 50 for sale

Copy number . 3 .

Fifteen copies printed on ordinary paper, for review use only, not to be sold

Review copy number ⌗ .

Figure 3.3. Three of Fifty. One of a limited run of hand-colored copies of William Gates's 1937 translation of Landa's Account. Reproduced with the kind permission of Arthur Dunkelman.

YUCATAN

BEFORE AND AFTER THE CONQUEST

BY

Friar Diego de Landa

WITH OTHER RELATED DOCUMENTS, MAPS AND ILLUSTRATIONS

TRANSLATED WITH NOTES BY

WILLIAM GATES

THE MAYA SOCIETY
BALTIMORE 1937

made by Charles Bowditch from Brasseur's French translation, "then corrected" with the Rada y Delgado and Brasseur transcriptions of the Spanish original, with further "corrections and emendations" stemming from suggestions by five other contributors, including Tozzer. Only Eleanor Adams apparently looked at the original manuscript, but her input was limited mostly to the compilation and transcriptions of archival sources for the massive number of footnotes. Despite the claim to multiple "corrections," Tozzer relied heavily on Genet's 1928–1929 French edition, both for his translation and notes. As a result of all this, Anthony Pagden rightly judged Tozzer's translation to be "a near literal rendering which often makes nonsense in English where the Spanish, although syntactically obscure, is only freely conversational in style," while Michael Coe dismissed Tozzer's version as "unreliable, since it is based on a French translation of the Spanish."[22] Indeed, comparing Tozzer's and Gates's versions to the original manuscript, the fallibility of Tozzer's method becomes clear. Many passages are better glossed by Gates, despite Tozzer's damning of Gates's translation as "a free one."[23]

Nonetheless, Tozzer's edition was a major achievement. Its copious notes gave it an aura of scholarly depth and reliability that, unfortunately, its translation lacked. Although his edition soon went out of print, it retained a reputation for decades—to some extent, to this day—as definitive. Partly for that reason, no new editions emerged for thirty-five years. Another reason may have been the political climate in Mexico, where *indigenismo* became incorporated into the institutionalization of the Revolution, exposing figures like Landa more to dismissive conquistador and inquisitor stereotypes than real scholarly investigation. An additional factor may have been the failure of the endeavors in Yucatan by the Carnegie Institution of Washington to ignite an immediate continuation of scholarly investigation into the Indigenous and colonial literature of the peninsula after the Carnegie ceased its sponsorship (which declined in the 1950s and was terminated in 1958; the Carnegie's publications would, of course, eventually help inspire a great deal of archaeological work).

Related to this (a fourth possible reason) was the fact that Ralph Roys, the Carnegie-sponsored figure who wrote the most in English on sixteenth-century Yucatan, never held a university post and thus never created a school of students to continue his work. Yet another factor may have been the role played by Thompson in stifling the development of Maya epigraphy during these decades, as Coe has argued.[24] A sixth and final factor may be the further development of the study of colonial Latin American history in the early and mid-twentieth century, with its

---

[22] Pagden, *The Maya*, 21–22; Coe, *Breaking the Maya Code*, chapter 4, 106n9.

[23] Tozzer, *Landa's* Relacion, viii.

[24] Coe, *Breaking the Maya Code*, 123–44.

emphasis upon political events, major institutions, and, eventually, social history as based on demography.

The relevance of all these factors is supported by their changing situations in the 1970s, which was when interest in Landa and the Account returned. In that decade the PRI-built (Partido Revolucionario Institucional) system in Mexico entered a crisis of legitimacy, fostering a very gradual but steady opening up of the political system and stimulating new directions in Mexican scholarship. A new generation of anthropologists in all North American countries (from Canada to Mexico) returned to the work of Roys and his Carnegie-sponsored colleagues in order to build upon it, while colonial Latin American historiography took a dramatic turn towards new social and cultural topics and concomitant methodologies. Finally, in 1975, J. Eric S. Thompson died. Within a few years Maya epigraphy experienced a series of breakthroughs, in part due to the Account, that would lead to the decipherment of most Maya hieroglyphs by the early 1990s, an extraordinarily rapid development considering that scholars had been working on "breaking the code" for two centuries.

Landa's relevance to epigraphic history is of course his inclusion of an apparent Rosetta Stone to Maya writing, what he called an "A, B, C" of glyphic signs with phonetic values. Back in 1880, Bandelier had noted that "the merits of Landa are certainly very great, but the real import of his so-called 'A. B. C.' ('De sus letras forme aqui un a. b. c.,' pp. 316–319), has been misunderstood and correspondingly misrepresented."[25] Indeed, as is now well known, Landa's Mayan alphabet is not a Rosetta Stone—not, as Landa implied, the Spanish alphabet rendered in Mayan glyphs—but a partial syllabary based on how the letters of the alphabet are pronounced in Spanish (we return to this in chapter 7). But that fact, circulating as an argument since Bandelier's day, was not undisputed until the revolution in Mayan epigraphy began in the 1970s.[26] Although the Ukrainian scholar Yuri Knorosov had "cracked" the code of Maya phonetics in an earlier publication in the 1950s, its Russian-language text remained inaccessible in the West, blocked in its translation by Thompson until Coe hazarded a translation and publication of its revolutionary findings.[27] Nonetheless, such knowledge was *not* used as a stepping stone to rethinking how the rest of the Account was compiled and how it may have been misused; in fact, it almost had the reverse impact, with Mayanists breathing a collective sigh of relief that the Account was in fact invaluable, and only the *ABC* passages were proven to be problematic.

---

[25] Bandelier, *Notes*, 6.

[26] A fine summary is in Coe, *Breaking the Maya Code*, 104–5, 193–258; also see Stuart, "Glyph Drawings from Landa's *Relación*," 23–32.

[27] Coe, "Triumph of Spirit," 39–44.

In the year of Thompson's death, a new English edition of the Account appeared, the third to date. Composed by Anthony Pagden, it compared well to Tozzer and Gates, improving on their translations. But Pagden did not offer extensive notes, instead referring the reader to Tozzer. Nor did his edition remain in print. With the growth of Maya studies at Harvard through the 1970s and 1980s, Tozzer remained the translation of choice for Maya archaeologists and art historians. Pagden's translation may have brought renewed attention to the Account, possibly contributing to the decision by Dover Press to pick up Gates's version a few years later, but unfortunately it did not supplant Tozzer. Meanwhile, a more easily acquired Spanish version of the text that had come out earlier, an edition from the prolific Mexican press Porrúa with an introduction from the Mexican scholar Ángel María Garibay, went back into print, while another Spanish-language edition, edited by the Spanish Mayanist Miguel Rivera for the Historia 16 series, came out in Spain.[28] The Rivera edition was an improvement on the Porrúa version, but (as with the Pagden and Tozzer editions) the Porrúa edition—with its unreliable transcription and lack of notes or extensive introduction—persisted as the one most commonly cited. Furthermore, not a single one of the many editions of the work in Spanish and in English adequately reproduced the drawings and illustrations, which have either been partially omitted or poorly redrawn—as clearly demonstrated by George Stuart with respect to the glyphs. As Stuart remarks, "*none* of the existing editions of Landa's *Relación* fulfills *all* the needs of the scholar seeking the total context of the original manuscript."[29]

Interest in Landa and his work persisted during the 1980s and 1990s: Maya epigraphy and Maya studies in general became a veritable industry; the Yucatec events of 1562 were treated to a well-received study by Inga Clendinnen, which stimulated ongoing interest; colonial Yucatan in general received more attention than it had since Roys's day; a reappraisal of "the spiritual conquest" in Mesoamerica eventually turned to Yucatan; and renewed Mexican interest in Landa led to the best Spanish-language edition of the Account to date.[30] As a result, by the first decade of this century, Landa had never been so widely read and so frequently cited.

Meanwhile, what impact did all this have on Maya studies? Landa was increasingly referenced, but did perceptions of him shift among Mayanists? In our survey of twenty-eight textbooks on the Maya, stretching from Gann and Thompson into

---

[28] See our bibliographic section on Account publications for the 1959 Garibay / Pérez Martínez and 1985 Rivera editions.

[29] Stuart, "Glyph Drawings from Landa's *Relación*."

[30] See the items in our bibliography by Christensen, Chuchiak, Clendinnen, Hanks, Love, Quezada, Restall, and Solari. The best Spanish-language edition is by María del Carmen León Cazares.

the 2010s, we found a remarkable consistency in how Landa and his "book" were mentioned, with virtually no shift in tone or usage across the past century.[31] On the one hand, Landa has been harshly judged for his actions: he was "a fanatical and sometimes brutal bishop and inquisitor"; his "fanaticism" lead to "wanton destruction," the "spirit of the Inquisition burned brightly in the young cleric's determination" and on his "frequent crusades" among Maya villagers; he "presided over a horrible auto-da-fé" and his book-burning was "a holocaust." The "bibliophilic" bishop was "a severe and narrow-minded man, who appointed himself to lead the Inquisition in Yucatan and then carried out a notorious program of floggings and imprisonment."

On the other hand, "Bishop Landa, an impeccable source," is "our great authority on all aspects of Maya life." His book is "an encyclopedic treatise," an "encyclopedic account of native life in Yucatan," offering "critical keys to understanding Maya civilization." Consequently, he is typically quoted, uncritically, as an authority on various aspects of Maya culture (mostly the calendar and glyphic writing), usually in discussions of time periods prior to Landa's lifetime (often by many centuries, even a millennium or more): he "reports" and "describes"; "from Landa's pen comes the following," or "Bishop Landa explained"; "his careful and thorough description of the way of life of the Maya" is "invaluable," even "fascinating to the modern reader."

The awkward connection made between these two threads in most of these textbooks speaks directly to the Landa conundrum. The common assumption made is that his actions were so extreme during the extirpation campaign of 1562 as to prompt his arrest by the incoming first bishop of Yucatan, fray Francisco de Toral, who then sent Landa back to Spain to be tried. Thus, the disgraced friar—according to this common view—"wrote his *Relación de las Cosas de Yucatan* in 1566 while on trial for his abuses of power." Landa's so-called book was "prepared as part of his defense a background document describing the people whom he was accused of oppressing." In fact, as mentioned earlier, the investigation into Landa's actions did not constitute a trial; he was neither arrested nor convicted. The Account, being excerpts made several decades later with some sections written two centuries

---

[31] Textbooks surveyed included those by Elizabeth Benson, Frans Blom, Michael Coe, Arthur Demarest, Charles Gallenkamp, Gann and Thompson (cited above), Norman Hammond, John Henderson, Heather McKillop, and Sylvanus Morley. We paid attention to possible changes over time between and within books (Coe, *The Maya*, for example, underwent nine editions between 1966 and 2015; and Morley, *The Ancient Maya*, has seen six editions from 1936 to 2006, along with an evolution of authors). It would be tedious to list all the textbooks consulted and to provide specific citations to these quotes that follow, and the intention here is not to point fingers but to convey a consistent pattern, so suffice to note that the quotes in these paragraphs are drawn from twelve of the textbook editions consulted, published in English between 1936 and 2015.

afterward from a larger work compiled over many years, could not have been composed as a "defense." As a result, the conundrum was not resolved but perpetuated. As the author of one textbook on the ancient Maya insightfully remarked in 1967, "Landa appears as a very contradictory character in the history of Maya studies."[32]

*   *   *

Our purpose here is not to indict Maya studies; Mayanist textbook authors generally are neither ethnohistorians nor scholars of literature, and their focus is usually the ancient Maya rather than the sixteenth century. Above all, they (and we, as Mayanists) have drawn upon the existing body of scholarship, which is built overwhelmingly upon Brasseur's invention of Landa's book from fragmentary, complex, and contradictory writings. Scholars in adjacent disciplines have treated Landa no better. Literature scholars, for example, have tended to ignore the Account (fair enough). When Landa is given some attention, it is in similar ways to that given by Mayanists, with the difference being that such scholars are less impressed by the Account, whose "rough" prose hardly offsets the "cruelty" of his actions, with the book "a poor substitute for the countless codices he burned in 1562" (again, fair enough).[33]

Our purpose, then, is not to judge how Landa and the Account have been (mis)used, but to explain that history—and to make the case for a more nuanced and better-informed understanding of the friar and his actions, to clarify the nature of the Account, and to show why it needs to be handled gingerly.

---

[32] Benson, *Maya World*, 3.
[33] Lavrin, "Viceregal Culture," 308.

4

Landa's Intellectual Roots, Sources, and Informants

Before turning to the nature of the Account, and putting aside for a moment issues of structure and authorship, how might we see the Account—and by extension, the larger and long-lost *recopilación*—as an intellectual product? We suggested in our introduction that Landa is best understood as a man of his century (the sixteenth), rather than a medieval or modern figure. Our reference was to the scholarly debate over the work of a contemporary and fellow Franciscan of Landa's, fray Bernardino de Sahagún. The creator of the famous Florentine Codex has been lauded as the "father of modern anthropology" and "father of anthropology in the New World"; viewed, in other words, as an archetypal Renaissance humanist who anticipated modern ethnographic methods and concerns. The counterargument is that Sahagún was a medieval figure struggling with the breakdown of medieval hermeneutics and the transition to early modern thinking.[1] Can we not see some element of a similar struggle echoed in the Account?

To some extent, the Account does offer evidence of a medieval mind at work—in the sense that its author's purpose was not to generate or produce knowledge by using perspective or their own intellect in a modern sense. Rather the writer (or writers) viewed knowledge as "a preexisting, divinely ordained, unified corpus" (to borrow from Walden Browne's definition of "medieval").[2] This corpus of knowledge

---

[1] Browne, *Sahagún*; Schwaller, *Sahagún at 500*.
[2] Browne, *Sahagún*, 9.

https://doi.org/10.5876/9781646424245.c004

(or aspects of it, such as details of ancient Maya culture) could be revealed through the grace of God, for providential purposes (in Landa's case, the obvious purpose of proselytization). The method of revelation was memory and observation through the lens of observant and conventual Franciscan theological and exegetical rhetoric and literature. Like Sahagún, Landa would have drawn upon memory as much as on curiosity or observation, and less his own personal memory (which might be based on past observation) than the memory of informants and other authorities and sources (*auctoritas* in the scholastic tradition).[3] Certainly, there are some personal observations in the Account, but there is little of Landa himself in the text. His personal reactions or interactions are absent, or at best rare such as when he comments on the appearance of Maya women, and instances of hearsay greatly outnumber claims to have seen something himself. And he is, not surprisingly, absent from passages that he copied from other authors. As such, the manuscript does not read like a personal memoir or a summary of "field notes" made during the years that the friar traveled from village to village—indeed, there is no indication that Landa ever made such notes.

We would argue that Landa's method, while rooted in late-medieval practice, was typically sixteenth-century in many ways. Precisely how he harvested the memories of his informants is not as clear as it is in the Florentine Codex, primarily because Landa's larger *recopilación* is lost to us. But the references to sources that the Account does contain suggest that Landa's larger work compiled a mixture of written sources, oral testimony taken from informants under informal circumstances, and testimony more formally garnered from informants responding to a predetermined set of questions.

This last method—the use of a questionnaire—was the principal means whereby legal testimony was taken in the Mediterranean and Spanish-speaking worlds during the medieval and early modern periods. Questionnaires were used to create cued responses to royal inquiries such as King Philip II's *Relaciónes Geográficas* project.[4] In this case, a fifty-question "Instruction" was sent to all towns in the monarch's global empire, and local Spanish settlers were required to respond on topics such as growable crops, maritime access, local diseases, and the history of each region's Indigenous peoples. Similarly, set questions were used to gather testimony in criminal investigations, in the civil inquiries that pertained to *probanza* and *residencia* procedures, and in Inquisition cases.

This was the most common method of enquiry in Landa's day, and its influence on the Account is heavy, especially in two ways: most of the first half of the manuscript

---

[3]   On what Landa would have considered "*auctoritas*" in his work see Kuttner, "On Auctoritas."
[4]   Introduced earlier, cited by us as RHGY.

is written as a series of short-paragraph responses to an invisible questionnaire, each one starting with *Que*, literally "how" or "that," but also marking the next answer (almost as we might use a hashtag); and the same ghost author (or partially acknowledged guest author) wrote passages in both Yucatan's official *Relaciónes Geográficas* responses and in Landa's *recopilación* (and thus the Account)—Gaspar Antonio Chi (we shall return to Chi, who was introduced in chapter 1, in a moment).

Another way in which the methods and characteristics of Landa's writings are characteristic of the sixteenth century is their reflection of ancient Roman practices and perspectives—not reproduced wholesale but borrowed and reworked through Spanish traditions and colonialist attitudes.

For example, in terms of method, Landa's irregular (to us, jumbled) combining of first- and secondhand observations with written testimony based or copied (to us, plagiarized) from other sources can easily be found in both ecclesiastical and ancient Latin texts. Julius Caesar's *Gallic War*, for example, primarily a personal narrative of Caesar's conquest of Gaul, is punctuated by digressions on natural history, geography, and local cultures and customs, probably copied by the Roman general from "books, maps, or hearsay, and not from Caesar's personal observation."[5] According to Cicero and Hirtius, Caesar saw his account "not as a finished history but as a collection of material for the use of future historians."[6] This might be how Landa regarded his *recopilación*: not as a finished study or history, but as a compendium of information that would help future Franciscans in Yucatan continue the work of proselytization. As a result, both *Gallic War* and the Account have a similarly dispassionate, matter-of-fact tone (although Caesar's clear, coherent style far surpasses the mess that the copyists who created the Account made of Landa's work).

In terms of the substantive characteristics of the texts, Landa's apparent ambivalence towards both the business of conquest and the nature of his Indigenous subjects is closely paralleled by Roman texts on the invasion of ancient Gaul, Germany, and Britain. We are thinking in particular of *The Agricola* and *The Germania* by Tacitus (both completed in AD 98), as well as Caesar's *Gallic War* of the previous century. Neither Tacitus and Caesar nor Landa ever question the fundamental premise of the invasions and their accounts of them—namely that the invading people are civilized (more than that, they are the quintessential representatives of civilization) and the invaded people are not; as Tacitus wryly remarks, "one must remember we are dealing with barbarians."[7]

Yet Tacitus and to some extent Caesar, like Landa, are sympathetic to their "barbarian" subjects. Their sympathy is more subtle than overt, and it is often disguised

---

5   Nardo, *Julius Caesar*, 103.
6   Nardo, *Julius Caesar*, 101.
7   Mathisen and Shanzer, *Romans, Barbarians, and the Transformation*.

by unadorned descriptions of cultural practices (some of which are judged harshly), but it is nonetheless undoubtedly present. Furthermore, Tacitus (although not Caesar) and Landa express doubts over the methods used by the invaders, denouncing acts of atrocity and suggesting in various ways that conquest violence is counterproductive. There is never direct criticism of the entire endeavor of conquest and colonialism; criticism is indirect or focused on particular events or individuals. For example, Tacitus criticizes Roman campaigns against the Germans, Gauls, and Britons by placing in the mouth of Calgacus (a leader of the Britons) an eloquent four-page speech that historians agree must have been composed by Tacitus himself. Landa details atrocities committed by Spanish conquistadors in Yucatan (in fact, a copyist sums up what Landa apparently described) and mentions "acts of valor" by Maya warriors, but he emphasizes that the invasion's leader, don Francisco de Montejo, committed none of the atrocities and that he disapproved of them "but could do nothing" to prevent them.[8]

The purpose of this comparison between Landa and ancient Roman authors is partly to illustrate the deep roots of Landa's method and approach and partly to demystify his apparent ambivalence towards "the Spanish Conquest" and the Mayas. In other words, we should expect Landa to show both sympathy and antipathy towards Yucatan's Indigenous peoples; such a dichotomy had been central to the colonial discourse of Mediterranean civilization for many centuries. There may also have been a closer link between Landa and his Roman antecedents. As David Lupher has shown in detail, sixteenth-century Spaniards were quick to compare the Roman Empire both to Indigenous American empires (the Mexica and the Inka) and the Spanish Empire, with both comparisons ultimately flattering to Spain.[9] Less common, but nonetheless significant, were denunciations of Roman imperial expansion designed as a way of indirectly criticizing—and perhaps influencing—the policies of the Spanish crown. Juan Luis Vives, for example, offered trenchant versions of such criticism in 1519 and 1529, the latter example a treatise titled *De concordia et discordia in humano genere* and dedicated to the Emperor Charles V. In case his indirect message was not clear enough, Vives included reference to Spanish attitudes "towards those Indians whom they do not consider human."[10]

We cannot be sure how familiar Landa was with the original Roman texts or with the full range of sixteenth-century publications discussing Roman precedents and parallels. But it is very possible that Landa was directly influenced by Tacitus, as the publication of the Roman author's works began in the 1470s; by the time Landa was beginning to assemble his *recopilación* in the 1550s and 1560s, at least

---

[8]   Sec. 15, f. 12r.

[9]   Lupher, *Romans in a New World*, 111.

[10]   Vives, *De concordia et discordia*, book 2, f. G3.

twenty-five Latin editions of part or all of Tacitus's writings were published in various European cities. And although the proliferation of vernacular editions did not come until later in the century, Landa would have had access to—and been able to read—*The Agricola* in the original Latin.[11]

The Observant Franciscan order was hesitant to embrace the ideas of humanism, and few of the humanists' works found their way into Franciscan libraries in the early sixteenth century.[12] Nonetheless, there were exceptions—Dante's *Inferno*, a few of the classical histories, and the classical works of early humanists—to which Landa likely had access.[13] He certainly had access in Toledo to at least one important humanist work on Roman history, Benvenuto da Imola's *Romuleon*, a compendium of Roman history, as well as the chronicles of Eusebius and other Latin texts of rhetoric from the classical philosophers.[14]

Landa also made at least two documented trips to the library collections in the Franciscan convent in Alcalá and in the University in Alcalá de Henares, where he could have consulted many classical works.[15] In fact, an inventory of the library from 1565 has a shelf-by-shelf index of the works available at the time of his visit.[16] Although we cannot directly place Landa's fingers on any of these classical volumes, we can assume that he knew some of this literature, and he was certainly well aware of the tendency among his contemporaries to make Roman comparisons. Significantly, such comparisons are a favored theme of Francisco López de Gómara's *La Istoria de las Yndias*, to which Landa refers several times in the Account. When Landa does mention López de Gómara, it is as "our general historian of the Indies."

---

[11] There is evidence in the surviving inventories of the books in the convent library of San Juan de los Reyes that some of the more secular histories of the Romans, rhetorical texts of Cicero and Ovid, and other classics existed at his disposal; see the catalogue in Castaño, *Noticia y defensa de los escritos.*

[12] According to Roest, "ceaseless warnings by medieval Franciscan theologians against undue studies of the pagans" had impacted the Observants' encounter with humanists' texts, always examining them with "the necessity to subsume pagan learning to Christian wisdom" (*History of Franciscan Education*, 169).

[13] A description of part of the San Juan de los Reyes collection catalogue is in Abad Pérez, "La Biblioteca Franciscana de Toledo," 25.

[14] See the humanist volumes in the catalogue published in Castaño, *Noticia y defensa de los escritos.*

[15] This is discussed in a chapter titled "Landa at Court: Madrid, Toledo, Ocaña, and Alcalá de Henares, 1564–1569" in a book manuscript in progress by Chuchiak, with the working title of "Spiritual Conquistador: A Life of Fray Diego de Landa—Friar, Inquisitor and Bishop, 1524–1579."

[16] See *Inventario de censos, libros y bienes muebles del Colegio Mayor de San Ildefonso de la Universidad de Alcalá, realizado con motivo de la visita de Juan de Ovando*, 1565, AHN, Universidades, Libro 920, fs. 161r–230r.

This *La Istoria de las Yndias* was published in Landa's lifetime, and it was clearly read by him.[17]

Landa also had access to far more local literature—manuscripts and books by fellow Spaniards who served as influences and even as direct sources for his own compilation. It is possible, for example, that there are traces of the writings of Francisco Cervantes de Salazar in the Account. Salazar began work in 1560 in Mexico City on a history of New Spain, and, because he had become a ubiquitous presence at the viceregal court by the time Landa visited in 1576–77, he almost certainly would have met the Yucatec bishop. The similarities between parts of Landa's Account and a manuscript copy of Cervantes de Salazar's Crónica de la Nueva España suggest that the two might have exchanged written drafts of their work, or more probably that both copies were made by the same copyist (see our chapter 6).[18] Most notably, some of the oddly marked paragraph headings in the Account have direct parallels, though with slightly different texts, in Cervantes de Salazar's work (see table 4.1). That means that Landa would have brought copies of his writings with him to Mexico City, and that he was still putting his *recopilación* together in the final years of his life.[19]

*   *   *

It is worth examining further the connection between Landa's intellectual formation as an Observant Franciscan and the two libraries to which he had greatest access. Arguably, it was unfortunate for the Maya of Yucatan that he had professed and been educated in two of the most conservative Observant monasteries in Spain: San Juan de los Reyes and San Antonio de la Cabrera. What Franciscan chroniclers called the "*observantisimo*" convent of San Antonio de la Cabrera witnessed the birth in 1477 of the independence of the Observant branch of the Friars Minor, to which Landa belonged. The first chapter and Vicario Provincial of the Observant branch came from this convent.[20] Stark theological differences existed between the order's two branches: the Observant branch, epitomized by the convent of San Juan de los Reyes, allied itself with the Catholic Monarchs in the collaborative extermination of heresy and the conversion of "the infidels." It is no coincidence that some of the most

---

[17]   In our notes to the Account, we discuss the possibility that the "general historian of the Indies" reference was to Oviedo; however, note that Landa would not have had access to Oviedo's second volume of his *Historia general de las Indias*, which treated the discovery and conquest of Yucatan, and while he might have had access to his previously published first volume (1535), it did not mention Yucatan at all, only covering the period up to 1517.

[18]   See Cervantes de Salazar, Crónica de la Nueva España—the handwritten copy of the manuscript in BN (MSS/2011), with additions and annotations made in the handwriting of Antonio de Herrera, the Cronista mayor de las Indias.

[19]   See Restall and Chuchiak, "A Re-evaluation," 665n3.

[20]   See Rojo, *Historia de San Diego de Alcala*, f. 417.

TABLE 4.1. Comparison of the several marked "paragraphs" in Landa's Account and their similarities to chapters in Francisco Cervantes Salazar's *Crónica de la Nueva España*

Landa's Account	Francisco Cervantes de Salazar Crónica de la Nueva España (1575)	Source	Natural History Topics
Paragraph VII. *On the kinds of serpents there are and other poisonous animals*	Capítulo XI *De las serpientes y culebras y otras sabandijas ponzoñosas que hay en la Nueva España*	Landa, Account (Sec. 46, f. 56r) Cervantes, Cronica (Tomo I, f. 23v)	Treats of the snakes, serpents, and poisonous lizards
Paragraph VIII. *Of the Bees and Their Honey and Wax*	Capítulo VI *De las semillas y hortalitas que se dan en la Nueva España, así de Castilla como de la tierra*	Landa, Account (Sec. 47, f. 56r–56v) Cervantes, Cronica (Tomo I, f. 15r)	Treats of aspects of agriculture, honey, and wax production

important preachers who called for an Inquisition against the crypto-Jewish *conversos* were Observant Franciscans.[21] Anti-Jewish preaching campaigns were "especially associated with the Observant Franciscans."[22] As Mark Davis has argued, the virulent anti-Semitism of the Observants is reflected in passages in the Account—with Jewish-assigned defects and sins, such as the repudiation of legal wives and the sacrificing of children, identified as Maya vices—and may help to explain "the singular violence of Landa's convictions" and the "vehemence of his adherence to his mission."[23]

Moreover, the Observant Franciscans, with their messianic and millenarian prophetic tradition, saw their alliance with the Spanish Crown as a means of expanding their evangelical mission, especially after the opening of the New World. The major polemic between the two branches focused on very different conceptions of the role of conventual life: the conventual or cloistered life, which was more tolerant and relaxed; and the Observant ideal, with its ascetic and rigorous evangelical goals and its intolerant persecution of heterodoxy. These two Franciscan ways of life clashed even in the pastoral mission of the friars, their administration of their convents and how they dealt with the people in their communities. The Observant Franciscans, with their Toledo convent of San Juan de los Reyes founded by the

---

[21] On the Observants' anti-Semitism, see Debby, "Jews and Judaism"; and Davis, "Evangelical Prophecies."

[22] "Once the Jews have been expelled," as Dorin puts it, adding "as exemplified by the indefatigable and indomitable Bernardino da Siena" (Dorin, "Once the Jews," 353).

[23] Davis, "Evangelical Prophecies," 87, 89; also see Enríquez, "Exuberant Imagination."

Catholic Monarchs, enjoyed the backing of the Crown, giving them preference in the early missions. In return, they aided the monarchs in their Inquisition and the rigorous punishment of heresy and heterodoxy among the Jewish *conversos*, and by extension the backsliding new converts of the New World.[24]

The nature of the Observant Franciscans and the role of education in their reform impacted greatly Landa's formation as a friar. The Observants remained "very critical towards higher academic learning, and in particular towards the pursuit of higher degrees for their own sake," and their vows of poverty mitigated against even the private ownership of books, considered inappropriately "precious objects."[25] As late as 1532, the Observant Franciscans' provincial chapter also prohibited the pursuit and use of academic degrees, arguing that their use ran in opposition to "the observance of a stricter life of religious perfection."[26] As we mentioned in chapter 2, Landa emphasized that his lack of formal academic titles was a result of Order policy, not his lack of training, which was extensive; he was a *lector*, equivalent to a professor of theology and religious instruction, in both San Juan de los Reyes and San Antonio de la Cabrera—before being elected Guardian of the latter convent. Pope Gregory XIII even addressed him as a "Professor of Theology" in a later papal bull.[27]

Despite their suspicion of formal university education and its system of titles, Franciscan Observants in Spain nonetheless followed a structured program of studies, so that Landa received training in "practical theology." This included learning to read and interpret the Scriptures on the basis of literal and moral commentaries by Franciscan and Dominican theologians, as well as education in "doctrinal matters and moral theology with the help of straightforward confession manuals, short compendia of dogmatic theology, small *summulae* of moral theology, handbooks for administering the sacraments, and preaching instruments for the making and presentation of sermons."[28] Landa would have learned that "copying" texts was a worthy enterprise, as it taught discipline, and he would have spent considerable time "copying exemplary sermons and suitable moral theological texts."[29] His public and private documents show that he copied in his own hand, rather than using scribes, later putting this ascetical labor of *sapientia* and *simplicitas* to work as a

---

[24] As Phelan argued, "the apostolic kingship" of the Catholic Monarchs encouraged friars like Mendieta and Landa to believe that a close alliance with "the Spanish monarchs might more effectively implement the apostolic mission inherent in all Christian kingship" (*Millennial Kingdom*, 10–13, quotes on 12).

[25] Roest, *History of Franciscan Education*, 167, 198.

[26] See Andres, *La teología española en el siglo XVI*, 142–50.

[27] *Bula de exoneración del Papa Gregorio XIII*, 16 de noviembre, 1572, AGI, Patronato, 3, no. 16, ramo 2, 1 folio.

[28] Roest, *History of Franciscan Education*, 167.

[29] Roest, *History of Franciscan Education*, 234.

missionary in Yucatan, dutifully copying from and adding to the great Maya grammar begun by fray Luis de Villalpando.[30]

When he was back in Spain in the 1560s, Landa served as the Master of the novitiate in Toledo, meaning that he was a professor of theology and rhetoric for the young novices, with unrestricted access to the impressive library collection of the Convent of San Juan de los Reyes.[31] The collection was heavy with volumes on canon law, on commentaries on ecclesiastical laws and jurisdictions—including important works such as a manuscript copy of Juan de Bromiard's Tratado de derecho canónico y civil (known as the Opus Trivium), and other compendia on the nature of ecclesiastical justice and the Order's inquisitorial powers and privileges. When Landa prepared his responses to the charges against him in 1565, he claimed that he had not usurped any powers, citing the papal bulls which conceded certain powers to his Order.[32] Landa presumably made the certified copy he presented to the Council of the Indies from the copies of the papal bulls and concession documents found in the library, which included an item called Bulario franciscano holding more than seventy papal bulls and privileges granted to the Order.[33] He was well aware of the powers of the bishops and their jurisdiction, as well as the powers subdelegated to the friars' prelates, who acted as bishops when none existed, as he could consult the anonymous manuscript with the title De los privilegios de los obispos.[34] He also had access to specific canon law treatises and other works on the jurisdiction in cases of heresy and the papal apostolic delegation of these cases in the jurisprudence of ecclesiastical law found in two other anonymous treatises in the library: the Explanación de Papae Inoc. IV sobre la injuria leve, and De los casos en que dispensa solamente el Papa.[35] Landa thus rightly claimed that as an ordinary inquisitor

---

[30] See Chuchiak, "Sapientia et Doctrina."

[31] Ayeta, *Último Recurso de la Provincia*, f. 21r–21v. The Observants had a strict policy on using the libraries, and without being a Provincial, Guardian, Lector, or the Maestro de Novicios, access to the library would have been restricted. Most often a friar only gained permission for the use of one or two books at a time. Even personal copies of books a young friar may have brought with him would need permission "in order to keep them for personal use" (Roest, *History of Franciscan Education*, 224).

[32] *Respuesta de fray Diego de Landa a los cargos hechos por fray Francisco de Guzmán*, AGI, Escribanía de Cámara, 1009A, 40 folios.

[33] Bulario franciscano, Tomo II, 85 folios, Ex Convent of San Juan de los Reyes Collection, Manuscript 3840 in the Biblioteca Nacional de España (see description in Abad Pérez, "La Biblioteca Franciscana de Toledo," 32).

[34] Anonymous, De los privilegios de los obispos, Ex Convent Collection of San Juan de los Reyes, Codex Y 51, 108 folios (fourteenth century) (see description in Abad Pérez, "La Biblioteca Franciscana de Toledo," 26–27).

[35] Anonymous, Explanación de Papae Inoc. IV sobre la injuria leve, and Anonymous, De los casos en que dispensa solamente el Papa, Ex Convent Collection of San Juan de los Reyes,

in 1562 he had proceeded "with the authority of the Pope," arguing, "I did this by law as I could and should have done, and this I did in order not to relinquish my rights to proceed in those cases nor abrogate those rights to another."[36]

In terms of his lifelong obsession with extirpating Maya "idolatry," Landa's early readings on millenarian Franciscan theology and anti-heretical treatises surely influenced his iconoclasm and his zeal for eradicating heretical beliefs and destroying Indigenous "idols." He would have had access to the works of the Catalan Dominican fray Raimundo Martín—his Lucha cristiana para yugular la perfidia de los impíos, and a volume on millenarian ideas of the Second Coming of Christ.[37] In some ways, fray Raimundo may have served as a model and inspiration for Landa, especially after his return from Yucatan in 1564, as the Dominican had gone with "a missionary zeal to convert the Muslims, and learned Arabic, Hebrew, and Syriac and had written among other things a *Summa* in refutation of the Koran, and preached the gospel among the infidel in Tunisia."[38]

Similar treatises against infidels and heresy were also found in the library, including the work of the Dominican fray Riccoldo da Monte di Croce, Contra legem Sarracenorum (c. 1320)—a perfect example of an exegetical critical treatise against the Islamic religion using specific examples of Islamic practices, along with their refutation.[39] Landa may well have modeled his own *recopilación* on either this manuscript or others which chronicled the errant practices of the infidels and then refuted them with Christian doctrine. Monte di Croce's dogmatic approach offered "a double perspective" chronicling the daily life of the Muslims and then condemning their theology.[40] A work well consulted by the friars in Toledo, his treatise offers a juxtaposition very reminiscent of the Account: "direct observation with passages about their piety which the Muslims manifested, their prayers, and their charity

---

Codex Y 51, 108 folios (fourteenth century) (see description in Abad Pérez, "La Biblioteca Franciscana de Toledo," 26–27).

[36] *Fray Diego de Landa responde a los cargos que el padre Guzmán me hace allende de las cartas*, AGI, Escribanía de Cámara, 1009A, fs. 16v–17r.

[37] See Fr. Raimundo Martín, Lucha cristiana para yugular la perfidia de los impíos; en su segunda parte se habla de la venida del Mesías, Ex Convent Collection of San Juan de los Reyes, Codex Y 75, 145 folios (fifteenth century) (see description in Abad Pérez, "La Biblioteca Franciscana de Toledo," 27).

[38] Simonet, *Glosario de voces ibéricas y latinas*, clxiv.

[39] Monte di Croce, Contra legem Sarracenorum, part of Codex Y 75, 145 folios (fifteenth century); see description in partial catalogue in Abad Pérez, "La Biblioteca Franciscana de Toledo," 27.

[40] Monte di Croce's Contra legem Sarracenorum (c. 1300) would have been a model for how members of the mendicant orders interpreted and "perceived cultural contact with the writing systems, laws and customs of other religions in a missionary context" (Ferrero Hernández, "Lectio et Disputatio," 141–55).

toward the poor, and their hospitality, and their respect for God" was then countered with brutally critical descriptions of their laws and religion, categorized with terms like *confusa, occulta, mendacissima, irracionabilis et violenta.*[41]

For example, in its section dealing with the daily life of the Maya "infidels," the Account goes on to chronicle their abhorrent religious practices and their "idolatry," which the author categorizes as their "vices and bad ancient customs" (Sec. 39, f. 33v) and a "great cruelty" (Sec. 43, f. 51r). Just as Monte di Croce claimed to have deep knowledge of the Islamic practices and the Arabic language he learned in Baghdad, which he used to preach and argue for the irrationality of Islamic religious beliefs and practices, so too the author of the Account used his knowledge of the culture and the Mayan language to refute their own religious practices. He may even have indirectly referenced Monte di Croce's work when he compared the Maya concept of baptism and its benefits of obtaining "the delight that they hoped for" to the concept of Islamic baptism in which "according to Mohammad, they had enjoyed delicacies and drinks" (Sec. 26, f. 20r); the parallel to Monte di Croce's description of Islamic practices like ritual cleaning and baptism is notable.[42] Moreover, Monte di Croce frequently uses exhortations imploring God to aid him in his work of conversion and extirpation, similar to the discursive style of appeals and exhortations to God from the Psalms seen in the Account, particularly in the epilogue on f. 50v (Sec. 43). Unfortunately, the Account does not contain a copy of the original prologue, but it likely also featured a scriptural appeal to the Psalms (see table 4.2). Both friars, one Franciscan and one Dominican, wrote their treatises in the style of sermons, a technique commonly employed by friars in their written sermons and treatises.[43]

A millenarian approach to the necessity and urgency of the conversion and forced expulsion of the Jews is also evident in some of the works that Landa had access to at San Juan de los Reyes. Included most prominently among them were those of the Observant Franciscan preacher Giovanni da Capestrano (1386–1456), whose sermons revealed a decidedly millenarian and anti-Jewish tone.[44] Capestrano practiced the type of evangelizing Landa later emulated, called "conversionary sermon,"

---

[41]   Monte di Croce, Contra legem Sarracenorum, 318.

[42]   Concerning Monte di Croce's views on the irrationality of many Islamic practices, such as ritual purification and their style of baptism with water, see Contra legem Sarracenorum, Chapter VIII, "On the Irrationality of their practices which are not of the Laws of God," fs. 14r–16v.

[43]   The use of exhortations to the Psalms was a common technique of these types of mendicant treatises (Bériou, "Les prologues des recueils de sermons latins," 395–426).

[44]   Giovanni de Capistrano's oratory skills and charisma enabled him to preach large public sermons against the Jews, and oftentimes these were followed by pogroms. Both he and fray Bernardo de Siena were personally rebuked by Pope Martin V for their anti-Semitism, and he issued a papal bull against them (Roest, "Giovanni of Capestrano's Anti-Judaism").

TABLE 4.2. Comparison of the *"auctoritas"* of Scripture and the Psalms as discursive elements of the exegetical treatises of Monte de Croce and extracts from Landa's Account

Passage	Source	Scriptural Knowledge or Psalms Referenced
By chance, Lord, do you ignore the capacity of my cup, the quantity of my limbs, and the quality of my strength? In fact, Lord, are you absent from my labors? Are you not the helpful father to whom I spoke, you the holy prophet in the psalm, "with him I am the tribulation and the labor, and I will free him from it, and I will glorify him?"	Landa, Account (Sec. 43, f. 50v) (possible Epilogue)	Psalm 91: 15 "... with him I am the tribulation and the labor, and I will free him from it, and I will glorify him."
How many are the days of your servant? When will you make judgment against those who pursue me? The evil ones tell me fables, but according to your law. All your commandments are true. Help me lord, they have persecuted me unjustly.	Monte di Croce, Contra legem Sarracenorum (folio 1v) (Prologue)	Psalm 119: 84–86 "How many are the days of your servant? When will you execute judgment on those who persecute me? The wicked have told me fables: Which is not according to Your law. Help me lord, they have persecuted me unjustly."

commonly used by Observant Franciscans. It was aimed at convincing Jews, and in Landa's case the Maya, of "the truth of Christian doctrine, with exegetical arguments to prove that Jesus Christ was the Messiah" and that the Maya, with their supposed prophetic belief in the imminent return of Kukulcan (Sec. 6, f. 5r–5v), held "an erroneous understanding of their own Scriptures."[45]

The references to the Jews and their conversion in various sections of the Account seem to hearken back to this "conversionary sermon" genre. For instance, in asserting, as other early Franciscans had done, that the Maya may have descended from the Jews, the author subtly lays claim to Spain's just titles and those of the Church. Such a declaration would justify his inquisition against the Maya by reminding the reader of the need to separate them from their errant Jewish origins. The author invokes this observant Franciscan tone when he recounts:

> Some of the old men of Yucatan say that they have heard from their ancestors that this land was populated by certain people who came from the east, whom God delivered by opening for them twelve roads through the sea. If this were true, it necessarily follows that all of the peoples of the Indies are descended from the Jews, because after passing through the Straits of Magellan they must have spread out over more than two thousand leagues of land which today Spain governs. (Sec. 5, f. 4r)

---

[45] Roest, "Giovanni of Capestrano's Anti-Judaism," 132.

Franciscan anti-Judaic treatises and sermons most often used imagery like this with "recourse to exegetical and apocalyptical genres, theological questions, canon law collections, designated *adversus iudaeos*–treatises, and *meditationes vitae Christi* literature."[46]

Evidence of the Account's author absorbing the often apocalyptic and prophetic works of Old Testament prophets also is scattered across the manuscript. For example, when he references a "commentary on Ezekiel" (f. 33v), he is likely thinking of the commentary from the manuscript Expositio super Ezechielem, available to him in the convent library.[47] For other references to the Old Testament prophets (Sec. 48, f. 58r; Sec. 51, f. 65v), the author may have consulted the voluminous work of Andreas de Sancto Victore's Expositionem super duodecim prophetas, a copy of which he had access to in Toledo.[48] He also included references and commentaries on the Psalms (Sec. 43, f. 50v) with personal appeals such as "Are you not the helpful father to whom I spoke, you the holy prophet in the psalm," perhaps derived from his consultation of the manuscript named Expositio optima super Psalmos David regis.[49] He refers particularly to the evangelical prophesies about Jerusalem found in apocalyptic texts, such as Expositio super Apocalipsim, likewise referred to in St. Paul's letter to the Romans:

> For this we could say we have completed the evangelical prophesies about Jerusalem, which our enemies besieged and stained with blood. They will grip it so much that they overthrew it by land. And this God has permitted according to who we are, and as such his church and all of it cannot be missing for it is said, "*Nisi dominus religuisset semen, sicut sodoma fuissemos.*"[50]

---

[46] Roest, "Giovanni of Capestrano's Anti-Judaism," 120. See also Davis, "Evangelical Prophecies."

[47] See Expositio super Ezechielem (fourteenth century), fs. 143r–97v, in Tomo V of the eighteenth-century collection catalogue of fray Poncio Carbonell, Ex Convent Collection of San Juan de los Reyes, Manuscript Núm. 449 (Est. II-4). For a detailed description, see Castaño, *Noticia y defensa de los escritos*, 85.

[48] Expositionem super duodecim prophetas (fourteenth century), 144 folios, in Tomo VI of the eighteenth-century collection catalogue of fray Poncio Carbonell, Ex Convent Collection of San Juan de los Reyes, Manuscript Núm. 450 (Est. II-4). For a detailed description, see Castaño, *Noticia y defensa de los escritos*, 93–123.

[49] Expositio optima super Psalmos David regis (fourteenth century), 280 folios, in Tomo III of the eighteenth-century collection catalogue of fray Poncio Carbonell, Ex Convent Collection of San Juan de los Reyes, Manuscript Núm. 446 (Est. 11-4). For a detailed description, see Castaño, *Noticia y defensa de los escritos*, 24–29.

[50] Sec. 39, f. 34r. Expositio super Apocalipsim, with Carta dedicatoria al arzobispo de Toledo Juan *de Aragón (1319–28)* (fourteenth century), fs. 94r–141v, in Tomo VII of the eighteenth-century collection catalogue of fray Poncio Carbonell, Ex Convent Collection of San Juan de los Reyes, Manuscript Núm. 450 (Est. II-4). For a detailed description, see Castaño, *Noticia y defensa de los escritos*, 124–54.

Here the author appeals to the *auctoritas* of Saint Paul's warnings to the new Christian Romans regarding the calamities of their time. He no doubt took this quote from the Franciscan commentaries on the Pauline letters in the manuscript Expositio super Epistolam Pauli ad Romanos.[51] In the Observant apocalyptical tradition, he saw his mission to convert the Maya as a "good thing" for "remedying in our era" and hastening the apocalyptic return of Christ.[52] By expressing his aversion and fear of the ongoing Maya "idolatry," he warns Christian readers that the prophecy may not be fulfilled, just as fray Martin warned in his writings on Muslim conversion campaigns: "They return to their miseries and iron bonds . . . the household devils turning on their souls, where with laborious care we have tried to cast them out, cleansing themselves of it, and sweeping away their vices and bad ancient customs."[53] The author reveals his close reading of fray Martin's and fray Monte di Croce's exegetical treatises when he cautions the Christian reader of the need for further extirpation of idolatry: "It doesn't take a lot to see the ruin that had happened for so many years in the great and very Christian Asia, and in the good, Catholic, Augustinian Africa, and the miseries and calamities that today are happening in our Europe, in our nation."

Finally, the author also seems to have read and absorbed in the two convent libraries some of the major works of rhetoric and moral theology, as well as some basic texts on classical philosophy. We know for certain that he had access to a summary edition of the sayings and works of classical philosophy in the Compendio sobre la vida y dichos de los filósofos, which he may well have used as a source for several quotations and allusions to the classical philosophers in the Account.[54] He may also have turned for inspiration to Nicolás de Biard's Sermones de tempore et de sanctis, for its sermon-like admonitions and exhortations. He also had access to the Latin translation of the lives and sayings of the ancient philosophers by the Italian Humanist, Ambrosius Traversarius, Vidas, opiniones y sentencias de los filósofos más ilustres (1545).[55]

---

[51] Expositio super Epistolam Pauli ad Romanos (fourteenth century), folios 1v–32r, in Tomo VIII of the eighteenth-century collection catalogue of fray Poncio Carbonell, Ex Convent Collection of San Juan de los Reyes, Manuscript Núm. 448 (Est. 11-4). For a detailed description, see Castaño, *Noticia y defensa de los escritos*, 155–87.

[52] Sec. 39, f. 33v.

[53] Sec. 39, fs. 33v–34r. See parallels in the account of fray Raimundo Martin about similar attempts to eradicate the heresies of the infidels, fs. 4r–5v.

[54] Sec. 50, f. 54v; Sec. 51, f. 65v. Compendio sobre la vida y dichos de los filósofos (fourteenth century), 200 folios, Ex Convent Collection of San Juan de los Reyes, Codex Y 122 (see description in Abad Pérez, "La Biblioteca Franciscana de Toledo," 28).

[55] Nicolás de Biard, Sermones de tempore et de sanctis (fourteenth century), Ex Convent Collection of San Juan de los Reyes, Codex Y 20, 107 folios (see description in Abad Pérez, "La Biblioteca Franciscana de Toledo," 26).

Many friars who knew Landa attested to his excellence as an orator and an evangelist, asserting that he displayed erudition in his grasp of theology, Latin, canon law, and the classics. Fray Agustín de Moragón—apparently his close friend—marveled at Landa's oration, stating that on one occasion in the convent of Cifuentes, Landa spoke to "a great congregation of the people, to their great contentment, his sermon so well received that they begged him to preach other sermons on festival days when he should return."[56] Other friars agreed that Landa enthralled his listeners when he preached and sermonized on the major feast days.[57] Such skills were apparently the result of intensive preparation, as fray Juan de Medina testified that Landa "never climbed the pulpit to preach without hours of study before."[58] In recognition of this reputation, the Inquisitors in Mexico City, Alonso Hernandez de Bonilla and Alonso Granero Davalos, asked Landa during his visit to the viceregal capital to give the important "sermon of the faith" for the second major auto-da-fé held at the Franciscan convent of San José de los Naturales on March 6, 1575.[59] His sermon on the evils of heresy and idolatry was remembered as mesmerizing the audience.[60] It must have also inspired renewed zeal in Landa, as upon his return to Yucatan he launched a major visitation and campaign of extirpation against "witchcraft" and "idolatry" among the Chontal Mayas of Tabasco.[61]

*　*　*

Of greater significance, however, are the Account's uncited Maya sources, though there are tantalizing hints in several passages. The most likely informant on the general culture, government, and society of the Maya was Gaspar Antonio Chi, who has long been assumed to be Landa's principal informant. As explained earlier (in

---

[56] See Testimonio de fray Agustín de Moragón, 19 de julio., 1572, AHNob, Condado de Almodovar, Caja 40, doc. 8, f. 23r.

[57] Fray Juan de Yepes noted that he had often heard him preach sermons and that he "always preached the Holy Gospel and the Word of God with much erudition and good doctrine" (*Testimonio de fray Juan de Yepes, fraile del convento de la Santa Cruz*, 18 de junio, 1572, Condado de Almodovar, Caja 40, doc. 8, f. 26v).

[58] *Testimonio del Reverendo Padre Fray Juan de Medina, fraile del convento de la Santa Cruz de Cifuentes*, 18 de junio, 1572, Condado de Almodovar, Caja 40, doc. 8, fs. 27v–28r.

[59] *Relación de los inquisidores del auto de fe celebrado el 6 de marzo*, 1575, AGI, Audiencia de México, 278, 5 folios.

[60] *Relación del auto de fe celebrado en la ciudad de México, 6 de marzo*, 1575, AHN, Inquisición, Libro 1064, fs. 64r–70v.

[61] See Ayeta, *Último recurso de Yucatan*, fs. 22v–23r. The chroniclers claimed that the "Indians" in Tabasco, suffering under his harsh campaign of extirpation, conspired to kill and drown him as he attempted to cross a narrow bridge; Ayeta and Cogolludo both stated that an "angel went ahead of him, threatening the natives with a sword of fire" (Ayeta, *Último recurso de Yucatan*, f. 23r; Cogolludo, *Historia de Yucathan*, Libro 6, Capítulo 17, f. 358).

chapter 1), Chi is a good candidate for such a role because he was the nobleman son of a Maya priest-scribe (and a Xiu on his mother's side), he was educated by Franciscans, and he worked closely with Landa for many years—both as his personal assistant and later as the colony's chief Indigenous interpreter and notary. Chi, well versed in Yucatec history (Maya and Spanish), was surely not only a strong influence on Landa, but was influenced by him as well; their personal intellectual interactions were paralleled in a kind of intertextual influence.

One obvious and specific example of that process has been introduced already: Chi's own lost *relación*, parts of which survived in roughly half of the *Relaciónes Geográficas* reports turned in by Merida's encomenderos in 1579–1581. Chi surely drew on material in his *relación* written prior to this, material that also reflected his interactions with recently deceased Bishop Landa and which thus ended up surviving in slightly different form in the Account.[62] Still, while Chi may have been an expert on the dynastic histories of the Maya, and their affairs of state, he would have had less intimate knowledge of precontact religious and calendrical practices. For this, Landa would have relied, as mentioned earlier, on two other important Maya informants: don Juan Cocom of Sotuta and don Francisco Euan of Caucel.

Landa himself tells us that don Juan Cocom had shared with him "many ancient things, and showing him a book, which had belonged to his grandfather, the son of the Cocom whom they killed at Mayapan."[63] Landa wrote that he was very familiar with Juan Cocom and that he was "very learned in their affairs and very wise and knowledgeable about the natives."[64] Similarly, in an Account passage describing Maya religion, Landa mentions that "a principal Indian lord, a native of the town of Caucel, called Francisco Euan, attested to this practice."[65] Euan had been an *ah kin*, or priest, as well as hereditary ruler, in Caucel, and following his conversion became close to the Franciscans. According to Cogolludo, "he was more than fifty years old, and of a very good intelligence and capacity, with which he was able to learn to read and write."[66] In Lizana's telling, Euan became a "very faithful assistant of the religious friars in the conversion of his other native peers, [and] due to his good persuasion he spoke to the other natives teaching them some things of our faith." By the seventeenth century, Euan had become something of a legend among

---

[62] *Relación de la Ciudad de Mérida* (by Martín de Palomar and Gaspar Antonio Chi, Feb. 18, 1579) in RHGY, Vol. I: 44–45; reflected in f. 8r–8v (sec. 11) of the Account. *Relación de Tiab-y-Tec y Tisculum* (by Juan Bote and Chi, Feb. 20, 1581) in RHGY, Vol. I: 288–89; reflected in f. 11r (sec. 14) of the Account.

[63] Sec. 11, f. 8v.

[64] On Cocom, see our notes to the Account; and Pérez Heredia and Bíró, *La Casa Real de Cocom*.

[65] Sec. 44, f. 53v.

[66] Cogolludo, *Historia de Yucathan*, Libro V, Capítulo VI.

the Franciscans: he was held to be "very wise among them in their sciences, since he had been a high priest of their idols before the friars arrived, and they believed it to be true what he told them; [thus] many flocked to the doctrine because of his work as a teacher among them."[67]

Additional Maya noblemen not mentioned in the Account, but strong candidates to have served as informants and sources of some kind, were of the Nah and Pech dynasties. One of the earliest élite converts was don Diego Nah, the young ruler of Campeche. He took instruction from the Franciscans, apparently composing compilations and historical chronicles of precontact Maya history, the wars of the Spanish conquest, and the religious conversion of their people. These included a chronicle titled "Apuntamientos históricos sobre la llegada de los frailes," written in the 1550s, reportedly consulted by several later friars as a source for their own works, but long since lost. With respect to the Pech, it is possible that Landa consulted two noblemen of this ruling lineage, both of whom wrote historical chronicles, and one of whom traveled to Spain and back. A number of Maya caciques, with several Pech nobles among them, traveled to Spain as an embassy in 1543 in the company of Alonso López, the Adelantado Montejo's brother-in-law.[68] They were presented at court in Toledo just after Landa had completed his novitiate at San Juan de los Reyes. The precontact ruler of the town of Chacxulubchen, Ah Nakuk Pech, later baptized as don Pablo Pech, wrote a history of his people through to the arrival of the Spaniards. His Crónica de Chac Xulub Chen was written in the 1550s (after his return from Spain), while his relative, don Alonso Pech, authored an overlapping account known as the Crónica de Yaxkukul.[69]

Of course, the discrete separation of Spanish and Maya sources simplifies what was in reality a complex interaction—with Maya noblemen and Franciscan missionaries influencing each other's perspectives as they sought to learn of each other's culture and history. The threads of *auctoritas* in the Account were multidirectional. For example, among the four sources that Gaspar Antonio Chi cited for his own historical and geographical information was Francisco Domínguez y Ocampo, a Portuguese cosmographer; as Domínguez happened to be working on his cosmography at the same time that Landa was compiling his great work, the cosmographer

[67] Lizana, *Historia de Yucathan*, 51r.
[68] On the visit of don Pablo Pech and others to the Royal Court, see Chuchiak, "Anhelo de un escudo de armas," 305–6.
[69] These histories are attributed to these Pech rulers, but their authorship is far more complex; they are variants on a common text that was copied from precontact codices, each copy then localized and recopied over the centuries, with extant versions dating from the eighteenth and nineteenth centuries; see Restall, *Maya Conquistador*, 104–28, and Hanks, *Intertexts*, 251–70. Early transcriptions are Pech and Pérez Martínez, *Historia y crónica de Chac-Xulub-Chen*, and Pech, *Crónica de Yaxkukul*.

was likely also a source of information about natural history.[70] Another was fray Gaspar de Najera, mentioned by Chi and a contemporary of Landa's, a speaker of Yucatec Mayan, and the author of a similar *relación*—a work also long lost (but possibly sitting undiscovered in Spain). Given the absence of the Najera *relación* we cannot prove that in addition to him being a source for Chi, fray Gaspar also may have authored parts of the Account. Nor can we disprove it either, for it is surely certain that Landa had access to Najera's own manuscript, and as a good Observant Franciscan he would have copied and included salient parts of Najera's manuscript into his own. Chi also mentions his own personal additions. Finally, and teasingly, Chi describes a "*recopilación* which the most reverend don Diego de Landa, who was bishop of these provinces, made of this land."[71]

*   *   *

Ecclesiastical sermons, philosophical texts, biblical commentaries, polemical exegetical treatises, Roman parallels, Renaissance debates, medieval roots, and Maya ghostwriters are thus additional ingredients to be added to the potage of multiple sources, ambiguous authorship, "plagiarized" passages, copyists' errors and omissions, and the mistreatment by editors that constitutes the Account. It is, in the end, a complex and messy compilation that should be handled as gingerly as, say, one of the colonial Maya compilations known as the Books of Chilam Balam. In the words of one scholar of the Franciscans: "The Friars Minor, whether Observant or not, did not aim for literary prowess per se, but instead tried to reach the populace at large. They took study very seriously, but it was a means to an end, not an end in itself."[72]

---

[70] Domínguez y Ocampo arrived in Mexico in 1571, as the companion of Francisco Hernández, the royal physician who came on the first scientific expedition to New Spain on the orders of King Philip II: Restall and Chuchiak, "A Re-evaluation," 653, 663; Rodríguez Sala, "Francisco Domínguez y Ocampo"; Madrid Casado, "Compás, mapa y espada."

[71] RHGY, Vol. I: 142–53.

[72] Roest, *History of Franciscan Education*, 171.

5

Gender and the Account as a Colonialist Reverie

The Account has been read by generations of Mayanists as a relatively unproblematic ethnographic description of sixteenth-century Yucatec Maya life. That is hardly surprising, considering that it is filled with tantalizing details of daily practice from Landa's memory, as well as from firsthand observations by him and others. However, one aspect of that putative ethnography is particularly deceptive, problematic, and revealing and thus deserves further attention: the portrayal of women and children in the Account.

In his writing about Maya women and children, Landa's anxieties and desires are fully exposed; his words reveal as much about his own values as they do those of the Maya.[1] Arguably, then, Landa's work is best understood as a gendered colonialist reverie, a highly selective reconstruction of those elements of Yucatec Maya life burned into the friar's memory. Some of those elements likely derived from his own experiences, others from stories told to him by Maya informants. We must exercise the utmost caution and care when using Landa's description of women's lives, especially when we attempt to decipher something so deeply ingrained in cultural expectations as gender and age categories. The depiction of Maya women and children we read today in the Account is not purely imaginary; it is—arguably—a

---

[1] As John Coakley notes in the case of friars' perceptions of women, "historical evidence of the way groups or societies have perceived and articulated sexual difference—have constructed gender—may therefore take us beyond matters of sexuality per se to wider revelations about the perceivers' sense of themselves" ("Gender," 445).

selective product of Landa's cultural conditioning and anxiety over his failed conversion of the Maya.

During his years both in Yucatan and Spain, Landa, like most Spanish ecclesiastics, had little personal experience with women or children, outside of his official pastoral duties. In both societies, the daily activities of most women and men were largely segregated along gendered lines. When he was evangelizing in Maya villages, and dependent upon local hospitality, Landa would have been permitted little access to the world of Yucatec women. The Maya domestic world where children and women spent a great deal of time, gardening, crafting, and tending small animals was a private space, administered by elders, and inhospitable to men from outside the extended kin group, much less foreign men. Furthermore, Franciscan attitudes toward women, who were seen as childlike and in need of governance under idealized codes of conduct, did not provide a suitable context for Landa to understand the complementarity of Maya gender roles, nor the power exercised by many Maya women.[2]

When women and children appear in the Account, most frequently it is in the context of Landa's desperate attempts to salvage his spiritual mission—suggesting strongly that such passages were authored by Landa himself, either written or revised after his return to Spain in 1563 rather than during his immersion in the Maya world of the 1550s. He chose to portray Maya women largely as natural allies in his spiritual wars and fellow victims of secular Spanish abuse. That illusory sympathy can also be read in the frank expressions of physical desire that lurk behind his descriptions of the behavior of younger Maya women and condemnation of their licentiousness. This obsession with sexual behavior and the decadence of Maya women even entered into the Franciscan's dictionaries. There are markedly more terms pertaining to female sexuality and perverse (to the friars) sexual practices in Franciscan grammars and dictionaries of Yucatec Mayan than comparable works on other Indigenous languages. Nevertheless, unraveling Franciscan theology as it touches on sexuality and gender is a complex undertaking. The writings of sixteenth- and seventeenth-century Franciscans focused on the notion that the human body was like a temple, and notions of corporal purity dominated their conceptions of sex and gender. Franciscan scholars believed that amoral practices rendered the body incapable of receiving Christian conversion; perverse bodies yielded perverse doctrine and incomplete conversions.[3]

Franciscans' rejection of Indigenous gendered practices and obsession with conversion are obvious in their curt but scathing critiques of the participation of Maya

---

[2] On Spanish clerical attitudes toward Indigenous women, see Socolow, *Women of Colonial Latin America*, 68; Kellogg, *Weaving the Past*, 73. For more on Indigenous Maya gender complementarity, see Ardren, *Social Identities*, 117–52; "Gender and Sexuality"; Joyce, *Gender and Power*, 3–89; and Klein, *Gender in Pre-Hispanic America*, 109–42.

[3] See Chuchiak, "The Sins of the Fathers," 87–94.

women in the religious and ceremonial life of Yucatecan villages, where women continued to perform long-standing ritual roles in more active and profound ways than expected within Christian practice of the time. Landa looks more fondly upon the children of colonial Maya society, whom he describes as healthy and well loved, although despite recording the Maya rationale in the Account, he was utterly unable to explain the persistence of child sacrifice. This may be yet another indication of multiple authorship or simply the inability of the friar to see how age could be understood differently in Maya society. As discussed in other chapters, the entire topic of human sacrifice as depicted in the Account must be read critically, as it was deployed in a strategy to advance Franciscan agendas of legitimization and conversion.

The 1562 auto-da-fé in Mani was the pinnacle in Landa's journey toward a complete rejection of native Maya ideology. In his excessive fervor, we can also see it as his acknowledgment that the Maya similarly rejected his ideology of Christian monotheism, as demonstrated in the persistence of Indigenous religious and social practices. Given these experiences, it is curious that Landa has anything positive to say about Maya women and children at all. As sections of the Account may have been written or revised as part of a defense against charges of excessive violence in conversion attempts, one might assume that Landa's motivations were defensive—and thus that he would depict the Maya as without redeemable characteristics. And while the statements made within the Account about Maya women in particular certainly could not be considered balanced, overall Landa chose to describe women sympathetically, as often reluctantly drawn into idolatry, as hardworking, and as chaste, submissive, and kind. Statements such as "They are prudent, polite, and sociable, with those who understand them, and they are extremely generous. They are not secretive, and they are very clean personally, and in their houses, with how much they wash like ermines" (f. 26v) are clearly complimentary, conveying a sense of admiration and appreciation on the part of Landa (or his coauthors and informants).

Why does the Account portray Maya women in this way, or more to the point, why did Landa and his informants depict them this way in his writings? There is ample evidence from the precontact material record, as well as from his own writing, that there were many components of Maya conceptualizations of the female gender that produced anxiety for Landa and other Spanish missionaries. Several of these aspects were not included in Landa's description of the lives of sixteenth-century Yucatec Maya women, and their omission is a potent clue to understanding the motivations behind the Account. The realization that the conversion process was not only being rejected but manipulated by Maya elites and commoners alike surely caused a form of trauma for Landa, a loss of innocence that we glimpse in the final pages of the Account when the author begs God for an explanation of his struggles:

Oh Lord, my God, the light, being, and life of my soul, holy guide and true path of my habits, consolation of my afflictions, inner joy of my sorrows, refreshment and rest from my labors! Why do you command me, Lord, to do what is better called work than rest? Why do you oblige me to do that which I cannot complete? (f. 50r)

If Landa wrote this passage while in isolation in Spain, as is often assumed (and discussed earlier), the friar may have returned to Franciscan teachings of compassion and empathy with Indigenous people. If so, he reconfigured at least one segment of Maya society as his ally, the segment he likely knew the least about, and with which he likely had the least negative interactions: commoner women. His Spanish understanding of gender compelled him to consider women as childlike and in need of protection—from other men, from their weak nature, and from the Devil. Thus, his role as spiritual protector might be made whole by focusing on a population that he knew little about but could imagine to be vulnerable and sympathetic to his mission and goals.

In the hyper-hierarchical social framework of Spain and New Spain in which Landa lived, women, like children, were subject to men. Just as Landa believed ardently that secular Spanish authorities should subordinate themselves to his greater spiritual authority, he believed that Mayas should also subordinate themselves to him and allow his paternalistic control of their spiritual lives. Casting Maya women as compliant with this vision was not only an obvious reflection of his particular Observant Franciscan understanding of gender ideologies; it was a strategic move to justify what might be considered a failure on his part to achieve the conversion of Yucatan.[4]

To accomplish this gendered depiction—this reimagination of Maya women as devout, chaste, pliant, and vulnerable—Landa had to forget major components of the lives of actual Maya women. Nowhere in the Account does one find mention of the essentially dual-gendered nature of the Maya cosmos; the resultant political and spiritual authority of many Maya women; the economic independence of Maya women and their dominion over household production, which was the cornerstone of the Maya economy; or the agency granted many Maya women to choose and control their personal relationships, including when and with whom they married, had children, or lived. On this last point Landa is consistent with other missionary writers in early New Spain who saw female agency only when women were wicked, as he bemoaned the ease with which Maya women (and men) initiated divorce.[5]

This highly selective depiction of Maya women as passive, in need of his protection, and even generous to him (when surely most Maya were not, or only

[4] See Wade, *Missions, Missionaries, and Native Americans*, 35–41.
[5] Reff and Kelly, "Saints, Witches, and Go-Betweens," 239.

pretended to be) can be read as a fictionalized account by a man longing for acceptance and purpose. If Maya women were "prudent, polite, and sociable, with those who understand them" (f. 26v), clearly Landa, in his particular understanding of what he was told by Maya informants, is making a claim to be among those who do. When he says, "They were so given to their idolatrous prayers that in times of necessity even the women, boys, and girls did this by burning incense and praying to God to free them from evil and repress the devil that had caused them it [the affliction]" (f. 22r), Landa is not only reinforcing the simpleminded nature of all non-men; he is asserting that even the simpleminded see the self-evident need to turn to God, underscoring his success with those he understood as most susceptible to evil. The painful longing for an ally is evident in a passage like the following, illustrating the time spent gazing at Maya women from a distance, an attention to their physical appearance and a consideration of how this makes the author feel:

> The Indian women of Yucatan are in general better put-together [*dispusicion*] than Spanish women, larger and well formed, lacking the large haunches of Black women. Those who are beautiful pride themselves on it, and on the one hand, they are not ugly, [although] they are not white, but of a brown color, caused more by the sun and by constant bathing than from their nature. They do not make up [*adoban*] their faces as our nation does, considering this trivial. (f. 25r)

This statement expresses an aesthetic in which Landa attempts to justify his appreciation of Maya beauty (dark-skinned only because of their time in the sun, more modest than Spanish women). This was a sensation that likely caused him much cultural and spiritual anxiety. On one aspect of Maya beauty all Spaniards could agree—the female body was a site on which power relations could be exercised. On another level, Landa was no different from other Franciscans in believing that women's sexual promiscuity was a dangerous harbinger of disorder; overt female sexuality was an instrument of social dissolution, and female corporeal beauty was a temptation and danger—even for the friars, thus threatening the social fabric of mission societies in places like Yucatan. While Landa likely did not beat or sexually assault Maya women in the manner of his secular brethren, nonetheless he exercised power over their bodies by his frank expressions of desire (Maya women's breasts are mentioned ten separate times in the Account) and his reimagination of these bodies as compliant with his other desire, their authentic conversion.[6]

---

[6] Socolow, *Women of Colonial Latin America*, 38; Restall, *Maya World*, 141–47; Chuchiak, "Sins of the Fathers," 77–87. Breasts are mentioned in the Account on folios 25v, 4v, 12r, 25r, 25v (3 times), 26v (3 times). While there is no evidence that Landa assaulted Maya women, many other Franciscan friar confessors accused of the crime of solicitation in the confessional did appear to share an obsession with Maya women's breasts.

This is not to say that Landa's depiction is purely fantasy. Certain ethnographic aspects of commoner womens' lives are depicted in the Account much as we see them in the precontact material record and historic ethnographies.[7] More importantly, the depiction of Maya women as allies of Landa may be derived in part from the efforts of Maya women to shape Spanish encounters in ways that would be advantageous to them and their families. Maya cultural values of respect for rank and religious authority surely contributed to the nature of Landa's social interactions. His proclivity to favor certain Maya families over others, or to persecute the idolatry of certain families while overlooking others, clearly would have been a consideration for the Maya women with whom Landa interacted.[8]

The ability of Maya women to shape Spanish perceptions of their families has its roots in cultural values of the precontact period. Prior to European contact, Maya women acted as cultural mediators, diplomats, or "go-betweens" who literally bridged the interactions of different kin or cultural groups.[9] Elite Maya women of the Classic period were often depicted on painted vases attending or assisting in palace meetings with visiting dignitaries, and marriage alliances cemented hierarchical relations between dynasties. In Yucatan in particular, elite Maya women had a long history of marrying incoming foreigners in order to build political and economic alliances, as attested in the inscriptions of Chichen Itza.[10] These diplomatic skills persisted in the colonial period, as women provided food to visiting foreigners, hosted guests, and served in important ceremonial roles for pan-community rituals like New Year's observations—according to the Account (fs. 24r, 30r). As long as interaction with non-family members occurred within acceptable cultural parameters, Maya women were (and continue to be) expected to provide social mediation and a subtle form of leadership in the realm of diplomacy.[11] Scholarship is abundant on the many Indigenous women of the New World who served in peacekeeping roles, such as translators and guides during the contact period and beyond, and their sisters who mediated through the diplomacy of cross-cultural sexual servitude.[12] Landa's imagination may therefore have been subtly shaped by

---

[7]   For an overview of elite and commoner women's lives in the precontact period, see Ardren, *Ancient Maya Women*, 1–11; "Gender and Sexuality." For early twentieth-century ethnographic descriptions of commoner Maya women's lives, see Elmendorf, *Nine Maya Women*; Redfield and Villa Rojas, *Chan Kom*, 68–104.

[8]   For specific examples of how Maya women manipulated the Spanish courts and priests, see Chuchiak, "In Servitio Dei," and "Sins of the Fathers," 96–110.

[9]   See Ardren, "Strange and Familiar Queens," for an extended discussion of women's essential roles in the maintenance of Classic-period kinship and dynastic systems.

[10] Krochock, "Women in the Hieroglyphic Inscriptions," 155–62.

[11] Martin, *Discarded Pages*.

[12] Karttunen, *Between Worlds*; "Rethinking Malinche"; Metcalf, *Go-Betweens*, 1–16; Restall,

the calculated performances of Maya women coping with a societal crisis beyond any other in their history.

* * *

A further way to view how Landa imagined or constructed Maya women and children is to highlight what he left out of his gendered colonialist reverie. Three omissions in his description of the lives of Maya women and children stem in part from the well-known inherent biases with which Spanish ecclesiastics viewed Indigenous culture.[13] But it is worth pointing out that when considering the ethnographic value of the Account, certain common Maya practices were invisible to someone like Landa, while other practices were the source of an anxiety that led them to be forgotten, or omitted, from his writings.

While Landa discusses the daily activities of commoner Maya women, including their preparation of foodstuffs and child-rearing skills, he made no mention of the lives of higher-ranking Maya women, who likely owned land, received tribute, and may not have spent their days performing domestic chores.[14] Landa interacted frequently with the Maya elite, and one of his chief informants for the Account (effectively his partial coauthor) Gaspar Antonio Chi, was born into a house of high-ranking Maya women. These women were occasionally literate; held political and religious offices of great significance, including military offices, as recently as the end of Mayapan in the fourteenth century; and prior to European contact, amassed personal wealth, either through skills particular to the elite, such as feather-work textiles, or through familial tribute.[15]

A bilateral kinship system was one of the primary bases for the wealth and influence held by some higher-ranking elite Maya women, a kinship system the Spanish shared. In Spain, laws protected the inheritances of women, and while the Maya likewise placed great emphasis on the descent lines of high-ranking women, and power-holding dynasties existed for hundreds of years prior to European arrival, the Account provides no description of the lives of these women who, likewise, would have been shielded from inappropriate contact with foreign men whenever possible.

Seven Myths, 3–24, 82–88; *When Montezuma Met Cortés*, 184, 287–93, 363; Townsend, *Malintzin's Choices*; *Fifth Sun*, 93–95, 99–106.

[13] A good examination of these biases can be found in the many confessional manuals created by the clergy; for relevant discussion, see Marcos, "Indigenous Eroticism," and on the nature and dangers of the female Indigenous body for the mendicant friars, see Frechette, "Danger in Deviance."

[14] Restall, *Maya World*, 98–140; Christensen and Restall, *Return to Ixil*, 120–33.

[15] Chuchiak, "Sins of the Fathers"; Harrison-Buck, "Coin of Her Realm"; Hunt and Restall, "Work, Marriage and Status"; Kellogg, *Weaving the Past*; Socolow, *Women of Colonial Latin America*; Valckx, Stanton, and Ardren, "Mujeres en la Guerra."

There is a risk, then, of using the Account to reconstruct the lives of all women, since it describes only the commoners Landa may have been able to observe during his travels, or the common women his elite male Maya informants deemed appropriate to discuss. Those same informants likely chose to shield their elite female relatives from Franciscan scrutiny whenever possible.

Landa's understanding of the economic lives of Maya women was likewise limited to what he could observe from a distance—he focused on the ubiquitous preparation of corn and the husbandry of small animals, both native and introduced. Despite the importance the Spanish placed on Maya cotton cloth, the enormous amount of time commoner women spent preparing mantles for tribute is hardly mentioned, perhaps because this work occurred in areas that were less visible to a friar. In contrast, Landa mentions animal husbandry (perhaps because this was a more publicly visible activity or perhaps because he was so focused on women's breasts). While it is tempting to see Landa's fantasies run amok in his description of Maya women nursing fawns, iconographic evidence from the Classic period and modern ethnographic examples of women providing breast milk to small mammals in other parts of the world suggest that this passage may not have been a complete fancy.[16]

Another omission from Landa's description of Maya life is any acknowledgment of the spiritual potency of children. Likely this concept was beyond the grasp of Franciscans, who completely rejected the rich Indigenous religious life of their local hosts. In Landa's ideology, where women lacked agency or capability, children were even less likely to be granted the ability to influence their families or society, despite large numbers of illegitimate children who raised themselves, and the occasional child accused of demon possession who was viewed as an otherworldly threat.[17] By the standards of today, colonial Spanish parents were capable of extreme violence toward their children, and there were few guarantees of support for many Spanish children in a society in which illegitimate births were nearly as common as legitimate ones.[18] Landa noticed the very different experience of childhood in Maya society—the care lavished on Maya children, their relative lack of responsibilities when very young, and the elaborate rituals through which infants were literally molded into family members:

> On the fourth or fifth day after birth they placed the newborn stretched out on a little bed made of wooden rods. Face down [alli boca], they placed their head between

---

[16] A precontact clay figurine of an elite Maya woman nursing a fawn is in the collection of the Lowe Art Museum, University of Miami; see Ardren, *Jaguar's Spots*, 80. An overview of this practice around the world is Simoons and Baldwin, "Breast-Feeding."

[17] Hamman, "Child Martyrs and Murderous Children," 203–31.

[18] Powers, *Women*, 117, 133.

two boards, one at the back of the head and the other on the forehead. Between them they squeezed their heads tightly, and they left them there for several days enduring it, until their heads remained flat and modeled, like all of them used to be. So great was the distress and the danger to the poor children, that some were placed at risk of their life. The author of this [account] saw the head of one pierced behind the ears and this must have occurred to many. They were raised entirely naked [*en cueros*], except at the age of four or five they gave them a small mantle for sleeping and several cloth strips to cover their private parts like their parents. [f. 20r]

In addition to these passages, he spends a great deal of time describing the so-called "baptism" or *caput-sihil* ceremony, which lasted nine days and involved an entire cohort of children who were celebrated and welcomed into their adult names (which would change again when they married). In these sections, Maya children are likewise depicted as allies in his conversion mission, compliant and subject to a ritual Landa saw as equivalent to Christian baptism.

The many bodily modifications described by Landa and seen in the precontact material record are materializations associated with changes in the social identity of Maya individuals.[19] Children in Maya society went through many transitionary rituals that gradually brought them into adulthood and which acknowledged their potency and agency from at least the moment of birth. Maya rituals of infancy and childhood, such as the *hetzmek* still practiced today, center on the concept that the newborn is filled with divine grace that must be directed toward appropriate purposes and actions.[20] The *caput-sihil* ritual as described by Landa introduced the children to a gendered life of complementary tasks and to the adult practice of reciprocal offerings to the gods. The linkage of these two components is important—in Maya cosmology it is the correct performance of gender and age-appropriate work (including daily tasks but also ritual observances) that proves an individual's good character and pleases the gods such that balance is maintained. Explicit in the *caput-sihil* ceremony is an acknowledgment that prior to assuming gender appropriate tasks, such as weaving or hunting, children need neither make offerings of food or incense to the gods, nor work to maintain balance.

A further indication of the spiritual grace Maya children embodied is their occasional offering as sacrifices to the gods.[21] Landa struggled with the fact that the most devout would apparently offer their own children into the cenote at Chichen Itza, which indeed contained the skeletal remains of young children of both sexes.[22]

---

[19] Tiesler, "Becoming Maya," 117–32.
[20] Twentieth-century descriptions of the *hetzmek* ceremony can be found in Fortuny Loret de Mola, "Transnational Hetzmek," 214–16; and in Redfield and Villa Rojas, *Chan Kom*, 189.
[21] Ardren, "Empowered Children."
[22] Recent reanalyses of the materials recovered from the Great Cenote can be found in Anda,

Along with these remains were other highly prized materials such as heirloom carved jades, rare gold plates, and huge balls of incense.[23] Landa mentions that the children were painted blue, like the other precious substances, and that those who offered their children expected to see them again on the third day, clear documentation of the enduring divine capital of the dead that was part of Maya ancestor worship. What Landa never grasped was that a child offered in sacrifice was certainly sorely missed, but the child's passing from the world of humans was, for the Maya, mediated by the certainty that the child continued to exist and exert influence upon family members as part of an extended network of ancestral relations.

A third and final lacuna is referenced in a rare passage from the Account that acknowledges the pleasures of a Maya woman's life: "They raise birds for their own pleasure" (f. 26v). This unusual statement aside, the general omission is likely due to the anxiety overt expressions of pleasure provoked in Landa, given his cultural perspective on the dangers of physical contentment. The Account describes the ease with which Maya women could initiate and thrive after divorce, a phenomenon that did not exist in Landa's value system; in the early modern Spanish world, *divorcio* merely meant permission to live in separate households, and it was extremely difficult to procure.[24] Landa preferred his imagination of the Maya past, invoked by a reference to Mayapan, when adultery was punishable by death (f. 24v). But the Account includes multiple and contradictory statements about how adultery was treated, likely due to multiple authors, and Landa acknowledges that in his own time adultery was often forgiven in Maya communities, a response that was likely impossible for him to accept.

On the sexual violation of women, Landa found common ground with Maya values—there were strict punishments for the rape of free Maya women (slaves were not granted this protection). Maya people initiated legal cases that grew out of a culture in which the sexual act was not a locus of shame but rather a form of social discourse that, like other activities such as planting *milpa* or weaving cloth, kept the universe in motion. Prior to European contact, most Maya women had no cause for shame over sexual desire or pregnancy—both aspects of life over which Spanish culture sought strict control. Like in most Indigenous American cultures, Maya female sexuality and fertility were also controlled, but through measures such as marriage alliances, ritualized arenas for female-male interaction, and a vast herbal apothecary.[25] These measures left more control in the hands of individual women

Tiesler, and Zabala, "Cenotes, espacios sagrados y la practica del sacrificio humano en Yucatan," and in Beck and Sievert, "Mortuary Pathways."
[23] Tozzer, *Chichen Itza.*
[24] Socolow, *Women of Colonial Latin America*, 12.
[25] We know very little about how precontact Maya women managed their reproductive lives,

or their female relatives than did Spanish Christian concepts of family honor and paternalism.

Spanish conceptualizations of masculinity included a strong emphasis on protecting female bodies—both daughters and wives—primarily from other men.[26] Male sexuality was understood to be uncontrollable, hence the general tolerance of prostitution, and Landa's pity for rather than condemnation of Maya "public women" (f. 24v). This gender ideology produced an extreme paternalism and anxiety over female honor, which Spanish women were expected to embody through chastity, obedience to male relatives, and an absence of visible pleasure, even within the sexual relations of married partners. Maya conceptualizations of masculinity were radically different, and they centered on the proper performance of gender-specific tasks and correct partnership. The creator couple at the heart of Maya cosmology, Itzamna and Chak Chel, worked together, each with their specific skill set, to bring about creation.[27] While hardly ensuring the equality of women within Maya society, this ideological emphasis on both partnership and procreation provided a conceptual space where Maya women brought a unique and essential contribution to society. Landa was likely highly anxious to reshape Maya women, from individuals with a lack of shame over sexual pleasure and an ability to obtain this in the appropriate venues, to women who performed modesty and inhibition even within marriage.[28]

Social identities are constructed in a myriad of ways, often with materialized objects and daily habits as props to assist in the maintenance or circulation of shared ways of understanding. Normalization of identities takes place in the repetition and familiarity of these habits, and thus can be very difficult to change. Maya people used ornaments and body modifications to mark infants and children as socially meaningful humans embedded in family and kin networks. Maya women shared proficiency in gender-specific household tasks that contributed to family economies. Female power was acknowledged and controlled in ways that benefited the larger social collective in both Maya and Spanish society, although in vastly different ways.

Landa and the Franciscans thus found themselves surrounded by women who were allowed a much wider sphere of social discourse than their culture would allow.

---

but see Knowlton and Dzidz Yam, "Perinatal Rites," 721–44; and Roys, *Ethno-botany of the Maya*, 14–20. For more on precontact Maya reproductive politics, see Ardren, "Strange and Familiar Queens."

[26] Powers, *Women*; Socolow, *Women of Colonial Latin America*.

[27] Bassie-Sweet, *Maya Sacred Geography*, 53–57; Vail and Stone, "Representations of Women."

[28] See, for discussions of marriage and clerical ideas of the proper role of sexuality, Chuchiak, "Sins of the Fathers," 89–104.

And yet in the Account we see that Landa came to admire and perhaps desire these women, despite their dangerous habits. The friar resolved this by reimagining Maya women as his partners in the struggle against sin, a vision that certain women may have fostered in their own self-interest. Such a vision was also surely pleasurable to Landa, once he was sequestered far away from actual Maya women. In his depiction of devout and vulnerable women, the Account reveals the Spanish desire for power and control over an imagined Maya less resistant to messages of salvation.

At the root of the Landa conundrum (as we have termed the paradoxes surrounding his actions and writings) lies a frustration over his inability to understand and command, shape and control, the Maya. Having infiltrated and invaded their communities, the friar desperately wanted to believe that Maya families should, could, and were being converted and colonized. Reality was less reassuring. As Landa came to realize that fact, whilst remaining in denial over his ability to change the Maya, his conflicted attitudes towards Maya women and children were thrown into relief. As his gendered anxieties sharpened, so did he become more intransigent and violent—while all along clinging to his colonialist reverie.

6

The Nature of the Account

Its Irregularities and the Mystery of Its Copyists

The irregular nature of the Account manuscript is obvious to anyone reading it. The historical reasons for its nature have already been explained. We have also mentioned that previous editors of the manuscript have responded to its irregularities by mishandling it, attempting to turn it into something it has never been—a coherent book. In this chapter, then, we analyze those irregularities, categorizing and further detailing them. We then summarize the manuscript by its thematic segments. We conclude the chapter by suggesting solutions to the mystery surrounding the extraction of the passages that comprise the Account, further discussing the possible identities of the authors of certain passages and of the copyists who created the Account from Landa's larger, lost *recopilación*. Our intention is to better understand, rather than alter or disguise, this complex series of documents.

The manuscript's irregularities fall into four categories: purpose (its inconsistent focus and intent); authorship (its multiple sources, authors, and copyists); structure (its ambiguous sequencing); and style (the disjunctive way in which it was written and presented).

If the purpose of Landa's long-lost *recopilación* was to provide Franciscans in Yucatan with encyclopedic information on the province's history, Indigenous peoples, and early conversion to Christianity, it must have succeeded in a scattershot kind of way; that is, future friars would have found something on almost any topic, even if it took them a while to delve through numerous non sequiturs and red herrings. That at least is the impression given by the Account, whose

https://doi.org/10.5876/9781646424245.c006

creators nonetheless accentuated what we presume was the disjointedness of the *recopilación*.

That ambiguity is evident in the Account from the very start—from the title page (see figure 3.2 in chapter 3). There the inscription reads:

> Relacion de las cosas de Yucatan sa-
> cada de lo que escrivio el padre fray
> Diego de Landa de la orden de St Fran-
> Cisco——
>
> ["Account of the things of Yucatan
> taken from the writings of the padre fray
>   Diego de Landa of the order of St. Francis"]

A little below this and to the side is written:

> Esta aqui otra relacion de las
> cosas de la china
>
> ["Here is another account of the
>   things of the Far East"]

Both editors of previous editions, and Mayanists using those editions, have tended to take this as evidence that Landa wrote a longer work called the Relación de las cosas de Yucatán, from which the extant manuscript is an excerpt or set of excerpts. But the inscription does *not* state that this is an excerpt from a work of Landa's that he himself composed with such a title; it only states that the excerpt is, in substance, an "account of the things of Yucatan" taken from a body of writings by Landa (literally "what he wrote down"; presumably some writings that he authored but others copied out).

Moreover, there is no evidence or indication that the inscription goes with all the material in the manuscript, which was copied in different hands and at different times. In addition, the reference to "another account" and to *la china*, "China" or "the Far East," strongly suggests that the copyists were part of the large-scale effort by the office of the Cronista Mayor de las Indias to write a comprehensive history of the Philippines and of Spanish activities elsewhere in East Asia—an effort mandated by various Royal Cedulas starting with King Philip II's interest in sending the first embassy to the Emperor of China in 1564 and continuing into the eighteenth century.[1]

---

[1]   As we will see below, the only Cronista of the Indies who actually wrote such a history—a History of the World, with detailed accounts of the Spanish missions in China and Japan, as well as a now lost History of China (1598), and who also translated another Franciscan

What we have here, then, is three layers of purpose: Landa's intent when he compiled his *recopilación* (uncertain, as the manuscript is long lost); the intent of the copyists (whose identities and dates were previously unknown but are discussed below); and the intent of whoever saved these excerpts and gave them a title and a cover (also discussed shortly). With respect to the latter, we explore in this chapter the apparent confusion in the collecting of reports by Franciscans on mission activities going back into the sixteenth century. As we shall explain, a notary or historian's assistant confused the late-sixteenth- and early-seventeenth-century copy of some Landa material (i.e., this Account) with other *relaciones* by Franciscans, and he mistakenly placed it among the source reports for this project. In this way, the Landa manuscript may have been taken from where it had been sitting since the seventeenth century, perhaps within the royal archives in Simancas, or in the archives of the Council of the Indies in Madrid, where it lay until the king had all of the papers of the Cronistas of the Indies transferred and deposited in the library of the Real Academia de la Historia in Madrid in 1744 (where Brasseur de Bourbourg found the Account). It is thus by sheer accident that we have any of Landa's larger manuscript at all.

The second irregular feature of the manuscript is that of its ambiguous authorship, the multiple hands of its copyists, and the confusing dates of its paper, content, and the extant object itself. That object resembles a small handwritten book, consisting of sixty-six numbered folios containing text written on both sides and thus offering 132 pages of writing. In addition, there are a title page folio (not numbered) and two folios with maps (not numbered, but we refer to them as fs. 67–68). As these sixty-nine folios were bound with five blank folios at the front and five at the back, the grand total is seventy-nine folios, all sized 21 by 14.5 centimeters (but cut unevenly). The folios were bound with a leather cover and marbled endpapers colored red, green, blue, and yellow, thereby dating the binding to the late eighteenth century.[2]

When one of us (Restall) first studied the manuscript in the 1990s in the small library where it survives, Madrid's Real Academia de la Historia, he found adjacent to the Account copies made in 1778 of other sixteenth-century manuscripts (such as copies of the Vienna originals of Cortés's letters to the king). That fact, combined with the appearance of the cover and binding, led to Restall's impression that the handwriting appeared seventeenth-century in parts and eighteenth-century in others, and to the opinion on the handwriting and watermarks of another of us, who viewed the original in 1996 (Chuchiak), all of which resulted in our conclusion that a significant part of the Account "dated to the later colonial period."[3] We

---

account by the Jesuit Luis de Guzmán in 1601—was Antonio de Herrera.

[2] Kettunen, "Observations," 56; confirmed by three of us (Chuchiak, Restall, and Solari) in the RAH.

[3] Restall and Chuchiak, "A Re-evaluation," 661.

TABLE 6.1. Dating the compositional stages of the Account

Manuscript/object	Author/creator	Date
Recopilación, possibly two variants or copies made, one left in Spain, one in Yucatan (both lost since late seventeenth century)	Landa, his Maya informants, various Spanish authors, composed and assembled in Yucatan and Spain	1549–1579
Paper on which the Account was copied	Manufactured in Spain	1548–1591
The Account	Two main copyists and up to five additional scribes	Mostly c. 1571–c. 1620s. Some mid- to late-seventeenth-century later minor additions, or words copied as late as the early eighteenth century
The binding and cover of the Account, as deposited in the RAH	Unknown royal officials	Late eighteenth century

were wrong! As a result of two more decades of sporadic study and discussion, the input of the other authors of this book (Solari and Ardren), and the recent, skilled examination of the manuscript's watermarks and paper by Harri Kettunen, along with a re-evaluation of the paleography and scribal hands of the manuscript, we have determined the following chronological aspects of the various elements of the Account as an object.

The original *recopilación* was written, copied, and compiled by Landa between 1549 (when he arrived in Yucatan) and 1579 (when he died there) (see table 6.1). The only date of apparent composition is atop the first folio—MDLXVI (1566 in Roman numerals)—and it thus seems likely that the *que* half of the manuscript (fs. 1–27; *que* is explained below) is copied from a larger portion of the *recopilación* that was assembled by Landa, but not all authored by him, when he was in Spain. He was there between 1564 and 1573, but a substantial portion of the *recopilación* must have been written or assembled over a two-year period starting with Landa's arrival in Spain in October of 1564.[4] On February 13, 1565, the Crown ordered copies made and sent to

---

4   The Crown officially recalled Landa in February of 1564, but the previous March he had already resolved to return to Spain to give the king "face to face" his "account of the things of this land" (in Lizana's telling of it; *Historia de Yucatán*, 66v). The journey, however, took eighteen months, as Landa fell ill soon after leaving Campeche, spending several months recuperating in Santo Domingo, and was subsequently adrift at sea for a while, "chased by a Moorish corsair vessel," and even briefly "a castaway" (Lizana, *Historia de Yucatán*, 66v; *Real cedula al alcalde mayor de Yucatán que Fray Diego de Landa, Fray Pedro de Ciudad Rodrigo, Fray Miguel de la Puebla, y Fray Juan Pizarro de la orden de San Francisco sean enviados a*

the Provincial of the Franciscans of "information, testimonies, and other documents" on Landa; in response to formal charges filed against him on March 6, he put together "other papers and *memorias*" which, "if Your Majesty should be served, I will submit, and they will greatly help in knowing and inquiring about the truth of these things."[5] The following year, he asserted that Maya were "very evil idolaters and filled with evil things and abominations, which can be confirmed in the summary information that I presented before the Council."[6] At least one bundle of papers submitted by him and assembled in the case against him amounted to 321 folios (642 pages).[7] No doubt such documents originally were part of the *recopilación*, as it existed in 1566, and thus a version of the lost manuscript went to the Council of the Indies in that year. But the history of the *recopilación* did not end there.

Then, in 1573, Landa took most of his writings back to Yucatan, where he continued to add to them. That version of the *recopilación* remained in Merida after his death in 1579, surviving there for about a century, until its disappearance. As we speculated earlier, it seems likely that there was a second version of the *recopilación* in Spain—either left there by Landa in 1573 or sent there by him later in the 1570s. But it too apparently did not survive the seventeenth century. Generations of scholars have hunted for the lost *recopilación*, all in vain.[8] The likely culprit? Fire. One possible resting place for the *recopilación* was the royal palace library at El Escorial, where a great fire in 1671 consumed many of the writings of the royal *cronista* Juan López de Velasco (to whom we shall return shortly), the original manuscript by Tomas López Medel, and countless other manuscripts and maps.[9] More likely, the *recopilación* remained in the archives of the Council of the Indies, and was thus in the library of the royal palace of Madrid in 1734 when a fire burnt most of the building to the ground, destroying numerous original copies of manuscripts—as well as

---

    estos reinos con la informaciones y autos en contra de ellos, 26 de febrero, Barcelona, 1564, AGI, Escribanía de Cámara, 1009A, 4 fs.; *Memorial de Fray Diego de Landa sobre su llegado a corte y su negocio con el Consejo de Indias*, 1565, AGI, Escribanía de Cámara, 1009A, 16 fs).

[5] *Cédula de su Majestad para que el Provincial de San Francisco haga justicia en el negocio de Fray Diego de Landa*, 13 de febrero, 1565; and the Memorial cited above; all in AGI, Escribanía de Cámara, 1009A.

[6] See *Respuesta de Fray Diego de Landa a los cargos hechos por Fray Francisco Guzmán*, 1566, AGI, Escribanía de Cámara, 1009A, 2 fs.

[7] See *Inventario de los papeles que existen en la Escribanía de Cámara del Consejo de Indias y causas que en él tuvieron origen y se fenecieron, Volumen 1,1547–1738*, AHN, Códices, Libro 1135, f. 136r.

[8] France Scholes claimed he searched the archives of the Franciscan convents in Toledo and Cifuentes where Landa had worked; Tozzer concluded that the entire manuscript went to Yucatan and was lost there; see Tozzer, *Landa's* Relación, vii; Pagden, *The Maya*, 20; Restall and Chuchiak, "A Re-evaluation," 653–55.

[9] Amo Horga, "El gran incendio de 1671," 598–603.

paintings and other artwork—from the time of the Hapsburgs. Perhaps the signs of water damage to the Account show that it was rescued from the fire, while the larger *recopilación* was lost.[10] Just ten years later, the remainder of the manuscripts were transferred to the Real Academia de la Historia.

Now we turn to the dating of the copied material that comprises the extant Account. Thanks to Kettunen's analysis of transillumination photographs of the manuscript, which revealed watermarks hitherto invisible, the paper of fs. 1–68 can be dated to 1548–1586, with the paper on the blank pages made in 1561–1591.[11] Royal government stocks of paper might have sat for decades, but not centuries, so that means the copyists did their work in the late sixteenth (after the 1571 establishment of the post of the Cronista Mayor) or early seventeenth centuries. The handwriting looks to us to date from anywhere from the last three decades of the sixteenth century to the early seventeenth century—as indeed it did to the French scholars Brasseur and Genet, who dated the copying to "about thirty years after [Landa's] death" and to "around 1616," respectively.[12] The exception is fs. 50–58, whose handwriting looks later (an *italica bastardilla* book-hand style of the early to mid-seventeenth century); but as the paper of the entire Account manuscript was manufactured in the late sixteenth century, that means any mid- to late-seventeenth- or early-eighteenth-century copyists just added material (perhaps not even drawn from Landa's *recopilación* or any of his writings) on some of the blank pages. Later still, when the manuscript was bound, those folios ended up inserted between the folios that were later numbered 1–49 and 59–66.

With respect to the copyists, none of the earlier scholars who examined or published the manuscript knew who they were, nor did they hazard any hypotheses on their identities or how many there were—let alone when they did their work and over how many days or years it was done. However, it appears that two principal compilers created the Account, with the assistance of several additional copyists and illustrators (see table 6.2). So, there were at least three contributing copyists, and there may have been as many as seven if all of the addenda and other notations are taken into account. Pagden made the insightful suggestion that part of the manuscript may have been dictated.[13] This would certainly explain irregularities such as errors of syntax and repeated words or phrases, as well as the fact that a second hand

---

[10]   Evidence of water damage is on the lower parts of fs. 11r–11v, 17r–27v, and 31r–33r, and at the top of fs. 34r–45r and 49r–51r. The fire is described in Castaño Perea, "La Real Capilla del Alcázar de Madrid," 181–83.

[11]   Kettunen, "Observations," 61–63.

[12]   Brasseur, *Relation* [1864], III, n3 (*une copie faite trente ans environ après sa mort*); Genet, *Diego de Landa* [1928], I, 10 (*Vers 1616, un inconnu fit unabrégé défectueux*).

[13]   Pagden, *The Maya*, 19.

TABLE 6.2. Pieces of the Puzzle (part 1): Identifying the various transcribers of the Account

Primary Scribes	Folios in the original MS	"Chapters" or "sections"	Possible date of handwriting
Scribe A	18r–45r	XXIII–XLI	Late sixteenth to early seventeenth century
	1r–17v	I–XXIII	Late sixteenth to early seventeenth century
	46r–49v	XLI–XLII	Late sixteenth to early seventeenth century
	59r–66v	XLVIII–LII	Late sixteenth to early seventeenth century
Scribe B	50r–58v	XLIII–XLVIII	End of sixteenth to mid-seventeenth century
	55v–56r (paragraph headings)		End of sixteenth to mid-seventeenth century

Secondary Scribes	Folios in the original MS		
Scribe B (notation hand) or Scribe C	3v–4r (13-line inserted passage)		
	4v–7r (inserted phrases and names)		
	11v (inserted lines)		
	11r (six-line inserted passage)		
	20v, 21v, 26r (inserted lines)		
	23r, 23v, 24r (marginalia)		
	26v–45r (inserted names)		
	34r–43v (calendrical inserts)		
	46v, 47r, 48v (drawings with captions)		
	67–68 (maps)		
Scribe D	15v–16r, 16r–16v (inserted passages)		

went back over the manuscript adding in Maya personal and place names; based on name-insertion evidence alone, about a third of the Account seems to have been sporadically copied from an original source consulted various times, or perhaps created through dictation.

In the passage where the so-called Landa Alphabet appears (f. 45r; Sec. 41), the first scribe to write on the page (we have called him Scribe A) made four or five errors in the Maya syllables, which another notary (Scribe B) went in and corrected.

TABLE 6.3. Pieces of the Puzzle (part 2): Sequencing the manuscript segments of the Account

Pagination in bound manuscript	**Sequence of** folios in Brasseur edition	**Sequence of** folios in Tozzer, Gates, Garibay editions
18r–45r, 1r–17v, 46r–68r	1r–49v, 58, 63	1r–68r

Note: Tables 6.2 and 6.3 are expanded and corrected versions of the tables in Restall and Chuchiak, "A Reevaluation."

Scribe B and perhaps a Scribe C made various corrections and added omitted words in the margins, including adding "p" and the rabbit glyph in the right margin; Kettunen commented that as the rabbit was trickster and scribe in precontact Maya art and mythology, this could be "the final trick of the Trickster Rabbit."[14]

The third irregular feature of the manuscript is its structure—specifically the sequence of its folios. The original manuscript is bound in one sequence, but Brasseur reordered the folios in a difference sequence (see table 6.3). Later editors followed Brasseur, most of them filling in what he had left out, while also making their own editorial decisions. None simply transcribed or translated the manuscript as they found it; they all sought in some way to improve it or enhance its readability. At worst, they all exercised a kind of editorial vandalism, attempting in vain to disguise the nature of the Account and transform it into something it is not. At best, they gave parts of it some structural or narrative coherence, giving it the semblance of a start and end, with a rhythm of imaginary chapters in between—but ultimately only adding further layers of inconsistency and ambiguity.[15]

---

[14] Kettunen, "Observations," 72; he also describes the "17 small puncture holes" made in this page, probably to hold it in place to make copies or photographs.

[15] Although we have judged Brasseur de Bourbourg for his editorial intrusions, he did clearly state that the Account is a flawed and incomplete copy (*Relation* [1864], III, n3); Kettunen makes a good point in remarking that Brasseur "is not so much to blame for the confusion as are the subsequent (twentieth-century) editors, translators, and commentators" ("Observations," 57). Here are just some examples of such decisions made by previous editors, from 1864 to 1975 (see the separate section of the bibliography listing these editions): Brasseur stopped at f. 49v (his last chapter was XLII [48]); Genet made it only through what Brasseur had numbered XLI [41], despite publishing his edition in two volumes; most later editors extended the invented chapter structure through the manuscript, although the 1900 CDI edition omitted all the calendrical material (eight "chapters" were simply skipped; fs. 28r–45r [secs. 34–41]); Gates included all the material but reorganized Chapter XL (40) (he relabeled them "sections," thus it was Sec. XL, "Months and Festivals of the Yucatecan Calendar"), so that the calendar does not start in January (as Landa had it) but in July (when the Maya New Year begins); Tozzer followed Gates with respect to "Sec. XL," although he was alone in not using chapter and section names and numbers; Tozzer also omitted most of the calendrical drawings, and his bizarre translation method (mentioned earlier) created numerous errors, some serious; Pérez Martínez repeated one set of day-sign drawings throughout the calendar section, and he also reorganized the "Landa Alphabet" by inserting the "p" in

The original binding of the folio sequences them in a manner that pays little attention to narrative or thematic order; as tables 6.2 and 6.3 indicate, that bound sequence does not even follow the folio numbering. But a "correct" sequence of sections is made apparent neither by reading the manuscript as it is bound, nor by reading it according to the sequence of its folios. Part of the problem is that we do not know who bound the manuscript, nor who numbered its folios; indeed, Brasseur probably added those numbers after he shuffled the sheets of paper in the order that he thought made sense (but he only published part of the manuscript, stopping where Scribe B begins on f. 50; Sec. 43). Other editors have followed the Brasseur sequencing of the segments of the document; we have done the same, simply because we cannot be sure that the unknown binder of the manuscript brought us any closer to coherence or an "authentic" structure than the person who wrote the folio numbers (whether that was an eighteenth-century Spanish copyist or Brasseur).

The fourth irregular feature of the manuscript is its disjunctive style. This is apparent from published editions, but it is highlighted by the coincidence of the most blatant breaks in narrative and topic with shifts in hand, paper, and the inclusion of small gaps between passages in some parts of the manuscript. There are also several abrupt breaks between folios as well as mismatched folios out of order. In addition, there are passages where Landa is referred to in the third person (as detailed in our notes to the translation). It may not be coincidence that the three such passages in the first half of the book all cover topics on which we might have expected Landa to be more expansive: his Maya informants; the violent methods of the Spanish conquistadors; and his return to Spain to defend his actions of 1562 (Secs. 11, 15, and 19). In other words, Landa surely did write more on these topics, but such passages were abbreviated and summarized by a copyist; indeed, based on early modern criteria of authorship, we might reasonably classify those passages as actually edited by the copyist, albeit one drawing from lost material by Landa.[16] Considering how crucial those passages are to how Landa has been imagined as an historical figure, that ambiguity of authorship is significant. Once again, Landa is less the author of the Account than previously assumed.

---

the wrong place; Garibay and Pagden repeated the day-sign error, and Garibay repeated the "p" placement error; Garibay generally followed Brasseur, Gates, and Tozzer, except in two ways—he invented a chapter on "Iguanas y Lagartos" (his Chapter XLVI) and then folded Chapters LI and LII [51 and 52] into a single Chapter LII; Pagden completely invented his own chapters (numbered I–XXXII [1–32], unrelated to the chapter and section numbers in the Brasseur and Gates editions), but included the whole Landa manuscript and even sequenced the calendrical material according to Landa.

16 See Chuchiak and Kettunen, "A New Understanding of the Structure, Composition, and Copyists of Diego de Landa's *Relación*."

Previous scholarly editions addressed few or none of these inherent structural problems. Moreover, previous editors attempted to "patch up" the manuscript in order to make sense out of several sections, yet they failed either to address the implications of disjuncture in style or to bring overall coherence to the manuscript. For example, the segment of the manuscript written by Scribe B (50r–58v; Secs. 43–48) suggests, by the dating of its style of handwriting, that it was copied many decades later than the rest of the Account; not only that, but other features also highlight its identity as an odd fit. On three folios in this segment, there are gaps in the writing, filled with headings that read, respectively:

[f. 50r]   Porque coſas hazian otros sacrficios los Indios.
[f. 56r]   Parrapho VII: de la manera d/ay de ferpientes y otros animales ponçoñofos.
[f. 56v]   Parrapho VIII: de las auejas y su miel y cera.

The second two of these headings are either written by a different hand, or they are written in a different handwriting styled by the same compiler. Either way, the creation of these headings and their orthography—an imitation of print, with such features as unjoined letters and an initial *s* resembling an *f* without a truncated horizontal stroke—was an early-seventeenth- through eighteenth-century convention used in the preparation of a manuscript for publication (an example is Lizana's abovementioned 1633 *Historia*, republished in facsimile in 1893). This feature is disguised in almost every edition, as Brasseur renumbered the two sections as chapters 46 and 47, and subsequent editors tended to follow suit. So why does this largely hidden feature exist in the manuscript?

One explanation is that some part of Landa's original work, perhaps his entire *recopilación*, was not only prepared for publication with this scribal "typesetting," but part or all of it may have been actually typeset or prepared for binding. It is also possible that the work was published, although no listing of it appears in the guide to the works published in Madrid in the sixteenth and seventeenth centuries.[17] Still, other regions in Spain had presses, and less documented information about these lesser presses (mostly in university towns) exists.

Indeed, there are a few further chapter references that might support that theory. For example, at various points, the text refers readers to specific chapters—"Chapter 1" (fs. 44r, 52r), "Chapter 10" (f. 42r), "Chapter XCVI" (96; f. 39v), "Chapter LXXXXIX" (99; f. 66r), "Chapter 100" (f. 29v), "Chapter CI" (101; fs. 37v, 66r),

---

[17] No work about Yucatan or by Landa appears in Gutiérrez Iglesias, *Catálogo de incunables y obras impresas del siglo XVI.*

"Chapter 110" (f. 33r), "Chapters 113, 114, 115, 116" (f. 34r), and "the last chapter," with no number, but paragraphs XV [15] and XIII [13] are cited (f. 66r)––none of which are in the Account. Many of these passages (and thus their parent "chapters") detail Maya religion and its deities, a topic not of interest to the royal Cronistas, and indeed a prohibited topic to put into print after 1577 (hence the lack of a colonial-era publication of Sahagún's great compendium, known to us as the Florentine Codex).[18] The Account also refers to marked line numbers in at least one passage. The fact that there are notations at the foot of some of the manuscript pages, letters and symbols which could be printers' marks, further suggests the small but tantalizing possibility that the copyists were working from a printed edition of Landa's *recopilación*. If such a book had been printed, one would expect at least one subsequent reference to it; even if no copies survived, a local press in Spain might have produced a dozen or so copies, with a trace of them waiting to be discovered in an obscure Iberian archive.

We propose an alternative, more likely, explanation, however: that the section of the Account from which "paragraph 7" and "paragraph 8" come was not written by Landa at all. The evidence for this is threefold. First, our supposition explains why this section of the book was "typeset" and yet there is no other evidence of a Landa publication. Second, this explains why the section is on a topic unrelated to the rest of the Account, namely the natural history of Yucatan, a significant clue as to the possible identity of one of the copyists. Third, the larger body of historical evidence on Landa's life—his letters and commentary about him by contemporaries—confirms a passionate interest in Maya history and culture, as well as the conversion campaign or "spiritual conquest," the topics of the rest of the Account. But there is little evidence that he had any interest in natural history.

So, if Landa did not write this part of the manuscript, who did? One good candidate is Francisco Domínguez—mentioned earlier as a contemporary of Landa's who spent time in Yucatan, who wrote on such matters in the peninsula, and whose 1576 cosmography was one of the sources mentioned above for one of the answers to the colony's 1579–1581 *Relaciones Geográficas* questionnaires.[19] Or, as discussed below, the source could be the treatise on natural history written by the visiting judge in Yucatan, Tomás López Medel, and published in 1570 as *De los tres*

---

[18] An increase in New World campaigns of extirpation of "idolatry" and direct complaints from bishops like Landa prompted Philip II to order the Council of the Indies to collect all manuscripts like Sahagún's, and to prohibit others from being published, so as not to perpetuate the memory of the old gods among the "Indians" of his realm. Landa may have indirectly been behind this prohibition against recording Indigenous culture and religion, as the king consulted with him on the question of extirpation of "idolatry" following a personal meeting in 1572 (shortly before Landa returned to Yucatan).

[19] Restall and Chuchiak, "A Re-evaluation," 662; RHGY; AGI, *Patronato*, 261, ramo 9.

elementos: Tratado sobre la naturaleza y el hombre del nuevo mundo. However, we believe there are two better candidates, one for Scribe A and the other for Scribe B.

*   *   *

Before discussing who Scribes A and B were, let us view the irregular features of the manuscript once more, by categorizing them according to topical or thematic sections. In a sense, that is what Brasseur and his successors tried to do in creating chapters, complete with invented numbers and titles. But, of course, that added to, rather than explicated, the manuscript—disguised, rather than exposed, its composite nature.

Here, then, is another perspective on the manuscript, sequenced according to its folio numbers (and our translation in part I of this book), with eleven thematic segments described (which we labeled A–K below).

Segment A (fs. 1r–12v; Secs. 1–16): The segment that begins the manuscript, as per Brasseur's reshuffling, comprises a dozen folios (twenty-four pages of text; the first sixteen of Brasseur's chapters, which Gates called sections and which we refer to as "Sec."). The segment opens with a brief description of Yucatan's geography, followed by an early history of contact and conquest (fs. 1r–4v; Secs. 1–4), before switching to precontact Maya history (fs. 4v–8r; Secs. 5–10), and then back to the Spanish invasion and colonization (fs. 8r–12v; Secs. 11–16); these passages on Yucatan's history are discussed above in our chapter 1.

The *que* style begins at the top of folio 1r and runs through all this segment—and indeed through to the end of segment C (which ends at the foot of f. 27v; Sec. 33). The *que* style means that each paragraph begins with *Que* or *que*, which can sometimes be translated as "how," but generally is better left untranslated (as we have done), treated as a paragraph marker, and as the point where a question is being answered. In other words, segments A–C were likely created through the questionnaire method that characterized how early modern Spaniards gathered information or evidence (including legal testimony in court proceedings). The questions are missing, but they are implied by the rhetorical style of each answer. Much of this segment closely follows—even partially or entirely paraphrases—the passage on the same topic in volume 4, chapter 98 of the *Historia General* by Bartolomé de Las Casas.[20] In other words, the implied question might have been, "What does fray Bartolomé tell us about this topic?" Other possible sources are the so-called Second Letter or *carta de relación* by Hernando Cortés, from which there seems to be some paraphrasing; and Francisco López de Gómara's *Conquista de México* (first published in 1552), from where Landa seems to have copied the letter that Cortés wrote to Jerónimo de Aguilar—unless one

---

[20] Las Casas, *Historia de las Indias*.

of the later copyists inserted it from López de Gómara, as it is written in a different hand (from the bottom of f. 3v to the top of f. 4r).

Segment A continues with a passage similar in length (fs. 4v–8r; Secs. 5–10) to the previous one and, likewise, in *que* style. The focus is the precontact political geography, a brief foray into ancient building design, and the history of the Yucatec Maya, possibly also paraphrasing Las Casas (the spelling of Quetzalcoatl as *Cezalcouati* is a clue there) or perhaps, but less likely, Oviedo.[21] The primary copyist here was clearly unfamiliar with Mesoamerica, and he left small gaps for a second copyist—one who knew New Spain—to fill in the Indigenous toponyms and appellations.

The final passages of this segment (fs. 8r–12v; Secs. 11–16), again similar in length to the previous two and continuing the *que* style, turn more specifically to the Spanish invasions of Yucatan. Landa is, for the first time, identified as being "the author of this book [*el autor deste libro fray Diego de Landa*]" (f. 8v; Sec. 11),[22] and again (on f. 11v; sec. 14): "this Diego de Landa says [*dize este Diego de Landa*]." This segment may therefore have been extracted from a part of Landa's *recopilación* that had been prepared for possible (but unrealized) publication. A different hand intrudes on f. 11v (the start of Sec. 15), just for four lines; this passage closely follows the accusations of cruelty that were leveled against Francisco de Montejo in his *residencia* investigation.

Some editors altered the pronominal perspective of such passages; Gates, for example, changed "this Diego de Landa, he says that he saw" to "I, Diego de Landa, say that I saw."[23] This change matters, as Landa did not in fact see atrocities such as the hanging of Maya women from trees; years later, he just saw the tree in Yobain where such an incident was said to have occurred. It seems probable that such brutality took place, but a series of small steps created a leap to two things that did not take place (Landa seeing those hanging bodies, and him writing "I saw . . ."). A letter coauthored by Landa in 1559 was likely included in his *recopilación*, and this passage is thus probably redacted by a copyist from that. Parts of this segment (fs. 12r–12v; Sec. 16) may have also been drawn from López de Gómara (or, unlikely but possible, copied from the unpublished manuscript by Oviedo which the copyists had access to, especially in its final folios).[24]

---

[21] As detailed below, Herrera and López de Velasco (Scribes B and A) both had access to Las Casas's works and all of his papers.

[22] This is evidence that the scribes were transcribing from a *libro* or handwritten book, not a simple *relación* or *recopilación* or other type of collected papers; as will be clear below, these copyists knew well the difference between those genres and a *libro*.

[23] Sec. 15; f. 11v; Gates, *Yucatán*, 25.

[24] Also see Tozzer, *Landa's* Relación, 60.

Segment B (fs. 12v–15r; Secs. 17–20): This segment is relatively short (fs. 12v–15; Secs. 17–19), essentially a continuation of the previous one, likewise employing the *que* style, and written by the same scribe (although note that the letters listed on f. 14r, Sec. 18, may have been inserted later). Its topic is the Franciscans and their "spiritual conquest" efforts in Yucatan. This segment probably also came directly from the *recopilación*, as it contains local or inside knowledge that would have been restricted to Landa and his fellow friars of the time.

Segment C (fs. 15r–27v; Sec. 20–28): This segment is relatively long, turning in detail to the topic of Maya culture (Secs. 20–33; a total of twenty-five pages of text). It is also in *que* style; note that this means that the first 40 percent of the manuscript (twenty-seven folios) is structured in the *que* style. At first, Segment C continues in the same hand as segments A and B. However, one page into the segment, the hand changes (on f. 15v; Sec. 20, with "They did not grow their beards"), but then the original hand returns (on f. 16r; Sec. 21), with the second returning again at the foot of that same folio. That second hand adds further ethnographic detail to the descriptions started by the first hand; the hand change takes place at a shift from the topic of food to that of tattoos (fs. 16r–17v; Secs. 21–22). Passages in this segment appear to be generically Mesoamerican (and thus taken from Las Casas or another source), but other passages seem specifically Maya (and so could be taken from writings by Landa—the passage, for example, on honey-based drinks). A long marginalia passage on f. 23r (Sec. 28) describes Indigenous practice in a style different from the main text. Gates and other editors simply embedded the marginalia into the main text, thereby eliding its distinctiveness.[25] As with previous theme segments, spaces were left for Maya toponyms to be inserted later (by apparently the same hand that writes in the captions on the architectural drawings).

Segment D (fs. 28r–45v; Secs. 34–41): Here the manuscript turns to the topic of the Maya Calendar. This is by far the longest segment so far (fs. 28r–45v; Secs. 34–41; some thirty-four pages of text, with glyphic drawings on twenty-five of those pages). We suspect it was copied wholesale from Landa's *recopilación*. The segment is written in the first person, right from the start (f. 28r; Sec. 34; see figure A.9 in part I of our book). The deity names (and anything in Mayan) were added in later by a different hand (as in previous segments), the same copyist who in f. 33r (Sec. 39, on the left side; figure A.13) added marginalia with a correction. It is possible

---

[25] Gates, *Yucatán*, 49. This marginalia passage prompted debate among us: two of us (Restall and Solari) became convinced that the passage describes Aztec or Mexica practice, and it was thus mistakenly added into the margin; one of us (Chuchiak) insists that the marginalia is in the hand of the scribe we suspect was Antonio de Herrera, who consulted sources on the Aztecs such as Tovar and Cervantes de Salazar, and who would not therefore have made such a mistake. One of us (Ardren) wisely chose neutrality.

that there is a change in handwriting starting on f. 34r (Sec. 40; figure A.15), for the *"Kalendario"* passage. The level of ethnographical detail in this segment is so precise that all sources must have been familiar with Yucatan—such as Francisco Domínguez; Gaspar de Najera; the Maya informants Francisco Euan, Juan Cocom, and Gaspar Antonio Chi; and of course, Landa himself. That said, we read this section as overwhelmingly originating with the friar's elite Maya informants—Euan, Cocom, and Chi.

Segment E (fs. 46r–49v; Sec. 42): This relatively brief segment on Maya architecture (Sec. 42) is a continuation of the previous segment in terms of hand and style (there are architectural drawings on three of its eight pages of text). Like segment D, segment E is laden with highly specific local knowledge, and so it could only have been composed by someone resident in the peninsula.

Segment F (fs. 50r–58v; Secs. 43–48): This nine-folio (eighteen-page) segment is dramatically different from the rest of the manuscript. Scribe A dominated the rest of the Account, but he is absent here, replaced completely by Scribe B (see table 6.2 above). But despite being copied by a single scribe, the segment is muddled in terms of style and content. It begins with the topic of Maya sacrificial rituals (fs. 56v–60v; Sec. 43; note that Brasseur's Chapter XLIII is only the first half of this section, as he stopped mid-section and never translated the rest of the manuscript). The topic is given a single page, and is highly polemical in tone, exaggerated and judgmental; it is followed somewhat jarringly, but in the same zealous tone, by a Christian prayer that runs for over two pages. The prayer was written either by Landa himself or by a fellow friar. Even more jarring is the shift that follows, to a series of paragraphs on various aspects of Yucatan's geography and natural history—its soil, metals, water, marine life, serpents, bees, and flora (fs. 51v–58v; Sec. 44 through half of Sec. 48).

There are thirteen gaps or spaces in this segment, large enough to accommodate a subheading or chapter title; and, indeed, three of those spaces (including the first, atop f. 50r) contain such subheadings (the other two are on fs. 55v and 56r) (see discussion below).

Segment G (fs. 59r–68r; Secs. 48 and maps): The manuscript then continues in a different hand (Scribe A has resumed the task), and without any subheadings or spaces for them to be added. However, the previous topic—not just natural history, but specifically trees—is continued as if Scribe A was copying from the same part of the *recopilación* as Scribe B had been. The treatment of trees runs four pages (fs. 59r–60v; second half of Sec. 48), then rolls into an eight-page description of birds and animals (fs. 61r–64v; Secs. 49–50). The entire run of paragraphs on Yucatan's natural history was likely not originally composed by Landa himself (Secs. 44–50), although it combines first-person with third-person observations made in Yucatan, as well as comments made in Spain. The disjointedness in style might be explained not only by the copyists' methods, but by Landa making small editorial changes as he himself redacted passages from another source into his *recopilación*.

The closing folios of Segment G and of the whole manuscript further give the impression of a grab-bag or cut-up sequence of copied paragraphs that began with f. 50r. The final two passages of text are short, being a closing statement of sorts (f. 65r–65v; Sec. 51), then a page and a half in which the author or copyist debates some points with the "Historian of the Indies" (likely López de Gómara; fs. 65v–66v; Sec. 52). It is in this last section of text that the abovementioned references are made to chapters "101" and "49," as well as to paragraphs "15" and "13" (all using Roman numerals), probably references to parts of Landa's own lost *recopilación*. At the very end of the manuscript are the two maps of the Yucatan peninsula and the Gulf coast (fs. 66v–68r; see our chapter 7 to follow).

*　*　*

A manuscript such as Landa's would not have been accessible to notaries or scribes from outside the closed and controlled circles of the Council of the Indies. Its archives were tightly controlled, and even the cronistas and the secretaries of the Council and of the Crown had restricted, recorded access—all designed, in the phrases of royal law, "to prevent their being seen or read by anyone not in possession of the secrets of the Council."[26] When the position of Cronista y Cosmógrafo Mayor was created in 1571, this culture of secrecy was extended to his office; the Cronista had to make his own notes and copies, to be "organized, kept and held in total secret without communicating them, nor allowing anyone else to see them," and those notes filed in "the secret archive at the end of every year before [the Cronista] can be paid the last third of his salary."[27]

Juan López de Velasco was Cronista y Cosmógrafo Mayor from 1571 until his promotion in 1591 to the prestigious position of the personal secretary of King Philip II.[28] Not only was López de Velasco given privileged access to the Council's archives, but he was specifically charged with "compiling, copying, and making the General History of the Indies." Such a history was to include "descriptions of the

---

[26] *Recopilación de las leyes de Indias*, Lib. II, Tit. 2, Law 55 (Vol. 1, p. 245); Ley 90: "Que ay libro donde se asienten los que sacaren del archivo," in *Ordenanzas reales sobre el Consejo de Indias*, Valladolid: Imprenta del Licenciado Varez de Castro, 1603, f. 16v.

[27] *Recopilación de las leyes de Indias*, f. 22r; *Siendo conveniente la separación de los oficios de cosmógrafo y cronista mayor de Indias*, Madrid, 12 de febrero, 1596, AGI, Indiferente General, 743, N. 209, 2 fs.

[28] Velasco's successful career made him well known and very wealthy; on his appointment, see *Real Provisión concediendo a Juan López de Velasco el título de cronista y cosmógrafo mayor de Indias, especificando sus derechos y obligaciones*, Madrid, 20 de octubre, 1571, AGI, Indiferente General, 426, Libro 25, folios 126r–27v.

said Indies"; "the deeds and memorable things that have been done in those parts"; and "things concerning the natural history worthy of knowing." To achieve this, the Cronista "should review and examine the histories written by other persons," for which he was given and handed over all of the histories, relations, and information, *memoriales*, letters, and other such books and papers that exist, and may be necessary to comply with the duties of this said office.[29]

Velasco thus had access to Landa's manuscript: his years of service and access to the documentation of the Council of the Indies immediately followed the years when Landa's *recopilación* was assembled and deposited with the Council. Furthermore, the date range of the paper used by Scribe A of the Account, with its mean of 1574, likewise coincides with López de Velasco's time in office. So, was López de Velasco Scribe A? One of us (Chuchiak) carried out a handwriting analysis study, concluding that the probability is very high. A comparison of documents written by López de Velasco over a thirty-year period and the script of Scribe A in the Account reveal a commonality of characteristic brush strokes, inclination, and curvature. The regularity of spacing and the shading—that is, evidence of pressure placed on the quill—is noticeably similar.[30]

Further evidence that López de Velasco was Scribe A comes from his use of paper. In the 1570s and early 1580s, the Cronista ordered some sixteen thousand sheets of paper, which came from Toledo and Madrid papermakers in *resmas* or reams, to be folded and sewn in the binding process. Sets of folded folio pages, known as "quires," were marked in order to ensure they would be bound properly.[31] As mentioned earlier, the Account has quire markings, letters every 4, 8, or 16 pages, which were either copied from the lost, larger manuscript or made at the time of copying in anticipation of a possible future publication. Those quire letters appear to be in López de Velasco's handwriting.

The first four Cronistas who succeeded López de Velasco did not last long in the position; he was a tough act to follow. In 1596, the Council decided to split the roles

---

[29] *Real Provisión concediendo a Juan López de Velasco el título de cronista y cosmógrafo mayor de Indias*, Madrid, 20 de octubre, 1571, AGI, Indiferente General, 426, Libro 25, fs. 126r–127v.

[30] On paleographic analyses of early modern Spanish handwriting, see Villasana Haggard and McLean, *Handbook for Translators*, 8–21; on forensic handwriting analysis, see Huber and Headrick, *Handwriting Identification*.

[31] Each time López de Velasco wished to buy paper he had to have a royal order to approve his purchase; examples are in *Carta acordada del Consejo de Indias a Antonio de Cartagena, su receptor, dándole orden de pago de 80 reales a Juan López de Velasco, cosmógrafo y cronista por 4 resmas de papel para imprimir ciertas instrucciones para la observación de eclipses*, Madrid, 27 de agosto, 1580, AGI, Indiferente General, 426, Libro 26, f. 214v; and *Carta acordada del Consejo de Indias a Antonio de Cartagena, su receptor, dándole orden de pago de 12 ducados a Juan López de Velasco, cosmógrafo y cronista mayor, por 6 resmas de papel*, Madrid, 12 de agosto, 1583, AGI, Indiferente General, 426, Libro 27, fs. 60r–60v. On quires, see Diehl, *Bookbinding*, 14.

of chronicler and cosmographer, and in March, Antonio de Herrera y Tordesillas became the new Cronista Mayor.[32] Like López de Velasco, Herrera was conscientiously committed to the post, and would prove to be highly productive, holding the office until his death in 1625 or 1626 (see figure 6.1). He even wrote an Historia general del mundo (completed in 1601), the only Cronista Mayor to attempt such an undertaking. It was that ambition that suggested to us that he might be Scribe B; after all, Scribe B came after A, wrote or copied significant portions of the Account, added marginalia, and made other corrections. Significantly, he also wrote the seemingly strange title page identifying the pages of the Account as "another account of the things of China"; Herrera also wrote a (now long lost) history of East Asia, or la China.[33]

Herrera was bound by the same rules of archival access and compositional method that López de Velasco had followed, meaning that he himself was obliged to make the initial notes and drafts of his book. Only then would secondary copyists work from Herrera's writings, shielding them from his original sources, all classified as secret.[34] Therefore, as in the case of López de Velasco as candidate for Scribe A, we would expect that if Herrera used Landa's writings, his own hand would be on the Account. Again, one of us (Chuchiak) made a close study of the handwriting of Herrera and Scribe B, especially the use and direction of the quill, and the relative height of capital and lowercase lettering.

Our conclusion was not only that Herrera was Scribe B, but that he may also have been Scribes C and D (see table 6.2 above). His prolific pen and skill enabled him to develop several scribal hands, four of which are seen in the Account: a rapid transcription hand (fs. 3v–4r, 4v–7r, 11r–11v, 15v–16r, 16r–16v, 20v, 21v, 26r); a sloppier annotation hand (fs. 15v–16r, 16r–16v, 66r); a more polished transcription and marginalia hand (fs. 23r, 23v, 24r, 26v–45r); and his more polished formal book hand (textual fs. 50r–58v; headings fs. 55v–56r).

---

[32] *Consulta del Consejo para informar a Antonio de Herrera de las condiciones puestas por su majestad para hacerle merced del oficio de cronista de Indias*, Madrid, 28 de marzo, 1596, AGI, Indiferente General, 743, N.229BIS, 2 fs.

[33] Also see Vol. II, Book I of Herrera's *Historia general del mundo* (1601), especially Chapter XIX, "De la descripción del gran Reino de la China por la relación de Fray Martin de Rada," fs. 47–50; Chapter XVIII, "De las cosas del reino de China," fs. 43–47; and Chapter XVIII, "De la entrada que los Castellanos hicieron en la China," fs. 40–43.

[34] This is confirmed by records of payments to the copyists who later rewrote Herrera's drafts of the *Historia general*; *Carta acordada del Consejo librando a su receptor Diego de Vergara Gaviria, con cargo al fondo de penas de estrados. 40 ducados a abonar al cronista mayor de las Indias, Antonio de Herrera, para pagar al escribano que le copia la obra*, Valladolid, 27 de noviembre, 1604, AGI, Indiferente General, 427, Libro 31, f. 240r ("a copyist being paid for the transcription of a clear pre-publishing copy of volume 3 of Herrera's work completed and printed in 1605").

Figure 6.1. Ghostwriter. The only known image of Antonio Herrera y Tordesillas (1549–1625 or 1626), published on the title page of his *Historia general del mundo* (1601); he was Cronista Mayor from 1596 until his death, and was likely Scribe B of the Landa-attributed Account.

Although we have not uncovered smoking-gun evidence—such as Herrera specifically stating that he copied excerpts from a Landa *recopilación*—the sum of the indirect evidence is compelling. For example, Herrera annotated a manuscript copy of Francisco Cervantes de Salazar's work; it survives in Spain's National Library, and the handwriting is a virtual match for Scribe B of the Account. His other hands—those we dubbed C and D—can also be seen in notations he made in his defense against lawsuits from relatives of conquistadors offended by his frank telling of atrocities committed against Indigenous populations.[35] In addition, in 1597

---

[35] Chief among his detractors who sued Herrera for his negative portrayal of their relatives were the descendants of Pedrarias Dávila, governor of Panama, who had executed Vasco Nuñez de Balboa (see *Colección de papeles impresos y manuscritos sobre las diferencias que tuvo don Francisco Arias Dávila y Bobadilla, Conde de Puñonrostro, con el cronista Antonio de Herrera sobre que quitase de su Historia General de Indias ciertos artículos que había puesto en ella*

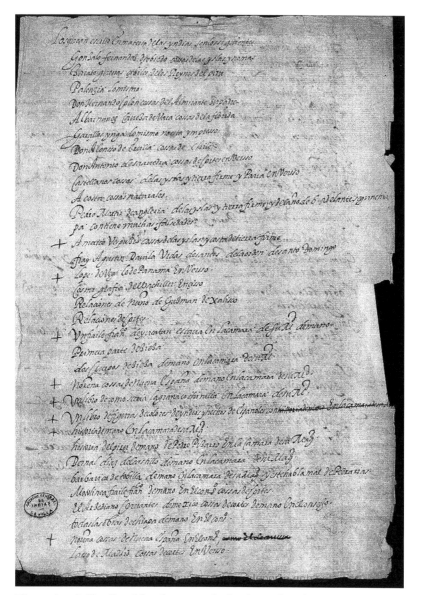

Figure 6.2. A Clue. Possible reference to the Landa-attributed Account in Antonio de Herrera's sources for the second volume of his General History (*Memorial del cronista Antonio de Herrera sobre los fuentes y documentos que usó para su Historia General de los Hechos de los Castellanos en las Indias*, 1603, AGI, Patronato, 170, ramo 19, f. 1v).

López de Velasco was ordered by the Crown to turn over papers pertinent to the office of the Cronista to Herrera, and these papers included entire collections by friars—such as Bartolomé de Las Casas.[36] Five years later, Herrera noted that he had been given access to "many fragments and relations written by ecclesiastics writing by means of a history in matters pertaining to the spiritual order which came to the Council."[37] He came tantalizingly close to naming Landa, when he remarked that he had consulted "a handwritten account by a Franciscan friar from Yucatan which was in the *Escribanía de Camara* of His Majesty" (see the twentieth line in figure 6.2).[38] That friar, surely, was none other than Diego de Landa.

---

contra su abuelo, Pedrarias Dávila, AGI, Patronato, 170, ramo 19, f. 1v).

[36] See *Real cédula a Juan López de Velasco, secretario, ordenándole entregar al secretario del Consejo de Indias, Juan de Ibarra, los libros y papeles del obispo de Chiapa que estaban a su cargo procedentes de San Gregorio de Valladolid, con ficha firmada de recepción por Antonio de Herrera, cronista mayor de las Indias*, 24 de septiembre, 1597, AGI, Indiferente General, 427, Libro 31, f. 29r.

[37] See *Memorial del cronista Antonio de Herrera sobre los fuentes y documentos que usó para su Historia General de los Hechos de los Castellanos en las Indias*, 1603, AGI, Patronato, 170, ramo 19, f. 1r.

[38] *Memorial del cronista Antonio de Herrera*, f. 1v.

7

The Nature of the Account

Its Visual Components and a Conclusion

This final chapter is a close sequel to the previous one, likewise on the nature of the Account, but with a focus on its visual material—its drawings of buildings, calendrical depictions, glyphs, and maps. Scholars have tended to make more use of the manuscript's textual descriptions to reconstruct precontact lifeways—in part because so many editions fail to reproduce in full the visual components of the Account. But the author relied on visual realizations to communicate to his intended audience of fellow Franciscans more fully. This is particularly evident in the discussions of calendrics, language, and, perhaps most dramatically, architectural design and geography.

The twenty-two-page-long exposé of Maya calendar systems includes thumbnail sketches of nearly four hundred hieroglyphs repetitiously representing months of the 260- and 365-day calendars, and the syllabary furnishes an additional thirty-seven icons. That syllabary is the Rosetta Stone mentioned in the previous chapter—except, of course, that it only *appears* to be a Rosetta Stone or key to unlock the code of Maya writing (f. 45r; Sec. 41; see figure A.37 in part I of our book). By describing the syllabary of Maya glyphs thus—"here begins their *ABC* [*su a.b.c.*]"—the authors of the Account misled early Mayanists, who imagined Landa meant "their alphabet [*su abecedario*]." These Maya "characters or letters [*caracteres o letras*]" had been created by Landa, or one of his colleagues, by asking a Maya informant how to write in glyphs each Spanish sound, "a, b, c," and so on (f. 44v). The informant naturally heard each Spanish letter as a Maya syllable. For example, imagine Landa asking his Maya informant how to write the letter *b*: Landa would pronounce it *beh*, which a

https://doi.org/10.5876/9781646424245.c007

Figure 7.1. To Beh or Not To Beh. The Maya glyph for *beh*, "path" or "road," depicting a bare (walking) foot, from the Dresden Codex, f. 39a (*left*), compared to the *be* glyph on f. 45r of the Account (*right*; detail from figure A.37).

Maya speaker would hear not as a letter but as a syllable or even as the word *be* (as it was written in the colonial period), meaning "road, path, way"; sure enough, in the first row of glyphs in figure A.37, the fourth glyph is a pictogram of *be*, depicting a human footprint on a path (see figure 7.1, right). A precontact example of the glyph can be found in figure 2.3, at the bottom of the glyph column that inhabits the upper right corner of the left-hand page. Writing a syllabic alphabet (with letters written as they were pronounced, rather than as a list of single vowels and consonants) would have made sense to colonial-era Spaniards, so the cultural disjuncture between the author and the Maya informant was not as great as is often assumed.

However, it was several centuries before scholars attempted to use the Account's Maya "characters" to read precontact hieroglyphic texts. Its relation to the ancient Maya writing system was sufficiently right and wrong enough to confuse generations of modern would-be epigraphers—whose task was made all the tougher by the woeful quality of published reproductions of the glyphs, a problem not clearly outlined until fairly recently.[1] In Thompson's short *Maya Hieroglyphs without Tears*, published a few years before his death, he devoted one of his six chapters to "Landa's alphabet and the task of decipherment." Although he emphasized that Landa's putative Rosetta Stone "gave, not the *sounds* of the ABC, but the *names* of the letters," meaning that it was not in fact the key to the code, his attention to Landa reflected the importance given to the Account in twentieth-century Mayanist studies.[2] Although it soon became clear how far Landa's *ABC* was from being a Rosetta Stone, his "alphabet" nonetheless contained the phonetic clues that

---

[1] See Stuart, "Glyph Drawings."
[2] Thompson, *Maya Hieroglyphs*, 31, 47.

enabled epigraphers, no longer hampered after 1975 by Thompson's overbearing domination of the field, to decipher the glyphs.

*   *   *

In contrast, the manuscript's renderings of buildings and other structures, which only total three images, are different than these linguistic icons in that they perform a more interpretive role within the context of the manuscript. It is also worth noting that this section of the manuscript (Sec. 42, fs. 46r–49v) comprises a distinct project; in terms of style, it is a clear and sudden disjuncture from the *que* style, as described in our previous chapter, in what we call section G of the Account. Viewers are intended to read text and image in conjunction with one another; a reader cannot get "the full picture" without having the text and associated imagery right at their disposal. The same could be said of the two maps of Yucatan (to which we turn shortly), albeit to a lesser degree.

The description in the Account of precontact Maya architecture begins with the declaration—understandably often quoted by archaeologists—that "In Yucatan there are many buildings of great beauty, which is the most remarkable thing that has been discovered in the Indies" (Sec. 4, f. 4v). This sentence neatly summarizes what must have been the author's goal in composing this quasi-treatise on Maya architectural design: to convince readers, whomever they were intended to be, of the architectural sophistication of Yucatan's ancient cityscapes. Why would the author be so concerned with stressing this aspect of Maya cultural history? Perhaps he believed that promoting the ancient Maya would by extension promote his work among them, that the grander their temple-pyramids, the grander would appear his convent-churches and entire conversion process, built atop those same pyramids.

The manuscript's highly schematic images rely on multiple perspectives, textual glosses, and additional alphabetic descriptions located in the body of the text. The drawing in the Account of Izamal's largest structure, referred to as the Kinich Kakmo in Lizana's *Historia de Yucatán* of 1633, is fully incorporated into the body of the text, with the author's words filling all available blank space around the mass of the structure's representation (see figure 7.2, and figures A.38–39 for the full pages). This differentiates this first architectural illustration from the two that follow (f. 47r in figure 7.3, and f. 48v in figure 7.5), which are simply banded by blocks of text. It suggests that at least in the case of the Izamal pyramid image, the author or scribe drew the structure first, and then used the remaining margins for the descriptive text.

During the Preclassic and Early Classic periods, the region's monumental structures were marked by a style defined by rounded corners, as can still be seen in the recently reconstructed upper walls of the Kinich Kakmo (see figure 7.4). As a means to represent this regional style, the Account's image (see figure 7.3) relies on

Figures 7.2, 7.3, and 7.4.
Monumental Maya Mound.
Upper temple of the Kinich
Kakmo structure, Izamal,
Yucatan (details from fs.
46v–47r of the Account;
photograph by Amara
Solari).

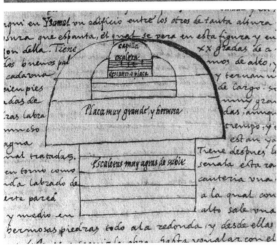

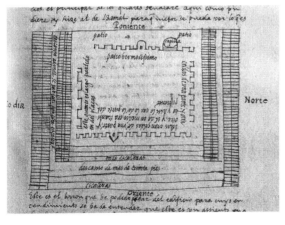

an overhead, or bird's-eye, perspective for the back (northern) section of the structure and the terrace that surmounts it. The text that surrounds the sketch clarifies that the stones "had been carved as rounded, as shown by this round line" (f. 46v). Additionally, the top portion of the massive base is viewed from above and labeled with the gloss: "Plaza, very large and beautiful." The author rendered the remaining architectural details using a frontal perspective: the monumental staircase that leads from the plaza located on the structure's southern side; the stairs that leave the aforementioned raised plaza and end at the top of the second raised terrace (figure 7.3); and finally, the smallest set of stairs that mount the diminutive structure that sits at the apex of the pyramid. This small, enclosed space is glossed as a "chapel." Unfortunately, nothing remains today of this uppermost building.

The Account's next architectural rendering depicts one of the largest structures of Tiho, the city upon whose ruins early Spanish colonists established the city of Merida in 1542 (see figure 7.5, and figure A.40 for the full page). As detailed earlier, Landa arrived in the province in 1549, at which point this building had already undergone a fair amount of reconstruction. His mentor, friar Lorenzo de Bienvenida, saw the structure in its untouched state and wrote a lengthy account of it. Either the author of these pages had a copy of Bienvenida's account, or their predecessors orally relayed the structure's original design. Like the rendering of the Kinich Kakmo, the *Relación*'s Tiho building illustration relies on multiple perspectives, similarly a bird's-eye view and a frontal view. The author notes that the rectilinear form was approximately twenty-eight to thirty strides in length, or nearly ninety feet long.

The Account repeatedly insists that the Maya living in the peninsula in the sixteenth century had "no memory of the founders" of these older structures (f. 46v, Sec. 42), a phrase that is also used in Section B ("These buildings of Izamal numbered eleven or twelve all together, without there being any memory of their founders"; f. 4v, Sec. 4). While this would appear to support the common, but incorrect, claim adopted by many colonists in New Spain that people other than the Indigenous "Indians" were responsible for the wondrous architecture observed throughout the Americas, the author of the Account uses extant architectural evidence to make the opposite claim: that predecessors of the Mayas were in fact the builders of these impressive structures. Looking at the stucco sculptures that adorned the monumental edifices of Izamal, then extant but now sadly lost, the author observed that the humans depicted there—albeit at a larger-than-life scale—were the same people as those living in the peninsula in the sixteenth century. In other words, the contemporary Indigenous population may not have been aware of this history, but, according to the author, he himself was.[3]

---

[3]   As Davis notes ("Evangelical Prophecies," 91–92), we should not rush to follow Tozzer (*Landa's* Relación, 113) and praise Landa's "stand" on this issue, as the friar twists the point to insult the Maya of his time: the construction may have been demonstrably "done by Indians,"

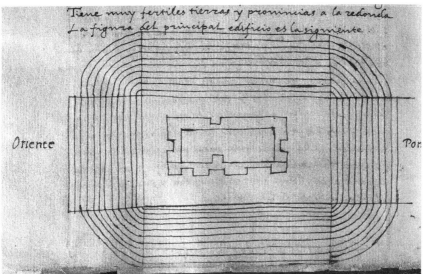

Oriente

Por

Tiene muy fertiles tierras y prouincias a la redonda
La figura del principal edificio es la siguiente.

Figures 7.5 and 7.6. Temple of Kukulkan, Chichen Itza (detail, f. 48v of the Account; photograph by Amara Solari).

*   *   *

The final genre of visual material in the manuscript consists of two geographical renderings—two maps—tucked into the very end of the collation. Different in scale, they both schematically represent the Gulf Coast region, but with varying emphases.

Taking up an entire folio sheet, the first map (see figure 7.7) furnishes a closer geographical perspective, seemingly drawn to emphasize the region's water sources. Oriented towards the north, the image pivots around the "Gulf of Cortés or Mexico [*Golfo de Cortes o Mexicano*]" (figure 7.8 provides helpful orientation). The map's artist outlined the southern coastline of Cuba and what would eventually become the coastal line of northeast Mexico, Texas, Louisiana, Mississippi, Alabama, and Florida, although only referred to as "La Florida," which was "discovered by Panuco." Great attention is paid to the riverine access to New Spain's gulf coast, as the mapmaker clearly delineated the mouths of the "Rio de Alvarado," "Guaza," "Rio de Grijalva o Tabasco," "Chapon Rio," and another two unnamed river mouths. Two ports are identified, those of Tabasco and the "Puerto Real" of northern Yucatan. Additional waterways include the Xicalango Lagoon, the "Mazatlan" River, the rivers of "TaItza" (Tah Itza), a lake located in Chiapas and another lagoon and some straits in "Salamanca" (the colonial town of Salamanca de Bacalar, which would soon become known permanently as just Bacalar, a Hispanization of its original Mayan name, Bakhalal).

Little circles scattered through the peninsula's southwest represent small islands in the swampy region of Acalan-Tixchel; the large island of Tixchel is clearly labeled. Some cultural information is also provided, such as the territory of the Indigenous Lacandon Maya (in what is now the state of Chiapas). Although the relative locations of these topographical features and cultural groups are vaguely correct, the cardinal points of the map are slightly skewed.

The primary human settlements are shown, connected by thin lines representing the route of the *camino real*. The port city of Campeche is rendered in a square-shaped cartouche on the western coastline, linked via a diagonal line to "Calkini." The road then leads to Merida, from which two additional roads spring. One to the south links the provincial capital to the "ancient city of Ychpa" and then on to Mani. "Ychpa" was Mayapan, which, according to the Account, "The Indians [today] call Ichpa, meaning 'Within the Enclosures.'" As we have found no other early colonial map of Yucatan that includes Mayapan as "Ychpa" or "Ichpa" (if there were any, therefore, they were rare), this detail contributes to the impression that the map was drawn by a copyist using the text of the Account (or the larger *recopilación*) as a source. It is possible that the copyist was redrawing a sketch map made by Landa, but the handwriting is evidence that if such a map ever existed, this is not it.

---

yet "if they were indeed the builders, they were a superior people than those of today, and of much larger, stronger bodies" (fs. 45r–46v; see also figure A.38).

The other Merida road on the second map (see figures 7.9–7.10) went east, running through Izamal, Ticoch, Chichen Itza ("ancient city inhabited by the Adelantado Montejo"), and finally into Valladolid. This central Spanish Yucatecan town then had a road leading south to Salamanca, which was also linked to Mani via a northwest route, thus closing the circuit of the camino real. The map provides an explanatory gloss:

> From the point of Catoch to the Royal Port is 130 leagues in length. The Point of Catoch is in less than 20 degrees. The mouth of the Royal Port in more than 23 degrees from Yucatan to the Island of Cuba, 60 leagues. Cozumel is an island 15 leagues in length and 5 in width, and it is 20 degrees from this part of the "equinythial." The Isla Mujeres is 13 or 14 leagues below Point Cotoch, appearing to measure 2 leagues. Chichen Itza is 10 leagues from Izamal and 11 from Valladolid. (f. 68r; figure 7.11)

Who drew these maps in the Account? We have already discounted Landa himself: while the geographical details of both maps seem to suggest someone familiar with the region, the unsure hand makes certain that they were not drawn by someone who had spent considerable time in the province. We suspect that the opacity of authorship of the maps is very similar to the same issue with the text; Landa did not draw these maps any more than he simply wrote the Account, and multiple authors and copyists have created filters and errors. But we have already suggested that Scribe A of the Account was none other than the Cronista y Cosmógrafo Mayor of 1571–1591, Juan López de Velasco, who was also a well-known cartographer. So, did he sketch or copy the maps (or schematic drawings) in the Account?[4]

Finding the cartographic materials in the archives of the Council of the Indies lacking, López de Velasco helped to create and send to the Indies a more streamlined questionnaire to acquire the exact type of historical, geographical, and natural resource information he needed to be able to compile his required Historia general de las Indias. These questionnaires gave rise to the Relaciones Histórico Geográficas, and, as one of us (Solari) previously noted, it was López de Velasco who "created a detailed Instrucción consisting of fifty questions asking for textual summaries of local culture, history and ecology"; every provincial governor was also asked to "provide a pictorial representation of his town" with a "civic plan detailing the layout [and] other notable urban features."[5] López de Velasco's "remarkably unified vision

---

[4]   He did, according to the argument that follows, which was authored primarily by one of us (Chuchiak), and viewed as a theory very much worth airing by two of us (Ardren and Restall), but not accepted by the art historian among us (Solari). Solari's objection is based on the rough nature of the maps; Chuchiak counters that these are merely schematic drawings, rough by nature, not intended to be polished maps.

[5]   Solari, "Relación Geográfica Map of Tabasco," 38; RHGY.

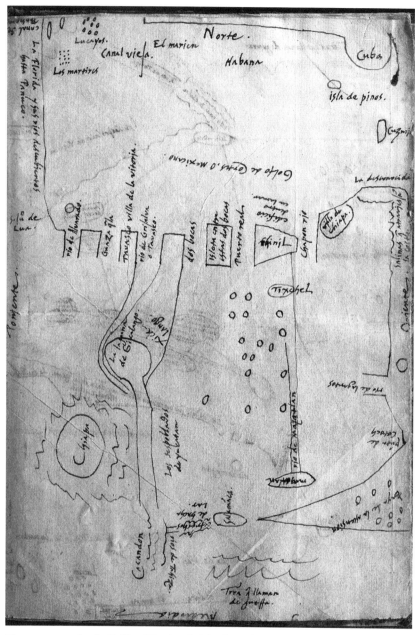

Figures 7.7 and 7.8. Gulf and Peninsula. The first of two maps depicting the Gulf of Mexico and the Yucatan peninsula, included at the end of the Account (f. 67r); the image on the right is taken from Google Earth.

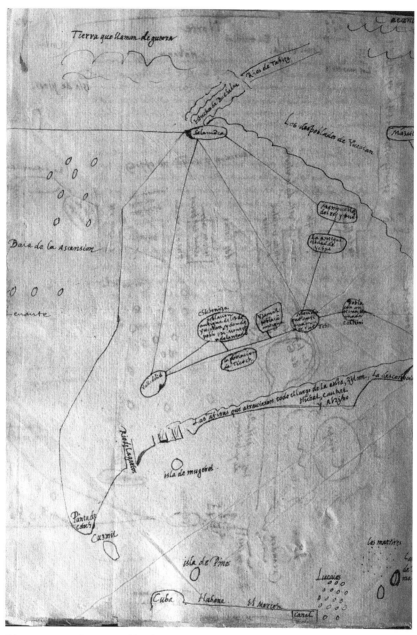

Figures 7.9 and 7.10. Gulf and Peninsula. The second of two maps depicting the Gulf of Mexico and the Yucatan peninsula, included at the end of the Account (fs. 67v–68r); the image on the right is taken from Google Earth.

TABLE 7.1. Comparison between Landa's Account and Juan López de Velasco's *Demarcación de las Indias* (1578)

The Account	López de Velasco's Demarcación de las Indias (1578)
"Yucatan is not an island nor a headland that enters into the ocean, as some have thought, but rather it is the mainland." f. 1r	"... it was taken to be an island at first, because it was surrounded almost completely by the sea." f. 26r
"Coming from Veracruz towards the headland of Cotoch, it is less than twenty degrees, and near the mouth of Puerto Real it is more than 23, and it extends from one headland to the other over 130 leagues in length in a straight line." f. 1r	"It extends some hundred leagues north to south in a straight line from the coast facing north to the part where it joins up with the provinces of Guatemala, and from there across it stretches for about 25 leagues ..." f. 26r
"This land is very hot, and the sun burns fiercely even though there is no lack of fresh air such as the breezes and easterly winds that prevail there, as well as the afternoon sea breeze." f. 1r	"[The land] is very hot and humid and with good breeze, although there is no river or running water in all of it, for water they have shallow wells ..." f. 26r

of the Spanish empire" (as map historian David Buisseret put it), inspired him to convince the king that it would be possible to create "detailed maps of the whole empire."[6] López de Velasco was "given great contentment," as he excitedly told the king's chief secretary, that his *Demarcación de la Indias* would serve as a "general book of the descriptions of the Indies"—as the Crown ordered—to "be placed and used in the Council for reference."[7]

Unwilling to wait while the answers to the Relaciones Histórico Geográficas drifted into Madrid from all corners of the empire, López de Velasco drew upon the manuscripts he had at hand—including Landa's. Completed in 1578, López de Velasco's Demarcación de la Indias cited notes he had taken from Landa's writings, composing descriptions of Yucatan that reveal the close relationship between the two (see table 7.1).[8] López de Velasco also sketched maps, including one of the coastlines of New Spain, appearing to make use of the similar map in the Account; in fact, the handwriting on the map in the Account is so close to López de Velasco's—already identified as likely to be Scribe A—that it is similarly likely that López de Velasco himself drew the maps in the Account (see figure 7.11).

---

[6] Buisseret, "Spanish Colonial Cartography, 1450–1700," 1146, 1171.

[7] Ruan, "Cosmographic Description," 461; Ley 117, "Las tablas de la cosmografía de las Indias que ha de hacer el cosmógrafo," in *Ordenanzas reales sobre el Consejo de Indias*, 1603, f. 21r.

[8] *Demarcación de las Indias*, 1578, f. 26r, BNE, Mss/2825. López de Velasco's massive map book remained unpublished until 1894 (López de Velasco and Zaragoza, *Geografía y descripción*).

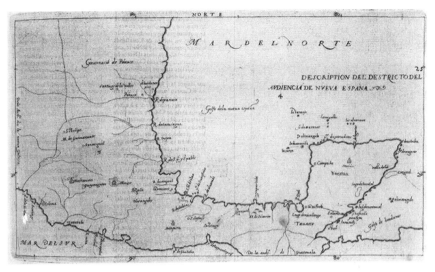

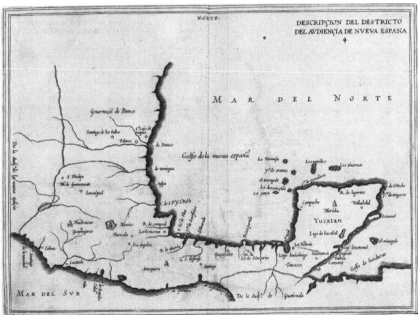

Figures 7.11a–b. Mapping Evidence. Compare the map drawn by Juan López de Velasco (c. 1578) (*top*) with the redrawn version by Antonio de Herrera y Tordesillas (1601) (*bottom*) and with the schematic geographical diagram on f. 67r of the Account (probably drawn c. 1571–1578) (*Figure 7.7 above*).

Further analysis of lettering strengthens this argument, both by comparing how words such as *Norte* are styled in the maps in the Account and the Demarcación, and by comparing specific letters in those two sources and other López de Velasco manuscripts.

There is a further twist of handwriting-based evidence. We have argued that López de Velasco probably drew the maps at the back of the Account (as Scribe A); we have also argued that Herrera annotated and added to parts of the Account that López de Velasco had copied; and we know that López de Velasco later passed on to Herrera, as his successor, manuscripts and notes. All of which offers context to a comparison of maps of Yucatan created by these two cronistas (figures 7.11a–c), the origins of which were surely the maps in the Account that López de Velasco copied, and that—in the case of the second map (figures 7.9 and 7.10; fs. 67v–68r)—Herrera annotated. In the first edition of his *Historia general*, Herrera simply reproduced López de Velasco's map of Yucatan; in subsequent editions, he redrew the lettering as the basis for a lithographic copper plate.[9]

* * *

In sum, the manuscript of the Account is a somewhat arbitrary collection of material on various topics—almost all related to the history and culture of Yucatan in the sixteenth century, before and after contact with Spaniards—created by multiple authors, compilers, and copyists at different times during Landa's lifetime and long after it. The excerpts were taken from either a larger multivolume work of Landa's (possibly already "typeset" for publication—which would explain why it was left behind in Madrid for future publication), or a collection of writings by Landa that did not comprise anything we might grant the integrity of a book (the very definition, indeed, of a *recopilación*).[10]

Portions of the manuscript were almost certainly not written by Landa, as we have seen above, including the maps appended at the end of the Account. The assumption that Landa wrote every word of the Account is a misguided, modern one with its own long history. His *recopilación* was likely transparent in its references to its sources, and to passages copied from manuscripts or books by other authors. The copyists who created the Account must have unwittingly or without concern drawn from Landa's papers—meaning both writings by him and writings

---

9   See *Carta acordada del Consejo librando a su receptor Diego Ruiz Osorio, con cargo al fondo de penas de estrados, 44 ducados, a abonar a Juan Peyron, por unas tablas de geografía y planchas de cobre hechas por orden de Antonio Herrera, cronista mayor de las Indias*, Madrid, 27 de marzo, 1599, AGI, Indiferente General, 745, N.248, 2 folios.

10   One of the earlier scholars of the manuscript, Jean Genet (*Relation*, vol. 1, 10) also believed that the original manuscript in its original form was intended for publication.

by his informants and contemporaries that were collected by him. Consequently, the Account cannot be treated as an authentic window onto only Landa's thoughts and feelings of the 1560s. Clendinnen described the Account as "a tender remembrance of beloved things past"; she conceded that it was "a very odd document" that we have in "defective form," but she believed it contained "allusions, omissions and emphases which could reveal something of Landa's tacit response to the terrible events of 1562."[11] Her evaluation may be eloquent and tempting, but ultimately it must be seen as speculative and ill-supported. Nonetheless, the Account is an extremely rich source of information and insight into the turbulent political and cultural world of sixteenth-century Yucatan—and, by extension, into the transformative and conflictual experience of invasion and colonization.

---

[11] Clendinnen, *Ambivalent Conquests*, 119.

Bibliography

ARCHIVAL SOURCES AND THEIR ABBREVIATIONS

AGI: Archivo General de las Indias, Seville, Spain

AGN: Archivo General de la Nación, Mexico City, Mexico

AGS: Archivo General de Simancas, Simancas, Spain

AHN: Archivo Histórico Nacional, Madrid, Spain

AHNob: Archivo Historico de la Nobleza, Toledo, Spain

ARCV: Archivo de la Real Chancillería de Valladolid, Spain

BNE: Biblioteca Nacional de España, Madrid, Spain

CDI: *Colección de documentos inéditos relativos al descubrimiento, conquista y organización de las antiguas poblaciones españolas de Ultramar, tomo XIII*. Madrid: Real Academia de Historia, 1900.

DHY: *Documentos para la Historia de Yucatán*. France V. Scholes, Carlos R. Menéndez, Juan Ignacio Rubio Mañé, and Eleanor B. Adams, eds. 3 vols. Merida, Yuc.: Compañía Tipográfica Yucateca, 1936–38. Also listed below under Scholes, et al.

DQAY: *Don Diego Quijada, Alcalde Mayor de Yucatán, 1561–1565: Documentos sacados de los archivos de España y publicados por France V. Scholes and Eleanor B. Adams*. 2 vols. Mexico City: Editorial Porrúa, 1938. Also listed below under Scholes and Adams.

https://doi.org/10.5876/9781646424245.c008

LoC: Library of Congress, Washington, DC

RAH: Real Academia de la Historia, Madrid, Spain

RHGY: *Relaciones Históricos Geográficas de Yucatán*, in *Colección de documentos inéditos relativos al descubrimiento, conquista y organización de las antiguas posesiones españoles de ultramar*, 2nd series, Vols. 11, 13. Madrid: Real Academia de Historia, 1898–1900.

TULAL: Latin American Library, Tulane University, New Orleans

EDITIONS OF LANDA'S ACCOUNT (LISTED CHRONOLOGICALLY)

Brasseur de Bourbourg, Abbé. *Relation des choses de Yucatán de Diego de Landa*. Paris and London: Arthus Bertrand and Trübner and Co., 1864.

Rada y Delgado, Juan de Dios de. *Relación de las cosas de Yucatán: Manuscrito de Diego de Landa tomada directamente del único ejemplar que se conoce y se conserva en la Academia de la Historia*. Madrid: Manuel Tello, 1881.

Landa, Diego de. *Relación de las cosas de Yucatán*. In *Colección de documentos inéditos relativos al descubrimiento, conquista y organización de las antiguas poblaciones españolas de Ultramar*, tomo XIII [cited as CDI], vol. 13, II: 265–408. Madrid: Real Academia de Historia, 1900.

Genet, Jean. *Diego de Landa: Relation des choses de Yucatán: Texte espagnol et traduction française en regard*. 2 vols. Paris: Les Editions Genet, 1928–1929.

Gates, William. *Yucatán before and after the Conquest by Friar Diego de Landa with Other Related Documents, Maps and Illustrations*. Baltimore: Maya Society, 1937 [reprinted New York: Dover, 1978].

Rosado Escalante, José E., Favila Ontiveros, and Alfredo Barrera Vásquez. *Relación de las cosas de Yucatán*. Merida, Yucatan: Triay e Hijos, 1938.

Pérez Martínez, Hector. *Relación de las cosas de Yucatán, por el P. Fray Diego de Landa, Obispo de esa diocese*. México: Editorial Pedro Robredo, 1938. [Merida, Yucatan: Ediciones Dante reprinted an incomplete edition, 1983, further reprinted in various abbreviated editions with uncredited translations in various languages through at least 2011].

Tozzer, Alfred M. *Landa's* Relación de las cosas de Yucatán: *A Translation*. Papers of the Peabody Museum of American Archaeology and Ethnology, vol. XVIII. Cambridge, MA: Harvard University Press, 1941.

Knorozov, Yuri. *Diego de Landa, Soobshcheniye o Delakh u Yukatanye, 1566G*. Moskva-Leningrad: Izdatel'stvo Akademii Nauk SSSR, 1955.

Garibay K., Ángel María. *Relación de las cosas de Yucatán, por el Padre Fr. Diego de Landa, Obispo de esa diócesis*. México: Porrúa, 1959 [one of many Mexican editions that reused the transcription published by Pérez Martínez in 1938].

Pagden, Anthony R., trans. and ed. *The Maya: Diego de Landa's* Account of the Affairs of Yucatán. Chicago, IL: O'Hara, 1975.

Silvini, Giorgio. *Relazione sullo Yucatán*. Roma: Edizioni Paoline, 1983.

Rivera Dorado, Miguel, ed. *Diego de Landa: Relación de las cosas de Yucatán*. Crónicas de América 26. Madrid: Historia 16, 1985.

León Cázares, María del Carmen, ed. *Fray Diego de Landa: Relación de las cosas de Yucatán*. Mexico City: Consejo Nacional para la Cultura y las Artes (CONACULTA), 1994.

Ershova, Galena. *Frai Diego de Landa: Drevnie maiia: uiti, chtoby vernut'sia. Istoki Predstavlenii O Modeli Mira*. Moscow: Institut arkheologii RAN, 2000.

Landa, Diego de. *Relación de las cosas de Yucatán: La cultura maya según el testimonio del Obispo de Yucatán en 1566*. Mérida, México: Dante S.A., 2003.

Kovač, Milan. *Správa o veciach na Yucatáne, ktorú napísal brat Diego de Landa, z rádu sv. Františka roku Pána 1566*. Bratislava: Slovenský archeologický a historický inštitút, 2010.

Landa, Diego de. Prologue by Raphaël Espiñeira Lavandeira. Translated by Jean Genet. *La fin du monde Maya: Relation du Yucatán*. Saint-Martory, France: Éditions Futur luxe nocturne, 2011.

Nevaer, Louis E. V. *Yucatán at the Time of the Spanish Encounter = Relación de las cosas de Yucatán*. Coral Gables, FL: Hispanic Economics, Inc., 2013.

Baldy, François. *Relation des choses du Yucatán: 1566*. Paris: Les Belles Lettres, 2014.

Kunzmann, Ulrich. *Bericht aus Yucatán*. Stuttgart: Reclam, 2017.

PUBLISHED PRIMARY AND SECONDARY SOURCES

Abad Pérez, Antolín. "La Biblioteca Franciscana de Toledo (1284–1808)." *Anales Toledanos* 20 (1984): 9–36.

Acosta, José de. *Historia natural y moral de las Indias*. Mexico City: Fondo de cultura económica, 1940 [1589].

Acuña, Rene. "Escritos Mayas inéditos y publicados hasta 1578: Testimonio del Obispo Diego de Landa." *Estudios de Cultura Maya* 21 (2001): 165–79.

Alberola Fioravanti, Maria Victoria. *Guía de la Biblioteca de la Real Academia de la Historia*. Madrid: Real Academia de la Historia, 1995.

Álvarez, Diego. *Memorial illustre de los famosos hijos del real, grave, y religioso convento de Santa Maria de Jesús*. Madrid: Imprenta de doña Maria Garcia Briones, 1753.

Amo Horga, Luz María del. "El gran incendio de 1671 en el Monasterio de San Lorenzo del Escorial y sus repercusiones en la arquitectura." In *Monasterio del Escorial y la Arquitectura: Actas del Simposium*, edited by Francisco Javier Campos y Fernández de Sevilla, 595–620. Alicante and Madrid: Biblioteca Virtual Miguel de Cervantes and the Biblioteca Nacional, 2010.

Anda, A. G., Vera Tiesler, and P. Zabala. "Cenotes, espacios sagrados y la practica del sacrificio humano en Yucatán." *Los Investigadores de la Cultura Maya* 12, Tomo 2. Campeche: Universidad Autónoma de Campeche, 2004.

Anderson, E. N., and Felix Medina Tzuc. *Animals and the Maya in Southeast Mexico.* Tucson: University of Arizona Press, 2005.

Andres, Melquiades. *La teología española en el siglo XVI.* Madrid: Biblioteca de autores cristianos, 1976.

Andrews, Anthony P. "El antiguo puerto Maya de Conil." *Estudios de Cultura Maya* 22 (2002): 137–49.

Andrews, Anthony P. *Maya Salt Production and Trade.* Tucson: University of Arizona Press, 1983.

Antochiw, Michel. *Historia Cartográfica de la Península de Yucatán.* Campeche, Mexico: Gobierno Estatal de Campeche and Comunicaciones y Ediciones Tlaquilco, 1994.

Ardren, Traci, ed. *Ancient Maya Women.* Walnut Creek, CA: AltaMira Press, 2002.

Ardren, Traci. "Empowered Children in Classic Maya Sacrificial Rites." *Childhood in the Past* 4 (2011): 133–45.

Ardren, Traci. "Gender and Sexuality." In *The Maya World*, edited by Scott R. Hutson and Traci Ardren, 147–63. London: Routledge, 2020.

Ardren, Traci. *The Jaguar's Spots: Ancient Mesoamerican Art from the Lowe Art Museum, University of Miami.* Published in conjunction with an exhibition of the same title, organized by and presented at the Lowe Art Museum, University of Miami, June 26–October 31, 2010.

Ardren, Traci. "Mending the Past: Ixchel and the Invention of a Modern Pop Goddess." *Antiquity* 79, no. 306 (2006): 25–37.

Ardren, Traci. "Procesiones y *sacbeob* de las Tierras Bajas del norte en el Clásico maya." *Arqueología Mexicana* 22 (2015): 22–27.

Ardren, Traci. "Savanna Products and Resource Abundance: Asking the Right Questions about Ancient Maya Trade and Urbanism." In *Abundance: The Archaeology of Plentitude*, edited by Monica L. Smith, 117–37. Boulder: University Press of Colorado, 2017.

Ardren, Traci. *Social Identities in the Classic Maya Northern Lowlands: Gender, Age, Memory, and Place.* Austin: University of Texas Press, 2015.

Ardren, Traci. "Strange and Familiar Queens at Maya Royal Courts." In *Faces of Rulership in the Maya Region*, edited by Patricia McAnany and Marilyn Masson. Cambridge, MA: Harvard University Press, forthcoming.

Ardren, Traci, and David Hixson. "The Unusual Sculptures of Telantunich, Yucatan: Phalli and the Concept of Masculinity in Ancient Maya Thought." *Cambridge Archaeological Journal* 16, no. 1 (2006): 7–25.

Ardren, Traci, T. Kam Manahan, Julie K. Wesp, and Alejandra Alonso. "Cloth Production and Economic Intensification in the Area Surrounding Chichen Itza." *Latin American Antiquity* 21, no. 3 (2010): 274–89.

Ares Queija, Berta. *Tomás López Medel, De los tres elementos. Tratado sobre la naturaleza y el hombre del Nuevo Mundo*. Madrid: Alianza Editorial, 1990.

Astor-Aguilera, Miguel. "Maya Rites, Rituals, and Ceremonies." In *The Maya World*, edited by Scott Hutson and Traci Ardren, 648–68. London: Routledge, 2020.

Atolaguirre, Ángel de. "Titulo de cronista general de Indias a favor de la Real Academia de la Historia." *Boletín de la Real Academia de la Historia* 78, no. 5 (1920): 449–52.

Avendaño y Loyola, Andrés de. *Relación de las entradas que hize a la conversion de los gentiles Ytzaex y Chehachez*. Edward E. Ayer Collection, Ayer MS 1040. Chicago: Newberry Library, 1696.

Ayeta, Francisco de. *Último recurso de la Provincia de San Joseph de Yucathan*. Madrid, 1695.

Bacci, Massimo Livi. *Conquest: The Destruction of the American Indios*. Cambridge, UK: Polity, 2008.

Bandelier, Adolph F. *Notes on the Bibliography of Yucatan and Central America. Proceedings of the American Antiquarian Society, October 21, 1880*. Worcester, MA: Charles Hamilton, 1881.

Bardawil, Lawrence W. "The Principal Bird Deity in Maya Art: An Iconographic Study of Form and Meaning." In *Proceedings of the Second Palenque Round Table*, vol. 3, edited by M. G. Robertson, 195–210. Pebble Beach, CA: Pre-Columbian Art Research Institute, 1976.

Baron, Joanne. "Making Money in Mesoamerica: Currency Production and Procurement in the Classic Maya Financial System." *Economic Anthropology* 5, no. 2 (2018): 210–23.

Barrera-Osorio, Antonio. *Experiencing Nature: The Spanish American Empire and the Early Scientific Revolution*. Austin: University of Texas Press, 2006.

Bassie-Sweet, Karen. *Maya Sacred Geography and the Creator Deities*. Norman: University of Oklahoma Press, 2008.

Batalla Rosado, Juan José. "Estudio codicológico del Códice Mendoza." *Revista Española De Antropología Americana* 40, no. 2 (2010): 229–48.

Batun Alpuche, Adolfo Ivan. "Agrarian Production and Intensification at a Postclassic Maya Community, Buena Vista, Cozumel, Mexico," PhD diss., University of Florida, 2009.

Baudez, Claude, and Sydney Picasso. *Lost Cities of the Maya*. New York: Abrams, 1992.

Baudot, George. *Utopia and History: The First Chroniclers of Mexican Civilization (1520–1569)*. Niwot: University Press of Colorado, 1995.

Bautista, Francisco, and J. Alfred Zinck. "Construction of a Yucatec Maya Soil Classification and Comparison with the WRB Framework." *Journal of Ethnobiology and Ethnomedicine* 6, no. 7 (2010): 1–11.

Beck, L., and A. Sievert. "Mortuary Pathways Leading to the Cenote at Chichen Itza." In *Interacting with the Dead: Perspectives on Mortuary Archaeology for the New Millennium*, edited by G. Rakita et al., 290–304. Gainesville: University Press of Florida, 2005.

Benson, Elizabeth P. *The Maya World*. Rev. ed. First published 1967. New York: Cromwell & Co., 1977.

Benzoni, Girolamo. "*Historia del Mondo Nuovo*." In *Americae pars quinta nobilis & admiratione plena Hieronymi Bezoni [sic]*, edited by Theodor de Bry. Frankfurt, 1595.

Bériou, Nicole. "Les prologues des recueils de sermons latins, du XIIe au XVe siècles." In *Les prologues Médiévaux*, edited by Jacqueline Hamesse, 395–426. Turnhout: Brepols, 2000.

Bienvenida, Lorenzo. "Carta a S.A. el Principe Don Felipe." In *Cartas de Indias*, 70–82. Madrid: Ministerio de Fomento, 1877.

Blom, Frans F. *The Conquest of Yucatán*. Cambridge, MA: Riverside, 1936.

Bracamonte, Pedro. *La memoria enclaustrada: Historia indígena de Yucatán, 1750–1915*. México: CIESAS, 1994.

Brasseur de Bourbourg, Charles Étienne. *The Manuscript Hunter: Brasseur de Bourbourg's Travels through Central America and Mexico, 1854–1859*. Edited and translated by Katia Sainson. Norman: University of Oklahoma Press, 2017.

Bricker, Victoria, Eleuterio Po'ot Yah, and Ofelia Dzul de Po'ot. *A Dictionary of the Maya Language as Spoken in Hocabá, Yucatán*. Salt Lake City: University of Utah Press, 1998.

Brinton, Daniel G. "Critical Remarks on the Editions of Diego De Landa's Writings." *Proceedings of the American Philosophical Society* 24, no. 125 (1887): 1–8.

Browne, Walden. *Sahagún and the Transition to Modernity*. Norman: University of Oklahoma Press, 2000.

Buisseret, David. "Spanish Colonial Cartography, 1450–1700." In *Cartography in the European Renaissance*, edited by David Woodward, 1143–1171. Chicago, IL: University of Chicago Press, 2007.

Butler, Alban. *Lives of the Saints: For Every Day in the Year*. 1878. New York: Benziger Brothers, 1955.

Butterfield, Marvin Ellis. *Jerónimo de Aguilar, Conquistador*. University of Alabama Studies 10. Tuscaloosa: University of Alabama Press, 1955.

Bynum, Carolyn Walker. *Christian Materiality: An Essay on Religion in Late Medieval Europe*. New York: Zone Books, 2011.

Caesar, Julius, *The Conquest of Gaul* [52 BC]. London and New York: Penguin, 1951.

Canedo, Lino G. "Fray Lorenzo de Bienvenida, O.F.M., and the Origins of the Franciscan Order in Yucatan: A Reconsideration of the Problem on the Basis of Unpublished Documents." *The Americas* 8, no. 4 (1952): 493–510.

Carrillo y Ancona, Crescencio. *El Obispado de Yucatan: Historia de su fundación y de sus obispos desde el siglo XVI hasta el XIX*. Merida, Yucatan: Ricardo B. Caballero, 1895.

Castaño, Vicente Manuel. *Noticia y defensa de los escritos del minorita catalán fray Poncio Carbonel*. Alcalá: Imprenta de don Joseph Antonio Ibarrola, 1790.

Castaño Perea, Enrique. "La real capilla del Alcázar de Madrid, Analises de la documentación grafica existente para completar una reconstitución grafica." *EGA: Revista De Expresión Gráfica Arquitectónica* 17, no. 19 (2012): 180–89.

Castellanos, M. Bianet. *A Return to Servitude: Maya Migration and the Tourist Trade in Cancun*. Minneapolis: University of Minnesota Press, 2010.

Catalina García, Juan. "Investigaciones históricas y arqueológicas en Cifuentes, villa de la provincia de Guadalajara, y sus cercanías." *Boletín de la Real Academia de la Historia* 16 (1890): 57–64.

Cerezo, Prometeo. *Alonso de Veracruz y el derecho de gentes*. México: Porrúa, 1985.

Cervantes de Salazar, Francisco. *Crónica de la Nueva España*. 2 vols. Madrid, 1914.

Cervantes de Salazar, Francisco. *Crónica de la Nueva España, su descripción, la calidad y temple de ella, la propiedad y naturaleza de los indios*, 1575 Manuscript Copy, Biblioteca Nacional de España, MSS/2011.

Chamberlain, Robert S. *The Conquest and Colonization of Honduras, 1502–1550*. New York: Octagon Books, 1966.

Chamberlain, Robert S. *The Conquest and Colonization of Yucatan, 1517–1550*. Washington, DC: Carnegie Institution of Washington, 1948.

Chamberlain, Robert S. "The Governorship of the Adelantado Francisco De Montejo in Chiapas, 1539–1544." *Contributions to American Anthropology and History* 9 (1948): 163–207.

Checa, Fernando. *El Real Alcázar de Madrid: Dos siglos de arquitectura y coleccionismo en la corte de los Reyes de España*. Madrid: Nerea, 1994.

Christensen, Mark Z. *Nahua and Maya Catholicisms: Texts and Religion in Colonial Central Mexico and Yucatan*. Stanford, CA: Stanford University Press, 2013.

Christensen, Mark Z. *The Teabo Manuscript: Maya Christian Copybooks, Chilam Balams, and Native Text Production in Yucatan.* Austin: University of Texas Press, 2016.

Christensen, Mark Z., and Matthew Restall. *Return to Ixil: Maya Society in an Eighteenth-Century Yucatec Town.* Louisville: University Press of Colorado, 2019.

Chuchiak, John F. "*Ah Mak Ikob yetel Ah Pul Yahob*: Yucatec Maya Witchcraft and Sorcery and the Mestizaje of Magic and Medicine in Colonial Yucatán, 1570–1790." In *Sorcery in Mesoamerica*, edited by John M. D. Pohl and Jeremy D. Coltman, 135–166. Louisville: University Press of Colorado, 2020.

Chuchiak, John F. "Anhelo de un escudo de armas: La falta de concesiones de escudos de armas indígenas mayas y la iconografía apócrifa de la heráldica colonial en Yucatán." In *Los escudos de armas indígenas: De la colonia al México Independiente,* edited by María Castañeda de la Paz and Hans Roskamp, 273–308. Zamora, Michoacán: Instituto de Investigaciones Antropológicos, UNAM y El Colegio de Michoacán; Zamora, Michoacán: Colegio de Michoacán, 2013.

Chuchiak, J. F. "The Burning and the Burnt: The Transformative Power of Fire, Smoke, and Flames in Conquest and Colonial Maya Ritual, Warfare, and Diplomacy." In *Smoke, Flames, and the Human Body in Mesoamerican Ritual Practice,* edited by Vera Tiesler and Andrew Scherer, 151–88. Washington, DC: Dumbarton Oaks, 2018.

Chuchiak, John F. "'*Ca numiae, lay u cal caxtlan patan lae*': El tributo colonial y la nutrición de los mayas, 1542–1812: Un estudio sobre los efectos de la conquista y el colonialismo en los mayas de Yucatán." In *Iglesia y sociedad en América Latina colonial,* edited by Juan Manuel de la Serna, 107–218. Mexico City: Centro Coordinador y Difusor de Estudios Latinoamericanos, Universidad Nacional Autónoma de Mexico, 1998.

Chuchiak, John F. *El castigo y la represión: El juzgado del Provisorato de Indios y la extirpación de la idolatría maya en el obispado de Yucatán, 1563–1763.* Mexico City: Instituto de Investigaciones Jurídicas, Universidad Nacional Autónoma de México; Jalapa, Veracruz: Universidad Anahuac Xalapa, 2022.

Chuchiak, John F. "Caves of Life and Caves of Death: Colonial Yucatec Maya Rituals and Offerings in Caves and Cenotes, 1540–1750." In *Maya Cosmology: Terrestrial and Celestial Landscapes,* edited by Milan Kovac, Guido Krempel, Harri Kettunen, 77–90. Acta Mesoamericana, 29. Markt Schwaben, Germany: Anton Saurwein Verlag, 2019.

Chuchiak, John F. "Colonial Maya Religion and the Spanish World: The Role of 'Idolatry' in Inter-Ethnic Relations in Colonial Yucatán, 1545–1820." *Axis Mundi: Journal of the Slovak Association for the Study of Religion* 9, no. 1 (2014): 47–66.

Chuchiak, John F. "La Conquista de Yucatán, 1517–1542." In *Historia General de Yucatán,* edited by Sergio Quezada, Ines Ortiz Yam, and Jorge Castillo Canché, 29–57. Merida, Yucatan: Universidad Autónoma de Yucatán, 2014.

Chuchiak, John F. "*De Descriptio Idolorum*: An Ethnohistorical Examination of the Production, Imagery, and Functions of Colonial Yucatec Maya Idols and Effigy Censers, 1540–1700." In *Maya Worldview at Conquest*, edited by Timothy Pugh and Leslie Cecil, 135–58. Boulder: University Press of Colorado, 2009.

Chuchiak, John F. "*De Extirpatio Codicis Yucatanensis*: The 1607 Colonial Confiscation of a Maya Sacred Book: New Interpretations on the Origins and Provenience of the Madrid Codex." In *Sacred Books, Sacred Languages: Two Thousand Years of Ritual and Religious Maya Literature*, edited by Rogelio Valencia Rivera and Geneviève Le Fort, 113–40. Acta Mesoamericana, 18. Markt Schwaben, Germany: Anton Saurwein Verlag, 2007.

Chuchiak, John F. "Documentos Históricos-Pilares de la Memoria: La Fundación de la ciudad de Mérida." *Ichcanzihó: Revista Trimestral del Patrimonio Arqueológico y Natural*, no. 9 (2001): 13.

Chuchiak, John F. "Entre la cooperación y la usurpación. La Orden Franciscana y la jurisdicción eclesiástica sobre la extirpación de la idolatría maya en Yucatán, 1570–1650." In *El ídolo y las hogueras. Idolatría y evangelización en América virreinal, siglos XVI–XVIII*, edited by Gerardo Lara Cisneros y Roberto Martínez González, 123–49. Mexico City: Instituto de Investigaciones Históricas, Universidad Nacional Autónoma de México, 2021.

Chuchiak, John F. "'*Fide, Non Armis*': Franciscan Reducciones and the Maya Mission Experience on the Colonial Frontier of Yucatán, 1602–1640." In *Francis in America: The Franciscan Experience in the Americas*, edited by John F. Schwaller, 119–42. Berkeley, California: Academy of American Franciscan History, 2006.

Chuchiak, John F. "Forgotten Allies: The Origins and Role of Native Mesoamerican Auxiliaries and Indios Conquistadores in the Conquest of Yucatán, 1526–1550." In *Indian Conquistadors: Native Militaries in the Conquest of Mesoamerica*, edited by Michel Oudijk and Laura Matthew, 122–97. Norman: University of Oklahoma Press, 2007.

Chuchiak, John F. "Human Plunder: The Role of Maya Slavery in Postclassic and Early Conquest Era Yucatán, 1450–1550." Presented at the 82nd Annual Meeting of the Society for American Archaeology, Washington, DC, 2018 (tDAR id: 443637).

Chuchiak, John F. "La iglesia evangelizadora: El provisorato de Indios y la extirpación de las idolatrías en Yucatán, 1571–1761." In *Historia General de Yucatán*, edited by Sergio Quezada, Ines Ortiz Yam, and Jorge Castillo Canché, 177–263. Merida, Yucatan: Universidad Autónoma de Yucatán, 2014.

Chuchiak, John F. "The Images Speak: The Survival and Production of Hieroglyphic Codices and Their Use in Post-conquest Maya Religion, 1580–1720." In *Continuity and Change: Maya Religious Practices in Temporal Perspective*, edited by Daniel Graña Behrens, Nikolai Grube, Christian M. Prager, Frauke Sachse, Stefanie Teufel, Elisabeth

Wagner, 71–103. Acta Mesoamericana, 14. Markt Schwaben, Germany: Anton Saurwein Verlag, 2004.

Chuchiak, John F. "The Indian Inquisition and the Extirpation of Idolatry: The Process of Punishment in the Provisorato de Indios of the Diocese of Yucatán, 1563–1812." PhD diss., Tulane University, 2000.

Chuchiak, John F. *The Inquisition in New Spain, 1536–1819*. Baltimore, MD: Johns Hopkins University Press, 2012.

Chuchiak, John F. "*In Servitio Dei*: Fray Diego de Landa, the Franciscan Order, and the Return of the Extirpation of Idolatry in the Colonial Diocese of Yucatán, 1573–1579." *The Americas* 61, no. 4 (April 2005): 611–45.

Chuchiak, John F. " 'It is their drinking that hinders them': Balché and the Use of Ritual Intoxicants among the Colonial Yucatec Maya, 1550–1780." *Estudios de Cultura Maya* 24 (Fall 2003): 137–71.

Chuchiak, John F. "Pre-conquest Ah Kinob in a Colonial World: The Extirpation of Idolatry and the Survival of the Maya Priesthood in Colonial Yucatán, 1563–1697." In *Maya Survivalism*, edited by Ueli Hostettler and Matthew Restall, 135–60. Acta Mesoamericana 12. Markt Schwaben, Germany: Verlag Anton Saurwein, 2001.

Chuchiak, John F. "*Sapientia et Doctrina*: The Structure of Franciscan Education in San José Province and the Teaching of Alphabetic Literacy among the Yucatec Maya, 1545–1650." In *The Franciscans in Colonial Mexico*, edited by Thomas M. Cohen, Jay T. Harrison, and David Rex Galindo, 127–55. Norman: University of Oklahoma Press; Oceanside, CA: Academy of American Franciscan History, 2021.

Chuchiak, John F. "The Sins of the Fathers: Franciscan Friars, Parish Priests, and the Sexual Conquest of the Yucatec Maya, 1545–1808." *Ethnohistory* 54, no. 1 (2007): 69–127.

Chuchiak, John F. "Toward a Regional Definition of Idolatry: Reexamining Idolatry Trials in the *Relaciones de Meritos* and Their Role in Defining the Concept of *Idolatria* in Colonial Yucatán, 1570–1780." *Journal of Early Modern History* 6, no. 2 (2002): 1–29.

Chuchiak, John F. "Writing as Resistance: Maya Graphic Pluralism and Indigenous Elite Strategies for Survival in Colonial Yucatán 1550–1750." *Ethnohistory* 57, no. 1 (Winter 2010): 87–116.

Chuchiak, John F. "Yaab Uih Yetel Maya Cimil: Colonial Plagues, Famines, Catastrophes and Their Impact on Changing Yucatec Maya Conceptions of Death and Dying, 1580–1794." In *Jaws of the Underworld: Life, Death and Rebirth among the Ancient Maya*, edited by Elizabeth Graham, 3–20. Acta Mesoamericana, 16. London: British Museum, 2006.

Chuchiak, John F., and Harri Kettunen. " '*Que los indios de Yucatán merecen que el rey les favoresca*': A New Understanding of the Structure, Composition, and Copyists of Diego de Landa's *Relación de las cosas de Yucatán*." *The Mayanist* 4, no. 1 (2022): 25–50.

Clayton, Lawrence A. *Bartolomé de las Casas*. Cambridge, UK: Cambridge University Press, 2012.

Clendinnen, Inga. *Ambivalent Conquests: Maya and Spaniard in Yucatan, 1517–1570*. 2nd ed. First published in 1987. Cambridge, UK: Cambridge University Press, 2003.

Cline, Howard Francis. "The *Relaciones Geográficas* of the Spanish Indies, 1577–1586." *Hispanic American Historical Review* 44 (1964): 341–74.

Coakley, John. "Gender and the Authority of Friars: The Significance of Holy Women for Thirteenth-Century Franciscans and Dominicans." *Church History* 60, no. 4 (1991): 445–60.

Códice Franciscano, in *Nueva colección de documentos para la historia de México, siglo XVI*, 55–72. Mexico City: Editorial Salvador Chávez Hayhoe, 1941.

Coe Michael D. *Breaking the Maya Code*. Rev. ed. New York: Thames and Hudson, 1999.

Coe Michael D. *The Maya*. 9th ed. First published in 1966. New York: Thames and Hudson, 2015.

Coe Michael D. "A Triumph of Spirit: How Yuri Knorosov Cracked the Maya Hieroglyphic Code." *Archaeology* 44, no. 5 (September–October 1991): 39–44.

Coe, Michael D., Stephen Houston, Mary Miller, and Karl Taube. "The Fourth Maya Codex." In *Maya Archaeology*, vol. 3, edited by S. Houston, C. W. Golden, and J. Skidmore, 116–67. San Francisco, CA: Precolumbian Mesoweb Press, 2015.

Coggins, Clemency C. *Artifacts from the Cenote of Sacrifice, Chichen Itza, Yucatan: Textiles, Basketry, Stone, Bone, Shell, Ceramics, Wood, Copal, Rubber, Other Organic Materials, and Mammalian Remains*. Cambridge, MA: Peabody Museum of Archaeology and Ethnology, 1992.

Coggins, Clemency C. *Cenote of Sacrifice: Maya Treasures from the Sacred Well at Chichén Itzá*. Austin: University of Texas Press, 1984.

Cogolludo, Diego López de. *Historia de Yucathan*. Madrid: J. Garcia Infanzon, 1688.

Coppens d'Eeckenbrugge, Geo, and Jean-Marc Lacape. "Distribution and Differentiation of Wild, Feral, and Cultivated Populations of Perennial Upland Cotton (Gossypium hirsutum L.) in Mesoamerica and the Caribbean." *PLOS One* 9, no. 9 (2014). https://doi.org/10.1371/journal.pone.0107458.

Covarrubias Reyna, Miguel, and Rafael Burgos Villanueva. "Investigaciones arqueológicas en la región centro-norte del Estado de Yucatan." In *The Archaeology of Yucatan*, edited by Travis Stanton, 207–42. Oxford, UK: Archaeopress, 2014.

Cuesta Domingo, Mariano. *Antonio de Herrera y su obra*. Segovia: Colegio Universitario de Segovia, 1998.

Cuesta Domingo, Mariano. "Los cronistas oficiales de Indias. De López de Velasco a Céspedes del Castillo." *Revista Complutense de Historia de América* 33 (2007): 115–50.

Cuesta Domingo, Mariano. *Estudio crítico de Antonio de Herrera*. Madrid: Biblioteca Virtual Ignacio Larramendi de Polígrafos, 2015.

Cuesta Domingo, Mariano, José Luis de Rojas, and José Andrés Jiménez Garcés. *Antonio de Herrera y Tordesillas, historiador acreditado*. Cuéllar: Caja Segovia, 2009.

Cypess, Sandra Messinger. *La Malinche in Mexican Literature: From History to Myth*. Austin: University of Texas Press, 1991.

Daniel, E. Randolph. "The Desire for Martyrdom: A 'Leitmotiv' of St. Bonaventure." *Franciscan Studies* 32 (1972): 74–87.

Davis, Mark Evan. " 'The Evangelical Prophecies over Jerusalem Have Been Fulfilled': Joachim of Fiore, the Jews, Fray Diego de Landa and the Maya." *Journal of Iberian Medieval Studies* 5, no. 1 (February 2013): 86–103.

Daza, Antonio. *Qvarta parte de la Chronica general de nu[es]tro padre, San Francisco y su apostolica orden*. San Francisco de Valladolid: Por Juan Godines de Millis y Diego de Cordoua, 1611.

Debby, Nirit Ben-Aryeh. "Jews and Judaism in the Rhetoric of Popular Preachers: The Florentine Sermons of Giovanni Dominici (1356–1419) and Bernardino Da Siena (1380–1444)." *Jewish History* 14, no. 2 (2000): 175–200.

Díaz, Juan, and Jorge Gurría Lacroix. *Itinerario de la armada del Rey Católico a la isla de Yucatán en la India el año 1518 en la que fue por comandante y capitán general Juan de Grijalva*. México: Editorial Juan Pablos, 1972.

Díaz del Castillo, Bernal. *The Conquest of New Spain*. New York: Penguin, 1963.

Diehl, Edith. *Bookbinding: Its Background and Technique*. Mineola, NY: Dover Publications, 1980.

Dine, Harper, Traci Ardren, Grace Bascope, and Celso Gutierrez Baez. "Famine Foods and Food Security in the Northern Maya Lowlands: Modern Lessons for Ancient Reconstructions." *Ancient Mesoamerica* 30 (2019): 517–34.

Dorin, Rowan W. " 'Once the Jews Have Been Expelled': Intent and Interpretation in Late Medieval Canon Law." *Law and History Review* 34, no. 2 (2016): 335–62.

Ducornet, Rikki. *The Fan-Maker's Inquisition: A Novel of the Marquis de Sade*. New York: Henry Holt & Co., 1999.

Dunning, Nicholas P. *Lords of the Hills: Ancient Maya Settlement in the Puuc Region, Yucatan, Mexico*. Madison, WI: Prehistory Press, 1992.

Dunning, Nicholas P., and Stephen Houston. "Chan Ik': Hurricanes as a Destabilizing Force in the Pre-Hispanic Maya Lowlands." In *Ecology, Power, and Religion in Maya Landscapes*, edited by Christian Isendahl and Bodil Liljefors Persson, 57–67. Markt Schwaben, Germany: Verlag Anton Saurwein, 2011.

Early, John D. *The Maya and Catholicism: An Encounter of Worldviews*. Gainesville: University Press of Florida, 2006.

Elmendorf, Mary. *Nine Maya Women: A Village Faces Change.* Cambridge, MA: Schenkman, 1976.

Enríquez, Alejandro. "The Exuberant Imagination: Blood Libel and the Myth of Maya Ritual Murder in the 1562 Sotutua Confessions." In *Journal of Medieval Iberian Studies* 10, no. 2 (2018): 276–94.

Enríquez, Alejandro. "Theaters of Rule, Theaters of Resistance: Franciscan Discourses of Spiritual Conquest in Colonial Yucatán, 1541–1688." PhD diss., University of Minnesota, 2010.

Enríquez, Alejandro. "Writing Violence in Seventeenth-Century Yucatan: Fray Bernardo de Lizana's Devocionario de nuestra Señora de Izamal y Conquista espiritual de Yucatán (1633)." *Colonial Latin American Review* 24, no. 3 (2015): 383–405.

Enríquez Ordóñez, Alfredo. "Borraduras y omisiones: Dos intentos frustrados en la Relación de las cosas de Yucatán (1606?)." PhD diss., State University of New Jersey, 1994.

Escalante Carrillo, Eduardo Andrés. "Reconocimiento y Análisis Arqueológico de Superficie para la Conservación del Patrimonio Arqueológico en Áreas Urbanizables de la Ciudad de Mérida, Yucatán." Thesis Licenciatura, Merida: Universidad Autónoma de Yucatán, 2010.

Fernández, Rafael Diego. "La visita al Consejo de Indias de Juan de Ovando y la Nueva España." *Revista Chilena de Historia del Derecho.* Estudios en honor de Bernardino Bravo Lira 22, no. 1 (2010): 445–457.

Fernández-Armesto, Felipe. "'Aztec' Auguries and Memories of the Conquest of Mexico." *Renaissance Studies* 6, nos. 3–4 (1992): 287–305.

Ferrero Hernández, Cándida. "Lectio et Disputatio en el prólogo del Contra legem Sarracenorum de Riccoldo da Monte di Croce." *Mélanges de la Casa de Velázquez* 49, no. 1 (2019): 141–55.

Fitzsimmons, James L. *Death and the Classic Maya Kings.* Austin: University of Texas Press, 2009.

Flores, José Salvador, and Jesús Kantún Balam. "Importance of Plants in the Ch'a Chaak Maya Ritual in the Peninsula of Yucatan." *Journal of Ethnobiology* 17, no. 1 (1997): 97–108.

Folan, William J., David D. Bolles, and Jerald D. Ek. "On the Trail of Quetzalcoatl/Kukulcan: Tracing Mythic Interaction Routes and Networks in the Maya Lowlands." *Ancient Mesoamerica* 27 (2016): 293–318.

Folan, William J., Abel Morales López, Raymundo González Heredia, José Antonio Hernández Trujeque, Lynda Florey Folan, Donald Forsyth, Vera Tiesler Blos, María Jose Gómez Coba, Aracely Hurtado Cen, Ronald Bishop, David Bolles, Geoffrey Braswell, Jerald Ek, Joel D. Gunn, Christopher Götz Gerardo Villanueva, Alicia Blanco,

Tomas Arnabar Gunam, María del Rosario Domínguez Carrasco, and Trenton Noble. "Chakanputun, Campeche 3,000 Años de Sustentabilidad." In *Arqueología de la Costa de Campeche La Época Prehispánica*, edited by Rafael Cobos Palma, 97–123. Merida: Universidad Autónoma de Yucatán: 2012.

Fontaneda Berthet, Cristina. *Ampudia 1606–2006: IV centenario del otorgamiento en la Villa del traslado de la Corte de Valladolid a Madrid*. Palencia: Institución Tello Téllez de Meneses, 2006.

Fortuny Loret de Mola, Patricia. "Transnational Hetzmek: From Oxkutzcab to San Francisco." In *Religion at the Corner of Bliss and Nirvana: Politics, Identity and Faith in New Immigrant Communities*, edited by Lois Ann Lorentzen, Joaquin Jay Gonzalez III, Kevin M. Chun, and Hien Duc Do, 207–42. Durham, NC: Duke University Press, 2009.

Frechette, Mariel. "Danger in Deviance: Colonial Imagery and the Power of Indigenous Female Sexuality in New Spain." Undergraduate Thesis, Scripps College, 2013.

Gabbert, Wolfgang. *Becoming Maya: Ethnicity and Social Inequality in Yucatán since 1500*. Tucson: University of Arizona Press, 2004.

Gann, Thomas, and J. Eric Thompson. *The History of the Maya: From the Earliest Times to the Present Day*. New York: Scribner's Sons, 1931.

García, Gregorio O. P. *Origen de los indios de el nuevo mundo*. Valencia, 1607.

García Bernal, Manuela Cristina. *La sociedad de Yucatán, 1700–1750*. Seville: Escuela de Estudios Hispano-Americanos, 1972.

García Bernal, Manuela Cristina. *Yucatán: Población y encomienda bajo las Austrias*. Seville: Escuela de Estudios Hispano-Americanos, 1978.

Garcia Carraffa, Alerto y Arturo. *Diccionario heraldico y genealogico de Appellidos Españoles*. Madrid, 1923.

Garcia Icazbalceta, Joaquin. *Colección de documentos para la historia de Mexico*. Mexico: Andrade, 1858–1866.

Garcia Targa, Juan. "Analisis histórico y arqueológico del asentamiento colonial de Tecoh (estado de Yucatan, Mexico) siglo XVI." *Ancient Mesoamerica* 11 (2000): 231–43.

Gómez Canedo, Lino. *Evangelización y Conquista: Experiencia Franciscana en Hispanoamérica*. México: Editorial Porrua, 1977.

Gómez Canedo, Lino. "Mexican Sources for the History of the Far East Missions." In *30th International Congress of Human Sciences in Asia and North Africa*, edited by Ernesto de la Torre, 7–19. México: El Colegio de México, 1976.

Gomez Robledo, Antonio. *El magisterio filosófico y jurídico de Alonso de la Vera Cruz*. México: Porrúa, 1984.

Gonzaga, Francesco. *De origine Seraphica Religionis Franciscana ejusque progressibus, de regularis observancia institutione [. . .]*. Rome: Dominicus Basa, 1587.

González Cicero, Stela Maria. *Perspectiva religiosa en Yucatán, 1517–1571, los franciscanos y el primer obispo fray Francisco de Toral*. México: El Colegio de México, 1978.

Grijalva, Juan de. *Intinerario de la armada del rey católico a la isla de Yucatán, en la India, el año de 1518*. Mexico: Editorial Juan Pablos, S.A., 1950.

Grube, Nikolai, and Ruth Krochock. "Reading between the Lines: Hieroglyphic Texts from Chichen Itza and Its Neighbors." In *Twin Tollans: Chichen Itza, Tula, and the Epiclassic to Early Postclassic Mesoamerican World*, edited by Jeff Karl Kowalski and Cynthia Kristin-Graham, 205–50. Cambridge, MA: Harvard University Press; Washington, DC: Dumbarton Oaks, 2007.

Gubler, Ruth. *Yerbas y Hechicerías del Yucatán*. Izamal, Yucatan: Secteraría de Educación del Estado de Yucatán and UNAM, 2014.

Guenter, Stanley P., and David A. Freidel. "Warriors and Rulers: Royal Women of the Classic Maya." In *Gender in Cross-Cultural Perspective*, 4th ed., edited by Caroline Brettell and Carolyn F. Sargent, 74–80. Upper Saddle River, NJ: Prentice Hall, 2005.

Gutiérrez Iglesias, Felisa. *Catálogo de incunables y obras impresas del siglo XVI*. Santander: Institución Cultural de Cantabria, Consejería de Cultura, Educación y Deporte, Diputación Regional de Cantabria, 1985.

Haines, Helen R., Philip W. Willink, and David Maxwell. "Stingray Spine Use and Maya Bloodletting Rituals: A Cautionary Tale." *Latin American Antiquity* 19, no. 1 (2008): 83–98.

Hamman, Byron E. "Child Martyrs and Murderous Children: Age and Agency in Sixteenth Century Trans-Atlantic Religious Conflicts." In *The Social Experience of Childhood in Ancient Mesoamerica*, edited by T. Ardren and S. Hutson, 203–32. Boulder: University Press of Colorado, 2006.

Hanks, William F. *Converting Words: Maya in the Age of the Cross*. Berkeley: University of California Press, 2010.

Hanks, William F. *Intertexts: Writings on Language, Utterance, and Context*. Lanham, MD: Rowman & Littlefield, 2000.

Haring, Clarence H. *The Spanish Empire in America*. New York: Oxford University Press, 1947.

Harrison-Buck, Eleanor. "The Coin of Her Realm: Cacao as Gendered Goods among the Prehispanic and Colonial Maya." In *The Value of Things*, edited by Jennifer P. Mathews and Thomas H. Guderjan, 104–23. Tucson: University of Arizona Press, 2017.

Herrera y Tordesillas, Antonio de. *The General History of the Vast Continent and Islands of America*. Los Angeles, CA: AMS Press, 1973 [reprint from the 1740 edition].

Herrera y Tordesillas, Antonio de. *Historia general de los hechos de los castellanos en las islas i tierra firme del Mar Océano*. 9 vols. Madrid: En la Emplenta [*sic*] Real, 1601–1615 [1726–30 edition also consulted].

Herrera y Tordesillas, Antonio de. *Historia general del mundo de XVII años del tiempo del señor Rey don Felipe II el Prudente*. Vol. 1. Valladolid: Godinez de Millis, 1606.

Herring, Adam. *Art and Writing in the Maya Cities, A.D. 600–800: A Poetics of Line*. Cambridge, UK: Cambridge University Press, 2005.

Hill, Roscoe. "The Office of Adelantado." In *Political Science Quarterly* 28, no. 4 (1913): 646–68.

Hillerkuss, Thomas. "Los méritos y servicios de un maya yucateco principal del siglo XVI y la historia de sus probanzas y mercedes." *Estudios de Historia Novohispana* 13 (1993): 9–39.

Hoggarth Julie A., Matthew Restall, James Wood, and Douglas J. Kennett. "Drought and Its Demographic Effects in the Maya Lowlands." *Current Anthropology* 58, no. 1 (February 2017): 82–113.

Houston, Stephen D. "A Splendid Predicament: Young Men in Classic Maya Society." *Cambridge Archaeological Journal* 19, no. 2 (2009): 149–78.

Hsia, Ronnie Po-Chia. *The Myth of Ritual Murder: Jews and Magic in Reformation Germany*. New Haven, CT: Yale University Press, 1998.

Huber, Roy A., and A. M. Headrick. *Handwriting Identification: Facts and Fundamentals*. Boca Raton, FL: CRC Press, 1999.

Hunt, Marta Espejo-Ponce, and Matthew Restall. "Work, Marriage and Status: Maya Women of Colonial Yucatan." In *Indian Women of Early Mexico*, edited by S. Schroeder et al., 231–54. Cambridge, UK: Cambridge University Press, 1997.

Hurst, Heather. "Maya Mural Painting." In *The Maya World*, edited by Scott Hutson and Traci Ardren, 578–98. London: Routledge, 2020.

Hutson, Scott R., and Traci Ardren, eds. *The Maya World*. London: Routledge, 2020.

Izquierdo, Ana Luisa. *Acalán y la Chontalpa en el siglo XVI: Su geografía política*. Mexico City: UNAM, 1997.

Jakeman, M. Wells. *The "Historical Recollections" of Gaspar Antonio Chi. An Early Source-Account of Ancient Yucatán*. Publications in Archaeology and Early History 3. Provo, UT: Brigham Young University, 1952.

Jones, Grant. *The Conquest of the Last Maya Kingdom*. Stanford, CA: Stanford University Press, 1998.

Jones, Grant. *Maya Resistance to Spanish Rule: Time and History on a Colonial Frontier*. Albuquerque: University of New Mexico Press, 1989.

Joyce, Rosemary. *Gender and Power in Prehispanic Mesoamerica*. Austin: University of Texas Press, 2000.

Joyce, Rosemary. "A Pre-Columbian Gaze: Male Sexuality among the Ancient Maya." In *Archaeologies of Sexuality*, edited by Robert Schmidt and Barbara Voss, 263–83. New York: Routledge, 2000.

Justeson, John S., and George A. Broadwell. "Language and Languages in Mesoamerica." In *The Legacy of Mesoamerica: History and Culture of a Native American Civilization*, edited by Robert M. Carmack, Janine Gasco, and Gary H. Gossen, 379–406. Upper Saddle River, NJ: Prentice Hall, 1996.

Karttunen, Frances. *Between Worlds: Interpreters, Guides, and Survivors*. New Brunswick, NJ: Rutgers University Press, 1994.

Karttunen, Frances. "Rethinking Malinche." In *Indian Women of Early Mexico*, edited by Susan Schroeder, Stephanie Wood, and Robert Haskett, 291–312. Norman: University of Oklahoma Press, 1997.

Kashanipour, Ryan Amir. "A World of Cures: Magic and Medicine in Colonial Yucatán." PhD diss., University of Arizona, 2012.

Kellogg, Susan. *Weaving the Past: A History of Latin America's Indigenous Women from the Prehispanic Period to the Present*. Oxford, UK: Oxford University Press, 2005.

Kettunen, Harri. "Observations Based on Transillumination Photography of Diego de Landa's *Relación de las Cosas de Yucatán*." *The Mayanist* 1, no. 2 (2020): 53–74.

King, Eleanor. "Maya Commerce." In *The Maya World*, edited by Scott Hutson and Traci Ardren, 443–58. London: Routledge, 2020.

Klein, Cecelia, ed. *Gender in Pre-Hispanic America*. Washington, DC: Dumbarton Oaks, 2001.

Knowlton, Timothy W. "Filth and Healing in Yucatán: Interpreting Ix Hun Ahua, a Maya Goddess." *Ancient Mesoamerica* 27, no. 2 (2016): 319–32.

Knowlton, Timothy W. *Maya Creation Myths: Words and Worlds of the Chilam Balam*. Boulder: University Press of Colorado, 2010.

Knowlton, Timothy, and Edber Dzidz Yam. "Perinatal Rites in the Ritual of the Bacabs, a Colonial Maya Manuscript." *Ethnohistory* 66, no. 4 (October 2019): 721–44.

Kobayashi, José María. *La educación como conquista (empresa franciscana en México)*. Mexico City: El Colegio de México, 1974.

Krochock, Ruth. "Women in the Hieroglyphic Inscriptions of Chichén Itzá." In *Ancient Maya Women*, edited by Traci Ardren, 152–170. Walnut Creek, CA: AltaMira Press, 2002.

Kunow, Marianna A. *Maya Medicine: Traditional Healing in Yucatan*. Albuquerque: University of New Mexico Press, 2003.

Kuttner, Stephan. "On Auctoritas in the Writing of Medieval Canonists: The Vocabulary of Gratian." In *Notion D' Autorité Au Moyen Âge: Islam, Byzance, Occident*. Edited by Georges Makdisi, Dominique Sourdel, and Janine Sourdel-Thomine, 69–81. Paris: Presses Universitaires de France, 1982.

Las Casas, Bartolomé de. *An Account, Much Abbreviated, of the Destruction of the Indies* [1552]. Edited by Franklin Knight. Translated by Andrew Hurley. Indianapolis, IN: Hackett, 2003.

Las Casas, Bartolomé de. *Historia de las Indias*. 3 vols. México: Fondo de Cultura Económica, 1995.

Las Casas, Bartolomé de. *Historia de las Indias, escrita por Fray Bartolomé de Las Casas . . . ahora por primera vez dada á luz por el marqués de La Fuensanta Del Valle y D. José Rayon*. Madrid: Impr. de M. Ginesta, 1875.

Las Casas, Bartolomé de. *Tratados de Fray Bartolomé de las Casas*. Prologue by Manuel Giménez Fernández and Lewis Hanke. Transcription by Juan Pérez de Tudela y Bueso. Translation by Agustín Millares Carlo and Rafael Moreno. México: Fondo de Cultura Económica, 1965.

Las Casas, Bartolomé de. Edited by Manuel Serrano y Sanz. *Apologética historia de las Indias: De Fr. Bartolome de las Casas*. Madrid: Bailly, Bailliere e hijos, 1909.

Lavrin, Asunción. "Viceregal Culture." In *The Cambridge History of Latin American Literature*, edited by Roberto González Echevarría and Enrique Pupo-Walker, 286–335. Cambridge, UK: Cambridge University Press, 1996.

Lee, Julian C. *The Amphibians and Reptiles of the Yucatan Peninsula*. Ithaca, NY: Comstock, 1996.

Lentz, Mark. *Murder in Mérida: Violence, Factions, and the Law*. Albuquerque: University of New Mexico Press, 2018.

León Cázares, María del Carmen. "Diego de Landa." In *Historiografía novohispana de tradición indígena*, edited by José Rubén Romero Galván, 259–80. Mexico City: UNAM, 2003.

León-Portilla, Miguel. *Hernán Cortés y la Mar del Sur*. 1985. Madrid, Algaba Ediciones, 2005.

Lhuillier, Alberto Ruz. *La costa de Campeche en los tiempos prehispánicos*. Mexico, D.F.: Instituto Nacional de Antropología e Historia, 1969.

Lizana, Bernardo de. *Historia de Yucatán, Devocionario de Nuestra Señora de Izamal y conquista espiritual*. 1633. México: Museo Nacional, 1893.

Looper, Matthew G. "Women-Men (and Men-Women): Classic Maya Rulers and the Third Gender." In *Ancient Maya Women*, edited by T. Ardren, 171–202. Walnut Creek, CA: AltaMira, 2002.

Lopes Don, Patricia. "Franciscans, Indian Sorcerers, and the Inquisition in New Spain, 1536–1543." *Journal of World History* 17, no. 1 (March 2006): 27–49.

López Austin, Alfredo. *La Educación de los Antiguos Nahuas*. Mexico, DF.: Consejo Nacional de Fomento Educativo, 1985.

López Austin, Alfredo. *Educación Mexica: Antología de Textos Sahaguntinos*. Mexico, D.F.: Universidad Nacional Autónoma de México, 1985.

López de Cogolludo, Diego. See Cogolludo, Diego López de.

López de Gómara, Francisco. *La Conquista de México*. Zaragoza: En casa de Agustín Millán, 1552.

López de Gómara, Francisco. *La Istoria de las Yndias*. Zaragoza: En casa de Agustín Millán, 1552.

López de Velasco, Juan. *Demarcación de las Indias*. Biblioteca Nacional de España, Manuscript Mss/2825, 1578.

López de Velasco, Juan. *Ortografía y pronunciación castellana*. Burgos: Imprenta Real, 1582.

López de Velasco, Juan, and Justo Zaragoza. *Geografía y descripción universal de las Indias, recopilada por Juan López de Velasco, desde el año de 1571 al de 1574*. Madrid: Tip. de Fortanet, 1894.

Love, Bruce. "Que son los Libros de Chilam Balam?" *Arqueología Mexicana* 28, no. 166 (January–February 2021): 36–43.

Love, Bruce, and Shigeto Yoshida. *Chilam Balam "Prophecies" and the Maya-Franciscan-Spanish Alliance That Produced Them*. Denver: University Press of Colorado, forthcoming.

Lupher, David A. *Romans in a New World: Classical Models in Sixteenth-Century Spanish America*. Ann Arbor: University of Michigan Press, 2004.

MacEvitt, Christopher. *The Martyrdom of the Franciscans: Islam, the Papacy, and an Order in Conflict*. Philadelphia: University of Pennsylvania Press, 2020.

Macleod, Murdo J. "Self-Promotion: The Relaciones de Méritos y Servicios and Their Historical and Political Interpretation." *Colonial Latin American Historical Review* 7, no. 1 (1998): 25–42.

Madrid Casado, Carlos. "Compás, mapa y espada: La cosmografía novohispana en los siglos XVI y XVII." *Cuadernos Hispanoamericanos* 836 (2020): 31–43.

Magaloni, Diana. "El arte en el hacer: Técnicas de pintura mural." In *Fragmentos del Pasado: Murales Prehispanicos*, edited by Maria Teresa Uriarte, 88–109. Mexico, DF.: Universidad Nacional Autónoma de Mexico: 1998.

Marcos, Sylvia. "Indigenous Eroticism and Colonial Morality in Mexico: The Confession Manuals of New Spain." *Numen* 39, no. 2 (1992): 157–74.

Marianus de Orscelar. *Gloriosus Franciscanus redivivus sive chronica observantiae*. Ingolstadt: Ex officina Wilhelmi Ederus, 1625.

Marks, Philippa J. M. *The British Library Guide to Bookbinding History and Techniques*. London: British Library, 1998.

Martin, Kathleen. *Discarded Pages, Araceli Cab Cumi, Maya Poet and Politician.* Albuquerque: University of New Mexico Press, 2007.

Martir de Angleria, Pedro. *Decadas del Nuevo Mundo.* Tomo I. Mexico: Jose Porrúa e Hijos, Mexico, 1965.

Masson, Marilyn A., and Carlos Peraza Lope. *Kukulkan's Realm: Urban Life at Ancient Mayapán.* Boulder: University Press of Colorado, 2014.

Masson, Marilyn, David Freidel, and Arthur Demarest, eds. *The Real Business of Ancient Maya Economies: From Farmers' Fields to Rulers' Realms.* Gainesville: University Press of Florida, 2020.

Mathisen, Ralph W., and Danuta Shanzer. *Romans, Barbarians, and the Transformation of the Roman World: Cultural Interaction and the Creation of Identity in Late Antiquity.* London: Routledge, 2016.

Matsumoto, Mallory, and Nicholas P. Carter. "Recent Developments in Ancient Maya Writing." In *The Maya World*, edited by Scott Hutson and Traci Ardren, 599–623. London: Routledge, 2020.

McAnany, Patricia. *Ancestral Maya Economies in Archaeological Perspective.* Cambridge, UK: Cambridge University Press, 2010.

McKillop, Heather, and Kazuo Aoyama. "Salt and Marine Products in the Classic Maya Economy from Use-Wear Study of Stone Tools." *PNAS* 115, no. 43 (October 23, 2018): 10948–52.

Medina, José Toribio. "Fray Diego de Landa Inquisidor de los Indios en Yucatán." In *Proceedings of the XVIII International Congress of Americanists*, vol. 2, 484–96. London: Harrison & Sons, 1913.

Metcalf, Alida. *Go-Betweens and the Colonization of Brazil, 1500–1600.* Austin: University of Texas Press, 2005.

Mignolo, Walter. *The Darker Side of the Renaissance: Literacy, Territoriality, and Colonization.* Ann Arbor: University of Michigan Press, 1995.

Millares Carlo, Agustín. *Apuntes para un estudio bibliográfico del humanista Francisco Cervantes de Salazar.* México, 1958.

Millares Carlo, Agustín. *Cartas recibidas de España por Francisco Cervantes de Salazar.* México: Porrúa, 1946.

Millet Cámara, Luis, and Heber Ojeda M., Vicente Suárez A. "Tecoh, Izamal: Nobleza indigena y conquista española." *Latin American Antiquity* 4, no. 1 (1993): 48–58.

Millspaugh, Charles Frederick, Agnes Chase, and Paul Standley. *Plantæ Yucatanæ and Flora of Yucatan.* Plants of the Insular, Coastal and Plain Regions of the Peninsula of Yucatan, Mexico. Botanical Series, vol. 3, no. 3. Chicago: Publications of the Field Museum of Natural History, 1904.

Miranda, Luis de. *Exposición de la regla de los frayles menores de la Orden de San Francisco.* Madrid: Imprenta Artus Taberniel, 1609.

Molina Solís, Juan Francisco. *Historia del descubrimiento y conquista del Yucatán con una reseña de la historia antigua de esta peninsula.* Mérida de Yucatán: Imp. y Litografía R. Caballero, 1896.

Monte di Croce, Fray Riccoldo da. *Improbatio Alcorani: Libellus fratris ricoldi ordinis fratrum predicatorum sacre theologie professoris contra legem saracenorum prohemium.* [In Codex Y 75 in Ex Convent Collection of San Juan de los Reyes.] Hispali: per Stanislaum Polonum, 1500.

Morales, Carlos, Félix Labrador Arroyo, Santiago Fernández Conti, and Ignacio Ezquerra Revilla. "El servicio de las Casas castellanas del emperador y de su familia." In *La Corte de Carlos V*, vol. 2, edited by José Martínez Millán, 85–152. Madrid: Sociedad Estatal para la Conmemoración de los Centenarios de Felipe II y Carlos V, 2000.

Morley, Sylvanus. *The Ancient Maya* [1936]. 6th rev. ed. Stanford, CA: Stanford University Press, 2006.

Nardo, Don. *Julius Caesar*. San Diego, CA: Greenhaven Press, 2002.

Nava Rodríguez, Maria Teresa. "La Real Academia de la Historia como modelo de unión formal entre el Estado y la cultura (1735–1792)." *Cuadernos de Historia Moderna y Contemporánea* 8 (2018): 127–55.

Nesvig, Martin Austin. *Forgotten Franciscans: Works from an Inquisitional Theorist, a Heretic, and an Inquisitional Deputy.* University Park: Pennsylvania State University Press, 2011.

Nielsen, Jesper. "How the Hell? Thoughts on the Colonial Demonization of the Maya Underworld." In *Maya Cosmology: Terrestrial and Celestial Landscapes: Proceedings of the 19th European Maya Conference*, edited by Milan Kováč, Harri J. Kettunen, and Guido Krempel, 241–49. Munich, Germany: Verlag Anton Saurwein, 2019.

Nueva colección de documentos para la Historia de México, siglo XVI. Mexico City: Editorial Salvador Chávez Hayhoe, 1941.

Okoshi Harada, Tsubasa. "Los Canules: Análisis Etnohistórico del Codice de Calkiní." PhD diss., Universidad Nacional Autónoma de México, 1992.

Okoshi Harada, Tsubasa. "Otra lectura de la 'Memoria de la distribución de los montes (1577)' de los Papeles de los Xiu de Yaxá, Yucatán." In *Los maya de ayer y hoy: Memorias del primer congreso internacional de cultura maya*, edited by Alfredo Barrera Rubio and Ruth Gubler, 778–91. Mérida: Universidad Autónoma de Yucatán, 2006.

Okoshi Harada, Tsubasa. "Relación de las cosas de Yucatán de fray Diego de Landa: Un crisol de intereses." In *Creación y consumo de imágenes étnicas de los mayas: Memoria del simposio en el VI Congreso Internacional de Mayistas*, edited by Shigeto Yoshida, 43–58. Sendai, Japan: Universidad de Tohoku Press, 2004.

Ordenanzas reales sobre el Consejo de Indias. Valladolid: Imprenta del Licenciado Varez de Castro, 1603.

Orique, David Thomas. *To Heaven or to Hell: Bartolomé de Las Casas's Confesionario*. University Park: Pennsylvania State University Press, 2018.

Orique, David T., and Rady Roldán-Figueroa, eds. *Bartolomé de las Casas, OP: History, Philosophy, and Theology in the Age of European Expansion*. Leiden: Brill, 2019.

Oviedo y Valdes, Gonzalo Fernández de. *Historia General de las indias, islas y tierrafirme del mar océano*. Vol. 3. Madrid: Real Academia de Historia, 1853.

Oviedo y Valdes, Gonzalo Fernández de. *Historia general y natural de las Indias islas y tierra firme del mar océano*. 4 vols. Madrid, Imprenta de la Real Academia de la Historia, 1851–1855.

Pagden, Anthony R., ed. *Hernán Cortés: Letters from Mexico*. New Haven, CT: Yale University Press, 1986.

Palka, Joel W. *Maya Pilgrimage to Ritual Landscape: Insights from Archaeology, History, and Ethnography*. Albuquerque: University of New Mexico Press, 2014.

Palou, Francisco. *Relación histórica de la vida y apostólicas tareas del Venerable Padres Fray Junípero Serra [. . .]*. Mexico City: Zúñiga y Ontiveros, 1787.

Paris, Elizabeth H. "Metallurgy, Mayapan, and the Postclassic Mesoamerican World System." *Ancient Mesoamerica* 19, no. 1 (2008): 43–66.

Paris, Elizabeth H., Stanley Serafin, Marilyn A. Masson, Carlos Peraza Lope, Cuauhtémoc Vidal Guzmán, and Bradley W. Russell. "Violence, Desecration, and Urban Collapse at the Postclassic Maya Political Capital of Mayapán." *Journal of Anthropological Archaeology* 48 (2017): 63–86.

Parish, Helen Rand, and Bartolomé de Las Casas. *Las Casas as a Bishop: A New Interpretation Based on His Holograph Petition in the Hans P. Kraus Collection of Hispanic American Manuscripts = Las Casas, obispo: una nueva interpretación a base de en su petición autógrafa en la Colección Hans P. Kraus de manuscritos hispanoamericanos*. Washington, DC: Library of Congress, 1980.

Parry, J. H. *The Discovery of South America*. New York: Taplinger, 1979.

Patch, Robert W. "The (Almost) Forgotten Plants of Yucatán." In *The Lowland Maya Area: Three Millennia at the Human-Wildland Interface*, edited by Arturo Gómez-Pompa, Michael F. Allen, Scott Fedick, and Juan J. Jiménez-Osornio, 561–70. Binghamton, New York: Food Products Press, 2003.

Patch, Robert W. *Maya and Spaniard in Yucatán, 1648–1812*. Stanford, CA: Stanford University Press, 1993.

Patel, Shankari. "Caves and Pilgrimage on Cozumel Island." In *Stone Houses and Earth Lords: Maya Religion in the Cave Context*, edited by James E. Brady and Keith M. Prufer, 91–112. Boulder: University Press of Colorado, 2005.

Pech, Ah Nakuk, and Héctor Pérez Martínez. *Historia y crónica de Chac-Xulub-Chen.* Mérida, Yucatán: Nuevos Talleres de la Cia. Tipográfica Yucateca, 1936.

Pech, Ah Naum. *Crónica de Yaxkukul.* Edited by Juan Martínez Hernández. Mérida, Yucatán: Nuevos Talleres de la Cia. Tipográfica Yucateca, 1926.

Peraza Lope, Carlos, Marilyn A. Masson, Timothy S. Hare, and Pedro Candelario Delgado Kú. "The Chronology of Mayapan: New Radiocarbon Evidence." *Ancient Mesoamerica* 17, no. 2 (2006): 153–75.

Pérez de Heredia, Eduardo, and Péter Bíró. *La Casa Real de Cocom: Una historia de Yucatán.* Self-published, Academia.edu, 2020. PDF.

Perry, Eugene, Guadalupe Velazquez-Oliman, and Richard A. Socki. "Hydrogeology of the Yucatan Peninsula." In *The Lowland Maya Area: Three Millennia at the Human-Wildland Interface,* edited by A. Gomez-Pompa, Michael F. Allen, Scott Fedick, and Juan Osornio, 115–38. Binghamton, NY: Food Products Press, 2003.

Phelan, John L. *The Millennial Kingdom of the Franciscans in the New World.* 2nd ed. Berkeley: University of California Press, 1970.

Pollock, H. E. D., Ralph L. Roys, Tatiana Proskouriakoff, and A. Ledyard Smith, eds. *Mayapan, Yucatan, Mexico.* Washington, DC: Carnegie Institution of Washington, 1962.

Pope, Kevin O., Adriana C. Ocampo, Gary L. Kinsland, and Randy Smith. "Surface Expression of the Chicxulub Crater." *Geology* 24, no. 6 (1996): 527–30.

Powers, Karen Viera. *Women in the Crucible of Conquest.* Albuquerque: University of New Mexico Press, 2005.

Proskouriakoff, Tatiana. "Civic and Religious Structures of Mayapan." In Pollock et al., *Mayapan, Yucatan, Mexico,* 87–164. Washington, DC: Carnegie Institution of Washington, 1962.

Quezada, Sergio. *Maya Lords and Lordship: The Formation of Colonial Society in Yucatán, 1350–1600.* Norman: University of Oklahoma Press, 2014.

Quezada, Sergio. *Los pies de la república: Los mayas peninsulares, 1550–1750.* México: CIESAS, 1997.

Quezada, Sergio. *Pueblos y caciques yucatecos, 1550–1580.* México: El Colegio de México, 1993.

Quezada, Sergio, and Tsubasa Okoshi Harada. *Papeles de los Xiu de Yaxá: Yucatán.* México: UNAM, 2001.

Quezada, Sergio, and Anabel Torres Trujillo, eds. *Tres Nobles Mayas.* Serie Silvio Zavala documentos para la historia colonial de Yucatán, vol. 1. Mérida: Instituto de Cultura de Yucatán, 2010.

Real Academia Española. *Diccionario de autoridades, 1726–1739.* Facsimile ed. Madrid: Gredos, 1979.

Redfield, Robert, and Alfonso Villa Rojas. *Chan Kom, a Maya Village*. Washington, DC: Carnegie Institution of Washington, 1934.

Reff, Daniel T., and Kelly, Courtney. "Saints, Witches and Go-Betweens: The Depiction of Women in Missionary Accounts from the Northern Frontier of New Spain." *Colonial Latin American Review* 18, no. 2 (2009): 237–60.

Remesal, Antonio. *Historia de la prouincia de S. Vicente de Chyapa y Guatemala*. Madrid: Francisco de Angulo, 1619.

Reséndez, Andrés. *The Other Slavery: The Uncovered Story of Indian Enslavement in America*. New York: Houghton Mifflin Harcourt, 2017.

Restall, Matthew. *The Black Middle: Africans, Mayas, and Spaniards in Colonial Yucatan*. Stanford, CA: Stanford University Press, 2009.

Restall, Matthew. "Creating 'Belize': The Mapping and Naming History of a Liminal Locale." *Terrae Incognitae* 51, no. 1 (February 2019): 5–35.

Restall, Matthew. "Gaspar Antonio Chi: Bridging the Conquest of Yucatán." In *The Human Tradition: Social Order and Disorder in Colonial Latin America*, edited by Kenneth Andrien, 13–31. 2nd ed. Wilmington, DE: Scholarly Resources, 2013.

Restall, Matthew. "Invasion: The Maya at War, 1520s–1540s." In *Embattled Bodies, Embattled Places: Conflict, Conquest, and the Performance of War in Pre-Columbian America*, edited by Andrew Scherer and John Verano, 93–117. Washington, DC: Dumbarton Oaks, 2014.

Restall, Matthew. "The Landa Conundrum." In *The Franciscans in Colonial Mexico*, edited by Thomas M. Cohen, Jay T. Harrison, and David Rex Galindo, 109–26. Norman: University of Oklahoma Press; Oceanside, CA: Academy of American Franciscan History, 2021.

Restall, Matthew. *Maya Conquistador*. Boston, MA: Beacon Press, 1998.

Restall, Matthew. *The Maya World: Yucatec Culture and Society, 1550–1850*. Stanford, CA: Stanford University Press, 1997.

Restall, Matthew. "The People of the Patio: Ethnohistorical Evidence of Yucatec Maya Royal Courts." In *Royal Courts of the Ancient Maya*, vol. 2, edited by Takeshi Inomata and Stephen Houston, 335–90. Boulder, CO: Westview Press, 2001.

Restall, Matthew. *Seven Myths of the Spanish Conquest. Updated Edition*. New York: Oxford University Press, 2021.

Restall, Matthew. "The Trouble with 'America.'" *Ethnohistory* 67, no. 1 (January 2020): 1–28.

Restall, Matthew. "The Wars of Invasion in the Caribbean and Mesoamerica, 1492–1547." In *Cambridge World History of Violence*, vol. 3, edited by Caroline Pennock, 138–55. Cambridge, UK: Cambridge University Press, 2020.

Restall, Matthew. *When Montezuma Met Cortés: The True Story of the Meeting That Changed History*. New York: Ecco/HarperCollins, 2018.

Restall, Matthew, and Florine Asselbergs. *Invading Guatemala: Spanish, Nahua, and Maya Accounts of the Conquest Wars*. University Park: Pennsylvania State University Press, 2007.

Restall, Matthew, and John F. Chuchiak. "A Re-evaluation of the Authenticity of Fray Diego de Landa's *Relación de las cosas de Yucatán*." *Ethnohistory* 49, no. 3 (Summer 2002): 651–69.

Restall, Matthew, and Wolfgang Gabbert. "Maya Ethnogenesis and Group Identity in Yucatan, 1500–1900." In *"The Only True People": Linking Maya Identities Past and Present*, edited by Bethany J. Myers and Lisa LeCount, 91–130. Boulder: University Press of Colorado, 2017.

Restall, Matthew, and Amara Solari. *2012 and the End of the World: The Western Roots of the Maya Apocalypse*. Lanham, MD: Rowman and Littlefield, 2011.

Restall, Matthew, and Amara Solari. *The Maya: A Very Short Introduction*. Oxford, UK: Oxford University Press, 2020.

Restall, Matthew, and Amara Solari. *The Maya Apocalypse and Its Western Roots*. Lanham, MD: Rowman and Littlefield, 2021.

Reyes-Foster, Beatriz. "He Followed the Funereal Steps of Ixtab: The Pleasurable Aesthetics of Suicide in Newspaper Journalism in Yucatan, Mexico." *The Journal of Latin American and Caribbean Anthropology* 18, no. 2 (2013): 251–73.

Reyes-Foster, Beatriz M., and Rachael Kangas. "Unraveling Ix Tab: Revisiting the 'Suicide Goddess' in Maya Archaeology." *Ethnohistory* 63, no. 1 (2016): 1–27.

Riesco de Iturri, María Begoña. "Propiedades y fortuna de los condes de Cifuentes: La constitución de su patrimonio a lo largo del siglo XVI." *La España Medieval* 15 (1992): 137–59.

Ringle, William M., and George J. Bey III. "Post-classic and Terminal Classic Courts of the Northern Maya Lowlands." In *Royal Courts of the Maya*, vol. 2, edited by Takeshi Inomata and Stephen D. Houston, 266–307. Boulder, CO: Westview Press, 2001.

Roa-de-la-Carrera, Cristián. *Histories of Infamy: Francisco López de Gómara and the Ethics of Spanish Imperialism*. Boulder: University Press of Colorado, 2005.

Robelo, Cecilio A. *Diccionario de pesas y medidas Mexicanas Antiguas y modernas y de su conversión*. Cuernavaca, Mexico: Imprenta "Cuauhnahuac," 1908.

Robinson, James R. *The Landa Alphabet Reconsidered: A Phonetic Theory for Deciphering the Mayan Hieroglyphic Script*. Phoenix, AZ: J. R. Robinson, 1981.

Rodríguez Sala, María Luisa. "Francisco Domínguez y Ocampo, geógrafo y cosmógrafo." In *El eclipse de luna: Misión científica de Felipe II en Nueva España*, 67–84. Huelva: Universidad de Huelva, 1998.

Roest, Bert. "Giovanni of Capestrano's Anti-Judaism within a Franciscan Context." *Franciscan Studies* 75 (2017): 117–44.

Roest, Bert. *A History of Franciscan Education (c. 1210–1517)*. Leiden: Brill, 2000.

Rogers, Rhianna. *From Ichcanzihoo to Merida: Documenting Cultural Transmission through Contact Archaeology in Tihoo, Merida, Yucatan*. Oxford, UK: Archaeopress, 2011.

Rojo, Fray Antonio. *Historia de San Diego de Alcala: Fundacion y frutos de santidad que ha producido su convento de Santa María de Jesús de la orden de N.P.S. Francisco de la Observancia de la Santa provincia de Castilla*. Madrid: En la Imprenta Real, 1663.

Roys, Ralph L. *The Ethno-botany of the Maya*. New Orleans, LA: Middle American Research Institute, 1931.

Roys, Ralph L. *Political Geography of the Yucatan Maya*. Washington, DC: Carnegie Institution of Washington, 1957.

Ruan, Felipe E. "Cosmographic Description, Law, and Fact Making: Juan López de Velasco's American and Peninsular Questionnaires." *Colonial Latin American Review* 28, no. 4 (2019): 450–77.

Rubio Mañe, Jorge Ignacio. *Notas y acotaciones a la historia de Yucatán de Diego López Cogolludo*. Mexico: Editorial Academia Literaria, 1957.

Ruppert, Karl. *The Caracol at Chichen Itza, Yucatan, Mexico*. Washington, DC.: Carnegie Institution of Washington, 1935.

Russell, Bradley. "Fortress Mayapan: Defensive Features and Secondary Functions of a Postclassic Maya Fortification." *Ancient Mesoamerica* 24, no. 2 (2013): 275–94.

Ruz Lhuillier, Alberto. *La costa de Campeche en los tiempos prehispánicos: Prospección cerámica y bosquejo histórico*. México: Instituto Nacional de Antropología e Historia, 1969.

Ruz Lhuillier, Alberto. *Costumbres funerarias de los antiguos mayas*. México: UNAM. Seminario de Cultura Maya, 1968.

Sabloff, Jeremy A. "It Depends on How We Look at Things: New Perspectives on the Postclassic Period in the Northern Maya Lowlands." In *Proceedings of the American Philosophical Society* 151:1 (2007): 11–26.

Salazar y Castro, Luis de. *Historia genealógica de la casa de Silva: Donde se refieren las acciones más señaladas de sus señores las fundaciones de sus mayorazgos y la calidad de sus alianças matrimoniales*. Madrid: Por Mateo Llanos y Guzman, 1685.

Salisbury, Stephen. *The Mayas, the Sources of Their History. Proceedings of the American Antiquarian Society of April 26, 1876*. Worcester, MA: Charles Hamilton, 1877.

Saville, Marshall H. *The Discovery of Yucatan in 1517 by Francisco Hernández de Córdoba*. New York: American Geographical Society, 1918.

Serano y Sanz, Manuel. "Vida y escritos de Fray Diego de Landa." In *Archivo de la historia de Yucatán, Campeche y Tabasco*, 2 vols., edited by Rubio Mañé, Jorge Ignacio, and Manuel Serrano y Sanz, 429–51. México, D.F.: Aldina, Robredo y Rosell, 1942.

Serano y Sanz, Manuel. "Vida y escritos de fray Diego de Landa." *Revista Archivos, Bibliotecas y Museos* 1, no. 2–3 (1897): 2:54–60, 3:109–17.

Scholes, France V. "Franciscan Missionary Scholars in Colonial Central America." *The Americas* 8, no. 4 (1952): 391–416.

Scholes, France V., and Eleanor B. Adams, eds. *Don Diego Quijada, Alcalde Mayor de Yucatán, 1561–1565.* 2 vols. Mexico City: Editorial Porrua, 1938.

Scholes, France V., and Ralph L. Roys. "Fray Diego de Landa and the Problem of Idolatry in Yucatan." In *Cooperation in Research* #501 (1938). Washington, DC: Carnegie Institution: 585–620.

Scholes, France V., and Ralph L. Roys. *The Maya Chontal Indians of Acalan-Tixchel: A Contribution to the History and Ethnography of the Yucatan Peninsula.* Norman: University of Oklahoma Press, 1968.

Schütte, Josef Franz. "Dokumente zur japanischen Kirchengeschichte im Archivo General de la Nación, México." *Archivo Historico de la Sociedad de Jesus*, no. 40 (1971): 4–66.

Schwaller, John F., ed. *Sahagún at 500: Essays on the Quincentenary of the Birth of Fr. Bernardino de Sahagún.* San Francisco, CA: Academy of American Franciscan History, 2003.

Schwartz, Stuart B. *Sea of Storms: A History of Hurricanes in the Greater Caribbean from Columbus to Katrina.* Princeton, NJ: Princeton University Press, 2015.

Shailor, Barbara A. *The Medieval Book: Illustrated from the Beinecke Rare Book and Manuscript Library.* Toronto, ON: University of Toronto Press, 1991.

Shore, Maxine, and M. M. Oblinger. *Hero of Darien: The Story of Vasco Núñez De Balboa.* New York: Longmans, Green and Co., 1946.

Simonet, Francisco Javier. *Glosario de voces ibéricas y latinas usadas entre los mozarabes.* Madrid: Atlas, 1982.

Simoons, Frederick J., and James Baldwin. "Breast-feeding of Animals by Women: Its Socio-Cultural Context and Geographic Occurrence." *Anthropos* 77, nos. 3–4 (1982): 421–48.

Smailus, Ortwin. *El maya-chontal de Acalán: Análisis lingüístico de un documento de los años 1610–12.* Mexico City: UNAM, Coordinación de Humanidades, 1975.

Socolow, Susan M. *The Women of Colonial Latin America.* Cambridge, UK: Cambridge University Press, 2000.

Solari, Amara. "The Contagious Stench of Idolatry: The Rhetoric of Disease and Sacrilegious Acts in Colonial New Spain." *Hispanic American Historical Review* 96, no. 3 (2016): 481–515.

Solari, Amara. *Idolizing Mary: Maya-Catholic Icons in Yucatán, Mexico.* University Park: Pennsylvania State University Press, 2019.

Solari, Amara. *Maya Ideologies of the Sacred: The Transfiguration of Space in Colonial Yucatan.* Austin: University of Texas Press, 2013.

Solari, Amara. "The *Relación Geográfica* Map of Tabasco: Hybrid Cartography and Integrative Knowledge Systems in Sixteenth-Century New Spain." *Terrae Incognitae* 41, no. 1 (2009): 38–58.

Solari, Amara, and Linda K. Williams. "Maya Blue and Franciscan Evangelism." *Latin American and Latinx Visual Culture* 3, no. 4 (Summer 2021): 49–71.

Stone, Erin Woodruff. *Captives of Conquest: Slavery in the Early Modern Spanish Caribbean*. Philadelphia: University of Pennsylvania Press, 2021.

Strecker, Matthias, and Jorge Artieda. "La relación de algunas costumbres, 1581, de Gaspar Antonio Chi." *Estudios de Historia Novohispana* 6 (1978): 89–108.

Stuart, David. "Maya Time." In *The Maya World*, edited by Scott R. Hutson and Traci Ardren, 624–47. London: Routledge, 2020.

Stuart, George. "Glyph Drawings from Landa's *Relación*: A Caveat to the Investigator." *Research Reports on Ancient Maya Writing* 19 (1988): 23–32.

Tacitus, Cornelius. *The Agricola and The Germania* [AD 98]. London: Penguin, 1970.

Taube, Karl A. *The Major Gods of Ancient Yucatan*. Washington, DC: Dumbarton Oaks Research Library and Collection, 1992.

Tedlock, Dennis. "Torture in the Archives: Mayans Meet Europeans." *American Anthropologist* 91, no. 1 (March 1993): 139–52.

Thompson, J. Eric S. *Historia y religion de los mayas*. Mexico, DF: Siglo Veintiuno, 1997.

Thompson, J. Eric S. *Maya Hieroglyphs without Tears*. London: British Museum, 1972.

Thompson, J. Eric S. *Maya History and Religion*. Norman: University of Oklahoma Press, 1970.

Thompson, J. Eric S. *The Moon Goddess in Middle America*. Contributions to American Anthropology and History, no. 29. Washington, DC: Carnegie Institution of Washington, 1939.

Thompson, J. Eric S. "Sixteenth and Seventeenth Century Reports on the Chol Mayas." *American Anthropologist* 40, no. 4 (October–December 1938): 584–604.

Thompson, Philip C. *Tekanto: A Maya Town in Colonial Yucatán*. New Orleans: MARI, Tulane University, 1999.

Tiesler, Vera. "Becoming Maya: Infancy and Upbringing through the Lens of Pre-Hispanic Head Shaping." *Childhood in the Past* 4 (2011): 117–32.

Tiesler, Vera. *The Bioarchaeology of Artificial Cranial Modifications: New Approaches to Head Shaping and Its Meanings in Pre-Columbian Mesoamerica and Beyond*. New York: Springer, 2014.

Timmer, David E. "Providence and Perdition: Fray Diego de Landa Justifies His Inquisition against the Yucatecan Maya." *Church History* 66, no. 3 (September 1997): 477–88.

Tokovinine, Alexandre. "Bundling the Sticks: A Case for Classic Maya Tallies." In *The Real Business of Ancient Maya Economies: From Farmer's Fields to Ruler's Realms*, edited by Marilyn Masson, David A. Freidel, and Arthur Demarest, 276–95. Gainesville: University Press of Florida, 2020.

Toral, Francisco de. *Avisos del Obispo Fr. Francisco de Toral* [1563]. In *Documentos para la Historia de Yucatán*, vol. 2, edited by France V. Scholes, Carlos Menéndez, J. Rubio Mañé, and Eleanor Adams, 25–34. Mérida, Yucatan: Compañía Tipográfica Yucateca, 1938.

Torquemada, Fray Juan de, and Miguel León Portilla. *Monarquia Indiana de los veinte y un libros rituales y monarquia Indiana, con el origen y guerras de los indios occidentales, de sus poblazones, descubrimiento, conquista, conversión y otras cosas maravillosas de la mesma tierra*. 7 volumes. Mexico City: Universidad Nacional Autonoma de Mexico, 1983.

Townsend, Camilla. *Annals of Native America: How the Nahuas of Colonial Mexico Kept Their History Alive*. New York: Oxford University Press, 2017.

Townsend, Camilla. *Fifth Sun: A New History of the Aztecs*. New York: Oxford University Press, 2019.

Townsend, Camilla. *Malintzin's Choices: An Indian Woman in the Conquest of Mexico*. Albuquerque: University of New Mexico Press, 2006.

Tozzer, Alfred M. *Chichen Itza and Its Cenote of Sacrifice*. Memoirs of the Peabody Museum, Harvard University, Vols. 11–12. Cambridge, MA: Peabody Museum of Harvard, 1957.

Tozzer, Alfred M. "A Spanish Manuscript Letter on the Lacondones in the Archives of the Indies at Seville." In *Proceedings of the International Congress of Americanists*, 497–509. London: Harrison and Sons, 1912.

Trejo, Antonio de. "Report on the Missions by the Franciscan Commissary General of the Indies, 1612." *The Americas* 2, no. 4 (April 1946): 489–97.

Vail, Gabrielle. "The Gods in the Madrid Codex: An Iconographic and Graphic Analysis." PhD diss., Tulane University, 1996.

Vail, Gabrielle. "Yearbearer Rituals and Prognostications in the Maya Codices and Landa's *Relación de las cosas de Yucatán*." In *Text and Context: Yucatec Maya Literature in a Diachronic Perspective*, edited by Antje Gunsenheimer, Tsubasa Okoshi Harada, and John F. Chuchiak, 53–82. Bonner Amerikanistische Studien, 47 Aachen: Shaker Verlag, 2009.

Vail, Gabrielle, and Maia Dedrick. "Human-Deity Relationships Conveyed through Balche' Rituals and Resource Procurement." In *Her Cup for Sweet Cacao: Food in Ancient Maya Society*, edited by Traci Ardren, 334–65. Austin: University of Texas Press, 2020.

Vail, Gabrielle, and Andrea Stone. "Representations of Women in Postclassic and Colonial Literature and Art." In *Ancient Maya Women*, edited by T. Ardren, 203–28. Walnut Creek, CA: AltaMira Press, 2002.

Valckx, Aimee, Travis Stanton, and Traci Ardren. "Mujeres en la Guerra: Una Vista desde la Arqueología." *Anales de Antropología* 45 (2011): 123–52.

Valenti, Maria. *Saggio di una bibliografia delle edizioni di tacito (nei secoli XV–XVII)*. Rome: Edizione de "L'Italia Che Scrive," 1951.

Valls i Subirà, Oriol. *La filigrana del peregrino*. México: Instituto de Estudios y Documentos Históricos, Claustro de Sor Juana, 1982.

Valverde, Roldán, and Kym Rouse Holzwart. "Sea Turtles of the Gulf of Mexico." In *Habitats and Biota of the Gulf of Mexico: Before the Deepwater Horizon Oil Spill*, vol. 2, edited by C. Herb Ward, 1189–1352. New York: Springer Nature, 2017.

Vázquez de Ágredos Pascual, Maria Luisa, Teresa Doménech Carbó, and Antonio Doménech Carbó. "Resins and Drying Oils of Precolumbian Painting: A Study from Historical Writings, Equivalences to those of European Painting." *Arché: Publicación del Instituto Universitario de Restauración del Patrimonio de la Universidad Politécnica de Valencia* 3 (2008): 186–90.

Verrill, Hyatt A. *Great Conquerors of South and Central America*. New York: New Home Library, 1929.

Villasana Haggard, Juan, and Malcolm D. McLean. *Handbook for Translators of Spanish Historical Documents*. Austin: Archives Collections, University of Texas, 1941.

Vives, Joan Luís. *De concordia & discordia in humano genere* [. . .]. Lugduni: Ex officina Melchioris & Gasparis Treschel fratrum, 1532.

Von Hagen, Wolfgang. *The Aztec and Maya Papermakers*. New York: J. J. Augusten, 1944.

Wade, Maria F. *Missions, Missionaries, and Native Americans*. Gainesville: University Press of Florida, 2008.

Wallace, Geoffrey H. "The History and Geography of Beeswax Extraction in the Northern Maya Lowlands, 1540–1700." PhD diss., McGill University, 2020.

Werner, Michael S., ed. *Encyclopedia of Mexico: History, Society and Culture*. Chicago, IL: Fitzroy Dearborn, 1997.

West, Delno C. "Medieval Ideas of Apocalyptic Mission and the Early Franciscans in Mexico." *The Americas* 45, no. 3 (January 1989): 293–313.

Whitehead, Neil L. *Of Cannibals and Kings: Primal Anthropology in the Americas*. University Park: Pennsylvania State University Press, 2011.

Index

Account of the Things of Yucatan, The (*Relación de las Cosas de Yucatán*): anti-Semitic passage in, 283; assembled between last decades of sixteenth century and turn of seventeenth century, 262; comparison with work by Monte di Croce, 288; conclusion regarding authors and content of, 19; content of, 7; copyists' decisions on content of, 231; description of authorships, inconsistencies, and sources in, 18–19; diverse *auctoritas* in, 293; as ethnography of the Maya, 7; fifty-two sections in, 22–24; first Spanish edition of (1884), 267; Gaspar de Nájera as possible contributor to, 294; integrates three Maya consultants, 234; involved three to seven copyists, 312; limited integrity as a cohesive book, 262; Maya calendar sources for, 320–21; messy and mysterious production and history of, 19–20; methods in collecting memories of informants not clear, 278; missing facts about, 18; most scholars miss the contradictions in, 267; multiple authors of, 8, 16, 18, 262; no evidence that Landa saw, 15–16; not a source on the Maya or Spanish invasion, 241; numeration of folios within sections of, 22–24; paltry Landa biographical information, 278; persistence of inaccurate editions of, 274; possible contributors to, 19; possible use of a questionnaire, 278–79; promotes three royal Maya lineages (Chel, Cocom, and Xiu), 234–39; refers to Maya women's breasts ten times, 299, 299n6; a rich source of contributors and Maya consultants, 241; scholars' interpretation of intent of, 256; similarities with the work of Francisco Cervantes de Salazar, 282–83; single date of authorship (1566) within, 16; Spanish edition also relied on Brasseur de Bourbourg's edition, 267; standard reference on Maya history, 19; tendency to use the manuscript as a bible or encyclopedia on the Maya, 267; two principal compilers, 312; uncertainty of Landa's sole authorship of, 16; a widely cited early writing in Latin America, 19; written at different times, 262. *See also* sections in Landa's Account

Acalan (Acalan-Tixchel), 29n19, 29n20, 42n58, 334

Acantunes/Acantun (four devils, idols), 160. *See also* Chacacantun; demons/devils; Ekelacantun; Kanalacantun; Zacacantun

Acanum Zuhuyzipi tabai (Acan Zum, Zuhuy Zip, and Ah Tabay; Maya gods of the hunt), 149

adelantado: defined, 171n340, 219; as sanctioned Spanish conquistador, 56, 219. *See also* Montejo, Francisco de (Adelantado)

Adrian IV, Pope, 58, 58n118, 59, 75, 76n172

Africa/Africans, 86n197, 130, 290; enslaved, 105n245. *See also* enslavement

agriculture, 23, 87n201, 197n395, 266, 283

Aguilar, Gerónimo (Jerónimo) de (interpreter for Cortes), 22, 30, 30n22, 31n27, 31n28, 58, 319

Aguilar, Hernando de (Spanish conquistador, killed in Maya Revolt of 1546), 67*n142*

Aguilar, Juan de (Spanish encomendero, 1580), 210*n433*

Aguilar, Pedro Sánchez de (Spanish Priest, author of *Informe contra idolorum cultores*), 91*n211*

ahau (Maya term for ruler; letters of the month), 124*n295*, 136, 136*n309*, 160, 161

Ahau Can May (*Ahuacanmai*), 47

Ah Bolon Dzacab (Schellhas God K, K'awil), 117*n280*

Ahbulucbalam (demon, devil, idol), 126. *See also* demons/devils

Ah Cambal (Maya *chilan*), 56, 56–57*n110*. *See also chilan*

Ahcanuolcab (demon, devil, idol), 126. *See also* demons/devils

Ah Chel (*Achchel*; Maya nobleman), 54

Ahcitzamalcum (Maya god of fishing), 154

Ahkaknexoc (Maya god of fishing), 154

ah kin (*ah kinob, ah kulel*; Maya priest), 44*n66*, 47*n77*, 48*n78*, 72*n157*, 122*n290*, 160–61*n320*, 188–89*n375*, 236, 292; Cutz, 31*n28*; may (*achkinmai, ahuacanmai*), 47, 127*n300*, 161*n322*, 235

Ah Kin Chel (lineage), 60, 239; lineage resided in Izamal (Ytzamal), 54

Ahpua (Maya god of fishing), 154

Ah Tabay (Ah Tabai; Maya god of the hunt), 149

Aixchel. *See* Ixchel

Alaminos, Antón de (pilot for the expeditions of Hernandez de Córdoba, Grijalva, and Cortés), 32, 35, 36

Albalte, Nicolás de (Franciscan friar who recruited Landa), 250, 250*n24*

Alcalde Mayor (Chief magistrate/Provincial Governor), 13*n25*, 74, 232*n32*

Almanac: in Madrid Codex, 196*n393*

alphabet of Landa, 165*n324*, 273, 314–15, 328–330

Alvarado, Pedro de (Captain of Cortés expedition, later conquistador of Guatemala), 35*n41*, 220, 223, 224*n13*, 230; transfer of Honduras to, 221; Xochimilco encomienda, 221

Álvarez, Pedro (conquistador of Yucatan), 240*n47*

Am (divinatory stones), 149

amber (stone), 107, 107*n251*

ancestors, 34*n37*, 39, 50*n88*, 52, 84, 160*n318*, 189, 215, 234, 288, 304

anointing (smearing): with black soot, 131, 148; with blood, 98, 99, 100, 121, 123–26, 154, 160; with blue color, 99, 100, 137, 149, 155; with red color, 107

appease, 124, 136

architecture, 332; differences within Maya communities, 49–50*n86*; Izamal's colonial, 253; Maya, 321, 330; Maya achievements in, 222; Maya source of Chichen Itza, 45*n70*; Mayapan monumental, 46*n72*; perceived similarities between Chichen Itza and Tula in, 45*n70*; Puuc-style, 52*n97*; Tecoh precontact, 174*n342*

artisans/artists: artistic production, 31*n25*; craft specialist/crafting, 48–49*n81*, 192; lifelong ties to crafted ritual objects, 155; *los oficiales* (tattooing), 82; Spanish Christian personages not crafted by, 97*n229*; women and, 296. *See also* body modification

Ascension Bay, 25, 35; named by Juan de Grijalva, 29

ashes: cremation, 23, 43, 43*n62*, 111, 168; Maya women's use of, 197; to ripen fruit, 204

Asia, 131, 290, 308, 324

astronomy/astronomical, 46*n72*, 113*n267*, 116*n269*, 222

Audiencia (Colonial District Court), 75; de los Confines–Guatemala, 62, 62*n127*, 68*n145*, 71, 189, 189*n377*; de México, 67

auto-da-fé (act of faith), 74, 74*n165*, 74*n166*, 76, 76*n172*, 275, 291, 291*n59*

Avila, Alonso López de (brother-in-law of the Adelantado Montejo), 108, 293

Axcocahmut (Yax Cocay Mut), 124, 124*n293*

axe, 51, 101

Ayeta, Francisco (Franciscan friar), cited Landa's *Arte y gramática*, 17. *See also* friars

Aztecs/Mexica: Culhua, Maya term for, 36*n45*; prophecies of Spaniards' arrival, 56; residents in Mayapan, 51–52, 54; spared from Maya vengeance, 54

plaster, 48–49*n81*, 168, 168*n328*, 175, 175*n348*, 200

plates, 121, 142, 143, 154, 185; gold, 304

platform. *See* architecture

polish, 42, 42*n58*, 48, 200; stone, 171

Ppap Hol Chac (pyramid): Christian convent built on, 168*n330*, 252–53

pottery/potters, 86, 95*n222*; ceramic wares, 43*n59*, 196*n393*, 205. *See also* vases

prayers/preaching, 94, 94*n221*, 96, 109, 117, 123, 125, 131, 137, 142, 148, 149, 154, 155, 182*n355*, 183, 299

priests (Ah Kin/*chilan*/*chilam*), 44*n66*, 46, 47, 47–48*n77*, 48, 50, 50*n89*, 53–55, 60, 66, 72, 72*n157*, 74, 78, 89, 90, 91, 92–97, 99–100, 110, 116–17, 120, 122, 122*n290*, 124*n296*, 125, 131, 136–37, 142–43, 148, 149, 154–55, 160, 160–61*n320*, 161, 161*n322*, 179, 185, 191, 192, 232, 235, 236, 239, 292–93

property, 87, 87*n203*, 89, 183

prophets/prophecies (Maya), 48, 56, 56*n109*, 232, 236, 239, 288

Puebla, Miguel de la (Franciscan friar), 13*n25*, 253, 310*n4*. *See also* friars

Puerto Real (Yucatan), 25, 334, 340

punishments (Maya): adulterers, 23, 50, 51, 51*n91*, 104, 104*n244*, 105, 304; death by dogs, 108; death for homicide, 104; enslavement as possible punishment for theft, 104; stoning of rapist of a virgin, 50

purification, 93, 287*n42*

pustules: and pestilence, 55

puuc (*puuk*; hill), 26*n5*, 26*n8*, 184*n362*, 187*n372*; as idiosyncratic mosaic patterning on monumental structures, 26*n5*, 52, 52–53*n97*; as region/area around Uxmal, 49–50*n86*

pyramids, 43–44*n62*, 124, 174*n342*, 178*n350*, 330. *See also* architecture; festivals/rituals; idols; idolatry; sacrifices

Quijada, don Diego de (Alcalde Mayor of Yucatan, 1561–1565), 232*n32*, 253–54

Rada y Delgado, don Juan de Dios de la (author of first Spanish edition of Landa's Account), 267, 272

rain, 26, 27, 49, 52, 77, 87, 123, 137, 187–88

residencia: described, 67*n144*; judicial review of official conduct, 67, 68, 229, 278

ropes: and dogs for fishing crocodiles, 192; for fishing, 190

Rosado Escalante, José E.: co-editor of Landa's Account in Spanish (1938), 269. *See also* Ontiveros, Favila

sacbeob ("white roads," Maya roads), 120*n281*, 170*n334*, 251–52

sacrifices: and animal blood, 136; animal sacrifices, 179; by arrow (*asaetadas*), 99; bloodletting, 124–25, 136, 154, 179; blood sacrifice, 99, 100; Campeche building representation, 33; dog sacrifice, 142; and ears, 120, 123, 160; and human blood, 74; other sacrifices, 179, 181–184; and penises (*xicin poy*), 98, 98*n234*; representation of child sacrifices in, 44*n67*; and body modifications, 97–100, 102; self, 97, 183

Sahagún, Bernardino de (Franciscan friar): debate over, 8; dual characterization of, 277; as early ethnographer, 277; and The Florentine Codex, 19, 268, 277, 278, 317; method of memory and observation by, 278; study of the Mexica/Aztecs, 267

Salisbury III, Stephen: collector of Maya artifacts, 266; president of the American Antiquarian Society, 266; relied on the Brasseur de Bourbourg's edition, 266; spoke on the value of the Landa's *Relación*, 266; viewed the *Relación* as a corroborated eye-witness account, 266; as wealthy Massachusetts male, 266. *See also* friars

Saint Augustine, 212, 212*n436*

Saint Gregory, 211

Salamanca (Bacalar, de Bacalar, Bachalal/Bakhalal), Yucatan, 26, 29, 32, 42, 53, 226, 228, 335; founded in Yucatan by Francisco Montejo (Adelantado), 64; Francisco Montejo named seven towns after, 224*n12*; Francisco Montejo native of Spanish, 57; Hispanization of Maya name, 334; in Spain, 62, 68; Spanish University of, 75

sambenito (san benito, saco bendito): Landa imposed on Maya idolaters, 74*n165*;